NORTHWESTERN UNIVERSITY
A HISTORY
1850-1975

NORTHWESTERN UNIVERSITY

A HISTORY
1850-1975

HAROLD F. WILLIAMSON

AND

PAYSON S. WILD

Research Associates: Gail F. Casterline,
Helen C. Lee, Timothy G. Walch

NORTHWESTERN UNIVERSITY
EVANSTON, ILLINOIS

This history is dedicated to

DR. J. ROSCOE MILLER

Chancellor Emeritus
Northwestern University

Library of Congress Catalog Number: 76-19476

Editor: Fannia Weingartner
Designer: Mirjana Hervoic

Printed in the United States of America

CONTENTS

Preface   xi

Part One: VISIONS AND STRUGGLES
             1. Laying the Foundation 1850-1876   1
             2. Affiliation and Expansion 1876-1890   43

Part Two: A UNIVERSITY FOR THE MODERN AGE
             3. Building a University 1890-1900   71
             4. Years of Transition 1900-1920   101

Part Three: TOWARD A GREATER NORTHWESTERN
             5. Times of Plenty, Times of Trial 1920-1939   143
             6. A Decade of War and Peace 1939-1949   205

Part Four: "A UNIVERSITY OF THE HIGHEST GRADE"
             7. The Miller Years 1949-1974   253
                Carrying Forward 1974—   355

Appendixes: A. Presidents of the Board and the University   361
            B. Charter   363

Notes   369

Bibliography   383

Indexes: General   387
         Tables   402
         Illustrations   403

PREFACE

This illustrated volume traces the 125-year history of Northwestern University's evolution from a small traditional liberal arts college into a major university of national stature. Given the limitation imposed by space, it was clearly impossible to identify the successive generations of faculty members whose talents and devotion as teachers and scholars served to fulfill the high purpose the founders set for the university. Nor was it possible to give more than a general account of the major curricular developments in the individual schools over this long period. Our primary objective has been to focus on what seemed to be the most significant features of Northwestern's history: the goals and vision of the founders; the role of trustees and friends in providing the financial support essential for survival and expansion; the growth in the endowment and physical facilities and the changing patterns of income and expenditure; the proliferation of associated professional schools; the development of two campuses—Evanston and Chicago; and the emergence of an academically integrated university.

The arrangement of the book into four sections is chronological. Section one, "Visions and Struggles," describes Northwestern's founding and survival in the face of the Civil War and recurring booms and depressions up to 1890. The second section, "A University for the Modern Age," deals with the university's expansion and adaptation to the needs of a changing society up to 1920. Section three, "Toward a Greater Northwestern," carries the account forward through the boom years of the 1920's, the depression of the 1930's, and the impact of World War II and its aftermath on the university. The final section, "A University of the Highest Grade," relates the development of Northwestern's physical and academic capabilities in the economically and intellectually supportive climate of the post-Sputnik era and the university's response to the student unrest of the late 1960's and early 1970's.

Credit for the establishment of the history project must be given to Chancellor Emeritus J. Roscoe Miller who, a year prior to his retirement, decided that an up-to-date history of Northwestern was greatly needed, and appointed John E. Fields, vice president for development, to be "publisher," with duties commencing with the engagement of the writers and ending with the publication and distribution of the book.

Only four published accounts dealing with the university's past were available: *Northwestern University: A History, 1855-1905*, a four volume collection of essays edited by Arthur Wilde, published in 1905; a one volume survey by Robert D. Sheppard and Harvey B. Hurd which came out in 1906; Estelle Ward's popular and somewhat impressionistic work, *The Story of Northwestern University*, published in 1924; and *A Pictorial History of Northwestern University, 1851-1951*, edited by Franklin D. Scott for Northwestern's Centennial celebration in 1951.

Initially the authors' plan was to concentrate on the history of Northwestern since 1939, but once the project was under way it became apparent that recent decades could not be properly treated or understood without an account of what had happened in earlier years. Accordingly, it was decided that the history should encompass the life of the university from its inception until 1975.

The authors are most grateful to the many individuals who assisted in the preparation of this history. We are particularly indebted to our associates Gail Casterline, Timothy G. Walch, and Helen C. Lee for their research assistance and substantive contributions to the manuscript.

Fannia Weingartner, as editor, contributed immeasurably to the organization and readability of the final product. Her skill in bringing the manuscript into consistent form proved to be invaluable. She also served as project coordinator under Vice President Fields.

We are deeply indebted to University Archivist Patrick M. Quinn, with whom we worked closely throughout the history project. Without his knowledge of the holdings of the archives and the assistance given by him and his staff members— Katherine H. Giese, Mary S. Moss, and Sarah L. Good—in making these records available, our task would have been infinitely more difficult. Ms. Moss also assumed major responsibility in finding illustrations for the first three parts of the history.

No meaningful discussion of the university's finances would have been possible without John Serva's careful synthesis and analysis of the various types of reports submitted by the Northwestern treasurers over the years. The Index is the work of Elizabeth Garber.

University Relations staff members involved in the production of the book include: Jack O'Dowd, director; Mary Buzard, publications manager; Eulalee Birchmeier, production coordinator; Mirjana Hervoic, who was responsible for the book's graphic design and layout; William S. Ricker, who did final proofing; Gregory W. Casserly and Marylou Sanders, who contributed special promotional material; and Lee Kovacsevics, who assisted in researching illustrations for the last part of the history.

Others who gave generously of their time and counsel include: Leslie B. Arey, Harold H. Anderson, James E. Avery, Robert H. Baker, Leon A. Bosch, Peter Byrne, Doris Corbett, Mikell C. Darling of the Evanston Historical Society,

Rolf H. Erickson, Katharine George, Charles H. Gold, Thomas A. Gonser, Paul H. Hass, Robert B. Hatter, Frances B. Holgate, Phill Issen, Paul E. Klopsteg, William S. Kerr, Franklin M. Kreml, Susan D. Lee, Richard W. Leopold, Brunson MacChesney, James C. McLeod, Claudine V. Mason, Joe W. Miller, Laurence H. Nobles, Walter Paulison, Moody E. Prior, Richard A. Rubovits, Leland M. Roth, Arthur T. Schmehling, Michael L. Sedlak, J. Lyndon Shanley, Jean Skelly, Alice W. Snyder, William H. Thigpen, Rosemary Westphal, Michael C. Weston, Raymond E. Willemain, Arline H. Williamson, Jeremy P. Wilson, and Barbara H. Young.

And to the many Northwestern alumni, whose pride and interest in their alma mater prompted them to share with us cherished personal photographs and memories of their college days, we are truly grateful.

Harold F. Williamson
Payson S. Wild

John Evans, physician, businessman, territorial governor and prime mover in the founding of Northwestern University

Part One

VISIONS AND STRUGGLES

1850—1890

Founder Grant Goodrich, active in law and church work

Founder Orrington Lunt, merchant engaged in politics and philanthropy

Old College, the university's first building, completed in 1855

1

LAYING THE FOUNDATION
1850—1876

When the founders of Northwestern University decided in 1850 to establish an institution of higher learning, their aim was to serve the people of the original Northwest Territory. Created by act of Congress in 1787, this included the area from which the states of Ohio, Indiana, Illinois, Michigan, Wisconsin, and part of Minnesota were later carved. The geographic scope of their venture supplied the name which the university carries to this day, even though its students now come from all fifty states and numerous foreign countries as well.

When the early pioneers pushed westward they settled first in the river valleys, so that when Illinois entered the Union in 1818 its population was concentrated at its southern tip and in towns along the Ohio and Mississippi rivers. What is now Chicago was a remote, muddy settlement surrounding a military fort. Within the next three decades its location along the southern shore of Lake Michigan led to the transformation of this settlement into a bustling mercantile center of nearly 30,000. By 1850 Chicago had become the focus of a cluster of important economic activities including meat packing, grain trading, shipping, railroading, and the production of farm implements.[1]

William B. Ogden, Chicago's first mayor, seemed to speak for both his city and its people when he boasted, "at fourteen I fancied I could do anything I turned my hand to, and that nothing was impossible, and ever since . . . I have been trying to prove it, and with some success."[2] In this spirit of optimism, Chicagoans set about providing their city with such cultural amenities as schools, churches, and newspapers. But the capstone on progress was still lacking, for no sizeable community considered itself complete unless it could boast academies, colleges, and a university.

The mid-nineteenth century witnessed the founding of hundreds of colleges in the United States since the federal laissez faire attitude toward education empowered the individual states to grant college charters at will. As a result, America became a land of many small colleges rather than of a few centralized national institutions of the kind traditional in most European countries. By 1860 over 800 colleges had been founded although only about 180 of these had succeeded in gaining a permanent foothold.[3] What prompted this feverish proliferation? One reason was that in the 1800's transportation was expensive and time-consuming, particularly in the West, so that it was both more efficient and more economical to provide education close to home. That one's children—especially males—should be educated was part of the democratic creed; there was nothing particularly exclusive about these numerous small colleges. In 1850, Henry Tappan, a future president of the University of Michigan, observed, ". . . we have multiplied colleges so as to place them at every man's door."[4]

By 1840 Illinois had twelve colleges. Though some were short-lived and little better than high schools, others—like McKendree in the southern part of the state, Illinois College at Jacksonville, and Knox College at Galesburg—were institutions of collegiate rank. Adjacent areas also had their colleges: Indiana Asbury (later DePauw), which opened at Greencastle in 1837; the University of Michigan, chartered the same year; the University of Wisconsin, chartered in 1848; and Beloit and Lawrence in southern and eastern Wisconsin, chartered in 1846 and 1847. Yet Chicago and northeastern Illinois had no degree-granting institution at all.[5]

Organizing a University for the Northwest Territory

At this point the needs of a prosperous and flourishing city attracted the concern of a group of men inspired by a combination of civic and religious zeal. Most of the American colleges of this period owed their existence primarily to denominational enterprise, the Presbyterians and Congregationalists being the most active in sponsoring academies and colleges up to the 1830's and the Methodists joining them thereafter. The Methodist General Conference at this time decided to subsidize colleges, both to raise the quality of ministerial training and to discourage its young people from attending schools controlled by rival denominations. Between 1830 and 1860, the Methodist Church and associated lay groups founded thirty-four permanent schools of higher learning.[6] Of these, Wesleyan University at Middletown, Connecticut, was the oldest and best known.

As elsewhere, Methodist fervor enlivened the religious life of Chicago where, from 1848 to 1870, Methodists outnumbered all other Protestant denominations.[7] The leading Methodist congregation in the city was the Old Clark Street Church which counted many prosperous, accomplished, and public-spirited citizens among its communicants.[8] It is therefore not at all astonishing to find that it was members of this congregation who took the initiative in founding a university to make higher education available to the Methodist youth of the Northwest.

The Founders' Meeting of May 1850

On May 31, 1850, nine men gathered in a law office over a hardware store at Lake and Dearborn streets in Chicago. Young, devout, and energetic, they included a physician, John Evans; three lawyers, Grant Goodrich, Henry W. Clark, and Andrew J. Brown; two businessmen, Orrington Lunt and Jabez Botsford; and three clergymen, Richard Haney, Richard H. Blanchard, and Zadoc Hall.[9] Evans, Goodrich, Clark, Lunt, and Botsford were members of the Old Clark Street Church, where Haney was pastor. Blanchard and Hall served the city's other two Methodist churches, the Canal Street Church and the Indiana Street Chapel. Goodrich lent his office for the meeting; Botsford owned the hardware store in which it was located. Several of the group had studied at seminaries; others had learned their trades through apprenticeship. John Evans was the only one who had attended college.[10]

At this first meeting the men knelt in prayer to ask for guidance and blessing, and then resolved that ". . . the interests of *sanctified* learning required the immediate establishment of a University in the northwest, under the patronage of the Methodist Episcopal Church." A committee was appointed to prepare a draft of a charter of incorporation. Though committed to the establishment of a Methodist institution, the founders determined at the outset that this would be a lay undertaking with a private endowment. They were very clear about the economic benefits to be derived. According to John Evans's estimate, "It would cost at least a thousand dollars less for each son we may educate in the proposed university than to send him to Yale or Cambridge."[11] Thus the founders expected to solicit support from many sources and not merely from the Methodist Church. Some of the founders were experienced and avid promoters to whom the nurture of a university promised an outlet for a creative and benevolent use of their talents and energy. One of Evans's biographers recognized that "On a grand scale Northwestern was one of those children of the heart that men call hobbies."[12] Three of the original sponsors—Evans, Lunt, and Goodrich—played especially important roles in the subsequent history of the university.

The most prominent of these was John Evans, from whom the future university community would take its name. Born in 1814, Evans was the oldest son of a Waynesville, Ohio, merchant and entrepreneur. He studied at Lynn Medical College in Cincinnati, from which he was graduated in 1838. After getting married, Evans set up his practice in Attica, Indiana, and soon became active in state politics. He worked for the establishment of a state asylum for the insane in Indianapolis and then served as its superintendent from 1845 to 1848. It was there that he became familiar with many aspects of institutional management. During the same three years, Evans held a professorship at Rush Medical College in Chicago, to which city he moved in 1848. Here he achieved professional eminence as the editor of a medical journal, as the inventor of a surgical aid, and as a researcher on cholera. He also helped organize the Chicago and Illinois Medical societies.

John Evans

As a diversion from his professional pursuits, Evans relished speculating in land and acquired a considerable fortune, first in real estate and later as a railroad builder. In 1853 and 1854 he served as city alderman. Eventually his business and political activities took up so much of his time that in 1857 he gave up his medical practice altogether. In 1864, when President Lincoln appointed him governor of the Colorado Territory, he moved to Denver where he spent the rest of his life and helped found the University of Denver. Even then John Evans continued to devote time, energy, and money to Northwestern, serving as chairman of the board until his death in 1897.[13]

Born in 1815 in Bowdoinham, Maine, Orrington Lunt received little formal education and started to work in his father's store at the age of fourteen. Ambition

Orrington Lunt

drove the young storekeeper West in 1842 to the boom town of Chicago, where he began a new career as a commission merchant to the grain trade. Lulled into excessive confidence by initial success, "he bought boldly and lost in a single season all that he made," a friend later recalled, adding, "He took the lesson to heart. He never speculated again, and was afterward noted for his cautious and conservative sagacity."[14]

In 1853 Lunt retired and thereafter channeled his efforts and resources entirely into political and philanthropic causes. During the 1850's he was a committee member of the Board of Trade; a Chicago Water Commissioner; a director of the Chicago and North Western Railway Company; a founder of the Chicago Orphan Asylum; a director of the Homeopathic Hospital; and a trustee of the Dearborn Observatory. He also subsidized the Quinn Chapel, a Methodist church for Chicago blacks.

Grant Goodrich   The third major founder was Grant Goodrich. Born in Milton, New York, in 1812, he had been educated at an academy and trained in a law office in Westfield, New York. At the age of twenty-two, he moved to Chicago where he opened a real estate and law office.[15] Goodrich was an active temperance crusader and helped plan the Washingtonian Home of Chicago for Alcoholics. He also organized public schools. From 1859 to 1864 he was a Judge of the Superior Court of Chicago. Through his legal practice he became acquainted with Abraham Lincoln whose policies he later supported.

Of the laymen among the founders, Goodrich was the most involved in church work, organizing the city's first Bible society and serving as vice president of the American Bible Society.[16] Goodrich also helped found the Garrett Biblical Institute in 1853. Through his efforts, the First Methodist Church acquired its valuable tract at Clark and Washington streets in Chicago.[17] Given Goodrich's devotion to the church it was to be expected that he would urge that Northwestern be established as a Methodist institution.

The remaining founders were also newcomers to Illinois, having moved to Chicago in search of new opportunities. Botsford, for example, started a hardware store and gradually expanded his business to include wholesale as well as retail operations. He was a city councilman and, with Lunt, an organizer of the Chicago Orphan Asylum. Brown and Clark became successful attorneys, while Blanchard, Haney, and Hall served the Methodist Church in various capacities throughout Illinois.[18]

The Search   The group appointed to prepare the charter was also directed to ask the regional
for Support   Methodist conferences to share in the "government and patronage" of the university. Another committee, composed of Haney, Blanchard, and Evans, was appointed to solicit funds for the construction and endowment of the university. Over the summer, this committee found that about $25,000 could be raised locally, including pledges from the founders.* Lunt and Evans made the first subscription

---

*The first entry in the university ledger, dated September 22, 1853, itemizes subscriptions totaling $20,000. These pledges could be paid in installments over three years, which perhaps explains why the trustees initially had no money to work with.
First Ledger of the University, July 1853–June 1859, Book I, N.U. Business Office, N.U.A.

to Northwestern, each for $5,000. By the trustees' meeting of June 14, the charter committee had prepared the Act of Incorporation which designated the school as "The North Western University."*

Six Methodist conferences were sent notices on behalf of Northwestern: Rock River, Wisconsin, Michigan, North Indiana, Iowa, and Illinois. The notice, known as a memorial, did not explicitly request funds but asked each conference to choose four representatives to serve on the university's board of trustees, making explicit the founders' goal of establishing a regional, rather than a local university. The founders pointed out that because of the extensive nature of their proposed university, "but one such institution can . . . be sustained in a large district of country under the patronage of our denomination." Chicago was an appropriate place for this institution, said the letter, for the locale was "favourable for securing the means of endowment and support" and "for receiving extensive patronage." The memorial went on to spell out the founders' commitment to high educational standards in a religious atmosphere. It expressed their conviction that "the regenerate heart must be accompanied and directed by an enlightened intellect to give man the full image of his Maker." The founders foresaw Northwestern as fostering all branches of learning, particularly those preparing students for "the practical duties of life" in chosen vocations. "Our church ought to have plenty of laborers," stated the memorial, pointing out that individuals needed training to assume a useful place in society.[19] The conferences responded by electing the designated number of trustees.

During the first session of the Seventeenth General Assembly, the Illinois state legislature approved Northwestern's Act of Incorporation, which was signed into law by Governor Augustus C. French on January 28, 1851.[20] Under the terms of the charter, a self-perpetuating board of thirty-six trustees was granted the power to administer the university's business affairs, organize a faculty, adopt by-laws and grant degrees. A provision reflecting the strong religious sentiments of the founders stated that twenty-four trustees were to be appointed by the various Methodist Episcopal conferences in the Old Northwest. However, no particular religious faith was required of students or faculty. The 1851 charter also stipulated that the university should not, except on a temporary basis, hold more than 2,000 acres of land.†

Incorporation, January 28, 1851

In February of 1855, an act to amend the charter was introduced into the legislature. Like the original charter, section 2 of this act expressed the founders' Methodist convictions. It prohibited the sale under license or otherwise of any "spiritous, vinous or fermented liquors within four miles of the location of the said university." Because temperance was already a local political issue by the 1850's, the introduction of this amendment initiated a heated debate between the wets and

Prohibition Amendment of 1855

---

*This title appeared in the university's records and publications until February 1863, when "North" and "Western" were combined to form a single word in the university *Catalogue*. Thereafter, this became the official title of the university, though the earlier spelling continued to appear in newspapers and magazines for many years.

† The university's peak holdings of land in Illinois came between 1854 and 1867 when approximately 680 acres were acquired. As of October 1974, the total owned was 325 acres—249 in Evanston, 45 in Chicago, and 31 in other parts of the state. Of this total all but 69 acres were devoted directly or indirectly to educational and related uses.

drys of the state legislature. By way of compromise, the amendment was approved, provided that "so much of this act as relates to the sales of intoxicating liquor within four miles of the said university may be repealed by the general assembly whenever they think proper." However, the establishment of a "four mile limit" within which liquor was prohibited made Evanston a choice haven for temperance advocates for the next hundred years.

Highly important was section 4 of the 1855 amendment, which stated that "all property of whatever kind and description belonging to or owned by the said corporation shall forever be free from taxation for any and all purposes."[21] McKendree College enjoyed a similar exemption, as did several colleges founded subsequently, including Monmouth College, chartered in 1853, and Lake Forest University (formerly Lind) and the original University of Chicago, both chartered in 1857.[22] The granting of tax exemptions was as far as the state legislature was willing to go to support private institutions of higher learning. But this indirect help proved crucial to their survival.

By spring 1851 the requisite number of trustees had been recruited and on June 14, the board convened at the Old Clark Street Church. The first order of business was the appointment of John Evans as president of the board. The trustees then chose an executive committee, including Evans, Goodrich, and Brown to suggest a plan of operation for the university, to develop a faculty, and to find a president. As a first step the board decided to organize a preparatory school which would ready students for the proposed university. Apparently the board feared that the existing secondary schools in the area were inadequate for that purpose. Evans and Lunt were assigned the task of finding a suitable site.

Purchase of the La Salle St. Property

According to Evans, immediately after this first meeting of the board he was approached by P. F. W. Peck, one of Chicago's leading real estate dealers and offered land at the corner of La Salle and Jackson streets.* Although Evans warned Peck that "we haven't a red cent," he then went out and "raised a subscription of two thousand dollars, which was the first payment on sixteen lots. My friends came in liberally and we raised the money."[23] The contract for the sixteen lots was signed in September 1852, and the balance of $6,000 scheduled to be paid off during the following three years.[24]

Even though a site was now available the trustees could not proceed further with the preparatory school, let alone the university, because they lacked money. By June 23, 1853, however, the executive committee was ready with a plan to raise $200,000, half by donations and half by the sale of perpetual scholarships. The latter was a common device for raising money in the pre-Civil War period and offered the double advantage of providing a source of income and a ready-made student body. [25] The terms suggested by the executive committee were highly attractive—for $100 a perpetual scholarship would entitle three generations (the purchaser, his son, and his grandson) to free tuition.

President Hinman

At the same meeting the trustees took the very important step of appointing one of their number, Clark T. Hinman, a Michigan Conference representative, as the

---

*This property is still owned by Northwestern which leases it to the Continental Illinois National Bank and Trust Company as a site for its headquarters building.

6

Clark Titus Hinman, President 1853-54

Henry Sanborn Noyes, Acting President 1854-56 and 1860-67

Randolph Sinks Foster, President 1856-60

Erastus Otis Haven, President 1869-72

university's first president. Though only thirty-two years old, Hinman already enjoyed a considerable reputation as a scholar and administrator. Originally from New York, he was a graduate of Wesleyan University and had taught at the Methodist Conference Seminary in Newbury, Vermont, before becoming principal of the Wesleyan Seminary and Female Institute at Albion, Michigan.[26]

The circumstances of Hinman's election were unusual. As an out-of-state conference representative, Hinman had been impressed by the resolution of the board to establish Northwestern as the central Methodist university in the region. But when he realized that the board planned to begin by building a preparatory school on the freshly purchased Chicago site, he minced no words. As Evans recalled many years later, Hinman declared, "You keep these grounds but do not build on them. If you are going to build an academy or high school for the city of Chicago why I haven't any business here, but our idea was that you were going to build a university for the Northwest." As an alternate plan Hinman suggested that the founders go "into the suburbs on the line of some of the roads that are being built in here, buy a farm and locate your institution, lay off a village to help build the institution and sell the lots." Apparently both the plan and Hinman impressed the board for, according to Evans, when the young man concluded, "we immediately elected him President of the University and decided to locate it out on some of the lines. . . ."[27]

Orrington Lunt was appointed to head the committee which would pursue the search for a suitable location. At this time, the city of Chicago comprised the area bounded by Thirty-first Street on the south, Western Avenue on the west, and Fullerton Avenue on the north.[28] Outside these perimeters lay farms and wooded lots, with small villages clustered around major thoroughfares and railroad stops. In exploring these areas, Lunt and his committee went south as far as the Indiana border and as far north as Winnetka. They had finally settled on some property near Jefferson Park[29] when Lunt joined a friend on a drive up the North Shore. As he later recalled:

"We Had Found the Place"

. . . we drove nearly to Lake Forest. Coming back, late in the afternoon, [my friend] said he wanted to see a farmer (Mr. Snyder) who lived east of the ridge. He drove east about where Davis Street is, until he came to the old shore road, Chicago Avenue, which had been formerly the main road, but which, owing to washing away by the lake, had been abandoned to the north. He drove south to Mr. Snyder's, and found him at home. While he was employed with him with his business, I took a stroll over to the lake through the wet land, and I well remember walking over logs or planks on a portion of it.

In looking south, it was wet and swampy; looking north, I noticed the large oak forest trees. The thought first struck me that here was where the high and dry ground began. Going through the woods to the lake shore and looking north, I saw the high, sandy bluff perpendicular as at present. . . .* It continued in my dreams of that night and I could not rid myself of the fairy visions constantly presenting themselves in fanciful beauties—of the gentle waving lake—its pebbly shore—the beautiful oak openings and bluffs beyond. The impression it

*South of the Evanston waterworks at Sheridan and Lincoln.

made settled in my mind that I would not vote to accept the option for Jefferson until the committee should make another trip north. The Executive Committee were to meet that morning to close the trade. In accord with my request, it was laid over and a number of the Executive Committee went to examine it. It was a pleasant, sunny August day. We drove into what is the present campus, and it was just as beautiful as now in its natural condition. We were delighted—some of the brethren threw up their hats.—We had found the place.[30]

The owner of the land was a Dr. John H. Foster, whom Evans described as "a rich, close man." When the board approached him, Foster, who owned 400 acres on the lake shore responded, "I will not sell it for any human price, and I have an idea of starting a female academy there myself." But as Evans would later recall, he did not allow himself to be discouraged by this response. Instead, he asked Foster: "Now we want to know what you will take and [whether you will] give us [a] long time, ten years' time." Foster replied that "he would take $25,000, if we would pay one thousand down and then give him our personal security for the balance, and give us ten years time at six per cent interest, and we took it."[31] But Evans first took the precaution of finding out whether the projected line of the Chicago-Milwaukee Railroad would run through the area to which Northwestern was about to commit itself. When the answer proved affirmative, the board went ahead and in October 1853 acquired a deed to 379 acres of Dr. Foster's lakeshore farm. Evans personally put up the $1,000 down payment and assumed responsibility for the mortgage covering the balance. He and Lunt were the first to build themselves homes in what the trustees decided should be called Evanston, in honor of the man who had been the prime mover in the whole undertaking.

Purchase of the Foster Farm

The purchase of the Foster farm gave impetus to the endowment drive. According to the financial report submitted to the trustees at their annual meeting on June 21, 1854, Northwestern's financial resources now totaled almost $250,000, of which approximately $159,000 was represented by real estate and subscriptions, and the remainder by the proceeds from the sale of perpetual scholarships. The trustees offered "devout praise to God and their sincere thanks to the friends of education for the present financial success and the future prospects of the University" and proceeded to plan the organization of a College of Literature, Science and the Arts. They explained this course as follows:

As the institution is designed to be a university—at least in the full American sense of the term—with its different departments, it might appear an oversight to confine our organization to the faculty of a single department, viz.: the College of Literature, Science and the Arts; but we judge this arrangement best adapted to the wants of the country.

Organizing the College

In the Department of Medicine the various institutions already established, particularly the Rush Medical College of this city with its able faculty and efficient organization, will undoubtedly keep pace with the demands of the profession. For the present at least, this precludes the necessity of such a department in the University.

The Department of Law will be organized at no distant day in connection with our present faculty.

Thus the trustees explicitly linked the establishment of professional schools to the needs of the Chicago community. Although the new institution was also intended to serve practical ends, Evans stressed that the major benefit to be derived from the university would be its "influence intellectually and morally . . . upon the character of our city and its youth, and upon the reputation of both abroad."[32]

Founding of Garrett Biblical Institute

No provision was made for the education of women or the training of ministers at Northwestern. The trustees assumed that Garrett Biblical Institute, founded in 1853 under the auspices of the Methodist Episcopal Church, would take on the latter responsibility. The second Methodist theological school in the United States, Garrett owed its existence chiefly to the benefaction of Eliza Clark Garrett, widow of Chicago mayor Augustus Garrett. Mrs. Garrett was a member of the Old Clark Street Church, as was her attorney, Northwestern trustee Grant Goodrich. It was Goodrich who arranged for the Institute to be established in Evanston. John Dempster became its first president and encouraged a close relationship between the Institute and Northwestern. From the outset, Garrett occupied a portion of the Evanston campus under perpetual lease. Its students were encouraged to attend Northwestern classes and for thirty years the boards of the two institutions were virtually an interlocking directorate.[33]

The purchase of a site brought the establishment of the university closer and President Hinman threw himself wholeheartedly into the planning of a course of study and the search for faculty. An eloquent and persuasive speaker, he had been remarkably effective in the endowment drive, and was credited with the sale of $63,000 worth of scholarships. Then, in October 1854, Hinman was struck down by a fatal illness.[34]

Hinman's death was a severe blow to the morale of Northwestern's founders. Nevertheless, at the annual board meeting of June 14, 1855, the trustees decided to proceed with their plans for "the erection of a frame building on some portion of the University grounds for temporary purposes." Although the cornerstone did not arrive in time, on June 15, 1855, a ground-breaking ceremony did take place at the northwest corner of Davis Street and Hinman Avenue. Trustees, Methodist brethren attending a Garrett Biblical Institute conference, and a sprinkling of spectators were on hand for the occasion.[35]

Construction of Old College

Completed in November 1855 at a cost of just under $6,000, the three-story frame structure, known familiarly as Old College, was

> a building about fifty feet in width and forty feet in depth, three stories in height with an attic and a belfry. It contained six classrooms, a chapel, a small museum and halls for two literary societies, with three rooms in the attic where, with a little oatmeal for food, a few aspiring students might board themselves and compensate the university for their rent by ringing the college bell.[36]

Official Opening November 5, 1855

The official opening of Northwestern University took place on November 5, 1855, five and a half years after the meeting in Grant Goodrich's office. No formal exercises honored the realization of the founders' plan. Professor Godman later recalled that the dozen or so townspeople present included "Mr. Danks who kept the hotel; and an eccentric man by the name of Wilbur."[37]

Of the ten students who would make up the first class, only four were present to be examined by Professors Noyes and Godman, who constituted the faculty (see page 17). To the men who had labored for so many years to bring this event about, the day must have seemed anticlimactic: Northwestern lacked a president; students and faculty combined numbered fewer than twenty; and most of Foster Farm remained a swampy wilderness. Little distinguished the newborn institution from numerous similar educational ventures that would soon come to grief except the resourcefulness, experience, and dedication of its founders. All these qualities would be called on in the days ahead.

University Leadership

When the founders met to plan a university they did not concern themselves with the details of the administration and division of responsibility in the management of the prospective institution. During the more than five years that intervened between their first meeting and the opening of the university, however, they made all the major decisions concerning the financing and form and content of the university and selected its first president from their own ranks. While the trustees clearly took into account and, indeed, adopted Hinman's recommendations for the location and financing of the university, his death so soon after his appointment once more returned all responsibility to their hands.

Typically, Northwestern's board was not a resident body and met only once a year to decide on matters of broad policy. Unlike other governing boards, however, it delegated its authority to a resident executive committee consisting of the president and vice president of the board and three elected members. Empowered by a change of the original by-laws at the annual meeting of 1854 "to conduct and manage the financial concerns and business of the institution in interim of the meetings of the Trustees," the executive committee met quarterly and later monthly, and, in effect, wielded direct control over all university affairs.

The life of an antebellum college president was hectic, according to historian Frederick Rudolph. He "lived at the college, was not absent for long periods of time, probably taught every member of the senior class, knew most of the students by name, indeed probably made a practice of calling on them in their rooms."[38] Northwestern's early presidents performed all of these functions and also examined prospective students for admission. Yet there was a significant difference between the role of the president at Northwestern and at other institutions. At most colleges, Rudolph notes, "the development of non-resident control helped to change the president from being either first among equals or spokesman or leader of the faculty into something far different—representative of the governing board with significant power in his own right." At Northwestern the existence of a resident executive committee led to the retention of authority by the trustees.

This situation was less the product of a conscious policy on the part of the trustees than of circumstances. Indeed, Clark T. Hinman had been chosen as president because he was a decisive and outspoken man capable of devising workable plans for the future of the institution and the trustees followed his suggestions readily. But Hinman's death in 1854 and the creation of the executive committee in the same year changed the pattern of shared power that had begun to develop during the first president's brief administration.

*Election
of President
Randolph S.
Foster*

For the next fourteen years the university was directed almost exclusively by the executive committee, there being no president at all for eleven of those years. To begin with, the trustees took almost two years to select a successor to Hinman and even then their choice was not unanimous. Randolph Sinks Foster, the leading candidate, accepted the presidency in June 1856 on condition that he might spend his first year on leave. Born in Williamsburg, Ohio in 1822, Foster had received his formal education at Augusta College in Kentucky, and had served in a number of mountain pastorates in West Virginia before achieving a national reputation with the publication of *Objections to Calvinism* in 1849. From 1850 to 1856 he preached in two New York churches and continued to write on religious topics. He seemed a natural choice for the presidency of a Methodist university.[39]

Foster took up his duties during the depression of 1857 when Northwestern's major problems were financial and the university very much needed leadership in temporal as well as spiritual matters. But Foster—as Isaac McCaskey of the Class of 1862 recalled—spent most of his time talking of another world: "He seemed to delight to dwell on the attributes of God, the creation, the universe and kindred topics . . . and his grasp of such themes was marvelous. . . ."[40] The presidency of Northwestern, however, demanded qualities Foster did not have and in June 1860, as noted in the trustees' minutes for that month, he returned to the pulpit in New York. During his time in office it fell to the executive committee to keep Northwestern afloat.

*Leadership of
Henry S. Noyes*

Before the trustees could find a suitable replacement for Foster, the country was at war. This did not make the search any easier and, indeed, for the entire duration of the Civil War the university was led by the executive committee in concert with Henry S. Noyes, professor of mathematics and one of the first two faculty members appointed by Hinman. In fact, Noyes acted virtually as a one-man administration. In addition to being acting president, he also served as financial agent, treasurer of the faculty, secretary of the executive committee, and, by no means least, as professor of mathematics and Greek. One alumnus remembered Noyes writing business letters while he listened to his students recite their Greek.[41] Ironically, Noyes had come to Northwestern because he disliked administration, his first love being teaching. While he handled the mundane and time-consuming tasks of university administration, the executive committee continued to manage financial affairs. By June 1862 its members were so pleased with the progress of the university that they spoke of tentative plans "to enlarge our educational facilities and keep pace with the growing demands of the country."

But Noyes could not do the job of ten men forever and by the end of the war he was exhausted. At their annual meeting of July 11, 1866, the trustees received both student and faculty petitions asking for the election of a new president. The board was divided over the issue of whether to elect a president in 1866 or whether to wait until the next annual meeting. The majority voted for an immediate election, with the new president to take office September 1, 1867. At their September 1866 meeting, the trustees unanimously elected Charles H. Fowler, a Chicago minister, to the presidency of Northwestern. But their haste proved ill-advised, for Fowler indicated that he was not interested in the position. Rather desperately the trustees asked Noyes to continue, but by midwinter it was clear that his health was deteriorating seriously and in June 1867, the board accepted his resignation. At the same meeting the trustees asked the faculty to serve as a board of government and to elect one of their number to serve as an executive officer for the following year. The faculty selected David H. Wheeler, professor of English, to serve as acting president, which he did for the next two years.

When the board of trustees once again took up the appointment of a president at its annual meeting of June 1869, it selected Erastus O. Haven, a man of extensive experience in many fields. Born in Boston in 1820, Haven had become a Methodist while an undergraduate at Wesleyan University. After an early career first as a teacher and then as a minister in Massachusetts and New York, Haven had become a professor of Latin, English literature, and history at the University of Michigan in 1853. After three years he had left this post for a dual career as editor of *Zion's Herald*, a Boston Methodist weekly, and as a Massachusetts state senator. He had pursued his interest in education by serving on the Massachusetts State Board of Education and on the Board of Overseers of Harvard University and had been responsible for the law which established the Massachusetts Agricultural College. In 1863 he had returned to the University of Michigan as president of that institution, and had succeeded in holding it together during six years of personal and institutional difficulties.[42]

Election of President Erastus O. Haven

The trustees had every reason to congratulate themselves on having succeeded in bringing a man of such wide-ranging experience and accomplishments to the presidency of Northwestern. Haven had encountered good and bad times at Michigan and had handled both with tact and grace. He was a man of the cloth, yet a practiced and seasoned administrator. Unfortunately, however, he came to Northwestern under the mistaken impression that he would have plenty of money for expansion. "I now believe it was an error of judgment to leave as strong an institution [as Michigan]," he later wrote in his autobiography, "where everything had assumed the form of stability and yet where there was so good an opportunity for expansion. Still in those days of pecuniary inflation when the atmosphere was full of hope and speculation, it appeared an easy thing to command money enough near Chicago to make Northwestern University equal to any in the country."[43]

Whatever his later reservations may have been, Haven's inaugural address was visionary and spirited. His ambition for Northwestern was to see it become a university in the fullest sense. "A university," he pointed out ". . . should not be a mere college for young men presenting only one inflexible and limited course of study. It should embrace all the highest departments of investigation, philosophy, and science and all investigations and studies required for the learned professions should be prosecuted in such an institution." Conceding that Northwestern had a strong foundation, Haven went on to point out that it still "had not one quarter of the resources that a first class university could use." In a fervent plea, Haven implored his audience to support the university as never before. "I call upon you, men and women of wealth," he concluded, "I call upon you men and women not wealthy but full of enterprise and hope and Christian zeal. Remember us in your prayers . . . in your wills disposing of your property and resolve through this avenue

"Remember Us in Your Prayers in Your Wills"

REGULATIONS.

I. Every student is required to be punctually in his place at all stated exercises. In all cases where the necessity of absence can be foreseen, excuse must be rendered beforehand. In case of failure to prepare the whole or any part of an exercise, excuse may be rendered at the close of the exercise; but the fact of the want of preparation must be reported before the exercise.

II. A record of standing shall be kept according to a scale, in which the maximum credit for each exercise shall be as follows :—

For a Recitation	10
For a Composition	40
For a Select Declamation	40
For an Original Declamation	80
For a Term Examination	100

For every excused failure to prepare an exercise, the mark shall be *one-half of the maximum* belonging to the exercise. For every unexcused failure, the mark shall be *zero*. For absence, if excused, the mark shall be *zero*. For absence, if unexcused, a deduction of *ten* shall be charged. In rare cases, by permission of the Faculty, omitted exercises may be made up; they shall then be credited, according to merit, on the record

No student who shall fail to maintain a standing equivalent to an average of *five*, on a scale of *ten*, shall be advanced with his class.

III. There shall be a register of unexcused delinquencies, according to the following scale :—

For absence from recitation, reading compositions, declamation, or church, there shall be four marks charged; for absence, though excused, one mark shall be charged, unless the excuse be presented beforehand; for absence from prayers, two marks; for tardiness at any exercise, one mark. The charge for going out from any exercise shall be the same as for absence. Also, for violation of study hours, or impropriety of conduct in chapel, at recitation, or elsewhere, a number of marks may be charged, varying with the nature of the offense.

When the marks of any student amount to sixteen, he shall be admonished, and written notice of the fact shall be given to his parent or guardian. When they amount to thirty two, he shall again be admonished, and written notice shall again be given. When they amount to forty-eight, he shall be removed from the University.

At the beginning of the second and third terms of the year, the marks of each student, after twelve have been deducted, shall be charged over to him on the register of the new term; but no such charge shall be made at the commencement of a new year.

IV. Any student, who shall fail to be present at the beginning of a term, shall be charged for his absence, both on the record of standing and on the register of delinquencies, in the same manner as in the case of absence occurring during the course of a term.

V. Smoking on the premises of the University, or in public places; drinking or keeping spirituous liquors; playing at cards; profane, rude, or indecent language; noise, or any irregular conduct tending to disturb the peace of the community; and all practices opposed to morality and good order, or unbecoming a gentleman, are strictly prohibited, and shall be visited with penalties at the discretion of the Faculty. The operation of this rule shall not be suspended during any vacation.

VI. Study hours are from 9 A. M. to 12 M.; from 2 to 5 P. M., and all the evening after 7. During these hours, students are expected, when not at recitation, to be in their own rooms, applying themselves diligently to their studies.

VII. Students are required to observe the Sabbath sacredly, and attend Divine Service in the morning, and in the afternoon or evening.

VIII. No student shall be allowed to go out of Evanston without the permission of the President, or, in his absence, of some other member of the Faculty.

Northwestern University, December, 1866.

David Hilton Wheeler, Acting President 1867-69

Trustee Philo Judson, financial agent from 1852 to 1858

University Hall, completed 1869, and Garrett's Heck Hall as published in Harper's Weekly, *September 20, 1873*

to bless the world long after you have ceased to labor and plan in your present life."[44]

Eloquent though he might be, Haven's efforts to raise money for expansion proved of no avail. On the one hand the trustees retained their control over endowment income, thereby limiting the president's ability to reallocate the available assets of the university. On the other hand, the Chicago Fire of 1871 crushed any possibility of raising funds in that city. Disappointed and unable to see any hope for the future, Haven resigned in the summer of 1872 to take on the secretariat of the Methodist Board of Education. A Northwestern faculty member, Oliver Marcy, reported that the president "withheld his resignation hoping that means would be provided through which the university would be placed in a superior and independent condition. But seeing no prospect of immediately realizing these hopes, he chose the broader field of immediate usefulness to which he had been elected."[45]

Election of President Charles H. Fowler

Meanwhile, having learned that Charles H. Fowler, who had declined the presidency in 1867, was prepared to reconsider this decision, the trustees renewed their offer to him. At the October 1872 meeting of the board, his election as Haven's successor was made official. Fowler was a dynamic young Chicago minister who, in contrast to his predecessor, had had no experience in higher education. Yet the trustees believed that he had other qualities that were of greater importance. Raised in Newark, Illinois (though born in Canada in 1837) Fowler was well acquainted with the Chicago area, having studied for the ministry at Garrett after graduating from Genesee College in Lima, New York. Fowler received his degree from Garrett in 1861 as valedictorian of his class and went on to serve in various pastorates in Chicago during the 1870's.

The trustees were drawn to Fowler because of his reputation as a powerful speaker and fund raiser. In a national campaign for funds to rebuild Chicago after the great fire, Fowler touched both the souls and pocketbooks of eastern Methodists. He mesmerized audiences with his tales of the devastation. Fowler's reputation was further enhanced at the Methodist General Conference of 1872 when the young preacher narrowly missed being elected editor of the *Christian Advocate*, a national weekly of some prestige. When he became president of Northwestern Fowler was only thirty-five years old, ambitious and energetic, and held in high regard by the Methodist Church. Undoubtedly the board hoped that the new president would build a lifelong association with the university. By the mid-1870's, however, it became obvious that the economic depression which followed the panic of 1873 would make it impossible for the trustees to provide financial support for Fowler's long-range plans. By their annual meeting of June 1876, the trustees had received Fowler's resignation together with the news that he had been appointed editor of the *Christian Advocate*.

Once more disappointed by a president from whom they had had every reason to expect a great deal, the trustees proceeded with caution. From the ranks of the faculty they selected Oliver Marcy, who had come to Northwestern as professor of natural history in 1862, to become acting president.

The realization of the university's educational goals was left to the president and the faculty within the guidelines set down by the trustees in their early deliberations. As Methodist ministers, the presidents of Northwestern regarded moral rectitude

16

and religious faith as primary qualifications for faculty members. Nor were they unique in this respect. The presidents of most antebellum colleges recruited men for whom the teaching of liberal arts was synonymous with the service of religion.[46] Hinman and his successors assumed that their faculty would offer not only knowledge but moral and spiritual guidance to the young students who came to Northwestern.

The Faculty and the Curriculum

In setting down the qualifications for faculty members at their June 1854 meeting, the trustees noted that they "expected" the applicants ". . . to devote a year or more to travel in Europe, and to study in the best Eastern University, comparing their own modes of instruction and profiting by the society of the ripest scholars of the age." The faculty was to establish a curriculum designed to graduate well-rounded Christian gentlemen and to that end professors were required to set a good example by their own conduct. Interestingly enough, though all the trustees were Methodists and devoted to their church, they resolved in June 1855 "that the character and policy of Northwestern University leave the Trustees free to elect professors without reference to church connections."

Choosing a Faculty

Nevertheless, in his search for faculty Hinman naturally turned to the established Methodist institutions. His choice for the professorship of Greek language and literature, William Godman, had graduated from Ohio Wesleyan in 1846, served in the ministry in the North Ohio Conference and returned to Ohio Wesleyan in 1848 as principal of the "academic department." The following year he had become principal of The Worthington Female College. He was still there in 1854 when Hinman, who had known him at Ohio Wesleyan, invited him to Northwestern.[47]

Hinman had also known the man he selected as professor of mathematics, Henry Sanborn Noyes. Indeed, Noyes had been Hinman's student at Newbury Seminary before going on to Wesleyan University. Noyes had returned to Newbury as a teacher of mathematics and Greek, eventually becoming principal of the seminary. Hinman appointed Noyes in June 1854, but by the time the latter took up his position the following June, Hinman had died.[48]

The president's sudden death left the faculty incomplete and the curriculum unformulated. Until a new president was elected, the trustees assumed responsibility for these important matters. In June 1856 they appointed a young Yale tutor, Daniel Bonbright, to be professor of Latin. Bonbright had attended Dickinson College in his native state of Pennsylvania before going on to Yale from which he received both his baccalaureate and master's degrees. He agreed to accept the Northwestern offer on condition that he be allowed to study in Europe for two years before taking up his post. His request was granted and as a result his arrival was delayed until 1858. Bonbright was to remain at Northwestern for fifty-four years.[49]

Planning the Curriculum

The trustees were confident that the appointment of Godman, Noyes, and Bonbright, would enable Northwestern to provide students with a classical education. The faculty, however, urged that the study of science be included in the curriculum. The prevailing view at the time was that "science was a useful tool in demonstrating the wonderous ways of God"[50] so that the chief function of the professor of science differed somewhat from what it would be in years to come.

Nevertheless, James V. Z. Blaney, whom the trustees appointed as professor of chemistry in June 1857, was a man of considerable accomplishments. A graduate of Princeton University and Jefferson Medical College in Philadelphia, Blaney was a professor of chemistry and *materia medica* at Rush Medical College in Chicago, and thus a colleague of John Evans. Blaney's commitment to science had led him to take an active part in founding the *Illinois and Indiana Medical Journal* and the Chicago Academy of Science. One of his associates at the Academy, Robert Kennicott,* was invited to help establish a Museum of Natural History at Northwestern.[51]

By 1858, the trustees had reason to rejoice. Randolph S. Foster had filled the vacancy left by Hinman's death and the roster of the faculty had been completed with the appointment of Blaney. But their joy was short lived. In 1860, following the departure of President Foster, Godman decided to return to his alma mater, Ohio Wesleyan, and, following the outbreak of the Civil War, Blaney joined the Union Army as a surgeon. Thus, in 1861, only Noyes and Bonbright remained to teach the forty-three students in the college.

As a replacement for Blaney, the board hired yet another graduate of Wesleyan University, Oliver Marcy, who had taught at Wilbraham Academy, Massachusetts, and Amenia Seminary, New York, before coming to Northwestern in 1861. Some years later Marcy would earn a national reputation as the government geologist in a survey for a federal road from Idaho to Montana. In the course of his career he would examine and record over 73,000 specimens in botany, zoology, geology and anthropology and give his name to two paleontological species and a mountain peak.[52] As a faculty member and, for a time, as acting president, Marcy contributed in manifold ways to the university's development.

The Preparatory School

One of the problems that the founders had anticipated even before Northwestern opened its doors was finding students qualified to undertake college work. Although Hinman had succeeded in discouraging them from building a preparatory school first, the board and faculty did concur in the decision to establish a preparatory department in which students could spend up to three years before entering the college. The first classes began informally in 1856 and were immediately successful. Many of the parents who had purchased scholarships sent their children to Evanston for both preparatory and college instruction.

By 1859 enrollment in the preparatory department had reached fifty and at their June meeting of that year the trustees decided that the venture was capable of paying for itself. The department was reorganized as a self-sustaining school with its own principal and listed as such in the *Northwestern Catalogue* for 1860-61. This specified that applicants for the preparatory school had to be at least ten years old and had to have "some acquaintance with the elementary English branches." It is rather startling to realize that some of the students proceeding on to the college were only thirteen years old. Apparently this presented problems

*Kennicott later achieved fame for his scientific exploration of Alaska, which contributed to American interest in that territory.

18

for by 1869 the age for entering college had been raised to fourteen, and by 1873 to sixteen. Presumably, the entrance age for the preparatory school had been adjusted accordingly. In 1869 enrollment in the preparatory school was 132, almost twice the number registered in the college; by 1873 it had risen to 355 and still outnumbered the registration of 275 students in the college; by 1875, the preparatory school had 472 students and the college 345 (see Table 1-1).[53]

TABLE 1-1

N.U. STUDENT ENROLLMENT 1855-1876

Academic Year	College	Medical	Law	Preparatory	Total
1855-56	10	—	—	—	10
1856-57	21	—	—	—	21
1857-58	22	—	—	—	22
1858-59	29	—	—	—	29
1859-60	36	—	—	50	86
1860-61	43	—	—	49	92
1861-62	31	—	—	56	87
1862-63	31	—	—	60	91
1863-64	39	—	—	87	126
1864-65	39	—	—	94	133
1865-66	40	—	—	114	154
1866-67	31	—	—	105	136
1867-68	50	—	—	132	182
1868-69	71	—	—	132	203
1869-70	109	75	—	153	337
1870-71	122	100	—	185	407
1871-72	NA	NA	—	NA	NA
1872-73	145	109	54	317	625
1873-74	275	125	59	355	814
1874-75	NA	NA	NA	NA	NA
1875-76	345	147	134	472	1098

SOURCE: Northwestern University Catalogs, 1855-1876.

Admission and Degree Requirements in the College

The establishment of a preparatory course of study allowed the faculty to set high standards for admission to the college. As early as 1855-56, entrance requirements at Northwestern were comparable to those at Harvard, Yale, and Wesleyan and in the years that followed the college continually raised the requirements for entering freshmen. From the outset students were expected to demonstrate a knowledge of advanced English grammar and of mathematics through algebra as well as a reading knowledge of Greek and Latin. The faculty also required elementary knowledge of American history and, by 1866, an equivalent knowledge of Greek and Roman history. In 1868 plane geometry and quadratics were added to the list of requirements.

Once admitted, students faced a rigorous classical curriculum. When the trustees, in June 1854, devised the instructional plan for the university, they brushed with broad strokes. "In connection with the usual textbook instruction pursued in American colleges generally," they wrote, "lectures will be delivered by all the professors in their respective branches to the undergraduate classes, thus combining as far as practicable the university lecture system with collegiate textbook instruction." At the same meeting, the trustees made plans for professorships in fourteen fields including moral philosophy and logic, rhetoric and English literature, mathematics, Latin and Greek languages and literature, and natural history.*

From the beginning Northwestern offered more than one course of study. The classical course, described as the equivalent of the typical offerings in other American colleges, required four years of both Latin and Greek as well as instruction in the sciences, mathematics, philosophy, and history. The scientific course—contrary to what might be expected—differed from the classical only in that it substituted modern languages for Latin and Greek. The elective course followed an innovation at Brown University and the University of Virginia which allowed students to choose among a prescribed range of subjects in addition to meeting the requirements of the classical course. These requirements remained in force with few changes during the university's first quarter century.

The pedagogical backbone of these courses was the library and the board acknowledged this early in the university's history by authorizing an annual expenditure of $1,000 for the purchase of books in 1856. By 1870 the library had grown to 3,600 volumes. In that same year, trustee Luther Greenleaf financed the purchase of over 20,000 books—mainly in the classics—from a member of the Prussian Ministry of Public Instruction. The acquisition also included dissertations in philosophy, philology, fine arts, general history, and education, written in German. Other trustees and friends of the university also donated books during the 1870's. These included 800 volumes on business and politics given by William Deering and Lyman Gage and housed in Old College. Even though the library's holdings were not as extensive in scope or depth as those of the established eastern colleges they were yearly becoming more substantial.

The Acquisition of Professional Schools

In providing Northwestern with the means for establishing a college of liberal arts the trustees did not neglect the founders' initial goal of creating a university. With Charles S. Eliot of Harvard and the presidents of other eastern schools, Northwestern's presidents transformed the term "university" from an honorific title for liberal arts colleges into the designation for an institution which included professional as well as undergraduate curricula among its offerings. The establishment of the professional schools in the early 1870's signaled the beginning of Northwestern's status as a genuine university.

In 1869 the trustees approached the Chicago Medical College and proposed that it become affiliated with Northwestern University. Founded in 1859 it had functioned as the medical department of Lind University until the latter's removal to the suburbs.† In March 1870 the Chicago Medical College and Northwestern reached an affiliation agreement.

The Medical College

Under the terms of the contract the Medical College retained its corporate identity and title to property, continued to manage its own financial affairs, and kept its control over faculty and curriculum. Northwestern agreed to contribute

*The remaining professorships were to be in intellectual philosophy, political economy and philosophy of history; natural philosophy, astronomy and civil engineering; Latin language and literature; chemistry and its application to agriculture and the arts; geology, mineralogy, botany, and zoology; German, French, and other modern languages and literature; Hebrew and other Oriental languages and literature; fine arts and arts of design; comparative anatomy and physiology.

†At which time it changed its name to Lake Forest University.

Nathan Smith Davis, founder and first dean of the Medical School

Henry Booth, founder and first dean of the Law School

The Chicago Medical College at Prairie Avenue and Twenty-Sixth Street, forerunner of the Northwestern University Medical School, 1870-93 (Courtesy Medical School Library)

$15,000 toward the construction of a new medical building on a site in Chicago and to pay $1,000 annually toward the salary of a professor of chemistry who would also teach on the Evanston campus. There would be no tuition charge for Northwestern students who enrolled in the medical department and the university would grant all medical degrees upon the recommendation of the medical faculty. Finally, Northwestern could at any time in the future take over complete control of the Chicago Medical College with the payment of an additional $5,000. The trustees were pleased with this agreement because it secured an established medical school for Northwestern at a minimal financial risk. At this time the Medical College had a registration of 75; by 1876 this number had almost doubled (see Table 1-1).[54]

By the time of the merger the Chicago Medical College had already acquired a reputation for innovations in medical school curriculum. In fact, Nathan Smith Davis, a faculty member at the Rush Medical College, had organized Chicago Medical because he was dissatisfied with the quality of medical education in the region. At Rush, for example, formal instruction consisted almost entirely of a single set of lectures spread over a two year period. Graduation came after a three year stewardship with a "respectable physician," the presentation of a thesis, and the successful completion of examinations in "all branches."[55] In place of this, Davis proposed a curriculum which provided for a completely graded three year program with the first year devoted to elementary science, the second to more advanced courses, and the third to clinical instruction in a hospital.

Davis had advanced this curriculum in 1850 in a book entitled *The History of Medical Education and Institutions in the United States*. "If we take a glance at the vast field of medical science," he wrote, "and reflect on the discipline of the mind which ought to be brought to the task of its successful acquirement, and also on the important collateral bearing that almost every other branch of science has on it, we shall readily see that the standard recommended is defective and inadequate."[56] Davis had fought for changes in medical education at the annual meetings of the American Medical Association during the 1850's. The establishment of his own medical school in 1859 and its subsequent affiliation with Northwestern fulfilled his dream.[57]

Union College
of Law   In 1869 the trustees also began negotiations with the University of Chicago* which had had a department of law since 1859. Henry Booth, the founder of that department and still its dean, was anxious to expand the curriculum but needed additional resources to do so. After lengthy discussion Northwestern and the University of Chicago finally reached an agreement in 1873 for the joint support of what would be known as the Union College of Law, to be located in Court House Square in Chicago. In order to place "the said law department on a secure and substantial basis financially," each group of trustees agreed to contribute $2,000 per annum toward its support. If either institution failed to pay its share of the expenses for longer than six months, the department would become the exclusive property of the university not in default.[58]

---

*Not to be confused with the present institution of the same name. The first University of Chicago, founded in 1856 on the south side of the city as a Baptist institution, closed down after 30 years due to financial difficulties.

The merger gave Booth the means he needed to hire new faculty and expand the course of study from one to three years. The augmented program and a rise in admission standards raised the level of the Union College of Law in a remarkably short time. By the mid-1870's its standards and curriculum were comparable to those of Yale, Michigan and Harvard. Between 1873 and 1876, enrollment grew from 54 to 134 students (see Table 1-1). The fact that Union College remained independent of its supporting institutions was by no means unusual; most law schools were at least partially independent of their parent universities until the 1890's.[59]

The trustees directed their next effort in expanding professional education to founding the College of Technology in June 1873, with the purpose of providing quasi-professional training at an undergraduate level for students entering the fields of applied sciences and engineering. The course of study emphasized laboratory work in chemistry and physics, mechanical drawing, and techniques of construction, as well as calling for extensive reading in the sciences. "The great variety of ends which students may desire to attain," wrote Dean Oliver Marcy in his June 1874 report, "is proposed to be secured by permitting the students to give special attention to any one of the studies taught in the last two years of courses." *The College of Technology*

Neither the minutes of their meetings nor contemporary newspaper accounts give any indication that the founders intended Northwestern to be coeducational. Yet in June 1869 the trustees voted to admit young women to university classes "upon the same terms and conditions as young men," the details to be worked out by incoming President Haven. What had brought about this change? *Coeducation*

Private colleges and seminaries for women had been in existence as early as the 1830's, but many of these offered only a limited curriculum. The first coeducational institution in America was Oberlin College which opened its undergraduate program to men and women on an equal basis in 1837. But Oberlin remained very much the exception. It took the Civil War to bring about a radical change in the attitude to higher education for women. As would happen again, the exigencies of wartime propelled women into new roles and showed that they were capable of doing work previously reserved for men. Moreover the same loss of manpower that drained the labor force also diminished college enrollments. Whether for economic motives or because of more liberal attitudes, several institutions of higher learning began to admit women during and after the Civil War.

Interestingly enough, the movement toward coeducation began in the state universities in the West, possibly because fewer established traditions stood in the way of change there than in the eastern institutions. The University of Iowa had become coeducational as early as 1858, to be followed by Wisconsin in 1863 and Michigan in 1870. Northwestern might well have admitted women earlier had it not been for the existence in Evanston of another institution, the Northwestern Female College and Preparatory Department, founded in 1855 by two brothers, William P. and J. Wesley Jones. *Northwestern Female College*

William Jones had acquired the land for the school from Philo Judson, Northwestern's business manager, and had lost no time in erecting a building at Greenwood and Chicago avenues. By the fall of 1855 the school offered classes in "business," "academic," and "ornamental branches,"[60] with William, a frail, scholarly man, serving as principal and teacher. Wesley, a bombastic Indian fighter and gold miner, meanwhile raised funds by exhibiting his daguerreotypes of the Far West. The public's comparative interest in Evanston's educational institutions at the time might be surmised from the enrollment figures of 1855: Northwestern University, ten students; Garrett, four; the Jones's school, eighty-four.[61] The trustees of the university seemed disgruntled by the Jones's good fortune and what they saw as a usurpation of their name. In July 1856 they insisted that the school be renamed. William Jones, who had already distributed catalogs and brochures, refused.[62]

Evanston College for Ladies

By the late 1860's a group of Evanston women, possibly encouraged by the success of the Jones brothers' venture, decided to embark on the establishment of a college offering more advanced education for women. In the fall of 1868 these women—including Mrs. Andrew Brown, Mrs. Henry Noyes, and Mrs. L. L. Greenleaf—met to form the board of the Evanston College for Ladies. They persuaded the village of Evanston to set aside a block of land between Orrington and Sherman avenues as a building site and by March 1869 had acquired a state charter for the college.[63]

Admission of Women to Northwestern

It is surely curious that the trustees of Northwestern should have chosen this very moment, when plans for the Evanston College for Ladies were clearly under way, to vote in favor of admitting women to Northwestern. This vote was taken at their meeting of June 23, 1869, the same occasion on which they elected Erastus O. Haven to the presidency of the university, and it may well be that these two actions were connected. Both as a professor and later as president of the University of Michigan, Haven had been a champion of coeducation at a time when others considered the very idea "wild and insane," and had been instrumental in bringing women students to that institution.[64] It may well be that Haven made coeducation at Northwestern a condition of his acceptance of the presidency.

The trustees' decision was by no means arrived at without opposition. As reported in the *Chicago Tribune* of June 24, 1869, the debate was spirited. Judge Bradwell, one of the trustees, noted that he "was credibly informed that the faculty were opposed to the admission of women." Responding to this, Professor David Wheeler, head of the faculty committee, explained the faculty's anxiety over the fact that "girls required looking after, and 'police' arrangements would have to be made to keep them out of mischief." The belief that women students required special care and supervision was widespread and largely unquestioned. On this occasion Grant Goodrich cautioned that a hasty move one way or another would create a "popular *furore*" and suggested that the trustees "consult the new president [Haven], who knows all about it."

Two months later the Western College Association met at Northwestern and heard Professor Wheeler deliver a paper on "The Joint Education of the Sexes." While he remained convinced that the mingling of male and female students on equal terms and under the same conditions detracted from study and decorum, Wheeler accepted the principle that higher education should not be denied to women. To overcome the objections usually raised against coeducation he proposed the following compromise:

> Suppose that every college should organize a girl's home which should be under its general supervision and oversight, but as far as possible made a separate property interest, and put it under a special control, under which the girls would have a substitute for home oversight and direction, the rules of which should be the same as those of a good Christian home.[65]

Thus the university would provide education for women but would not assume responsibility for their conduct and character.

In the meantime the organization of the Evanston College for Ladies continued and in June 1870 President Haven reported that its board had proposed a union with Northwestern "so that lady students might have all the advantages of a university education." In effect, the Ladies' College was proposing a merger before it had even opened its doors. The trustees of Northwestern responded favorably, but made the condition that the Ladies' College secure a building to house its students. However, they showed their enthusiasm for the venture by promising to help obtain at least $50,000 for the building fund.

By February 1871, the Ladies' College board had appointed a president, Frances E. Willard, then thirty-one years old. A strict Methodist who had grown up in the Wisconsin farm belt, Frances Willard was a strong believer in intellectual and moral discipline and in the virtues of hard work. Her selection as president of the Evanston College for Ladies was no doubt aided by the fact that she had distinguished herself as a student at the Northwestern Female College and by her familiarity with the Evanston community. By the time she came to the Ladies' College she had held a number of teaching jobs. *Appointment of Frances E. Willard*

Soon after Frances Willard's appointment, the Ladies' College had made arrangements to rent the building which had previously housed the Northwestern Female College—William Jones having decided to accept a diplomatic post in China and having transferred the charter of his school to the Evanston College for Ladies. However, fearful that the College for Ladies might lose its option on the site donated by the village of Evanston because the land had been granted on condition that by 1874 at least $25,000 would have been spent on construction, Frances Willard decided to raise money to start building. She was joined in this effort by President Haven.

In April 1871 the sponsors of the Ladies' College began addressing local groups and sending circulars throughout the country.[66] These fund-raising activities were climaxed by a gigantic picnic held in Evanston on the Fourth of July, at which time the cornerstone for the new building was laid. The event, attended by nearly ten thousand, garnered pledges of approximately $30,000 to add to earlier commitments totalling $25,000.[67] The following year a group known as the Women's Educational Aid Association of Evanston purchased a cooperative boarding house, College Cottage, to accommodate women students of limited means.[68] The Evanston College for Ladies seemed off to an auspicious start.

From the time of her arrival Frances Willard and Haven worked together to further the interests of both of their institutions. Thus at the very first registration held at the Evanston Ladies' College, qualified students were able to enroll in

Charles Henry Fowler, President 1872-76

Frances E. Willard, dean of the Woman's College 1873-74

Woman's College of Northwestern University, circa 1879, later Willard Hall residence, then Music Administration Building

Old First Methodist Church, Evanston

Centennial Celebration in Fountain Square, Evanston, July 4, 1876

courses at Northwestern. Total registration at the Ladies' College that fall numbered 236, with 38 enrolled in undergraduate courses at Northwestern; 62 attending Northwestern's preparatory school; and the remaining 136 enrolled in courses given by the faculty of the Ladies' College.[69]

Frances Willard, who had resented the strict discipline imposed on her at the Northwestern Female College, introduced a system of student self-government at the Ladies' College which proved highly successful. Under this program, college women—despite the protests of alarmed parents—were permitted to become active members of the Hinman and Adelphic Literary Societies at Northwestern and to attend meetings with faculty chaperones. According to President Haven, "Here more than in the recitation room young men will learn that young women are their peers. It will break down the prejudice against women's public speech and work; it will refine the young men and develop intellectual power in the girls, precisely what each class most needs."[70]

The cooperative arrangement worked to everyone's advantage. As Haven told the board in June 1872, the fact that the Ladies' College provided "good home accommodations for young ladies" attracted more women to Northwestern than to other universities in the region. For the former, access to Northwestern classes and extracurricular activities proved equally valuable in broadening the scope of its offerings.

Nevertheless, the College for Ladies found itself in trouble when prospective donations to the building fund vanished in the flames of the Chicago Fire of 1871. As Frances Willard recalled, the fire "shrivelled our generous Fourth of July subscription list, impoverishing some of our most trusty friends . . . We furled our sails and went scudding as best we could before the blast."[71] Not only was work on their new structure discontinued but by the spring of 1872 the Ladies' College was having difficulty paying rent for its temporary quarters. At this point Haven left Northwestern and Frances Willard turned to the university's new president, Charles Fowler, for assistance.

Evanston Ladies' College Becomes Woman's College of Northwestern University

It was clearly not in the interests of Northwestern to have the Ladies' College go under, since it had supplied both the university and the preparatory school with a substantial number of students. The only feasible solution that presented itself was a merger. On June 24, 1873, the Evanston Ladies' College became the Woman's College of Northwestern University. The university trustees took over the Ladies' College's property and assumed its financial obligations, including the completion of its building. The presiding officer of the Woman's College was given the title of dean and a professorship in the university. Another clause stipulated the membership of no fewer than five women on the Northwestern board of trustees. The incorporation gave Northwestern control over the Woman's College, except for certain powers explicitly vested in the dean. As described in the 1873-74 university catalog, the college aimed to "provide a *Home for Young Women* where morals, health, and manners *can* be constantly under the special care of women."

The union had not been achieved without difficulty. Whereas Frances Willard had worked amicably with Haven, she was at odds with Fowler from the start. It appears that during the early 1860's the two had been engaged to marry and the clash of personalities which had changed their minds then came into play again at Northwestern a decade later. Fowler believed that women should be free to enroll directly at the university and live where they chose. Frances Willard maintained that the Woman's College had committed itself to supervising the women students both in the incorporation agreement and in the catalog that went out to parents. Fowler did not share this view.[72] The argument intensified when the Woman's College gave up its temporary quarters and students were forced to board with Evanston families in the fall term of 1873. To fulfill her supervisory obligations, Dean Willard devised a self-policing system consisting of thirteen rules. The Chicago papers got wind of this and pilloried Frances Willard as a tyrannical "female Bluebeard." Neither Fowler nor the faculty came to her defense.[73]

When the Woman's College building was finally completed in April 1874, Fowler and the faculty met to discuss "Home Rules for the Woman's College." Frances Willard was indignant that the faculty should usurp what she regarded as her responsibility and reduce her role to meting out discipline on their advice. Moreover, she was angry that the faculty had ignored her recommendation that women students be required to live in the college building, as well as disturbed by the faculty's decision to allow women students to attend "weekly religious services" and "university outings" with escorts.[74] What was at issue was who should have final authority in regulating the lives of women students—the faculty or Dean Willard. The possibility that President Fowler's action in reducing her power was personally motivated was not calculated to soothe Frances Willard's ruffled feelings.[75]

In a letter to the faculty dated June 16, 1874, Frances Willard made her position clear. She stated that she frequently talked to parents who "contemplate entrusting their daughters to the care of the Faculty, and who are not entirely disabused of old-time prejudices against mixed schools." Such parents, she said, wanted assurance that their daughters' social relations would be regulated. With the faculty in charge, she continued, regulations and discipline were not systematically enforced: "I have found it extremely difficult, indeed impossible, to impress [the young ladies] with the dignity and importance of such exceptions to the general rule as the Faculty has seen fit to make." As an example she noted that women students were interpreting "university events" in the broadest manner and accepting escorts for all types of social activities without seeking permission. She felt that she no longer had the power to take necessary measures in dealing with discipline problems and found herself personally compromised when mothers asked her "if this were not a strict school." While her idea of supervision was not "the old-fashioned boarding-school system, which I never advocated" she believed that the university should frankly state its policies to inquirers and patrons. As her current situation conflicted with previous understandings with the administration, the faculty, and parents, she found herself with no alternative but to resign.[76]

Dean Willard's Resignation

Frances Willard went on to become a leading figure in the Woman's Christian Temperance Union. Though she appeared in a conservative role in her conflict with the president and faculty of Northwestern, she was, in fact, an ardent advocate of woman's suffrage and active participation in political life. She continued to live in Evanston and maintained an interest in the university.

Curiously her successor at Northwestern, Ellen Soulé, seems to have been more conservative than Frances Willard regarding social life for women students. Before assuming her post she insisted that the literary societies be completely segregated. A former principal of a women's school and a student of French culture, Ellen Soulé had come to Northwestern from New York.[77] That Fowler would grant Dean Soulé's conditions when he had provoked Frances Willard into resigning over much milder issues suggests that their dispute went beyond their personal differences to the broader question of how much power the dean of women should exercise. Once Frances Willard left, the university was free to assert full control over the Woman's College.

The Conservatory of Music

Northwestern's first women students were free to enroll in all of the undergraduate classes of the university. Many of them, however, confined themselves to the study of literature and the fine arts. The Evanston College for Ladies had previously staffed its own departments in art and music—pursuits considered most appropriate for women. During its brief existence, the Ladies' College department of music, headed by Professor A. O. Mayo, had gained a particularly favorable local reputation. As a result of the 1874 merger this department became the Northwestern University Conservatory of Music, forerunner of the present School of Music. For many years the Conservatory, which was located on the top floor of the Woman's College building, continued to draw a student body consisting largely of women. Mayo remained its director until 1876.

Women and the Professional Schools

The entrance of women into the two university-affiliated professional schools proceeded more slowly. Though the Union College of Law placed no restrictions on coeducation, its first women students did not enter until the 1880's. Because of conventional notions of propriety, the medical profession resisted training men and women in the same classrooms. For a brief period, in 1868, the Chicago Medical College had admitted women, but when the faculty complained that mixed classes were "disruptive," the idea was abandoned.[78]

Student Life in Early Evanston

By current standards Northwestern students led a very confined life during the university's first two decades in Evanston. The faculty and administration exercised strict authority and kept undergraduates occupied with prodigious recitations and frequent attendance at chapel. But there were compensations. Because of their sparse numbers, students, faculty, and townspeople became well acquainted, and Evanstonians shared in the extracurricular activities that brought variety to the students' lives. By contrast, students at the medical and law schools in the city divided their time between home and school and devoted most of their attention to their future careers.

The College of Literature, Arts and Sciences began offering courses at all four levels of undergraduate instruction in Evanston in the fall of 1858, but a nationwide depression, followed by the Civil War, combined to prevent any marked expansion in the student body during the succeeding decade. Enrollment in the college did not reach a total of 50 students until the fall of 1867, then rose rather rapidly aided by the acquisition of the Woman's College in 1873. By 1876 there were 345 students in the college (see Table 1-1).

Though envisioned by the founders as an institution which would serve primarily the states of the Northwest, the university soon began to attract students from other regions. Undoubtedly the midwestern Methodist conferences represented on Northwestern's board encouraged their young people to attend the institution and various missionary groups must also have promoted the new university. Of the forty-three students who registered for the 1860-61 academic year, for example, two each were from Michigan, Pennsylvania, New York, and Maryland and one each came from Indiana, Ohio, Wisconsin, Canada, and England.[79] In spite of the distance, Northwestern also had a group of students who commuted daily from Chicago. Since all students were required to observe the Sabbath, the faculty resolved that "day students from Chicago were to remain in Evanston on Sunday except by permission on special occasions."[80]

For students not on perpetual scholarships, tuition for the three-term academic year was $45; the library fee $3; and incidental expenses $6. Other expenses varied according to the habits of the students. Parents having minor sons were advised to entrust their funds to a member of the faculty, "who will attend to the payment of their bills and render an accounting thereof regularly, charging for the service a commission of three percent. By this course one of the strongest temptations of the young to vice will be avoided."[81]

That vice lay forever in wait for the university students was taken for granted by the faculty, who spent many of their meetings discussing discipline problems. Nor is this to be wondered at for students were confronted by a formidable list of rules. To begin with, no student could leave Evanston without the president's permission. Smoking, drinking, card-playing, profane language, noise, and other practices "unbecoming a gentleman" were forbidden. Three hours every morning, another three in the afternoon, and all evenings after seven were set aside for study, during which time students were "expected, when not in recitation, to be in their own rooms applying themselves diligently to their studies."[82] Their academic standing—as well as absences from recitations, daily prayers, or the two Sunday religious services— were recorded and made available to parents.

For a student's view of life at Northwestern we have Lewis Elmer Sims's weekly letters to his parents from the fall of 1874 to the spring of 1877. "They have the most examining here," complained Sims at the end of his first term, "and they are terrible hard. Folks need not say that this is not a good school." By the following term, Sims was near rebellion: "a student is a slave, a slave to his studies. He leaves home and has to work hard and anxiously or if he doesn't he will have to drop out." As he finished his sophomore year, Sims was still feeling hard-pressed. "I have now only two studies, but I am behind in both and it makes me study. I believe that they are worse about giving long lessons than they used to be."[83] And he may well have been right, for as noted, the aim during these years was to raise standards both in the preparatory school and in the college. In a rather bleak assessment of student life at Northwestern at that time, Professor Daniel Bonbright some years later

"They Have the Most Examining Here"

Baseball team which won the College Champion of the West title in 1875

Old Gym, which opened in 1876 (Courtesy Evanston Historical Society)

commented: "I suspect there was little escape from lonely isolation save in the self-forgetfulness of hard work."[84]

Despite the substantial increase in enrollments in the college during the early 1870's, the Northwestern student body remained a close-knit group. Students who entered college at the same time were generally taught as a group throughout their four years at college, and this practice made the class unit the single most cohesive organization among students. Inevitably some students found an outlet for their energy and high spirits in pursuing class rivalries. Sims wrote his parents about several freshman-sophomore skirmishes, one of which led to the suspension of one of the participants.[85] A more constructive manifestation of this competition was the presentation of class gifts to the university. The Class of 1872 attained a certain distinction when it presented the university museum with an eleven-foot elephant skeleton.

The focus of student social life was to be found in the undergraduate debating societies to which most students belonged. The Hinman Society was founded during the first year, in 1855; the Adelphic Society in 1860; and the Ossoli Literary Society for women in 1874. The weekly debates offered by the societies ranged over a wide field of subjects. Among the topics debated at Hinman Society meetings, for example, were the propositions that: capital punishment should be abolished; secret societies should be prohibited; property should be made a qualification for the exercise of political suffrage; the moon and planets are inhabited; the mind of woman is inferior to that of man; and, President Andrew Johnson should be impeached.[86] *Debating and Literary Societies*

Since university courses took the form of lectures and recitations, it was the debating societies which gave students the opportunity to develop their skills in formulating and expressing their own ideas and encouraged their interest in contemporary public issues. By the 1870's the debating societies began to engage in intramural debates and oratorical contests and in 1872 a Northwestern team met a University of Chicago team in the first intervarsity debate.[87]

Before long the debating societies broadened their scope to include music and literature in their programs and eventually became as much literary as debating societies. In January 1871 the Hinman and Adelphic societies undertook the joint publication of a monthly magazine, the *Tripod*. Typical of articles published during the first year were: "Geological Rambles"; "Why Do We Study the Classics"; and "The Howling Dervishes of Constantinople." It does not appear to have been a frivolous publication.

In 1859 a chapter of Phi Delta Theta was formed at Northwestern only to disappear when its members enlisted in the Union Army. The first of the Greek letter societies had sprung up in the East during the antebellum period and had aroused some opposition from educators and others because their secret codes and rituals were perceived as undemocratic and potentially subversive in character.[88] The Northwestern faculty, however, seems to have posed no objections to the establishment of Greek letter societies on campus. A Phi Kappa Psi chapter was formed in 1864, a Sigma Chi chapter in 1869, Phi Kappa Sigma in 1872, and Beta Theta Pi in 1873.[89] In the course of the next few years conflicts began to develop *Greek Letter Societies* between the Greek letter societies and other campus organizations.[90] Undoubtedly competition for membership played a part in arousing the opposition of the established student societies, but the Greek letter fraternities had come to stay.

Athletics Students also sought relief from their studies in athletic activities, especially baseball. From informal beginnings the game developed into an organized team sport at the university during the 1870's. During this decade the Northwestern team played other regional colleges as well as professional teams, such as the "Chicago Acmes" and "Chicago White Stockings," and in 1875 won the title of "College Champion of the Northwest."[91] Football, a newer game, was relatively unknown at Northwestern at this time.

Social Diversions The programs offered by the Hinman and Adelphic societies, athletic activity, and the opportunity for friendships afforded by the fraternities provided some relief for men students from the long hours of study described by Sims and Bonbright. For women the opportunities for diversion were somewhat more limited. Few of their names are found in *Tripod* reports on student affairs and few seem to have sought positions of leadership on campus. On the other hand, the Woman's College had its own schedule of teas, receptions, dinners, and musical recitals and even invited men to some of these events. There were also other functions that brought men and women students together—though always under watchful eyes—including class parties, sleigh rides in winter, boat rides on Lake Michigan in summer, and occasional dances.

Lewis Sims has left an account of the mores at a Woman's College reception in a letter he wrote his parents in April 1876. "Firstly get acquainted with some lady and secondly promenade with her until you or she gets tired and then take another one and so on until you or she gets completely tired out and then go home. As for myself, I got acquainted with a few young ladies, but not as many as I would wish for, but I did not do much at promenading." From other Sims letters it appears that literary games, puzzles, and music might also contribute to the evening's entertainment.[92] As Mrs. Andrew Brown, the trustee's wife, admitted in later years, "our ingenuity was sometimes taxed to the utmost to provide amusement for young people who might not indulge in card playing or dancing."[93]

Living Conditions The Woman's College building, later named Willard Hall, was one of two university residence halls on campus. First occupied in the spring of 1874, it was described by reporters as built in the American-Italian style. It was, in fact, designed in the baroque style then popular in France. Constructed of brick and stone it sported a mansard roof with ornate dormers. In addition to accommodations for 135 students, it contained a chapel and public rooms. Men students for the most part boarded with families or in rooming houses throughout Evanston, often in poorly heated and ill-lit rooms which made studying uncomfortable. A handful lived in the only other campus residence, Dempster Hall, which Northwestern took over from Garrett in 1868 following the latter's construction of a larger facility. Dempster served as a Northwestern dormitory until it burned down in January 1879. From time to time an outbreak of an epidemic forced the university to take special measures to protect its students. In 1863, for example, the university quarantined students housed in a local hotel where smallpox had broken out.[94]

Since students lived very much as part of the Evanston community, the university administration took great care to stress the high moral tone of the town. The *Catalogue* of 1858-59 noted:

> We have never seen a community anywhere in which so large a preponderance of opinion was strictly moral and religious. . . . Parents may send their sons here with the utmost confidence that they will be placed at a distance from temptation and be brought under the most wholesome influences.

"We Knew Everyone in Town"

The administration could speak with such confidence because Evanston had been planned and had developed as a college community. Originally laid out by John Evans, Andrew Brown, and Philo Judson, the village of Evanston had 831 inhabitants by 1860.[95] Many of these were affiliated with Northwestern, Garrett or the Female College and developed a way of life that reflected shared interests. Students were part of this life and mingled freely with local residents. "Those were happy days," remembered Thomas Strobridge, a theological student of the early 1860's. "We knew everyone in town, and all the Christians in the place filled up the meeting house."[96]

There was a distinctly religious tone to life in Evanston. As might be expected, the Methodists were the largest and most prominent sect, but by 1873 nearly a dozen denominations were represented as well.[97] Some observers found the town oppressively self-righteous: "A first visit . . . is like entering the holy precincts of a cloister, where one is afraid to laugh, or speak, or smoke, for fear of committing some horrible impropriety, and shocking the sensibilities of the Sisters." But on further acquaintance the same commentator decided that despite their outward austerity, Evanstonians were "kindly, hospitable, and courteous."[98]

Impact of the Civil War

Evanston had been founded at a time of great national stress and the political events of the late 1850's engaged the interest of the entire community. Northwestern students debated the resolution: "Judging from the Political Course of the Two Men, Stephen A. Douglas is more worthy of a seat in the United States Senate than Hon. Abe Lincoln."[99] The decision in this case was in the affirmative. Lincoln himself visited Evanston the year before the war and was honored by a reception.[100] When President Lincoln called for 75,000 volunteers to defend the Union following the fall of Fort Sumter, the Evanston community responded with fervor. Students at the Female College resurrected a flag which they proudly displayed over their building.[101] Methodist Bishop Matthew Simpson, a strong supporter of the antislavery cause, delivered a sermon that Frances Willard later described as:

> an assault upon heaven for the overthrow of human bondage and the triumph of our Union Arms as no soul among us had ever thought to hear from human lips. The very air seems surcharged with the thunder and lightning of God's wrath against secession and slavery.[102]

The response of Northwestern students was reflected in enrollment figures. Of the thirty-six students registered in 1859-60, twenty-three took part in the war, most of them serving in various Illinois regiments. The graduating class of 1863 was reduced to two, one of whom had enlisted and the other of whom had been rejected for physical disability. Three of the five graduating seniors in the class of 1864 were

Meeting place of the Hinman Literary Society in University Hall, a focus of student social life

Library in University Hall, 1875

excused from delivering their commencement orations because they were already in the army. Altogether a total of eighty-three Northwestern graduates, undergraduates, and preparatory students—including two who enlisted in the Confederate army—took part in the conflict. Seven of these lost their lives, as did Alphonso Linn, tutor in Latin, and one of the two faculty members to serve in the war.* The diary of Merritt C. Bragdon, a student in the preparatory school, brings home the sadness that hung over the community during these years:

> This evening about five o'clock Willie Pratt, a returned soldier, died. He had been in a rebel prison and they had *starved* him. . . . Oh, this war is dreadful— it has taken away *so* many who were so good. Among the number are Prof. Linn of whom I thought so much. He was my teacher and friend. And Mr. Lyford—he too was so good.[103]

Evanston also honored the heroism of Edward Spencer, a Northwestern student who conducted a valiant rescue operation when the excursion steamer, *Lady Elgin*, was wrecked off the coast of Wilmette in 1860. Though several hundred people perished in the accident, Spencer single-handedly saved the lives of seventeen.† The drama of the disaster attracted national attention and led to the establishment of a lifeboat station some years later. In 1871 the United States Navy supplied Northwestern with a lifeboat to be manned by a university officer and student crew. The heroic implications of their duties gave crew members considerable status on campus.[104]

Edward Spencer and the Wreck of the Lady Elgin

In the early years of their existence Evanston and Northwestern were inextricably bound together by an identity of interests. Since the university's chief asset consisted of Evanston real estate, the town fathers—who were also the university's founders—were bent on developing the town to its fullest potential. As early as 1855 they began a program of drainage works to bring more of the low, swampy land into use. By 1870 the population of Evanston had risen to 3,062.[105] The following year a gas utility brought street lighting to the town, and in 1874 the Evanston Water Works was established. [106]

Town and Gown

Evanston community leaders took the occasion of the Chicago Fire of 1871 to recruit new residents from among the displaced families. The *Evanston Index*, founded in June 1872 as the town's first newspaper, led this movement by announcing: "There can be no question, that, as a place of residence, Evanston has no superior and few equals anywhere in the West."[107]

Early Evanston was in many ways self-contained but from the outset its development foreshadowed its evolution as a suburb. As early as 1855 the Chicago and Milwaukee Railroad established a depot on Davis Street and John Evans became one of the first commuters as he "rode back and forth on the cars" each day to his office in Chicago.[108] By 1873 service had expanded to ten round trips daily. Remarked the *Index*, Evanston's "convenience to Chicago enables its residents to do business in the city."[109]

---

*The other was Dr. J. V. Z. Blaney, professor of chemistry.

† As a result of over-exertion and exposure, Spencer's health was permanently damaged and he had to forego both his education and his plan for a career in the ministry. A plaque in his honor was dedicated in September 1935 at Patten Gymnasium. It bears the words which Spencer reportedly uttered as he collapsed from exhaustion: "Did I do my best?" *Edward Spencer file, N.U.A.*

Thus in its first two decades the university community grew much as Northwestern's founders had intended. Gradually the university developed a life of its own while the town that had grown up around it developed its own civic character and interests. Town and gown remained close, but Evanston had become more than merely the site of Northwestern University. Indeed so much was this the case that Evanstonians began to fret over the university's tax-free status, and in 1874 Evanston initiated the first of many unsuccessful attempts to have the courts remove the university's exemption from taxation of its property and facilities.

And what of the graduates of the Northwestern of those early decades? The founders had hoped that an education at Northwestern would foster Christian attitudes and prepare its recipients for a life's work. By 1876 Northwestern had awarded bachelor's degrees to 213 men and women. A survey at the turn of the century showed that a third (72) of these had entered the ministry; another third was engaged in business (35), law (23) and medicine (13). The remainder of the group included 23 in education, 14 in politics and government service, 11 authors and editors, 2 druggists, 1 chemical scientist, 3 agriculturists, and 2 temperance workers.* The university was justifying the hopes of its founders.[110]

Finances At the annual meeting of the trustees in June 1857, Philo Judson, Northwestern's financial agent, reported that the finances of the university were ". . . in a most healthy condition. Seldom, if ever, has it been the good fortune of an institution, unless endowed by very liberal bequests, to present in its infancy such a pecuniary basis as is shown by the Exhibit herewith submitted."

The Exhibit referred to by Judson indicated that Northwestern in 1857 had assets valued at $344,244.00, two-thirds of which were in the form of real estate. All but a small fraction of the rest was represented by pledges of gifts and contracts for the balance due from the purchasers of scholarships, both of which were payable in installments. With liabilities totalling $28,399.00, including the mortgage of $24,000 owed on the purchase of the Evanston campus, the university could boast of an impressive net worth of $315,845.00.

The trustees were sufficiently encouraged by Judson's report to inaugurate a building program. This plan, outlined in the university's *Circular* for 1858-59, stated that anyone contributing $10,000 would have the privilege of endowing and naming a museum, library, or other permanent building. Anyone willing to give $5,000 could endow a professorship bearing his name with a guarantee by the trustees that they would appropriate property worth $15,000 to ensure its permanent support.† Recognizing that the *Circular* was not an appropriate place for such an appeal, the trustees nevertheless concluded, "We trust that God will move some noble hearts to undertake this great work! Who will accept the opportunity, and do with the gifts of a gracious providence as bestowed upon him, a deed worthy of the noble and good? . . . Let those who are seeking the right place for the investment of their funds look this way."

* Five of the remainder listed no careers and nine died shortly after graduation.

† One feature of the proposed plan was the provision that anyone who subscribed $5,000 or $10,000 could retain the principal "for any length of time, provided always that it is satisfactorily secured and subject to an annual interest of ten per cent."

Unfortunately, the campaign was launched during the depression that followed *Panic of 1857* the panic of 1857 and was therefore largely unsuccessful. Meanwhile the trustees' *and Depression* concern over the lack of permanent buildings gave way to the more immediate need to avoid deficits on the university's current operation. A resolution adopted by the board on June 29, 1859, stated:

> We are imperatively required in the discharge of our trusts to bring the current expenses of this Institution within its available income and the executive committee [is] instructed to adhere strictly to this principle.

In order to meet the deficit of $3,000 for the academic year 1958-59 all the members of the faculty, including President Foster, agreed to accept unproductive real estate in lieu of a portion of their salaries. The trustees added the proviso that when the income of the university was sufficient to pay the faculty in cash, such property could be sold back to the university. Six of the trustees also purchased land at this time on the latter basis.

The income and expenditure data for this period are not available, but apparently within two years the worst of the financial pressure was over. On June 18, 1862 the Trustees' Auditing Committee reported to the board:

> We find our financial affairs in a prosperous condition, and believe if the policy instituted two years since of keeping our annual expenses within our income be adhered to, we shall soon be able to realize sufficient [revenue] from sales and rent of our large landed property to enlarge our educational facilities and keep pace with the growing demands of the country.

A continued improvement in the university's financial prospects in the post-Civil War period allowed the trustees to turn their attention to the construction of the university s first permanent building. In July 1865, they appropriated $15,000 for a building fund to which an additional $10,000 was to be added from the sale of non-income producing property. They also appointed a financial agent to secure additional pledges. Construction would begin as soon as enough subscriptions had been obtained to underwrite the building. In September 1866 the executive committee was authorized to settle with the members of the faculty "for all arrearages of salary in former years and if the funds of the university will allow to pay each professor an addition of $500 to the present salaries." Two months later came the announcement that John Evans was donating $25,000 for the endowment of a chair of mental and moral philosophy.

The prospects for an increase in the university's income from rents were greatly enhanced when the La Salle Street property—acquired by Evans in 1852—was leased to a small group of Chicago businessmen in March 1867. Three years later this group formed the Pacific Hotel Company which undertook the construction of the Grand Pacific Hotel on this site. In drawing up the lease, the trustees shrewdly anticipated a rise in Chicago property values and arranged for a sliding scale of payments based on a re-evaluation of the property at four ten-year intervals beginning in 1880.*

---

*The arrangement called for fixed annual rentals of $3,000 during 1867-71; $4,000 during 1872-74; and $6,000 during 1875-79. Thereafter annual payments were to be 7½ per cent of the value of the property as determined at the beginning of each re-evaluation period. *Trustees' Minutes, March 4, 1867.*

Construction of the campus building was begun in 1867 and completed two years later. It was named University Hall. Describing its dedication in the *Chicago Republican* of September 9, 1869, a reporter wrote approvingly:

> The edifice is somewhat irregular in plan and is equivalent to about 70 by 100 feet, has a basement, three full stories and an attic story under the roof. The basement is fitted with laboratory and lecture room, closets, etc. On the main floor is a large classroom, though it will be temporarily used for chapel purposes. The second story is divided off into professors' and class rooms. The story above contains class rooms, library, reading and professors' rooms. The attic will be devoted to a museum and dormitories. The style of the edifice is gothic with steep roofs. It is surmounted with towers, turrets, mansards, etc. which add much to its picturesqueness. In the main tower, at an elevation of 120 feet, is a lookout from which may be seen on a clear day the towers and spires of Chicago, twelve miles distant. The building is admirably constructed of brick and stone—the latter being rock-face, which gives it a rich, massive and substantial appearance, comparing notably with any university structure in the land.

Local pride aside, the concluding sentence reveals that the provision of much needed classrooms, offices, and facilities was only part of what University Hall had to offer. Also important was the symbolic value of its "rich" and "substantial" appearance, which suggested that Northwestern had left behind its early struggles and was here to stay.

TABLE 1-2
N.U. BUDGETED RECEIPTS AND EXPENDITURES: 1869-1876
(In Thousands of Dollars)

Year	1869-1870	1870-1871	1871-1872	1872-1873	1873-1874	1874-1875	1875-1876
Receipts							
Tuition	$4.8	$6.1	$5.6	$8.3	$13.1	$15.7	$16.6
Rents[a]	8.1	10.6	10.3	17.2	20.2	18.2	15.7
Interest[b]	7.1	5.5	7.4	6.6	6.5	8.3	2.4
Gifts and Subscriptions[c]	1.6	2.6	0.3		0.7		
Total	21.6	24.8	23.6	32.1	40.5	42.2	34.7
Expenditures							
Instruction	$18.9	$18.7	$19.5	$17.9	$36.3	$35.0	$26.9
Library	0.5	0.1	0.6	0.4	—	0.1	0.4
General Administration[d]	4.0	5.7	6.9	8.8	8.6	9.4	11.1
Interest	2.9	4.8	6.2	5.5	5.1	15.6	15.8
Physical Plant	0.8	0.5	—	—	—	0.1	0.7
Other[e]	1.3	—	0.4	—	—	—	—
Total	28.4	29.8	33.6	32.6	50.0	60.2	54.9
Surplus (deficit)	(6.8)	(5.0)	(10.0)	(0.5)	(9.5)	(18.0)	(20.2)

Source: Northwestern University Treasurer's Reports, 1870-1876

[a] Income from leases on university owned property.
[b] Income from mortgages and securities held by university.
[c] Contributions for special purposes, including salary supplements and current deficits.
[d] President's office, cost of catalogs and advertisements.
[e] Miscellaneous expenses.

There was every reason to view the future with optimism. Between 1865 and 1871 the university's income had increased from $8,800 to $24,800 (see Table 1-2). Anticipation of continued growth in the value of the university's productive real estate holdings had encouraged the trustees to borrow the funds for an ambitious program of expansion, including construction of the Medical College, University Hall, and the Woman's College.

Then came the panic of 1873 followed by a major depression and the university's financial prospects took an unexpected turn. As Table 1-3 shows, the value of productive real estate began to decline instead of rising. Equally serious for Northwestern was the fact that by 1876 interest payments were absorbing almost half of the university's income of $34,700. Northwestern's financial position was further threatened by a suit instituted in 1874 by the city of Evanston to collect taxes on the real estate held by the university in the city. At their annual meeting in June 1875 the trustees expressed confidence that the suit would be settled in favor of the university. Nevertheless, the amount of taxes claimed by the city for the two years, 1873 and 1874, was alarming, amounting to over $10,000.

Panic of 1873 and Its Aftermath

TABLE 1-3
N.U. RESOURCES AND LIABILITIES, 1868-1876
(In Thousands of Dollars)

Year	Physical Plant[a]	RESOURCES Productive Property[b]	Non-Productive Property[c]	Gross	LIABILITIES[d]	NET
1868	$140.7	$328.5	$279.0	$748.2	$44.0	$704.2
1869	178.3	282.5	300.0	760.8	38.1	722.7
1870	150.0	319.7	360.6	830.3	51.0	779.3
1871	257.0	462.7	521.4	1,241.1	65.4	1,175.7
1872	282.0	549.8	503.6	1,335.4	66.6	1,268.8
1873	276.5	678.3	490.8	1,445.6	60.0	1,385.6
1874	380.5	723.2	522.1	1,625.8	142.6	1,483.2
1875	412.7	666.5	593.0	1,672.2	182.2	1,490.0
1876	413.4	623.9	621.1	1,658.4	185.5	1,472.9

Source: Northwestern University Treasurer's Reports, 1868-1876.

[a]Value of property used for educational purposes.
[b]Capitalized value of income producing property.
[c]Estimated value of non-income producing property, chiefly unimproved real estate.
[d]Bonds, notes and accounts payable.

Because of their anxiety over the university's declining financial condition, the trustees appointed a special Ways and Means Committee to develop a policy to balance the budget. During this period of depression there was little immediate prospect of raising enough money through real estate sales to pay off the university debt and so reduce the mounting interest payments. As the Ways and Means Committee gloomily predicted in April 1876,

> This year will prove to be the worst one that we have passed through since 1858, from present indications, so far as relates to the selling or leasing of our property. And in this regard we but keep company with most or all of the prominent real estate owners of Chicago and vicinity.

Northwestern's situation was not unique; at this time even well-established schools like Harvard and Yale found themselves short of funds.[111] Indeed, the devastating impact of the panic was just one more indication of the lack of stability in university financing across the country. From the founding of Northwestern in 1851 until the crisis in the mid-seventies, the trustees had followed a conservative plan for expansion; frivolous spending was hardly the style of these men. Yet, as this situation showed, even the most cautious university expansion was vulnerable in a national depression.

*Oliver Marcy, Acting President
1876-81*

*Joseph Cummings,
President 1881-90*

Law School, Class of 1877, Dean Henry Booth seated at desk to the right

2

AFFILIATION AND EXPANSION
1876—1890

The pattern of university leadership established during Northwestern's first *Leadership* quarter-century remained virtually unchanged during the next fifteen years. The trustees continued to deal with all financial matters while the presidents concerned themselves with faculty, curriculum, and student affairs. But in many ways their responsibilities overlapped. The economic crisis of the mid-1870's forced the trustees to tighten their control over all university operations and inevitably their financial decisions affected educational policy. Meanwhile the presidents were pressed to devise means of attracting and keeping students without lowering academic standards. Much hinged on the energy and talents of the trustees and administrators during this difficult period.

While founders John Evans and Orrington Lunt continued to play a leading role in the affairs of the university—Evans remaining president of the board until 1894 and Lunt succeeding him and holding that position until 1897—several of the men who joined the board during the 1870's and 1880's went on to become highly influential in guiding the fortunes of the institution. In the course of long years of service they provided a continuity and stability of leadership which helped offset the somewhat rapid succession of presidents.

Among the most active of these board members were William Deering, trustee *The Board* from 1875 to 1913, and president of the board for the last 16 of these years; Thomas Hoag, trustee since 1864, treasurer from 1865 on, and agent as well from 1876 to 1892; and Frank P. Crandon, trustee from 1883, assistant secretary from 1886 to 1891, and secretary and auditor from then on until 1919.[1] Deering would become a dedicated benefactor who contributed both his experience as a businessman and entrepreneur and his money to the university, while Hoag and Crandon devoted much time to the financial and technical management of the university.

A former dry goods merchant, Deering had become one of the most enterprising and successful manufacturers of harvesting equipment in the country.[2] Thomas Hoag had built a successful wholesale grocery business before becoming the president of an insurance company and, later, the founder of what is now the State

43

National Bank in Evanston.[3] Frank P. Crandon came from a somewhat different background. A former school principal and veteran of the Union Army, he had served as superintendent of a government bureau for refugees, freedmen, and abandoned lands in Virginia before returning to Illinois in 1873 to become tax commissioner of the Chicago and North Western Railway. When he became a trustee of the university, Crandon had already served as a village trustee and member of the board of education of Evanston.[4]

Such were the men who would help steer the university through the troubled years that followed the financial panic of 1873. They were fortunate in the caliber of the two administrators with whom they shared their task, Oliver Marcy and Joseph Cummings.

Acting President Marcy

When Oliver Marcy agreed to become acting president in 1876 his powers were sharply circumscribed not only by the economic distress in which the university found itself but also by the interim nature of his appointment. But this in no way deterred him from expressing views with considerable vigor. In his annual reports—models of well-organized and clearly formulated observations, criticisms and ideas—Marcy reminded the trustees of their obligation to maintain and improve the quality of education at Northwestern.

Summarizing the "very unfavorable" circumstances under which his first year as acting president had begun, Marcy, in his report for 1876-77, emphasized the difficulty of maintaining an adequate academic program in the face of a financial crisis which made it impossible to replenish a reduced faculty. Graphically he outlined the faculty's dilemma:

> To the faculty that remained was given the task of maintaining with its reduced means, the character of the institution for good instruction. This was hardly possible. To place Logic in the hands of the professor of natural history and Rhetoric in the charge of the professor of civil engineering, and have the work done well could not reasonably be expected. But the circumstances compelled us to do this. We are glad to be able to say that notwithstanding this educational absurdity we heard no complaints from the students.

Turning to the question of how such crises might be avoided, Marcy urged that the trustees and faculty develop clear and consistent educational policies. The failure to do so in the past, he thought, had led to haphazard decisions. As he explained, "The varying conditions of our finances have given rise to times of great depression of interest and activity, and again to times of inordinate hope, expansion and unjustifiable debt." He was particularly distressed that during the early 1870's the number and variety of courses had been allowed to increase beyond the university's capacity to give them adequate financial support. He urged the trustees "to place the support of the essential departments on a financial basis that cannot be altered or jeopardized."

A clear example of overexpansion was the founding of the College of Technology in 1874. It fell to Marcy to announce the failure of this venture in his report for 1876-77, by which time it had become obvious that the university lacked the financial means to supply the laboratories, equipment, library facilities, and faculty essential for the success of this undertaking. Since the state universities were in a position to provide the facilities necessary for technical courses Marcy urged Northwestern to stay out of this field unless it could obtain a large endowment to support a curriculum in technical education.

The associated professional schools survived the financial crisis of the mid-1870's in spite of some decline in enrollments. Transmitting reports from the heads of these schools to the trustees, Marcy noted an enrollment of 147 in the Medical College in 1875-76, but only 126 students the following year. Nevertheless, by 1880-81 this figure had risen to 195. In the Union College of Law, a sharp decline continued, from 134 students in 1875-76 to 101 in 1880-81 (see Table 2-1). But the school remained financially sound.

Enrollment was also one of Marcy's chief concerns on the Evanston campus. *Competition* Indeed, the crucial question was how to increase the size of the student body without *for Students* lowering standards. Between 1876 and 1877, registration in the college had dropped from 345 to 242, while the number of students in the Preparatory School had declined even more sharply, from 472 to 227. Competition among the burgeoning number of educational institutions had become intense, and Northwestern was particularly vulnerable because of the propinquity of several fine tuition-free state universities.

Recounting this situation to the trustees, in his report for 1878-79, Marcy pointed out that in their desire to attract students many colleges were beginning to use "means to secure large attendance that a few years ago would have been thought to be beneath the dignity of educational institutions." A number of the state schools, for example, competed with privately supported colleges by using money derived from taxes to advertise the merits of their respective institutions. Even some of the denominational colleges had "adopted the custom of sending out runners to solicit patronage and make special bargains with individual students." Competition for students in the region was further intensified when Harvard, Yale, Vassar, Princeton, and Wesleyan University all announced in 1879 that they were scheduling entrance examinations to be held in the City of Chicago.

Recruitment of students for the college was complicated by the difficulty of attracting applicants who were properly qualified. There were no good private preparatory schools in the Midwest other than those attached to universities, whereas the East abounded with "prep schools." This meant that aside from its own preparatory school, Northwestern was largely dependent on the public high schools for students. In an attempt to increase the number of public school applicants the faculty decided in 1874 to "admit students of all first class high schools upon the examination certificates of the principals and give the students credit for the work they had done."[5] But this measure did not procure the desired results. As Marcy noted in his 1879-80 report, "In practice we found that we could not delegate to others the authority to examine and at the same time maintain a good grade of scholarship. We have withdrawn the proposition."

In his 1879 report Marcy had emphasized the university's need "to secure the interest and sympathy of the children of the church, for the educational institutions of the church." Noting that the state normal schools and colleges attracted many Methodist students "because of convenience in locality or free tuition," he warned

NAME, *Lodilla Ambrose*.   LATIN ⬥ SCIENTIFIC C...

BIRTHPLACE, *Ann Arbor Michigan*   DATE OF BIRTH, *June 17th 1865* AGE, *18*
NAME OF PARENT OR GUARDIAN, *James Clement Ambrose*
POST-OFFICE OF SAME, *Evanston Illinois*
PLACE OF PREPARATION, *Evanston High School*
ADMITTED TO *Freshman Class*   TERM, *First*   YEAR, *1883*
RESIDENCE, *Evanston Ill.*

Hours per Week	FRESHMAN.	Standing	Hours per Week	SOPHOMORE.	Standing	Hours per Week	JUNIOR.	Standing	Hours per Week	SENIOR.	Standing
5	Latin,	91	3	Latin,	94	2½	Metaphysics,	97	4	Ethics,	92
5	Mathematics,	95	3	French,	94	4	Chemistry,	93	4	Political Economy,	90
4	French,	97	5	German,	87	2½	English Literature,	98	3	Physics,	92
1	Drawing,	85	2	Elocution,	96	1	Composition,	94	4	Geology,	100
1	Ancient Art,	—	1	Composition,	92	2	German E	87	2	Orations,	94
				N. Hist	100	3	French (no 2)	94			
5	Latin,	94	2½	Latin,	96	4	Physics,	94		Christian Evidences,	94
5	Mathematics,	95	5	Mathematics,	96	2½	Logic,	100	2	Political Economy,	
4	French,	95	2½	German,	87	4	Natural History,	100	2	Astronomy	90
1	Natural History,	—	2½	Mediæval History,	95	1	Composition,	94	2½	History of Civilization,	
1	Drawing,	95	1	Natural History,	100	2	German E	87	3½	Constitutional Law,	100
			2½	English Literature,	99					Orations,	92
				Essay	91				4	Chemistry	95
			2	French	92				2	Eng Lit	95

Student Record of Lodilla Ambrose, who later became Northwestern's first full time librarian

Class of 1879 gathered around the old oak tree, a pre-1900 landmark

that "if these children are not lost to the church they are lost to the educational interests of the church." It was characteristic of Marcy that he looked beyond immediate problems to the long-range issues involved.

Nowhere is this more clearly demonstrated than in his discussion, in 1878, of coeducation at Northwestern. Brushing aside the superficial objections to coeducation as being of "minor importance," he focused instead on the fact that women students came to Northwestern "with little or no idea of the difference between a good college and a seminary" with the result "that the majority of young women do not remain long with us." Nor did he blame the students for this. The real problem was a "confusion" not only in public "opinion" but also among the educators as to "what is the best provision for the higher education of women." His concluding statement shows how mistaken today's reader would be to assume that by "coeducation" even enlightened educators meant "the same education" for men and women. Marcy did not question the ability of women to deal with a rigorous course of study, but he tied women's education to the place they would be expected to occupy in society:

Coeducation: "Civilization Demands That Distinction Be Made"

> Say what you will, civilization demands that distinction be made between young men and young women in everything that is not purely religious, literary or scientific. And in giving instruction in these, distinctions are frequently demanded, for good reasons, in regard to methods, to the books used, and the phases of literature and science which it is best for them to study.

It would be some time before the majority of educators and the public at large would accept the fact that these distinctions were not essential to the preservation of civilization!

In general, Marcy believed that in order to attract well-qualified students Northwestern would have to meet two conditions. It would have to have a scholarly faculty with sufficient time to do research as well as to teach, since no one "can instruct well who is not engaged in research along the line in which he gives instruction." In addition, it would have to have the kinds of libraries, equipment, and laboratories essential for a high standard of research and instruction. Both conditions required adequate financial support. As he told the trustees in 1881, to the extent to which these conditions were met and maintained "a good college was possible anywhere; without them a good college was impossible."

The financial situation during the late 1870's had made impossible the kind of improvements Marcy advocated. During the academic year 1876-77, the deficit had been reduced by cutting the funds allocated to maintenance and faculty salaries to an irreducible minimum. But interest payments on the university's debt from 1878 through 1880 absorbed over 50 percent of the average annual income of approximately $31,000 (see Table 2-2).

Although he devoted his full powers to carrying out the duties of acting president, Marcy told the trustees as early as 1877:

> . . . it is a bad thing for us that we change our presidents so frequently and with him our inside work and presentation to the world outside. . . . *Character is the growth of years.* As long as the occupant of the presidential chair is changed each three years, the institution must lack character.

Acting on this conviction, Marcy tried to resign to bring his point home to the board. "Please make provision for some other person to do the executive work of the faculty," he wrote in June 1878. "I have been intending to say to the Board at the proper time that I cannot serve next year."[6] But the board remained deaf to his entreaties and Marcy reluctantly continued in office. By 1880, however, he had become impatient. In blunt words he informed Orrington Lunt that in the absence of a permanent president Northwestern was becoming a second rate institution. "If we are destined to become fixed in a lower grade," he added, "I need not longer do work which I dislike to do. Almost any man will fill the place as well."[7] In his annual report of June 1881, he reiterated his belief that "the most essential part of the faculty was a president who knows his business . . . the college cannot rise higher than the man who is kept at its head."

By spring 1881 the gloomy outlook of the 1870's began to give way to a rising spirit of optimism among the trustees and faculty. Several factors contributed to this change. First, there was a general improvement in the state of the economy. Secondly, the suits for back taxes brought against the university by the city of Evanston in 1874 were settled in favor of Northwestern by the Supreme Court of the United States.[8] But the most encouraging news came from a meeting called by John Evans on April 18, 1881. Evans offered to donate $25,000 to the First Debt-Paying Fund provided that others would contribute the $75,000 needed to bring the total to $100,000. Moreover, he offered to contribute an additional $25,000 to a Second Debt-Paying Fund of $100,000 under the same conditions.[9] To help secure the pledges needed to take advantage of Evans's offer, the trustees appointed one of their number, the Reverend Robert H. Hatfield of Evanston.

This positive development in the university's financial prospects was followed by a further affirmative step when the trustees, in June 1881, elected the Reverend Joseph Cummings as president.

Election of President Joseph Cummings

At the time of his election Cummings had already distinguished himself as a minister, teacher, college administrator, and effective fund raiser. Born in Falmouth, Maine, in 1817, Cummings was a graduate of Wesleyan University. He had served as principal of the Amenia Seminary and president of Genessee Wesleyan College in New York state, before returning to Wesleyan as president in 1857. After 18 years in that post, Cummings resigned the presidency but remained on the faculty for another three years. In 1878 he left academe to devote his time to the ministry. He was sixty-four when he took the presidency of Northwestern in 1881.[10]

At a reception for him in Evanston later that year, Cummings explained that he had accepted the presidency because he believed that by rebuilding and strengthening the departments already established, Northwestern could achieve its potential as an ideal educational institution.[11] He realized that no plans for the future could be implemented until there was a substantial improvement in the university's finances. Since the obvious first step was to reduce the burden of the institution's accumulated debt of over $200,000, Cummings agreed to assist the Reverend Robert Hatfield in securing pledges for the $75,000 needed to take advantage of Evans's offer to donate $25,000 toward a debt-paying fund.

Cummings and Hatfield achieved their goal within a year. At the annual meeting in June 1882, the trustees thanked Evans for the initial gift and urged the two fund raisers to search for the additional $75,000 to meet the conditions of Evans's second offer. Again they were successful. As noted by the trustees in June 1883, "Under the blessings of Providence the means have been provided by generous and liberal friends to substantially extinguish the indebtedness which has so long weighed upon the Institution." They once again expressed gratitude to John Evans for his wise forethought but went on to point out that the second drive would not have been successful without the untiring effort of President Cummings and the generosity of Brother William Deering, who had offered to give $50,000 of the $75,000 required to meet the proposition of Governor Evans.

Financial Policies

William Deering's pledge in 1883 assured the ultimate success of the drive to eliminate the bulk of the university's fixed indebtedness and heavy interest payments. It did not, however, provide any immediate relief since his pledge, like those of most subscribers, was to be paid in installments extending over several years. In view of this the trustees, in June 1883, instructed the executive committee and the president not to increase the expenditures of the institution in anticipation of future receipts until the entire debt had been canceled, and so far as possible to keep the university's current expenses within current income. It was clear that if Northwestern was to grow as Cummings hoped, additional income would have to be found.

The president's immediate reaction was to launch a campaign that would increase income by attracting more students. As he reported in June 1884, a series of advertisements designed to acquaint prospective students with the advantages of attending Northwestern were placed in a number of church papers and selected periodicals. At Cummings's suggestion the faculty agreed to try once more to attract applicants by not requiring holders of certificates from accredited secondary schools to take entrance examinations.[12] These measures, coupled with a recovery of the economy, were largely responsible for a marked rise in the combined college and preparatory school enrollment—from 506 in 1880-81 to 804 in 1886-87 (see Table 2-1).

TABLE 2-1
N.U. STUDENT ENROLLMENT 1876-1890

Academic Year	College	Medical	Law	Pharmacy	Dental	Preparatory	Total
1876 - 77	242	126	101	—	—	227	696
1877 - 78	251	153	124	—	—	247	775
1878 - 79	225	151	105	—	—	185	666
1879 - 80	265	188	93	—	—	191	737
1880 - 81	303	195	101	—	—	203	802
1881 - 82	350	189	130	—	—	251	920
1882 - 83	358	171	139	—	—	245	913
1883 - 84	344	123	101	—	—	239	807
1884 - 85	310	123	134	—	—	231	798
1885 - 86	352	127	152	—	—	247	878
1886 - 87	444	132	143	67	—	360	1,146
1887 - 88	480	159	148	159	9	434	1,389
1888 - 89	496	183	137	121	13	510	1,460
1889 - 90	492	214	138	200	24	590	1,658

SOURCE: Northwestern University Catalogs, 1876-1890.

Meanwhile President Cummings had become increasingly unhappy with the trustees' conservative financial policy. Contributions to the two debt-paying funds were used between 1882 and 1886 to retire Northwestern's bonded debt of $70,000 and to reduce the mortgage account by $25,000. There was an accompanying decline in interest payments over the same period from $14,500 per annum to $6,700. This debt reduction, however, did not bring about any increase in the university's current receipts. These, as shown in Table 2-2, actually declined between 1882 and 1883 and did not move up again until 1886. Expenditures followed a similar pattern with the result that the amount budgeted for salaries in 1885 was only $1,500 more than it had been in 1882.

In his report to the trustees in June 1884, the president warned:

> . . . to hold the rank claimed for it, [the university] must have more instructors, more apparatus, additional buildings and must reduce the expenses of education. The necessity for these changes is becoming very urgent and the peril of losing influence great. A few years ago the university had a larger number of instructors and more extended and various courses of study while expenses were less. We cannot secure additional students or retain the number we have unless such measures shall be adopted.

Cummings's Recommendations

In searching for new resources Cummings stated that it would "not be well to trust the spontaneous gifts of the Church." Instead, he recommended the appointment of a special agent to secure funds and otherwise promote the interests of the university. He explained, moreover, that the trustees should not expect a president to serve in this capacity, since the administrative duties of that office were so demanding that he could not possibly devote the time and energy needed to do an effective job. In conclusion Cummings pointed out that he had "been greatly embarrassed by the limited available funds of the university" and urged the trustees to reconsider their settled policy "not to incur a debt" and to anticipate to some degree at least a future increase in resources.

The trustees accepted the recommendation that a special agent be employed to solicit donations and in the fall of 1885 arranged for the Reverend Mr. Hatfield once again to serve in this capacity. This decision may well have been prompted by the fact that illness forced President Cummings to take a two month leave at this time. They were not prepared, however, to follow his suggestion that they provide funds for expansion by going into debt. Thus it was not until the university's income began to rise sharply after 1886—thanks to a combination of increased enrollments and higher rents—that Cummings could begin to carry out his plans for expansion.

Additions to the Evanston Campus

Robert Hatfield's great ability as a fund raiser was demonstrated early in 1886 when he reported that an anonymous donor had agreed to contribute a sum of $45,000 to Northwestern to be used in the construction of a hall of science which would accommodate the departments of chemistry and physics. This gift was most welcome since the physics department had been confined to two small recitation rooms in University Hall, while the chemistry laboratory was quartered in the basement. Small wonder that President Cummings in June 1886, hailed the gift as "the most important and encouraging event of the year."*

It was not until his death in 1890 that it became known that the donor was Daniel B. Fayerweather, a wealthy resident of New York City who was interested in supporting educational institutions. The gift was prompted by a letter which Hatfield sent to a friend in Connecticut outlining Northwestern's plans for a science building and asking for a donation.[13] The friend passed the letter on to Fayerweather who, though he had never heard of Northwestern, was sufficiently impressed with the proposal not only to contribute the funds for the building but to provide in his will for an additional bequest of $100,000.†

Dedicated in February 1887, the completed Science Hall was hailed by the press in an outburst of regional pride as "an epoch in the history of science at Chicago. It is the first building especially erected for instruction in these sciences in the city or the suburbs." A committee of students from the college met a special train that brought students from the professional schools in Chicago to take part in the ceremonies. The program ended with a banquet and dedication service at the Methodist Church which featured the singing of hymns especially written for the occasion.[14]

Science (Fayerweather) Hall

During his two years as special agent, Hatfield was also responsible for persuading some sixty-nine friends of the university to contribute a total of just under $12,000 to be used for the construction of a men's dormitory on campus. Completed in time for the opening of classes in the fall of 1889, the building had accommodations for about thirty students. It represented a modest but important step toward providing badly needed housing facilities for men students.[15]

President Cummings seems to have played an important role in the events leading up to the second—and last—major addition to the educational facilities on the Evanston campus during his administration. This was the Dearborn Observatory, which came to Northwestern as a result of negotiations with the Chicago Astronomical Society, which had been organized in 1862 by a group of Chicago businessmen interested in having an observatory in the city. Early in 1863 the group learned that a telescope manufactured by a firm in Cambridge, Massachusetts, was available. The instrument with an 18½ inch lens—the largest in the world at that time—had been ordered initially by the University of Mississippi some time prior to 1860, but because of the outbreak of the Civil War it had not been delivered. Purchased by the Chicago Astronomical Society, the telescope was installed in 1866 in an observatory tower located on the campus of the original University of Chicago.**

Acquisition of Dearborn Observatory

Two subsequent developments led the Chicago Astronomical Society to transfer the telescope to Northwestern University. One was the Great Chicago Fire of 1871

---

* Under his original agreement with Northwestern, Hatfield was to receive ten percent of such sums as he might secure for the university. Following the receipt of the $45,000 bequest for the new hall of science, however, the agreement was revised so as to give him a two-year contract at an annual salary of $2,500. *Trustees' Minutes, April 10, 1886.*

† Unfortunately litigation held up the bequest until 1897, when Northwestern finally received $128,347 from the estate. *Trustees' Minutes, June 14, 1898.*

** At the suggestion of J. Y. Scammon, who financed the construction of the tower, it was named the Dearborn Observatory in memory of Mrs. Scammon whose maiden name was Mary Haven Dearborn and who was related to General Henry Dearborn for whom Fort Dearborn was named. *In* Annals of the Dearborn Observatory, *(1915), pp. 1-3, N.U.A.*

Grand Pacific Hotel, Chicago, circa 1887, on land purchased by the founders in 1852, now site of the Continental Illinois National Bank and Trust Company (Courtesy Chicago Historical Society)

Fayerweather Hall of Science, completed 1887, hailed as "an epoch in the history of science at Chicago"

which, though it did not damage the observatory, did virtually bankrupt the Astronomical Society. The second was the prospect of having to vacate the observatory tower when it was learned that the University of Chicago was going to close down because of financial difficulties.

By mid-1887 negotiations were completed for the transfer of the telescope to the Evanston campus.* A gift of $25,000 from James B. Hobbs, a close friend of President Cummings and a Northwestern trustee, enabled the building for the new observatory to be completed in June 1889 on a site on the campus overlooking Lake Michigan.[16] George Washington Hough, formerly in charge of the Dearborn Observatory of Chicago, was named director of the observatory and appointed the first professor in the newly established astronomical department. He was to serve the university for 20 years, during which time he became an authority on the planet Jupiter and came to be known as Jupiter Hough.

While the administration struggled to reduce the institution's debt and fortify the endowment, gradual changes were taking place in Northwestern's educational program. In the decades following the Civil War the traditional concept of the college as embodied in a paternalistic faculty and rigid curriculum began to crumble. In an early effort to meet the needs of a more technological age research centers such as The Johns Hopkins University, responsive multipurpose state universities such as the University of Michigan, and specialized institutions like Yale's Sheffield Scientific School, developed alternative modes of higher education. Northwestern was in no position to espouse any grand plans but in small ways it began to borrow ideas from these other institutions.

College Faculty and Curriculum

Both Marcy and Cummings adhered to the vision of Northwestern as primarily a liberal arts college in federation with relatively autonomous professional schools. Neither inaugurated any clear break with past policies. The course of Marcy's term as acting president was virtually predetermined by lack of funds. With improved economic conditions in the 1880's, however, Northwestern's educational offerings became both stronger and broader. At the undergraduate level, the Cummings years brought the addition of more faculty, new courses, and better facilities, particularly in the sciences. The curriculum became more versatile with the introduction of electives and honors programs.

The resignation of Charles Fowler in 1876 combined with the financial crisis to depress faculty morale and led to a temporary decline in the quality of instruction. His departure, which left vacant the Evans chair of moral and intellectual philos-

---

*In January 1961 Dr. Miller received a letter addressed to "The President of Northwestern University, Cleveland, Ohio" from Mrs. Russell C. Tolbert of Hazelhurst, Mississippi, suggesting that the telescope in the Northwestern Observatory really belonged to the University of Mississippi. Citing an article in the *Oxford Eagle* for August 1957 as her authority, Mrs. Tolbert claimed that the telescope had been installed in the observatory at the University of Mississippi prior to 1860 but had been stolen by the Union Army during the Civil War and moved to Northwestern. She wrote, "Now that the war is over and we all love each other and perhaps a lot of us have almost forgot which side we were on, I guess there is not only sentiment felt by individuals, but also by Institutions. Your University could not possibly hold the sentiment for that old telescope that 'Ole Miss.' does. . . . Perhaps there are few if any in your University that know the history of this telescope—but wouldn't it be a magnanimous venture if you would use your influence as President to have the telescope returned to Chancellor J. D. Williams, Oxford, Mississippi?" In the absence of any further correspondence it may be assumed that the letter from the Northwestern Information Services explaining the purchase of the lens in 1863 by the Chicago Astronomical Society convinced Mrs. Tolbert of her mistake. *Mrs. Russell C. Tolbert to the president of Northwestern University, January 18, 1961; and Robert C. Cramm to Mrs. Russell C. Tolbert, February 14, 1961; Dearborn Observatory Records, N.U.A.*

Evanston in 1880, Davis Street looking east from Benson Avenue, taken by the noted photographer Hesler

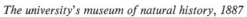

The university's museum of natural history, 1887

ophy, was soon followed by the resignation of David Wheeler in English history, Joseph Allyn in chemistry, and Ellen Soulé, professor of French and dean of the Woman's College. Responsibility for teaching the courses thus left open was divided among the remaining professors, instructors, and preparatory school staff.

Although this situation was not without its incongruities, Marcy regarded the reduction of faculty as only part of Northwestern's educational problem. On numerous occasions he compared Northwestern's programs to those of state-supported and privately-endowed universities and found "many points . . . which so contrast with the management of this institution that they challenge our attention."[17] Among other reforms, he encouraged a greater specialization within subject areas, lighter teaching loads to allow for more faculty research, and a thorough review of academic policies and goals.

Handicapped by lack of money Marcy was able to do little more than theorize. But he kept alive even in these most difficult times the ideal of a liberal arts education. To that end his administration changed the designation of the College of Literature and Science to the College of Liberal Arts. As his report for 1880-81 made clear, the change affirmed his and the faculty's commitment to the principle that, "To teach the trades, to make artisans, engineers, book-keepers, merchants and farmers is not directly the purpose of this College."

"To Teach the Trades . . . Is Not the Purpose of This College"

Confronted by competition from the state universities which offered practical training, Northwestern strove to retain its character as an institution of broad learning. This accorded with what Marcy perceived as Northwestern's unique mission: the preparation of individuals for Christian leadership and for the ministry. In his 1878 report he expressed the view that teaching in the secular university lacked "the tone and influence of the instructions of that professor whose standpoint is an intelligent, superintending Providence."

Both Marcy and Cummings were anxious to restore and enlarge the liberal arts faculty. To fill the position of Woman's College dean and professor of French language and literature, the university in 1877 hired Jane Bancroft, who held advanced degrees in French history from Syracuse University. In June 1881 two Northwestern alumni were added to the faculty—Robert Baird as professor of Greek language and literature, and Charles W. Pearson as professor of English literature and history. In 1885 the trustees approved the appointment of Robert D. Sheppard, a former Northwestern trustee and minister with degrees from the University of Chicago and Garrett to the newly created post of professor of political economy and history. The chemistry professorship was filled in 1886 by Abram Young, who had trained at Johns Hopkins and Harvard; and in 1887, Charles E. Cook from Dartmouth was appointed professor of physics. Two years later the university recruited James Taft Hatfield, son of the Reverend Robert Hatfield and a Northwestern graduate, to fill a second new chair in German language and literature. By 1890 the permanent teaching staff of full professors had grown to sixteen.

Faculty salaries were relatively stable throughout this period. The Trustees' Minutes for 1876-77 reveal that for that year President Marcy received a salary of

$2,500; the other professors, $2,000 each; and the dean of women, $1,200.* Ten years later, these salaries remained the same and the faculty petitioned the trustees that "the need of advance in salaries . . . is most urgent." Some adjustment according to tenure was then made. Cummings's salary was raised to $3,000, while full professors received from $2,000 to $2,500 annually.[18]

Addition of Electives
As earlier, students in the college pursued a classical, scientific, or literary course of study. The major change between 1876 and 1890 was an effort to make these curricula more flexible and varied. Nevertheless, Northwestern's steps in this direction were timid compared to the massive elective program started by President Charles W. Eliot at Harvard and attempted elsewhere during the 1880's. At Northwestern the traditional, classical curriculum continued to attract the majority of the students, but Cummings believed in allowing some freedom of choice. Beginning in the fall of 1883, the number of required courses of Latin and Greek was lowered and more electives, particularly in history, science and German were added. Freed from some of the required courses, qualified students now had an opportunity to work for "special honors" in a field of their choice. Two years earlier, the public reading of students' grades and class rank, a custom practiced since the first years of the college, had been abandoned on Cummings's initiative.[19]

The inauguration of an elective system at Northwestern University indicates the extent to which a greater number of disciplines were becoming a part of accepted undergraduate study. Moreover, the appointment of specialists in these fields demonstrated the university's willingness to accord the new disciplines equal status with the traditional ones. But as at other universities the first significant departure from the first classical curriculum came with the expansion of offerings in the physical sciences. By 1890 Northwestern's courses in this area had become one of the college's chief attractions.

Robert McLean Cumnock
Another example of this trend was the status accorded to the teaching of elocution and rhetoric. In 1869 Robert McLean Cumnock had joined the College of Liberal Arts as an instructor in elocution, becoming a professor of elocution four years later. He was an exceptionally energetic and able teacher as well as a splendid performer on the public platform and soon established a fine reputation both for himself and for his field. To meet a growing demand for teachers of elocution, Cumnock in 1878 introduced a special course in elocution comprising a two year curriculum. Students who completed this course were awarded a certificate by the university.

The acquisition of new faculty and facilities added substantially to the college's academic standing. In 1889 the National Phi Beta Kappa Society granted Northwestern a charter, thereby according it the distinction of becoming one of the first colleges in the West to have a Phi Beta Kappa chapter on its campus.[20]

Like his predecessor, President Cummings was not involved directly in the administration of Northwestern's affiliated Chicago Medical College and Union College of Law, both of which continued to function under the supervision of their own deans and faculties. During the 1880's the Medical College created a number of

---

*The per annum scale for the Harvard University faculty in 1879-80 was: full professors up to $4,500; assistant professors, $1,500 to $4,000; instructors, $250 to $1,500. *Seymour H. Harris*, The Economics of Harvard (*McGraw-Hill Book Company, 1970*), *p. 157.*

new departments and staffed them with practicing specialists. Classroom procedure began to entail more clinical and laboratory work and the study of new fields such as bacteriology. As a result the faculty grew from 19 in 1876 to 29 in 1890.[21] Over the same period enrollment grew from 126 to 214 (see Table 2-1).

With the closing of the first University of Chicago in 1886, the Union College of Law came under the sole sponsorship of Northwestern in accordance with the agreement of 1873. The change caused little disruption in the program of instruction. The faculty remained at six, but the two-year course of study was broadened to include more oral exposition and the drawing of legal papers. Enrollment followed an upward trend, from 101 students in 1876 to 138 in 1890, with some fluctuations between (see Table 2-1). *N.U. Becomes Sole Sponsor of College of Law*

President Cummings did, however, play an active part in negotiations which led to the association of two new professional schools with Northwestern. The first had its origin in 1886 when a group of Chicago druggists, headed by Dr. D. R. Dyche, a Northwestern trustee, proposed to found a pharmacy college to be affiliated with the university. The trustees responded favorably to the proposal with the result that in June 1886, the Illinois College of Pharmacy became a department of the university. As in the case of Northwestern's other affiliated professional schools, the new college had its own board of trustees responsible for its finances and administration.[22] Their choice of dean for the new college was Oscar Oldberg, a Swedish pharmacist who had settled in the United States in 1865. At the time he accepted the Northwestern appointment, he was professor in the Chicago College of Pharmacy.[23]

Although it admitted anyone over sixteen years of age with a "good common public school education," the Illinois College of Pharmacy provided a much higher standard for pharmaceutical training than was currently available in other schools by more than doubling the average amount of time spent in classes, by making a substantial number of laboratory classes compulsory, and by discouraging concurrent drug store employment.[24] Despite these strict requirements, the course proved attractive, as indicated by the rapid growth in the number of students enrolled in the school, from 67 during 1886-87 to some 200 during 1889-90 (see Table 2-1). *College of Pharmacy*

In December 1886 the board appointed a committee to consider "the question of adding a dental department to the university." By the following spring a charter had been obtained for a College of Dental and Oral Surgery to start operations in the fall.[25] Most of the classes were held in the medical school buildings and many of the courses were taught by members of the medical faculty. As in the case of the College of Pharmacy, responsibility for the finances and administration of the Dental College was assumed by its own board of trustees. John S. Marshall became the first dean of the school. *College of Dental and Oral Surgery*

The sponsors of the Dental College proposed to raise the requirements for the profession, which at the time typically consisted of a sequence of two courses, each lasting six months. By contrast, graduates of the Northwestern college were required to complete three courses of seven months each. The curriculum included lectures and clinical instruction, requirements that according to the Northwestern catalog "were in harmony with a resolution regarding dental education recently passed by the American Medical Association."[26] Graduates of the school were also offered the opportunity of obtaining an M.D. degree by continuing their studies for a fourth year.

The Northwestern Dental College was the first in the country to set such a high standard for graduation. The result was that enrollment stayed low—only twenty-four students in 1889-90. Fearful that the school would be unable to continue operation with such a limited number of students, the faculty in 1890 moved to make the third year of instruction optional.

Campus Life

Student interests and activities during this period continued to center largely around such organizations as the Students' Christian Association, the literary clubs, and the Greek letter societies—the latter two groups tending to dominate campus life.

"My Daughter Applies Herself Too Closely to Her Studies"

Northwestern coeds faced special circumstances in their efforts to obtain an education. Collegiate education for women was still fairly new and there were many, including parents, who feared that prolonged mental exertion would defeminize young women and unsuit them for marriage and motherhood. Consequently, though the university set the same academic requirements for men and women, the latter were subject to a much higher degree of personal supervision. Pressure for this supervision came largely from parents who bombarded the dean of women with queries about their daughters' companions, emotional states, conduct, and, particularly, their health. One mother considered withdrawing her daughter because the girl had developed poor posture and the habit of biting her nails; other parents worried that their daughters worked too hard. One anxious father wrote, "My daughter . . . applies herself too closely to her studies and does not take sufficient rest at night, which event certainly would impair and undermine her health which is *paramount* to everything else."[27]

Dean Bancroft tried to calm parental worries and at the same time moved to protect the physical well-being of her charges by enlisting Dean Nathan Davis of the Medical College to conduct health inspections of the women's quarters. She arranged for the employment of a resident physician for the Woman's College and persuaded the trustees that they should install an elevator in the building to "avoid broken constitutions among the students."[28] The dean also devoted considerable energy to raising the aspirations of young college women. To this end she began a placement service to find teaching jobs for women graduates and, in 1883, founded the Western Association of Collegiate Alumnae, a regional forerunner of the American Association of University Women.[29]

Northwestern coeds were fortunate in being able to live on campus. By contrast, the men had to find lodgings and meals in the town. Some students organized cooperative dining clubs such as the Velvet Tops. They hired a cook to prepare meals at a reasonable rate, but unfortunately the members' appetites outran their budget and the plan had to be abandoned after three months.[30] By the mid-1880's many students were complaining about the exorbitant charges for rooms in Evanston which, including maid service, ranged from six to fourteen dollars a week.[31] The completion of a men's dormitory in 1889 provided some relief, but

Members of the tug-of-war team which won the
1890 championship

Women athletes, 1880

Women's dormitory room, 1880's (Courtesy Evanston Historical Society)

since the building accommodated only thirty or so students the majority remained dependent on boarding houses in the town.

Greek Letter Societies

Three more chapters of national fraternities were organized at Northwestern during these years: Phi Kappa Psi, 1878; Phi Delta Theta, 1887; and Delta Upsilon, 1888. In 1881 Alpha Phi became the first sorority to establish a chapter on campus. Others rapidly followed suit: Delta Gamma and Kappa Kappa Gamma, 1882; Kappa Alpha Theta, 1887; Gamma Phi Beta, 1888; and Alpha Chi Omega, 1890.

In the absence of chapter houses, the sororities customarily met on Monday evenings in rooms assigned for their use on the top floor of the Woman's College. On Friday afternoons they would gather at the home of a Chicago or Evanston member for what were commonly known as "cozies," informal parties that offered such entertainment as tableaux, "chocolataires" and bean bag contests.[32]

The Monday evening meetings of the fraternities were usually held at some conveniently located rented quarters in Evanston. One alumnus recalled that:

> . . . the custom was inaugurated of having peanuts, doughnuts and cider after the regular meetings. Sometimes oysters were served. These simple, happy occasions were more to us than one can now imagine. They were the scenes of fervent, joyful outbursts of feeling known only to kindred spirits. The flow of wit, the hearty laugh, the eloquent words, all found a pleasant abode within these halls. It was just such fun as a student free from all care and trouble can have.[33]

The Greek letter societies' emphasis on social activities and amusements proved more attractive to many students than the more austere pursuits of the literary societies.[34] This trend became a matter of some concern. One undergraduate in an article in the April 13, 1882 issue of *The Northwestern* entitled "Use and Abuse of College Fraternities," commented that while fraternities could provide a good opportunity for intellectual growth, often ". . . we find some chapters of some fraternities making no claim to literary improvement, and making their meetings times for general hilarity and fun, not unfrequently enhanced by the exhilaration of the 'flowing bowl'." The writer, W. A. Evans, himself a fraternity member, was also critical of the spirit engendered by interfraternity competition: "This bigoted spirit being rife engenders unhealthy rivalry and envy, leads to unmanly and unchristian acts, causes prejudice to thrive and fosters the growth of deceit and hypocrisy." Pleading for reform of the fraternity system, he proposed: "Let the various fraternities come together by delegations and draw up a code of laws by which they will be governed in their rivalry of one another as Christian men should be governed." Evans's article suggests the ambivalence with which many students regarded the growing influence of the Greek letter societies.

Student Publications

News and editorial comments on events and activities on both campuses were covered in *The Northwestern*, the student paper that began as a biweekly publication in 1881 and after 1887 was issued weekly. Faculty, alumni, and students all contributed articles to the paper. In 1884 the graduating class published Northwestern's first yearbook, the *Pandora*, a slim volume with a portrait of President Cummings, lists of faculty and students, and descriptions of various student organizations. It was superseded a year later by the more formal and elaborate *Syllabus*.

In contrast to the carefree tenor of the social life built around the Greek letter societies was the program sponsored by the Students' Christian Association. Founded in 1880, the Northwestern S.C.A. enjoyed the support of President Cummings who led many of its discussions on religion and ethics. But the interest of S.C.A. students went beyond theoretical issues to such practical concerns as temperance and missionary work, and they offered both financial and moral support to those who planned to devote their lives to these undertakings. In 1880 the Students' Christian Association voted to transform itself into a campus branch of the national Y.M.C.A. and Y.W.C.A. movement.[35]

Religious Life

Though religious life on campus flourished, decorum in chapel was clearly on the decline. In 1882 *The Northwestern* noted, "Dr. Cummings has repeatedly made the request that disorder during chapel exercises should be discontinued. . . . We know what a temptation it is to send a hymn book flying at the uplifted head of some irreverent Soph. But a moment's reflection will convince any gentleman of the manifest impropriety of this and all similar acts."[36] Several years later the student paper reported that President Cummings was unhappy with chapel attendance and went on to explain that "by presenting a reasonable excuse, any student can be exempt from these duties." The editor concluded, "Would it be sacrilegious to suggest that chapel exercises be made more attractive?"[37]

Many Northwestern students attended local churches, though not always for purely spiritual reasons. "I went to the Presbyterian church today," wrote Florence Call in 1883 to a friend, "to let the congregation see my blue silk. The Methodists had seen it before and I wanted to be perfectly fair." In a letter to her family written shortly after her arrival on campus, Florence explained what was expected of students in the way of religious exercises:

"The M.E. Church Is The Church of This Place"

> We are all required to attend church somewhere once on Sundays. You know the catalogue says 'the spirit of the college is not denominational but it is the desire that it shall be distinctly Christian' and that means that they tell us that there are various churches—probably good ones—in town but the *M.E.* Church is *the* church of this place. The church certainly is fine and they have a large pipe organ and some splendid singers. The Pastor doesn't amount to much but he fills the pulpit.[38]

Florence's letters give a sense of the peaceful, indeed bucolic, setting of the Evanston campus in the 1880's. Looking out of her front window at the Woman's College she could see "the top of the University—the lake—a few of our shade trees and the North-Western Cow pastures."[39]

Students in the Chicago professional schools inhabited a different world. While the Evanston city council discussed such matters as "the protection of song birds from small boys with slingshots," and the problems caused by "the driving of cows to and from pasture through the streets"[40] of the town, Chicagoans faced the social and environmental consequences of massive industrialization and rapid urban growth. With a population that numbered over one million by 1880, Chicago had become the second largest city in the United States. It had also become the world's greatest market for corn, cattle, and timber, as well as the site of a large number of financial, industrial, and commercial enterprises. In this setting students at Northwestern's professional schools were exposed to many aspects of the world in which they would soon be pursuing their life's work.

Northwestern students in both locations sensed the disparity between their educational experiences and during the 1880's pressed for closer ties. Their concern led to the establishment in 1886 of University Day as an annual affair to which all students, faculty, and deans were invited. Writing for *The Northwestern*, one student commentator expressed the hope that the program "might make us feel that we are of one family and . . . that we belong to a University."[41]

The construction of Sheridan Road in the late 1880's providing a direct carriage route between Chicago and the North Shore municipalities, accelerated Evanston's growth as a metropolitan suburb and eventually brought the two Northwestern communities closer together.[42] Though the impact of the new thoroughfare was not immediately felt, its coming signalled the end of the founders' hope of keeping the Evanston undergraduates insulated from the temptations of urban life.

Athletics Athletics, operated under student direction and supervision, remained popular. This was especially true of baseball. The Northwestern team, as a member of the Western College Baseball Association organized in 1883, competed with rivals from Chicago, Wisconsin, Michigan and Racine, winning the championship in 1883 and 1889.[43] Billy Sunday, the well known evangelist, coached the team during the 1888 season. A member of the professional Chicago White Stockings, Sunday was simultaneously enrolled at Northwestern where he studied oratory with Professor Cumnock and coached the baseball team in return for tuition.[44] The team finished the season of 1888 with a record of six wins and four defeats. Sunday's subsequent career as a preacher suggests that Cumnock's instruction was by no means wasted.

Although far from matching the enthusiasm for baseball, there was a growing interest in football during these years despite the fact that there was no organized league and contests with other institutions were infrequent and informal. Indeed, the game seems to have been played entirely on an intramural basis until 1882, when Northwestern held its first scheduled intercollegiate contest with Lake Forest. No further intercollegiate games were scheduled, however, until 1888 when rivalry with Lake Forest was renewed. In the following year the Northwestern-Notre Dame series began, and Notre Dame won the first game by a score of 9-0. Later in the season, Northwestern defeated a group called the Chicago Wanderers 24 to 0.

The results of the season seemed sufficiently encouraging to prompt *The Northwestern* of December 13, 1889, to editorialize,

> Foot ball has established itself as the popular fall sport, and next year we may expect it to be fully as popular as a fall game as base ball is a sport for spring and summer, and especially since the latter is rent with civil strife . . . it has been proposed that a league be formed consisting of Ann Arbor, Madison, Minnesota and Northwestern. Arrangements are now being made by correspondents and convention for the completion of the scheme. A final foot ball game is now *the* society event of the season in New York and Chicago, and we think we see signs showing that our faculty are beginning to recover from their unaccountable prejudice against the noble game.[45]

One unique Northwestern organization—the lifesaving crew—deserves further

Baseball team, winner of the 1889 championship in the Western College Baseball Association

First Lifesaving Station, circa 1890, home of the campus heroes

Lifesaving Crew mention here. In 1871 the United States Navy furnished a fully-equipped lifesaving boat and in 1876 provided a permanent station located east of what is now Fisk Hall for use by the crew. In 1880 Captain Lawrence Lawson was appointed keeper of the station, supervising the crew until 1904. During the 1870's the crew had no calls to action, and members used the boat for recreation and entertaining coeds. In the 1880's, however, the Northwestern crew participated in rescue operations following several major lake disasters. The most notable of these was the wreck of the steamer *Calumet* near Highland Park in November 1889. So crucial was the Northwestern crew's role in saving passengers from the capsized ship that the Secretary of the Treasury awarded the captain and each member a gold medal.[46] Though only a handful of students made up the lifesaving squad, it enjoyed a great deal of prestige. Its members were the early campus heroes.

Between 1876 and 1890, Northwestern University awarded 388 baccalaureate degrees. By far the largest proportion of graduates, 102, chose a religious calling of some kind, including the ministry, missionary work or religious education. The second largest number, 79, were drawn into teaching; 53 into law; 44 into business; and 31 into medicine. The remainder chose a variety of careers including writing and editing, the civil service and—not the least important—homemaking.[47]

"Sound the Praises of Northwestern" By 1881 there were enough alumni with a strong commitment to Northwestern to form the first alumni association. Three years later, Frank H. Elliott, president of the alumni association, reported a membership of 227. Commenting on the "stern economy" measures to which the university had been driven, he concluded:

> It seems evident, therefore, that the hope of the University, for the next few years at least, lies in the Alumni Association. Not that it can provide any money for the university, except in an indirect way, but that it can exert a live and substantial interest in its behalf. . . . It is the duty as well as the privilege of our graduates to sound the praises of Northwestern and send students to it.[48]

In the spring of 1890, President Cummings had good reason to be pleased with Northwestern's progress since 1877. Total enrollment at the university had reached an all-time high of 1,658. Taken together, the college and the preparatory school accounted for 1,082 of this total. Addressing the trustees on June 18, 1889, Cummings had cautioned against evaluating educational institutions merely by the size of their student bodies, but added that he found it "pleasant to have large numbers" since this was the test that most people used to measure the standing of a college.*

Finances The improvement in Northwestern's finances was particularly gratifying. The expansion in the total annual receipts from their low point of $31,000 during 1878-1880 to $64,000 in 1890,† made it possible to increase the allocation of money for the addition of new faculty and the raising of salaries in the college and the preparatory school. The budget for instruction rose from a low of $16,200 in 1880 to an impressive $47,100 in 1890. The combined college and preparatory school

---

*In 1890 enrollment at the University of Illinois was given as 387, at University of Wisconsin as 877, and at Michigan University as 2,370. On the east coast Yale had 1,254 students, Columbia 1,526, and Harvard 2,370. *From the* Report of the Commissioner of Education (1890-91), *U.S. Government Printing Office (1894) II: 1398-1413.*

†Additional tuition from the expanding enrollment in the college and preparatory school accounted for the major portion of this increase in income.

faculty rose from fourteen in 1876-77 to twenty-nine in 1889-90. Over the same period enrollment in the college more than doubled from 242 to 492, while registration in the preparatory school grew from 227 to 590 (see Table 2-1). At this time the university appointed its first full-time librarian, Lodilla Ambrose, a Northwestern alumna, class of 1881.[49]

TABLE 2-2
N.U. BUDGETED RECEIPTS AND EXPENDITURES: 1877-1890
(In Thousands of Dollars)

Academic Year	1876-1877	1877-1878	1878-1879[b]	1879-1880[b]	1880-1881	1881-1882	1882-1883	1883-1884	1884-1885	1885-1886	1886-1887	1887-1888	1888-1889	1889-1890
RECEIPTS														
Tuition	$13.5	$12.8	$13.2	$13.5	$14.2	$18.3	$18.4	$17.1	$17.6	$18.5	$24.3	$25.3	$27.8	$28.9
Rent	19.0	16.5	16.5	15.8	22.0	21.0	21.4	21.6	21.9	22.1	24.9	21.4	25.6	26.1
Interest	2.7	0.8	1.0	0.9	1.3	1.5	0.9	4.4	3.3	1.1	0.9	2.3	3.0	5.3
Gifts	7.1	0.5	0.2	0.4	0.5	7.6	3.7	0.5	1.4	2.8	0.3	1.8	3.6	1.9
Woman's Hall Bd. Acct. Net[a]	0.3	0.4	1.0	0.6	0.4	0.4	0.5	0.1	0.2	(0.2)	1.5	(1.2)	0.5	1.8
TOTAL	42.6	31.0	31.9	31.2	38.4	48.8	44.9	43.7	44.4	44.3	51.9	49.6	60.5	64.0
EXPENDITURES														
Instruction	19.1	17.7	17.7	16.2	21.7	27.8	29.0	29.6	29.3	30.6	34.2	38.7	44.0	47.1
Library	0.3	0.3	0.4	0.1	—	—	—	—	—	—	0.3	0.1	0.4	0.4
Administration	—	—	—	—	—	—	—	—	4.3	3.4	2.9	3.4	3.3	3.4
Physical Plant	1.5	1.1	1.1	1.0	1.8	0.2	1.7	0.7	3.2	3.0	2.0	3.2	2.9	2.8
Other	5.8	4.5	5.3	6.9	4.1	6.6	5.4	5.6	2.5	3.1	5.7	7.2	5.9	6.8
Interest	15.5	16.0	15.5	16.0	14.5	14.5	13.6	11.7	8.6	6.7	7.1	6.8	6.8	7.0
TOTAL	42.2	39.6	40.0	40.2	42.1	49.1	49.7	47.6	47.9	46.8	52.2	59.4	63.3	67.5
Surplus (Deficit)	4.4	(8.6)	(8.1)	(9.0)	(3.7)	(0.3)	(4.8)	(3.9)	(3.5)	(2.5)	(0.3)	(9.8)	(2.8)	(3.5

Source: Northwestern University Treasurer's Reports, 1877-1890.

[a]Gross income from board and room, minus operating expenses.
[b]Estimated

As Table 2-2 shows, annual deficits between 1880 and 1890 were relatively minor (except for 1888) and well within the range which business manager Hoag and the trustees considered manageable, given the increase in the value of the university's net assets from $1,069,000 in 1877 to $2,380,800 in 1890 (see Table 2-3).

TABLE 2-3
N.U. RESOURCES AND LIABILITIES: 1876-1890 (Selected Years)
(In Thousands of Dollars)

Year	Physical Plant	Productive Assets	Non-Productive Assets	Other[a] Assets	Total	Liabilities	Net
1877	$296.7	$ 451.7	$504.9	—	$1,253.3	$184.3	$1,069.0
1881	266.0	388.2	500.0	—	1,154.2	209.8	944.3
1884	335.0	734.2	500.0	113.5	1,682.7	143.1	1,539.6
1887	379.5	1,013.0	506.2	79.8	1,978.5	139.0	1,839.5
1890	511.0	1,497.0	510.3	30.5	2,548.8	168.0	2,380.8

SOURCE: Northwestern University Treasurer's Reports, 1876-1890.

[a]Miscellaneous assets including cash, tuition notes, bequests and legacies.

Dearborn Observatory during and after construction in 1889, built to house the world's largest telescope, donated by the Chicago Astronomical Society; Professor Oliver Marcy in foreground at top

Promising as this improvement in the university's financial situation might be, President Cummings, in his report for 1889, nevertheless emphasized that Northwestern was still badly in need of "more officers of instruction and enlarged facilities in the way of buildings, apparatus and libraries." Some of these could be financed from a further growth in enrollment and a rise in income from the university's rental properties, but if Northwestern was to rank "among the best colleges in the land" it must increase its endowment.

Prospects for raising funds were encouraging. Many large fortunes had been amassed during the years following the end of the Civil War. What Northwestern needed was someone who could present its plans for the future to potential donors. This responsibility, Cummings conceded, could be assumed by the president, but only if he were free to "attend to the general interests of the university, to visit its patrons and attend conventions and general educational meetings."

President Cummings's urging that the university's endowment be raised and his outline of how the president might assist in bringing this about reflected his lengthy experience as an administrator and money raiser. But these recommendations to the trustees were to be his last. The following spring, on May 7, 1890, he was stricken by a heart attack and died. Shortly before his death he had begun to draft his annual report to the board. Its opening words were prophetic, "Men die but institutions live on."

"Men Die but Institutions Live On"

Patten Gymnasium, dedicated 1910, used for commencement and other events

Part Two

A UNIVERSITY FOR
THE MODERN AGE

1890-1920

Annie May Swift Hall, completed 1895 for use by the Cumnock School of Oratory

Henry Wade Rogers, President 1890-1900

Fisk Hall, built to house the Academy and made possible by the "munificent generosity" of William Deering

3

BUILDING A UNIVERSITY
1890-1900

At a special meeting following the death of President Cummings, a trustees' committee headed by William Deering was appointed to conduct a search for his successor. The committee had the benefit of the very thoughtful advice Cummings had incorporated into his last report. Noting that Northwestern's custom of appointing a philosopher-minister as president was unrealistic in the face of the coming era in higher education in America, he stressed the importance of choosing a man of "broad intellect and sympathies" who was "first of all a man of good executive ability." The next president would need to have this talent so that he could administer effectively all the colleges of the university. He must also have a strong will since he "must command the respect of the ardent, exuberant, keen and critical but often wrong-headed and misjudging young men and women with whom he will have to deal." In addition, "he must be a man in whose judgment businessmen will have confidence. He must be a leader, a leader among men who are accustomed to lead."[1]

"A Leader among Men... Accustomed to Lead"

This injunction to select an experienced administrator and powerful personality seemed all the more timely given the competition that Northwestern would soon face from the newly rechartered University of Chicago headed by President William Rainey Harper and supported financially by John D. Rockefeller. On September 1, 1890, Deering reported to the trustees the committee's success in finding someone "eminently qualified" to fill the "high office for which he is named." Henry Wade Rogers, dean of the Law School at the University of Michigan, appeared to possess all the qualities for leadership prescribed by Cummings.

Then thirty-seven years old, Rogers had graduated from the University of Michigan in 1874 and after studying and practicing law had become a member of the Law School faculty in 1877. Two years later he had been appointed dean and had gone on to transform the Law School into the largest in the United States.

Henry Wade Rogers

A noted lecturer and author of several major legal treatises, Rogers had also published articles in various literary periodicals. Both he and his wife, Emma, the daughter of a Methodist minister, were active in the Methodist church. Mrs. Rogers was a leading member of the Methodist Woman's Home Missionary Society, a prohibitionist, and a supporter of woman's suffrage. She was, as well, a cultivated and gracious woman who warmly supported her husband's efforts.[2]

"Wise Conservatism" Rogers's inauguration took place on February 18, 1891 at Evanston's First Methodist Church before a crowd of 1500 interested spectators, representatives of regional universities, and members of the Northwestern community. The occasion was marked by a somewhat pointed exchange between trustee Orrington Lunt and the new president. As Lunt presented the keys of office to Rogers he expressed the view that "The seats of learning ought to be as essentially conservative as they ought to be slow to run risks or enter on dangerous experiments." Rogers responded that although "wise conservatism" had its merits "we must . . . not hesitate to make such changes in the established order of things as the demands of the progress of the age shall show to be wise and good."[3]

In an immensely lengthy and learned inaugural address on educational theory and practice in various parts of the world from ancient times to the present, Rogers left no doubt that he meant to make changes that would move Northwestern into the modern age. Though he recognized that the university was "governed by the principle that Christianity is true, that it is the basis for our civilization, and the beginning of wisdom," he went on to state ". . . I do not believe that it was ever intended by the founders of this institution of learning that it was to be narrowly sectarian. . . ." Their purpose, he reminded the assembly, was to provide means for the study of "every description of knowledge that, rising above mere handicraft, could contribute to train the mind and faculties of man."

Rogers noted that many people were dissatisfied with universities because of "a deep-seated conviction that they (are) not performing the work necessary to prepare men for the various activities of modern life, so different from the life their fathers lived half a century ago." He urged that Northwestern expand its offerings to remedy this lack. The College of Liberal Arts, for instance, should add the comprehensive study of economics and political science to its program to prepare men for careers in financial administration and government. And a school of civil, mechanical and electrical engineering should be established to educate specialists in these fields.

The new president was quick to point out, however, that changes in curriculum would serve little purpose unless the university had a good faculty. Such a faculty must have the opportunity and facilities to do more than teach, since "a university whose professors simply teach classes realizes only in part the purpose of its being." To be a place "where the boundaries of knowledge are to be enlarged, where original investigation and research are to be carried on, and the sum of human knowledge increased," Northwestern would need a sizeable and comprehensive library. This and other necessary facilities called for a large endowment.

Inadequate Endowment The new president compared the financial resources of Northwestern to those of the major institutions of the East, and concluded that if it wished to take its

72

place among their ranks, the university must increase its endowment more rapidly than they were increasing theirs:

> ... We will not call an institution rich whose property is valued at less than three millions, and whose income does not exceed $100,000, when we recall that Harvard has property valued at over $11,000,000 and an income of over $800,000 a year, that Columbia has $8,000,000 of property and an income of $530,000; Johns Hopkins has between $5,000,000 and $6,000,000, an income of a quarter of a million; that Cornell has $7,500,000 and an income of over $377,000; that Yale has an income of $336,000. . . .

If the trustees were inclined to be complacent about the improvement in Northwestern's financial outlook during the preceding few years these figures told them how far the university was from commanding the financial support necessary to build and maintain a major center of learning. Moreover, since Rogers—unlike Cummings—came to Northwestern from a state-supported institution, he did not assume that it was his responsibility to raise money. He would provide leadership on educational policies but the board would have to shoulder the burden of finding the resources to realize these policies. But money was not the only problem. Rogers saw a need for fundamental changes in the organization and administration of the university if Northwestern wished to meet the lofty aims he set for it.

Creating One University

Until now relations between the College of Liberal Arts in Evanston and the affiliated professional schools of medicine, law, dentistry, and pharmacy had been nominal at best. Not only were the latter all located in Chicago but each had its own board of trustees and each operated under its own budget. The president's attention had been largely devoted to the College of Liberal Arts. "While this relationship persists," Rogers noted in his report for 1892, "the University can hardly be considered a university except in name."

From the outset Rogers made it clear that he intended to be president of the whole university in fact as well as in name. On his recommendation the trustees created the new post of dean of the College of Liberal Arts and appointed Oliver Marcy to fill it, leaving the president to deal with university-wide issues. Defying the tradition which had placed the president on the Evanston campus, Rogers established an office in Chicago. This offended some Evanstonians "who were accustomed to having the president in their midst," but it allowed him to meet others—especially merchants and lawyers who joined him on the early morning train to Chicago.[4] Rogers welcomed the opportunity to establish contact with men who were influential in the life of the city, for he was determined to link the future of Northwestern to the needs and fortunes of the great metropolis.

Consolidation of the Professional Schools

By the summer of 1891 Rogers's plan for the consolidation of the professional schools was ready and the trustees authorized him to carry it out. Within a year he was able to report that, "The separate boards of trustees formerly governing these schools have surrendered their powers to the trustees of the University together with the property of their respective institutions." All expenditures were to be handled by a newly established central business office. The four affiliated colleges became the Northwestern University Medical School, Law School, Dental

School and School of Pharmacy. These changes, Rogers predicted, would do much to "make the University better known and . . . identify it more closely with the city of Chicago."[5]

Creation of the University Council

To strengthen the bonds among the schools, the trustees authorized the creation of the University Council. Composed of the president, the five deans, and a faculty representative from each school, the Council was empowered "to consult and advise on any subject that pertains to the University as a whole and to communicate to the Board of Trustees in writing its views."[6] Although the Council's power was limited, it represented the first attempt to provide a forum for discussion among administrations and faculty representatives from all parts of the university.

The same purpose prompted the decision to hold a joint commencement in 1895. Since the First Methodist Church—at which the college commencement had traditionally been held—was too small to accommodate all those who might wish to attend the joint commencement, the university rented the Chicago Auditorium for this occasion.[7]

As a result of the consolidation Rogers was much more involved in the growth and development of the professional schools than his predecessors. This was particularly true of the Law School. Shortly after the plans for integration were completed, Henry Booth, the school's founder and only dean, decided to retire. When Henry W. Blodgett, his successor, left after a year, the trustees called on Rogers to serve as acting dean, a position he continued to hold until 1898.[8]

Law School

Rogers took an active role as dean. In 1892 he reorganized the faculty by increasing the number of resident or full time professors from one to four. In June 1895 he asked the trustees to accept the recommendation of the Law School faculty to raise the standards of the school by requiring a three-year course of study. As always he wished Northwestern's standards to equal those of the institutions of national stature, observing that it hardly seemed in keeping "with the dignity of Northwestern" to confer the degree in law at the end of two years when institutions such as Harvard, Columbia, Yale, Cornell, Michigan, and Wisconsin had already or were about to adopt a three-year curriculum. At their June 11, 1895 meeting the trustees responded by voting to adopt the new requirement for the LL.B. degree as of 1896-97. As anticipated, enrollment fell off following the adoption of the new requirement, but by 1899-1900 all of this loss had been recovered. Additions to the law faculty included professors from Cornell, Harvard, Yale, and the Boston University Law School. Among the new faculty was John H. Wigmore, who thus began an association with the Northwestern Law School that lasted until 1929.

The temporary decline in enrollment was more than compensated for by a dramatic improvement in the quality and qualifications of the students who were now drawn to the school. By 1900 Rogers would report that:

> The school . . . has become recognized as one of the foremost law schools of the United States. . . . Of those enrolled this year, 10 held degrees from Harvard, 10 from Yale, 10 from our own University, and 15 from Chicago University. The degree men represented thirty-five colleges, including, in addition to the institutions already named, Amherst, Bowdoin, Brown, Dartmouth, Princeton, and the Universities of Michigan and Wisconsin. Ten years ago there was but

one graduate of our College of Liberal Arts enrolled in the Law School. Harvard was not represented at all, although Yale was represented by three.

It is worth noting that at a time when discrimination against racial minorities and women was very much a matter of course, the Northwestern Law School had an openly expressed policy of "making no distinction on account of sex or color."[9]

The School of Pharmacy also made changes in curriculum during this period. The original course of study had emphasized the practical needs of the pharmaceutical profession and had required its students to complete at least three years on-the-job training in drug stores. Applicants were required to have the equivalent of a grammar school education. In its 1895-96 catalog the school announced that it could no longer "assume responsibility for the training which the students may have had in drug stores" and that "a course of special education . . . should precede the practice of pharmacy in the store in order to render the drug store experience safe, intelligent, and effective."[5] This course, which called for more theoretical training in the classroom, led to the degree of Pharmaceutical Chemist. The immediate result of these more rigorous requirements was a sharp drop in attendance the following year—from 373 to 183. There was some talk of closing the school but by 1900 enrollment was again on the upswing. After 1892 the school admitted women.

Pharmacy

In the Dental College, the decision to adopt a three-year course of study when most other dental schools required only two may well have been responsible for the enrollment of only thirty students during 1890-91. When it became obvious that tuition would not cover expenses, the eight man faculty resigned.[10] The permanent loss of the Dental College was averted when a group of Chicago dentists approached the trustees with a proposal to reorganize the college and reopen it as the Northwestern University Dental School. The trustees accepted the proposal and a contract with the group of dentists was signed in July 1891.

Reorganization of the Dental College

The reorganized school reopened with forty-six students. At this time the National Association of Dental Faculties instructed affiliated schools to adopt a three-year course of study. Once the Northwestern Dental School no longer had to compete against schools offering a shorter course enrollment rose rapidly, more than doubling by 1895 (see Table 3-1). The consolidation of the professional schools made it possible for the dental students to take their courses in anatomy, chemistry, general surgery, histology, and physiology in the Medical School.[11]

The scope and size of the Dental School was expanded substantially with the acquisition of the American College of Dental Surgeons in 1895. Founded in 1885 as a private institution, the college was owned by a leading Chicago dentist, Dr. Theodore Menges. The need for a larger faculty and more administrative expertise prompted Dr. Menges to ask Northwestern to consider the possibility of a merger. The board reacted favorably and at its meeting of March 2, 1896 agreed to the consolidation of the two schools. Under this new arrangement the Dental School faculty became sufficiently large to assume responsibility for all the courses required by its students and the previous arrangement with the Medical School came to an end. In 1897 Dr. Greene Vardiman Black was appointed dean and charged with the task of further systematizing the school's operations. He was to hold that office

Dental School, late 1890's

Dental Clinic, 1890's

Dr. Greene Vardiman Black, founder and later dean of the Northwestern University Dental School

The Medical School

for the next twenty years. The school continued to expand and enrollment reached a total of nearly six hundred students by 1899-1900.[12]

In spite of the consolidation of the professional schools, the president had relatively little to do with the administration of the Medical School which—under its contract with the university—retained control over policy, finances, and faculty appointments throughout the 1890's.[13] The terms of the agreement no doubt reflected the reluctance of Dean Nathan Smith Davis, Sr., founder and chief administrator of the school, as well as a member of the university board of trustees, to relinquish his control.

But neither Rogers nor the board had reason to regret this arrangement since the school continued to maintain a high place among the medical colleges in the United States. In 1892 the faculty voted to follow the example of the Harvard, Pennsylvania, and Michigan medical schools by making the completion of a four-year course of study a requirement for graduation.[14] As in the case of the other professional schools, the raising of requirements led to a temporary decline in enrollment (see Table 3-1). In 1893 the school moved into a new five-story building on South Dearborn Street, complete with an amphitheatre, a lecture hall, and numerous laboratories.

TABLE 3 - 1
N. U. STUDENT ENROLLMENT, 1890 - 1900

Academic Year	1890-1891	1891-1892	1892-1893	1893-1894	1894-1895	1895-1896	1896-1897	1897-1898	1898-1899	1899-1900
EVANSTON CAMPUS										
College	383	379	481	487	498	547	498	551	537	572
Graduate		18	31	19	33	27	23	36	38	42
Music						70	101	112	114	149
Total	383	397	512	506	531	644	622	699	689	763
Academy (Preparatory)	692	701	600	497	534	547	487	531	497	507
Total	1075	1098	1112	1003	1065	1191	1109	1230	1186	1270
CHICAGO CAMPUS										
Medical	240	271	274	252	269	316	328	356	301	325
Woman's Medical		122	137	115	116	130	120	98	79	69
Law	145	264	180	139	191	203	188	141	166	211
Dentistry	30	46	66	94	111	582a	513	478	478	594
Pharmacy	273	360	385	462	388	373	183	115	247	235
Total	688	1063	1042	1062	1075	1604	1332	1188	1271	1434
Grand Total	1763	2161	2154	2065	2140	2795	2441	2418	2457	2704

aIncludes 402 students in the American College of Dental Surgeons.
SOURCE: Northwestern University Catalog 1890-1900.

Some faculty suggested that it would be "consonant with the University's dignity" to raise the requirements for admission above the level adopted in 1889, which merely called for graduation from high school. Others advanced the more persuasive argument that such a move "was both unnecessary and undesirable," because it might seriously reduce the number of applicants. While prospective students were strongly advised to complete at least two years of college before applying for admission, the basic requirement of a high school graduation remained intact. Between 1895 and 1900 enrollment in the Medical School averaged well above three hundred students.[15]

The administration of the Medical School changed in 1898 with the resignation of Dr. Davis from the deanship. His successor, Dr. Frank D. Johnson, served for only one year because of ill health, and in 1899 the trustees named Dr. Davis, Jr., to the position so long occupied by his father.[16]

In 1892, Northwestern's professional schools were augmented by the acquisition of the Woman's Medical School of Chicago. Organized in 1870 at a time when medical schools generally did not admit women, the Woman's Medical School had survived the Chicago fire of 1871, the financial pressures of the 1873 depression, and prejudice against women doctors, to take its place among the respected medical schools in the Chicago area. Its admission standards and four-year course of study were essentially the same as those required of the male students enrolled in the Northwestern Medical School.[17]

Woman's Medical School 1892-1902

The trustees' decision to acquire the Woman's Medical School may well have been influenced by the fact that the Medical School's refusal to admit women ran counter to the university's policy of encouraging coeducation. But if this was a consideration it was a secondary one, for above all it was assumed that like the other professional schools the Woman's Medical School would pay its own way so that its acquisition would enlarge the university without making any additional demands on its resources.

During the first five years of its association with Northwestern, the school prospered with its enrollment reaching a peak of 137 in 1892-93 and remaining high until 1896. After that enrollment began to dwindle rapidly until in 1900 only 69 students registered (see Table 3-1). In large part this drop was due to the decision of several Chicago medical colleges to admit women students. Graduation from a coeducational medical school promised a higher professional standing for women physicians and as a result the demand for a Woman's Medical School declined. In an attempt to reduce costs and save the institution Rogers tried to convince the Northwestern Medical School to admit women to its first and second year classes, but the Medical School faculty declined. On February 17, 1902 the board of trustees voted to close the Woman's Medical School and sell its property to the American College of Physicians and Surgeons.

Rogers did not let his concern with the professional schools keep him from taking an active interest in developments on the Evanston campus. Indeed, in what was to be his last presidential report, he affirmed that the College of Liberal Arts should "in any university . . . take the leading place." Indeed, one of his major objectives was to strengthen and enlarge the faculty of the college, most of whose sixteen members were the sole teachers in their respective fields. By 1900 the list had grown to include thirty-one full professors, one associate professor, two assistant professors, fifteen instructors, and four assistants. These faculty appointments—spread over all the disciplines—substantially raised the level of intellectual life for both students and faculty. The former were offered greater opportunity for advanced and specialized training, while the latter enjoyed the stimulus supplied by a larger circle of colleagues with a broader range of interests than Northwestern had provided until now.

Liberal Arts Faculty

Prior to 1890 the Liberal Arts faculty was largely composed of graduates of Wesleyan and other Methodist institutions. Prominent among the newcomers were six scholars trained at The Johns Hopkins University, one of the pioneers in graduate education in America: Henry Crew in physics; Edwin Conklin in zoology; John A. Scott in Greek; Omera Floyd Long in Latin; James Alton James in history; and Ulysses S. Grant in geology. They were joined by colleagues with doctorates from other American and European universities: in political economy, John H. Gray from the University of Halle; in mathematics, Henry White and Thomas F. Holgate from Clark; in zoology, William A. Locy from the University of Berlin; and in philosophy, George Coe also from the University of Berlin. These men formed a community of scholars interested in research as well as teaching, who focused their lives around the university and became nationally known in their respective fields. Rogers lent support to their research efforts by carefully listing for the trustees the titles of books faculty members had published as well as taking note of their contributions to periodical literature and the papers they had delivered at meetings of learned societies.

Interest in German Studies

With these additions to the faculty, Northwestern came closer than it had ever been to the ideal of an institution where all branches of learning are taught. One of the more striking changes was the decline in emphasis on classical studies and a flowering of interest in the German language and literature. In addition to translating important works, students majoring in this subject held informal meetings in the course of which they conversed in German and read original papers on topics taken up in their classes. Interest in this field was no doubt stimulated by the fact that in 1890 close to 15 percent of Chicago's population was German or of German descent. Since German was widely taught in the public schools, some teaching candidates had a practical reason for learning the language.[18] The college showed interest in German culture by hosting gatherings of German-American associations such as the Germania Maennerchor and the Chicago Germania Club.[19] In his report for 1898, the president announced that members of Chicago's German community made a contribution of $1,000 to the university for the purchase of a large collection of rare books from a private library in Leipzig.

English Studies

It may surprise present-day readers to learn that as early as 1892 the faculty prescribed remedial courses for students with demonstrated grammatical problems.[20] The regular curriculum in English language and literature was comprehensive, including an intensive seven-term program devoted to "the examination of literary masterpieces from the earliest period of our literature to the present day." All candidates for the baccalaureate degree were required to do some work in oratory, the object being to teach "the management and regulation of the breath; the proper use of the body in the development of vocal energy; the most advanced knowledge of English Phonation" and "the most approved methods of acquiring a distinct articulation." Special attention was devoted to "how exhaustion in speaking may be overcome; how sore throat . . . may be avoided: how harsh quality of voice may be removed (and) how awkwardness in gesture may be conquered."[21] Such training was particularly valuable for students preparing for teaching or the ministry.

BUILDING A UNIVERSITY

The president's interest in the social sciences was reflected in a wider range of courses in political science and history. Though previous presidents had taught moral philosophy and theology, Rogers taught constitutional and international law to undergraduates in the college. Courses in medieval, English, modern European and American history became part of the standard curriculum, as did classes in political economy. The catalog for 1894-95 announced a year-long seminar in that field devoted to the following two topics: The Policy in Regard to the Issue of Paper Money in the United States, Past, Present, and Future, and The Saloon Question in Chicago, from a Financial Administrative and Political Standpoint.

The Social Sciences

Students interested in science could choose courses in natural history, chemistry, physics, or astronomy. The emphasis in these courses tended to fall on methods of scientific investigation and experimental work in the laboratory. The teaching of scientific theories raised certain problems at a Methodist institution during this period of heated debate over the validity of Darwin's theory of evolution. There is no record of any open dispute over this question at Northwestern, but in general the sciences appear to have challenged the religious convictions of some of the students. Addressing himself to this question, Professor Oliver Marcy delivered a special lecture in which he attempted to reconcile the two points of view. "There can be no conflict between science and religion," he reassured the students, "true religion is in harmony with the laws of the universe."[22]

The Sciences

The magnitude of curricular expansion in the College of Liberal Arts during Rogers's administration becomes clear in a comparison of course offerings. Whereas the catalog for 1889-90 listed 35 full year courses, within a decade this number had increased to 117. Moreover by 1900 approximately 75 percent of the students were majoring in modern languages and literature and the natural and social sciences rather than in classics. Rogers's pledge in his inaugural speech to modernize the curriculum had been fulfilled.

In his report for 1897 the president indicated that by vote of the faculty it had been decided to introduce a semester system to replace the three-term academic year in effect since 1855. He noted that this change, which added one week to the summer vacation, was a distinct advantage to "the large class of students who earn their own living and can make good use of the extra week in the summer earning money to defray the expenses of their next year." Moreover, he added that members of the faculty had felt that under the old system too much time had been spent on examinations. Rogers concluded with the observation that the semester plan was "the system under which the larger number of the leading universities of the country are working."

Introduction of Semester System

Between 1890 and 1900 the number of undergraduates registered at Northwestern grew from 383 to 763 (see Table 3-1). Few American institutions, the president reported, could match this record. He added that attendance in the college had "increased proportionally more than at Harvard, Yale, Columbia, Johns Hopkins, Michigan, or Princeton during this period."

By waiving entrance examinations for certified students from accredited schools, Northwestern continued to attract applicants from midwestern public high schools. School boards interested in having their schools placed on the university's accredited list were urged to apply directly to the president who would arrange for an inspection of the school by a committee of the faculty.[23]

The Academy However the most important source of undergraduates during this period continued to be the university's preparatory school—renamed the Academy in 1892. In his report for 1893-94, for example, Rogers noted that over half the students enrolled in the college were graduates of the Academy, while a third of the remainder were sent to the Academy to make up certain deficiencies after they had been admitted to the college.

The Academy was plagued by its own success. Housed in Old College it could no longer accommodate adequately the 701 students in attendance by 1891-92. In spite of the importance of the school to Northwestern, the trustees apparently considered that the university's resources were inadequate to finance a new building. They did, however, encourage the principal of the school, Herbert Fisk, to solicit funds for this purpose. In 1896 he reported to the president that a new building "to which reference has been made in every report for eight years, is soon to be supplied through the munificent generosity of Mr. William Deering."[24] Named Fisk Hall in his honor, the building was ready for occupancy in January 1899. Built at a cost of $70,000, the three-story structure included offices, classrooms, laboratory space, a library and a chapel seating 800.* In his contribution to the President's Report for 1898, Professor Fisk praised the hall as being "in architectural features worthy of its place among other noble and beautiful structures that adorn the city of Evanston." Although enrollment dropped sharply between 1892 and 1894, the Academy continued to provide training for an average of close to 500 students per year to the end of the decade (see Table 3-1).

Coeducation A firm believer in higher education for women, Rogers took the occasion to defend coeducation at Northwestern in his report of 1893. The issue, he noted, was not whether women could do as well in classes as men without endangering their physical well being. It was, rather, whether they were entitled to an equal education. If the answer was affirmative, then the reason that justified Northwestern as a place for the education of men would seem to justify the extension of the privilege to women on equal terms. "For until there exists in this part of the country a university for women, as well equipped as those for men, the principle of coeducation must be applied or women will be discriminated against in their efforts to secure an education." He dismissed the argument that Northwestern should not be coeducational because women from the West could attend Vassar, Wellesley or Smith. As he pointed out, it could also be said that because men from the West could go to Harvard or Yale there was nothing to justify the existence of Northwestern. He concluded his discussion of coeducation by pointing out that between 1883 and 1893 the proportion of women in the College of Liberal Arts averaged about 38 percent of the total.†

*According to Edwin A. Greenlaw in "The Academy" (in Arthur H. Wilde's *Northwestern University 1855-1905*), the move into Fisk Hall raised the question of what should be done with Old College, occupied by the Preparatory School since 1860. Rumors that it was to be destroyed apparently brought so many protests from students and alumni that the trustees decided to move the building to the rear of Fisk Hall and to remodel it for classroom use by the College of Liberal Arts. It was finally demolished in 1973 when a lightning storm revealed that it was in danger of collapse because of damage from dry rot.

†At this time women accounted for 33 percent of the student body at Michigan, approximately 50 percent of Oberlin's students, and 66 percent of the enrollment at Boston University. *Rogers's Report of 1893.*

BUILDING A UNIVERSITY

Both in his inaugural address and in his first annual report to the trustees in June 1891, Rogers had expressed the hope that someone would provide Northwestern with a library worthy of a university. Shortly thereafter Orrington Lunt responded with an offer to contribute $50,000 toward the erection of a suitable library building, provided that an equal amount could be raised from other sources. By early 1893 pledges had been received for an additional $15,000 and the university itself set aside $35,000 from its endowment to bring the total to the $100,000 needed to cover the cost of the proposed building.[25]

Northwestern was badly in need of the new library. As Rogers pointed out in his report for 1893, the university's holdings of some 27,000 volumes and 18,000 pamphlets were crammed into every conceivable space on the third floor of University Hall, while the small reading room, capable of accommodating no more than fifty students, was always crowded.

By fall of 1894 the Orrington Lunt Library, named in honor of the principal donor, was completed and ready for occupancy. A distinguished group attended the dedication ceremony including President William Rainey Harper of the University of Chicago, President Charles Kendall Adams of the University of Wisconsin, and Dr. Justin Winsor, Librarian of Harvard University.

Orrington Lunt Library

Stacks, offices, and a reading room with 120 seats were located on the main floor of the three-story building. Documents and newspaper files were put in the basement.* An auditorium seating 500 and a suite of rooms occupied the second floor, while the German department was moved into seminar rooms on the third.[26]

With the promise of better library facilities and the addition of a number of research-oriented staff members, the college faculty moved to improve and expand the graduate training program. During the 1860's the university had started awarding a master's degree to alumni of three years standing† provided they could give evidence of having a good moral character and pay a fee of $5.00.[27] Under the rules adopted a decade later, the M.A. or M.S. degree was limited to graduates who spent an extra year taking a course of study approved by the faculty.[28]

In 1891 the faculty changed its requirements for postgraduate degrees to conform with regulations "prescribed by the universities of the highest grade."[29] In the future only students with bachelor's degrees in arts, philosophy, science, or letters would "receive the corresponding master's degree on the completion of a course of advanced study equal in amount to the work of one full college year." This work was to be done in residence, and the degree would be granted after an examination and the completion of "a thesis of not less than 4,000 words on an approved subject pertinent to the course of study."[30]

Graduate Studies

The major step in developing Northwestern's graduate program, however, was taken in 1891 with the establishment of a doctoral program. Requirements for this degree included: a bachelor's degree equivalent to Northwestern's; two years of resident work; a reading knowledge of French and German; the preparation of a

---

*The new library was expected to accommodate 100,000 volumes, but was so designed that with the addition of extra wings it could house 1,000,000 volumes.

†It may be noted that this practice was not unique to Northwestern. Until the early 1870's graduates of both Harvard and Yale could also receive the master's degree three years after graduation merely upon the payment of five dollars. *Brooks Mather Kelley*, Yale: A History (*New Haven; Yale University Press, 1974*), p. 258.

thesis; and satisfactory completion of written and oral examinations. The latter were conducted by a committee composed of the president of the university, the dean of the College of Liberal Arts, the heads of departments, and three other persons invited by the president.[31]

Although fluctuating on a year-to-year basis, the number of graduate students grew from the eighteen registered during 1891-92 to forty-two in 1899-1900 (see Table 3-1). During this period a total of ninety-five students received master's degrees and four were awarded their Ph.D.'s.* This growing emphasis on graduate study and research no doubt enhanced the university's scholarly reputation. But at a price. When fifty-three-year-old Henry Cohn, assistant professor of German, suffered a sudden, fatal stroke in March 1900, his colleagues were fairly certain as to the cause.[32] In a memorial statement they noted:

> It is very easy to deplore the fact that Professor Cohn 'over-worked,' and yet it was not his choice to be continually under the lash of urgent haste: his nature inclined to sociability, and to relaxing, at proper intervals, the close bonds of strenuous effort. His life was, indeed, only one more illustration of that unnoticed tragi-comedy which is ever taking place in American academic communities: it was an example of the feverish struggle which men of high organization are so often compelled to maintain, in order to do even approximate justice to the more ideal demands of their high calling.[33]

President Rogers's plans for the unification of the university brought important changes in two departments on the Evanston campus: the Cumnock School of Oratory and the Conservatory of Music. Like the professional schools these departments had previously functioned autonomously and had enjoyed what was essentially a nominal relationship with the rest of the university.

Cumnock School of Oratory   Thus, under an agreement with the university reached in 1878, Robert McLean Cumnock, as professor of elocution and rhetoric, had contracted to teach certain classes in elocution required of Northwestern students, as well as offering special training to those interested in becoming teachers of elocution or public readers.[34] By 1892 it was obvious that the single room in University Hall assigned to the department could no longer accommodate the growing number of students applying for admission.[35] Faced with this situation Cumnock suggested to the trustees that the university erect a building which he would lease for the department.[36] After two years of considering this proposal, the trustees informed Cumnock that they were unable to provide the financial resources for such a building but that they would grant him "permission to erect on the campus a building which shall be known as Cumnock Hall."[37]

At the same meeting the trustees elevated the department of elocution to the status of a School of Oratory and appointed Cumnock as its director. But the change was

---

*Two candidates completed their Ph.D.'s in 1896: Vernon James Hall, whose dissertation was entitled "A Study of Iron and Zinc Hydroxides in Precipitation"; and Francis Cummins Lockwood, whose topic was "Emerson as a Philosopher." The two who received their Ph.D.'s in 1898 and 1899 were Charles Hill, who wrote on the topic "Primary Segmentation of the Vertebrate Brain"; and Alice Gabrielle Twight, whose topic was "Women of the French XVII Century Classic Theatre." *N.U. Catalogs 1896-97, 1899-1900.*

more nominal than real. The school remained essentially a privately owned and operated institution. Cumnock determined its policies, received all income from tuition and fees, and was responsible for the salaries of his staff.

Thanks largely to the assistance of Gustav Swift, wealthy Chicago meat packer, Cumnock was able to finance a new building for the school which was completed in the spring of 1895. It was named Annie May Swift Hall in memory of Swift's daughter, who had died while a student at Northwestern. *The Northwestern* for May 23, 1895, described the building—located northeast of University Hall—as consisting of a first floor on which were to be found an office, reception room, and auditorium seating 300; a second floor housing fifteen classrooms; and a basement to be used for a gymnasium. Cumnock assumed financial responsibility for maintenance of the hall.

Annie May Swift Hall

The situation of the Conservatory of Music was somewhat different. In 1891 Oren Edwin Locke, its director since 1876, resigned suddenly. During the preceding three years enrollment had steadily decreased. Locke's departure left the school in such a "disorganized and chaotic condition" "that there was a strong feeling in favor of discontinuing" the conservatory among the trustees.[38] Fortunately the board yielded to the pleas of Cornelia, daughter of Orrington Lunt, and trustee James Raymond, and decided to continue the conservatory under a new director. Their choice fell on Peter Christian Lutkin, organist at Chicago's St. James Episcopal Church and a member of the American Conservatory faculty.

The new director was remarkably successful in recruiting staff and reorganizing the music program. Indeed before long the prospects for the future looked so encouraging that the trustees agreed to relieve Lutkin of the financial responsibility for operating the conservatory and transformed it into the department of music in the College of Liberal Arts.[39] Lutkin actively promoted an interest in music both on campus and in the larger Evanston community. He organized the University Glee Club, the a capella choir and the Evanston Musical Club and scheduled numerous concerts and recitals.[40] These varied activities helped to enhance the reputation of the department.

In his report to the trustees in 1895 President Rogers informed them that the university had "a Department of Music that is in every way creditable and which receives the heartiest commendation of those who are competent to judge in such matters." He went on to say that the department had "now attained so good a standing . . . as would seem to justify its changing its name to that of a School of Music." At their meeting of June 26, 1895, the trustees voted to accept this recommendation and named Lutkin dean of the School of Music.

The School of Music

In accordance with its new status the school expanded its program to offer professional training in "the higher branches of music-study either as a theoretical, practical, or creative art." Provision was also made for the continued study of music as "a part of general culture or as an accomplishment." Full time students were given two options: one a two-year course designed especially for teachers, the other a four-year program which would train performers for the concert stage.[41] The number of students registered for the full time courses leading to a certificate or a diploma increased from 70 in 1895-96 to 149 in 1899-1900 (see Table 3-1).

With an increasing enrollment there was growing pressure to move the school from its location on the top floor of the Woman's College. In 1897, Rogers reported that the women students housed in the building resented "the discomfort and extreme annoyance of listening throughout the day and often into the night to the sounds of many instruments" coming from the various practice rooms. Although in no position to finance the $50,000 structure visualized by President Rogers, the trustees did authorize the construction of a one-story building on a site near the Woman's College to be used exclusively by the School of Music. As noted by the dean, the school then had "an abode where we were free to propagate as many sound waves as we wished without disturbing the liberal arts students." He continued, "Although the new building was neither large nor pretentious, it was a source of gratification and encouragement to those interested in the Music Department of the university for it implied permanency and the active interest of the Executive Board."[42]

The University Guild
While the president initiated changes within the university, Emma Rogers turned her efforts to improving relations between Northwestern and the Evanston community. In the summer of 1892 she brought together representatives from each and set afoot the subsequent formation of the University Guild.[43] The objectives of the Guild were both social and cultural. Its meetings, which generally featured talks and programs dealing with the arts and letters, gave university people and local residents an opportunity to become acquainted under informal circumstances.

The first president of the group was Cornelia Lunt, representing the town. She was succeeded by Mrs. Rogers, thus establishing the tradition of rotating the office between town and gown. The first project undertaken by the group was to establish an art collection. At Mrs. Rogers's suggestion, a number of artifacts—mainly fine pottery and porcelain—were acquired at the close of the Columbian Exposition in 1894.[44] These were put on display in the meeting rooms assigned to the Guild in the suite of rooms on the second floor of the Orrington Lunt Library.*

In 1898 Mrs. Rogers became interested in a settlement house located in rented quarters on the near north side of Chicago. Founded in 1891 by Charles Zeublin, a Northwestern alumnus, the settlement was concerned with improving the living conditions of the Polish and German immigrants in this neighborhood. Mrs. Rogers made a major contribution to the project by sponsoring the incorporation in 1898 of the Northwestern University Settlement Association. With its own board of trustees the association had no official connection with the university, but members of the Northwestern community were active in the association as officers and fund raisers. President Rogers served as the first chairman of the board and was later succeeded by Mrs. Rogers. William Deering, Robert D. Sheppard, and Milton H. Wilson were also active on its board.[45]

Campus Life
The mere fact that on the Evanston campus enrollment rose considerably during the 1890's changed the character of undergraduate life. Most striking was the growth in the number and variety of extracurricular activities. Special interest clubs proliferated: the Circle Français, composed of French majors; the Historical

---

*In 1923, when the library found itself short of space, the collection was put in storage. When new Guild rooms became available in Scott Hall in 1940, the collection was put on display there.

Association; the Social Science Club; the Linnaean Society; the Mineralogical Journal Club; and the Glee, Banjo and Mandolin clubs. The Coffee Club was organized in 1892 to "counteract and minimize the evil effects that inevitably attend the existence of college fraternities in any institution, in the way of clannishness and the undue development of 'cliques'."[46] Both faculty and students attended Coffee Club meetings at which literary works not included in the students' courses were discussed.

During this period students began to show a greater interest in politics, perhaps as a result of an increased emphasis on current events in the curriculum. A Prohibition Club had been organized in 1891; a mock Republican convention was held on campus in May 1892; and the issues of the 1896 presidential campaign led to a series of spirited debates between the University Sound Money Club and the University Bimetallic League.[47] A university-sponsored lecture series brought to Evanston a number of distinguished speakers, including Sir Edwin Arnold, William Dean Howells, General John B. Logan, and Hamlin Garland. Alumni efforts brought Ohio Governor William McKinley to the campus in 1895 to address the students on "The Relation of Education to Citizenship."[48] *Student Interest in Political Issues*

Enthusiasm for debating revived during the Rogers era. In its first intercollegiate debate since 1877, Northwestern answered the challenge of the University of Michigan in 1894 and sent a faculty-selected three-man team to Ann Arbor. Debating the resolution "That the policy of the federal government ought to be to bring about the annexation of the Hawaiian Islands," Northwestern won the contest. The following year Northwestern again debated Michigan, this time in Evanston, and took the negative on the question: "Should the United States government own and control the Nicaragua Canal?" Again Northwestern won. The students held a victory parade through Evanston, then composed themselves enough to state: "Having clearly outclassed the University of Michigan it would seem to be no presumption now for Northwestern to challenge Harvard, an institution claiming the championship in debate in the East."[49] Intercollegiate debating became a regular part of life at Northwestern, especially following the formation of the Central Debating League in 1897 which arranged regular meetings with Wisconsin, Michigan, and Chicago.[50] *Debating*

Oratorical contests also became popular. In 1890 Northwestern joined the Northern Oratorical League, which represented a number of midwestern universities and colleges. By 1900 Northwestern had won two of the annual championships. In 1897 a group of students organized the Rogers Literary Society "to develop in its own members the power of oratory and debate" and "to promote the same activity in other students of the University."[51] Newspaper accounts suggest that the collegiate forensic style of the nineties was characterized by florid language and melodramatic delivery. In the 1899 League contest, for example, Northwestern's representative delivered an oration entitled "The Saxon or the Slav?" which warned against the menace of Russian power: *Oratorical Contests*

> The proposition from St. Petersburg looking toward universal disarmament is but a move to hide the true intent and to cover the advance of the Russian Bear. Those shaggy paws now lifted in supplication will soon descend; the

Women's tennis team in the 1890's

Jesse Van Doozer and Albert Potter, Northwestern's All Western halfbacks, 1896

Senior class play, "The Holy Grail," June 1894

watchful eyes will blaze with innate savagery; and . . . the huge brute will strike a swift and terrible blow, whose results even a century will not efface.

The young man who gave this fearsome address was awarded third prize.[52]

During the 1890's much of the social life on campus continued to revolve around the fraternities and sororities which were still growing in membership and prestige.* By 1895 the Greek letter societies had attracted approximately thirty percent of the 328 men and thirty-six percent of the 219 women enrolled in the College of Liberal Arts. Membership in the fraternities also included twenty-two university faculty members, nineteen students from the Medical School, seven from the Law School, and three from the Dental School.

Fraternities and Sororities

Reactions to the fraternities and sororities remained mixed. Defenders claimed that these societies provided a wholesome and helpful environment for students and encouraged the development of an *esprit de corps*. Proponents also maintained that fraternities and sororities promoted high standards of scholarship and, in general, contributed to the intellectual, moral, and social development of their members. Critics asserted the very opposite, accusing the Greek letter societies of distracting members from their studies and of fostering false social values and bad habits, including extravagance and dissipation.[53]

By 1890 objections to the influence of the fraternities led to the organization of the Massasoits—a group of men pledged not to join a Greek letter society while they were in college.† This group proceeded to cause a stir on campus by publishing a weekly newspaper, *The Northwestern World*, and an annual entitled *The Arrow*, which competed with the fraternity controlled publications, *The Northwestern* and *The Syllabus*.[54]

Although they did not form an independent organization, at least some women felt the stigma of non-sorority status. Describing some new residents of her boarding house, one girl wrote her mother, "I like them all well enough, one of them very much, but they are not at all our style. They are all society—and all fraternity. That means a good deal."[55]

In general the university authorities were favorably inclined toward fraternities and sororities. Although it was many years before the fraternities could take advantage of the offer, the trustees in June 1895 indicated their positive attitude by setting aside a section on the campus for the future location of chapter houses. Rogers himself was rather noncommittal.**As he put it, there were fraternities whose influence was not altogether wholesome, but there were others which were "to a high degree in every way helpful and to which it is an honor for any man to belong."[56]

*Local chapters of the national groups organized during this period included three fraternities: Delta Tau Delta (1893), Sigma Alpha Epsilon (1894), and Sigma Nu (1898); and two sororities: Pi Beta Phi (1894), and Delta Delta Delta (1898).

†The members of *Massasoit* were apparently less disturbed by the evils of fraternity life than they were by the fact that they did not belong to any of the existing Greek letter societies. Within two years interest in the organization had waned, and when some of its leading lights left to organize new chapters of national fraternities on campus, the society disintegrated. *James Alton James, "History of Northwestern University," typescript, Chapter XIV, p. 11, N.U.A.*

**Northwestern's fraternity rivalries during this period inspired the first novel written about the university, William C. Levere's *'Twixt Greek and Barb*, published in Evanston by William C. Lord in 1900. It recounted the dissolution of a lifelong friendship between a loyal fraternity man and the leader of the campus's independent faction.

Rogers was more disposed than any of his predecessors to grant students freedom to pursue their own interests. As part of his plan to develop Northwestern as a Chicago institution, he relaxed the rules governing visits to the city. Northwestern's catalogs had always drawn attention to the high moral tone of Evanston, advertising this as one of the institution's most favorable features. But now a new phrase was inserted: "The village is near enough to the city of Chicago to secure many of the advantages . . . of city life."[57] In describing the School of Music the catalog stated: "The great series of orchestral concerts at the Chicago Auditorium, together with the Apollo Club concerts and the frequent appearances of world-renowned artists are all within easy access from Evanston."[58]

"Too Much Social Gaiety"

But Rogers had little sympathy for students whose conduct was questionable. After a year in office he had observed enough of student life at Northwestern to be concerned by the tendency toward "too much social gaiety and a somewhat too free intermingling of the sexes."[59] Whether such conditions had produced any scandals—even minor social infractions caused much talk—can only be surmised, but in 1897 the faculty adopted a strict set of regulations governing the conduct of women students. Under these rules all women enrolled in the College were required to sign a pledge: not to leave Evanston in the evening without a chaperone approved by the dean of women; to live only in quarters approved by the faculty; and to receive calls from gentlemen only on Friday and Saturday evenings, "and then only from such persons as approved by the parents in a letter addressed to the dean."[60] Violations were subject to review by the faculty. Additional regulations passed several months later provided that no campus organization was to hold more than one mixed social a year, and that such events were to end by 11 p.m.[61] These rules applied to both men and women students.

Religious Life on Campus

The rise of numerous secular campus organizations did not noticeably alter Northwestern's image as a sectarian institution. In 1892 the publication of the national young people's society of the Methodist Episcopal Church, the *Epworth Herald*, carried a feature article on Northwestern, which, it stated, "stands in the front rank of the higher educational institutions of Methodism and must, therefore, be of greatest interest to the thousands of Epworth Leaguers who are preparing for university entrance."[62] Actually the President's Report of 1898 indicated that only 47 percent of the students in the college were Methodist. The college chapters of the Y.M.C.A. and Y.W.C.A. attracted students of all faiths and kept alive the school's religious character. In 1895 about 30 percent of all undergraduates belonged to one of these organizations.[63]

To give students an opportunity to listen to representatives of different sects, the faculty in 1892 inaugurated a monthly series of sermons by preachers from various evangelical churches. In 1895 they relaxed the rules requiring all students to attend daily chapel and church service on Sunday. Students were now "expected to attend public worship" on Sunday at a church of their choice and, unless otherwise excused, required to be present at three of the five daily chapel exercises each week.[64]

A decline of interest in careers associated with church work and a rise of interest in the field of education is indicated by a survey of Northwestern students who graduated between 1891 and 1900. Of the 615 graduates surveyed, 211 or over

34 percent chose careers in education, while only 102, or 17 percent, chose to go into the ministry or related work.* This was a striking reversal of the pattern for the period from 1876 to 1890.

Rogers was much in favor of student athletics on several counts. Observing that *Athletics* "They afford a vent through which the excess of animal spirits find an outlet," he claimed, in his report for 1894, that "since these sports have become so prominent, the college 'pranks,' that, in former years, were so common and so annoying a feature of college life, have largely ceased to be a disturbing element in the administration of college affairs." He believed that athletics could improve student health as well as "teach self-mastery, the ability to control one's temper, and to work with others. They demand steadiness of nerve, coolness, self-reliance, the subordination of animal impulses."

At the same time the president thought that athletic activities should be regulated so that they did not interfere with studies, become an end in themselves or be carried to the point where they became dangerous to life and limb. "In the West," he noted, "college athletics have never been carried to the excess that has characterized the eastern institutions." †

A faculty committee was appointed in 1891 to consider the entire question of the conduct and control of athletics at Northwestern. The following year the committee adopted rules which forbade competition with professional teams, required players to meet certain academic standards, called for committee endorsement of the list of players, and increased administrative control over the scheduling of games.[65] A year later supervision was tightened further with the appointment of a Committee on the Regulation of Athletic Sports made up of three alumni and three undergraduates.[66]

In January 1895 Rogers joined the presidents of the universities of Chicago, *Evolution of* Wisconsin, Michigan, Minnesota, Illinois, and Purdue at a conference in Chicago *The Big Ten* to consider the regulation of intercollegiate athletics. The outcome of this meeting was the adoption of what became known as the Presidents' Rules. These stated that each college was to have a supervisory athletic committee; each contestant was to be a bona fide student of six months' residence; no coach, trainer, or professional athlete could compete; players had to meet academic standards and could receive no pay for their participation; and all games were to be played on grounds owned by one of the colleges.[67]

The following year representatives of the seven universities met in Chicago to create a permanent faculty organization to supervise intercollegiate sports among their respective institutions. Named the Intercollegiate Conference of Faculty Representatives, this board was subsequently enlarged and became The Western Conference also known as The Big Ten.**

---

*Other fields which attracted substantial numbers were law, 54; business, 48; homemaking, 42; medicine, 38; and journalism, 11. *Noted in* College Alumni Record, *pp. 213-331.*

† In December 1895, however, Rogers became sufficiently concerned about brutality in football games to ask the faculty to consider whether football should not be prohibited altogether. Nothing came of this move.

** Indiana and the University of Iowa became members of the Conference in 1899 and Ohio State was admitted in 1912. The University of Chicago withdrew officially in 1946 and was replaced by Michigan State in 1949.

The old oak, though down, still a favorite meeting place on campus in 1898

Lakefront in the late 1890's at the south end of the campus

The record of Northwestern's teams in intercollegiate competition during the 1890-1900 period was not particularly distinguished. Except for 1894, when it enjoyed a fifteen-game winning streak, the baseball team suffered more losses than victories in contests that were marred by disputes over the eligibility of players and accusations of professionalism.[68] In football, the results were somewhat happier. During the 1896 season, the first to be played under the new Conference rules, Northwestern came close to the championship but tied Wisconsin when a victory was needed to win the title. Earlier in the season Northwestern had scored a stunning victory over Chicago 46 to 6 at the latter's Marshall Field.[69] Shortly thereafter the team went to Urbana with a "crowd of 300 roaring supporters on a special train to give Illinois its first defeat on home grounds, 10 to 4."[70] In 1898 Northwestern once again had a Conference win when Minnesota was defeated 11 to 5 on its home field before 3,000 spectators, the largest crowd up to that time to view a football game in Minneapolis and the first Northwestern triumph over Minnesota in four years.

Basketball was first played at Northwestern in 1898 when a group of coeds organized a team which played a series against "young ladies from Austin High School." The following year a men's team was organized primarily to provide conditioning exercises for football players. Evidently it was a rough sport. The uniforms consisted of football pants and padded shirts, and, since dribbling was not permitted, a player simply tucked the ball under his arm "and ploughed a deep furrow through his opponents to the far end of the gym, leaving his path littered with the still breathing bodies of all who got in his way."[71]

Sheppard Field

The growing interest in intercollegiate athletics focused attention on the need for better playing facilities. Teams had traditionally played on what became the site of Orrington Lunt Library, but in September 1891 the trustees set apart a field on the north campus where the fraternity houses are now located. A fund-raising drive among citizens, students, and alumni made possible the construction of a grandstand. The facility was named Sheppard Field in honor of Robert D. Sheppard, who contributed the lumber for the fence enclosing the area.[72] At the dedication of the grandstand in 1892 Rogers praised the benefits of manly competition and dismissed the charge that universities were "inculcating a new religion which enjoined its disciples above all things to fear God and run a mile in four minutes and a half."[73]

Two further events associated with the development of athletics during the decade should be mentioned. One was the decision in 1892 to make royal purple—rather than purple and gold—the official color of the university.[74] The second came in 1894 when Northwestern athletes "were given the privilege of wearing a white N on a purple sweater."[75]

Finances

Early in 1892 Thomas C. Hoag, Northwestern's business manager and treasurer since 1865, announced his resignation.* He was succeeded by Professor Robert D. Sheppard, a faculty member since 1886 and donor of the fence for the athletic field. Sheppard's reputation among the trustees as a "man of affairs" who had been very successful in the management of his family estate made him a logical

---

*Hoag continued to serve as a member of the Northwestern board of trustees until 1900 when he moved from Evanston to Pasadena, California.

choice for the position. The new business manager played an important role in the financial affairs of Northwestern during the remaining years of Rogers's presidency.

TABLE 3-2
N.U. BUDGETED RECEIPTS AND EXPENDITURES: 1890-1900

(In Thousands of Dollars)

Academic Year	1890-1891	1891-1892	1892-1893	1893-1894	1894-1895	1895-1896	1896-1897	1897-1898	1898-1899	1899-1900
EVANSTON SCHOOLS										
RECEIPTS										
Tuition	$ 32.5	$ 39.1	$ 43.8	$ 43.6	$ 47.9	$ 50.6	$ 60.7	$ 66.9	$ 64.7	$ 73.6
Rent	70.2	70.9	74.3	80.7	83.0	21.7	43.8	107.2	109.5	115.7
Interest	6.4	2.7	3.2	13.2	11.8	5.8	11.8	11.5	10.5	12.5
Other[a]	0.7	1.1	1.0	0.8	0.5	0.2	0.6	0.5	0.6	0.6
Woman's College Boarding Account; Net	0.4	2.2	1.0	3.1	0.8	4.4	0.4	0.3	2.2	0.2
Total	110.2	111.6	123.3	141.4	144.0	82.7	117.3	186.4	187.5	202.6
EXPENDITURES										
Instruction	53.8	67.5	73.4	83.2	95.2	83.5	102.7	109.1	106.5	118.7
Library	1.2	1.9	1.6	1.6	5.6	3.4	5.7	7.2	8.8	7.9
Administration	8.8	9.2	10.1	13.0	10.4	4.1	7.2	8.9	9.5	8.1
Physical Plant	12.9	6.3	7.5	4.3	9.8	7.6	10.6	8.0	9.8	10.3
Other	14.8	20.5	17.1	2.7	17.3	9.9	9.0	23.4	18.7	20.9
Interest	13.6	5.9	7.1	12.3	10.9	7.8	21.2	29.5	16.0	25.3
Total	105.1	111.3	116.8	117.1	149.2	116.3	156.4	186.1	169.3	191.2
Surplus (deficit)	5.1	0.3	6.5	24.3	(5.2)	(33.6)	(39.1)	0.3	18.2	11.4
CHICAGO SCHOOLS[b]										
Receipts	48.8	68.9	90.0	93.1	96.1	106.0	138.7	148.4	133.5	112.4
Expenditures	38.0	57.1	90.8	101.5	103.6	86.0	143.7	130.9	126.4	127.4
Surplus (deficit)	10.8	11.8	(0.8)	(8.4)	(7.5)	20.0	(5.0)	17.5	7.1	(15.0)

SOURCE: Northwestern University Treasurer's Reports, 1890-1900.
aMiscellaneous including dormitories and gymnasium.
bData on receipts and expenditures of Chicago professional schools included in treasurer's reports beginning in 1890-1891.

TABLE 3-3
N.U. RESOURCES AND LIABILITIES: 1890-1900 (Selected Years)

(In Thousands of Dollars)

Year	Physical Plant	Productive Assets	Non-Productive Assets	Other Assets	Total	Liabilities	Net
1890	$ 511.0	$1,497.0	$510.0	$ 30.5	$2,548.5	$168.0	$2,380.5
1892	1,012.0	1,593.9	801.6	40.4	3,447.9	125.3	3,322.6
1894	1,424.0	1,710.1	691.0	21.3	3,846.4	266.7	3,579.7
1896	1,470.0	2,092.7	708.6	160.3	4,431.6	556.3	3,875.3
1898	1,575.0	2,334.6	720.0	231.1	4,870.7	599.2	4,271.5
1900	1,659.0	3,089.8	721.5	191.0	5,661.3	618.0	5,043.3

SOURCE: Northwestern University Treasurer's Reports, 1890-1900.

As shown on Table 3-2 the annual budgeted income for the schools on the Evanston campus rose from approximately $110,000 in 1890-1891 to over $202,000 in 1899-1900. From 2 to 10 percent of these totals came from interest and close to 30 percent from tuition. By far the largest portion, however, was derived from rents on the university's real estate holdings. The most important of these was the property on La Salle Street in Chicago, occupied by the Grand Pacific Hotel.

Just how significant this particular holding was for the state of the university's finances was dramatically illustrated in April of 1895, when the Grand Pacific Hotel Company canceled the lease it had held on this land since 1867.[76] The immediate consequence for the university was a loss of the annual rental of $53,400 which the lease had been yielding since 1890.* A second consequence was that with the termination of the lease, ownership of the hotel building passed to Northwestern. This acquisition proved to be of doubtful value since the building had not been adequately maintained.

Importance of Grand Pacific Hotel Lease

After discussing various alternatives for well over a year the trustees, in June 1896, decided that the most economical solution would be to raze the old hotel and erect a commercial building on the site. At their December 12 meeting that year they authorized Sheppard to accept an offer from the Equitable Assurance Society of New York to lend Northwestern $475,000 for a period of twenty years at an annual interest rate of 4½ percent.

The trustees were willing to incur this sizeable debt because they had in the meantime concluded an agreement with the Illinois Trust Safety Deposit Company to lease the land and proposed building for a period of ninety-nine years. The terms of the lease specified the payment of an annual rent of $70,000 for the first ten years, of $80,000 for the next twenty, and of $90,000 for the remainder of the term.[77] With the completion in May 1897 of what the president described as "the finest bank building in America" the university was assured of a substantial source of income for many years to come.†

At a meeting on June 16, 1896, the trustees paid a special tribute to the president and business manager for the "skill with which the financial affairs of the institution have been conducted and the vigor and success with which the serious conditions resulting from the decreased revenue of the university have been grappled with and accommodated."

The loss of approximately $100,000 in income due to the cancellation of the La Salle Street lease led to a temporary retrenchment in 1896 (see Table 3-2). Nevertheless, the trustees were sufficiently encouraged by the university's long-range financial prospects to resume an impressive expansion of educational programs soon thereafter. Especially noteworthy was the increase in the amounts allocated to instruction on the Evanston campus from just under $54,000 in 1891 to almost $119,000 in 1900 (see Table 3-2). To an essentially conservative board of trustees it must have been a source of satisfaction that Northwestern operated at a deficit only during the three years when little or no income was being derived from the La Salle Street property.

---

*This rental was based on the 1890 appraised value of the property as provided for under the terms of the 1867 lease.

† Over the long run, however, the terms of the lease worked out to Northwestern's disadvantage because the agreement failed to provide for any adjustment of the rent to rising urban land values during the sixty-nine year span from 1925 to 1994.

Despite the fluctuation in the fortunes of the Chicago professional schools, their aggregate receipts often exceeded their aggregate expenditures for this period (Table 3-2). The major exceptions were the School of Pharmacy and the Woman's Medical School which experienced financial difficulties in 1900.[78]

Northwestern University in 1900

In his report to the trustees in June 1900, Rogers prefaced his comments on what efforts must still be put forward to make Northwestern an institution of the first rank by reviewing what had already been accomplished, noting that "in the contemplation of the many and pressing needs to be provided for, there is danger sometimes of overlooking the things for which gratitude is due. In reflecting upon what was the condition ten years ago and what is the condition now we may find reason for greater courage and greater determination to meet the problems of the present."

Overall enrollment had grown from just over 1,700 in 1890 to 2,700 in 1900. Measured by the number of full time students, Northwestern now ranked third among all of the American universities—with only Harvard and Michigan ahead and Pennsylvania, Cornell, Yale, Columbia, and Princeton following. Acknowledging that size was not necessarily a reflection of quality, Rogers nevertheless saw this development as testimony to the university's growing reputation. Further confirmation of this was to be found in the fact that Northwestern's student population was being drawn from far afield as well as from the local area, with students from forty states and sixteen foreign countries now enrolled at the university.

In reviewing the financial record, the president was pleased to report that the net value of the university's property had increased from two million dollars to over five million dollars in the course of the decade (see Table 3-3). Although most of this growth was due to an increase in the value of Northwestern's real estate holdings—especially the La Salle Street property—gifts totaling $659,850 represented an important contribution to the total. The major donors were William Deering, $375,000; the Fayerweather Estate, $129,000; and Orrington Lunt, $50,000. The university had expended approximately $475,000 during this period on permanent improvements, including the construction of the Orrington Lunt Library, the Medical and Pharmacy schools, Swift Hall, Fisk Hall, and the purchase of the Woman's Medical School facilities.

In the final section of his report the President noted that Northwestern had for the first time in its history issued an appeal for funds to the Methodist Church and the general community which the university had "served and enriched for nearly fifty years." The immediate inspiration for this appeal had been an announcement in 1899 by the bishops of the Methodist Church of their plan to launch a program to raise $20 million, half of which was to be devoted to education. The coincidence of this announcement with the "deepening consciousness of Northwestern's needs" and the university's impending semi-centennial anniversary made it "not only the privilege but the duty of the Northwestern administration to urge its own claims upon the attention of the Church and the friends of education." Although Northwestern was financially the strongest educational institution associated with the Methodist Church, its buildings and income were still inadequate to meet the needs of a great school.

As he had done from the outset, Rogers compared Northwestern to the major state universities, Michigan and Wisconsin, as well as to the neighboring University of Chicago and the privately endowed institutions of the east and west coasts. And, as usual, he found Northwestern's resources inadequate not only relative to theirs but also relative to its own great need for more buildings and facilities.

He hoped that the appeal would raise a total of two million dollars. Of this amount, roughly $500,000 would be spent for the construction of a new gymnasium, a chapel, men's dining halls and a natural science and museum building. The remainder was to be devoted to enlarging the library and improving its administration and to strengthening the faculty.

The president concluded by announcing that at the request of the executive committee of the board he had agreed to assume responsibility for conducting the fund-raising drive. He appealed to all who were sincerely interested in seeing that Northwestern become the great institution it could be to lend him their enthusiastic support and effort—"without which no attempt to enlarge Northwestern's financial resourses could succeed."

This personal commitment to help raise funds was delivered at the conclusion of the morning session of the trustees' meeting on June 10, 1900. It proved to be premature. Shortly after the board reassembled for the afternoon session William Deering read a letter from Rogers resigning from the presidency of Northwestern. The letter offered no explanation for Rogers's action other than the statement: *Rogers's Resignation*

> All that I had hoped to accomplish has not been attained but I have the satisfaction of knowing that the University is in excellent condition. The time has now come when in my judgment it is best for me to retire. I therefore ask that my resignation be accepted to take effect July 15.

A motion to accept the resignation was adopted unanimously without further debate.

The announcement of Rogers's resignation made the headlines in the Chicago and Evanston press and elicited a certain amount of editorial comment and speculation. Although there had been rumors that some of the trustees were dissatisfied with Rogers's administration his resignation apparently took everyone else completely by surprise. The president of the board, William Deering, was quoted as saying, "There had been dissatisfaction for some time among some of the trustees concerning Dr. Rogers, a feeling that his administration had not been altogether what it should. When Dr. Rogers became convinced that such a feeling existed among a considerable number, he decided to resign."[79] When asked why he had made the decision Rogers himself minced no words. "There was opposition on the part of certain trustees that made it utterly impossible for me to carry out my policies. They worked against the plans I wished to adopt to such an extent that I could not even begin my work." He went on to explain that he had not intended to resign at this meeting but when he learned that certain members of the board were planning to introduce a resolution calling for such action he decided to quit rather than cause an unpleasant crisis.[80]

Rogers's
Differences
with the
Board

The names of Rogers's critics on the board remain unknown. Rogers himself refused to identify his opponents while none of the trustees would admit belonging to the faction which wanted to remove him from office. Nor would any of the board members be drawn into a public statement explaining why they did not consider him to be a good president. But there was widespread speculation that the chief reason for the opposition to Rogers was his outspoken stand on a heated political issue of the day, namely, the American annexation of the Philippines following the end of the Spanish-American War of 1898.

Rogers had made his position quite public, presiding over an anti-imperialist rally in Chicago in 1899 at which, so one account said, he had expressed "rabid anti-expansionist sentiments" which offended "a number of board members who had previously staunchly supported him."[81] An editorial comment in another paper pointed out that Rogers's anti-imperialist position "was not in accord with the views of the Methodists of the United States as a body." This, the editor commented, was most unfortunate since for Northwestern to achieve success it was necessary "that its head should be in general sympathy with the great church of which it is the educational representative."[82] In answer to those who argued that politics had not and should not influence the choice of the president of an educational institution, the editor of the *Evanston Index* replied that there could be "no doubt that a large majority of those who are most influential in Northwestern would prefer at the head a man who is a staunch Republican."[83]

Some weeks later the *Evanston Index* reported that some alumni groups had been opposed to Rogers because of his strong support of coeducation. They claimed that during his administration the emphasis on coeducation had been carried to the point where women students dominated the student body to such an extent "that athletics, scholarship and social life had been permanently injured, the last-named through abuse and the former through a lack of virility."[84]

A number of commentators suggested that Rogers would have done much to regain the favor of those who opposed him if he had been more successful in gathering money for the university. In this regard it was pointed out that the University of Chicago, "which had made such rapid strides during the decade of the nineties, owed much of its financial strength and vigor to the money-hustling qualities of Dr. Harper." Some of the trustees were said to have stated that "a man of similar type was what was wanted at Northwestern."[85] The *Chicago Daily News* shared this view, pointing out that "there are millions—awaiting the Northwestern, as well as the Chicago university if only somebody goes after them in a proper way—the Dr. Harper way, for instance." But in fairness to the presidents of other institutions, this commentator, in an obvious reference to John D. Rockefeller, acknowledged that "it will be many a day before another university is placed in as favorable a position as to securing the funds for its enlargement and growth as that of which Dr. Harper is the head," adding, "if Methodism has a man of many millions who is ready to cover every dollar given to Northwestern with another then the comparison would be fair."[86]

"The Result
of Conspiracy"

By far the most dramatic explanation of Rogers's resignation, however, was advanced in a letter to the *Chicago Evening Post* from a Northwestern trustee who wished to remain anonymous. He claimed that the resignation should be recognized as "the result of conspiracy" by certain members of the Executive Committee, "whose main object was the elevation of Professor Robert D. Sheppard to the president's chair of the university." Because of this group's effectiveness in blocking Rogers's plans for the advancement and betterment of the university, the writer continued, "the president was often charged with possessing narrow views, an inclination to economic management approaching niggardliness, and in many instances condemned for a policy which he never approved and which he was powerless to obstruct."[87]

Since the latter part of this explanation, at least, accords with Rogers's more restrained statement to reporters, it deserves some attention. Though there is no evidence of an actual conspiracy to replace Rogers with Sheppard, the latter was, by all accounts, widely considered the heir apparent to the Northwestern presidency. His training for the ministry and his strong support of the American policy in the Philippines no doubt made him especially attractive to those who were outraged by Rogers's stand on this issue. Others were impressed by his record as Northwestern's treasurer and business manager, trustee H. H. C. Miller being quoted as saying, "Everything Dr. Sheppard touches turns to gold," and board president William Deering being quoted by the same source as stating that "Dr. Sheppard is a splendid businessman and colleges need at their heads nowadays men of business ability as well as of scholarly attainments."[88]

Rogers's Aspirations for Northwestern

Undoubtedly all the factors mentioned in these contemporary speculations on the reasons for Rogers's sudden resignation contributed to make his position difficult. But one additional reason is worth considering, namely, that the scope of Rogers's ambition for Northwestern exceeded that of some of the trustees and even of some of the faculty. His frequent exhortations that Northwestern must model its standards and curriculum after those of Harvard, Yale, Columbia, and Princeton and must secure resources equivalent to those available to these privately endowed institutions, may well have grated on those trustees who believed that Northwestern had, all things considered, done remarkably well in the less than fifty years of its existence. Similarly Rogers's recruitment of a new generation of highly trained scholars may have disturbed some of the older faculty who felt themselves hard pressed to emulate their younger colleagues. The faculty's memorial to Professor Henry Cohn certainly suggests some discontent with the demands made on its members during this period.

In any case Rogers left before he had achieved all his great plans for Northwestern. His own subsequent career gives the measure of the man. After leaving Northwestern he accepted an offer from the Yale Law School on whose faculty he remained until 1921, serving as dean from 1903 to 1916. In 1913 President Woodrow Wilson appointed him Judge of the United States Circuit Court of Appeals in New York City, a position he retained until his death in 1926.[89]

Daniel Bonbright,
Acting President
1900-02

Edmund Janes James,
President 1902-04

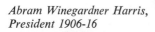

Abram Winegardner Harris,
President 1906-16

Lynn Harold Hough,
President 1919-20

Thomas Franklin Holgate,
Acting President
1904-06 and 1916-19

4

YEARS OF TRANSITION
1900—1920

Those who had expected Business Manager Robert D. Sheppard to succeed Rogers *University* as president of Northwestern were disappointed. Opposition to Sheppard's can- *Leadership* didacy had been sufficiently strong to discourage the search committee from appointing him. His critics considered his training and experience inadequate for the post and stressed his lack of academic stature. As one graduate put it, "If a local hero, no matter how sweet and lovable his temper, no matter how notable his ability to raise and care for funds, is put in the president's chair, no self-respecting alumnus will ever again reveal the name of his backwoods college mother."[1] When the committee proved unable to agree on any other candidate either, the trustees, at their meeting of July 19, 1900, appointed Daniel Bonbright, dean of the College of Liberal Arts, as acting president.

During his nineteen months in office, Bonbright continued to wrestle with *Acting* problems that had plagued the university for many years. Chief among these was *President* ensuring a flow of qualified applicants to the college. Though its own preparatory *Daniel* school supplied the college with students, their number was not sufficient to allow *Bonbright* for continued expansion. To widen the scope of the university's recruitment, Bonbright, in his report for 1902, recommended that Northwestern follow the example of other institutions which kept representatives in the field to inform parents and potential students of the merits of their programs. He also persuaded the trustees to award tuition scholarships to outstanding Illinois students who chose to attend Northwestern. In a further attempt to gain access to a pool of well prepared students, Northwestern acquired a financial interest in two Illinois preparatory schools that were on the verge of bankruptcy: the Grand Prairie Seminary at Onarga and the Elgin Academy at Elgin. In return for its financial support the university obtained the right to control the policies and programs of these schools.[2] Northwestern's relationship with the Grand Prairie Seminary continued until 1918; its contract with the Elgin Academy remained in force until 1924.[3]

Fear of a "Feminine Image"

Another problem which concerned Bonbright was the rise in the proportion of women students on the Evanston campus during the preceding decade, from 36 percent of the total student body in 1891 to 50 percent in 1900. It will be remembered that some of Rogers's opponents had attacked him for his fervent support of coeducation and Bonbright himself appears to have viewed the increase in the number of women students with some alarm. Reporting to the trustees in 1901, he expressed the fear that this development might give Northwestern a "feminine image" and discourage young men from seeking admission. Though he suggested that "the enrollment of young women might be wisely limited to the capacity of the buildings supplied for their residence," the trustees failed to follow this advice.

The most important development during Bonbright's administration was the university's purchase of the Tremont Hotel Building at the corner of Lake and Dearborn streets in Chicago. Acquired at a cost of $800,000 the remodeled structure, known as the Northwestern University Building, was ready for occupancy by the fall of 1902 and provided space for the Law, Dental, and Pharmacy schools.[4]

President Edmund J. James

By their meeting of January 10, 1902, the trustees had found an acceptable candidate for the presidency of Northwestern in Edmund Janes James. A native of Jacksonville, Illinois, James had spent one year at Northwestern and another at Harvard before going to Germany where he received his doctorate from the University of Halle in 1877. On his return to the United States that year he became principal of the Evanston Township High School and, two years later, of the Model High School in Normal, Illinois. In 1883 he joined the faculty of the Wharton School of Finance at the University of Pennsylvania where he remained until 1895 when he became a professor of political science at the University of Chicago. It was from this post that he came to Northwestern in March 1902 at the age of forty-seven.[5]

In the course of negotiating with James on behalf of the board, trustee Milton H. Wilson informed him that Northwestern needed a strong and dynamic president and that the board would give him a free hand in directing the university. He did add, however, that "there is one limitation which we have placed upon ourselves, to wit, that indebtedness shall not be created for current expenses. We cannot believe that on this proposition your judgment will disagree from our own." Responding with enthusiasm, James reaffirmed Rogers's prediction that Northwestern would soon rank among the leading centers for scientific research and successful instruction without losing any of its high reputation for moral and religious training.

In April 1902, a month after his arrival on campus, James proposed several long-range objectives. He urged that Northwestern recognize the importance of technical and professional education in the modern university curriculum by expanding its offerings in the fields of engineering, business, and education. He stressed the need for more facilities, including an expansion of the library and the construction of a natural science building, an engineering building, a gymnasium, a number of residence halls, a dining hall, a student center, and a university chapel. To free the faculty for more important work he suggested the hiring of clerical help to deal with bureaucratic details.

But there were other problems to be faced as well, among them the uneasy relationship between the university and the Evanston community. In January 1902 the *Evanston Press* had published an essay on inaccuracy and myth in the Bible. The author of this article was Charles W. Pearson, professor of English at Northwestern for nearly thirty years.[7] The Methodist community was outraged and demanded that Pearson be dismissed. Since this crisis erupted during the period between the appointment of James as president and his assumption of office, the trustees decided to handle the matter themselves.

Town and Gown

Summoned to appear before the executive committee of the board, Pearson was informed that his article had "in the judgment of the executive committee discredited some of the essential truths of the Christian religion." The keeper of the minutes of this meeting recorded for posterity that a "friendly discussion ensued" as a result of which Pearson voluntarily resigned, accepting a year's salary as severance pay.* "Friendly" as the discussion may have been, the incident caused a furor in the national press and proved embarrassing to the university.[8]

Yet another controversy developed several weeks later when a stinging editorial in the *Evanston Press* criticized Northwestern faculty members for staying aloof from the civic and social life of Evanston. "They have drawn themselves down to narrow limits," noted the editors, "and beyond a more or less active association in church work are not known outside of school circles. The university faculty needs a shaking up that will pull it out of its ruts."[9] The editorial was too much for James Taft Hatfield, professor of German. The following week he lashed out at Evanston society while lauding the contributions of the faculty to the life of the community. He noted that the university was one of the few redeeming features of the town and certainly "worth more to the community than the custards, high-balls, and ping pong of so called 'social Evanston'." He ended, "I have long since come to the conclusion that the barrier lies not in the exclusiveness and selfishness of the gown but in a certain vulgarity of standards on the part of the town."[10] Even though Hatfield later apologized for the harshness of his remarks, the incident understandably set university-community relations on edge.[11]

Town and gown made up their differences to give a hearty welcome to President Theodore Roosevelt when he visited Evanston in April 1903 in the course of a goodwill tour of the West. In June 1893, when he was still United States Civil Service Commissioner, Northwestern had awarded Roosevelt his first honorary degree. Now, on the occasion of his 1903 visit, he referred to himself as a son of Northwestern. Describing the grandeur of Roosevelt's arrival, the *Chicago Journal* of April 2, commented, "Not only were the gowns and caps and formalities of Northwestern in evidence, but Fort Sheridan furnished federal troops as an escort, besides a military band and a battery of artillery for the presidential salute of twenty-one guns." A reception committee led by Mayor James A. Patten, a Northwestern trustee, met the presidential train. After welcoming Roosevelt, the *Journal* reported, Patten described the community as "a city of homes of families who have come here to educate their children at our great university, and of men who are

President Theodore Roosevelt's Visit

---

*Upon leaving Northwestern, Pearson became pastor of the Unitarian Church in Quincy, Illinois, where he remained until his death three years later. *Pearson Family file, N.U.A.*

President Theodore Roosevelt visiting Northwestern's campus, April 1903, in the course of a goodwill tour of the West.

William Jennings Bryan, the "Great Commoner" and an alumnus of the Law School, speaking on campus, July 1903

engaged in business in the great city of Chicago." Roosevelt responded with a speech on the value of higher education in building the American character.

Diverting and pleasant as this much publicized visit might be, it did little to help President James's efforts to raise the endowment needed to support his plans for expansion. Believing that the basic financial resource of any private university is a dedicated body of alumni, James encouraged the organization of alumni associations and reunions.[12] He also persuaded the trustees to establish a Jubilee Memorial Fund as part of Northwestern's celebration of its semicentennial in 1905. James also attempted to interest Andrew Carnegie in various building and research projects at Northwestern. His efforts were unsuccessful, largely because Carnegie objected to the university's religious affiliation.[13] However, when James turned to the Methodist Church for help he found an abundance of sympathy but a paucity of funds.

After two years in office James became discouraged. Not only did his prospects for raising the endowment substantially seem dim, but he saw himself as spending most of his time on petty administrative matters rather than on building a "new Northwestern." When he was offered the presidency of the University of Illinois in the spring of 1904 he accepted with little hesitation.[14] His chief reason for leaving Northwestern, he later explained, was that, "with each passing year the opportunity of my doing large things was diminishing."[15] It is possible that, like Rogers, James appeared overly ambitious to some of the trustees. For example, William A. Dyche (who had succeeded Robert Sheppard as business manager in 1903), wrote, "I sometimes feel that James's wide horizon and his eagerness to plan for the years ahead were, from a practical standpoint, a source of weakness. Possibly if he had not had so many things in mind, each of which was beyond criticism, he might have been better satisfied with his labors."[16]

Nevertheless, the trustees could hardly have been pleased at having to resume their search for a president once more. When Bonbright declined to become acting president because of failing health, the board, on September 27, 1904, selected Thomas F. Holgate, dean of the College of Liberal Arts, to serve as president *ad interim*. Holgate was thoroughly familiar with the university, having come to Northwestern as a member of the mathematics department in 1893, immediately after earning his Ph.D. at Clark University. A Canadian by birth, he had received his B.A. and M.A. degrees from the University of Toronto. Holgate had been acting dean for a year before becoming dean of the college in 1903, a post he retained until 1916.[17]

Acting President Thomas F. Holgate

Holgate shared his predecessor's view of the importance of science in the curriculum of a modern university. As he informed the trustees in his report for 1905, "In our future development, it should be in my judgment, our immediate aim to enlarge the work of the scientific departments along practical lines so as to furnish young men more and more with facilities for entering upon commercial pursuits with adequate knowledge."

Because of his prior association with the university, Holgate was keenly aware of some of the discomforts suffered by students and eager to remedy them. For the particular benefit of men who were not members of a fraternity he recommended the construction of a dining hall where they could secure healthful food at reasonable rates "with comfortable and attractive club rooms where men can come together for meals and to spend an idle hour in chat." He was also disturbed because a lack of dormitory space forced a considerable number of women students to live in boarding houses scattered about town. Continuing growth of the student body had led to a lack of adequate classroom and laboratory space.

The possibility of providing for these needs was somewhat improved when the $1,000,000 target set for the Jubilee Memorial Fund was reached in June 1905. In Holgate's view the completion of the drive was even more significant for the university than the amount of money added to its resources, large as that sum was. He predicted in his 1905 report that, "the inspiration which comes to faculties, alumni and trustees from this task accomplished, and the confidence developed by increased strength will be felt in all the work of the university, both financial and educational for many years to come." He expressed the hope that because all but a small fraction of the one million dollars had been pledged by the trustees, friends of the university outside the board would be inspired to contribute to its future support.

Administration of Abram W. Harris

Holgate served as interim president until September 1, 1906, when Abram Winegardner Harris took office as the new president of Northwestern. The board had taken its time in making a choice, having been burned by James's speedy departure and wanting the assurance that the next president would be content to work within the resources available to the university. As William Deering, president of the board, told a fellow trustee, "I do not want any more 'kite flyers' because we can't afford it. A few years at the cost of Dr. James would greatly add to a floating debt already too large."[18]

Deering need not have worried, Harris proved to be the most experienced and practical administrator to come to Northwestern since Rogers. Born in Philadelphia in 1858, he had graduated from Wesleyan University in 1880 and had received his M.A. there three years later. After several years of teaching at Wesleyan and at Dickenson Seminary, Harris became an assistant director in the United States Department of Agriculture in 1888. Five years later he was appointed president of Maine State College, which he helped transform into a university by 1901. His next post was as director of the Jacob Tome Institute in Maryland, where he remained until he came to Northwestern in 1906.[19]

In his new position, Harris made a point of keeping the president of the board apprised of his plans and actions. In February 1907, for example, he informed Deering of an unsuccessful attempt to interest Andrew Carnegie in contributing funds for the construction of "a recitation building for the department of natural sciences." The philanthropist's reaction to this second appeal from Northwestern had once more been negative, but this time on the grounds that Carnegie's "field was the small and needy college not the great university with its thousands of students and millions of endowment." Happy though Harris may have been to see Northwestern so characterized, he was also puzzled by this response, for he had just read in the press that Carnegie had given substantial amounts of money to Yale, Syracuse, and Princeton, none of which could be construed as being "small and needy." Encouraged rather than depressed by this contradiction, Harris vowed to approach Carnegie again at an opportune time.[20]

Fortunately the new president was more successful elsewhere. In the course of the next six years he raised enough money to remedy many of the lacks he had drawn attention to in his first report to the trustees in June 1907. On that occasion he expressed deep concern about living and working conditions for students on the Evanston campus. He deplored overcrowding in classrooms and the library and strongly urged the construction of a new gymnasium. Pointing to one of the major discomforts suffered by male students—most of whom had to find board and lodging in the town—Harris advocated the erection of on-campus living quarters for men. The board of trustees gave the president substantial backing in working toward these goals.

One of the most important developments during Harris's administration was the realization of Rogers's cherished hope, namely, the reestablishment of a school of engineering at Northwestern. This was made possible by a gift of $150,000 from the Gustav Swift family for the construction of the Swift Hall of Engineering. Completed in May 1909, the four-story stone building provided space for laboratories, classrooms, offices, a small library, and study rooms. *Swift Hall of Engineering*

The following year, 1910, saw the dedication of Patten Gymnasium, financed by a $310,000 gift from Northwestern trustee, James A. Patten, a highly successful grain merchant. This beautifully designed building included an indoor track, a swimming pool, exercise rooms, and a baseball practice area that could be converted into an auditorium seating an audience of 4,500.[21] Located in the area preempted in 1939 by the Technological Institute, Patten Gymnasium became the traditional site of the university's commencement exercises and the North Shore Music Festival. *Patten Gymnasium*

By 1911 plans had been drawn up for the construction of men's dormitories to be located north of Patten Gymnasium. Harris wrote the national secretaries of the Greek letter fraternities on campus urging their support of the project. As he told one representative, "In the interest of University unity and college spirit the dormitory campus should be the home of all students, not only of the non-fraternity men. Such a location is in the interest of the fraternities because it saves them the cost of land and because it brings them in close touch with the general student community."[22] A number of the fraternities responded to the university's offer of a free building site and assistance in securing long term financing by launching special building fund drives among their alumni. In February 1914, eleven units—seven affiliated with fraternities and four open houses—were ready for occupancy. The buildings were arranged in quadrangles, with each unit accommodating thirty to forty students. *Men's Quadrangles*

The last major addition to the Evanston campus during President Harris's administration came with the dedication in December 1915 of Harris Hall. The building, located just south of University Hall, was named in honor of Norman Wait Harris, prominent Chicago banker and Northwestern trustee, who contributed $150,000 toward its construction.[23] Designed for use by the departments of history, political science, and economics, the three-story limestone structure *Harris Hall*

Interior of old Patten Gymnasium, site of the annual North Shore Music Festival; the organ was later rebuilt and moved to Lutkin Hall (Courtesy N.U. alumnus W. Curtis Hughes)

Alumni luncheon in 1907 (left side, front to back) President Abram W. Harris, Mrs. Harris, Mrs. William A. Dyche, Business Manager Dyche and (right side, front to back) Dean Thomas F. Holgate, Professor Daniel Bonbright, Mrs. Holgate, and Mrs. William F. McDowell wife of trustee Bishop McDowell

Harris Hall, completed in 1915, built to house the social sciences

contained seminar and classrooms, offices, a social hall, and an auditorium with a seating capacity of 300.[24]

But President Harris was more than a practical and energetic administrator; he was also a reflective man deeply concerned with the question of how the university could reconcile the demands of the modern world with the aspirations of its founders. In yet another letter to Deering, composed shortly after his arrival at Northwestern, he wrote, "I have given much thought to our church relations and am trying to fix the principles that ought to govern the administration in relation to religious matters and religious questions. Doubtless it ought not to be sectarian in any offensive sense nor narrowly denominational, but it ought to be religious and it ought to do some things the state universities cannot be expected to do."[25]

Like Rogers, Harris wished to see Northwestern go beyond the narrow limits of sectarianism without rejecting the religious values that had inspired its founders. The circumstances surrounding the resignation of Professor Charles W. Pearson following the publication of his article on myth in the scriptures only five years earlier, had underscored the potential for conflict between scholars and supporters of the sectarian position during this period when many traditional views were being questioned. With an eye to the university's standing in the larger world, Harris, in his 1908 report to the trustees, stressed: "It is vitally important that an institution like Northwestern should not be misrepresented in its character in such a way as to offend either the denomination which gave it birth or the great community which is becoming interested in it without respect to denominational considerations." Difficult though it might be to achieve this delicate balance, Northwestern did in fact succeed in doing so until its official severance from the church in 1972.

The Tax Question   Harris had proved equally adept at dealing with the resurgence of yet another sensitive issue soon after his arrival. In 1907 the city of Evanston once again brought into question the tax exempt status of the university's property holdings. The president responded by pointing out that the exemption was based on an irrevocable trust between the founders of the university and the state which should not be violated. Moreover, he demonstrated that the amount of revenue lost to the city as a consequence of the exemption was paltry compared to the benefits the university conferred on the city. Indeed, the mere presence of Northwestern in Evanston increased the value of all property in the city. "It is the charter that excluded the saloons," he wrote, "and the university atmosphere" that gave Evanston its "peculiar charm." Finally, he called attention to the fact that the university not only provided education for many Evanston residents, but also spent nearly a million dollars each year in the city on goods and services. The effectiveness of Harris's argument might be measured by the fact that the issue immediately dropped from the pages of the press.[26]

The sporadic town-gown conflicts were only part of the story, however, for there were many occasions which brought the two communities together for common pleasures. After 1909, for example, the campus became the site of one of the most eagerly anticipated annual events—the North Shore Music Festival. The most distinguished musical artists of the time participated in the festival and drew audiences from far away. The organizer and director of the festival was Dean Peter

Lutkin of Northwestern's School of Music, who headed the Evanston Musical Club (founded in 1894) and the Ravenswood Musical Club (founded in 1896). He combined the musical resources offered by these clubs with those of the Chicago Symphony Orchestra to present what would become a series of the most important musical events in the area. The first festival concert was given in Patten Gymnasium on June 5, 1909, shortly after the building had been completed.[27] The festival continued to draw enthusiastic audiences for over two decades. Discontinued in 1930, it was revived in 1937. The final performances of the festival were given in 1939 at Dyche Stadium.

Evanston Campus

During the first two decades of the twentieth century enrollment in the College of Liberal Arts more than tripled—from 603 to 1,909 (see Tables 4-1 and 4-2). Keeping pace with this increase in students, the college faculty grew from 57 to 165. The addition of a large number of young instructors permitted the college to offer a greater number and variety of courses than ever before.

Early in this period admission requirements had been liberalized in accordance with the guidelines set down by the Committee on College Entrance Requirements of the National Education Association. The new regulations asked for a minimum of four units in foreign languages, two units of mathematics, two of English, one of history, one of science, and six units of electives. They reflected a further shift away from the classical curriculum to one which acknowledged the value and importance of modern languages, history, and science.[28]

The growing emphasis on professional education which had become apparent during Rogers's administration continued under his successors, in part because it coincided with a national trend in higher education. In his report for 1904, President James planned to expand Northwestern's offerings in engineering, business, and education. As a consequence of his sudden departure, however, it fell to his successors to carry these plans forward.

In 1906 Holgate transformed the department of pedagogy into the department of education. In his report for that year he announced that a full time assistant professor had been engaged to expand the course offerings and students could henceforth choose a program that would instruct them in "the art of teaching and school management."

Reestablishment of Engineering

The trustees on April 9, 1907, discussed plans for the reestablishment of a school of engineering, made possible by the Swift family's funding of Swift Hall. The four-year curriculum leading to a Bachelor of Science degree included courses in civil, mechanical, and electrical engineering. A fifth year of specialized study led to a more technical degree. The president emphasized that the Northwestern program would turn out well rounded graduates. He added, "Such students as ours having greater general training would look for their success not in manual skill but in more important and more highly paid positions calling for administrative and theoretical ability." The new College of Engineering was officially opened in 1909 under the direction of John F. Hayford, professor of civil engineering and formerly chief of the Geodetic Division of the U.S. Coast and Geodetic Survey. By 1916 the Engineering College had an enrollment of 100 students and had established itself as an important center for engineering studies in the Middle West.

Graduate School   Harris was also instrumental in reorganizing graduate studies. In 1910, acting on his recommendation, the trustees voted to replace the loosely structured graduate program that had existed since the 1890's with a more formally organized graduate school. A Board of Graduate Studies composed of twenty-one faculty members chosen by the president was to administer the school.[29] In the course of the next ten years enrollment in the Graduate School rose from 83 to 162. In 1917 James Alton James of the history department became the first Graduate School dean. The successful development of graduate studies at Northwestern received outside recognition[30] that same year when the university was unanimously elected to membership in the Association of American Universities.*

Establishment of Summer School   There were several other organizational changes to be noted on the Evanston campus during the latter part of Harris's administration. The School of Oratory, which had been under the direction of Robert M. Cumnock since its founding in 1894, came under the direct control of the university's board of trustees in 1913 at Cumnock's request. The following year, Harris and the board formally organized Northwestern's first summer school in response to a growing demand for a more flexible academic calendar.[31]

The School of Music continued to flourish under the dynamic leadership of Dean Lutkin, who made many friends for the university through his active participation in the musical life of the North Shore. Between 1900 and 1916, enrollment in the school rose from 162 to 480 (see Tables 4-1 and 4-2).

University Library   In 1908 Dr. Walter Lichtenstein, curator of the Hohenzollern collection of German history at Harvard, accepted the position of university librarian at Northwestern. He found the fourteen-year-old Orrington Lunt Library badly overcrowded and poorly funded. Under his energetic leadership the resources and services offered by the library increased substantially. Over the next ten years the number of volumes grew from 70,000 to 116,000 and the staff was enlarged from eight to fifteen. A major organizational change occurred in 1911 when the library severed its relationship with the College of Liberal Arts and became a separate department of the university serving all of the schools on the Evanston campus.[32]

The Chicago Schools   The growing complexity of the professional fields and a demand for higher standards led to a marked rise in admission requirements in all of Northwestern's professional schools during this period. In 1900, for example, applicants to the Medical School had only to present evidence of secondary school graduation or "sustain an examination on subjects required for admission to the College of Liberal Arts." By 1920 they had to have two years of college instruction as well as a "certificate of moral character." In the Law School, the requirements changed from "high school equivalency" to a college education or being twenty years of age and having a high school diploma. The Pharmacy and Dental schools also raised their entrance requirements. In every case the schools realized that these changes would lead to an immediate decline in enrollment and an accompanying

---

*The Association of American Universities had been founded in 1900 by ten of the major universities "for the purpose of consideration of matters of common interest relating to graduate study." Membership in the AAU was considered a form of accreditation. *Donald B. Tresidder, Stanford University*, AAU Proceedings, *October 1947, Princeton University Press.*

TABLE 4-1
N.U. STUDENT ENROLLMENT 1900-1910

Academic Year	1900-1901	1901-1902	1902-1903	1903-1904	1904-1905	1905-1906	1906-1907	1907-1908	1908-1909	1909-1910
EVANSTON CAMPUS										
College	603	603	726	796	818	854	882	1,088	997	872
Graduate	40	35	43	51	61	59	54	57	82	84
Music	162	218	268	352	344	363	328	321	384	338
Oratory						187	194	234	148	224
Engineering										57
Academy	477	407	485	569	537	512	600	554	544	578
Total	1,282	1,263	1,522	1,768	1,760	1,975	2,058	2,254	2,155	2,153
CHICAGO CAMPUS										
Medical	345	462	607	586	591	579	593	684	658	470
Woman's Medical	63	67								
Law	195	162	184	223	225	239	287	274	322	333
Dental	500	535	571	515	454	403	355	357	269	346
Pharmacy	176	205	238	283	252	208	169	160	156	217
Commerce									255	314
Total	1,279	1,431	1,600	1,607	1,522	1,429	1,404	1,475	1,660	1,680
Grand Total	2,561	2,694	3,122	3,375	3,282	3,404	3,462	3,729	3,815	3,833

SOURCE: Northwestern University Catalogs, 1900-1910.

TABLE 4-2
N.U. STUDENT ENROLLMENT 1910-1920

Academic Year	1910-1911	1911-1912	1912-1913	1913-1914	1914-1915	1915-1916	1916-1917	1917-1918	1918-1919	1919-1920
EVANSTON CAMPUS										
College	1,118	980	1,045	1,125	1,246	1,315	1,469	1,272	1,973	1,909
Graduate	91	83	95	100	119	125	132	111	62	162
Music	384	378	440	475	575	480	694	448	281	372
Oratory	221	196	254	278	173	208	192	229	217	181
Engineering	54	57	59	82	88	100	104	86	196	141
Commerce										463
Academy	461	448	480	394	376	337				
Total	2,329	2,142	2,373	2,454	2,577	2,565	2,591	2,146	2,729	3,228
CHICAGO CAMPUS										
Medical	533	259	200	181	196	236	241	286	297	413
Law	283	314	309	330	357	341	386	234	292	281
Dental	384	432	555	631	640	688	738	530	481	301
Pharmacy	194	181	194	134	77	71	59			
Commerce	508	488	507	647	762	917	1,076	951	1,016	2,598
Total	1,902	1,674	1,765	1,923	2,032	2,253	2,500	2,001	2,086	3,593
Grand Total	4,231	3,816	4,138	4,377	4,609	4,818	5,091	4,147	4,815	6,821

Summer School (selected years)   (1912) 66   (1916) 406   (1920) 666

SOURCE: Northwestern University Catalogs, 1910-1920.

Evanston's livery stable, operated by Henry Butler in the days before World War I

Junior Class Day, circa 1908

School of Pharmacy's student parade, 1903

loss of income from tuition. Yet they believed that in the long run these actions would bring them more and better students.[33]

The Medical School changed both its admission and graduation requirements in several stages. In 1908 applicants were for the first time expected to have completed one year of college; three years later this requirement was raised to two. Northwestern was somewhat ahead of the American Medical Association, for the latter took until 1914 to recommend a minimal one year of college as a prerequisite and until 1918 to raise this to two years.[34] *The Medical School*

In 1915 the Northwestern Medical School became one of the first half dozen in the United States to add a compulsory fifth year of internship to the four year course of study for the M.D. degree. Four years earlier, in October 1911, the trustees had approved a six year course of study leading to both a Bachelor of Science and an M.D. degree as a mode of encouraging adequate premedical training for students.

All in all these changes and innovations served to enhance the Medical School's standing, but their immediate effect was to reduce enrollment from 470 in 1909-10 to a low of 181 in 1913-14. Over the ensuing six years, however, the situation improved substantially and by 1919-20 registration was up to 413 (see Tables 4-1 and 4-2).

Conflict between Dean Nathan Davis, Jr., and a conservative faculty group which had opposed the 1907 proposal to raise entrance requirements had led to the dean's resignation in that year. He was followed by Dr. Arthur R. Edwards, a member of the faculty since 1897, who presided over the school during the very difficult period of falling enrollments. In 1916 Dr. Edwards returned to teaching and research and was succeeded by Dr. Arthur I. Kendall, who had come to the school as a professor of bacteriology in 1910.[35]

Oscar Oldberg continued to serve as dean of the School of Pharmacy until his retirement in 1913, at which time the trustees appointed John H. Long, professor of chemistry in the Northwestern Medical School as his successor. The school's insistence on maintaining high standards worked to its disadvantage. As Dean Oldberg explained in his 1906 report to the trustees: *Pharmacy*

> In nearly all the . . . states, the laws and rulings of the Boards of Pharmacy are such that special Pharmaceutical education is directly and decidedly discouraged by the fact that drug store training is declared sufficient and applicants for license to practice pharmacy can secure their licenses without any preceding systematic education.

This makes abundantly clear why the enrollment, which had been 252 in 1904-05, dropped to 208 the following year after the school raised the entrance requirement to include completion of at least one year of high school (see Table 4-1).

After reaching a low point of 156 in 1908-09, enrollment had risen to 194 by 1912-13 when the course for the degree of Graduate in Pharmacy was lengthened from three eighteen-week terms to two full scholastic years and the course for the degree of Pharmaceutical Chemist was extended from two to three scholastic years. At the same time, as the President's Report indicated, the minimum admis-

Tremont House at Lake and Dearborn in Chicago, home of Northwestern's Schools of Dentistry, Pharmacy, and Law between 1902 and 1926

Swift Hall of Engineering, completed 1909 to house the reestablished College of Engineering

sion requirement was advanced from one year of high school work to the completion of a four year high school course.

At the time President Harris acknowledged that the new admission requirement was considerably higher than that in force in most of the schools of pharmacy and possibly even "greater than ought to be enforced by all of them." But these decisions were based on the conviction that Northwestern should not "admit as candidate for any degree persons whose preliminary education is less than a full high school course." Harris added that while the number of students would undoubtedly be reduced at first, "the enhanced reputation of the school will attract a growing number of applicants for admission."

Only part one of his prediction proved correct. By 1916-17 enrollment had dwindled to fifty-nine. The trustees decided that the university could no longer maintain the school. In June 1917, an arrangement was made to transfer the "students and goodwill of the School of Pharmacy of Northwestern University" to the School of Pharmacy of the University of Illinois.[36]

Dental School

The Northwestern Dental School, under the leadership of Dean Greene Vardiman Black, maintained its position among the leading dental schools in the United States during this period. In 1901 the faculty moved to raise entrance requirements from one to two years of high school work. Beginning in 1906, this was raised to four years of high school. At the same time the scope of the three-year curriculum leading to the D.D.S. degree was expanded. The school was encouraged in these efforts by the passage of a State of Illinois law in 1905 which specified that only individuals who had graduated from "reputable dental schools" would thereafter be eligible for the examination for a license to practice in the state. In 1917, a fourth year was added to the curriculum leading to the D.D.S. degree.[37]

Though these changes undoubtedly raised the standards of dentistry practiced by graduates of the Northwestern Dental School, they also seriously reduced the number of students enrolled for the next few years—from 500 in 1900-01 to only 269 in 1908-09. From this low point enrollment began to move up again until it reached a record high of 738 in 1916-17 before falling off again toward the end of the decade (see Tables 4-1 and 4-2).

An important feature of the Dental School program during this period was the establishment of clinics at which members of the public could have dental work performed by students for a nominal fee. Students were expected themselves to recruit patients on whom to practice their skills. Dean Black believed that clinical experience under the supervision of a demonstrator would allow students to see a broader range of cases and acquire a higher degree of skill than could be developed in a lifetime of private practice. As the President's Report shows, in the course of 1905-06 alone a total of 36,163 clinical operations were performed on 6,688 individuals. By 1914-15 the number of operations had risen to over 96,000.

In the summer of 1915 Dean Black died, having earned an international reputation as the father of modern dentistry for his pioneering work in preventive and restorative dentistry and oral pathology. He was succeeded by Dr. Thomas L. Gilmer, who had been professor of oral surgery since 1891. Arthur D. Black, son of the former dean, was appointed junior dean. He was made dean following the resignation of Dr. Gilmer in 1918.

Law School   In 1898, after Henry Wade Rogers had served both as dean of the Law School and as president of the university for six years, the trustees appointed Peter S. Grosscup, a U.S. Superior Court judge, to head the Law School. When Dean Grosscup retired in 1901 the board decided that the school now needed the services of a full time administrator and selected John Henry Wigmore, a faculty member since 1893, for the position. Born in San Francisco in 1863, Wigmore had received both his baccalaureate and law degrees from Harvard. Following two years of private practice in Boston, he had spent three years as professor of Anglo-American law at Keio University in Japan before coming to Northwestern.[38]

Within two years of Wigmore's appointment as dean, the Northwestern Law School was threatened with the loss of its faculty when the two senior and four junior members of the teaching staff, who constituted the core of the faculty, were invited to join the newly organized Law School of the University of Chicago. As President James noted in his report for 1902-1904, sometime after the crisis was over, the board of trustees assured the Law School staff that it was "determined to do whatever was necessary to make and keep the Law School on a par with the very best institutions of its kind in the country." As part of this commitment the trustees "proposed to enlarge the faculty and increase the equipment, particularly of the library."

In the end only one member of the faculty left for the Chicago Law School. Meanwhile the trustees had agreed to the establishment of a nucleus of six faculty members who, as James explained, would give "practically all their time to the work of instruction in law, and to add to these six other professors in active practice who should be expected to give only a portion of their time."

In 1902 the Law School had moved to more spacious quarters in the remodeled Tremont Hotel. Around the same time, under the direction of Dean Wigmore, the school appointed its first librarian and began the systematic enlargement of its collections. In 1903 the school acquired the Gary Collections of Continental Law and in 1906-07 the Gary Collection on International, Ancient, Oriental and Primitive Law.* "The initial foreign collection [was] at that time unequaled in any other law library in the country with the exception of Harvard. . . ."[39]

Combined with the reorganization and expansion of the faculty, these developments contributed to a substantial growth in the size of the Law School. Enrollment moved up from 195 in 1900-01 to a high of 386 in 1916-17, then declined somewhat during the war and immediately thereafter (see Table 4-2). Though the school continued to accept applicants with no more than a high school education, Rahl and Schwerin note that by 1916 a majority had had college training, in many instances of three or four years.†

In that year, the Law School faculty decided to adopt a four-year curriculum with a prerequisite of at least three years of college. This seven-year course of study would lead to a new degree of Juris Doctor. Though there was some opposition to this because it would endanger enrollments, the faculty stood firm. The change was announced to take effect in 1918 but was delayed until the following year by

*Contributed by alumnus and trustee Elbert H. Gary.

†In their history, *Northwestern University School of Law.*

the war. However, candidates who entered Law School having already earned a bachelor's degree could still finish the law course in three years. These revisions led to a massive change in course offerings which, according to Rahl and Schwerin, grew from about twenty-five in 1900 to over sixty by the 1920's.

One of the most important developments during this period was the addition of another type of venture to the roster of Northwestern's schools in Chicago, namely, the School of Commerce, offering evening courses to part time students. The origin of the school was somewhat unusual, the impetus for its establishment coming from a group of young Chicago businessmen who met regularly to discuss business problems. They enlisted the services and enthusiasm of Willard E. Hotchkiss and Earl D. Howard, both professors of economics on the Evanston campus, who took the idea of founding a school of commerce to President Harris. Northwestern then approached interested members of the Chicago business community and proposed that if they would guarantee the school against financial loss for a period of five years, the university would sponsor the project and later assume responsibility. The businessmen agreed, and in the spring of 1908 they formed a Board of Guarantors representing all branches of business and three organizations: the Chicago Association of Commerce, the Illinois Society of Public Accountants, and the Industrial Club of Chicago.[40]

Establishment of the School of Commerce

Professor W. E. Hotchkiss was appointed dean of the school which opened in the fall of 1908 with six professors and 255 students. Success was immediate and before long the school was virtually self-supporting. It continued to grow at a phenomenal rate during the succeeding decade with new faculty members being added each year, including Walter Dill Scott, the future president of Northwestern. By 1916-17 the enrollment on the Chicago campus had risen to 1,076 and by 1919-1920 to 2,598 (see Tables 4-1, 4-2). Clearly the School of Commerce filled a great need in the Chicago area.

In October 1912, the trustees acted to introduce elementary commerce and accounting courses on the Evanston campus under the auspices of the department of economics. Under this program undergraduates were able to receive a Bachelor of Science in Commerce, and, if they spent their junior and senior year on the Chicago campus, a Bachelor in Business Administration as well. This arrangement proved so popular that it was decided to add further courses in commerce to the curriculum of the economics department in the College of Liberal Arts on the Evanston campus. By 1919-20 there were 463 students enrolled in these courses.

The growth of the Chicago professional schools and the increasing size of the university as a whole made it desirable to increase the number of faculty elected to represent each of the schools on the University Council. As a result of the reorganization carried out in 1909 the college was to elect three representatives, the Medical and Law schools two each, and the Dental, Pharmacy, and Engineering schools one each.

Expansion of the University Council

In his report for 1909-10, President Harris indicated that he was eager to have the Council play a more active role, noting that in the past it had "made little attempt to conduct business of importance" but that it "ought to furnish a forum for the discussion of matters relating to general University interest and that it ought to be endowed with some real authority. . . ." New responsibilities assigned to the Council at this time included control of "matters of general interest . . . such as meetings of the united faculties, the observances of University Day, the program for Commencement anniversaries" and, significantly, "changes in entrance requirements or programs of study for degrees. . . ." The latter provision in particular would insure university-wide monitoring of admission and graduation standards.

Proposal for a Chicago Campus

During the closing year of President Harris's administration, trustee Nathan William MacChesney presented the Committee on Endowment of the board of trustees with a proposal that would have far-reaching consequences. It called for the consolidation of all the Chicago professional schools on a single campus on the near North Side.[41] Though some of the faculty on the Evanston campus were disturbed by the possibility that too large a portion of the university's resources would be diverted to the Chicago venture, the majority of those interested in the university's future saw great value in the proposal. The preliminary plans for the project were getting under way in 1917 when America's entry into the war forced a postponement of further action.

On May 10, 1916, the *Daily Northwestern* reported a rumor that the national Methodist Conference meeting in Saratoga, New York, intended to ask Harris to become corresponding secretary of the Methodist Episcopal Board of Education. Within a few weeks the rumor was confirmed and he resigned effective July 1, 1916. After many years in highly demanding executive posts, Harris may well have been attracted by the less taxing nature of the position offered him by the Methodist Church.

In its July issue for that year, the *Alumni Journal* reviewed the impressive gains made by the university during the ten years of Harris's administration, noting especially a substantial increase in the size of the student body and a more than 30 percent increase in Northwestern's resources. Two new schools had been established, namely, Engineering and Commerce, and twenty new buildings added. As the *Daily Northwestern* had noted earlier, "Since his coming to Northwestern in 1906 the institution has gained largely in attendance, scholarship and in rank among the large universities in the country."[42]

Reappointment of Thomas F. Holgate

Caught unprepared once more, the trustees turned again to Dean Thomas F. Holgate and appointed him interim president. It would fall to Holgate to steer the university through the difficult period following American entry into the war ten months later.

In November 1903 the trustees announced that Robert D. Sheppard, Northwestern's business manager* since 1893, had resigned his position. His successor, William A. Dyche, was a Northwestern graduate of the class of 1882 and the son of trustee David R. Dyche, founder of the university's Pharmacy School. By the time of his appointment, William Dyche had had extensive experience in the family business and had also become active in banking circles, initially as a director and later as president of the Evanston State Bank and Trust Company. He was to remain the university's business agent until 1934.[43]

*He remained a trustee and member of the history department until 1906.

It was at this point that the university adopted a modern accounting system *Finances* which combined the accounts of the Chicago professional schools with those of the schools on the Evanston campus. As Table 4-3 shows, the total income of the university increased from $377,200 in 1900-01 to $991,700 in 1915-16. The proportions of income derived from tuitions, rents, interest and other specified sources remained roughly the same during this period, with tuition being responsible for nearly 60 percent of the receipts. Expenditures over the same period show the amount spent on instruction continuing to account for roughly 50 percent of the budget. The most striking jump in expenditure in one area occurred between 1900-1901 and 1902-03 when interest payments rose from $17,900 to $81,900.

This sudden and sizeable rise in expenditure, largely responsible for the first major deficits during this period, represented interest payments on $1,150,000 which Northwestern borrowed at the time. Of this amount, $350,000 was spent on the construction of a building on land owned by the university in Chicago. This building was then leased for fifty years to the Booth Packing Company at an annual rental of $35,500.[44] The prospect of a high yield in rental had persuaded the trustees that the initial investment would be worth making. The remaining $800,000 was spent, as previously noted, for the purchase and renovation of the Tremont Hotel to provide more adequate quarters for three of the Chicago professional schools.

By 1905-06, the university's income had increased sufficiently to catch up with expenditures, tuition receipts and rents being mainly responsible for this improvement in the financial situation. This situation was short-lived, however, and except for 1907-08, the university again experienced a series of deficits from 1906-07 through 1912-13. This time it was a sharp rise in the expenditure for instruction which caused the problem. Between 1906 and 1910 the teaching faculty grew from approximately 300 to over 500, an increase of almost 60 percent. The continued rise of the instructional budget over the next few years was also partly accounted for by modest increases in salaries.[45]

In his report to the trustees in 1912, President Harris commented on the difficulty of running a university without incurring deficits. To begin with, unlike commercial enterprises, the university up to this time had operated entirely without a reserve fund. In the second place, while roughly 95 percent of the university's expenditures —on such items as physical plant operations, instruction and administration— remained fixed, the major source of income, namely, tuition, was variable. On the one hand growing attendance required an increase in facilities and instructors, on the other, a drop in enrollment would leave the university·with sizeable amounts committed to these items but insufficient income from tuition to cover them.

The trustees had good reason to know that Harris's analysis was correct. For although enrollment continued to grow during this period, sudden fluctuations in registration in the professional schools caused by the raising of entrance and graduation requirements had created considerable financial difficulties from time to time. On June 16, 1903, for example, the Committee on the Law School reporting to the board stressed that deficits in the school's budget were the result of new equipment—above all the preparation of new quarters at the remodeled Tremont

TABLE 4-3

N.U. BUDGETED RECEIPTS AND EXPENDITURES: 1900 - 1910[a]

(In Thousands of Dollars)

Academic Year	1900-1901[b]	1901-1902[b]	1902-1903[b]	1903-1904	1904-1905	1905-1906	1906-1907	1907-1908	1908-1909	1909-1910
RECEIPTS										
Tuition	$207.4	$217.9	$265.0	$276.2	$280.5	$285.9	$295.6	$321.3	$370.2	$379.0
Interest	34.5	25.8	30.6	23.0	23.7	33.2	45.9	41.6	33.4	28.0
Rent	115.0	121.8	175.6	169.8	176.8	183.1	186.7	194.4	202.7	201.4
Gifts	—	1.3	—	—	—	—	1.8	6.0	1.1	21.0
Education Clinics	18.0	22.6	22.1	22.6	22.9	20.8	25.2	28.9	18.5	25.9
Other	2.3	0.7	2.2	6.8	2.2	9.2	6.5	4.9	6.1	5.8
Woman's College Boarding Account; Net	—	(2.6)	(1.4)	1.4	—	(0.8)	2.3	3.6	5.1	2.8
Total	377.2	387.5	494.1	499.8	506.1	531.4	564.0	600.7	637.1	663.9
EXPENDITURES										
Instruction	190.3	212.4	236.3	235.7	232.2	235.9	246.7	260.4	289.1	341.6
Library	9.3	9.0	7.1	9.3	9.1	15.0	10.6	14.8	15.9	16.4
Administration	25.4	19.9	57.5	55.8	55.0	63.5	73.8	76.6	79.0	77.0
Physical Plant	81.0	82.4	94.8	87.4	80.1	87.8	91.5	90.1	98.3	109.3
Student Aid	—	—	—	—	—	—	12.5	11.9	13.6	13.9
Other	42.0	45.6	54.2	52.9	52.1	46.8	55.2	52.9	61.1	69.2
Interest	17.9	65.6	81.9	81.2	80.0	80.3	88.2	85.0	85.0	76.1
Total	365.9	434.9	531.8	522.3	508.5	529.3	578.5	591.7	642.0	703.5
Surplus (deficit)	11.3	(47.4)	(37.7)	(22.5)	(2.4)	2.1	(14.5)	9.0	(4.9)	(39.6)

SOURCE: Northwestern University Treasurer's Reports, 1900-1910.
a All schools   b Estimated

Hotel. But a glance at Table 4-1 shows that during the preceding year there had also been a sudden drop in enrollments from 195 to 162, which undoubtedly contributed in a major way to the school's financial problems.

However, the committee also explained why it was worthwhile to incur deficits in order to maintain and build the professional schools. "All universities of recognized prominence and standing will be found to hold their reputation to a very considerable extent through the influence emanating from their law and medical departments," noted the report. And, indeed, desirous as the trustees were to avoid deficits, they continued to support the improvement of the professional school programs and facilities as best they could.

When the situation became pressing, the board resorted to its traditional policy of covering deficits by selling off the university's non-productive real estate in Evanston. And, like their predecessors, the presidents during this period continued to try to increase the size of the endowment so as to give the institution greater maneuverability and make possible long-range planning. As noted earlier, President James encouraged the establishment of alumni organizations and persuaded the trustees to initiate a Jubilee Fund Memorial campaign to celebrate Northwestern's semicentennial in 1905. The drive was completed during Holgate's service as interim president.

TABLE 4-4

N.U. BUDGETED RECEIPTS AND EXPENDITURES: 1910 - 1920

(In Thousands of Dollars)

Academic Year	1910-1911	1911-1912	1912-1913	1913-1914	1914-1915	1915-1916	1916-1917	1917-1918	1918-1919	1919-1920
RECEIPTS										
Tuition	$393.4	$388.8	$423.4	$528.6	$549.2	$607.7	$687.6	$608.3	$631.9	$705.9
Interest	31.1	22.7	34.0	52.2	59.1	58.7	98.8	122.5	119.1	133.1
Rent	211.0	215.0	187.6	215.7	214.8	223.5	275.1	217.6	223.9	250.1
Gifts	11.6	12.6	12.0	14.7	16.4	15.3	13.2	13.9	61.4	68.6
Education Clinics	30.6	28.8	38.9	47.7	45.3	54.5	68.4	87.8	60.9	68.0
Other	5.9	11.6	2.3	7.6	30.5	27.1	28.0	31.1	43.5	48.6
Woman's College Boarding Account; Net	2.7	4.0	6.4	7.5	5.4	4.9	4.8	6.0	4.7	0.2
Total	686.3	683.5	704.6	874.0	920.7	991.7	1,175.9	1,087.2	1,145.4	1,274.5
EXPENDITURES										
Instruction	356.3	367.6	374.3	457.0	480.0	548.1	629.3	597.2	559.6	622.5
Library	18.2	21.9	25.7	27.7	28.6	29.2	36.4	36.7	34.2	38.1
Administration	89.7	91.5	88.6	95.5	104.5	110.0	122.1	140.8	144.2	160.5
Physical Plant	114.1	107.8	111.6	120.3	118.3	123.8	140.3	154.8	161.5	179.7
Student Aid	15.9	16.2	18.8	20.3	23.7	25.4	25.6	24.6	23.1	25.7
Other	58.2	49.3	55.4	59.7	76.2	51.3	70.3	66.0	66.3	73.8
Interest	59.3	68.8	65.4	70.5	88.1	101.6	127.5	138.5	156.6	174.2
Total	711.7	723.1	739.8	851.0	919.4	989.4	1,151.5	1,158.6	1,145.5	1,274.5
Surplus (deficit)	(25.4)	(39.6)	(35.2)	23.0	1.3	2.3	24.4	(71.4)	(0.1)	—

SOURCE: Northwestern University Treasurer's Reports, 1910-1920.

Both James and Harris had approached Andrew Carnegie without success. But Harris was able to attract the financial resources required for the construction of the Swift Engineering School, Patten Gymnasium, and Harris Hall. He also helped negotiate the guarantee by Chicago businessmen which made possible the establishment of the School of Commerce, and initiated the campaign as a result of which the national fraternities erected housing facilities on Northwestern land.

Late in 1912 Harris, who had been warning the trustees of the dangers of continuing deficits, made one more attempt to increase the endowment. At his urging the board appointed a finance committee to undertake a million dollar endowment campaign. The group first applied to the General Education Board of the Rockefeller Foundation for $250,000. In May 1913, the Rockefeller Foundation offered the university $100,000 on condition that the rest of the million dollars were raised in the near future.[46] In June Harris and the board of trustees set July 1, 1914, as the target date for the completion of the fund drive. But the campaign seemed to have come at a bad time. The amount was not raised by mid-1914 nor even by 1915; indeed, by February 1916, the finance committee had raised only $480,000. At their meeting on the 21st of that month the trustees reluctantly decided to withdraw the university's application to the Rockefeller Foundation. It may well be that the failure to secure additional resources contributed to Harris's decision to accept the offer of a new position.

Miss Lodilla Ambrose (seated, center), assistant librarian, at the main desk of Lunt Library, 1904

Northwestern University Band, 1904 (Courtesy N.U. alumna Bonmilla P. Grobenkort)

During the first two decades of the twentieth century the student population *Student Life* on the Evanston campus grew from 1,282 to 3,228 (see Tables 4-1 and 4-2). Inevitably this increase in numbers wrought changes in the character of campus life. No longer was social activity confined to a few literary societies and clubs. Now students had available to them organizations and activities catering to a wide range of interests. Indeed, as Arthur Guy Terry of the history department observed in 1910, the Northwestern collegian's problem was no longer one of finding ways to escape the routines of study and to avoid the dangers of overwork; now it was extracurricular overexertion that had become the more prevalent threat to the students' well-being.[47]

Religious organizations, as earlier, retained an important place on campus. *Religious* Northwestern was still close enough to its Methodist roots to uphold its commit- *Activities* ment to a Christian education. In an article in the *Northwestern Christian Advocate* of August 16, 1902, Professor J. Scott Clark stated that the university's wholesome moral and religious atmosphere was one of its preeminent features and urged parents to send their children to this "training-place for mind and soul." While Clark took care to point out that "the bilious youth of monastic habits, who considers all fun sinful, is not to be found here," he noted that all the campus leaders "were also conspicuous for their moral and religious standing." Possibly Clark alluded to the popular local chapters of the Y.M.C.A. and the Y.W.C.A. In the fall of 1900 the college Y.M.C.A. rented a house on Orrington Avenue and proceeded to offer various services, including Bible classes, reading rooms, and an employment bureau. The upper floor of the "Association House" also served as a men's dormitory. Indeed, prior to the development of the men's quadrangles, the Y.M.C.A. functioned as the closest equivalent to a commons.[48]

In October 1901 the work of the University Settlement was given concrete *University* encouragement by a gift of $25,000 from Milton H. Wilson, which made possible *Settlement* the construction of a large permanent building at 1400 West Augusta Boulevard, near the corner of Chicago and Milwaukee avenues. The settlement was operated by an independent staff and board of directors, though the building and equipment were held in trust by the university.[49] Northwestern students volunteered their services at the settlement and by 1904 the student organization reported growing participation, especially by students in the School of Music. After 1906, students in the College of Liberal Arts raised funds to support at least one full time staff member at the settlement each year.[50]

The political interests of the campus became more focused when a Garrett *Politics* professor and some Evanston students formed a good-citizenship society, "Aleph Teth Nun," to discuss matters of public concern and to interest members in politics. The new group, formed in 1903, established an informal affiliation with the National Reform League in Washington, D.C. One of the major issues Aleph Teth Nun tackled was the political situation at Northwestern itself, where some students perennially complained about domination of campus life by Greek society alliances.[51] Eleven years after its founding Aleph Teth Nun was still trying to bring a conciliatory note into campus politics:

Forget your personal prejudices for a while and try to believe that others are going to do the same thing. We are not a pious lot of hypocrites nor a wild-eyed mob of reformers. We are simply trying to do a little here and a little there to make our school a bigger, finer, better place.[52]

Creation of the Student Council 1914
The formation of the first university student council in the spring of 1914 marked an important step forward in the students' assumption of responsibility for campus life. The students assembled and elected a committee to organize a central governing body to act as a go-between with faculty and administration on matters of politics, honor codes, and athletics.[53] There were other moves as well in the direction of student self-determination. Dean of Women Mary Rose Potter happily approved the replacement of the Faculty Social Committee—which for years had planned the annual schedule of events—by a board of nine students and five faculty members. As she noted, social life need no longer be regarded as "certain entertainments granted as concessions to frivolous youth by the powers that be."[54] Limited self-rule also spread to Willard Hall. During the 1902-03 academic year the coeds developed a constitution for a house executive council to determine matters of discipline not provided for by general university policy.[55]

Clubs
Many special interest clubs blossomed at Northwestern in the pre-World War I era. Scientifically-minded students could join the Science Club, and after 1904, the Engineering Club. Other organizations included a Poetry Club, a Chess Club, even a "Glee, Mandolin and Banjo Club." By 1903, Northwestern had a sufficient number of candidates for advanced degrees to warrant the formation of a graduate club to promote new friendships and provide opportunities for the reading of papers before fellow students.

As these new groups proliferated, the older literary clubs felt the impact of competing activities. By 1907 enthusiasm for forensics had lapsed to such a degree that Northwestern had difficulty finding good representatives to compete at intercollegiate oratory contests.[56] Northwestern debaters, though, made a distinguished record in regional meets, usually being strong contenders for the Midwest championship.[57] Why this shift in interest occurred is difficult to explain. It may be that on-the-spot analytical argumentation had come to be seen as generally more useful than the more formal style of oratory.

Athletics
Competitive athletics had never occupied such a prominent position in campus life as in the two decades after 1900. When President Theodore Roosevelt visited Northwestern in 1903, he praised "manly sport" and every form of rough, physical engagement with great enthusiasm.[58] The administration shared his view but with some reservations. The pattern for the control of athletics created in the 1890's continued with modifications during the following years. Within the university an athletic committee was established and in 1896 the Intercollegiate Conference of Faculty Representatives was set up to govern interuniversity sports. Football won out over baseball in becoming the king of college sports, as far as spectator interest and student participation were concerned. Basketball emerged as a third major sport when the Conference granted it full-fledged varsity status in 1906.[59]

According to the 1895 agreement of the seven university presidents, authority for athletic control was given over to faculty representatives through the Conference. Inevitably friction arose. On March 9, 1906, President James Angell of the University of Michigan called a special meeting to draft new regulations. This so-called "Angell Conference" issued rules which required one year of residency for eligibility, allowed only three years of competition and banned graduate students from participation. In addition, new rulings limited the football season to five games and the price of spectator tickets to fifty cents.

Turn-of-the-century football was brutal and exhausting. In its early form it emphasized running, prohibited the forward pass and allowed three downs to gain five yards. The physical dangers of the game loomed so large that in 1905 Northwestern took a drastic step and abolished it as an intercollegiate sport. Acting upon the recommendations of a special investigating committee headed by Dean Thomas Holgate, the trustees voted to suspend competitive football for a period of five years.[60] In the interim, intramural football flourished. President Harris reported to the trustees, "Fully four times as many students as under the old system have taken regular exercises and competed in various games."[61]

Two-Year Suspension of Intercollegiate Football

The suspension lasted only two years, but when the game resumed in 1908, the lack of experienced players led to several poor seasons. The first Conference win since 1904 came with the defeat of Purdue, 14 to 8, in 1909. There were several so-called "moral victories" when arch-rivals like Wisconsin and Chicago were held to low scores. The team fared much better by 1916, when—under the famous John "Paddy" Driscoll—Northwestern won six of seven games, including the first defeat of Chicago in fifteen years. The championship eluded the team that year when Ohio State administered a 23 to 3 defeat in the final game. The next season brought Northwestern its first victory over Michigan since 1892. Football continued during World War I, though the Conference temporarily suspended its activities as controlling body in 1918. During the war, the Northwestern team played many games with Conference rivals and with the Great Lakes Naval Training Center. After the armistice in November 1918, the Conference resumed its former authority.[62]

Although basketball became a Conference sport in 1906, Northwestern did not organize a team until the following year. In its early years the team's record was dismal. The Purple remained in the Conference cellar until 1913 when it had a first division team for the first time. As in football, the team then had a banner year in 1916 with nine wins—including the first ever over a Chicago basketball team—and only three defeats.[63]

The story of baseball paralleled that of football and basketball: a few wins, many losses, no championships and no real success until 1915. At this time Northwestern placed third in the Conference, but the following year the team again lapsed into defeat.[64] Though university teams were seldom victorious, student enthusiasm remained high. This was demonstrated by the almost immediate popularity of "Go U Northwestern," introduced in 1912. When Northwestern defeated Indiana that season, the band found itself in the embarrassing position of having no victory song to play. Theo. C. Van Etten, band member and pharmacy student, rose to the occasion and composed the words and music for the song which the band played at the Illinois game the next week and again at University chapel. Another football song dating from this era is "Rise Northwestern" formerly titled "The Northwestern Push On Song." Donald G. Robertson, Class of 1913, composed this song

"Go U Northwestern"

Botany field trip

Football team, 1903, on the steps of University Hall

Women's basketball team

Hard at play, circa 1903

Y.W.C.A. Central Student Conference at Lake Geneva, 1915 (Photos top left and bottom right, courtesy N.U. alumna and former faculty member Margery C. Carlson)

but withheld publication until 1916 to avoid conflict with "Go U Northwestern."[65]

Homecoming   In 1911 Homecoming was inaugurated as a regular fall event. Thereafter, alumni would return to campus to join the parade and other festivities that marked the weekend. For this first Homecoming the Alumni Association and the Evanston Commercial Association appropriated funds to cover expenses and President Harris sent a special letter of invitation to all alumni. Despite rain which dampened the parade and the fact that Northwestern was defeated by Chicago 9 to 3 on Saturday afternoon, the occasion was enthusiastically supported by students and alumni.[66]

The physical facilities for sports also received attention. In 1905 a new athletic field was developed on Central Street at the present site of Dyche Stadium. Costing about $25,000, the twelve-acre facility provided two football gridirons, a baseball diamond, a quarter-mile track and a wooden grandstand accommodating 10,000 fans.[67] Four years later members of the university community were delighted to learn that trustee James A. Patten had provided funds for a large athletic building. "With the completion of the new building," Dean Holgate assured the trustees, "we now have facilities which are unsurpassed."[68] Named for its donor, Patten Gymnasium was an architectural triumph which provided facilities for basketball, indoor track meets, and swimming and baseball practice. It was built on what is now the site of the Technological Institute and in addition to serving as a gymnasium it became the location for commencement exercises.

Following the end of World War I regular athletic competition was resumed under the aegis of the Conference. The record for football, basketball and baseball between 1900 and 1920 was anything but spectacular. Nevertheless, the university clung to its membership in the Conference, fielded teams which occasionally displayed exciting heroics in the face of challenging odds, and maintained loyal support from students, alumni, and administration. The addition of school songs, the institution of Homecoming, and the provision of improved facilities helped sustain an intercollegiate sports tradition.

The improvement of athletic activities at Northwestern was directly related to two larger concerns: the matter of coeducation and the need for better facilities for men students in general. While Northwestern's unimpressive athletic showing was partly due to a relatively small enrollment, there was nonetheless some feeling that the university failed to attract athletes because it had the public image of being overly soft and effeminate. Writing an article on "Virility at Northwestern" in the June 1905 issue of the *Northwestern Magazine*, one young man complained that no rugged esprit de corps could ever develop as long as the school lacked men's dormitories, commons, technical curricula, and a men's club. The issue was still alive in 1914 when another student discussed Northwestern's "stigma" of being a "girls' school."[69] Both James and Harris outlined plans for men's quadrangles and sports areas; as for the coeds, the main concern was not what they did, or were, but their number.

The Men's   As the editors of the student paper grumbled in the issue for February 19, 1903,
Dormitories   the need for men's dormitories "has been the theme of *The Northwestern*'s editorial thunder for something like a decade." Actually, some of the wealthier fraternities had started renting and buying chapter houses in Evanston during the 1890's,

though the non-fraternity men still found their own lodgings in boarding houses.[70] The eating situation was even more dire, for as one undergraduate protested, "there is a large proportion of students who subsist from hand to mouth at the local restaurants and lunch-counters, getting their living on cheap, greasy food, served in a noisome atmosphere, and among uncongenial neighbors."[71] Needless to say, when the first north quadrangle buildings opened for occupancy in 1914, they were quickly filled.[72]

One of the interesting aspects of the housing quadrangles was the cooperative planning between the administration and the fraternities. As early as 1903 President James had asked the faculty to explore the possibility of on-campus chapter houses.[73] Harris also wanted to involve the chapters in the overall architectural plan and, as noted, in 1911 he contacted fraternity representatives, offering the free use of sites on campus provided each group would share in building expenses.[74] In response to this offer most of the fraternities prepared special fund-raising brochures with which to approach their alumni. Once the dormitories and chapter houses were furnished, the overall effect was deluxe. According to a reporter writing in the March 27, 1919 issue of the *Evanston News Index:*

> On the first floor of each house is a big club room with an attractive fireplace. On the large table may be found copies of the latest magazines, and around the room are comfortable arm chairs and rocking chairs, settees, etc. The walls are panelled in oak, and a handsome rug covers the floor. Each house organization either buys or rents its own piano, victrola, and subscribes to a number of periodicals.

Women Students

The women continued to be housed on the south campus, either in Willard Hall, Pearsons Hall, or in Chapin Hall (built in 1901). Their activities probably varied as much as the hats they chose to wear for their annual *Syllabus* photographs, ranging from tight-fitting, practical little bonnets to the latest creations of the milliner's art. Some women attended college for the avowed purpose of preparing for a life's work; others were content to cultivate social graces and develop refined tastes. One student, Lydia Bartlett,* wrote serious and reflective essays on such subjects as the need for studying the Bible in public schools and the suitability of women for the profession of book reviewing.[75] A girl of quite a different type was Ethel Robinson, an oratory student in the class of 1912, who kept a scrapbook of her life at Northwestern in which she preserved engraved calling cards, invitations to teas and luncheons, and dance cards mostly filled with the signature of "XX," her anonymous but loyal beau.[76] Whatever their interests, all the girls seemed to enjoy an occasional ice cream sundae at Theobold's in downtown Evanston.

But all was not hearts and flowers for the women students; often they had to fight to be taken seriously. In 1905, for example, the female editorial staff of the *Northwestern Magazine* went on strike against their male editor-in-chief. The cause of the dispute was the girls' objections to producing love stories for the publication. As one indignant student related, "I wanted to write about the 'Influence of Present

*She died in 1908 while still a student at Northwestern.

*"Day of the
Clinging Vine
Is . . . Leaving
Us"*

Day Education on the Future of the Race' and he wanted me to write 'The Confessions of the Love Sick Co-ed.' Of course I wouldn't do that. . . . How should I know anything about what passed through the mind of one who was love sick? I have never had the experience, I am sure." The editor gave up and invited his staff back, letting them write on any topic they wished.[77] The incident reflected the coming of a new generation of college women—stronger and more determined than their predecessors. As the May 15, 1912 Woman's Edition of the *Daily Northwestern* boldly announced, "The day of the sweet but insipid 'clinging vine' is rapidly leaving us, and it is our business to show that the modern woman surpasses her in every way."

The ultimate purpose of all these activities—religious, political, athletic, coeducational and academic—was to make college life pleasant as well as useful. Yet some students had doubts about their place in the surrounding flurry, and speculated what their various involvements would amount to in the long run. When Owen Johnson's *Stover at Yale* was published in 1912, students at Northwestern began to question the motives of the big men on their own campus.[78] There is no doubt that by this time certain unwritten codes and customs had been established at Northwestern to foster the cultivation of useful contacts and allow those with social ambitions to impress the proper people, but this hardly distinguished this university's students from those on other campuses.[79]

Unfortunately, surviving diaries and letters of students of this era are few. The students might be known more personally through the fictional prototypes they created in the *Northwestern Magazine:* the "Fearless Fusser" who nervously mismanaged his dates; "Elmer Wilson," a thin, "seedly looking" freshman "with frayed collars and stringy neckties"; the lovely and adventurous "Betty" who challenged her boy friends to a race in her Mercedes.[80] These student types seemed to reflect the concerns of many Northwestern students of the period: gaining social acceptance and having a good time. If nothing else, student life at Northwestern just before the war was enriched by the students' capacity to enjoy themselves and each other while they struggled to solve the perennial problems which afflict young people, not the least being the use of their newly gained freedom.

*World War I
and After*

For many students "good times" on campus ended when the United States entered the war in April 1917. When the European conflict had first erupted in August 1914, few Northwestern students thought that their own lives would be affected. Like many of their compatriots they saw the conflict as Europe's war and certainly not a concern of the United States. However this attitude changed over the next two years. Courses in military training were introduced in September 1915 along with mock war games, and lectures on war preparedness became increasingly common.[81]

By March 1917, involvement in the war had become a matter of daily concern on campus as elsewhere. "Every student," wrote the editor of the *Daily*, "must commit himself to the service of his country, but at the same time endeavor to place himself where he is best fitted."[82] Within a short time over 1,000 undergraduates were in the armed services. It would be some time before campus life was back to normal.

Actual declaration of war in April 1917, brought about a major reorganization of academic life. As noted, some courses in military training and organization were already being taught before the declaration of war. In March, in answer to a plea from the International Committee of the Y.M.C.A., a group of some twenty-one Northwestern University and Garrett Biblical Institute students joined similar contingents from Princeton and Yale to serve as volunteer workers in prisoner of war camps in France and Great Britain.

When the Allies appealed for more hospital facilities, the Northwestern Medical School responded by organizing the Northwestern Medical Corps Hospital Unit No. 12 under the direction of Dr. Frederick A. Besley. Between May 1917, and April 1919, the Unit—staffed by 37 doctors, 199 non-commissioned officers and enlisted men, and 105 Red Cross nurses—treated some 60,000 servicemen at its field station in Etaples, France.[83]   *N.U. Hospital Unit*

Immediately following the American declaration of war the board of trustees voted to place the university's entire facilities—buildings, laboratories and personnel—at the disposal of the government. A committee of trustees, alumni, and faculty was organized to cooperate with the National Research Council in determining how the university might be of service. Professor John T. Hayford, of the College of Engineering, was quickly recruited to become a member of the National Advisory Board on Aeronautics in Washington, D.C., where he remained until the end of the war. The dean of the Law School, John H. Wigmore, was appointed to the Office of the Judge Advocate General with the rank of Colonel. There he helped draft the selective service legislation and the regulations for the Student Army Training Corps. Professor of Psychology Walter Dill Scott, on leave at Carnegie Tech, joined the Adjutant General's Office, where he set up a system for classifying army personnel according to their experience and aptitudes for particular duties. He also persuaded the Army to adopt a policy of promoting officers on the basis of a system that measured their efficiency rather than simply on the basis of seniority, which had been the long-accepted practice.[84] These were only the first of a total of some 121 members of the Northwestern faculty who took leaves of absence during 1917-1918 to serve the United States government either as civilians or as officers in the armed services.[85]

Meanwhile, the eagerness of students to volunteer for service following the United States declaration of war threatened to reduce the size of the Northwestern student body. But as President Holgate explained to the board, several factors continued to make for "deliberation in action." One was the passage in May 1917, of the Selective Service Act which provided for the registration and classification for military service of all men between the ages of twenty-one and thirty. At the same time government officials urged students to remain in school until they were called up by the draft. Meanwhile, according to the President's Report for 1917-19, the faculties of the various schools announced that anyone entering government service before the end of the college year would receive full academic credit for his or her course work. By the end of the second semester in June 1917, a total of 350 students had withdrawn from Northwestern to enter the services.

For those who remained the university organized what became known as "Lang's Army," comprising 500 draft-aged students who trained under the command of Lt. W. W. Lang, a disabled Canadian officer. By the time Lang returned to Canada   *Lang's Army and SATC*

*Recruiting for the infantry
on the Evanston campus*

Students' Army Training Corps (SATC) at Northwestern during World War I

in the spring of 1918, his "army" was able to join the Northwestern unit of the Students' Army Training Corps. The SAT Corps had been organized in 1918 following the lowering of the draft age from twenty-one to eighteen to encourage students to continue their education until they were actually called. As President Holgate explained in his report to the board for 1917-19, this was done so that "young men in college might be inducted into the army and remain at the college for study while living the life and receiving the training of a soldier." The colleges were asked to provide housing, food and academic instruction at a fixed price, while the army took care of military instruction and discipline and provided uniforms and rifles.

As one of the universities cooperating in the SATC program, Northwestern was required to adopt an army approved course of study for members of the Corps and to shift from the semester to the quarter system. All fraternity houses and dormitories were converted into barracks and new barracks and mess halls were built to take care of the 1,600 members of the Corps: 800 in Evanston; 500 in the Law and Dental schools; and 300 in the Medical School. The SATC was scarcely under way when the influenza epidemic hit the campus. Though scores of students were laid low there was only one reported death.[86]

Women Students' War Effort

The university also mobilized about 1,700 women students for service in the National Aid and Red Cross. Regular classes were formed to prepare surgical dressings and so-called "comfort kits" for men going into active service. The girls were also enrolled in courses in food and fuel conservation, principles of agriculture, and first aid—all designed to further the war effort. They took an especially active part in the war bond drives sponsored by the university.

In April 1918, the United States government Committee on Education and Special Training asked a number of colleges and technical schools, including Northwestern, to offer instruction in such skills as woodworking and sheetmetal work. Northwestern agreed to do so and, having installed the necessary equipment in the basement of Fisk Hall, hired a staff of skilled mechanics to conduct the classes. By October 1918 a course to train radio operators had been added to the list of offerings. During the same period the School of Commerce conducted courses for the training of ordnance officers; the Dental School provided training in oral and plastic surgery for a group of seventy officers assigned to the school by the Surgeon General; while another forty commissioned officers received training in osteopathic surgery at the Medical School.

The signing of the Armistice on November 11, 1918, brought the war to a close. The SATC was disbanded and all members of the detachment discharged. During the second term of 1918-1919 life at the university gradually returned to normal. As President Holgate reported in 1919, large numbers of those associated with Northwestern had actively participated in the war effort, including 121 members of the faculty, 1,017 undergraduates and 1,692 alumni. Of this group, 65 had lost their lives.

Closing of the Academy

Two permanent changes took place during the war years, namely, the closing of the Academy and, as noted earlier, the transfer of the Northwestern School of Pharmacy to the University of Illinois. In the course of almost sixty years of operation, the Academy had, as President Holgate acknowledged, trained most of the university's loyal alumni. But, as he went on to explain, the development of a growing number of public high schools capable of offering students adequate preparation for admission to college meant that the need for privately endowed and independent academies had become "greatly restricted." The Academy had been showing deficits—some as high as $10,000—since 1905 and in April 1917, the board finally voted to close it down and to turn Fisk Hall over to the College of Liberal Arts. By the time the Academy's final graduation came around in June 1917, the country was at war.

Transfer of Pharmacy to University of Illinois

The Northwestern School of Pharmacy terminated its operations, as noted earlier, for similar reasons. Competition from other schools had cut enrollment severely and by 1916-17 the school had an operating deficit of approximately $6,000. Since the School of Pharmacy conducted in Chicago by the University of Illinois was offering an equivalent program it was decided that "the two schools could be combined without loss of efficiency and without increased cost to either." This was done in June 1917.[87]

In 1918 the university's librarian, Walter Lichtenstein, was dismissed from his post, allegedly because his services were no longer required. There are those who claim that in fact his dismissal can be attributed to the wave of anti-German feeling that swept the country at this time, especially since a successor, Theodore Wesley Koch,was appointed shortly thereafter.[88] Koch had been educated at the University of Pennsylvania and Harvard and had also studied at the College de France of the University of Paris. By the time he came to Northwestern he had already had extensive experience as a librarian at Cornell University, the University of Michigan and the Library of Congress. He was to serve Northwestern for twenty-two years, in the course of which the total number of volumes in the library increased from 120,000 to 380,000.[89]

As the end of the war drew in sight, Holgate had asked to be relieved of his duties as acting president. In his closing report to the trustees some months later, he stressed his concern about the university's financial situation. As Table 4-5 shows, although the net resources of the university had grown from roughly $6,000,000 to over $10,000,000 since 1901, the income-producing assets remained

TABLE 4-5
N.U. RESOURCES AND LIABILITIES 1901 - 1920 (Selected Years)

(In Thousands of Dollars)

Year	Physical Plant	Productive Assets	Non-Productive Assets	Other Assets	Total	Liabilities	Net
1901	$2,549.5	$3,096.0	$ 724.4	$ 245.6	$6.615.5	$ 468.5	$6.147.0
1906	3,626.2	3,450.0	1,064.7	551.6	8,692.5	1,780.8	6,911.7
1911	3,776.1	4,005.0	1,267.6	586.0	9,634.7	1,058.6	8,576.1
1916	4,085.7	4,703.6	1,088.9	841.7	10,719.9	1,588.0	9,131.9
1920	3,769.7	4,722.1	1,290.3	2,179.7	11,961.8	1,804.0	10,157.8

SOURCE: Northwestern University Treasurer's Reports, 1901-1920.

under $5,000,000. It is therefore understandable why Holgate, like his predecessors, underlined the need for an increased endowment:

> A university so largely dependent on student tuition as Northwestern has come to be in recent years is peculiarly affected by sudden changes in student attendance, similar to those brought on by the War, and with rapidly advancing costs of operation added to reduced receipts from fees a deficit is inevitable unless additional funds are made from new and unanticipated sources. . . . Where plans are so largely contingent on income from student sources no far-reaching enterprises can be undertaken. The remedy lies in an increase of endowment without which the University cannot hope to maintain proper educational facilities and standards. As has frequently been pointed out, five million dollars added to the present endowment would not more than adequately support the work already in hand.

Responsibility for Northwestern's postwar development, however, would be undertaken by Holgate's successor.

Following the announcement that the trustees were engaged in a search for a *Election of* new president, the Alumni Association canvassed its members with 12,000 letters *President Lynn* asking them to demand a president of high caliber—"a Taft or Wilson, a Pershing *H. Hough* or a Wood, a MacAdoo or a Hoover." The board, however, more realistic in its assessment of what was possible, chose Lynn Harold Hough, professor of theology at Garrett Biblical Institute, and a well-known and widely traveled public speaker. A native of Cadiz, Ohio, Hough had been educated at Scio College and Drew Theological Seminary and had served in the ministry before coming to Garrett. He was forty-two when he accepted the presidency of Northwestern.

On May 17, 1919, the day on which the trustees selected Hough, the *Evanston News Index* commented on his stature as a public figure, noting that during the past year he had spoken before the students of practically "all the great universities of this country." The article went on to praise him for his "sterling character and high ideals that react (sic) as an inspiration upon the young men and women who come within the sphere of his influence." The *Index* included an enthusiastic editorial from the *Daily Northwestern* praising the imminent election of Hough alongside its own approving comments. It was assumed that the new president's tenure would be long and fruitful.

Undoubtedly the most important developments during Hough's administration were the launching of a major campaign to increase Northwestern's financial resources and the decision to go ahead and establish a North Side campus. The immediate incentive for the financial drive came in June 1919 when an anonymous donor—later identified as Milton H. Wilson—contributed $172,000 to be applied to the university's operating deficit for the year 1919-20. The gift was made on the condition that the trustees would at once start laying plans for an "earnest, scientifically conducted campaign" which would secure sufficient endowment to protect the university in its current operations and to provide for a further extension of its work.[90] A further incentive was the growing pressure on all university facilities

Rifle practice in the snow

Faculty wives working for N.U.'s American Red Cross chapter in Fisk Hall, 1917

arising from a postwar upsurge in enrollment. Between 1917-18 and 1919-20 overall enrollment jumped from 4,147 to 6,821.

A committee of trustees under the chairmanship of President Hough and includ- *Fund Drive* ing the business manager, William A. Dyche, was appointed to survey the financial needs of the university. The committee's recommendations submitted at a special meeting of the board on October 9, 1919 called for a campaign to raise approximately $25 million over a ten year period.

Although the amount of money demanded by the needs of the university was large, the members of the committee noted that it was no more than other institutions had obtained over the preceding decade. They optimistically suggested that a well-planned, well-directed campaign might obtain pledges for half of the $25 million goal by June 1920. The number one priority was the $4 million dollars needed to continue the university's current operations. The second was the $1,420,000 needed for the purchase of the proposed North Side campus.

Shortly before American entry into the war, the board had authorized the draw- *Purchase of* ing of plans for the proposed Chicago campus and had acquired an option on a *Site for the* tract of land at the corner of Chicago Avenue and Lake Shore Drive to be pur- *Chicago* chased at a price of $1,500,000.[91] The war had forced the proposal to be shelved *Campus* and it was not until late in the summer of 1919 that the trustees began to debate the question of whether Northwestern should exercise its option to buy this property. The debate continued until June 15, 1920, when President Hough recommended that the option be exercised and a majority of the board voted to accept his recommendation. Their decision was no doubt influenced by a letter from representatives of the Chicago professional schools strongly endorsing the purchase of the property. Trustee James A. Patten, however, who had vigorously opposed the idea of the Chicago campus, handed in his resignation at the conclusion of the meeting.

Two weeks later President Hough asked the board to relieve him of his duties as president. He indicated that "the cause of his retirement was due to lack of physical strength and the fear that if he continued to carry on the burdens of his office his health would suffer." On September 29, 1920 the trustees met once again to select a new president.

*Montgomery Ward Memorial Building,
built to house the Medical and Dental
Schools on the Chicago campus,
completed 1926*

Part Three

TOWARD A GREATER NORTHWESTERN

1920-1949

Major contributors who made possible the construction of the Chicago campus gathering around the president, for the ground breaking ceremony, May 8, 1925 (left to right) Mrs. Levy Mayer, Mrs. George R. Thorne, Mrs. Montgomery Ward, President Walter Dill Scott, Mrs. and Mr. George A. McKinlock, Mrs. and Mr. William A. Wieboldt, and Judge Elbert H. Gary

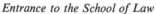

Entrance to the School of Law

5

TIMES OF PLENTY, TIMES OF TRIAL
1920-1939

Walter Dill Scott, Northwestern's tenth president, was the first alumnus and the first non-Methodist—being a Presbyterian—to be elected to the office. His background was also different from that of his predecessors in other respects. Born in Cooksville, Illinois in 1869, Scott had to work on his family's farm until he was nineteen before beginning his secondary education. In 1891 he won a competitive four year scholarship to Northwestern where he entered that fall.

As an undergraduate Walter Scott was a top-ranking student: elected to Phi Beta Kappa, he was also a leader in campus affairs. Among other things, he served as president of the Y.M.C.A., president of his senior class and, during his junior and senior years, played left guard on the varsity football team.[1] After three years of postgraduate studies at McCormick Theological Seminary in preparation for missionary work in China, Scott realized that his vocation lay elsewhere. In 1898 he married his former Northwestern classmate Anna Miller and immediately after, the couple left for Germany—he to study psychology at the University of Leipzig, she to study philology at nearby Halle.

By 1900 both Scotts had received their doctorates and were ready to return to the United States. They first went to Cornell University, where Scott taught for one year before coming to Northwestern as an instructor of psychology and pedagogy. Once there, he established and directed the university's psychological laboratory. By 1906 Scott was chairman of the psychology department of the college, and in 1909 he took on the added duties of professor of advertising in Northwestern's School of Commerce.[2]

Scott was especially interested in the application of psychology to the solution of problems in business and industry. His book, *The Theory and Practice of Advertising* (1903), was the first in its field and two subsequent volumes about advertising were also highly influential. Yet another work, *Increasing Human Efficiency in Business* (1911), presented his pioneering work in the application of psychology to personnel selection. In 1916 Scott was appointed visiting professor of applied psychology and director of a newly established Bureau of Salesmanship Research at Carnegie Institute of Technology in Pittsburgh, where he developed a series of rating scales designed for use in the selection and evaluation of salesmen. Upon American entry into the war a year later, Scott became director of the Committee on Classification of Personnel in the Army, which used the rating scales he had developed to assign officers and enlisted men to the duties for which they appeared most suited.[3] In 1919 he was awarded a Distinguished Service Medal for this work and in the same year he was elected president of the American Psychological Association.

Returning to Northwestern in the fall of 1919, Scott was quickly drawn into another venture. This was to serve as the president of the Scott Company of business consultants, organized that year by a number of his associates in the Army Classification Program. The company, with offices in Chicago, Dayton, and Philadelphia, was highly successful. But Scott's connection with the firm was short-lived.[4] In September 1920, he accepted the invitation of the Northwestern trustees to succeed Lynn H. Hough as president of the university.

Election of Scott as President

Scott accepted the appointment with considerable misgivings.* For some years there had been an annual deficit in the university's operating budget which members of the board of trustees, particularly James M. Patten and Milton H. Wilson, had made up out of their own pockets. The professional schools in Chicago were in cramped quarters, faculty salaries generally throughout the university were low, and housing facilities for students, especially in Evanston, were both limited and unsatisfactory. Finally, the bold program to raise $25,000,000 launched in 1919 was virtually at a standstill. In accepting the challenge of the office Scott did so with the stipulation that prior to a formal inauguration he be given a year in which to study the university's situation and devise plans for the future.[5]

Presenting to the trustees his views on Northwestern's role and obligations, Scott told them that he believed that there was nothing more "fundamental in advancing the aims of civilization than the type of service" institutions like Northwestern could render. He made it clear that he supported the Christian character of Northwestern's educational programs and noted with approval the extent to which the university had harmonized its religious commitment with the social, economic, and intellectual changes that had come about since the middle of the nineteenth century. A potential conflict between religion on the one hand and science and technology on the other had been resolved at Northwestern by an early recognition that the latter "not only gave man power over nature but provided him with a more adequate conception of his Creator." The development of the professional schools had in similar fashion reflected the awareness of the trustees and the faculty that however valuable culture, religion, and science were in themselves, they were "doubly valuable when used by a skilled practitioner as a means of service to mankind."

*According to Scott's biographer, he had turned down the offer to become president twice: once in 1919, prior to Hough's appointment, and again immediately following the latter's resignation. *J. Z. Jacobson*, Scott of Northwestern, *pp. 126-27.*

Scott was confident that a growing interest in the social sciences could be made a part of the university's educational goals. He was in complete agreement with Alexander Pope's dictum that "the proper study of mankind is man" and believed that Northwestern could and should become a leader in this area of investigation with its unlimited possibilities for development.[6]

As Scott prepared to assess Northwestern's prospects he could not help seeing many positive factors to counter the university's financial problems. The first steps had already been taken in bringing about the consolidation of the Chicago professional schools on a single campus. Both the Chicago schools and those on the Evanston campus enjoyed the leadership of a group of able and energetic deans. And, even though the immediate financial condition of the institution was poor, the long-range outlook for the economy as a whole was promising in this booming postwar period. Moreover, Scott had every reason to be confident that his own talents and background would enable him to attract widespread support from alumni, trustees, and faculty, many of whom he had known for a long time. And he also knew that in this, as in his previous endeavors, he could count on the help of his vibrant and highly talented wife.

Before the trial year had passed, Scott agreed to be formally installed. On the occasion of the inauguration—held on June 14, 1921—Scott observed that he believed he had been selected because the trustees were convinced that as a "son of Northwestern" he would provide the emphasis which they felt the university should continue to give to "human culture, to natural science, to religion, to professional skills and to the social sciences."[7]

The Search for Funds

The fundamental problem facing the university when Scott took office was financial, as was dramatized by the fact that although tuition rates had been raised and the General Education Board of the Rockefeller Foundation had made annual contributions of $35,000, the university's operating deficit for 1921-22 was approximately $113,000 (see Table 5-2).* As Scott pointed out to the trustees in his report for 1920-21, because of the rising costs associated with postwar inflation, Northwestern was confronted with a choice of either giving up certain of its "traditional responsibilities" or of increasing its resources. To abandon any of the university's current work, he maintained, was unthinkable, since it could only be interpreted as "a frank admission of defeat, as a last resource to save the whole university." But, he concluded, "Fortunately, we have not yet reached that stage."

In considering how resources and income might be increased, the president drew attention to the fact that the university derived its receipts primarily from three sources: return on endowment, gifts, and student fees. Despite the past generosity of donors, gifts, because of their uncertainty, could not be relied upon to cover current operations. There were also severe limits upon the possibility of expanding income from student fees. Any large increase in tuition rates, for example, would automatically exclude many desirable students. Nor was it feasible to increase total

*In obtaining these annual grants of $35,000 Northwestern was the beneficiary of a policy adopted by the General Education Board of the Rockefeller Foundation in 1919 to assist colleges and universities in raising faculty salaries which had generally failed to keep up with the rise in the cost of living between 1914 and 1919. *General Education Board*, Review and Final Report 1902-1960, *issued in New York in 1964.*

tuition income by expanding the size of the student body, since, as a result of a postwar increase in enrollment, the physical facilities of Northwestern were already taxed to the utmost. Thus he concluded that the only way to safeguard the work that the university was doing was to increase the endowment.

This, of course, had been the primary objective of the financial campaign launched in August 1919, which was intended to add $25,000,000 to Northwestern's resources over a ten year period. By mid-June 1920, however, the committee had received pledges totaling only a little over $2,000,000, of which $1,200,000 had been specifically pledged for the purchase of the land for the Chicago campus.* But with the onset of the sharp economic depression of 1920-21, it was decided to suspend further work on the campaign until business conditions were more favorable.

Establishment of a Publicity Department
The president concluded that in part Northwestern's failure to obtain more financial support, especially from the greater Chicago community, stemmed from the lack of a central agency for the collection and dissemination of authoritative information about the university's constructive activities. Accordingly, early in 1921, he established a publicity department headed by an experienced newspaper man. To strengthen the university's appeal to prospective donors, the board in 1922 selected James Gamble Rogers, widely known as the architect of Yale's Harkness Memorial, to plan the proposed Chicago campus. It was hoped that Rogers would be helpful in presenting the university's needs to potential donors.[8]

Interest in reviving the financial campaign was stimulated by the announcement that the General Education Board of the Rockefeller Foundation, rather than continuing to make annual grants, had offered to contribute $600,000 toward an endowment to be used by Northwestern to raise the salaries of the faculty and staff of the College of Liberal Arts, the School of Engineering, and the library. A condition of the offer was that Northwestern would, by the end of June 1924, obtain pledges for $1,400,000, which would bring the total endowment to $2,000,000.[9]

The board responded by appointing a financial campaign committee under the chairmanship of trustee Robert W. Campbell. Following consultation with the deans and faculty representatives from the various schools, the committee decided that in order to provide for the most urgent needs of the university they should attempt to raise $4,500,000 over the next two years. Of this amount, $1,400,000 was to be used to qualify for the General Education Board grant and $700,000 was to be spent for improvements on the Evanston campus, including new buildings for the Music and Speech schools as well as housing and recreational facilities for women students. The remaining $2,400,000 was to finance the construction and maintenance of the consolidated campus for the Chicago professional schools.[10]

---

*Included in these earmarked funds was a pledge for $250,000 made in June 1921 by a Chicago businessman, George A. McKinlock. In consideration of this gift, the trustees agreed that the official name of the new campus would be the Alexander McKinlock Memorial Campus in honor of the donor's son who had been killed during World War I. Between 1921 and the early 1930's, McKinlock contributed approximately $156,000 toward his original subscription. Of this amount, approximately $25,000 was spent for a memorial gate which was installed on the Chicago campus in 1929. Then came the depression and by the mid-1930's McKinlock's property had depreciated to such an extent that he found it impossible to pay the balance of his pledge. Under the circumstances Northwestern not only agreed to cancel the amount still due, but arranged to return the amount he had already contributed. At the same time the trustees, at Mr. McKinlock's suggestion, voted to rename the Alexander McKinlock Memorial Campus the Chicago Campus. *Trustees' Minutes, September 8, 1936 and April 3, 1937.*

Because of the disappointing results of the 1919-1921 campaign, the committee members decided to enlist expert advice and arranged to hire Robert Duncan, a member of the John Price Jones Corporation of New York (a professional fund-raising organization) to serve as the committee's executive secretary starting in January 1923.

The campaign conducted under Duncan's general supervision was impressive. Alumni meetings were held in various locations throughout the country. State and school committees were appointed to solicit donations from graduates and students. Pamphlets and brochures bearing such titles as "Endowing Higher Education," "Service," "An Investment for All Time," and "For a Greater Northwestern," were prepared and widely distributed. Lists were drawn up of wealthy Chicago and North Shore residents capable of responding to Northwestern's plea for financial assistance.

"For a Greater Northwestern"

What became known as the Campaign for a Greater Northwestern got off to a good start. As the President's Report for 1922-23 indicated, by mid-June 1923, the committee had received pledges totaling approximately $700,000. These included gifts of $100,000 from Judge Elbert H. Gary for the establishment of a Law School library bearing his name; $100,000 from John C. Shaffer to support a professorship in the College of Liberal Arts; and another $100,000 from a "friend" (Charles H. Deering) to endow a professorship of botany.

As a result of the intensive drive carried on between June 1923 and June 1924, the committee received nearly 9,200 subscriptions, bringing the total amount pledged to just under $8,500,000, or some 60 percent more than the campaign's initial goal. Though President Scott attributed this achievement to the inspired leadership of the committee plus the efforts of a large number of graduates and friends, according to committee chairman Robert W. Campbell, Scott was himself largely responsible for pledges amounting to between $5,000,000 and $6,000,000. "The President," he noted at the trustees' meeting of June 14, 1924, "had made himself available at any hour of the day or night for service in any phase of the campaign activities. He developed and carried through personally leads resulting in large gifts to the university's funds."

Although sufficient pledges were obtained to qualify for the General Education Board grant, the most noteworthy aspect of the campaign was that approximately $7,000,000 of the $8,500,000 had been raised for the buildings and endowment of the schools on the Chicago campus. Equally significant was the fact that this phase of the campaign owed its success primarily to three women who chose this means to commemorate the life and work of their husbands. As the trustees learned at their meeting of December 14, 1923, Mrs. Elizabeth Ward had decided to give $4,000,000 for the construction and endowment of the Montgomery Ward Memorial Building on the Chicago campus which was to house the Medical and Dental schools and to serve as a memorial to her husband, Montgomery Ward, founder of the company which bore his name. At their May 28, 1924, meeting the trustees heard that Mrs. Ward's sister, Mrs. Ellen M. Thorne, had followed suit with a gift of $250,000 to build an auditorium as a memorial to her late husband, George R. Thorne, cofounder with Montgomery Ward of the famous mail order

The Ward, Thorne and Mayer Gifts

house. The third major donation which had been announced at the trustees' meeting of October 30, 1923, amounted to $500,000, and came from Mrs. Rachel Mayer. It was to be used to erect a Law School building to be named in honor of her recently deceased husband, Levy Mayer, long prominent in Chicago legal circles.

To maintain the momentum developed in the course of the campaign, the board formed a Committee on Development at the conclusion of the drive. Thomas A. Gonser, class of 1924, who had served on the campaign committee while still an undergraduate, was appointed secretary of the new committee to provide continuity. To serve as chairman, the board appointed Melvin A. Traylor,* vice president of the First National Bank of Chicago and a widely known and respected figure in the financial community.[11]

Wieboldt and Gary Gifts The momentum of the 1922-24 campaign did in fact continue into the late 1920's especially as far as contributions for expanding the facilities on the Chicago campus were concerned. As noted in the trustees' minutes for April 28, 1925, the Wieboldt Foundation—headed by William A. Wieboldt, a prominent Chicago merchandiser and philanthropist—made a grant of $500,000 toward the cost of constructing Wieboldt Hall to be used by the Northwestern University School of Commerce. That same year Judge Gary pledged $150,000 for the erection of a building to be located next to the Levy Mayer Hall of Law, to house the law library which he had donated earlier.

At this time the university took a step important for the future of the Medical School by entering into an agreement with the Institute of Protestant Deaconesses, operators of the Passavant Memorial Hospital. As the President's Report for 1924-25 indicated, under this arrangement Northwestern was to provide space for the erection of a new hospital building by Passavant on the Chicago campus. It was further agreed that one-third of the beds in the new hospital were to be allocated to the Northwestern Medical School faculty. Both the Medical and Dental schools received an important boost in 1926 when, according to the trustees' minutes of March 12, 1926, Mrs. Elizabeth Ward donated an additional $4,000,000 to enable Northwestern to obtain "the highest quality of personnel for instruction and research" in those schools.

The major disappointment of the 1922-24 campaign was the failure to raise the amounts originally sought for the Evanston campus. It is true that by meeting the requirements of the General Education Board a total of $2,000,000 was added to the endowment of the Liberal Arts and Engineering colleges. But instead of the $7,000,000 thought to be absolutely necessary, less than $185,000 was pledged for the support of the Music and Speech schools and to provide facilities for women's housing and recreation.

Moreover, in reviewing the situation in his report for 1923-24, President Scott noted that because of rising costs and new educational demands it would require

*Other members of the committee included Mark W. Cresap, of Hart, Schaffner and Marx, one of the largest clothing firms in the U.S.A.; George Craig Stewart, Episcopal minister and president of the Northwestern University General Alumni Association; the Reverend J. Hastie Odgers, representing the Rock River Conference; and Mrs. Helen Babcock Latham, first member of the board to be elected by the General Alumni Association and head of the trustees' committee on women's buildings. The ex-officio members were President Scott, William A. Dyche and Robert W. Campbell, president of the board of trustees and chairman of the 1922-24 fund-raising drive.

$5,700,000 just to finance the construction of the new buildings needed on the Evanston campus, the estimated costs of which were: a library, $1,000,000; a chapel, $1,000,000; a women's building, $500,000; women's dormitories, $300,000; men's dormitories, $300,000; science laboratories, $600,000; School of Music, $400,000; School of Speech, $400,000; School of Education, $400,000; and a stadium, $800,000. Moreover an additional endowment of $2,000,000 would be needed for the maintenance of these buildings.

Experience with the 1922-24 campaign clearly indicated that it would not be advisable to launch another highly organized and intensive fund drive at this time. As President Scott pointed out, given the pledges made by alumni during that campaign it was unrealistic to expect any further significant contributions from them for years to come. Nor did he favor turning to the undergraduates for support. Not only had the costs of collecting the pledges made by students in the 1922-24 campaign been high, but he was convinced that the psychological effects of asking for contributions in addition to regular tuition and other fees were apt to work against whatever plans Northwestern might have for building up a loyal body of alumni.

The university could expect to generate some additional funds from an expanding demand for its rental properties and more favorable market conditions for securities. But as President Scott noted in his report for 1923-24, the campaign of the previous two years had demonstrated that the most promising way to increase the university's financial resources was to "appeal to those individuals within the general public who have the means and the interest in scientific and social advance and could be brought to an understanding of the university as a channel through which this advance has been secured in the past and will be secured in the future."

Under the circumstances, Thomas Gonser and the Committee on Development made no attempt to conduct an elaborate campaign for funds. As the chairman of the committee, Melvin A. Traylor, told the trustees in June 1926, their major objectives had been to "continue a quiet hunt for big Gift Prospects and to strengthen the ties between the university and the alumni as well as with the Methodist Church."

Committee on Development

In their continued search for donors, Gonser and the Committee on Development solicited and received suggestions from a variety of sources including students, alumni, trustees, and others interested in the future of the university. At one stage, Gonser developed a group of prospects by noting the license plate numbers of luxury automobiles parked at social events and checking the names of their owners through the state licensing bureau. Published lists of individuals who paid large income taxes were another source for prospects.[12]

By mid-June 1928, the Development Committee reported that its office was maintaining records on a selected group of 3,000 of the wealthiest prospects for the university. As names of prospects were suggested to Gonser, he would call on members of the Committee for advice on how to establish contact with these people. Scott, William A. Dyche, and Chairman Melvin A. Traylor were especially helpful in arranging introductions, writing letters, or making personal phone calls. New brochures outlining Northwestern's needs and future plans were prepared and distributed. President Scott made a point of visiting friends of the university who had retired or spent their winters in Arizona, Southern California, or Florida.

Yield of 1924-30
Fund Raising

The overall results of the fund-raising activities between 1924 and 1930 were impressive. In addition to the $4,750,000 contributed during 1925 and 1926 by Mrs. Ward, the Wieboldt Foundation, and Judge Gary, the value of the gifts received by the university during this period was over $16,750,000.[13] Of this amount, approximately one-third, or $5,600,000, was allocated to the professional schools on the Chicago campus and almost without exception came from previous donors. The Wieboldt Foundation, for example, gave $125,000 for the upkeep of Wieboldt Hall; Mrs. Rachel Mayer provided $300,000 for the maintenance of Levy Mayer Hall; while $50,000 from the estate of Mrs. Ward was set aside for Medical School scholarships.[14]

The campaign to raise funds for projects on the Evanston campus got off to a disappointingly slow start. From 1924 through 1927 the only important donations received by Northwestern not allocated to the Chicago campus were: $100,000 in 1925 from William Smith Mason, a long time member of the board of trustees, to endow a professorship in the College of Liberal Arts; an annuity of $100,000 in 1926 assigned to Engineering by Frederick A. Ingalls, an alumnus of the class of 1877; and a contribution in 1926 of $100,000 from the Carnegie Corporation to the School of Music to found a department of church and choral music. In 1928, however, came a welcome bequest of $500,000 from Charles Deering, which President Scott set aside to establish the Charles Deering library fund, hoping to attract enough additional money to construct a new library.[15]

Austin Scholars

The following year the university received three major donations. The first was a gift from Frederick Carlton Austin, a wealthy Chicago businessman, who presented the university with an office building located on West Jackson Boulevard in the heart of the Chicago business district valued at $3,000,000.[16] A long time friend of Judge Gary and William A. Dyche, Austin specified that the income from the property was to be used for full scholarships for "male persons of the Caucasian race, with no reference to nationality, religion or wealth for the purpose of fitting the recipients to attain proficiency in business and industrial pursuits having in mind the fitting of such persons for executive positions in large business and industrial enterprises." Though Austin was self-taught, he believed that business had become so complex that future executives needed the same quality of technical training as doctors and lawyers.[17] The program had a good start in the fall of 1929 when the first class of Austin Scholars—ten in number—arrived on campus to begin their studies.

Wilson Bequest

The President's Report for 1928-29 also carried the happy news that under the will of Milton H. Wilson, who had died in February 1928, Northwestern was to receive approximately $8,000,000. This, the largest single bequest the university had ever received, was not to be used to construct buildings but was to be added to the endowment of the College of Liberal Arts to make it "the best undergraduate school possible under the circumstances." After considerable discussion of how best to show their appreciation for the donor's generosity, the trustees in

January 1932 voted that "the south campus in Evanston extending from University Place to Willard Place be named the *Milton H. Wilson Campus . . . .*"*

Deering Bequest

Since neither the Austin nor the Wilson donation provided for the construction of buildings, Scott was particularly pleased to report to the trustees in November 1929, that Mrs. Marion Whipple Deering, widow of Charles Deering, and their two daughters, Marion Deering McCormick and Barbara Deering Danielson, had agreed to contribute "such sums as together with the original bequest . . . from Charles Deering . . . will amount to one million dollars." These grants were made with the understanding that the money would be used to erect the Charles Deering Memorial Library building on the Evanston campus. Immediately following confirmation of the agreement, architect James Gamble Rogers and university librarian Theodore Koch were instructed to plan the proposed structure.

Northwestern University Foundation

In June 1926 the Committee on Development in cooperation with the Alumni Association moved to enlist the continuing financial assistance of the alumni by organizing the Northwestern University Foundation.[18] As at Yale, which served as the model for this undertaking, the Foundation was dedicated to keeping alumni informed about Northwestern's educational plans and programs and to having "every living alumnus a contributor to the university every year irrespective of the amount."[19]

In an appeal to the alumni General Nathan William MacChesney, the first president of the organization, noted that unlike the graduates of a number of eastern institutions, Northwestern alumni were not generally wealthy. There was no intention of attempting to induce "a few wealthy alumni to make great sacrifices" but to get "a large number to contribute relatively small amounts on a regular basis." The possibilities of such a plan were impressive. There were at the time, some 26,000 alumni on record in the alumni office. If each could be persuaded to make an annual gift of ten dollars, for example, the result at a current interest rate of 5 percent would be equal to an increase in Northwestern's endowment of over $5,000,000. Although actual contributions averaged somewhat below $30,000 annually, according to the trustees' minutes of April 1932, the number of individuals contributing to the Foundation had grown from approximately 1500 in 1926 to over 5,400 by 1931.

Organization of Northwestern University Associates

What promised to be a highly effective means of establishing valuable contacts with potential supporters in the greater Chicago area grew out of a suggestion by Thomas Gonser that the Committee on Development form an organization designed to attract primarily non-alumni who would be interested in promoting the welfare of the university. The Northwestern University Associates were organized in 1928, with a membership drawn from a select group of men prominent in business and the professions. The general plan was for the Associates to hold monthly luncheon or dinner meetings during the school year and to be invited to attend occasional football games. From time to time members of the faculty or administration would report to the Associates on various developments at Northwestern.[20]

---

*At the same time the trustees also voted that "the north campus in Evanston, extending from the north line of the land leased to Garrett to Lincoln Street should be named the *James A. Patten Campus.*"

Thorne Hall, completed in 1932, providing two auditoriums and additional meeting facilities for the Chicago campus

Levy Mayer Hall and Elbert H. Gary Library, part of the Law School complex on the Chicago campus, completed in 1926

The School of Commerce moved into Wieboldt Hall on the Chicago campus in the fall of 1926

The organization started when some fifty-seven members, described as among the "most eminently successful and influential men in the whole country" held their first meeting early in February 1929. Much credit for getting these individuals interested in the organization was due to its first chairman, Silas H. Strawn. A member of the law firm of Winston, Strawn, and Shaw, legal counsel for a number of major corporations and a former president of the American Bar Association, Strawn was widely known and respected by the Chicago business and professional community. In outlining the purpose of the Associates, Strawn told the assembled guests that "the perpetuation of the university and its advancement" were a responsibility that every citizen should share and that by joining the Associates they were not only discharging their duties as citizens but were promoting the welfare of several activities in which they were personally engaged.[21]

President Scott worked closely with Gonser and the Committee on Development in promoting the growth of the Associates which, by mid-June 1931, had more than 100 members.

The Chicago Campus   Once financing was assured Northwestern moved quickly to develop the Chicago campus. Plans and specifications for the proposed buildings had already been prepared under the direction of James Gamble Rogers, and on May 8, 1925, in a ceremony attended by a large number of faculty, students, alumni, trustees, Chicago city officials, friends and donors, the Chicago campus was formally dedicated and ground was broken on the sites for the separate buildings. As a reporter for the *Chicago Tribune* described it in the May 10, 1925 issue, the scene was one of:

> Silver spades gleaming in the sunlight against the new black earth, purple robes and mortar boards of collegiate rank invading the downtown district, youth trailing at the heels of a group of elderly millionaires, planting the seeds of a future civilization, and on the wings of a song the chant of Northwestern's a capella choir in "Quaecumque Sunt Vera."

Construction progressed rapidly on all the buildings except Thorne Auditorium, the erection of which had to be postponed when it became clear that costs would exceed the original gift. But by the fall and winter of 1926, the four professional schools were able to move into their new quarters.

Montgomery Ward Memorial Building   Emulating the Gothic style of the Harkness Memorial at Yale, the group of buildings was dominated by Montgomery Ward Memorial Building, its fourteen stories surmounted by a five-story tower. The first seven floors plus the fourteenth were assigned to the Medical School while the Dental School occupied floors eight through thirteen. The tower rooms included an office for the president of the university, space for the alumni office, and meeting rooms for faculty members.*

Wieboldt Hall   Wieboldt Hall, located just to the east toward Lake Michigan, was eight stories high with a tower rising an additional six stories above the main portion of the building. The structure included some twenty classrooms with a combined seating

---

*The original plans for the Montgomery Ward building included only the Medical School. But President Scott, who felt responsible for seeing that all of the professional schools were transferred to the new campus, successfully argued that since the amount pledged by Mrs. Ward for the center was two and a half times the total funds originally set as goals for both schools, it seemed only reasonable for them to share the same building. *Leslie B. Arey*, Northwestern University Medical School, *p. 239.*

capacity of 1500, space for offices, and a research department and club rooms for men and women students. The most unusual feature of the building was that these facilities were situated above and around the heating plant for the Chicago campus which consisted of a boiler room and a huge stack over eleven feet in diameter that extended to the roof.[22] The School of Commerce happily moved into quarters in the newly completed building.

The Law School complex, immediately to the east of Wieboldt Hall, combined the Levy Mayer Hall and the Elbert H. Gary Library building—four stories in height and constructed around a landscaped courtyard. In addition to the library the building housed four lecture rooms—one modeled after the British House of Commons and another after a typical court room—faculty offices, a law journal office, space for a research department and, like Wieboldt Hall, study and meeting rooms for students.[23]

Mayer Hall and Gary Library

By spring of 1927 plans were already well under way for the construction of the Passavant Hospital to be located on a site adjacent to the Montgomery Ward Medical Center. As President Scott pointed out to the trustees in his report for 1926-27, if the training in the Northwestern Medical and Dental schools was to be effective, a number of conveniently located teaching hospitals were needed to serve as practical laboratories for the students. The trustees were obviously impressed by this argument, for early in July 1927, Robert W. Campbell, president of the board, announced that plans were being developed which over the next five to ten years would make Northwestern University and the city of Chicago the "greatest medical center in the country." This was to be achieved by building four new hospitals—in addition to Passavant—on sites to be provided by Northwestern on the Chicago campus. They were to include a general hospital, a training hospital for nurses, a maternity hospital, a children's hospital and a hospital for patients with industrial injuries.[24]

Passavant Hospital

It was quite apparent, however, that to provide space for the proposed new buildings the Chicago campus would have to be extended beyond its original nine acres. By July 1927 the university had purchased a five acre block of land immediately to the south of the Chicago campus from the Newberry Library at a cost of approximately $2,185,000. The Passavant Hospital was completed and ready for use by June 1929. The onset of the Great Depression soon thereafter, however, followed by the outbreak of World War II, postponed further development of the Medical Center for over thirty years.[25]

For Northwestern's Chicago based professional schools, the move into the new facilities on the Chicago campus during 1926 marked the realization of long cherished goals. As President Scott observed in his report for 1926-27,

The Chicago Schools

> The results of the move were immediately apparent, not only in the improved types of work which the new equipment enabled the schools to do but in the new work undertaken and in the general morale of the student body. For the first time it was possible to undertake the work of the schools in a proper university atmosphere and in inspiring surroundings. It is difficult to overestimate the quickening which has resulted through the whole personnel of the Chicago schools, both faculty and student.

Except for the addition of Journalism, the history of the schools on the Chicago campus during the 1920's was marked less by any major educational innovations than by a further evolution of policies which had been adopted earlier. The historian of the Medical School might well have been referring to Commerce, Law and Dentistry as well, when he stated that, "If developments affecting the Medical School during this period seemed less dramatic than in some others it was because so many basic problems had been conquered previously that the school was now entering a state of relative maturity."[26]

Medical School   Thus the Medical School saw no reason to modify the provision adopted in 1911 that only applicants who had completed two years of college would be considered for admission. Nor was there any change in the requirement added in 1919 that in addition to four years of course work candidates were to complete one year of hospital internship before receiving the M.D. degree.[27] Despite these relatively high requirements, however, the Medical School did not lack for prospective students. In 1925 there were over 600 applicants for an entering class of 111, four years later the first year class of 120 was selected from more than 2,000 applicants.[28] The size of the student body, however, increased much more slowly than the number of applicants because of the essentially conservative admission standards. Nevertheless enrollment rose from 438 in 1920-21 to 744 by 1929-30 (see Table 5-1).*

TABLE 5-1
N.U. STUDENT ENROLLMENT, 1920-1930

Academic Year	1920-1921	1921-1922	1922-1923	1923-1924	1924-1925	1925-1926	1926-1927	1927-1928	1928-1929	1929-1930
EVANSTON CAMPUS										
College	1,896	1,991	2,073	2,132	2,098	2,220	2,438	2,540	2,587	2,631
Graduate	227	289	319	347	360	441	503	496	516	585
Music	303	340	381	370	487	407	439	435	392	426
Speech	201	204	232	256	274	288	297	316	326	334
Engineering	160	163	151	169	180	205	243	271	279	305
Commerce	323	334	321	342	329	355	381	430	473	410
Journalism		38	36	65	61	72	76	85	72	79
Education							97	157	183	324
TOTAL	3,110	3,359	3,513	3,681	3,789	3,988	4,474	4,730	4,828	5,094
CHICAGO CAMPUS										
Medical	438	456	489	513	536	530	571	639	676	744
Law	201	217	220	211	243	246	277	324	353	419
Dental	700	578	489	386	227	242	340	418	435	556
Commerce (part time)	2,939	3,126	3,420	3,678	3,887	4,149	4,827	5,278	5,867	6,513
Journalism (part time)		180	278	327	275	283	278	263	276	369
Liberal Arts (part time)										691
Education (part time)										53
TOTAL	4,278	4,557	4,896	5,115	5,168	5,450	6,293	6,922	7,607	9,345
GRAND TOTAL	7,388	7,916	8,409	8,796	8,957	9,438	10,767	11,652	12,435	14,439
Summer School (selected years)	(1921) 808				(1925) 1,323					(1930) 1,533

SOURCE: Northwestern University Catalogs, 1920-1930

*Although comparable data for the Northwestern faculty are not available for 1920-21, this expansion in enrollment was accompanied by a growth in the school's teaching staff from a 6 full time and 161 part time faculty in 1921-22 to a 34 full time and 316 part time faculty in 1929-30. *N.U. Catalogs for 1921-22, 1929-30.*

One significant change was the readmission of women students to the Medical School which had adamantly excluded them since the end of its brief excursion into coeducation during 1869-70. The issue had finally come to a head in 1923-24 when Mrs. Montgomery Ward, in discussing her plans for the medical center with President Scott, expressed some astonishment that women were not admitted to the Medical School. Following this conversation, a committee which had been appointed earlier at Scott's suggestion to reconsider the school's policy toward coeducation, "suddenly came alive" and recommended that women be admitted on the same terms as men. The motion was adopted by a faculty vote of 13-3. As Professor Arey pointed out, "This was an act of policy rather than heart, since it was considered business-sense not to be unchivalrous under the circumstances."[29]

In 1924 Dr. Arthur I. Kendall, who had been dean since 1919, resigned. Dr. James Pearson Simmonds, professor of pathology, served as acting dean pending the arrival of Dr. Irving S. Cutter, who became dean in 1926. A graduate and later faculty member of the University of Nebraska College of Medicine, Dr. Cutter had served as dean of that school from 1915 until his appointment to Northwestern. His arrival in Chicago marked the beginning of a sixteen year career as head of the Northwestern University Medical School.[30]

Dental School

The Dental School retained its basic four year course of study for the D.D.S. degree, but raised its admission requirement to at least one year of liberal arts training starting in the fall of 1921.[31] The reaction was a sharp decline in enrollment from a peak of 700 in 1920-21 to a low of 227 four years later, followed by a gradual recovery to a total of 556 students in 1929-30 (see Table 5-1).*

Meanwhile the faculty, under the continued leadership of Dean A. D. Black, took several steps to implement their announced policy of promoting "every phase of dental education and service."[32] In 1920 Northwestern became the first dental school in the United States to offer a postgraduate course leading to a M.S. degree. Two years later the school pioneered the establishment of the first children's clinic in association with a newly established department of orthodontics and, in order to meet the growing demand for better trained technicians, also developed a curriculum for dental hygienists and dental assistants.[33]

In 1926, the school adopted a policy of encouraging graduates from dental schools outside the United States to enroll at Northwestern for graduate and postgraduate study. The response was encouraging. The dean reported that during 1929-30 applicants from Canada, Chile, Czechoslovakia, England, Finland, Greece, Haiti, Japan, Sweden and Syria were enrolled. The school was also proud of the work done in its dental clinics. In his report for 1920-21, the dean had noted the performance of 61,621 operations on 8,768 patients; by 1929-30 he reported that 9,946 adult patients had received treatments involving 80,349 operations and 3,056 children had received 7,121 operations.

As anticipated by the Law School faculty at the time, the adoption in 1919 of a four-year curriculum and the raising of entrance requirements from one to three

---

*Between 1921-22 and 1929-30 the number of full time faculty increased from seven to thirty-five while the number of part time members declined from fifty-seven to forty-six. *N.U. Catalogs for 1921-22, 1929-30.*

Law School   years of undergraduate work brought about a substantial decline in enrollment from a prewar peak of 386 in 1916-17 to 201 in 1920-21. Thereafter, however, registration grew steadily reaching a new high of 419 in 1929-30 (see Table 5-1).*

A significant era in the history of the Law School came to an end in the summer of 1929 with the retirement of John H. Wigmore from the deanship which he had held for twenty-eight years. Aggressive and hard driving, he had established a personal reputation as a scholar and administrator on the one hand and had helped raise the standing of the school by his indefatigable efforts on its behalf on the other.† Dean Wigmore's retirement came rather abruptly when the board of trustees voted a mandatory retirement age of sixty-five for all deans and other administrative officers, but he remained an active member of the faculty until 1934 and continued to write, to research, and give seminars until his death in 1943.[34]

Wigmore's successor to the deanship was Leon Green who had already earned a considerable reputation as a legal scholar by the time he came to Northwestern. A graduate of the University of Texas Law School, he taught there part time while carrying on a private practice until 1926, when he became the dean of the Law School at the University of North Carolina. The following year he joined the faculty of the Yale Law School where he remained until his move to Northwestern two years later.[35]

Two institutions conceived by Wigmore became important affiliates of the Northwestern Law School during the first years of Dean Green's administration. One was The Scientific Crime Detection Laboratory which began operations in July 1929. Supported by various groups interested in crime prevention, the laboratory carried on an extensive research program, rendered important services to various police departments throughout the United States, and developed a number of valuable investigative devices basic to police work, including the "lie detector."

The second of the affiliates sponsored by Wigmore was the Air Law Institute. Organized in August 1929, it was put under the direction of Professor Frederick D. Fagg, Jr., a graduate of the Law School and a member of the Northwestern economics department. An aviator during World War I, Fagg had done postgraduate work in the field of air transport in Germany. The *Journal of Air Law*, published by the Institute, kept its subscribers informed about laws and regulations affecting air transportation throughout the world.[36]

On Both Campuses: Commerce   The history of the School of Commerce under Dean Heilman was marked by an irrepressible expansion during the postwar decade. Enrollment in the late afternoon and evening classes in Chicago grew from 2,939 in 1920-21 to 6,513 a decade later. The full time upper division day school established on the Evanston campus in 1919 also proved popular, with registration increasing from 323 to 410 students between 1920-21 and 1929-30 (see Table 5-1).**

---

*The size and composition of the teaching staff remained essentially the same, with nine full time and thirty-six part time members in 1929-30. *N.U. Catalogs for 1921-22, 1929-30.*

†It was estimated that by 1943 Wigmore had produced 46 original books, 36 edited volumes, 16 works on Japanese law, plus 700 articles, papers and notes. *James A. Rahl and Kurt Schwerin*, Northwestern University School of Law, p. 42.

** A decline in the full time faculty of the school from 39 to 29 between 1921-22 and 1929-30 was accompanied by an increase in part time members from 41 to 132. *N.U. Catalogs 1921-22, 1929-30.*

In 1920 the school expanded its operations still further by introducing a graduate program leading to the degree of Master of Business Administration. Available to college graduates enrolled in either the Chicago or Evanston division of the school, the program required the completion of the equivalent of a full year of course work plus a thesis.*

Three years later, Northwestern acquired the Garrett Biblical Institute's Memorial Hall and converted it for use by the Evanston division of the School of Commerce. It was subsequently dubbed the Little Red Schoolhouse.

With over 4,000 registrants enrolled in the Chicago division of the school during 1926-27, it is small wonder that Dean Heilman welcomed the move into Wieboldt Hall on the new Chicago campus. As he reported to President Scott at the end of that year, the building provided a "modern, well planned and beautiful home for the work of the School of Commerce. The physical equipment and facilities may now be regarded as adequate not only for the present but for the anticipated future growth and development of the school."

The resources of the School of Commerce and the department of economics were enlarged in 1925 when the Institute for Research in Land Economics and Public Utilities became associated with Northwestern. Organized at the University of Wisconsin in 1920 by Richard T. Ely as a non-profit and independently financed corporation, the Institute was engaged primarily in formulating the principles governing land use and in analyzing problems of particular concern to public utilities. A founder of the American Economic Association and a member of the economics department at Wisconsin since 1892, Ely was appointed research professor of economics when the Institute was transferred to Northwestern.[37]

Under the affiliation agreement Northwestern provided housing for the Institute first in the Commerce building in Evanston and, after 1926, in Wieboldt Hall on the the Chicago campus, but the Institute continued to receive its financial support from outside sources. The presence of the Institute did much to strengthen the School of Commerce and the economics department, both in teaching and research. In addition to the *Quarterly Journal of Land and Public Utilities*, published under the Northwestern University imprint, Ely and his staff produced a steady flow of books and articles between 1925 and 1933. At that point, however, the affiliation between the Institute and Northwestern was terminated because of financial difficulties.[38]

The Medill School of Journalism, the first of the new schools to be added to the university during Scott's administration, evolved from a suggestion made in 1920 by a *Chicago Tribune* reporter, Eddie Dougherty. His initial idea was that the *Tribune* should publish a "little evening paper" to serve as a workshop for journalism apprentices, and since it seemed desirable to secure the backing of an educational institution for the program, Dougherty discussed the project with Dean Heilman of the School of Commerce. Heilman suggested that Dougherty wait until a new president was appointed but in the meantime agreed to develop a curriculum and prepare a budget estimate for the proposed department.

Medill School of Journalism

---

* Starting with an initial enrollment of 388 in 1920-21, the number of commerce graduate students reached a total of 810 by 1929-30. *N.U. Catalogs 1920-21, 1929-30.*

Shortly after Scott became president he met with Heilman, Dougherty, and Captain Joseph Medill Patterson and Colonel R. R. McCormick, co-editors and principal owners of the *Tribune*. Although the publication of a newspaper was deemed impractical, both Patterson and McCormick were much interested in Dean Heilman's suggestion for a journalism department and shortly thereafter the *Tribune* agreed to underwrite a school of journalism—set up as a department within the School of Commerce—by an amount not to exceed $12,500.00 a year from 1921 through 1925.[39] It was decided that the school should be named the Joseph Medill School of Journalism in honor of Joseph Medill, founder of the *Chicago Tribune*, a pioneer in the field of journalism, and grandfather of Captain Patterson. According to the latter, when Scott accepted the *Tribune* subsidy he stated that "he would take our money but that he would not take our advice." "Thus," said Patterson, "it started just as free as any school ever started."[40]

Northwestern chose H. F. Harrington, an experienced newspaperman and professor of journalism at the University of Illinois, to direct the new department and he provided the program with aggressive and innovative leadership. As outlined by Dean Heilman in his report for 1920-21, the main objective of the program was to provide "practical professional training" for those wishing to enter the field of journalism as well as for those already engaged in it. To this end the department developed a curriculum that would give students a broad background in the social sciences and literature; teach them how to express themselves clearly; and provide them with a knowledge of the processes and techniques of modern journalism.

Part time students who completed forty-eight semester hours of the courses offered by the school in Chicago were awarded the Diploma of Journalism. Candidates with credit for two years of college could enroll for the full time junior and senior courses offered on the Evanston campus leading to the degree of Bachelor of Science in Journalism.*

The Journalism faculty included members of the university faculty, practicing journalists, and special lecturers. Thanks to the cooperation of various Chicago newspapers, students were given the opportunity to observe both the working conditions and the actual process of getting out a newspaper. This part of the program according to Professor Harrington was considered "unique in the teaching of journalism" and created interest on the part of newspapers throughout the country.[41] For Northwestern, which was about to renew its endowment campaign, the news coverage of the founding of the Medill School was a welcome means of attracting the attention of prospective donors to the university's position as a major Chicago educational institution.

Undoubtedly the most popular addition to the curriculum of the School of Journalism was the course called "Contemporary Thought" introduced in 1923-24. It was taught by Baker Brownell whose background included a master's degree from Harvard University and experience as an editorial writer for the *Chicago Tribune*.

---

*Students holding bachelor degrees could qualify for a Master of Science degree by completing the equivalent of a full year of course work, plus a thesis and "six months satisfactory service in a newspaper office." *N.U. Catalog, 1924-25.*

Brownell believed that students all too often left college "with a lot of intellectual trinkets that have little relationship to one another and even less connection with the world of actuality." It was his goal to integrate "the intellectual and factual world" by bringing in controversial figures from the outside world to lecture to his classes. This brought criticism from some of Northwestern University's trustees but did not affect his career.[42]

During 1921-22, the first year of the school's operation, 180 students were enrolled on the Chicago campus and 38 in Evanston. By 1929-30 enrollment in Chicago had risen to 369 and in Evanston to 79 (see Table 5-1).

The Evanston Campus

From the very outset of his administration, Scott had called attention to the need for a stadium and for housing for women on the Evanston campus. Though he had a much longer list than this, these two projects were the first to get under way because they promised to be self-supporting.

Dyche Stadium

The first step towards the construction of the stadium were taken in December 1924, when, at the urging of William A. Dyche, Northwestern's business manager, the trustees appointed a special committee to work with James Gamble Rogers on plans for the proposed facility. On October 27, 1925, the committee reported that the stadium as designed by Rogers could be built at an estimated cost of $975,000. Rather than involve the university directly, it was decided to finance the project by forming the Northwestern University Stadium Corporation, a non-profit organization which would issue bonds valued at $1,250,000 to be retired over a period of fifteen years. Northwestern in turn agreed to lease the facilities from the Stadium Corporation at an annual rental which would cover the sinking fund requirements and interest charges of 5 percent on the bonds.[43] Named in honor of Dyche for his part in its promotion, the stadium with a seating capacity of approximately 47,000, was completed in the fall of 1926.

It had been assumed that the university would have no difficulty in meeting payments to the Stadium Corporation from the sale of tickets for football games and other athletic events to be held at Dyche. But the initial plan of avoiding direct responsibility for financing had to be abandoned rather quickly when it was discovered that the Stadium Corporation, unlike the university, was not exempt from taxation. As a result the Stadium Corporation was dissolved early in 1927 and its properties and obligations transferred to the university.[44]

Housing for Women Students

In a move designed to provide more housing facilities for women students, the trustees, on January 29, 1924, set aside a block of land at the south end of the campus to be used for dormitories and sorority houses. At the same time, James Gamble Rogers was commissioned to design the proposed buildings so that they would be substantially alike in size, cost, and appearance. The sororities were informed that as soon as they had raised an amount sufficient to cover 25 percent of the estimated cost of the complex of chapter houses, the university would arrange to lend them the balance to be repaid under a long term lease.

Early in 1927, fourteen sororities announced that they had raised the $250,000 needed for the down payment on the total cost of the chapter houses, estimated at just over $1,000,000. Construction moved ahead rapidly with the result that by the opening of the new school year in September 1927 the new houses with rooms for approximately 400 girls were ready for occupancy.*

What became known as the Women's Quadrangles were added to a year later with the construction by the university of two open dormitories with rooms for an additional eighty students. Financed by the university from endowment funds at a cost of about $140,000 each, the first of the new dormitories was named Rogers House in honor of Mrs. Henry Wade Rogers who had contributed so much to Northwestern during the ten years her husband was president. The second dormitory was named Hobart House in honor of Emily Hatfield Hobart, a Northwestern alumna who was serving as a missionary in China when she was killed in 1928 during an uprising in that country. Ten years later another dormitory was added to the west quadrangle. Built to house freshman women, it was dedicated on September 28, 1938, the ninety-ninth anniversary of Frances Willard's birth and named in her honor.[45] The new building replaced the dormitory facilities of the original Willard Hall (formerly the Woman's College) which was scheduled to be remodeled for eventual use by the School of Music.

The Evanston Schools

In his report to President Scott for 1920-1921, Dean Roy C. Flickinger of the College of Liberal Arts noted that thanks to the $35,000 grant from the General Education Board, plus more tuition revenue and the "generosity of certain trustees," it had been possible to raise the salary scale in the college and to increase the maximum salary offered from $4,000 to $5,000. This increase, he indicated, had served to avert what would otherwise have been a highly critical situation. He hoped that it might become possible to raise the maximum to at least $6,000.

The College of Liberal Arts

Of immediate concern to the dean were two problems posed by the increase in the size of the student body during the postwar period. The first was that the enrollment of just under 1,900 students for 1920-21—up nearly 50 percent from the prewar high—"represented nearly the maximum number who could be provided with living accommodations in Evanston." The second was that the increase in the size of the student body had not been accompanied by a corresponding increase in the size of the faculty so that the per capita teaching load in the college had become considerably heavier.[46]

In the spring of 1923 Flickinger resigned from the deanship in order to resume his teaching duties as a full time member of the classics department. Following an extended canvass of potential candidates, the trustees, in June 1924, named Raymond A. Kent, dean of the School of Education at the University of Kansas, as his successor.

The new dean turned his attention to several of the problems noted by his predecessor but also went on to deal with other aspects of the organization and operation of the college. He was concerned with the heavy per capita teaching load of the faculty and two related matters, namely, the large size of classes and the absence of personal contact between faculty and students. He was also critical of the rigid curriculum and the small choice of courses available at all levels from offerings to freshmen to those for graduate students.

*The sororities involved were: Alpha Chi Omega, Alpha Gamma Delta, Alpha Omicron Pi, Alpha Xi Delta, Chi Omega, Delta Delta Delta, Delta Gamma, Delta Zeta, Gamma Phi Beta, Kappa Alpha Theta, Kappa Delta, Kappa Kappa Gamma, and Pi Beta Phi.

However, the alarming statistic that immediately caught Kent's eye was that approximately half of the freshman class failed to return for their sophomore year. While some of this may have been due to the conditions described, Kent was convinced that the more important factor was the quality of the students admitted to the college. As a result, he persuaded the faculty that starting in the fall of 1926, only applicants who ranked in the upper half of their graduating class should be admitted to Northwestern without passing entrance examinations. The faculty also agreed with the dean that the college could attract more well qualified applicants by reducing the foreign language entrance requirement to two years of one language rather than two years of two languages or three years' study of one. The success of the new admission requirements in reducing the attrition rate was shown when only 25 percent of the students enrolled in 1926-27 failed to return the following year.[47]

To provide for closer personal relations between students and faculty the dean in 1926 arranged for students to be assigned to the same faculty advisers during their first two years in college. In the same year the faculty took an important step toward broadening the curriculum when it authorized the departments within the college to allow their junior and senior majors to register for an honors course calling for independent study. As the President's Report for 1927-28 indicated, under this plan students were encouraged to select a field for study which cut across traditional departmental lines. Working under the direction of a departmental adviser, each candidate for honors was required to take an oral examination covering his major field prior to graduation. In 1927 an orientation course entitled An Introduction to Social Science was introduced. A cooperative enterprise on the part of economics, history, philosophy, political science, and sociology, the course was designed to give students an appreciation of the content and methodology of these fields.

Broadening the Curriculum

What the dean in his report for 1925-26 described as a "genuinely significant administrative feature of the year" was an increase in faculty salaries made possible by the success of the drive to increase the endowment of the Liberal Arts and Engineering colleges by $2,000,000.* Noting that the College of Liberal Arts had been "pruned of faculty members from top to bottom," the dean expressed the hope that by raising the maximum salaries of professors from $5,800 to $6,400 and the minimum salaries of instructors from $1,200 to $1,800 it would be possible for the college to keep and promote its best men and to attract well-qualified candidates for positions as instructors.[48]

Faculty Salaries and Promotion Procedures

In reviewing the relations between the faculty and the administration, the dean was disturbed to discover that there was no clearly defined policy concerning the promotion of instructors. After meeting with departmental heads, he circulated a letter in October 1926 to all instructors stating that henceforth any one who had been an instructor for four consecutive years would only be recommended for reappointment if he were also being considered for promotion. Some months later, in a letter to all faculty members, he suggested that in recommending appoint-

*Though officially separated from the College of Liberal Arts in 1907, Engineering continued to function more like a department of the former than like an autonomous school.

ments or promotions, departmental chairmen should consider not only the applicant's scholarship and teaching ability but also his capacity to exercise "a strong, constructive influence upon the character development of his students."[49]

Evening Courses
An interest in adult education made Dean Kent an influential supporter of the liberal arts faculty's decision to open an evening division on the Chicago campus for the fall of 1928. From the outset the results were highly encouraging (see Tables 5-1 and 5-5).

Dean Kent's association with Northwestern came to an end in the spring of 1929 when he resigned to become president of the University of Louisville. As his successor, the trustees on August 27, 1929, appointed Clarence S. Yoakum, professor of personnel management at the University of Michigan.

In March 1930, Dean Yoakum made a long report to the trustees outlining the educational needs of the college and stressing the importance of establishing a salary scale that would attract distinguished scholars to the faculty. Referring to the magnificent bequest of $8,000,000 to the college from the estate of Milton H. Wilson, he asserted that this additional endowment presented the college with "an unusual opportunity to reconsider its place in the university and to restate its aims." But Yoakum did not remain at Northwestern long enough to provide significant leadership. At the end of one year he returned to the University of Michigan as a vice president. He was replaced by Addison Hibbard, dean of the College of Liberal Arts and professor of English at the University of North Carolina.[50]

Though many problems remained to be solved, the college had developed significantly in the course of the decade with the introduction of higher and more realistic entrance requirements, a more flexible curriculum, and better faculty-student relations. Equally impressive was the growth in enrollment during this period from 1,896 to 2,631 and an increase in the faculty from 166 (130 full time and 36 part time) in 1921-22 to 205 (191 full time and 14 part time) in 1929-30.[51]

School of Music
For Peter Christian Lutkin, dean of the School of Music, the fall of 1920 marked the completion of a twenty-nine year association with Northwestern that had begun at the time Walter Dill Scott entered the university as a freshman. With classes available to "all seeking instruction in music" the school over the years had offered training to those "wishing to become cultural amateurs" as well as those "wishing to prepare themselves for professional careers."[52] These objectives reflected in essence the dean's basic philosophy that the development of the moral and artistic senses was "just as important a part of education as the abstract development of the intellectual. In other words, it is quite as necessary to know how to live as how to get a living."[53]

The North Shore Music Festival, the university glee clubs, the a capella choir and the Symphony Orchestra were but a part of the dean's unremitting efforts to enhance the cultural atmosphere of the school, the university, and the North Shore community. Despite overcrowded facilities and inadequate financial resources, the School of Music continued to increase the range of its offerings. In response to a growing demand for teachers and music supervisors the school introduced extended courses in public school and community music leading to the degrees of Graduate in School Music and Bachelor of Music Education. As Dean Lutkin pointed out in his report for 1920-21, "We [now] offer quite the stiffest courses in this subject in the country and we are hoping to attract a superior grade of students in consequence."

The President's Report for 1924-25 announced a reduction of the five-year course of study for the Bachelor of Music degree to a four-year course. At the same time some of the liberal arts courses which had previously been optional for students for their degree in music were now made an obligatory part of the program for the Bachelor of Music degree.

Hailed by Lutkin as the "outstanding event" of the year for the Music School was a grant of $100,000 from the Carnegie Corporation in 1925-26 which enabled the school to realize Lutkin's ambition of establishing a department of church and choral music. Since the facilities of the school were already being used to capacity, the offer of classroom space from Garrett Biblical Institute—which had an obvious interest in the program—was gratefully accepted.

To provide professional guidance and to coordinate the activity of the university band and glee club, the school in 1926 appointed Glenn Cliffe Bainum professor of band organization and conducting. Professor Bainum became widely known for the fine performances of his marching and concert bands.

In the spring of 1928, having reached his seventieth birthday, Lutkin decided to give up the deanship and devote himself to teaching, composing and the North Shore Music Festival. Upon his recommendation, the trustees appointed Carl Beecher as his successor. Beecher, who in 1908 had received the first Bachelor of Music degree granted by the school, had spent several years studying music in Germany before returning to Northwestern in 1913 as professor of theory and composition.[54]

Early in 1930, it appeared that Lutkin's long cherished dream of adequate teaching facilities would be realized when the Presser Foundation of Philadelphia offered to donate $250,000 toward the cost of a new music school building, provided that Northwestern would raise a matching fund.* The university not only accepted the challenge but decided that an attempt should be made to raise enough money to make possible the construction of a building to cost $750,000 and to be dedicated to Dean Lutkin. By June 1930, sufficient funds had been pledged to meet the conditions of the Presser Foundation but not enough to meet the objective of $750,000. Under the circumstances, as the president explained in his report for 1929-30, it was decided to postpone construction of the proposed building until "times are more favorable for the securing of money."

Enrollment in the School of Music during this period rose from 303 in 1920-21 to 426 in 1929-30 (see Table 5-1). Though the size of the faculty appeared to have decreased—from forty-one to thirty-six—this statistic is somewhat deceptive since the drop represented primarily a reduction in part time faculty.[55]

---

*Organized in 1916 by Theodore Presser, head of a musical publishing firm, the Presser Foundation was interested in encouraging the study of music by undergraduates in colleges and universities and in popularizing the teaching of music as a profession. *See* The Foundation Directory, *4th ed. (New York: Columbia University Press, 1971).*

Among the more dynamic administrators inherited by Scott was Ralph B. Dennis, who had succeeded Robert McLean Cumnock as director of the School of Oratory in 1916. Dennis was thoroughly versed in the Cumnock tradition and appreciative of the latter's contributions, but he realized that the changes that had been taking place in the field of speech made it necessary for the School of Oratory to expand and modernize its program if it were to survive. His arguments proved persuasive. Early in 1921 the trustees authorized the introduction of a four-year program leading to the degree of Bachelor of Letters. And in recognition of the broader scope of the proposed program as well as to honor the school's founder they voted to change the name of the School of Oratory to the School of Speech Founded by Robert M. Cumnock.[56]

Under the new arrangement students could still qualify for the diploma in speech by completing a two-year course of study within the school. The four-year curriculum for the baccalaureate, however, required the equivalent of two years of courses in the College of Liberal Arts as well as the two-year program in Speech. Included in the latter were courses in voice and diction, fundamentals of expression, story telling, extemporaneous speaking, literary interpretation, play production, persuasion, public address, and speech education.[57]

By 1926 the school had become well enough established at the college level to warrant dropping the two-year diploma course and replacing the Bachelor of Letters degree with a Bachelor of Science in Speech. In addition a one-year graduate program leading to an M.S. in Speech was established. At the same time the title of the head of the school was changed from director to dean.[58]

Two years earlier the Children's Theatre—subsequently known as Theatre 65—had been launched by Winifred Ward. Nationally famous in the field of creative dramatics, Miss Ward was supervisor of dramatics in the Evanston elementary schools and had been a member of the School of Speech faculty since 1918. Begun with the enthusiastic support of the parents and children of Evanston the new theater became an immediate success. In 1929 the Evanston public schools joined with the university in sponsoring the project. Dean Dennis in his report for 1928-29 suggested that "probably no phase of the work of this school has won more praise and aroused more interest—and this all over the country—than the work of Miss Winifred Ward in the field of creative dramatics for children."

Also highly regarded and popular was the University Theatre, organized in 1926. Under the direction of Garrett Leverton, professor of dramatic production, the University Theatre by 1929 had assumed complete control over all dramatic activities on the campus including those of the two student sponsored groups, the Prentice Players and the Campus Players. Both the University Theatre and the Children's Theatre became integral parts of the curriculum of the School of Speech, serving as well-organized laboratories in which the students developed acting skills and learned the practical application of the theories of acting and stage production.[59]

One of the most important developments during this period was the organization in 1929 of the Speech Re-education Clinic (later renamed the Speech and Hearing Clinic) for the study and correction of speech defects. Directed by Clarence

T. Simon, who had joined Northwestern's faculty in 1922, the new clinic treated *Speech* such vocal handicaps as stammering, stuttering, lisping, and faulty articulation, *Re-education* and conducted research on the causes of and remedies for these defects. *Clinic*

This entry into the scientific aspects of speech enlarged the scope and potential of the school in immeasurable ways and set it on a path that would bring international recognition in the years ahead. Simon guided the clinic, one of the few of its kind in the United States, during these crucial years and also concerned himself with graduate education in general.

By 1930 Dennis had largely succeeded in achieving his original goal of making a modern school of speech out of the School of Oratory. Enrollment, as shown in Table 5-1, increased from 201 in 1920-21 to 334 in 1929-30, while the faculty grew from eight to eighteen full time members and from three to twelve part time members.[60]

Between its separation from the College of Liberal Arts in 1907 and 1920, the *Engineering* College of Engineering, under the direction of Dean Hayford, had increased its enrollment from 57 to 160. As noted earlier, however, in practice it had remained a department within the College of Liberal Arts. Admission requirements were identical and the five-year curricula leading to the degrees of Mechanical Engineer and Civil Engineer included a large number of non-technical courses selected to serve as a foundation for a broad, general education. With seven of the nineteen full time faculty holding joint appointments in liberal arts, stress was laid on mathematics, physics, and other sciences fundamental to engineering, while a minimum amount of time was devoted to shop work. Those in charge of the program assumed that a thorough grounding in the sciences was more important for this stage of training than the acquisition of technical skills.[61]

But President Scott was not satisfied that the College of Engineering was offering the kind of program that would make it the distinguished center for engineering education that it could be and that Chicago needed and appointed a committee to survey its status and needs. In 1926 the committee made suggestions for strengthening the program. First, its report urged that the curriculum be reorganized to include more technical training. Secondly, it recommended that the faculty should be predominantly oriented towards engineering rather than the pure sciences. And finally, it counseled that the Engineering College be made entirely autonomous.[62]

Responsibility for implementing the committee's recommendations was assumed by William C. Bauer, professor of electrical and mechanical engineering, who had been appointed director of the college following the death of Dean Hayford in March of 1925. Starting in the fall of 1926, a four-year course leading to a B.S. in engineering was adopted. Students who completed an additional year of more specialized work were, as before, awarded the degree of Civil Engineer or Electrical Engineer. During 1927 the trustees voted to rename the College of Engineering the School of Engineering and to make it entirely autonomous. Bauer was appointed dean. An engineering oriented faculty was insured by termination of the joint appointments with the College of Liberal Arts leaving the school with a full time faculty of nine members.[63] To conform with the graduation requirements of the Chicago high schools, the foreign language requirement was dropped.

Meanwhile, Bauer and the president had become involved in discussions on the feasibility of an affiliation with the Armour Institute of Technology. Negotiations had apparently been going on for some time when the *Chicago Tribune* on December 13, 1925, carried a story about this possibility. According to the *Tribune*, Scott had explained that

> pressure has been coming from members of the engineering profession in Chicago who want a local school that will be nationally recognized. At present, neither school is strong. A consolidation would give us an engineering institution comparable to our medical school.

J. Ogden Armour, president of the board of trustees of the Armour Institute, was quoted in the *Evanston News Index* on December 14, 1925, as being extremely hopeful "that the present negotiations would bring about the historical affiliation of the two schools."

Early in 1926 a contract calling for an affiliation between the Armour Institute and Northwestern University was drawn up. As noted in the trustees' minutes for January 12, 1926, it specified that the merger would not take place for the next five years and that during this interval both institutions would cooperate in raising the $10,000,000 considered "necessary to make possible a feasible and permanent affiliation." Instruction was to be given in new buildings designed by James Gamble Rogers for both the Evanston and Chicago campuses of Northwestern. The Armour faculty would be absorbed by Northwestern and the name Armour would be retained in the title of the new institution. Committees from both institutions were appointed to work together in raising funds and planning curriculum.

Agreement on a combined course of study proved difficult to achieve because of the fundamental differences between the existing curricula of the two schools. The Northwestern program up to this point had been highly theoretical in orientation; the Armour program had been highly technical. Though Northwestern was on the brink of placing more emphasis on technical training than it had in the past, the content of the curriculum proposed by the Armour faculty seemed to the Northwestern faculty to be more appropriate for a trade school than for a university school of engineering.

But when it was announced in March 1929 that the merger would not take place, the prime reasons were financial rather than disagreement about educational policies. There is no record of how much Northwestern had raised toward meeting its share of the goal of $10,000,000. But Philip Armour reported to President Scott that it would be impossible for members of the Armour family to provide even a small portion of the approximately $3,300,000 they had expected to contribute.[64]

President Scott and Dean Bauer appear to have been more relieved than disappointed at the failure of the proposed merger. The latter was particularly pleased with the development of engineering at Northwestern since 1926. Thanks largely to the removal of the foreign language requirement in that year, the school had attracted a growing number of well-qualified applicants from high schools in the Chicago area. This increase in the number of applicants had allowed the school to apply higher standards of selection than had been possible in the past. Limited classroom space and laboratory facilities forced the school to restrict enrollment, but as Dean Bauer noted in his report for 1929-30, Northwestern's School of Engineering with its registration of 305 students was equal in size to the engineering schools of Harvard, Johns Hopkins and Stanford.

An important development during the decade of the 1920's was the emergence of an independent School of Education. The first tentative step in this direction had been taken in 1920 when the education department—still within the College of Liberal Arts—was renamed the School of Education and given its own director. Under this arrangement, students majoring in education would complete two years of work in the College of Liberal Arts and then register as candidates for a certificate in education at the end of their sophomore year. Upon graduation two years later they would receive the certificate in addition to their bachelor's degree. These certificates were generally accepted by school superintendents and accrediting agencies as guarantees that their holders were qualified to teach in the public schools.[65]

Emergence of a School of Education

During the early 1920's the university came under increasing pressure to expand and strengthen its curriculum in education. In 1924 a meeting of the deans on the Evanston campus debated whether a "complete and separate School of Education" should be established without delay. But the general consensus was that however desirable this might be the personnel of the school was not yet "sufficiently strong in administrative abilities, in scholarship and in teaching ability to assure the success of a separate school."[66]

In April 1926, as pressure continued to mount, the trustees voted to establish the School of Education as a separate administrative unit in the university. Housed in Old College it was to have its own dean and a staff made up of faculty who had been teaching education courses in the college plus those who had been offering specialized teacher training to students enrolled in the schools of Music and Speech. The school was authorized to award the degree of Bachelor of Science in Education. However, it was not yet entirely independent since students were required to complete the equivalent of two years of work in the College of Liberal Arts before receiving the degree. To serve as the school's first dean, the board selected John E. Stout, professor of administration of religious education.

In his annual reports to President Scott for 1927-28 and 1928-29, Dean Stout emphasized the problems posed by operating the School of Education as a two-year senior college. To begin with, the education faculty had no jurisdiction over students who entered Northwestern with the intention of transferring to the School of Education at the end of their sophomore year. Indeed, not only was the school "debarred from contacts with graduates of high schools, but it was also handicapped in recruiting its students from the student body of Northwestern." An obvious complication arose when students in the College of Liberal Arts chose to major in subjects that were not taught in the public schools and then transferred to the School of Education for their last two years.

The dean stressed that the basic trouble was that no two-year program could be made adequate for the preparation of teachers because teaching was becoming a highly specialized vocation requiring well defined types of training. This was implicit in what was demanded by state legislation and required as well in the regulations affecting the employment, retention, and promotion of teachers, supervisors, and administrators of the public schools. As far as the dean was concerned, the only way that Northwestern could meet this challenge was to allow the school to organize and administer its own four-year curriculum. In May 1930, the board voted to give the School of Education complete autonomy as a four-year school authorized to establish its own admission and degree requirements.

From its initial organization as a two-year senior college in 1926 the School of Education had attracted an immediate following. Its enrollment—including part time students—rose rapidly from 97 in 1926-27 to 377 in 1929-30. The number of full time faculty grew from fifteen to seventeen and of part time from six to seven.[67]

Since Northwestern lacked its own laboratory school, the School of Education made arrangements for its students to do their practice teaching in the Evanston, Wilmette, and Winnetka public schools. By 1928 members of the faculty were offering special extension courses for teachers and school administrators in a number of nearby public school districts. The response was so encouraging that a year later similar courses were introduced on the Chicago campus. The future of the latest addition to the roster of Northwestern schools looked encouraging.

Summer School
By the early 1920's the Northwestern summer session had become an integral part of the university organization. In general, the offerings were equivalent to those taught in the regular academic year. The credit courses were designed for various types of students. These included students wishing to complete the requirements for admission to the college or the professional schools; regular students needing or wanting additional credits toward graduation; graduate students interested in completing their residence requirements; and teachers and school superintendents seeking advanced instruction in their professions. Non-credit courses were available to practicing doctors, dentists, lawyers, journalists, and businessmen interested in the latest developments in their special fields. An added feature of the summer session was an extensive program of lectures, concerts, and excursions. The courses offered, the extracurricular activities and the school's location on the shore of Lake Michigan combined to attract an enrollment in the summer session that grew from 666 students in 1920 to 1,533 in 1930.[68]

Graduate School
A significant educational feature of the 1920's was the growing emphasis by major American universities on graduate studies and research. James Alton James, dean of the Graduate School, was concerned to have Northwestern stay abreast of this development. In his reports to President Scott he stressed that having become a member of the Association of American Universities in 1917, Northwestern was under an obligation to expand its graduate offerings and provide financial support for research programs comparable to those already being sponsored by other universities. Attendance at the annual meetings of the AAU made Dean James acutely aware of the increasing competition for graduate students and the growing disparity between Northwestern's expenditure on graduate education and that of other Association members. Thus, in his report for 1923-24, he cited the example of a "leading university with a graduate student body but

little larger than our own" which in 1922 had awarded sixty fellowships and scholarships worth $35,000 to its graduate students. At Northwestern there were only two fellowships and scholarships valued at $5,500 available for graduate students. Along with his annual plea for more student aid and support for research, the dean, in his comments for 1927-28, also called attention to the school's need for an adequate library, housing for graduate students, and a university press which would publish the results of research by faculty members.

President Scott was not unmindful of the fact that the standing of a university was largely dependent upon the emphasis given to the work done in its graduate school. But he believed that research should be conducted primarily as a means to train students rather than for the sake of the professors.[69] In the end, however, the reluctance of the president and the trustees to provide more support for graduate education and faculty research stemmed from their belief that there were other more pressing needs to be met from the financial resources at their disposal. As a result James's pleas gained no more than a dozen additional fellowships and, as noted in the President's Report for 1929-30, the first grant for faculty research, namely $1,000, awarded by the Northwestern University Foundation.

Despite these limitations graduate student enrollment grew from 227 in 1920-21 to 585 in 1929-30 (see Table 5-1). However, relatively few of these students were doctoral candidates. Indeed, the records show that while Northwestern awarded 1,076 master's degrees during this period, it granted only 111 Ph.D.'s.*

Two developments toward the end of the decade encouraged James to hope that the Graduate School was on the eve of better things. The first was the large Milton H. Wilson bequest, much of which was to be used to raise faculty salaries. This would enable Northwestern to retain faculty with an interest in research and to attract eminent scholars from other institutions. The second was the approaching completion of Deering Library which would provide badly needed research facilities, especially for graduate students in the social sciences and the humanities.

Campus Life

After the great marshaling of energy and selflessness demanded by the war effort, the country returned—in President Harding's memorable phrase—to "normalcy." This turned out to be a strange blend of conservatism and rebellion: conservatism in matters political and economic; rebellion, especially on the part of women, in matters of dress and social behavior. The 18th Amendment, ratified in 1919, brought Prohibition; the 19th Amendment, ratified the next year, gave women the right to vote. The "engineer, the stockbroker, the salesman, the advertiser, and the movie star were the popular heroes," wrote Nevins and Commager in their *History of the United States*, but so were the gilded youth and the flappers "making whoopee."

Athletics

On the Evanston campus the various organizations—including the fraternities and sororities—which had flourished before the war resumed their activities with undiminished enthusiasm. Early in the 1920's both town and gown focused

---

*The number of Ph.D. degrees awarded by other midwestern universities during the 1920's were: Indiana, 85; Iowa, 390; Michigan, 375; Ohio State, 325; Minnesota, 359; Illinois, 431; Wisconsin, 475; Chicago, 1,243. *Lindsay R. Harmon and Herbert Soldz, "Doctoral Production in United States Universities, 1920-1962," National Research Council, Pub. #1142, Washington, D.C., 1963.*

their attention on the improvement of Northwestern's athletic program. The 1921 season had been disastrous. The football team failed to win a single Conference game; the basketball team won only two, and the baseball team, three. Critics began to wonder whether Northwestern was "masculine" enough to compete against major midwestern universities. "The questions on the lips of every interested person are these: 'What is the matter with Northwestern athletics? Is it not possible to do something to improve the situation?' " read the report of a committee of alumni and trustees appointed by the board to inquire into the athletic program.

The committee went on to assign responsibility for Northwestern's mediocre record to a variety of factors, including the abolition of football in 1906 and 1907, inadequate administration of the athletic program, frequent changes in the coaching staff (there had been eight different football coaches between 1908 and 1921) and a lack of college spirit. To remedy the situation they recommended a campaign among faculty, students, and alumni to stress the importance of intercollegiate athletics and to generate a "real university spirit." The alumni were also urged to use all legitimate means to persuade more athletically inclined young men to enroll at Northwestern. The committee conceded that although such an effort would not be easy, its value was so great that "no effort should be spared to secure it in fullest measure."[70]

Early in 1922 the trustees moved to strengthen Northwestern's football performance by hiring Glenn Thistlewaite, the university's first full time coach. Improvement was immediate, for the team finished the 1922 season with a respectable record of three wins and three losses. Enthusiasm within the university community ran high. President Scott regularly participated in the weekly pep rallies proudly wearing his 1893 varsity sweater and leading the student body in cheers. Another loyal attendant was General Nathan William MacChesney, the trustee, who often delivered brief talks on the value of athletics in building character.

The Wildcats Thistlewaite continued as football coach through the 1926 season when he was succeeded by Dick Hanley. Northwestern teams shared the Big Ten Conference title with Michigan in 1926 and again in 1930 on their way to an overall record of thirty-nine wins and twenty-five defeats between 1922 and 1930. It was the performance of the team in a 3 to 0 loss to arch rival Chicago in 1924 that prompted a sportswriter to suggest that the players should be known as the Wildcats rather than the Fighting Methodists (or simply the Purple).[71] Northwestern got its revenge at the formal dedication of the newly constructed Dyche stadium in 1926 by overwhelming its ancient maroon rival 38 to 7, the first win over Chicago in ten years.

The enthusiasm for football created two new types of campus celebrities—the football coach and the football hero. Thistlewaite and Hanley were easily among the most popular men on campus as were such outstanding players as Tim Lowry, Ralph "Moon" Baker, Leland "Tiny" Lewis, and Waldo Fisher.

There were some who did not share the enthusiasm for football. In the fall of 1926 the editors of the *Daily Northwestern*, in response to the rhetorical question of what the average student knew of culture, literature, history, art, and philosophy answered, "Nothing. The college student of today looks at the world through his or her bovine eyes and discerns only a dollar mark and outlines of a pigskin."[72]

Success on the gridiron was not matched by Northwestern in other sports. There were exceptions, of course. During the mid-1920's the swimming team won three consecutive Big Ten championships and, in 1925, the golf team also took Conference honors. But the basketball and baseball teams fared badly in competition with their Big Ten rivals.

For the socially minded there were such all university events as Homecoming, *Social Events* the Freshman Frolic, Sophomore Hop, Junior Prom, Senior Ball, and the prestigious Y.M.C.A.-Y.W.C.A. sponsored Spring Circus. In addition to smokers for the men and "cozies" for the women, the calendars of the fraternities and sororities were booked with informal get-togethers, dinner parties, and formal dances at a hotel or country club.

But by no means was campus life entirely social. The serious-minded undergraduates could join one of a dozen departmentally sponsored discussion clubs or one of a half dozen literary societies. Intercollegiate debating was popular. The Campus Players, Prentice Players, and Thalian Players attracted students in dramatics, as did the Waa-Mu spectacular. The name of the latter represented the combined initials of the Women's Athletic Association and the Men's Union,* members of which collaborated to produce the first Waa-Mu Show, entitled "Good Morning Glory," in April 1929. The Women's Athletic Association had been presenting its own musical show for several years but the founding of the Men's Union in 1928 made possible a much more ambitious joint effort. Director Joe W. Miller was then a senior in the School of Journalism but had already participated in several student productions. In the preface to the program of their first show the producers wrote hopefully, "If people come here and like the show, creating goodwill along the North Shore, it will carry on in years to come." It was one prediction destined to come true.

The Student Council, organized in 1914, continued to supervise the interests and activities of the undergraduates and to cooperate with the faculty in maintaining discipline. According to the President's Report for 1926-27, a survey made that year had shown that there were approximately 147 organizations of various kinds on campus with close to 600 officers and a total membership of over 3,500 students.

One traditional type of activity which the Student Council was unable to control *The Mount* was the class rush, which had degenerated into a massive brawl between the *Tragedy* freshman and sophomore classes, with most of the participants ending up in Lake Michigan. The rush of 1921 led to a grim episode in Northwestern's history: the disappearance and death of freshman Leighton Mount. When Mount, who had taken part in the "big scrap" on the evening of September 21, failed to return to his home the next morning, his parents notified Dean Flickinger and President Scott, who, in turn, called in the police. The massive manhunt that followed proved fruitless. It was nineteen months before his skeleton was discovered under the Lake Street pier in Evanston.

---

*The Men's Union was formed in 1928. It developed out of a series of Monday student-faculty lunches and was dedicated to working for a student union to serve "as the social center of the campus." *W.A.A. File, N.U.A.;* "*The Men's Union*" in Syllabus *for 1929.*

Bathing at Lincoln Street beach, circa 1921

N.U. Circus, 1928, an annual student event sponsored by the Y.M.C.A. and the Y.W.C.A.

The Roaring Twenties

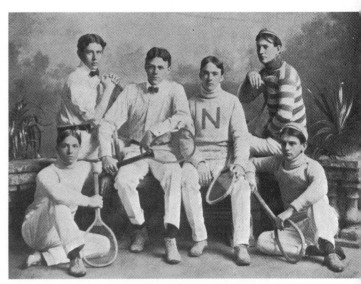

University tennis team, 1920's

Women's athletics: getting in shape, 1920's

Subsequent investigation by the Evanston police, the coroner, the state's attorney, and a Cook County Grand Jury failed to solve the mystery surrounding his death. Meanwhile Northwestern was sharply criticized by the nation's press for permitting such dangerous activities. President Scott defended the university's position and in his report for that year pointed out that prior to this tragedy, no one had ever suffered a serious injury as the result of a class rush. He did conclude, however, that Northwestern's interests would be best served by prohibiting all such activities in the future.

The serenity of student life was again disturbed in 1924 when Brent Allison, a well-known pacifist, came to speak on campus and persuaded a group of undergraduates to declare publicly that they would not, under any circumstances, take part in a war. Conservative groups on campus were outraged. Members of the ROTC urged the university to require every student to sign a pledge of allegiance to the Constitution. In this way "potential traitors" and "pusillanimous pacifists" could be identified and expelled. Several rallies were held to proclaim the "patriotism" of the majority of the students; those who did not attend were suspected of being pacifists.[73] This swell of patriotic sentiment was in keeping with the national temper which was to be suspicious of anything that smacked of the foreign or the radical. Within a few weeks the furor had died down. Pacifism would not become an issue again until the 1930's.

The Scrawl　　But there were also academic issues which stirred student reaction. In the mid-1920's a group of students concerned about the quality of intellectual life on campus formed a new campus literary magazine, *The Scrawl*. Beginning late in 1924 the editors hoped to stimulate students and faculty to write articles on important university issues. In May 1925, for example, the editors published an article on "Fraternities, Pro and Con," which criticized the lack of intellectual caliber of fraternity members. In a later issue contributors attacked the acritical atmosphere created by "The Greater Northwestern Campuses."[74]

The most important discussion generated by the *Scrawl* addressed itself to the question of intellectual freedom at Northwestern. In an essay entitled "Do Colleges Educate?" Isabella Tanes castigated the university for graduating large numbers of "insipid coeds" and male "fashion plates." Worse yet were faculty members who delivered ill-prepared, boring lectures. But the most serious problem at Northwestern as seen by the editors of *Scrawl* was the lack of intellectual freedom on campus. "Let us try to believe," appealed the editor, "that the final purpose of the university is to give the intelligent a chance to become truly educated. Perhaps in time, the college will live up to the expectation. We can become, if we will work toward that day, a university where no one is afraid of ideas, when anything may be said and where those who hear will weigh the worth of every utterance and judge it by its truth. On that day we will have seen a school worth studying in and worth fighting for."[75] *The Scrawl* continued publication until 1929.

Bernard DeVoto, a member of Northwestern's English department from 1922 to 1927, shared at least some of these views, though he did not confine his criticism to Northwestern. In an article published in *Harper's Monthly* he characterized the contemporary American college as:

> ... by and large ... a training school.... The man who comes to college today is not there to grow in wisdom, or to invite the truth to make him free, to realize his fullest intellectual possibilities, to learn the best that has to be said and thought. ... He is there to get through the prerequisites of a professional school or of business.

As suggested by the title of the article from which this comes—"The Co-ed: The Hope of Liberal Education"—DeVoto thought rather better of the women students:

> The whole point of this article ... is my discovery that the greater part of the education which the modern college manages to achieve, in the intervals between endowment campaigns, football championships, and psychological surveys, is appropriated by the very sex who presumably do not belong to the *educabilia* at all.[76]

It must surely have occurred to at least some of DeVoto's contemporaries that his view was not uninfluenced by the fact that he had married Helen Avis MacVicar, a coed who had sat in the front row of one of his freshman English classes.*

The religious atmosphere of earlier days remained in evidence in the postwar period. Religious exercises continued to be a part of student life on the Evanston campus. All students in liberal arts were expected to attend church on Sunday, and were required to attend at least one of the three half-hour chapel sessions held each week in Fisk Hall. Alumni remember the Chapel Hour as an occasion to gather around The Rock to meet their friends, exchange gossip, and arrange dates. The Y.M.C.A. and Y.W.C.A. flourished and continued to organize a variety of religious and social service activities. They were also joint sponsors of the traditional big dance which opened the social activities of the school year.

The university community in general accepted President Scott's notion that the well-rounded student life should include experience in education, in religion, in social and athletic activity, and in financial responsibility. For example, the high cost of college demanded that students economize; athletic contests underlined the value of competition and sportsmanship; social programs emphasized the importance of working in groups; religious exercises reinforced the students' belief in a Christian god; and educational programs provided the knowledge necessary for life's work.[77]

During the first decade of President Scott's administration the university made significant progress in improving conditions for the faculty. In 1924 the first steps were taken to encourage applications for sabbaticals when the trustees ruled that they would consider granting leaves of absence with half-pay for faculty members who had taught full time for seven years. Special consideration was to be given to applicants who applied for leaves for "the sake of carrying on research in which continuity of effort" was important.[78]

In Praise of the Coed

Religious Life

The Faculty

---

*The rumor that Northwestern dismissed DeVoto because of his critical comments about the university are quite unfounded. In fact, he had just been promoted to assistant professor when he decided to resign in September 1927, in order to devote himself fully to a writing career. *Wallace Stegner, in* The Uneasy Chair (*New York: Doubleday and Company, Inc., 1974*), p. 77.

Establishment of the University Senate

In 1928 the university moved to increase the voice of the faculty in the determination of general educational policies by replacing the University Council—originally organized in 1910—by a University Senate. The membership of this body was to be considerably more inclusive than that of the Council it replaced, for in addition to the president, the deans of all the schools, and the chairmen of all departments, it was to include all faculty members with the rank of full professor. In his report for 1927-28, the president expressed his belief that the Senate would "represent more fairly the various faculty points of view and become as a consequence a helpful forum as well as a legislative body for educational matters."

Retirement Plan for Faculty

Of particular importance was the introduction of a new policy on retirement income for faculty. Until the late 1920's Northwestern had no established policy on pensions or annuities for its faculty beyond a tradition of granting retirement allowances to individuals who had spent many years in its service. It was not until the spring of 1928, following a thorough investigation of various possibilities, that the trustees voted to adopt the Retirement Allowance Plan of the Teachers Insurance and Annuities Association, sponsored by the Carnegie Corporation.

The plan called for each full time faculty member or administrator over the age of 35 to contribute 5 percent of his salary to TIAA with Northwestern to contribute the same amount. It was expected that under this arrangement anyone who served twenty-five years or more at Northwestern would, upon retirement at age sixty-five, receive an income equal to 50 percent of his annual salary during the last five years of regular service. If a member who had retired was survived by his widow she was to receive one-half of his annuity payments during the remainder of her lifetime.* The trustees, having provided for retirement incomes once faculty members turned sixty-five, decided in July 1929 that this would henceforth be the official retirement age for all deans and professors in the university.

In part, these various decisions represented a recognition of the fact that as the faculty increased in size personal arrangements with individuals had to be replaced by rules and provisions which applied to all. And the growth of the faculty during this period was, indeed , considerable. In 1921-22 there had been 263 full time and 335 part time faculty; by 1930 this number had risen to 366 full time and 285 part time in all schools.†

The Record for the 1920's

In general, there was every reason to be pleased with Northwestern's growth and development during President Scott's first ten years in office. Thanks chiefly to the success of the fund-raising activities during these years the net value of the university's resources had grown from $10,195,000 to $44,047,000 (see Table 5-3). There had been an equally impressive expansion in the size of the total educational budget, from $1,727,000 in 1920-21 to $4,293,000 in 1929-30. And, although there had been deficits of varying amounts through 1925-26, income was sufficient to cover all operating expenses between 1926-27 and 1928-29 (see Table 5-2). Between

*To provide coverage for faculty members who were too old to meet the minimum service requirement set by TIAA, the university arranged to make such supplementary contributions as would provide them with a retirement allowance equal to that of teachers who had participated in the plan for twenty-five years or more. *President's Report, 1927-28.*

†The major concentration of the part time faculty was to be found in the Medical, Dental, and Law schools and in the Chicago division of the Commerce School.

1920-21 and 1929-30 student attendance nearly doubled from 7,388 to 14,439, while the number of degrees awarded grew from 621 to 1,510.

TABLE 5-2
N.U. BUDGETED RECEIPTS AND EXPENDITURES, 1921-1930

(In Thousands of Dollars)

Academic Year	1920-1921	1921-1922	1922-1923	1923-1924	1924-1925	1925-1926	1926-1927	1927-1928	1928-1929	1929-1930
RECEIPTS										
Tuition	$1,158	$1,175	$1,220	$1,352	$1,343	$1,461	$1,836	$1,892	$2,099	$2,358
Investments	220	272	296	341	391	424	639	772	725	744
Gifts	186	82	98	117	138	156	198	275	288	348
Clinics	68	103	156	141	84	90	84	138	168	191
Other a	91	104	153	180	213	257	251	460	709	622
TOTAL	1,723	1,736	1,925	2,131	2,169	2,388	3,008	3,537	3,989	4,263
EXPENDITURES										
Instruction	985	1,054	1,118	1,229	1,183	1,308	1,612	1,986	2,197	2,366
Libraries	56	67	66	72	87	103	140	176	186	222
Administration	237	242	265	314	354	397	470	515	568	634
Physical Plant	182	248	281	264	265	267	348	368	354	357
Student Aid	40	51	55	54	77	84	107	154	177	211
Other b	227	187	177	204	226	263	331	336	507	503
TOTAL	1,727	1,849	1,962	2,137	2,192	2,422	3,008	3,535	3,989	4,293
Surplus (Deficit)	(4)	(113)	(37)	(6)	(23)	(34)	—	2	—	(30)

aIncludes income from the operation of dormitories, athletics and student health services.
bIncludes interest payments plus costs of operating dormitories, athletics and student health services.

SOURCE: Northwestern University Treasurer's Reports, 1921-1930.

TABLE 5-3
N.U. RESOURCES AND LIABILITIES, 1921-1939 (Selected Years)

(In Thousands of Dollars)

Year Ending June 30	Physical Plant a	Endow- ment b	Other Assets c	Total	Liabilities	Net
1921	$ 2,675	$ 5,804	$5,020	$13,499	$3,304	$10,195
1925	3,688	9,048	9,254	21,990	2,264	19,726
1930	16,023	25,526	7,737	49,286	5,239	44,047
1935	17,917	21,782	1,543	41,242	4,000	37,242
1939	23,184	21,529	9,220	53,933	3,054	50,879

aEducational buildings, grounds and equipment, dormitories and athletic facilities.
bEndowment and other non-expendable fund accounts.
cCash, notes and accounts receivable, mortgages and unrestricted fund accounts.

SOURCE: Northwestern University Treasurer's Reports, 1921-1939.

Except for the failure to attract more nearby teaching hospitals for the training of medical and dental students, the development of the various schools on the Chicago campus made possible by the expansion of the university's financial resources was especially encouraging. A good start had also been made toward achieving the goals set by the president for the Evanston campus with the construction of the stadium, sorority houses, women's dormitories, the promise of a new library building, and the Austin gift and Wilson bequest. Still lacking was the financial support needed for the construction of a chapel, better laboratories, a women's recreational center, more student housing, adequate classroom facilities and endowments for the schools of Music, Speech, Education, Journalism and Engineering.

The Great Depression   It is worth noting that when President Scott delivered his annual report to the trustees in June 1930 the stock market crash of 1929 was already a matter of fact. Yet the long-range effects of that collapse were not fully apparent, for Scott concluded that the friends of the university would be no less loyal and generous in the future than they had been in the past. And, indeed, even by the following June the university seems not to have been seriously affected by the financial crisis, for the report for 1930-31 was brimful of encouraging statistics. Total registration for 1930-31 was the highest in the university's history, being just under 15,000, while the educational budget had reached a new high of $4,800,000 (see Table 5-4).

TABLE 5-4

N.U. BUDGETED RECEIPTS AND EXPENDITURES, 1931-1939

(In Thousands of Dollars)

Academic Year	1930-1931	1931-1932	1932-1933	1933-1934	1934-1935	1935-1936	1936-1937	1937-1938	1938-1939
RECEIPTS									
Tuition	$2,461	$2,369	$2,117	$2,035	$2,136	$2,287	$2,569	$2,800	$2,754
Investments	1,057	1,077	822	678	712	893	1,003	1,005	1,086
Gifts	283	160	110	84	88	87	98	159	186
Clinics	206	226	219	249	262	169	190	202	161
Other	799	804	681	549	578	869	976	1,137	1,240
TOTAL	4,806	4,636	3,949	3,595	3,776	4,305	4,836	5,303	5,427
EXPENDITURES									
Instruction	2,574	2,590	2,203	2,063	2,163	2,419	2,683	2,960	2,898
Libraries	225	226	220	171	179	192	213	228	225
Administration	684	661	577	341	357	423	469	525	472
Physical Plant	414	385	294	328	344	330	366	387	401
Student Aid	200	182	178	144	151	150	166	179	176
Other	709	672	587	653	685	841	934	1,010	1,091
TOTAL	4,806	4,716	4,059	3,700	3,879	4,355	4,831	5,289	5,263
Surplus (Deficit)	—	(80)	(110)	(105)	(103)	(50)	5	14	164

SOURCE: Northwestern University Treasurer's Reports, 1931-1939.

Moreover, work was about to start on the Charles Deering Memorial Library on the Evanston campus and the long delayed George R. Thorne Hall on the Chicago campus. The president also announced that a second group of ten Austin scholars had been enrolled in 1930-31 and that another group would be admitted in the fall of 1931.*

* As a result of a decline in the rental income from the Austin Building after 1929, the last of the original Austin Scholarships—five in number—were awarded in 1932. The building was operated at a loss until the early 1950's and no further awards were made until the fall of 1959 when the building was sold and the net proceeds of $321,000 were deposited to the account of the Austin Scholarship Foundation. *Northwestern University Financial Report, 1960, p. 57.*

There was one ominous note, however. Scott mentioned that a number of students had been forced to withdraw from the university because of financial reverses stemming from recent bank failures. Though he concluded by stating, "I do not anticipate that the work of the university will be endangered unless the general situation becomes unprecedented," he did foresee that a continuation of withdrawals by students would necessitate a resort to "radical economies."

President Scott's optimism proved unwarranted and the "general situation" did become "unprecedented." Once under way the downward spiral set off by the collapse of the stock market in 1929 swept out into the economy in an ever-widening circle. Between 1929 and 1933 the United States gross national product fell from $104 billion to $74 billion, unemployment rose from approximately 1,500,000 workers to nearly 13,000,000, thousands of investors lost their savings while thousands more of businessmen and farmers were thrown into bankruptcy. Bread lines, soup kitchens, and apple sellers became a part of the urban scene.

With patience growing thin at the failure of the Republican administration to stem the deepening depression, the nation's voters in 1932 turned to the Democrats and elected Franklin Delano Roosevelt president. In the course of the next three years Roosevelt's controversial New Deal policies stimulated economic recovery. A slide back into recession in 1937 proved temporary, and by 1939 the GNP reached a new high of $111 billion, though some 9,500,000 workers—accounting for over 17 percent of the labor force—still remained unemployed.[79]

By 1933 there was no longer any doubt that the depression was making itself felt at Northwestern. Between 1930-31 and 1933-34, as shown in Table 5-4, the university's annual income dropped 25 percent from $4,800,000 to just under $3,600,000. *Drop in Income* This was partially accounted for by a smaller return on investments and partially by a reduction in income from tuition as fewer students found it possible to begin or to continue their university education. Under these circumstances "radical economies" did, indeed, become necessary. Among them were two across-the-board salary cuts of ten percent for all university employees, the first during 1932-33 and the second a year later. A moderate reduction in the size of the faculty and staff was achieved by not filling positions vacated by death, resignation, or retirement. No new building was undertaken between 1931 and 1936, appropriations for books and research were curtailed, and even the purchase of essential equipment was postponed. With the imposition of these economies the university's budgets for 1933-34 and 1934-35 averaged over $1,000,000 below the 1930-31 figure, but because it had been impossible to decrease expenditures rapidly enough to offset the fall in income, there were a series of deficits between 1932 and 1936.

The upturn in the economy after 1933 was reflected in higher yields on Northwestern's investments and a rise in income from tuition as student enrollment—which had dropped from 14,714 in 1930-31 to 11,917 in 1932-33—moved up to over 18,000 after 1936 (see Table 5-5). As a consequence income rose from $3,595,000 in 1933-34 to a new high of over $5,400,000 in 1938-39. However, although there was a boost in salaries on a selective basis of $280,000 in 1935-36 followed by an across-the-board increase of ten percent a year later, expenditures tended to move up more slowly than income, with the result that 1936-37 marked the end of the deficits. To build up a reserve against future emergencies, those in control of university finances decided to maintain budget surpluses rather than to grant further salary increases or encourage promotions for the time being.[80]

New Buildings:
Thorne Hall

The construction of Thorne Hall on the Chicago campus, begun in the summer of 1931, was completed in October 1932. Designed by James Gamble Rogers in the modified Gothic style of the other Chicago campus structures, the new building contained two auditoriums—one seating 800 and the other 450—plus study rooms and a fully equipped kitchen. Used for exhibitions, club meetings, lectures, and social gatherings, Thorne Hall contributed much to life on the Chicago campus.[81]

Deering
Library

In December 1932, the Charles Deering Memorial Library was completed. The design as worked out by James Gamble Rogers in cooperation with Theodore W. Koch, the university librarian, called for the construction on the Evanston campus of a modified Gothic structure similar to those on the Chicago campus. So that it might serve as an architectural centerpiece linking the buildings on the north and south sides of the campus, the new library was located at the eastern edge of the meadow overlooking Sheridan Road.

The first floor of the completed building opened into a large lobby flanked by a Reserve Book Room on the left and the School of Commerce library on the right. Toward the back stretched five small seminar rooms. The basement was occupied by another four seminar rooms, a small reading room, and a documents room. On the second floor were to be found the combined Reading and Reference Room, a Periodical Room, and administrative offices. Finally, there was a six floor stack area with eighty-four carrels and studies and a storage capacity for a half million volumes. The aesthetic features of the library included "carvings in wood and stone [which] symbolize attributes associated with the world of learning, the owl, the hourglass, the open book, the pen and countless other fanciful creations." Medallions of colored glass executed by Diven Bonawit glowed richly in the great windows.[82]

On December 29, 1932, the new library was officially opened by Mrs. Chauncey McCormick and Mrs. Richard E. Danielson, both daughters of the late Charles Deering. As Scott had said earlier, this building met what had become "the greatest need on the Evanston campus."

The Proposal
to Merge
Northwestern
and the
University of
Chicago

At a meeting of the trustees' executive committee on June 13, 1933, President Scott reported the receipt of a letter dated May 24, from Robert Maynard Hutchins, president of the University of Chicago, requesting that consideration be given—in strictest confidence—to the possibility of merging the two universities. Scott characterized this suggestion, which he had already discussed informally with several trustees, as "the most important problem ever presented to the Board of Trustees." Upon his recommendation a special committee was appointed to consider the proposal. The committee, designated in the interests of secrecy as the Special Committee on an Important Problem—but later renamed the Committee on Chicago Merger—included Melvin A. Traylor, chairman, James Oates, and Vernon Louckes, with John H. Hardin, William A. Dyche, and President Scott serving *ex officio*. Thus began a nine-month period of investigation, argument, and deep soul-searching unmatched at Northwestern before or since.

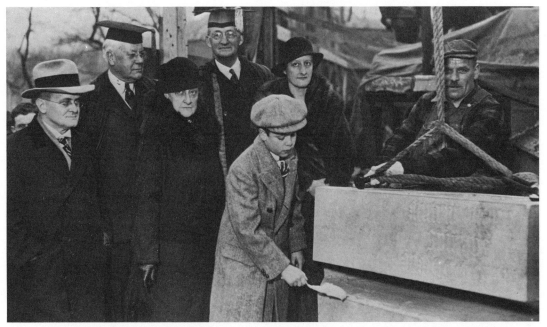

Laying the cornerstone of Deering Library, January 12, 1932 (left to right) Theodore W. Koch, university librarian, with Mrs. Charles Deering and her grandson Roger McCormick; (back row, left to right) John H. Hardin, president of the N.U. board of trustees, President Walter Dill Scott, and Mrs. Chauncey McCormick, daughter of Charles Deering

Charles Deering Memorial Library, designed by James Gamble Rogers to serve as an architectural centerpiece linking the buildings on the north and south sides of the campus

In a memorandum accompanying his letter to President Scott, Hutchins urged that insofar as legally possible Northwestern and the University of Chicago should operate as one institution. He based his recommendation largely on the following assumptions: first, the two universities as currently organized had reached the point where further economies could not be made without seriously damaging their educational and scientific effectiveness; second, because of the depression, it would be difficult to secure new money for education over the next few years; third, the operation of Northwestern and Chicago as one institution would produce the greatest educational enterprise in the world; and fourth, it would produce large economies without diminishing the effectiveness of the two institutions.[83]

Soon after their appointment the members of the Northwestern merger committee asked the two presidents to outline more specifically the educational changes and economies that might result from the proposed merger. In a confidential memorandum dated July 6, 1933, Scott and Hutchins indicated that under their plan there would be a complete unification of the educational administration of the two institutions with one dean, one registrar, one head librarian, one athletic director, a single health service, a single press, and one alumni organization. They also proposed to eliminate the duplication which currently existed between the two institutions in the fields of education, commerce, law, medicine, liberal arts, and the graduate schools. This was to be accomplished by concentrating graduate work on the South Side, undergraduate training on the Evanston campus, and professional education on the Northwestern Chicago campus. They estimated that a total savings of $1,700,000 annually might be achieved under this plan.[84]

At a joint meeting on July 19, 1933, between the Northwestern merger committee and a similar group representing the trustees of the University of Chicago it was agreed that there were four fundamental questions to be considered. One, was the merger educationally desirable? Two, was it economically desirable? Three, could it be entered into legally without affecting Northwestern University's tax free status under its charter? Four, was the mutual good will and competence of the two boards of trustees sufficiently strong to assure the success of the merger?[85] It was further agreed that consideration of the other three questions should be postponed pending a determination of the legal status of the proposal. Accordingly, legal opinions were sought from Leon Green, dean of the Northwestern Law School, and from three Chicago-based law firms.

The legal briefs received during late September and early October were by no means in agreement as to whether Northwestern would forfeit its tax free status under a merger. Despite this uncertainty, President Scott was sufficiently optimistic to recommend that the other implications of the merger should be considered. At their meeting of November 24, 1933, the trustees expanded the merger committee to include alumni and faculty representatives. The faculty group—nominated by the University Senate—was specifically charged with the task of determining the educational advantages and disadvantages of the proposal to each of the schools within the university.

Meanwhile the secrecy surrounding the discussions spawned a number of rumors regarding the motives behind the proposal and its possible implications. Although denied explicity by both presidents, some alleged that the primary objective of the plan was to permit the University of Chicago to share Northwestern's tax free status. Should this occur, these sources claimed, then the annual revenues of various tax gathering agencies in the state would be reduced immediately by some $300,000.[86]

An article by an anonymous writer in the *Evanston Review* for January 18, 1934, was headlined "Call Merger Rockefeller Plan to Wipe Out NU." According to the author an additional endowment of $25,000,000 would become available from the Rockefeller Foundation on the condition that there would be only one university in the Chicago area. The Rockefeller-Chicago interests, he stated, saw in the merger "a way of disposing of a competitor by swallowing it. The Rockefellers have followed this method often enough in other lines of business." A columnist for the *Evanston Review*, who wrote under the pseudonym of The Saunterer, noted in the December 28, 1933, issue that, "under the pending merger plan we learn from inside sources that alma materless waifs of what used to be Northwestern will be permitted to continue their immemorial candlelighting ceremony. On the condition, of course, that they burn nothing but 'Standard Oil Candles.' "

Opposition Forms: Evanston

The Evanston City Council and Chamber of Commerce went on record as opposing the merger. As one representative of the business community put it, Northwestern was the city's largest industry and a merger agreement with the University of Chicago would "deal a staggering blow to Evanston" through a decline in the volume of trade and a reduction of real estate values.[87]

By late fall the lines of opposition within the university community had also begun to form. With the exception of the Northwestern Medical School, students in both institutions generally adopted a wait and see attitude. Scott and Hutchins along with Melvin Traylor remained enthusiastic. Indeed at one point President Hutchins, a brilliant but highly controversial figure, offered to resign if this would allow the merger to take place.[88] There is little evidence, however, that University of Chicago alumni and faculty were involved in the merger discussions. The Northwestern faculty and alumni clearly were, and they increasingly expressed their objections.

Much of the alumni opposition was based on the fear that long cherished associations and loyalties to Northwestern would be lost if, as originally proposed, the name of the merged institution was to be The Universities of Chicago. Even the possibility of The Chicago-Northwestern University or the Northwestern-Chicago University was viewed with skepticism by many, including Northwestern trustee Bishop George Craig Stewart, who was certain that it would be only a matter of time before the Northwestern name was dropped completely.[89]

The strongest and the most outspoken criticism, however, came from Dean Cutter and the faculty and students of the Northwestern Medical School. Their objections were based primarily on differences in the educational philosophies of the two medical schools. Most of the Chicago medical faculty, for example, were full time and largely concerned with research and the teaching of the more theoretical aspects of medicine. Northwestern, by contrast, was primarily interested in teaching its students applied medicine. The last two years of their medical training

Medical School Protest

were spent in courses taught by practicing physicians who spent only a few hours a week in the classroom or laboratory. The attitude of the faculty was reflected in the reactions of the Medical School students who at a mass rally on the Chicago campus in November burned the effigies of Scott and Hutchins.[90]

During the early months of 1934 opposition to the merger began to mount. In their report presented on February 6, 1934, for example, the faculty committee appointed to consider the educational implications of the proposal stated that any positive educational advantages would be confined to the schools of Commerce, Law, and University College. The schools of Speech, Engineering, Music, Dentistry, and the College of Liberal Arts, they felt, would neither gain nor lose by the merger but there would be positive disadvantages as far as the work in the Medical, Education, and Graduate schools was concerned. Their conclusion, based on educational considerations alone, was that the proposed merger was not desirable.[91]

The Proposal Laid Aside   The final blow to the hopes of the pro-merger forces came on February 15, with the death of Melvin A. Traylor, chairman of the Northwestern merger committee. With the loss of his strongest ally among the trustees President Scott concluded that, since there was little chance that the board would vote for the merger, negotiations should be terminated. Hutchins agreed, and upon their joint recommendation the trustees of the two institutions voted on February 25, 1934 that "the proposal of the merger of the two institutions be laid aside and the committees discharged."[92]

The plan was a daring one and had it been adopted might have achieved great things. Both President Hutchins and President Scott were deeply disappointed with the outcome. In a letter to a member of the Northwestern board early in March 1934, Scott wrote, "The more I studied the merger the more desirable I found it to be. It is a great regret to me that conditions were such that it could not become a reality. In my judgment the merger will become a reality at some future date."[93] And in 1949 Hutchins stated, "I shall never cease to regret the failure of this plan for I regard it as one of the lost opportunities of American education."[94]

The Search for Endowment   In September 1934, William A. Dyche retired from his position as business manager. For some thirty-two years he had been primarily responsible for Northwestern's financial operations and—in the words of President Scott—"had won for the university that essential foundation of good will without which the recent development of Northwestern would have been impossible." As his successor the trustees elected Harry L. Wells, a 1913 Northwestern graduate, who at the time of his appointment was vice president and general manager of Bauer and Black, the well-known manufacturer of surgical supplies.

The new business manager took over at a difficult time. As was to be expected, the amounts received by Northwestern in the form of gifts and bequests had declined sharply from just under $870,000 in 1930-31 to a low of $331,000 in 1935-1936. Moreover, most of the $3,400,000 received during these years represented the yield of earlier pledges and bequests and was earmarked for specific purposes.

Shortly before Wells had been appointed, President Scott, working with a committee on development, had considered alternate modes of organizing the fund-raising work which had for the past twelve years been carried on by various alumni and development groups affiliated with the university. The committee, noting that there had been considerable overlap in the activities of these groups, urged that "all of these efforts should be knitted together in a correlated program."

The committee's report recommended that, "the Committee on Development of the Board of Trustees be continued in its present form but that it act as an advisory committee only. Development work for the university should be pursued full time by a Department of Development under the direction of an assistant to the president." To this department would be "delegated the entire responsibility of securing students, funds and prestige for the university." The report concluded, "We believe this is a very urgent and sound step for the university to take." The board of trustees accepted this recommendation and on March 28, 1933, voted to establish the Department of Development. Thomas Gonser was appointed director of the new department which was made responsible for public relations and publicity, the maintenance of alumni records and the recruitment of students. *Department of Development Established*

Northwestern's financial outlook was greatly improved in February 1936, when it was announced that Roger Deering, son of Charles Deering and grandson of William Deering, had died at his home in Albuquerque, New Mexico, leaving a bequest valued at over $6,000,000 to Northwestern. This bequest, as President Scott noted in his report for 1935-36, was the latest of a long series of gifts and services to the university from members of the Deering family. And because it was unrestricted it would make possible a resumption of the educational progress that had been interrupted by the effects of the depression.

The Roger Deering bequest accounted for all but $1,500,000 of the approximate $8,000,000 contributed to Northwestern during 1937 and 1938. A campaign was already under way, however, to raise money for a student union in Evanston and a decision had been made to build a skyscraper dormitory, to be known as Abbott Hall, on the Chicago campus.* In addition, President Scott and Gonser were in the process of negotiating with a prospective donor who would set a new high for the amount contributed to Northwestern by any one individual.

The depression affected the various schools in different ways, although all were faced with the common problem of adjusting their operations to the sharp decline in the resources available for their educational budgets. Least affected by the depression was the Medical School, which through the mid-1930's continued to hear from ten to twenty times the number of applicants who could be admitted to entering classes of approximately 125 students. *The Schools During the Depression*

As Dean Cutter and the faculty had made clear in their opposition to the proposed merger with the University of Chicago, the Medical School was deeply committed to training practicing physicians. This gave great importance to the outpatient department, which offered an ideal opportunity for clinical instruction and investigation, allowing students not only to observe but to participate in the examination and treatment of patients. In addition to its teaching value the outpatient department made a significant contribution to the social and economic welfare of the *Medical School*

---

*Abbott Hall was named in honor of Clara A. Abbott and her husband, Dr. Wallace C. Abbott, founder of Abbott Laboratories, from whose estate the money for its construction was received by the university.

Chicago community. Limited either to charity patients or those who could afford to pay only a small fee, the clinic handled well over 125,000 visits annually during the 1930's. According to the dean's report for 1930-31, if paid for on the basis of a moderate medical fee, the services rendered by the faculty at the clinic would have cost patients over $1,000,000 each year.

Dental School   The Dental School enrollment fluctuated during this period, reaching a low of 369 in 1938-39 (see Table 5-5). To some degree this was caused by the raising of

TABLE 5-5
N.U. STUDENT ENROLLMENT, 1931-1939

Academic Year	1930-1931	1931-1932	1932-1933	1933-1934	1934-1935	1935-1936	1936-1937	1937-1938	1938-1939
EVANSTON CAMPUS									
College	2,737	2,685	2,532	2,465	2,133	2,485	2,583	2,752	2,740
Graduate	680	691	683	644	638	983	1,403	1,481	1,562
Music	420	347	315	273	295	270	356	460	493
Speech	318	310	259	266	256	279	370	338	306
Engineering	313	317	291	261	252	249	247	277	264
Commerce	519	543	474	433	463	479	556	600	607
Journalism	106	110	104	148	133	129	153	154	93
Education	371	400	425	365	345	303	376	346	407
TOTAL	5,464	5,403	5,083	4,855	4,515	5,177	6,044	6,408	6,472
CHICAGO CAMPUS									
Medical	773	804	833	816	850	816	852	669	697
Law	420	372	317	304	269	276	250	265	229
Dental	459	500	393	412	358	397	390	394	369
Commerce (part time)	6,265	5,419	3,960	4,318	5,284	5,880	7,606	8,170	7,557
Journalism (part time)	374	378	353	359	438	447	473	460	431
Liberal Arts (part time)a	824	741	568	—	—	—	—	—	—
Education (part time)a	135	151	410	—	—	—	—	—	—
University College (part time)	—	—	—	1,216	1,830	3,876	3,086	3,284	3,196
TOTAL	9,250	8,365	6,834	7,425	9,029	11,692	12,657	13,242	12,479
GRAND TOTAL	14,714	13,768	11,917	12,280	13,544	16,869	18,701	19,650	18,951
Summer School (selected years)	(1931) 1,613				(1935) 1,996				(1939) 3,007

aLiberal Arts and Education students enrolled in University College after 1932-33.

SOURCE: Northwestern University Catalogs, 1931-1939.

entrance prerequisites from one to two years of college beginning in 1936. Yet a further cause, according to the dean, was the reluctance of practicing dentists to encourage prospective dental students in the face of their severely reduced incomes during this period.

There were no important changes in the curriculum or in the requirements for graduation during these years. An average of 90,000 operations were performed annually at no or nominal cost to patients in the adult and children's clinics maintained by the school. And because of the many contacts previously established outside the United States, the school, in spite of the depression, continued to attract students from a large number of foreign countries.

In December 1937, Dr. Arthur D. Black, who had served as dean since 1917, died. He was followed by Dr. Charles W. Freeman, an alumnus who had joined the faculty immediately following his graduation in 1912.

Enrollment in the Law School fell steadily from 420 students in 1930-31 to 229 in 1938-39 (see Table 5-5). Dean Green attributed this decline to the effects of the depression as well as to competition from state-supported or low tuition schools and a lack of student housing on the Chicago campus. Nevertheless, the school continued to maintain high admission standards and refused to accept transfers or dropouts from other law schools or applicants with below average collegiate records. In 1935 the school introduced a Bachelor of Law degree for candidates who completed a six-year course which combined three years of undergraduate work with three years of law.[95]

Law School

Throughout the 1930's the school continued to support the Air Law Institute and the publication of the *Journal of Air Law*. It also maintained the Crime Detection Laboratory until the summer of 1938, when, largely for budgetary reasons, the operation was transferred to the City of Chicago.

The period of the New Deal with its unprecedented and often controversial legislation was one in which various law school faculty members throughout the country were increasingly drawn into public debate on the legality and soundness of governmental actions. Under Dean Leon Green's influence, the Northwestern Law School had during this time enlarged the scope of its curriculum, changing from its traditional concentration on the judicial process of the courts to the study and analysis of the relationship between the law and the whole range of governmental and business agencies.[96]

Dean Green's legal philosophy drew him in 1937 into two famous controversies. The first involved Franklin D. Roosevelt's proposal to increase the number of Supreme Court Justices, the so-called court-packing bill. The second had to do with the legality of the tactic of the sitdown strike.

Dean Green and the New Deal

In an article entitled "Unpacking the Court" which appeared in the February 1937 issue of the *New Republic*, the dean argued that the President's proposal was not unconstitutional, that courts, including the Supreme Court, are made up of men and should not be permitted to remain insensitive to the needs, desires, and interests of the nation as a whole.*

The dean's position on sitdown strikes was outlined in a second article in the March 1937 issue of the *New Republic* under the heading "The Case of the Sitdown Strike." He did not in this article suggest that sitdown strikes were a good thing. He did, however, argue that because employees shared a vital interest with employers in an enterprise, the peaceful occupation of a plant by workers awaiting the adjustment of differences growing out of industrial relations was but an incident of industrial relations and in no sense unlawful.

The dean's public expression of these views in the midst of violent arguments over the relative merits and demerits of the New Deal inevitably produced much

---

*The dean was bitterly attacked, particularly by Senator Tom Connally of Texas, when he later repeated these arguments in testimony before the Senate Judiciary Committee. *Hearings on S1392, "Reorganization of the Federal Judiciary," 75th Congress, first session, 1937.*

criticism. There were strong rumors that some trustees had suggested he be asked to resign.* But the university's commitment to the principle of academic freedom was not violated and both the dean and the Law School survived the storm.

In his report to President Scott in the spring of 1939, Dean Green hailed the beginning of the construction of Abbott Hall as the most important event of the school year. Noting that the Law School was attracting more good students than ever before in its history he concluded that with the opening of the dormitory the following year, "we may expect the School of Law to take on a very vigorous growth."[159]

School of Commerce

The program established early in the 1930's by the School of Commerce remained essentially unchanged during the decade. The basic attraction of the school's offerings on the Evanston and Chicago campuses was demonstrated when total enrollment, after fluctuating from 6,784 students in 1930-31 to 5,747 in 1934-35, expanded to a record high of 8,164 in 1938-39 (see Table 5-5).

The school continued under the guidance of Dean Heilman until his death in February 1937. Following what was described as a painstaking canvass of the entire field of business education, the trustees in September 1937 appointed as dean Fred Fagg, Jr., of the Northwestern Law School, then serving in Washington, D.C. as director of the United States Bureau of Air Commerce.

Medill School of Journalism

In his annual report to President Scott covering the year 1930-31, Director Harrington was enthusiastic over the future of the School of Journalism. He was especially pleased that the *Chicago Tribune* in recognition of the contributions of the school to the field of journalism had announced a second gift of $125,000 to be expended over the succeeding ten years.† It was indicative of the school's continued popularity that in spite of the depression the combined enrollment on the Evanston and Chicago campuses reached more than 500 by 1933-34 and remained there throughout the 1930's (see Table 5-5).

Following the death of Harrington in 1935, Kenneth E. Olson, head of the journalism department at Rutgers University and an experienced newspaperman, accepted the position of director of Northwestern's School of Journalism. After a careful survey he concluded that the school's four-year curriculum did not provide the students with an adequate general background. As he pointed out in his report for 1937-38, modern journalism called for a thorough understanding of political science, economics, history, and sociology, as well as the ability to write well.

Following Olson's recommendation the four-year course leading to the Bachelor of Science in Journalism was discontinued in 1939 and replaced by a five-year program under which students completed three years of liberal arts work and two years of journalism for the degree of Master of Science in Journalism.[97] At the same time the school was removed from the general supervision of the School of

---

*At one point the dean was informed by Harry Wells that if he would resign, someone—whom the latter did not identify—had promised to finance the construction of the badly needed student dormitory on the Chicago campus. The dean promptly offered to hand in his resignation once the offer was made official, but nothing more came of the matter. *Letter, Leon Green to Harold F. Williamson, July 14, 1975, Green Biographical File, N.U.A.*

† The *Chicago Tribune* has since 1931 continued its decennial grant of $125,000 to the School of Journalism.

Commerce and made autonomous. Olson's title was changed from director to dean of the Medill School of Journalism.

At the conclusion of the academic year 1930-31 the prospects for the College of Liberal Arts seemed very good. On the basis of an expected income from the Milton H. Wilson bequest, the trustees had authorized the expenditure of over $100,000 to increase salaries of the faculty and staff. At the same time they had promised to make more funds available for faculty research and to increase the number of fellowships and scholarships. With salary scales more competitive with other institutions, Dean Addison Hibbard noted in his report for that year that he believed Northwestern would be able to retain its "best men." This, after years during which Northwestern "had been impoverished to benefit the faculties of other institutions" was especially satisfying. Hibbard's chief concern was the lack of adequate classroom and laboratory facilities for the more than 2,700 students enrolled in the college. *College of Liberal Arts*

In the early 1930's the college made several curricular changes. As indicated in the President's Report for 1931-32, a group of four interdisciplinary courses was introduced to "give more unity, sequence and coherence" to the work of the college as a whole. These included Man and his Past and Man and Society, open to freshmen and sophomores; Man and his Physical World, primarily for juniors; and Man and the World of Ideas, designed especially for seniors. At the same time fields of concentration replaced the former requirement that all students choose one major and two minors. As an incentive for students of exceptional merit, the faculty established an honors degree and expanded the possibilities for independent study.

The university-wide salary cuts in 1932 and 1933 and a decline in student registration to just 2,133 in 1934-35, forced a postponement of efforts to strengthen the faculty and expand the operations of the college. As Dean Hibbard noted in his report for 1935-36, although the "real work" of the college, the instruction of young people and the advancement of learning had gone on seriously and successfully, "the year had not been marked by any conspicuous progress or development for the college."

The situation remained essentially unchanged over the next three years. Although by 1938-39, enrollment had reached its predepression level of over 2,700 students, the dean noted rather sadly that he was unable to "paint a glorious future" or to announce "a grandiose plan for improving the College." "Reduced budgets," he concluded, "are not the food upon which progress thrives."[98]

Registration in the School of Music dropped from 420 in 1930-31 to under 300 in 1933-34 before rising again to a record high of over 490 in 1938-39. An important change in the administration of the school took place in the spring of 1936 with the resignation of Dean Beecher, who left the university to complete his study of the music and life of the South Seas. He was replaced by John W. Beattie, professor of music education and a member of the faculty since 1925. *School of Music*

Under Dean Beattie's guidance the School of Music expanded the scope of its graduate courses. In part this was a response to the continuing demand for elementary and high school teachers of music who could develop and conduct programs that went beyond the level required for an extracurricular activity. Locally the School of Music faculty and students maintained their cooperation with the Evanston public schools.

At the end of the 1938-39 school year Dean Beattie concluded his report to President Scott on a note of high optimism, stating that "we of the School of Music have courage to believe that in the not too distant future space and equipment at our disposal will be equal to those provided in any other institution of our type."

School of Speech As was generally true of the schools on the Evanston campus, variations in the enrollment in the Northwestern University School of Speech were closely related to changes in the economy during the 1930's, moving from 318 in 1930-31 to 256 in 1934-35 and back to 306 in 1938-39. Dean Dennis and his faculty saw no reason to change the basic structure and operation of the school during these years. Both the University Theatre and the Children's Theatre retained their popularity as did the Speech Re-education Clinic, which soon developed a long waiting list of patients. Members of the university debating teams, coached by Speech School faculty, distinguished themselves in intercollegiate debate.

An increase in the demand for teachers of speech after the mid-1930's was most encouraging to the school. A 1938 survey, for example, revealed that some 70 percent of the gainfully employed graduates of the school were teaching speech and 90 percent of these, in turn, were either full time teachers of speech or of one other subject only. It seemed highly likely that with a further improvement in general economic conditions after 1939 job opportunities for speech graduates would continue to expand.

School of Engineering Enrollment in the Northwestern University School of Engineering after declining from 313 in 1930-31 to 247 in 1936, began to climb again in 1937-38. In the early 1930's the school saw little reason to make any modifications in its entrance or graduation requirements since, according to Dean Bauer, it had experienced less of a decline in enrollment than other engineering schools. But this situation changed abruptly in 1937 when the newly formed Engineering Council for Professional Development, after completing a national survey of engineering schools, announced that Northwestern would be denied accreditation for 1937-38. Members of the Council had no criticism to make of the type of men who graduated from Northwestern. They were, however, critical of the fact that the four-year program leading to the B.S. degree in engineering, adopted in 1926, was still heavily weighted with nonprofessional courses in arts and sciences. Only by returning for a fifth year of study could students take engineering subjects which in most schools were a part of the undergraduate curriculum. Since very few engineering students returned for the fifth year of professional courses, the Council decided that Northwestern's program fell short of meeting the requirements for accreditation.

Following a study of the Council's report the members of the original survey team were invited by Northwestern to return to Evanston for consultations with both the administration and the engineering faculty. Two results emerged from these discussions. The first was the decision by the faculty to adopt a four-year curriculum along lines recommended by the Council. The second was authorization by the trustees of such additions to the faculty and improvements in the laboratory space and equipment as the Council and the engineering faculty considered necessary. The university was assured that once these steps had been taken the school would receive its accreditation.[99]

With the resolution of the crisis Dean Bauer, for reasons of health, asked to be relieved of his administrative duties. To take over responsibility for guiding the school on the road to what appeared to be a promising future, the trustees appointed Professor George A. Maney, a member of the Engineering School faculty since 1926. Meanwhile the administration was in greatest secrecy already negotiating with Walter P. Murphy, whose gift would make possible President Scott's long held dream of establishing an outstanding engineering school at Northwestern.

School of Education

A major development in the field of education in the United States during the 1930's was a growing number of states and accrediting agencies which required their teachers and public school administrators to complete a minimum amount of graduate work—in many instances an amount sufficient for a master's degree. The Northwestern School of Education reacted to this situation in two ways. One was to introduce a program in 1933 leading to a Master of Education degree. The second, largely for the benefit of in-service teachers and administrators, was to schedule more part time, evening, and Saturday morning classes on the Chicago campus and at conveniently located elementary or high schools in the greater Chicago area. Both programs proved popular. Enrollment in the school on the Evanston campus, as shown in Table 5-5, grew only moderately from 371 in 1930-31 to 407 in 1938-39. By contrast students on the Chicago campus majoring in education—included in the University College registration after 1932-33—rose from 135 to nearly 800. Equally impressive was the expansion in the number of education majors enrolled in the Graduate School from 102 in 1933-34 to 739 in 1938-39.[100]

Dean Stout continued to head the school until his retirement in the spring of 1934. Named as his successor was Ernest O. Melby who had joined the faculty of the school in 1928. By this time, Northwestern had moved very rapidly from being one of the smallest schools of education to being one of the largest. Dean Melby's chief concern was to ensure that the university would provide the school with the kind of support it needed to maintain its position of leadership. In his report for 1934-35 he pointed out that Northwestern was seriously handicapped by the lack of a laboratory school without which "no great school of education has been developed in this country," and urged that steps be taken at the earliest opportunity to provide adequate facilities for training teachers for both the elementary and secondary school levels.

The following year he suggested that the School of Education should operate an experimental teacher-education program modeled after that of the Teacher's College of Columbia University. To be effective, he maintained, it would need to have its own facilities and its own program and be free of the control of the faculty of any of the existing colleges on the campus. He was disturbed that teacher education at Northwestern was divided among a number of schools and departments and believed that this violated the intention of the board at the time that the School of

Education was created in 1926. The trustees wished to make the school solely responsible for the introduction and administration of all professional courses designed for the preparation of teachers and educational workers. More important was that many of the courses outside the jurisdiction of the school were ill-adapted to the needs of prospective teachers and were taught by faculty members with little or no interest in teaching techniques.

Dean Melby's Commitment to Progressive Education

Dean Melby shared the educational philosophy of the progressive movement in education. In common with other progressive educators during this troubled period when a world-wide depression and the rise of totalitarianism in Europe threatened the values to which America was committed, Melby believed that traditional education did not provide the kind of training required to preserve a democratic society. As he put it in his report for 1939-40, "We need an education which has effective social action as its goal. Failing in this goal, democracy is doomed."

To teach democratic values to their students the teachers must themselves have been trained in democratic ways. Such teachers must have a thoroughgoing faith in people, and this could only be developed by close association during their own training with staff members who respected individuals and in an institution which "literally radiated faith in people." The dean maintained that the only feasible way to provide such an environment was to turn over to the faculty of the School of Education sole responsibility for the education of teachers.

Dean Melby's suggestions did not elicit the desired response from the university administration, in part because of the continued shortage of financial resources and in part because the dean of the Graduate School, Franklyn Bliss Snyder, did not agree with Melby's educational philosophy.

University College

Northwestern's University College had its origin in the part time, late afternoon, and evening classes introduced on the Chicago campus in 1928 by the College of Liberal Arts and the School of Education. By 1932-33 these classes, supplemented by courses in music and speech, had attracted close to 1,000 registrants. Because of this expansion the trustees decided in the spring of 1933 to put all of Northwestern's part time work—except that offered by Commerce and Journalism—within a new school, which would be called University College. Samuel N. Stevens, assistant dean of the College of Liberal Arts, was appointed its director.

Students enrolled in the University College tended to fall into one of three categories. First were those taking undergraduate work leading either to the professional degree of Bachelor of Science in Education or Speech, or the nonprofessional degree of Bachelor of Philosophy. The second group consisted of graduate students, most often working for a Master's in Education. Finally, there were those whose primary interest was not in earning a degree but in expanding their intellectual and cultural horizons. The continued popularity of the programs offered by University College is shown by the growth in enrollment from 1,216 in 1933-34 to just under 3,200 in 1938-39 (see Table 5-5).

In his final report as dean of the Graduate School in 1931, James Alton James observed that a part of the vision of those who had organized the Graduate School some twenty years earlier had been fulfilled. But as he had repeatedly pointed out to President Scott, it would not be possible for the school to maintain its standing among the colleges from which it drew its students unless additional resources were *The Graduate* put at its disposal. These would include more scholarships and fellowships for *School* graduate students as well as dormitories to house them. It would also include more support for research and the services of a university press.

Dean E. O. Moulton, formerly a professor of mathematics, succeeded James. But he was no more successful than his predecessor in securing financial support and by 1933 asked to be relieved of his office. However, he agreed to serve on a three-member faculty committee which administered the school until the following year.

In 1934 Franklyn Bliss Snyder, a member of the English department since 1901, became dean of the Graduate School. He remained in this post until 1937 when he was appointed to the newly created office of vice president and dean of faculties. He was succeeded, in turn, by James W. Bell, who had joined the department of economics in 1923.

After a relatively minor drop from 680 students in 1930-31 to 638 in 1934-35, enrollment mushroomed to a total of 1,562 in 1938-39. Much of this growth, as already noted, resulted from a great influx of graduate students into the field of education. Even before this Dean Snyder had become concerned about the quality of graduate work offered on the Chicago campus, especially in education. His report for 1935-36 questioned whether many of the "so-called" graduate courses in that field met the standards of graduate instruction. "Were they conducted by mature and conscientious teachers? Were the classes open only to properly prepared persons? Were those who attended them really interested in professional training or only in a diploma which could be exhibited to some school superintendent?" He admitted that in many instances the answers to these questions would be in the affirmative. But he strongly suspected that in some cases at least the university was merely presenting large general lecture courses and encouraging the students to think that they were actually engaging in valuable graduate study. To this extent the master's degree was being cheapened and sooner or later students and alumni would become disillusioned. In opposition to what he interpreted as the School of Education's philosophy of "bigger and better," Snyder proposed a policy that would admit only those who had passed a rigorous entrance examination and would award a master's degree only to those who had reached a certain level of scholarly accomplishment.

The reaction to Snyder's recommendation was generally favorable and two steps *Strengthening* were taken to strengthen the standards of the Graduate School. In 1936 the degrees *Standards* of Master of Science in Education and Speech were discontinued and all graduate work in those fields placed under the jurisdiction of the Graduate School. Two years later a plan was put into effect whereby committees composed of representatives from both the School of Education and the relevant subject areas would develop programs of study which would fit prospective teachers for successful work in their chosen field. Snyder was highly gratified with the construction of this "pontoon bridge across the stream of prejudice and misunderstanding which so often separates faculties in American universities."[101]

Formation of
the Traffic
Institute

In 1933 the university, in cooperation with the Evanston police department, organized a special school for the training of police officers in the field of law enforcement and traffic safety. Instruction was based on the highly effective traffic safety program developed by Franklin M. Kreml, director of the Accident Prevention Bureau of the Evanston police department since 1929. In March 1936, the board of trustees approved the formation of the Northwestern Traffic Institute as an affiliate of the university under Kreml's direction. The Institute combined the Accident Prevention Bureau of the Evanston police department with the traffic division of the International Chiefs of Police, who had moved their headquarters to Evanston in order to participate in this program. Supported largely by grants from outside foundations, the Institute operated autonomously until 1959 when it was joined administratively with the Northwestern Transportation Center.

Campus Life
in the 1930's

Initially, the depression seemed to have little effect on student life as extracurricular activities continued to revolve around athletics, campus politics, and the social scene. Thus when the football team capped an undefeated Conference season by beating Wisconsin in the 1930 homecoming game, the students went on a celebration that lasted for several days before the 14-0 defeat by Notre Dame in the final game of the year. They took pride in the fact that the Northwestern marching band was the "biggest and best ever." Fraternities and sororities broke all records for the number of pledges. Each of the four classes organized themselves in the fall of 1930 to plan a variety of social events ranging from all-campus mixers to a grand charity ball. Literary societies, discussion clubs, theatrical groups, and the debating society continued to attract a large proportion of the student body.[102] A Men's Union had been founded in 1928 to offset all "the scattering forces of group organizations . . . [and] to help weld Northwestern into a unit of friendly feeling."[103] It was assigned quarters in the Coast Guard Lifesaving Station in 1931, where it remained until 1938.[104]

The students' relative indifference to national affairs began to change after the election of Roosevelt and the introduction of his New Deal program. Various speakers were invited to present their views on these developments, including Paul H. Douglas, University of Chicago economist, and Norman Thomas, the tireless presidential candidate of the American Socialist Party. A large crowd turned out for a debate early in 1934 over the probable effects of the National Recovery Act on the economy. Professor Ernest Hahne of the Northwestern economics department argued that enforcement of the N.R.A. codes would give a tremendous boost to the economy. Maynard Krueger of the University of Chicago claimed that the codes would serve only to restrict competition and prolong the depression.[105]

Isolationist
Sentiment

By 1935 the attention of students was drawn toward the international scene. A survey of attitudes toward international affairs conducted by the *Daily Northwestern* in February of that year revealed that the student body was predominantly isolationist, with some 57 percent opposing American participation in the League of Nations. Another 20 percent were adamant pacifists who indicated their unwillingness to fight, even if the United States were invaded. Talk of the growing possibility of war in Europe inspired a peace march in the spring of 1937 with over a thousand students attending the rally that followed.[106]

A number of speakers, including Thomas Mann and H. G. Wells, came to Northwestern during 1938 to discuss the question of war versus isolationism. In September 1938 the campus followed the press accounts of the Munich Conference between Neville Chamberlain and Adolf Hitler hoping that the meeting would secure peace in Europe.

In spite of the predominantly isolationist mood on campus, however, the Northwestern community was not indifferent to what was happening overseas. In 1939 income from the Lindgren Foundation, established in 1909 "for the promotion of international peace and interdenominational unity," was allocated to provide $1,000 in scholarships for refugee students at the university. At the same time the Northwestern branch of the American Student Union sent a wire to President Roosevelt to protest "the suppression of the civil liberties of German minority groups" and to urge "that German refugees be admitted to this country under the unused Russian quota."[107]

During the spring of 1939 the political crisis in Europe deepened and as the school year came to an end the prospect of armed conflict on that continent loomed large.

An important change in the administrative structure of Northwestern was introduced in the spring of 1937 when the board, upon the recommendation of its Committee on University Administration, voted to create the new position of academic vice president and dean of faculties. According to the memorandum sent out to all deans, directors, and departmental chairmen, the dean of faculties was to receive all reports and recommendations concerning faculty appointments, budgetary problems, and all other matters relating to the educational work of the university. These would, in turn, be transmitted to the president, accompanied by the dean of faculties' recommendations. As noted earlier, Franklyn Bliss Snyder, then dean of the Graduate School, was appointed to the new position. At the same time Business Manager Harry Wells was given the additional title of vice president.[108]

Changes in Administrative Structure

> We have a client who is much interested in the development in the United States of the science of engineering. This client is considering the matter of making either a substantial gift or bequesting a substantial legacy toward establishing or endowing a school of engineering in one of several outstanding educational institutions.[109]

The Mysterious Prospective Donor

This letter of February 2, 1936, to President Scott from attorney E. E. Cabell representing an unnamed client, marked the beginning of a series of negotiations which lasted for three years. In his letter, Cabell requested information about the current offerings in engineering at Northwestern, and asked what plans or ideas the university might have for training future engineers.

Cabell's letter was turned over to Thomas Gonser, executive secretary of the Department of Development, who, with the active cooperation of President Scott, launched an all-out drive to secure the bequest. At the time of the proposed merger with the Armour Institute, Northwestern had developed a detailed prospectus for the engineering school and this was immediately sent off to Cabell.[110]

In April the latter wrote Gonser on behalf of his client asking for a list of five or six engineers with whom he might confer about the possibility of establishing an engineering school. Gonser wrote back suggesting Charles F. Kettering, distinguished head of General Motors' Research Division. This was not a random choice. Some years earlier President Scott and Gonser had struck up a friendship with Kettering at an American Petroleum Institute meeting in Texas and in June 1935, Northwestern had awarded Kettering an honorary Doctor of Science. To make sure of Kettering's support, Scott and Gonser made a special trip to Detroit to "sell him" on the advantages of establishing an engineering school at Northwestern. Kettering responded enthusiastically to the possibility of introducing a new type of engineering education to the United States and indicated his willingness to go along with their plan.[111]

Kettering Proposal: Cooperation with Industry
On May 16, Cabell wrote Gonser that his client was impressed by Kettering and was "becoming more and more favorably" inclined toward Northwestern. Kettering's plan for an ideal engineering education called for a four or five-year course of study that would combine both theory and practice. The first two years would be given over to obtaining a thorough basic foundation in physics, chemistry, mathematics, and English. The last two or three years would be spent in the application of that basic foundation to the solution of practical engineering problems and this was to be done in cooperation with industry.[112]

Cabell wrote Gonser early in July that his client was much interested in Kettering's proposal for establishing a school on a cooperative basis with industry. He suggested that it would be helpful to know to what extent Northwestern believed in and would be interested in furthering such a plan. Gonser replied that Northwestern was both able and willing to put such a plan into effect.[113]

Meanwhile, at the suggestion of Kettering, Cabell and his client had contacted Herman Schneider, dean of the School of Engineering at the University of Cincinnati. As a result, Cabell informed Gonser on August 10 that his client had decided to go ahead with a plan to establish a cooperative engineering school; that Dean Schneider had been retained as a consultant to work out the details; and that he was prepared to establish the school at Northwestern if an arrangement satisfactory to all concerned could be worked out.[114]

The program as recommended by Dean Schneider called for training in the fields of civil, mechanical, electrical, and chemical engineering. The school was to operate on a quarter system in order that students might alternate three months in industry with three months on campus. A dean familiar with cooperative education was to be hired. Three new buildings plus dormitories were to be constructed and Swift Hall was to be remodeled.[115]

The Mystery Solved
Cabell's client finally allowed his name to be revealed August 27, at a meeting of the University Committee on Engineering. Gonser, who had long since guessed that Walter Patten Murphy was the prospective donor, was pleased to have his hypothesis borne out. Murphy was no stranger to Northwestern. He had made two contributions to the university's fund drives during the 1920's and in 1929 had

been asked to join the Northwestern Associates (an offer which he declined). He was also acquainted with two members of the board, Fred Sargent and Silas Strawn. Murphy's interest in cooperative engineering education was a natural outcome of his own experience. Unable to continue his formal education beyond one year at St. Louis University because he lacked the money to go on, he subsequently became highly successful as an inventor and manufacturer of equipment for railroad freight cars. By the late 1920's he was reputed to be among the richest men in the United States. In 1926 he had formed the Walter P. Murphy Foundation to handle his many philanthropies.[116]

Early in September the contract between the Walter P. Murphy Foundation and Northwestern University calling for the establishment of a cooperative engineering school was ready to be signed. Under its terms the Foundation was to make a grant of $6,310,000, of which $6,000,000 was to be spent on new buildings and equipment and the remainder used to pay operating expenses over a five-year period.[117] It was at this point that the project hit an unexpected snag. Dean Schneider in drawing up the proposal had not, as Murphy assumed, made any provision for the cost of maintenance. Northwestern which had a rule against accepting donations for buildings without an endowment of approximately 50 percent of their cost to cover upkeep, refused to sign. When Murphy balked at the idea of adding an extra $3,000,000 to the original amount, negotiations came to a halt. Although Scott and Gonser were assured by Cabell that Murphy had not lost interest in the project no further progress was made during the next two years. *Contract with the Walter P. Murphy Foundation*

Finally, in August 1938, Scott announced that Northwestern was willing to sign the original agreement with only a few minor changes. Negotiations were reopened with Murphy indicating his preference for locating the school just north of Patten Gymnasium. A consulting architect was employed to work out detailed construction plans and to review the 1936 cost estimates.*

At long last a contract differing very little from the original one was signed on March 20, 1939. Under its terms Northwestern received a gift of $6,735,000 from the Walter P. Murphy Foundation. The ground-breaking ceremony for the construction of the Institute building was planned for January 1940, while completion of the project was scheduled for the fall of 1941.[118]

Late in 1938 a group of Northwestern alumni and friends began to organize a memorial to President and Mrs. Scott in anticipation of the former's retirement. It was decided that this tribute should take the form of a building "which would fill a variety of needs, and serve as the center of university and community life for Northwestern and the North Shore district." The building was to be called Scott Hall.[119] *Retirement of President Scott*

The need for such a center had long been recognized and the Scott Hall Committee, under the chairmanship of alumnus Harold H. Anderson, found a ready response to its appeal for funds. Plans for Scott Hall were publicized in the *Alumni*

---

*When it became obvious that the site selected by Murphy was too small for the proposed building, the university decided to create the necessary space by razing Patten Gymnasium and building a new gymnasium to the north of the original one.

Men's Quadrangle (top left); Scott Hall and Cahn Auditorium, built to serve as the center of university and community life for Northwestern and the North Shore

News of February 1939 and by May 1 of that year—the date of President Scott's seventieth birthday—all was ready for the ground-breaking ceremonies.

One of the largest contributions came from the Women's Building Fund of the University Guild, whose money-raising efforts went back to 1911 when the Women's Athletic Association began to collect money for a women's gymnasium and student center by performing a variety of ingenious services. These included washing curtains, selling

Women's Building Fund

> . . . sandwiches, calendars, pencils, hair shampoos, doughnuts, Japanese prints, theatre tickets, phonograph records, hot dogs and any other devices that determined femininity might contrive—all for the women's building fund.[120]

By 1915 the organization had accumulated $3,000 and it was decided to set up a permanent Women's Building Fund under the presidency of Mrs. James Alton James. An annual minstrel show was later replaced by a county fair as yet another means of swelling the fund. Then came the announcement of the campaign to raise money for the Women's Quadrangles and the Women's Building Fund "recognized a more immediate need" and turned over $110,000 for this purpose. Thus, by 1920, its treasury was depleted and the fund raising had to begin anew.

In 1922 the Women's Building Fund became part of the University Guild and thereafter all the money-raising activities of the women's organizations were coordinated by the Guild. New ways of filling the treasury were devised by students, alumnae, and faculty wives, including a gift store and, for a while, a tea room named The Purple Oak, which raised $7,000. An annual spring musical show became, with cooperation from the Men's Union, the Waa-Mu show. The University Circle organized performances of plays and operas, the proceeds of which went to the fund. By 1939 fully $200,000 had been gathered and all of it was contributed toward the building of Scott Hall.[121]

Meanwhile the Scott Hall Committee had commissioned James Gamble Rogers, architect of the Deering Library and the Women's Quadrangles, to draw up plans for the proposed hall. A generous donation from trustee Bertram Cahn enabled the committee to plan for a large auditorium to be incorporated into the new building. The *Alumni News* of February 1939 indicated that Scott Hall would be:

> A T-shaped structure of lannon stone, it will harmonize with the collegiate gothic structure of the beautiful women's quadrangles, of which it will be an important and integral part. . . . As Deering Library, architecturally beautiful, is representative of the intellectual interests of the campus so Scott Hall, with the same architectural pattern, will represent the social center of the University.

The fund raising proceeded apace with more than 11,000 donors contributing the total $750,000 needed to complete and furnish the new building which would include thirty-five meeting rooms and lounges, a cafeteria, and a grill. The Cahn Auditorium, with facilities for staging plays and musicals, would seat 1,225. In appreciation of the generous contributions made by the women's organizations, certain rooms were set aside for their use including the University Guild Parlors and the Associate Alumnae Library. Behind Scott Hall, setting it off from the women's quadrangles, was to be the Anna Scott Garden given by Alpha Phi (Mrs. Scott's sorority) and the University Circle in her honor.[122]

Scott Hall Ground for Scott Hall was broken, as planned, on May 1, 1939, and the building was dedicated on September 24, 1940, by President Scott's successor. The facilities and opportunities for student and community activities offered by Scott Hall were indeed a fitting tribute to a man who believed that

> ... the fifteen or eighteen [hours a week] spent in the classroom form only a fragment of the time during which a university may contribute to the development of its students. ... We must break away from the traditional beliefs that the only place we can serve students is in the classroom; to that end progressive universities must increase their facilities to provide for the extra-curricular needs of individual students.[123]

Although Scott is best known for the great building programs undertaken during his administration, his contemporaries valued him for many other contributions to the quality of student and faculty life at Northwestern. Thus his professional interest and work in psychology made him unusually aware of the needs of both students and faculty. For example, he encouraged the establishment of a counseling system to help students with their financial, vocational, religious, and social problems and also advocated a tutorial system which provided students with free supplementary instruction in difficult subjects. As one observer wrote, "His studies of personnel relationships have made him markedly sensitive to the need of the individual for freedom, for personal responsibility and self-reliance and for personal expression."[124]

"Truth Is Permanently Strengthened by Freedom of Speech." Scott's defense of the importance of individual freedom was put to the test more than once, when alumni and friends of the university protested invitations to such controversial figures as Clarence Darrow and Norman Thomas to speak on campus. When, in the course of a nation-wide Red-scare, a bill was introduced in the Illinois legislature to force teachers to take a public loyalty oath, Scott strongly opposed the measure:

> ... I am a believer in capitalism, but I do not believe that adherence to capitalism is reduced by experiments in socialism. In religion, in politics and in economics the truth is not endangered by propaganda on the part of heretics. ... Error may temporarily be kept alive by censorship, but truth is permanently strengthened by freedom of speech.[125]

Although he was conservative in both political and personal matters, Walter Dill Scott was uncompromising on matters of academic freedom. It served Northwestern well to have such a man at its head in the highly charged political climate of the postwar years.

During the nineteen years of Scott's presidency the university made great strides. Budgeted expenditures for maintenance and instruction had tripled from $1,727,000 to $5,263,000 (see Tables 5-2 and 5-4). Meanwhile, as shown in Table 5-3, the net assets had grown from $10,195,000 to $50,897,000. This included a striking increase in the value of the physical plant, from $2,675,000 to $23,184,000, and an equally impressive growth in the total endowment and other assets from $10,824,000 to $30,749,000. It was a measure of Scott's success in obtaining the resources to carry out his plans that while the total gifts received by the university between 1851 and 1920 amounted to $6,800,000, contributions from 1920 to 1939 came to over $47,000,000.[126]

Three new schools had been added: the School of Journalism in 1921, the School of Education in 1926, and University College in 1934. The addition of the Scientific Crime Detection Laboratory, the Air Law Institute, and the Traffic Institute, had carried Northwestern into new fields of activity. Although full time enrollment at the university had grown from just under 4,600 to nearly 6,000 during Scott's administration, a careful screening of applicants for admission had ensured that the increase did not erode the university's academic standards. On the contrary, whereas 65 percent of the undergraduates in 1920 represented the upper half of their high school classes, by 1939 this percentage had risen to 90.

On the Evanston campus the Women's Quadrangles and the Deering Library fulfilled two long-recognized needs. The Chicago campus had brought together all the professional schools and housed them handsomely and well. Moreover, on June 1, 1939, construction was begun on the twenty-story Abbott Hall dormitory which would house 700 students when it was completed in the fall of 1940.[127]

It had been one of Scott's major accomplishments that he had succeeded in interesting prominent members of the Chicago community in the university. But his goals and achievements went beyond this to placing Northwestern among the nationally known universities.

*The calm before the storm: Trustees and Alumni Association officers lead
the traditional Alumni Day Parade, 1941 (top); Navy V12 trainees marching past the Technological Institute on their way to class, 1943*

6

A DECADE OF WAR AND PEACE—
1939-1949

In 1937 Walter Dill Scott had informed the trustees that he would like to retire by July 1, 1938. The board immediately asked its committee on university administration to begin the search for a new president. In the course of the next two years the committee interviewed both outside and inside candidates, Scott having agreed to serve another year when it became clear that a successor would not be named by the summer of 1938. Finally on March 3, 1939, the committee unanimously recommended to the board that Dean of Faculties Franklyn Bliss Snyder become the eleventh president of Northwestern University.

Snyder was named president on September 1, 1939, the day on which Germany invaded Poland. Thus his administration was shadowed first by the possibility of war, then by the problems of the war years themselves, and finally by the special demands made on the university by the flood of returning veterans during the early postwar years.

Born in Middletown, Connecticut, on July 26, 1884, Snyder had gone west to Beloit College for his undergraduate training and then on to Harvard where he completed his graduate work in English. Immediately after receiving his Ph.D. in 1909, Snyder married Winifred R. Dewhurst and then moved west again to take his first academic post as an instructor at Northwestern University. Noted as an eloquent and effective teacher, Snyder rose rapidly to become a full professor by 1919. His scholarly work also attracted favorable attention, especially *The Life of Robert Burns*, published in 1932 and *Robert Burns, his Life and Art*, published four years later. In 1934 Snyder was appointed dean of the Graduate School and three years later he became the first dean of faculties. As a result, by the time he assumed the presidency, Snyder was thoroughly familiar with most aspects of the institution.[1]

President Franklyn B. Snyder

At the same time that the board appointed Snyder president, it selected a highly experienced administrator, Fred D. Fagg, Jr., to succeed him as dean of faculties.

A Northwestern alumnus, Fagg had first come back to his alma mater in 1929 as a professor of law and had gone on to become the first director of the newly established Air Law Institute in 1933 and editor of the *Northwestern Journal of Air Law*. After an interlude as director of the United States Bureau of Air Commerce in Washington, he had returned to the university once again in 1937 to serve as dean of the School of Commerce. He, too, was familiar with the administrative workings of Northwestern.[2]

Franklyn Bliss Snyder was inaugurated as president of Northwestern University at the First Methodist Church of Evanston on November 15, 1939. The committee in charge of the ceremony presented him with a university seal attached to a gilt chain, which has been worn by the chief executive at all official ceremonies ever since. President Snyder also received a copy of the original university charter and its amendments. In the course of the ceremony, honorary degrees were conferred on Thomas F. Holgate, former president *ad interim*, as well as on retiring President Scott and entering President Snyder.

In his inaugural address Snyder affirmed the university's mission to dispel ignorance through teaching and research and stressed the need for scholars to have freedom to teach and pursue their scholarly interests without interference by state or university. At the practical level he emphasized the importance of maintaining and attracting a devoted faculty by offering higher salaries and improved facilities. He concluded on a universal note, pledging to carry on a campaign on behalf of the educated man whose attributes are those of intelligence, toleration, reverence, humility, a sense of humor, courage, and patriotism.

"The Quality of Distinction" Some of the basic tenets of Snyder's policy as president had been foreshadowed in his final report as dean of faculties in 1939. Commenting on the disparity in quality among the various schools within the university, Snyder had asserted "If there is one thing needful it is the quality of distinction in our total educational program" and had gone on to say, "I should like to see the next few years chiefly concerned with bringing all our Schools up to the level which the best have already attained." To this end he recommended the recruitment of eminent scholars and teachers and "the elimination of activities which do not support this goal."

A year later, in his first report as president, Snyder, having bluntly acknowledged that various surveys had given Northwestern "unpleasantly low" ratings, went on to give his own evaluation of the overall quality of the university. The College of Liberal Arts, the Graduate School and the School of Commerce were on "short rations," he stated, while the other schools had profited, and though he did not propose to cut the budgets of the other schools, he declared that new money "would be funnelled in large measure" to the College, the Graduate School, and Commerce "with a view to providing salary increases and an improvement in facilities for advanced study and research to those three areas."

The direction of Snyder's policy as president was thus set early: to attract and keep the best possible faculty. From this course he never deviated despite the intervention of troubled times and events.

More than two years elapsed between the outbreak of war in Europe and America's entry into the conflict following the attack on Pearl Harbor in December

1941. Nevertheless, the possibility of American involvement had become apparent *The Threat* long before then. Following the fall of France in June 1940, the United States *of War* increased the tempo of its national defense preparations and by September 14 of that year Congress had passed the Burke-Wadsworth Act providing that all men between the ages of twenty-one and thirty-six must register for an eventual year of military service within the limits of the United States.

These events on the national scene had their repercussions on the Northwestern campus. In the summer of 1940 President Snyder appointed a committee to co-operate with national defense agencies and asked its members to make a study of university facilities that could be made available for military use. For its part, the trustees' executive committee issued a statement to students endorsing selective service and put the university on record as being prepared to assist in national defense programs.[3]

The expression of Northwestern's commitment to national defense went beyond *V7 Reserve* mere words. The federal government had begun to make contracts for space facilities *Unit* and faculty services with various educational institutions in order to accelerate its training of armed services personnel. Northwestern now made space available in Abbott* and Wieboldt halls on the Chicago campus to accommodate a V7 Reserve Midshipmen's Training Unit.† The Medical School began to organize a base hospital unit. Anticipating the acceleration of defense preparations, the administration took a census of faculty who might be called for duty and put the university's scientists in touch with the Council for National Defense. When Congress passed the conscription act, the university provided offices for the administration of selective service.[4]

During the following year the university committed itself further to defense *NROTC* programs and designated Dean of Faculties Fagg as its coordinator of National *Increased* Defense Activities. The size of the NROTC was increased as was the number of defense-related faculty research projects; a civilian pilot training program was initiated and the Traffic Institute agreed to assist the army with traffic control. In-cluded in the list of defense measures was a cooperative arrangement between the psychology department and the army for the improvement of army and army air corps personnel selection.[5]

Following United States entry into the war in December 1941, the university *After* under Snyder's strong leadership geared itself to the fullest possible support of the *Pearl Harbor* war effort. Preparations had already been under way for this contingency and by the time the war came, there were 3,500 men in uniform on the two campuses. The V7 program had grown from 1,000 men to 2,000 and there had been a marked in-crease in classified research. Laboratories were made available for government purposes. In the course of the war the university would grant leaves of absence to over 400 faculty members to serve in the armed forces or in some other form of war-related activity directed by the government.[6]

---

*Completed in 1940.
†Known as the "ninety day wonder" school, the program transformed civilians into commissioned naval officers within a three month period.

Temporary buildings erected southwest of Dyche Stadium
to ease the housing shortage during and after World War II

Naval aviation cadets at mess, 1943

*Commencement June 18, 1947 (left to right) President Franklyn Bliss Snyder,
General of the Army Omar Bradley, General Nathan W. MacChesney*

Honoring World War II dead in memorial services on campus

As the federal government expanded its armed services training programs on campuses throughout the country, Northwestern became the site of several such undertakings. A Naval Radio Training School was established in the new Technological Institute building, and, to house and feed the 1,000 enlisted men in that school, both Lunt Hall (which had been the administration building) and Swift Hall of Engineering were remodeled. Foster House was converted into a sick bay and dispensary for those taking part in the armed services training programs on the Evanston campus. The university's administrative offices were moved to a business building and Pearsons Hall on Clark Street.

V12, CATS,   On July 1, 1943, the V12 Navy College Training Program opened on the Evans-
ASCT   ton campus with dormitories and fraternity houses being put to use to house this group. Looking ahead to the end of the war, the government established a Civilian Army Training School (CATS) on campus to train men who would staff the military government in occupied areas. Northwestern also provided facilities for an Army Signal Corps Training School. In his report for 1942-43, Dean J. Roscoe Miller of the Medical School noted that 85 percent of the school's students were in uniform, that a Nursing School had reopened at Wesley Hospital, and that a physical conditioning program had been organized at the request of the armed services.

As a result of all these developments, both campuses became in large measure military centers with regular civilian programs cut back sharply despite the president's determination to maintain some normal curricula. The number of civilian men dwindled drastically, particularly in the professional schools, and women became a distinct majority in the regular programs.

By the end of 1945 nearly 50,000 men and women had received some form of training related to the war effort at Northwestern, as the following figures show:

Navy Radio School, Evanston	6,210
Navy V12-ROTC, Evanston	2,338
Reserve Programs (Army, Navy, Marine), Evanston	1,317
Navy Flight School, Evanston	1,006
Army Signal Corps, Evanston	375
Army, Navy Medical Programs, Chicago	761
Army, Navy Dental Programs, Chicago	478
Army Civil Affairs Schools, Chicago	410
V7 Midshipmen's School, Chicago	24,570
Officer's Indoctrination School	2,000
Tuition-free instruction to civilians engaged in war work, under Office of Education	9,760
	49,225

In addition to the faculty members who left the campus for military and government service, more than 15,000 alumni and former students served in the armed forces. Of these, 300 died in uniform and two were awarded the Congressional Medal of Honor.[7]

As early as 1943 President Snyder began to anticipate the problems the university would need to solve when the war ended and in his report for the academic year ending that June he raised a number of questions about the federal government's *Preparing* future relations with universities. When the government cut back a number of *for Peace* military training programs in 1944, Snyder appointed an advisory committee to assist him in handling the transition from war to peace.

As the military programs began to be phased out, veterans, taking advantage of the G.I. Bill, not only replaced wartime trainees but pushed the enrollment figures to the highest in Northwestern's history. In 1939-40 there had been 19,691 students enrolled on both Northwestern campuses; by 1948-49 there would be 29,038 (see Table 6-1).* Snyder expressed his concern as he watched the registration figures

TABLE 6-1
NU STUDENT ENROLLMENT—1939-1949 (Selected Years)

Academic Year	1939-40 Full Time	Part Time	Total	1943-44 Full Time	Part Time	Total	1948-49 Full Time	Part Time	Total
EVANSTON CAMPUS									
College	2,706	196	2,902	1,768	227	1,995	2,868	178	3,046
Graduate	295	442	737	197	253	450	893	383	1,276
Music	378	143	521	343	192	535	689	129	818
Speech	349	30	379	407	61	468	866	29	895
Technological Institute	252	4	256	399	43	442	959	16	975
Commerce	557	8	565	324	22	346	1,629	6	1,635
Journalism	97	2	99	310	14	324	499	14	513
Education	392	57	449	303	27	330	459	8	467
TOTAL	5,026	882	5,908	4,051	839	4,890	8,862	763	9,625
CHICAGO CAMPUS									
Medical	710	119	829	745	3	748	767	10	777
Law	244	17	261	45	12	57	482	9	491
Dental	314	20	334	436	11	447	424	—	424
Commerce	—	7,876	7,876	—	2,863	2,863	891	9,631	10,522
Journalism	—	417	417	—	483	483	—	693	693
University College	44	3,331	3,375	6	3,420	3,426	31	5,843	5,874
Graduate	47	644	691	38	518	556	82	550	632
TOTAL	1,359	12,424	13,783	1,270	7,310	8,580	2,677	16,736	19,413
GRAND TOTAL	6,385	13,306	19,691	5,321	8,149	13,470	11,539	17,499	29,038
Summer School	(1940) 3,078			(1944) 3,957			(1949) 3,886		

SOURCE: Office of the Registrar.

grow, believing that the university could do justice to no more than 7,000 full time students. But given the university's sense of obligation to returning veterans, it was unthinkable to restrict registration at this time.[8]

Although the impact of World War II upon the university was obviously enormous, Snyder was determined to maintain regular academic programs for civilian students as far as possible and to carry forward his aim of increasing the scholarly stature of the faculty. Early in his term, he had appointed a joint committee of trustees, faculty, students, and alumni to study ways in which the intellectual life

*As Table 6-1 shows, the postwar enrollment typically included a large number of part time students.

of the university might be improved, and in his first president's report (1939-40) he expressed his pleasure that the committee's reports emphasized the importance of academic excellence and recommended elimination of extracurricular activities "which are juvenile and superficial."

Snyder's Educational Goals

During the most critical days of the war, in October 1942, Snyder addressed a memorandum to the faculty and trustees declaring ". . . we must never forget our responsibility to educate men and women for the peace that will return."[9] And in his annual report the following year he warned against manipulation of the curriculum to suit the fashions of the moment. The curriculum, he declared, should be what is best "not for years or decades but for centuries." It is therefore not surprising that throughout the difficult war years the university continued to develop long-range programs in the liberal arts college, in medicine, dentistry, education, music, speech, law, commerce, and journalism.*

Snyder was a firm proponent of the values of a liberal arts education and stressed the importance of maintaining a balance between new and established areas of study. On the one hand he thought that international affairs should receive more attention in the curriculum, on the other, he feared that the great surge of interest in the sciences would lead to a decline in the attention given to the humanities and the social sciences. But in all areas his chief concern was quality in both undergraduate and graduate education.

Northwestern's efforts to maintain academic programs in the midst of war were rewarded, for at the end of 1945 the president proudly reported that Northwestern had distinguished itself among a group of thirty major universities by losing the smallest number of students since 1939. Indeed, 7,000 had applied for admission as freshmen for the fall of 1945, though only 1,300 of these could be accepted.

In commenting on admission policies the previous year Snyder had taken note of developments at the University of Chicago where President Robert Maynard Hutchins had put into effect a plan for admitting students after only two years of high school and awarding the B.A. at the end of what would usually be considered the sophomore year. Snyder opposed this policy on the grounds that while the young students might be mature intellectually, they would be immature socially.[10] Several years later he returned to the theme of admissions, declaring that he was not so much interested in admitting geniuses and high school valedictorians as in having students who were well-rounded and well-adjusted people. Northwestern, he believed, offered the opportunity not only for intellectual development but for "a sane and gracious social life."[11]

It would be wrong, however, to interpret this comment as an attack on academic distinction. Quite to the contrary, Snyder bent considerable effort to fostering it. He believed that the way to do this was to strengthen graduate studies. In a report to a trustees' committee in 1948 he declared,

> No institution other than a college . . . can attain eminence if it concentrates its efforts largely on undergraduates. What is needed are scholars excited by research in every department and they need graduate students. The University

*See discussion of the individual schools.

of Chicago did not attain eminence concentrating on undergraduates. Greater eminence means research and graduate study. Greatness is not won by teaching alone.[12]

Using funds acquired by means of tuition raises, Snyder set about to recruit new faculty. To attract scholars he allocated money to improve library and other research facilities as well as providing financial aid for graduate students. At the end of 1944-45 he reported that the faculty had been increased by thirty and in his report for 1946-47, he noted the hiring of twenty-four additional assistant professors from such distinguished institutions as Harvard, Princeton, Johns Hopkins, the University of Chicago, Brown, Duke, and Michigan. *Faculty*

In planning his campaign to recruit and keep good faculty, Snyder recognized the importance of offering competitive salaries. By 1944, for instance, he had succeeded in raising the salary ceiling in the college from $7,200 to $9,000 and, working directly with the budget committee of the college, had selected several professors as recipients of this top salary. Operating on his own, he had gone further and broken that maximum by offering $9,500 to a prospective economics professor then attached to Duke University. In a frank letter to Dean Hibbard of the College of Liberal Arts describing these developments, he joyfully remarked, "Now for the first time that I have been on campus, I can look at the budgets of the Medical School and Law School with a happy smile."[13]

The appointment of Simeon E. Leland as dean of the College in 1946 brought to Northwestern an administrator who cooperated enthusiastically with the president to improve the quality of the College faculty and the Graduate School. Leland came from the University of Chicago where he had been chairman of the department of economics. He had also been a member of the board of the Federal Reserve Bank of Chicago and chairman of the Illinois Tax Commission.[14] The new dean fervently agreed with Snyder on the importance of paying competitive salaries. In his report for 1946-47, Leland pointed out that although the average professor's salary in 1947 was $6,964, this sum could purchase only $4,096 worth of goods and services, for while the cost of living had gone up 60 percent since 1939, salaries had risen only 30 percent during that time. He stressed that Northwestern's salary scale compared unfavorably with that of Columbia, Harvard, and Yale.

With the support of the deans—especially Leland—Snyder assigned funds for salary raises whenever possible. Yet he was far from satisfied with what he had been able to achieve in this area. In his final report as president he lamented that though faculty salaries were up, "they were by no means high enough." Nevertheless, the fact remains that through his efforts Northwestern had come a long way toward building a faculty of genuine merit. His stress upon scholarship, standards of excellence, research, and graduate training paid rich dividends. Many of the young faculty he brought to the university eventually became professors of national and international renown.

Snyder took a direct personal interest in all aspects of university life. Rather than delegate authority to the dean of faculties or the deans of the individual schools, he made all major decisions himself. He did not hesitate to overrule the salary *A Firm Hand* recommendations of the deans, nor did he let more minor items in the education budget go by without his scrutiny.[15] When Dean Fagg approved a budget for assistants in the science departments in a letter to one of the deans, the president initialed his own approval before the letter went out.

Given his concern about the quality of the faculty, it was natural enough that Snyder would take a keen interest both in promotions and in the reasons for the departure of faculty to other institutions. In a memorandum to Deans Fagg and Hibbard dated April 16, 1943, he wrote, "Before approving certain promotions discussed the other day, I wish to be sure that advancing these and passing over some assistant professors will not be construed as being unfair to certain undergraduate teachers. I will be more specific orally if you want me to."[16] Once the decisions were made, Snyder would write personally to those who had been promoted. From time to time he would take stock of departments as a whole. After examining such an evaluation of the college prepared by Dean Hibbard and the college board committee, he wanted to know how the departments stood compared to five years earlier, which were distinguished, and which most in need of improvement.

Snyder and Schilpp Because of his close personal supervision of salary adjustments and promotions Snyder was inevitably accused of violating academic freedom by withholding raises and advancement from faculty members whose views he found distasteful. Two cases in particular attracted considerable attention both within and outside of the university. The first of these concerned Professor Paul A. Schilpp, who had been appointed as lecturer in the philosophy department in 1936 and promoted to associate professor in 1938.

A teacher with a considerable following, Schilpp also came to enjoy an outside reputation as editor of the *Library of Living Philosophers*, which became a successful publishing venture.* In his earlier years at Northwestern Schilpp seemed to have been on amiable terms with Snyder who apparently persuaded him to stay at the university when he received an offer from Scripps College in 1940. "I shall do all in my power to see to it that you never regret your decision to remain with us," the president wrote to Schilpp at the time.[17] But within a year the situation had changed. Schilpp was an ardent pacifist and once the United States entered the war his open avowal of his position led a number of people to complain to the president. Responding to one such complaint Snyder wrote:

> . . . this confirms a growing impression that the instructor takes advantage of his position to promulgate his own personal beliefs. This is not in accordance with the best standards of the teaching profession. One of the necessary accompaniments of living in a free country is that we have to listen to a lot of nonsense which in a totalitarian state would be immediately suppressed.[18]

A copy of this missive went to Schilpp.

In an angry three and a half page retort to the president, Schilpp defended his right to teach his personal beliefs, particularly as a philosopher.[19] Rumors were

---

*Each volume presented the views of an eminent living philosopher as well as comments on them by other contemporary philosophers.

rife that Schilpp was about to be dismissed, though Snyder denied that North-western had any thought of firing the philosopher or of trying to silence him. Yet the situation remained uneasy and as late as 1946 students were still writing letters to Snyder in defense of Schilpp. Some made the point that Schilpp took a personal interest in students, others that though firm in his views, he allowed students to disagree with him.[20] Clearly they believed that Schilpp needed their support.

For one thing, between 1940 and 1948, Schilpp failed to receive a single increase in salary. His stipend remained $4,500 until it was raised to $5,000 in 1948 and then to $5,500 in the following year.[21] Moreover, for the entire period of Snyder's presidency, Schilpp was kept at the rank of associate professor in spite of his growing reputation as editor of the *Library of Living Philosophers*. In 1945 Dean T. Moody Campbell of the Graduate School had recommended his promotion, noting that though Schilpp's pacifism was troublesome, Northwestern was large enough to harbor persons of different views. But Dean Campbell's recommendation was ignored.[22]

Support of Schilpp's Scholarly Work

Why did Schilpp stay? Besides the fact that pacifism was no more popular at other institutions than at Northwestern so that Schilpp would not have had an easy time finding another job, there was a more positive reason for staying. Through-out the whole period of strain between Snyder and Schilpp, the president continued to make available university funds to forward Schilpp's scholarly enterprise. In 1940 Schilpp was authorized to appoint a secretary at university expense to assist him with the *Library of Living Philosophers*.[23] The following year he received a grant of $2,000 from the Carnegie Corporation contingent upon the receipt of an equal amount from other sources, and Snyder was ready to be one of the other sources.[24] In 1942 Snyder provided $300 from the president's fund and the follow-ing year he asked the College to grant Schilpp $500 from its fund for the publication of Volume V.[25] By 1947, after a review of university policy towards the series, Snyder informed Schilpp that he was prepared to accept a recommendation that the university assume some responsibility for the Library which had, in the mean-time, attracted an annual subsidy of $4,000 from the Owen L. Coon Foundation.[26] Obviously the relationship between Snyder and Schilpp was more complex than might be thought. On August 2, 1948, for instance, Schilpp wrote Snyder thanking him for a leave of absence with pay, stating that "in spite of our numerous differ-ences of opinion, I trust you will let me express my sincere appreciation for this great courtesy."[27]

Owen L. Coon, the prominent alumnus whose foundation eventually helped subsidize the *Library of Living Philosophers*, wrote Schilpp in 1944 stating that in his view Schilpp had not been denied academic freedom since he had received university support for his research and had not been released or silenced. Coon pointed out that as a radical, Schilpp must expect some opposition and that the university's delay in granting him a full professorship was understandable. However, he went on to assure Schilpp that the university needed "live wires" like him and urged him not to leave.[28] Schilpp did, in fact, stay and was promoted to full pro-fessor in 1950 shortly after J. Roscoe Miller became president.

Snyder and MacDougall

During the presidential campaign of 1948 Snyder once more had to deal with letters of complaint concerning the political views of a faculty member. Professor Curtis MacDougall of the Medill School of Journalism was campaigning vigorously on behalf of Henry A. Wallace and the Progressive Party ticket.* Some of the letters suggested that MacDougall was neglecting his academic duties in order to participate in political activity; others accused him of being pro-Communist and subversive. Snyder asked Dean Kenneth Olson of Journalism to inform MacDougall of the barrage of criticism and to warn him that his political activities were becoming troublesome.

In response, MacDougall wrote an indignant letter to Olson maintaining that his nonacademic activities in no way interfered with his teaching duties and did not embarrass the university.[29] His political views, he said, did not color his classroom teaching. Furthermore, he vehemently denied that he was a Communist "or anything resembling a Communist." He reaffirmed his intention of continuing to work for Wallace and submitted a batch of letters from students praising his teaching and scholarship.

On March 17, 1948, Olson wrote to Snyder saying that he had talked with MacDougall and was giving him unqualified support:

> You and I may not agree with his politics but as educators imbued with the American tradition of academic freedom we cannot but defend his right to say what he honestly believes. Voices like his were the first to be stifled in European universities by the Hitlers and Mussolinis.

To this Snyder responded the following day, explaining his position on issues of this kind:

> If a person impresses members of the university and of the public as being interested primarily in a political career, I think it is my duty to call that fact to the attention of his dean. That is what I was trying to do when you and I discussed MacDougall. I should be glad to have you or anyone else point out any instance in which the university has violated in any way the best traditions concerning academic freedom.[30]

Several weeks later, on April 11, the Illinois Progressive Party nominated MacDougall as its candidate for United States senator. Though initially he accepted, he withdrew from the race two weeks later. The *Daily Northwestern* for April 27, reprinted his letter of withdrawal which referred to "obstacles mostly of a personal nature." There was no suggestion that the university had exerted any influence in this matter. Indeed, MacDougall vowed to continue campaigning for the Progressive Party and carried out his promise for Snyder continued to receive indignant letters. The president's reply to one such letter suggests how misleading any hasty judgment of Snyder's stand on academic freedom would be. On October 14, 1948, responding to a complaint from a Lt. Colonel Edwin M. Hadley who had declared,

---

*The Progressive Party, newly formed in 1948, proposed the destruction of all atom bombs and the repeal of conscription as part of a foreign policy that would preserve peace with Russia. It also advocated fundamental domestic reforms. Henry A. Wallace had been Roosevelt's Secretary of Agriculture (1933-1940) and Vice President (1941-1944) but had broken with the Democratic Party under Truman.

"A man like Curtis MacDougall who is spreading the doctrine of Henry Wallace has no business being on the faculty," Snyder asked his correspondent:

> What would you suggest that I do concerning Mr. MacDougall and those other persons on the faculties whom you think to be thoroughly subversive? Much as I dislike the friendship which Henry Wallace seems to be showing for Russia, I do not think you or I would recommend Russian methods of liquidating people who disagree with us. So long as members of the university obey the law, and perform satisfactorily the tasks the trustees assign them, should they not have the rights guaranteed to American citizens by the Constitution?"[31]

Certainly Franklyn Bliss Snyder was not a man who could be easily characterized.

New Buildings

Although the impact of World War II inevitably restricted the amount of construction possible, a number of new buildings—some begun before the war—were completed during Snyder's term of office. On the Evanston campus these included the Technological Institute; Scott Hall and Cahn Auditorium; a new Patten Gymnasium; Lutkin Hall, and the Northwestern Apartments. It also included the remodeling of old Willard Hall for use by the School of Music. On the Chicago campus it included the erection of the Abbott Hall dormitory and the move of Wesley Memorial Hospital to new facilities adjoining the campus.[32]

Technological Institute

The Technological Institute, made possible by the Murphy gift of $6,735,000 was a major addition to the campus. Facing Sheridan Road, it housed not only all the engineering departments but also the college departments of chemistry and physics which hitherto had occupied inadequate quarters in Fayerweather Hall at the south end of the campus. The dedication ceremonies for Tech extended over two days, June 15 and 16, 1942, and included a special educational conference. Jesse A. Jones, United States Secretary of Commerce, gave the principal address and fifteen honorary degrees were conferred on this occasion.[33]

Opening of Abbott Hall

Abbott Hall, the Chicago campus dormitory, was opened early in 1940 and almost immediately half the space in the structure was occupied by the V7 Naval Reserve Midshipmen's Unit. When that unit expanded following the United States entry into the war, the entire building became a naval center. Funds for the hall had been provided by a gift of $1,662,745.05 from the Clara A. Abbott Trust. As graduates of the V7 School, thousands of young men who had lived in Abbott Hall became, in a rather special sense, "alumni" of Northwestern. Among them was John F. Kennedy, later President of the United States. Many of the V7 alumni returned to the university after the war to enroll as regular students.[34]

Completion of Scott Hall and Cahn

Scott Hall, on the Evanston campus, was ready for use during the early winter of 1941. It immediately became the center for a rich variety of university activities. The Scott Hall grill proved a popular gathering place for students and faculty, offering one of the few opportunities on campus for professors and students to meet informally over lunch and coffee. The second floor lounges were used for faculty meetings—especially by the College of Liberal Arts—as well as for university functions and receptions. And of course, they were also used by the University Guild and the University Circle, both of which had contributed generously to the building fund which made Scott Hall possible. Cahn Auditorium offered very much needed facilities for conventions, concerts, plays, and the famous Waa-Mu Show.

Northwestern Apartments, completed 1947 and initially designated for faculty and staff, later available to students

Lutkin Hall, dedicated in 1941 and named for the founder of the School of Music

Abbott Hall, the Chicago campus dormitory, completed in 1940 and used by naval midshipmen throughout World War II

Following the razing of Patten Gymnasium to make way for the Technological Institute, a new facility bearing the same name was constructed on the north campus

Dedication of   Lutkin Hall, named after the founder of the School of Music, was dedicated
Lutkin Hall   on November 4, 1941. Seating 408 people in a room designed specially for music, it was to be used for faculty and student recitals, organ lessons and practice, convocations and meetings of classes too large to be accommodated elsewhere on the music school premises. While other deans and administrators complained at length about the lack of space, Dean John Beattie of the Music School cheerfully announced at the end of the year, "With four buildings at our disposal, all on the same plot of ground, close to women's dormitories and administrative offices and classrooms (on) the Evanston campus, our School of Music is satisfactorily housed."[35] His satisfaction was short-lived, however; by 1945 he had joined the other deans in asking for more space.

Patten Gym   The new Patten Gymnasium became available in 1941 as did a new group of multiple-unit fraternity houses. Meanwhile on the Chicago campus the construction of Wesley Memorial Hospital marked a significant addition to the university's medical facilities.

The attack on Pearl Harbor virtually ended further construction on both campuses. As Snyder noted in his report for 1941-42, "We need a chapel, an administration building, new dormitories and a field house but we must await the clearing of the international storm clouds." In the meantime extensive remodeling was undertaken to accommodate the burgeoning military units on the two campuses. This was true especially on the Evanston campus where Swift, Lunt, Foster House, and many of the fraternities were taken over by wartime programs. Old Willard Hall was remodeled to accommodate the School of Music, and new laboratories were prepared for botany and zoology. A $16,000 addition to the Navy Building for use by the NROTC was also authorized. Following the transfer of chemistry and physics to the Technological Institute building, a wing of Fayerweather Hall was turned over to the School of Journalism.

During this same period the university received as a gift the Charles G. Dawes home in Evanston originally built by Robert Sheppard, former Northwestern business manager. In making the gift Mr. Dawes specified that if his wife survived him she was to be allowed to continue living in the house as long as she chose, and she did indeed remain there until her death in October 1957. Subsequently the university leased the house—located at 225 Greenwood Street—to the Evanston Historical Society for a nominal rent of a dollar a year.

Other   As the war drew to an end the influx of veterans and the increase in the size of
Additions   the faculty created a severe housing problem. To meet this crisis, the university built nine villages of metal Quonset huts and steelcraft houses as well as the Northwestern Apartments in Evanston, and some houses for faculty at the University Golf Course, a subdivision in Wilmette. This program cost in excess of $6,000,000.[36]

Nor were the physical needs of the Chicago campus neglected. In March 1946, Snyder announced that the trustees had approved a $100 million program for that campus. Ten of the proposed sixteen new buildings were to be dedicated to the development of a great medical center to be dominated by an institute of medical research. They included as well a cancer clinic, a urological institute, an eye hospital, a women's hospital, a school of nursing, a children's hospital, a university clinic,

an expansion of a general hospital and a neuropsychiatric clinic. A new building *Plans for the*
and an extension of the Gary Library were announced for the Law School, as well *Chicago*
as new homes for University College, for the School of Journalism's program on *Campus*
the Chicago campus and a great central library.[37] This program of expansion was
certainly ambitious when viewed from the vantage point of 1946. Yet within twenty-
five years many of the goals of that program had been achieved.

One of the first steps in realizing the plans for a medical center was taken during *Beginning of*
the academic year 1946-47, when the Medical School concluded an affiliation *the Medical*
agreement with Children's Memorial Hospital in Chicago. In addition, the Veterans *Center*
Administration announced a plan for a $10 million dollar hospital which was later
erected on the Chicago campus, while in 1946 Mrs. Joy Morton gave the university
$1,500,000 for a new hospital.[38] Subsequently President Snyder and Dean Miller
of the Medical School decided that this amount was inadequate for the construction
and endowment of a hospital, and during Miller's term as president the university
obtained authorization to build a medical research building—the Morton wing of
the Montgomery Ward building—instead.

TABLE 6-2
NU BUDGETED RECEIPTS AND EXPENDITURES, 1940-1949

(In Thousands of Dollars)

Academic Year	1939-1940	1940-1941	1941-1942	1942-1943	1943-1944	1944-1945	1945-1946	1946-1947	1947-1948	1948-1949
RECEIPTS										
Tuition	$2,906	$2,908	$2,871	$2,622	$2,423	$2,616	$4,054	$5,930	$6,092	$7,189
Investment	993	1,053	992	965	1,214	1,489	1,775	2,026	2,291	2,429
Gifts	203	248	240	210	223	216	281	448	590	996
Clinics	163	158	167	175	186	202	183	257	282	327
Govt. Contracts & Grants	—	—	299	1,203	3,275	2,584	1,099	573	992	916
Other	1,268	1,804	2,084	2,807	1,756	1,982	2,649	3,664	4,305	4,244
TOTAL	5,533	6,171	6,653	7,982	9,077	9,089	10,041	12,898	14,552	16,101
EXPENDITURES										
Instruction, Clinics & Research	2,976	3,123	3,310	3,753	4,200	4,462	4,749	6,487	7,691	8,514
Libraries	230	221	194	192	205	242	472	441	480	546
Administration	516	495	518	466	506	588	714	895	973	1,120
Physical Plant	383	384	457	545	630	746	946	1,114	1,257	1,187
Student Aid	192	216	201	181	124	140	199	273	315	376
Other	1,028	1,618	1,782	2,463	2,885	2,528	2,620	3,056	3,413	3,771
TOTAL	5,325	6,057	6,462	7,600	8,550	8,706	9,700	12,266	14,129	15,514
Surplus	208	114	191	382	527	383	341	632	423	587

SOURCE: Northwestern University Treasurer's Reports, 1940-1949.

During President Snyder's administration, Northwestern continued to operate *Finances*
within its budgeted income as it had since 1937 (see Table 6-2). In his first annual
report to the trustees, Snyder noted that by encouraging thrift, the university had
ended the year 1939-40 with a surplus. But he made the point that "thrift on the

part of the university is not an end in itself; should it be so considered only calamity would result! It is merely a means to larger ends: security against possible future adversity and provision for possible future development."

The following year concern about the probable effect on enrollment of the draft and other preparatory activities prompted by the possibility of war led the university to trim its budget for 1941-42. Expenditures for travel and entertainment were drastically curtailed and all but the most necessary building repairs and alterations were postponed.

In fact American entry into the war and the subsequent dislocations in university life did not have an adverse effect on Northwestern's financial situation. The anticipated fall in tuition income was more than offset by government contracts and grants. As a result, while budgeted expenditures for 1943-44 reached a new high of $8,550,000, the university's receipts for the year also reached a new high, amounting to just over $9,000,000 (see Table 6-2).

The university's income continued to grow during the war years and after, reaching a total of $16,101,000 in 1948-49, the last year of President Snyder's administration. While some of this growth stemmed from investments and auxiliary operations, most of it derived from an increase in income from tuition. Two factors were responsible for this: a rise in tuition from $100 to $140 per quarter in 1945-46, and a massive expansion in enrollment during the postwar years, reaching a peak of 11,539 full time and 17,499 part time students in 1948-49 (see Table 6-1).

Paralleling this favorable financial outlook was an accelerated growth in the university's budgeted expenditures, which reached a total of $15,514,000 by 1948-49. It was consistent with Snyder's basic policy of doing everything to attract and keep the best possible faculty that the amount spent on faculty salaries rose from $4,462,000 in 1944-45 to $8,514,000 in 1948-49.[39]

Murphy Bequest Gifts during this period totaled over $41,165,000. Of this, close to $28,000,000 came from the estate of Walter P. Murphy, who had died in December 1942, six months after the dedication of the Technological Institute which his earlier gift had made possible.*

In his report to the president for 1946-47, Vice President and Business Manager Harry L. Wells, reviewing the changes in the university's fiscal policies over the previous decades, noted that in the 1930's the university had changed its fund-raising philosophy from ". . . what was commonly called the deficit method to a conservative viewpoint where budgets were concerned." Wells went on to say that "when the university decided to live within its financial cloth, we discovered a new viewpoint on the part of donors. . . . Men in recent years have been giving to institutions which handle their finances on a sound business basis."

Significant and welcome as the Murphy bequest was, the publicity attending it created some curious problems for those engaged in raising funds for the university. In his report for 1945-46, Snyder speculated—possibly with tongue in cheek—that gifts would have been larger "had the university not acquired the reputation of having so much money that you don't know what to do with it." Most outsiders

---

*The funds became available over a period of years as money was realized from the estate. The final settlement yielded $28,000,000. *See* Northwestern Engineer, *March 1967.*

222

did not realize that the Murphy funds could be used only for the development of engineering and the principal sciences.

Though Northwestern ended 1948-49 with a surplus of $587,000, and assets which had doubled in the course of the previous decade, rising costs and the pressure put on all of the university's facilities by the rapid expansion of the student body in the postwar years meant that more resources would have to be found to cover the expenditures that would become imperative within the next few years.

TABLE 6-3
NU RESOURCES AND LIABILITIES, 1940 - 1949 (Selected Years)

(In Thousands of Dollars)

Year Ending August 31	Physical Plant	Endowment	Other Assets	Total	Liabilities	Net
1940	$24,234	$23,460	$ 9,319	$57,013	$ 3,275	$53,738
1944	28,492	31,571	3,246	63,309	2,216	61,093
1949	32,052	62,051	3,958	98,061	2,646	95,415

SOUCE: Northwestern University Financial Reports, 1940-1949.

Developments in the Schools

Four major issues confronted the schools of the university during the decade of Snyder's tenure: adjustment to wartime programs, 1940-1945; long-range curricular changes; the pressure of escalating numbers of students after 1945; and the shortage of space and teaching personnel.* The many special military programs offered by several of the schools in most cases required accelerated schedules and year-round academic calendars. Several of the schools, notably the College of Liberal Arts, Law, Speech, Commerce, and Education seized the opportunity afforded by changing educational conditions to make major revisions in their programs. The great mass of students applying to both campuses after 1945 brought both benefits and problems. On the one hand the university had the opportunity to become very selective in its admissions; on the other hand all its facilities were heavily taxed by the sheer numbers of students using them. The deans set up a perpetual cry for more faculty, more equipment, and more space.

Chicago Campus: the Law School

Taking into account national trends in legal studies, the Law School increased the number of courses dealing with administration, business, and institutions. This required the addition of faculty concerned with the social sciences. Early in Snyder's regime, Dean Leon Green had made the point that the Northwestern Law School had been severely handicapped during the previous twelve years by a combination of deficits, shrinking endowment, and reduced scholarship funds. Though the school had acquired a fine reputation as a pioneer in legal training, in seeking quality students it suffered from the competition offered by Harvard, Yale, and the low tuition law schools in the Middle West. Only if the university supplemented the school's income from general funds could it operate effectively, noted the dean in 1940-41. To help remedy the situation, he advocated an increase in enrollment without a lowering of standards, more alumni contributions for scholarships, and a part time day program.

*The sources for this section are the annual reports of individual school deans for 1939-49.

Before these recommendations could be acted upon, war broke out and cut Law School enrollments dramatically. Whereas the enrollment for 1939-40 had been 261 students, in 1943-44 the Law School had only 57 students (see Table 6-1). The ranks of the faculty had diminished equally dramatically from thirty-eight to only four full time and three part time instructors in 1943, many of the professors having departed for some form of military or government service. To help maintain enrollment the admission requirement was dropped from three years of college to two and an accelerated schedule of three full terms within a calendar year was adopted. In addition, a reduced program extending over four years was offered to prospective students. So desperate did the school's situation seem to the dean that he advocated the appointment of a committee of trustees and alumni to consider the problem of rehabilitating the school in the future.

By 1945-46 the situation had altered just as drastically the other way, the pressure for admissions becoming so great with the return of veterans and the availability of G.I. benefits that the school could afford to become highly selective. In 1947-48 the school began to use the Law School Admission Test.

In 1947 Leon Green resigned after eighteen years as dean of the Law School to become distinguished professor of law at the University of Texas. His successor, Harold Havighurst, had joined the Law School faculty in 1938, having received his baccalaureate degree from Ohio Wesleyan and his law degree from Harvard. During the war Havighurst served for a period of time with the Foreign Relief and Rehabilitation Organization before returning to the Law School. He was appointed dean in March 1948.

As the faculty returned from service the school developed a new curriculum with more logical groupings of required courses. The moot court system was reorganized with alumni help and, as an experiment, corporate group seminars were formed in which members of the bar confronted students with actual legal problems.

By 1947-48 the Law School had returned to a two semester calendar with a half-semester length summer session. Although much was done to refurbish the Law School buildings following their wartime use for military training programs, Dean Havighurst stressed the need for new buildings for the library and student housing.

Medical School   The general hospital unit which had been established during World War I was revived in 1940 as Unit No. 2. The following year, Wesley Memorial Hospital opened a nurses' training program. The Medical School itself instituted an accelerated three-year program which eliminated summer vacations. By 1941-42, when this program went into effect, 85 percent of the students were in either the Army or the Navy Reserve.

As the war drew to an end the accelerated program was modified in accordance with the gradual return to civilian life. But in the aftermath of war there were new medical needs to be met, and in 1946 the Northwestern Medical School cooperated with the University of Illinois Medical School to organize the Hines and Vaughan veterans' hospitals.

As noted earlier, the Medical School formed an affiliation with Children's Memorial Hospital in 1946-47 and established three new departments—one in experimental medicine, an institute of rheumatic fever, and a department of nutrition and metabolism. Curricular changes included a greater emphasis on personal instruction in the clinical departments.

In 1941, J. Roscoe Miller, an alumnus of the Northwestern Medical School and an assistant dean since 1933, succeeded Dr. Irving Cutter as dean of the Medical School. Dean Miller stressed the need for additional institutes, hospital facilities, and programs, including a central school for nursing. Many of these proposals were incorporated in the plan for a Medical Center announced by President Snyder in 1946.

At the time of America's entry into the war, Dean Charles W. Freeman of the *Dental School* Dental School expressed his concern that the Selective Service System failed to take into account the urgent need for dentists. Once it became apparent that 21 percent to 28 percent of draft rejections were due to dental problems the armed services recognized the importance of allowing dental students to complete their training. By 1942-43 most of the students were in uniform studying in an accelerated program similar to the one in effect in the Medical School. As the war proceeded, the shortage of teaching personnel became acute and those who remained were forced to carry extremely heavy teaching loads.

By 1945-46 the accelerated program had become optional and with the return of peacetime conditions the Dental School found itself overwhelmed with applicants for admission. As in the other schools the need for more full time faculty, space, hospital connections, and new equipment became acute. Dean Freeman continually stressed that notwithstanding attempts at rehabilitation, the facilities and equipment of the school were now obsolete and worn out. Despite this serious problem the school managed to exercise leadership in graduate training and research and resumed its tradition of training dentists from foreign countries.

Professor S. A. Hamrin of the School of Education became director of the *University* University College in 1939, serving until 1942, when he was succeeded by Professor *College* Rollin Posey of the political science department. During the latter's term of office the title of the head of University College was changed from director to dean. In 1948 Dean Posey resigned and was followed by Professor E. T. McSwain of the School of Education.

In 1940 University College and the schools of Journalism and Commerce concluded an agreement for joint registration on the Chicago campus and for joint advertising of the evening offerings. As far as administration was concerned these evening units remained separate and distinct, the dean of Commerce in particular being opposed to any merger between the evening divisions of his school and University College. In 1942, however, the Schaffner Library of Commerce was consolidated with the University College library.

While enrollment decreased during the war years, University College offered some practical new courses during this time, including mathematics as applied to warfare, blueprint reading, and secretarial techniques. In 1944 four out of five students were women, but by 1947, the enrollment included a large number of veterans. In that year the total number of students reached a peak of 6,907 compared to the 1939 peak of 3,375. Facilities on the Chicago campus were overtaxed and an annex for University College was opened in the Austin Building in downtown Chicago. To help alleviate the crowded conditions, some Saturday morning and afternoon classes were given beginning in 1947 and a program of afternoon classes for full time students, mainly veterans, was started in 1946 but liquidated after 1948.

Throughout the decade University College remained dedicated to providing courses for part time students who could enroll after their daytime working hours. Rather than organize a duplicate full time faculty in Chicago for evening courses, the college relied primarily upon part time teaching by faculty from the Evanston schools and upon joint appointments with departments in the College of Liberal Arts. By 1948 there were eighteen such joint appointments.

Evanston Campus: Liberal Arts

In 1944 the College of Liberal Arts faculty adopted a new B.A. program comprising sixteen units: six prescribed, six electives within a major field, and four free electives. This program in liberal arts attracted considerable attention both within and outside the university. Among the special features of the program was an experiment in language teaching which called for regular hours of oral practice in addition to more stress upon reading ability. Subsequent modifications made the B.A. program less rigid.

In 1946 Simeon Leland was appointed dean following the death of Dean Hibbard the previous year. Dean Leland urged that a single baccalaureate degree—rather than the B.A. and the B.S.—be awarded to all students. After a faculty committee had studied the proposal the faculty in 1948 approved a new program calling for a common freshman year in which students would choose one course from each of four groups, namely, English, languages, science or mathematics, and the social sciences. Other changes during this period included the elimination of the distinction between "pass" and "honors" degrees. Instead, all students became eligible to graduate with "distinction" or "highest distinction."

The size of the College faculty grew from 194 in 1939 to 218 by 1948. Minimum floors for faculty salaries were set at $6,000 for full professors, $5,000 for associate professors, $4,000 for assistant professors, and $3,600 for instructors. Though Snyder had raised the ceiling for College salaries to $9,500, Dean Leland maintained that in general the College faculty was underpaid and overworked. In common with his fellow deans he also asked for more classrooms and research space.

Graduate School

The character of the Graduate School changed markedly in the postwar years not only because of increased enrollment but also because of the increased interest in Ph.D. programs. In 1938 Northwestern had granted thirty Ph.D.'s; in 1948 this had tripled to ninety.

With the appointment of Arthur R. Tebbutt as the university's first full time graduate dean in 1945, the school acquired a strong spokesman and a continuity of leadership. Tebbutt had received his B.A. from Brown University and his Ph.D. from Harvard, and had taught at Brown before joining Northwestern's School of Commerce in 1939 as professor of business statistics. He served as dean of the Graduate School until 1951.

DECADE OF WAR AND PEACE

As the number of applicants for admission to graduate studies grew, the school found itself in a position to become highly selective. By 1948, for example, the school had 1,270 applicants of whom only 648 were admitted. The decision to use the widely employed Graduate Record Examination as an admission test made the selection process considerably easier and more effective.

The allocation of more funds for fellowships and research during Snyder's presidency led to a substantial strengthening of the graduate programs. In 1947 the trustees moved to enlarge the graduate faculty from 125 to 200—an important step in broadening the base of faculty interest in graduate studies. But much remained to be done. The lack of housing for graduates and of a center for graduate activities made it difficult to draw students from far away. Those who came lived in rooming houses or commuted from nearby areas and, having no place to gather, failed to develop the sense of community which is the basis for a graduate school of national stature.

The advent of war led to a sharp decline in the number of male students enrolled in the School of Music and directors of band and choral programs had to rise to the challenge this offered. Fortunately, the number of women students remained sufficiently high to keep the school active, especially during summer sessions. *School of Music*

While wartime conditions called for temporary adjustments, fundamental changes in forms of public entertainment led to long-range shifts in curriculum. The decline of Chautauquas and the increasing audiences for radio and movies, for example, changed the demand for certain kinds of musical training. During this period the School of Music broadened its curriculum to take account of new opportunities for musicians. As noted earlier, music education, which would prepare musicians to direct and teach music in the public schools was one of the important programs encouraged and developed by Dean John W. Beattie.

In 1946 the swell of postwar students raised enrollment at the school to 600 full time and 100 part time students. Dean Beattie's contentment with the space available for music students vanished. He complained bitterly about the lack of space, especially practice rooms. He was equally unhappy about the disparity between the teaching loads of his faculty and those of the other schools' faculties. Though he conceded that giving lessons involved a somewhat repetitious procedure requiring less preparation than that expected of a history professor in his classes, he nevertheless maintained that the difference had been exaggerated and that his personnel was very much overworked. As in the case of all the schools, the great flood of students in the postwar years presented problems as well as opportunities for the School of Music.

Throughout the years 1939-1949 Dean Homer B. Vanderblue never ceased to stress the urgent need for a new building and new facilities for the School of Commerce in Evanston. The Little Red Schoolhouse, as the Commerce building was called, had been woefully inadequate for some time and after 1945 the overcrowding became acute.* The postwar enrollment proved heavier than anticipated, *School of Commerce*

*In his report of 1945-46, Vanderblue mournfully noted that the building acquired from Garrett Biblical Institute in 1923 "can best be described as resembling an atrociously designed country court house in a small prairie town to which, as an afterthought, a jail was built in the rear."

Cloris Leachman in a University Theatre production of "Blithe Spirit"

STUDENT ACTORS

Paul Lynde (standing) and Charlotte Rae in the 1948 Waa-Mu Show, "See How They Run"

Charlton Heston in a University Theatre production of "Hedda Gabler"

comprising almost 1,500 undergraduates; a new graduate program limited to 50 students in Evanston; and 8,000 part time students in Chicago. To accommodate such numbers the Chicago campus offered Saturday morning and afternoon classes in addition to regular evening programs, while during the years 1946-1949 evening classes were also made available in Evanston. There was in addition a Day Division program for full time students on the Chicago campus.

In 1940 the program was broadened from what had been primarily technical courses to include new courses dealing with administrative statistics and managerial functions. In 1946 the undergraduate curriculum was completely revised to include core subjects for upperclassmen. Mathematics and American business history became required freshman courses and economics, geography, and accounting were required for sophomores. A revised and amplified graduate program was developed at the same time. Summing up these changes in 1948, Snyder noted that Commerce was no longer a two-year undergraduate program tacked on to a two-year College of Liberal Arts program, but had become a full-fledged four-year program with a full calendar year of study for the M.B.A.

Vanderblue, a Northwestern alumnus who received his graduate training at Harvard, served as dean from 1939 until 1948. When illness prevented him from carrying out his duties, Professor Paul H. Morrison was named as temporary chief administrative officer of the school. Dean Vanderblue retired in 1949.

Enrollment in the School of Journalism stayed relatively stable, even during the war years, the addition of a year of graduate training in 1937 having proved highly successful. In 1941 Dean Kenneth E. Olson noted that the Medill School was the largest professional journalism school in the country. Moreover, there were more calls for graduates than the school could supply. After 1945 the growth in enrollment continued at such a rapid rate that the number of admissions had to be limited. By 1943, when enrollment stood at 807, there had been five times as many applicants as could be admitted (see Table 6-1).

Medill School of Journalism

To accommodate to wartime conditions the School of Journalism introduced an accelerated schedule in 1942, using the summer as a full quarter. This made it possible for students to earn a B.S. degree in three years and an M.S.J. in four. In addition, a special one-year program was made available for those with a background of three or four years of college.

The curriculum received a complete overhaul in 1946, with the radio, advertising, and magazine sequences being greatly strengthened. A new departmental organization was created comprising six departments: advertising, magazine, news, radio, graphic arts, fiction and the Chicago evening division. In 1948 the school was accredited for the first time, receiving a very high rating.

During these years of successful development, Dean Kenneth Olson nevertheless stressed the need for further support, particularly for more faculty, scholarships, and space. In 1942 Journalism had moved from the Commerce building to Lunt and then, when chemistry and physics moved into the Technological Institute, to Fayerweather. Conditions in the latter, the dean pointed out, became virtually intolerable during the period of postwar crowding, and he urged with all the vigor at his command that a new building be made available for the school.

School of
Speech

Enrollment in the School of Speech not only did not shrink during the war years, but actually increased. By 1943 the number of students, 468, was the largest in the school's history, the greatest increase being in the areas of speech education, audiology, and speech defects. The school had a nationwide reputation and by 1946 the number of applicants was so large that selective admission became essential. At the graduate level the school came to rank fifth in the nation in the number of master's and doctoral degrees awarded.

Dean Ralph B. Dennis died in August 1942 and was succeeded by James H. McBurney, professor of forensics in the School of Speech. Under his guidance the school instituted a major curriculum revision in 1946. Six broad areas of study now became available to students: three in the humanities, social sciences, and physical sciences taught by the College faculty, and three in professional speech areas taught by Speech faculty. Like Journalism and Commerce the school was severely handicapped by lack of adequate space and equipment. When the school inaugurated courses in television in 1948, for example, the only way in which these could be offered was in cooperation with NBC which allowed the school to use its facilities.

The University Theatre flourished during this period, providing a training ground for several performers who would achieve fame in the years to come.

Dean McBurney constantly urged the university to provide a new building for the school. Together with his faculty he drew up plans for a building which would serve the manifold needs of the school, but no funds were available to transform these plans into reality. Nevertheless the school continued to enhance its reputation, its research in speech and hearing defects becoming particularly well known.

Technological
Institute

Ovid W. Eshbach became the first dean of the newly formed Technological Institute in September 1939. He came to Northwestern from the Bell Laboratories of the American Telephone and Telegraph Company, having previously served as assistant dean of engineering at Lehigh University. His task was not an easy one, for along with the magnificent Murphy bequest for the Technological Institute came grave responsibilities. In his will Murphy had stated, "It is my express desire that the Technological Institute shall become second to none in America, and the bequest is made for the purpose of enabling the trustees of Northwestern University to carry out my wishes in this respect." The phrase, "second to none," came to haunt Snyder, his administrative colleagues, the trustees, and the dean and faculty of the Institute. Against whom or what other institutions was quality to be gauged and how could it be measured?

The agreement of March 20, 1939, between Northwestern and the Murphy Foundation laid down the condition that the Institute adopt a work-study program —designated as cooperative education—for at least five years. Under this program students would spend the first year at Tech and subsequently alternate one quarter at the university with one quarter in industry. Moreover, the agreement specified that Dean Herman Schneider* of the University of Cincinnati, which already had

*Schneider died soon thereafter and was replaced by Dean Robert Disque of Drexel Institute.

The Technological Institute, completed in 1942, home of engineering and the college departments of physics and chemistry; main entrance showing some of the stone reliefs by Edgar Miller used throughout the building

such a program, be appointed as a consultant and advisor on all major appointments and policies for at least five years.[40]

In December 1943, an outside advisory committee of prominent businessmen and engineers appointed by the university in collaboration with the Murphy Foundation and headed by Charles F. Kettering,* reported on the Institute's potential. The committee noted that Tech had a "signal opportunity" to demonstrate the value of cooperative engineering education, to assume leadership in the field of engineering, and with "adequate funds to emphasize quality, not quantity." During these war years, however, when Tech facilities were largely at the disposal of the military, the possibility of launching long-range programs was rather limited.

"*Second to None*"   In a memorandum prepared for his own use, Snyder pondered the meaning of "second to none" as applied to the Institute. It is, he wrote, "more than a faculty or a building," more than "simply another School of the University." It is "a concept, a dream" which should be thought of "not in terms of today or ten years but of the next two centuries."[41]

Snyder also concluded that the provisions of the Murphy will which permitted the use of Murphy income for the "teaching of science," were intended to ensure that Tech not be "segregated . . . from the rest of the university"; that the Institute not be limited to the "narrow field of engineering"; and that instruction in science should be available not only to Tech students but "to all parts of the university."

In practice this meant that instead of setting up its own science departments, Tech paid the College of Arts and Sciences and, where appropriate, other schools, for teaching certain subjects to engineering students by means of a system known as cross tuition. While this seemed ideal in theory, in practice Tech faculty frequently complained that the College departments failed to provide the kind of applied science instruction desired by engineers and that Murphy funds were being exploited by these departments to build faculties more suitable for liberal arts than for the Institute. A counter argument stressed that an institute "second to none" needed distinguished science departments and that the use of Murphy money to raise the stature of the science faculty could not help but redound to the benefit of Tech.

Such differences of opinion as to whether the Murphy money was being properly used were bound to create unpleasant relations between the central administration on the one hand and the administration and faculty of Tech on the other. Snyder in no way allayed misgivings at Tech when in March 1947, he wrote to Dean Ovid Eshbach expressing the wish that the Institute's program could be more like that of MIT and the California Institute of Technology and could include more courses in the social sciences and humanities.[42] He concluded by inviting the dean to present his plans for the Institute to the board of trustees.

Eshbach's presentation to the board three months later merely served to increase Snyder's uneasiness about the direction the Tech program was taking and led him to ask the board to appoint a special trustees' committee to evaluate the situation.[43] The charge given to the three members of the special trustees' committee at the board meeting of December 17, 1947, was a comprehensive one. They were to

---

*At that time general manager of the Research Laboratories Division of General Motors, as well as a vice president and director of that corporation.

report on the progress of the Institute in discharging its specific responsibility under the terms of the Murphy will and in so doing they were to answer the following questions: What program had been formulated so that Tech could attain the stated ideal of being "second to none" and how long would it take to realize it? How did its curricula compare with those of other schools? What other schools used cooperative education? How had it worked at Tech? What did the Society for the Promotion of Engineering Education think of it? What was the responsibility of the director of Research? Was the faculty outstanding? And, of course, how did Tech compare to other institutions?

In its report, made February 26, 1948, the committee emphasized that the university was restricted in its administration of Tech by the stipulations of the Murphy Foundation and its appointed consultant. It noted that cooperative education, which was mandatory through 1948, was still experimental and might require a longer period to prove its value, but stressed that Tech should not accept the programs uncritically. While it found the faculty competent, the committee recommended that in addition to developing its promising younger faculty Tech should hire more men of established reputation. No new curricula should be added until the present ones achieved increased distinction. On the matter of expansion the committee was clear. Vigorously opposing any move to expend capital for plant and equipment, it stated that an outstanding faculty is more important than machines or buildings. The committee approved the marked concentration on undergraduate education but dodged the issue of comparisons with other institutions, stating that "chance comments have been noncommittal or negative."[44]

A Difference of Opinion

In his response to the report Eshbach stoutly maintained that Tech was progressing satisfactorily and defended the quality of the students, the faculty, and the curricula. The cooperative program, he claimed, was the best in the country and the curricula of the four departments compared favorably with those of the best five departments in the country. In electrical engineering, he stated, only MIT was superior and the other departments "could be brought along" to achieve distinction as well. The curricula, voted by the faculty, had been approved by the appropriate committee of the American Society of Engineering Education. When it came to graduate work and research, the dean cited the appointment of Dr. Paul Klopsteg as director of research and the fact that there were eighty-nine candidates for the Master of Science degree as proof of satisfactory progress. Though a Ph.D. program was under consideration, the dean obviously chafed under the rules of the Graduate School, believing that they were inappropriate for an engineering school.[45]

Both the trustee committee's report and Eshbach's response were read at the board meeting of March 30, 1948, after which the board voted to refer the matter to the president of the university who was "to report his recommendations to the board at a later date."

At an executive committee meeting on May 20, 1948, Snyder expressed his reaction to the committee's report, taking issue with some of its statements but agreeing with others. Commenting on the committee's endorsement of the stress upon undergraduate education, Snyder remarked tartly, "Yes, but if the educational program is limited to undergraduates, Tech will remain at the present level.

The trouble with Tech is that it was conceived on a low plane, and if the Institute is to receive a higher rating, research scholars as well as good teachers are essential." He concurred with the committee's statement that the university had not been free to develop Tech as it might have desired because the consultant appointed by the Foundation "kept the books, certified that we were operating within the terms of the agreement, and approved or vetoed all appointments."

In the end, neither the report nor the ensuing discussions resolved the differences between Tech and the central administration. When Snyder's successor took office in the summer of 1949 the issues raised by the report were still to be settled.

Changes Apart from these circumstances the most important developments at the Institute during this period involved a change in requirements and the expansion of opportunities for graduate work. In 1945 the academic requirements for the B.S. degree were raised from eleven to twelve quarters. Simultaneously the cooperative education— or on the job—requirement performed outside the school was reduced from seven to six quarters. The following year a committee headed by Dr. Paul Klopsteg, director of research, was appointed to coordinate policies and programs with the Graduate School. Greater emphasis was placed on the program leading to the M.S. degree, and evening classes for graduate work were organized on the Evanston campus. The opening of the Argonne National Laboratory* at nearby Lemont, Illinois, opened up opportunities for research for both faculty and students at the Institute.

The wave of applicants in the postwar years brought many highly promising students to the Institute. A Carnegie Institute study of freshman qualifications revealed that the class admitted to the Institute in 1945 tied for second place in ability among freshmen in engineering schools throughout the country. By the following year the number of students at Tech exceeded 1,000, of whom three-fourths were veterans. To prevent overcrowding it was decided to set a limit of 1,000 students for the Institute.[46]

School of Education As dean of the Graduate School and, later, as dean of faculties, Snyder had had strong reservations about the rapid expansion of the School of Education and had made clear his opposition to the educational philosophy and practices of Dean Ernest O. Melby.[47] When Snyder became president his attitude toward the school remained negative and the exchanges between him and the dean became less and less cordial.[48]

Whatever their differences on academic issues may have been, the final confrontation between the president and the dean developed over the disposition of resources. Melby had long thought that the School of Education should have more financial support for its programs and every year his reports stressed the need for larger allocations to his school. But Melby's requests for more funds coincided with Snyder's attempts to reduce spending during 1939-40 in anticipation of the possibility that the outbreak of war in Europe might eventually have an adverse effect on the university's financial situation. Starting in the spring of 1940 relations

*Established as a cooperative venture by a group of midwestern institutions with support from the federal government, Argonne was intended to provide a unique opportunity for nuclear research by engineering and science faculty and graduate students "under conditions and with equipment that could not be provided in any other way . . . ." *President's Report 1945-46.*

between the School of Education and the central administration began to deteriorate rapidly.[49]

The situation came to a head the following summer when Snyder ignored promotion and salary recommendations submitted by Melby who had consulted with the advisory committee of the School of Education elected by the Education faculty. In a reproachful letter, dated August 8, 1941, Melby indicated that:

> The Advisory Committee feels that the situation resulting therefrom will have an unfortunate effect upon the morale of our School. Recommendations made by me on the final budget were carefully considered by the Advisory Committee. Yet they were overruled by the President's Office without our being given a chance to discuss the matter or to present additional reasons, if desired, for the original recommendations.

The dean went on to detail yet another incident in which a member of the School of Education had been informed by the vice president that "no one of these six men whom the Advisory Committee and myself had recommended for reappointment could be certain of his reappointment." Melby added that since his salary recommendations had been "altered and no notice or reason given for such action" he felt justified in asking to be informed if the same was about to happen with the reappointment recommendations. He stressed that "the Advisory Committee and I think this matter is much more serious than the first."[50]

Conflict

Snyder made no apparent effort to smooth the matter over and on September 20, 1941, Melby tendered his resignation in a curt note to the president. Students in the School of Education protested vigorously and for many months thereafter Snyder's office continued to receive letters from administrators, teachers, and spokesmen for parents' and teachers' associations as well as from parents in surrounding school districts praising Melby's achievements and, in some cases, urging Snyder to appoint someone with similar convictions and goals to succeed him. Snyder selected a faculty member, James M. Hughes, as acting dean and appointed a faculty committee to make recommendation for a permanent dean.[51]

The search committee took a long time to agree on a list of prospects but when it finally submitted a number of names to the administration Snyder failed to act on its recommendations. Professor E. T. McSwain, a member of the search committee, wrote to the dean of faculties complaining about the administration's failure to cooperate with the committee, but to no avail.[52] Hughes continued as acting dean until March 1945 when Snyder appointed him dean.

Since the training of teachers was carried out not only in the School of Education but in several other schools as well, members of the university administration and the Graduate School had, since the late 1930's, worked with the dean of Education to coordinate the various programs by means of joint committees with the cooperating schools—the College, Speech, Music and Commerce. This system was developed even further in 1945 when the School of Education adopted an entirely new curriculum which used more fully the resources of these other schools. The new four-year undergraduate program was planned to provide a balanced blend of a liberal education, professional training, and courses in specialized professional subject matter. A required seven units of the college B.A. program underlined the liberal arts foundation of the Education program.[53]

In his reports Dean Hughes stressed the need for more specialized classroom space and more scholarship money. He was successful in obtaining a curriculum laboratory for the school located in the university library. In addition, a special science education laboratory was constructed for the School of Education.

The Library   University librarian Theodore Koch died in March 1941, five months before he was due to retire. The gardens of the library which he had planned were renamed Koch Memorial Gardens in his honor. In the course of his twenty-two years as university librarian, Koch did much to improve both the quality and size of the library. His enthusiasm and energy brought many gifts from book lovers and several important collections to Northwestern. During his stewardship the library's holdings grew from 120,000 to 377,000 volumes.

Following Koch's death Effie Keith, a staff member since 1916, was appointed acting university librarian. She exercised these responsibilities under the special circumstances created by the war and managed to deal successfully with shortages of staff and difficulties in securing books and periodicals from overseas. She resumed her post as assistant librarian in 1944 when Jens Nyholm was appointed university librarian. Educated at the University of Copenhagen and George Washington University, Nyholm came to Northwestern from the post of assistant librarian at the University of California in Berkeley.

Nyholm persuaded President Snyder that it would be both more economical and more efficient to establish a strong centralized library administration and in the course of the next few years the Music School and Technological Institute libraries as well as the remaining departmental libraries in the College of Liberal Arts (except for the Astronomy Collection) were incorporated into the central library system.

A Library Council consisting of the university librarian and the librarians of the four libraries on the Chicago campus was established in 1946. The circulation of a weekly bulletin, *The Northwestern Library News*, improved the flow of information among the libraries on the two campuses.

Several major collections were acquired during this period, and by 1949 the total library holdings on both campuses had grown to 987,956 volumes.*

Campus Life   At first glance student life at Northwestern at the beginning of the 1940's would seem to have been indistinguishable from that of the preceding decade. Fraternity and sorority life flourished. Student government came under attack in a column of the *Daily Northwestern* headed "Boys in the Back Room," which asserted that "student government at Northwestern University probably looks pretty good on paper. Actually we know it to be superficial and ludicrous."[54]

Intramural sports had become highly popular on both the Chicago and Evanston campuses and keen rivalry developed when championship contests were organized between the winners in basketball, baseball, badminton, tennis, and swimming on the two campuses.[55]

---

*The above material on the library is taken from Rolf Erickson's article "Northwestern University Libraries" published in the *Encyclopedia of Library and Information Science* (New York: Marcel Dekker, Inc.).

DECADE OF WAR AND PEACE

The *Daily* of January 14, 1941, carried the happy news that King of Swing Benny Goodman would play at the Junior Prom to be held in the Crystal Ballroom of the Stevens Hotel in Chicago. But a closer perusal of the student paper during the year before Pearl Harbor shows a growing concern over the possibility that America might become involved in the European conflict. Its columns and editorials reported and commented on the parade of prominent speakers who came to the campus to argue for and against American intervention.

When the Burke-Wadsworth Act providing for selective service was passed in the fall of 1940, the *Daily* took a poll on attitudes toward conscription and found students rather evenly divided with a slight margin in favor of conscription—51.6 percent for and 48.4 percent opposed. An editorial on this result accepted the need for selective service but expressed concern because conscription made it difficult for students to make plans for the future.[56]

Isolation versus Intervention

Three months later, on January 15, 1941, the *Daily* presented a column of pro and con views on the position of the Committee to Defend America by Aiding the Allies on the one hand, and of the America First Committee on the other. The next day's issue reported a debate held at Northwestern's Y.W.C.A. on "How Can America Best Defend Democracy?" One of the speakers, Oswald Garrison Villard, former editor of the *Nation* responded—"By staying out of Europe's war." The other, John Morrison, of the Committee to Defend America answered, "By all possible aid to Great Britain without impairing America's defense."

Student opinion at this time appears to have inclined towards isolationism rather than intervention. The *Daily* of January 17, 1941, reported that 1,370 students from forty-two houses on the Evanston campus had signed a petition opposing "any foreign war," a stance which the *Daily*'s editorial applauded heartily. In the spring several well-known figures came to the campus to join in the growing debate. Carl Sandburg filled Cahn Auditorium on April 1, for the Phi Beta Kappa lecture, and stressed the inevitability of "darkness in Europe or worse if Britain falls." Three weeks later students gathered at the auditorium once more to hear veteran socialist leader, Norman Thomas, oppose intervention in a debate with George Fielding Eliot, a CBS commentator and expert on military affairs, who urged intervention on the side of the Allies. Their subject was "What Must We Do to Obtain Peace?"[57]

War

By the winter such concerns had become irrelevant. On December 8, 1941, classes were dismissed so that the university community could hear the radio broadcast of President Roosevelt's address to Congress asking for a declaration of war against Japan. "Not since Northwestern defeated Notre Dame has this happened," noted the *Daily* nostalgically on December 9. In its editorial for the previous day the paper had urged students to rally behind the government:

> There will be a part for all of us in this war. The Northwestern student body can show its cooperation by a sincere backing of the government in all its policies, by a willingness to serve in whatever way is necessary.

On December 10, classes were dismissed once more for an All-University Defense Convocation in Cahn, planned by the Student Governing Board, the General Faculty Committee, and the Student Defense Committee. By the following day radio code, Red Cross first aid, lifesaving, and aviation ground school courses had been set up by the Student Defense Committee.

Yet it would be wrong to assume that every aspect of campus life was immediately transformed by these serious events. On February 11, 1942, a snowball fight involving four fraternities and three residences for independents led to the breaking of forty-six windows. Reporting on the event, Paul MacMinn, director of men's dormitories, explained that "the men regard this as a traditional activity and take great delight in it."[58] Nor was this the sole instance of "traditional" fraternity activity. Shortly after this incident President Snyder received an indignant letter from a fraternity pledge who complained that "Hell Week is brutal" and that despite the pledges against hazing taken by all students at registration he had been paddled until he was "black and blue, and bleeding." He concluded by asking President Snyder, "How would you like to be swatted until you were black and blue?" and threatened to make it "hot for Northwestern."[59]

But there was another side to fraternity life as well. On January 10, 1941, the *Daily* reported that the Panhellenic Council had voted unanimously to recognize Alpha Kappa Alpha, a black sorority, and invited it to membership on the Council. An item several days later announced that the Inter-Fraternity Council had voted $75 and Panhellenic had voted $50 as contributions to Better Understanding Week, to be held on campus the following month under the sponsorship of the Interracial Commission.[60] The speakers invited to the campus during that week were Clarence Dykstra, director of Selective Service (on leave from the presidency of the University of Wisconsin), Rabbi Stephen Wise of the Free Synagogue in New York City, and Dr. Ralph Bunche, then a faculty member at Howard University.

Housing Problems of Black Students

The Student Interracial Commission had been formed in 1940 as a reaction to the general attitude toward racial minorities at Northwestern. In 1941 there were thirteen black male students registered at the university and even this small number created a housing problem since the administration considered it unfeasible to house black and white students together.[61] When he found himself under pressure to provide housing for black students, Snyder strongly endorsed the policy enunciated by the director of dormitories, who explained that "the racial factor makes it impossible to divert rooms used by other students."[62]

Not everyone at the university shared this view, however, and in the summer of 1941 the administration found itself at odds with one of its own staff members, Mrs. Ruth O. McCarn, counsellor for women. Forthright and eloquent, Mrs. McCarn publicly advocated that the newly established black sorority, Alpha Kappa Alpha, be housed at 628 University Place and that deliberate efforts be made to improve the treatment of blacks and other minorities on campus. She was especially troubled by the scattered living arrangements for black women students in Evanston as well as being aware of the burden that fell on those who commuted from the south side of Chicago.[63] The situation for male students was not much better. They lived at the segregated Y.M.C.A. on Emerson and, like the black women students, could find few eating places other than Hoos's Drug Store or the Scott Hall grill to serve them. Mrs. McCarn's concern about such matters provoked unfavorable reactions from some of her colleagues. In a lengthy memorandum to

Snyder, one of these complained that Mrs. McCarn's "advocacy of interracial relations favoring Jews and Negroes" had brought protests from alumni "who will be disappointed, and the future welfare of our Department of Development and of our Alumni Foundation will be in jeopardy."[64]

In a long talk with Mrs. McCarn, Snyder reproached her for her preoccupation with race relations and asked her to pay more attention to other problems of student life such as drinking.[65] But she was not to be diverted from her concerns. When a student, Joyce O'Brien, prepared a petition to Snyder asking the university to open a hall for black women, to provide a cooperative house for white and black women, and to draw up a list of approved housing for black women, Mrs. McCarn strongly endorsed this appeal.

Snyder and Counsellor McCarn

Having studied the report, a member of the staff dealing with student housing responded in a memorandum to Snyder that an acceptable house for black women could not be found and that a cooperative house for black and white women would not be practical because it would require a subsidy from the university, a burden "which the university was not in a position to assume." The memorandum made note of the fact that in 1935-36 white male students living at Pearsons Hall had voted to admit black students but that their parents had created such a fuss that the experiment had had to be dropped.[66] Snyder assented to the position outlined in the memorandum and the relationship between Mrs. McCarn and the university administration became even more strained.

The advent of war did nothing to improve the situation. Attempts by interracial groups to go beyond the status quo quickly provoked adverse reaction from the administration which always referred to alumni protest as the reason for its stance. When the twenty-five member Interracial Group of Evanston—for the most part Northwestern students—held a "mixed" social at the John Evans Center in the summer of 1943, the university's response was immediate and hostile. An assistant professor at Tech had chaperoned the dancing and the beach party which followed and some alumni urged that he be dismissed. On the memorandum in which the dean of faculties reported the event to the president, Snyder scribbled "No such groups should be admitted to a university building."[67] Letters from alumni stated that they did not want their gifts to the university to be used in support of such activities.[68]

Mrs. McCarn continued to work for better conditions for racial minorities at Northwestern and continued to draw criticism for doing so. Relations between her and the central administration reached a breaking point in 1948, when, after seven years of friction, President Snyder finally asked her to resign.[69]

The crowding of the postwar years forced large numbers of students on the Evanston campus to seek lodging with private families. Given the conservative attitude of the majority of the white community, black students found themselves particularly disadvantaged in trying to find housing close to the campus. Eventually the handful of black male students—the majority of whom were athletes—found rooms with black families in Evanston. For black women students the only concession made by the university was the establishment of what was called International House on Orrington Avenue, in which some black women were housed

Informal entertaining at the Delta Gamma sorority house

Their finest hour: Rose Bowl rally

Women's Quadrangle, part of the complex housing coeds

along with a few white American women and some foreign students. Technically International House was university housing, but it was visibly segregated from the other units on campus.[70]

Situation on the Chicago Campus

There were racial difficulties on the Chicago campus as well as in Evanston. Dean Miller of the Medical School approved the admission of black students to the course in physical therapy and stated "We lean over backward to admit Negroes whenever we find one with the required qualifications." Snyder, however, indicated that black students would be denied admission to the physical therapy program "unless they were members of a public health nurses program which could supply Negro patients."[71]

The same principle applied in the Dental School. A black Air Force veteran wrote to Snyder complaining that he had been denied treatment in the dental clinic. He reported that he had been "informed that necessary work could not be done because I was a Colored Person." The white dental student to whom he had gone had agreed that the policy towards blacks was wrong, but was told by the dean's secretary that "Since the school had no colored students enrolled, white students were not asked to treat colored patients."[72]

Snyder passed this complaint on to Dean Freeman, who denied that his office had been discourteous and went on to say that "types of treatment which extend over a long period and are carried out entirely by the students are accepted only when we have an available student who can benefit by the procedure." In other words, since there were no black students and since white students could expect their future practices to be confined to a white clientele, there was no point in having a white student treat a black patient as part of his clinical training. The dean concluded by stating, "We never refuse any patient who is in urgent need of dental care to relieve pain or for the preservation of health, but we are refusing many patients because they are not of educational value and because we have no suitable students to whom the patient may be assigned." President Snyder passed Dean Freeman's explanation on to the veteran without any further comment or action.[73]

Effect of the War

The war years brought radical changes to student life on both campuses. On the Chicago campus most of the medical and dental students were in uniform and subject to military discipline, while by 1944 the number of law students had shrunk to a mere fifty-seven. On the Evanston campus most traditional activities were curtailed or suspended. The Waa-Mu Show was closed for the duration of the war when its director, Joe Miller, left the university to join the Air Force. The former all-university dances were discontinued. The Student Governing Board ruled that all groups sponsoring events which brought in revenue should donate 60 percent of any profits to a War Benefit Fund earmarked for scholarships for returning veterans.

The prewar "fun and games" atmosphere disappeared almost entirely. For the military trainees, the only free time permitted during the week was from 4:30 to dinner, after which came compulsory study hours with lights out at 10 p.m. Only on Saturday afternoons and on Sunday were those in uniform allowed to be off campus. To provide at least some entertainment, a Scott Hall Student Committee sponsored Sunday afternoon open houses for the trainees and encouraged informal get-togethers in the grill during recreation periods.

Of the civilian students, many women continued to live in sorority houses, but the men for the most part lived in private homes and apartments in Evanston, fraternity houses having been largely assigned to the military. Those fraternity groups which continued to function during the war years used Scott Hall for their meetings.[74]

A recognition of the need to coordinate the various aspects of student life led to the creation of the post of dean of students at this time. F. George Seulberger, who had joined the faculty of Tech in 1939 as professor of cooperative education, was appointed to this post in 1944. The responsibilities of this office included admission, student health, student affairs, housing, office of employee personnel, counsellor for veterans and university examiner.[75]

Following the surrender of Japan in August 1945, the influx of veterans to both campuses became very great indeed. "Ah, Peace—Ah, Men," cheered the women editors of the *Daily Northwestern* on September 27, 1945: *"Ah, Peace, Ah, Men"*

> Those strange 2-legged creatures wearing trousers which you may have seen around campus are MEN. Fraternities—still without houses—are coming out of hibernation. And for the feminine element, too, the lean years are over. Peace, its wonderful!

In the month that followed, the *Daily* detailed the imminent return of traditional events and activities: "Homecoming Again"; "Waa-Mu Back Home for Keeps"; "Purple and White, Fight, Fight cheers will mix with songs and engine whistles today when Northwestern students give the Wildcat eleven their biggest send-off in many years."[76] Fraternity and sorority activities resumed full scale. The Interfraternity Council and the Inter-House Council came back to life, and in 1947, three new fraternities were added to the Greek roster: Chi Psi, Zeta Psi, and Alpha Tau Omega.[77]

But the return of familiar peacetime pursuits was only part of the story. For several years the tone of student life was much influenced by the maturity and serious mindedness of the large number of veterans among the students. In the spring of 1948 there was a total of 10,704 veterans enrolled at Northwestern. Of these, 3,639 were on the Evanston campus. The Chicago campus had a registration of 1,807 full time and 5,248 part time veterans. The School of Commerce, the College of Liberal Arts, and the Technological Institute led in the enrollment of veterans in that order.[78] As the reports of Chester E. Willard, coordinator for veteran's education, to the president from 1945 to 1948 show, the veterans maintained a high level of academic achievement. They also remained deeply concerned about national and international developments. In an article in the *Daily* the chairman of the Anchor and Eagle veterans' group (founded in 1943) explained that the group had invited Robert Maynard Hutchins to speak on the Atom Bomb because "N.U. veterans are plenty disgusted! They're disgusted with the appalling mental slothfulness of American citizens concerning life and death issues before them."[79]

*"We Young
People Are
Afraid"*   An editorial in the *Daily* several days later confessed "We Young People Are
Afraid" and went on to say, "We're afraid we aren't strong enough to use our
own power right. We can still remember the scientific knowledge of the Hitler
gang and how it was used."[80] In April 1946, the campus celebrated U.N. week
with a mock United Nations conference at Tech. The *Daily* of April 23, described
the event with verve:

> Led by the uniformed Northwestern band, student representatives to the General
> Assembly shifted the campus observance of U.N. week into high gear with a
> parade up Sheridan Road to Tech. Following the parade and the greeting by
> President Snyder, the session was formally called to order by Frank Haiman,
> chairman of the General Assembly.

The final session was addressed by Senator Claude Pepper of Florida.

Religious Life   Among the groups that encouraged serious discussions on campus were the
various religious organizations. In 1939-40 representatives of trustees, students,
alumni and faculty were added to the Board of Religion which had been established
by the trustees in 1937. The role of this board was to cooperate with the churches
in Evanston in presenting campus programs and to assist the larger denominations
and religious organizations in finding housing near the campus. In 1940 monthly
vesper services were inaugurated, first in Cahn Auditorium and later in Lutkin Hall.

Efforts by the Board of Religion led to the creation of a Student Religious
Council in 1940. The Council represented thirteen campus religious organizations
in Evanston as well as the Association of the Religious Counsellors, designated
by the several denominations to serve the students on campus.[81] In 1943 the
university made the John Evans Center available as the headquarters for the Board
of Religion (previously housed in the Coast Guard building) and the Student
Religious Council. It was also made available for use as a counselling center by
the advisors to the religious organizations.[82] By 1947 there were ten student
groups cooperating through the Student Religious Council, and the Y.M.C.A. and
Y.W.C.A. joined the groups housed in the John Evans Center.[83]

The war years gave fresh impetus to those who favored the construction of a
university chapel. To begin with, Northwestern took the step of creating the position of university chaplain, appointing the Reverend James C. McLeod to this
post in 1946.[84] The chaplain engaged actively in counselling, taught courses in
religion, and in 1948 started a regular Sunday morning chapel service, accompanied by a student choir, in Lutkin Hall.

Athletics   In 1940 Northwestern's baseball team established a first by sharing the championship in a .750 tie with Illinois. This accomplishment was not repeated during
the remainder of the decade; nor did football and basketball bring home any championships for Northwestern in this period. However, the decade ended on a climactic
note when on January 1, 1949, Northwestern defeated California 20 to 14 in the
Rose Bowl, coming from behind in the fourth quarter to win the exciting contest.
Actually Northwestern had ended the 1948 football season in second place behind
Michigan, but in accordance with the Rose Bowl agreement, the latter was not

The John Evans Center, headquarters for the Board of Religion and the Religious Council during the 1940's

Snow blanketing the south campus on a winter night in 1945 (Photo by Evanstonian Glen E. Tardy)

eligible to go to Pasadena two years in a row, having defeated Southern California on January 1, 1948.*

During the 1948 season, Northwestern had lost only to Michigan 28 to 0 and Notre Dame 12 to 7. Victories over Purdue, Minnesota, Ohio State, Wisconsin, and Illinois assured a second place finish. Following the victory over Illinois, the students did not wait for the official confirmation of the Rose Bowl invitation but "unleashed a mass celebration immediately after the game." So great was the student pressure for calling off classes that President Snyder canceled classes for the following week, Thursday being the beginning of the Thanksgiving holiday anyway. As described by the *Daily Northwestern:*

> Conservative Northwestern literally stood on its head in a 24-hour Rose Bowl celebration. The festivities were marked by parades, pep rallies, a dance, open houses and no classes. . . . Even President Snyder was a guest at a midnight serenade during which a 'no school' sign was tacked on his front door. . . . More than 3,000 students paraded through Evanston behind the band. Nearly 500 more boarded "L" trains and invaded the Loop where they conducted a snake dance through Marshall Fields.[85]

The Rose Bowl   Thousands of students and alumni made the trip to Pasadena for the Rose Bowl game, the band traveling on a special train as guests of the Chicago and North Western Railroad. Unfortunately, on the return trip, the train carrying the band and other special trains were snowbound in Wyoming for nearly a week. "The end of a blizzard-enforced vacation for 275 stranded students was in sight as a special train pulled out of snow-covered Cheyenne, Wyoming."[86]

The war had had a serious effect on the Conference and intercollegiate sports between 1941 and 1945. In a series of decisions the Conference waived so many regulations because of wartime conditions that by 1943 only two eligibility rules remained: athletes had to be regularly enrolled students and they were not to receive compensation for athletic participation. In May 1945, Kenneth L. "Tug" Wilson, Northwestern's athletic director, became the Conference Commissioner. The following December 7, the Big Ten voted to return to the prewar rules.[87]

The End of an Era   During the closing years of his presidency, Snyder received recognition from many quarters. He was awarded eleven honorary degrees and in 1949 received the United States Navy Civilian Service Award acknowledging his long-standing interest in the Navy and his contribution to the naval training programs conducted at Northwestern during the war. A talented speaker, Snyder was invited to give a number of commencement addresses and in 1949 received the Freedoms Foundation's gold medal and prize for his commencement speech at Northwestern.

In the course of his many years of residence in Evanston, Snyder had taken an active part in the community, serving on the boards of various local institutions. Following his retirement from the Northwestern presidency in 1949, he became president of the board of managers of the Presbyterian Hospital in Chicago,

---

*The Big Ten had voted on September 1, 1946, to "enter into a five-year agreement with the Pacific Coast Intercollegiate Conference permitting a Conference representative to play a PCC representative in the January 1, Rose Bowl football game. This marked a singular exception to the Conference's stand against post season games." *From* The Big Ten Records Book, *p. 208.*

The 87th Annual Commencement, June 13, 1945 (left to right) Law School Dean Leon Green, President of the Board Kenneth F. Burgess, John Evans (grandson of Founder John Evans), ex-President Walter Dill Scott, Vice Admiral Randall Jacobs, Captain Charles J. Stuart, and Captain B. B. Wygant

Alumni Day, June 1946, brought back Dr. Eben P. Clapp, Class of '81

serving in that capacity until 1956. He continued his research and writing until his death in May 1958.[88]

Snyder's contributions to Northwestern have not always received appropriate recognition because of two circumstances surrounding his administration: his term of office was only ten years compared to his predecessor's nineteen years and his successor's twenty-five years; and nearly half of his tenure occurred during World War II when much of his energy necessarily was devoted to programs designed to assist the war effort. In addition, the strong flavor of his character and personality and a tendency to be abrasive served to obscure the full measure of his achievement.

As an administrator Snyder was not inclined to delegate authority. He gave the deans little leeway in running their schools. The exceptions were the deans of the Medical and Dental schools to whom he gave a greater measure of autonomy because he was less familiar with their fields. But in general he took the lead in making all major decisions and many minor ones as well. This often did not sit well either with other administrators or with faculty committees which saw their recommendations ignored or overruled.

With the trustees, particularly with the chairman of the board, Kenneth F. Burgess, Snyder early established a sound working relationship. The board members shared his conservative outlook and were pleased by the efficient way in which he conducted meetings with the trustees. He reported to them regularly on university affairs and carefully prepared in advance statements of policy for adoption by the board. He was orderly and unfailingly clear and cogent in his remarks and there was never any doubt as to where he stood or what he thought about an issue. His conservative views on social and political matters were also shared by many of the Northwestern alumni and parents, as their letters to him show.

Self-confident and assertive though he might be on academic matters, Snyder was not particularly concerned with financial administration, for the most part leaving the details of business management to Harry L. Wells, his vice president and business manager. While money raising was not his prime interest, as noted earlier, the university received gifts totaling over $41,000,000 during his administration. While 70 percent of this was accounted for by the Murphy bequest, Snyder supported the efforts of the Department of Development in raising the remaining $13,000,000.

In the course of Snyder's administration the university's net assets rose from just under $54,000,000 to more than $95,000,000. Particularly impressive was the growth in endowment from under $24,000,000 in 1940 to over $62,000,000 in 1949. Once again the major portion of this increase was accounted for by the Murphy bequest.

Snyder's chief contribution to the development of Northwestern, however, was as an academic leader. He believed that the university must attract a more distinguished faculty of scholars as well as teachers and must encourage more research and a greater emphasis on graduate studies. The very strength of his personality and his ability to move vigorously toward his goals enabled him to make Northwestern a far more impressive intellectual center than it had been.

Assessing Snyder's long service to the university, one of his former colleagues commented, "Snyder's career is rather interesting because whatever he was, he performed as though his commitment to that role was the one important commitment of his life." This was true of him as a professor of English, as a departmental chairman, as dean of the Graduate School, as the first dean of faculties and, finally, as president of the university.[89]

*Chancellor and Mrs. J. Roscoe Miller
at the 116th Annual Commencement*

Part Four

"A UNIVERSITY OF
THE HIGHEST GRADE"

*Objective of the Founders as Stated in the First
Annual Report of the Trustees, June 1854*

1949-1974

Dedication of the J. Roscoe Miller Lakefill Campus, 1964 (left to right) John G. Searle, president of the board of trustees, President and Mrs. Miller, and the Hon. Adlai E. Stevenson; (below) aerial view showing a decade of construction on the Evanston campus

7

THE MILLER YEARS

1949-1974

On September 28, 1948, the board of trustees after a year's search selected a successor to President Snyder in preparation for his retirement effective July 1, 1949. At the time of his appointment as twelfth president of Northwestern University, J. Roscoe Miller had been associated with the university for more than twenty years, first as a student, then as a teacher and administrator. A native of Murray, Utah, where he had been born in 1905, Miller had come to Northwestern to study medicine after receiving his B.A. from the University of Utah in 1925. While still a medical student he married a fellow graduate of the University of Utah, Berenice Johannesen. In May 1929, he received his Bachelor of Medicine from Northwestern, followed by his M.D. in 1930 and his M.A. in 1931. In that year he began to practice medicine part time while continuing to do research at the Medical School.

In 1933 Miller became both a member of the medical faculty's teaching staff and assistant dean of the school under Dean Irving Cutter. He continued his practice and became a well-known cardiologist. When Irving Cutter retired in 1941, Miller succeeded to the position of dean of the Medical School. With the exception of a leave of absence during World War II to serve as a commander in the Navy assigned to the Bureau of Medicine and Surgery—where his main concern was to arrange for the most advantageous placement of medical personnel in the various naval hospitals—Miller continued as head of the Medical School until his selection as president of the university. Having had sixteen years of administrative experience, fifteen of them at Northwestern, he was well prepared for the responsibilities he now faced.[1]

One of President Miller's first moves was to select a vice president and dean of faculties, his predecessor having left him free to choose a successor to Dean Fagg, who had moved to the University of Southern California in 1947. Miller's choice fell on Payson S. Wild, dean of the Graduate School of Arts and Sciences at Harvard. Born in Chicago in 1905, Wild had graduated from the University of

The Administration

253

Wisconsin in 1926 before going on to Harvard where he received his Ph.D. in 1931. Wild remained at Harvard as a member of the department of government, being promoted to full professor in 1946, when he also became graduate dean. A specialist in international relations and law, Wild had served on the staff of the U.S. Naval War College at Newport, Rhode Island, and as a member of a policy planning group associated with the Department of State. After becoming dean of the Graduate School he had participated in the establishment in 1948 of the Association of Graduate Schools as an offspring of the Association of American Universities. In the course of the next twenty-five years Miller and Wild developed a working relationship that was well nigh unique both in length and harmony.[2]

The nature of their collaboration stemmed from Miller's view of what it was possible and desirable for the president of such a complex institution to do. His experience as dean of the Medical School had taught him that the finest educational plans were useless unless the university could obtain financial backing to carry them out. In the years ahead he would devote the major part of his energies to procuring the means for the physical and intellectual development of the university and he would delegate to Payson Wild the responsibility of working with the deans in the administration of the schools.

A reorganization of the top layer of the central administration in 1969-70 led to the appointment of Dr. Miller as chancellor and Payson Wild as provost of Northwestern; Robert H. Strotz became president and Raymond W. Mack was appointed vice president and dean of faculties. This organization remained in effect until Provost Wild's retirement in 1973 and Chancellor Miller's retirement the following year (see page 321).

Business   In addition to creating the dual post of vice president and dean of faculties, the earlier reorganization of 1937 had added the title of vice president to that of the business manager. In 1949 this dual position was held by Harry L. Wells who had first become business manager during the administration of President Scott. James M. Brooks who, as an administrative assistant to President Snyder, had shown considerable talent for working on the budget, also stayed on to serve the new president. In 1954 Wells retired and was succeeded as business manager and eventually as vice president by William S. Kerr. The latter had been executive assistant to the president of the Burlington Railroad before coming to Northwestern. In World War II he had served as a lieutenant colonel in the United States Army in the China-Burma-India theater and had also been a member of the Joint United States-Brazil Economic Development Commission during 1952-53. Kerr worked closely with Arthur T. Schmehling, a Northwestern alumnus who had first become associated with the Budget Office in 1936. Subsequently Schmehling became assistant business manager, controller and, in 1969, vice president and controller.

Public Relations   The administration included, as well, Jay J. Gerber, a staff member since 1937, who succeeded Thomas Gonser as director of public relations in 1947 and as vice president in 1950. Three years later Gerber resigned and was replaced by Professor A. C. Van Dusen of the psychology department, who coordinated the academic portion of the 1951 Centennial celebration. Van Dusen served until 1956 but was not replaced by an administrator holding an equivalent position. For the next five years public relations were carried on by the Information Service Office of the Department of Development.

In 1961 a reorganization of administrative functions led to the creation of the position of vice president of planning and development. Franklin M. Kreml was appointed to this post, crowning a lengthy administrative career at Northwestern which included service with the Traffic Institute since its founding in 1936 as well as direction of the Transportation Center since 1955. He resigned in 1971, at which time the position was redesignated as that of vice president for development, and John E. Fields was elected to the post. Fields, an alumnus, had held various administrative positions at the university between 1936 and 1943. During World War II he was a division director of the Japanese language psychological warfare program and after the war he was with the United States State Department. He then served as vice president for development of the University of Southern California under President Fred D. Fagg, Jr., former vice president and dean of faculties at Northwestern. For fifteen years prior to his return to Northwestern, Fields headed several corporations engaged in manufacturing and finance.[3]

Development

Except for the Medical School deanship which he had vacated in assuming the presidency, Dr. Miller inherited a group of deans all of whom had been appointed before he took office. Dr. Richard H. Young became dean of the Northwestern Medical School in the summer of 1949. An alumnus of that school, he had been dean of the University of Utah Medical School before returning to Northwestern.

During the 1950's President Miller met periodically with what was known as the Administrative Council. This included, among others, the vice presidents, the school deans, the university librarian, and the university attorney. During the 1960's this Council was supplemented by a Council of Deans which met to coordinate the administrative and educational policies of the various schools. In addition, the president began to hold weekly meetings with his immediate staff to stay abreast of current developments. He believed that it would not be useful for him to become enmeshed in the details of everyday operations. Thus, he gave his colleagues in administration considerable leeway in acting on their own initiative. He expected to be kept informed and consulted about important matters, reserving for himself the final responsibility for making major policy decisions.[4]

Administrative and Deans' Councils

Within the structure of the university, Miller saw the presidency as a link between the administration, faculty, and students on the one hand, and the board of trustees on the other. The board which appointed Miller consisted of forty-four members, eight of whom were Methodist ministers chosen by their respective midwestern conferences. This church representation formally ended in 1972 (see page 349), reducing the number of trustees to thirty-six. In 1973-74 two alumni from recently graduated classes were added as non-voting trustees serving for two-year terms. All other board members were elected for four-year terms, with the exception of life trustees who were also non-voting members of the board.[5]

Board of Trustees

As a self-perpetuating body, the board elected new members nominated by its committee on nomination of trustees and officers. Meetings of this committee usually were held at Dr. Miller's home where he and the committee, a relatively small group of six or seven including the board president, would canvass the possibilities for new membership and prepare the nominations.

From the outset President Miller worked closely with the board, highly cognizant of the fact that legally the trustees were empowered to exercise final authority on most essential university matters. He made sure that they were kept informed about all important issues and developments. When first appointed, President Miller relied heavily upon the counsel of Kenneth F. Burgess, a distinguished Chicago lawyer and board president from 1937 to 1959. Burgess devoted a great deal of time and thought to university matters and exerted a highly significant influence over the course of events at Northwestern. President Miller also developed fine working relations with the subsequent board presidents: Wesley M. Dixon (1959 to 1964), John C. Searle (1964 to 1970) and Kenneth Zwiener (1970 to 1975). In 1972 the title of the head of the board was changed from president to chairman as part of the new by-laws adopted at that time.[6]

Miller and Burgess agreed fully on how the trustees should operate. They believed that board members should not be assigned to committees dealing with the problems of individual schools but should always regard themselves as being responsible for the university as a whole. Thus the trustee committees were organized around broader concerns such as educational policies, educational properties, and budget and development. An executive committee of the board—usually composed of around fifteen members—was authorized to act on behalf of the entire board between meetings. President Miller believed that the work of the board could be carried out most effectively through committees and that meetings of the full board should, in the main, be briefing and ratifying sessions only. In the course of the years this procedure worked very well except for times of unusual crisis.

"The School Must Hold the Scales in Balance" Although President Miller, like most members of the board, was a conservative in political matters, he never deviated from his commitment to the right of faculty members to hold whatever political and social views they wished and during the worst of the political turbulence on campus defended the principles of academic freedom against all who complained about the views of particular faculty members. To one such correspondent he wrote:

> A university is a repository for the thinking of the past; a forum for the thinking of the present. It must make certain that all sides of a question are heard, examined, and thought deeply upon. Its faculty and students may be as partisan as they feel is demanded by conscience and conviction; but the school as a corporate body, like justice itself, must hold the scales in balance.[7]

Some years earlier when a trustee had urged that one of the professors should be fired because of his radical views, the president had responded, "It is personally distressing (but) a big university contains all kinds, and the president has to grin and bear it."[8]

The president had very definite notions of what the respective responsibilities of the various groups within the university community should be. In academic matters he respected the faculty's right to determine the curriculum, set degree

*President Franklyn Bliss Snyder
with President-elect
J. Roscoe Miller*

*Mrs. Walter Dill Scott,
Mrs. Franklyn Bliss Snyder, and
Mrs. J. Roscoe Miller at the
inauguration of President
Miller, October 7, 1949*

Chancellor J. Roscoe Miller with President-elect Robert H. Strotz, July 1970

*President's
Views on
Division of
Responsibilities*

requirements, and make recommendations on faculty promotions and tenure. In administrative matters he was a staunch advocate of faculty participation in the selection of the school deans and in every instance asked an appointed faculty committee to recommend a list of candidates from which the administration made a choice for final approval by the board of trustees. Over the years this procedure was altered so as to give the faculty a greater part in the selection of the search committees charged with considering candidates for top administrative positions, including those of president and provost.

The changing times eventually brought faculty pressure for a voice in areas that had previously been considered the exclusive preserve of the administration. Though he occasionally had strong reservations about instances of what he considered "faculty interference," President Miller accepted the fact that the nature of university administration was changing. Increasingly faculty representatives began to take part in long-range planning: in guiding the physical development of the campus, including the planning of new buildings; in setting admission policies; and in discussing some aspects of the budget. However, the administration refused to relinquish its prerogatives in such areas as trustee relations and university housekeeping and finance. Decisions on the latter remained, as always, subject to the approval of the board.

*"One
University"*

From the very beginning Dr. Miller was committed to maintaining the record of balanced budgets going back to 1937, a goal that he succeeded in fulfilling for all except one of his twenty-five years as president. A firm believer in the "One University" concept, he contended that the university had an obligation to support and maintain each school according to its merits without undue concern for the sums it could produce in tuition or gifts on its own. In return, he expected the school deans, while exercising considerable autonomy, to operate within the concept of a single university and to follow through on their responsibility to the university's central officers, especially to the dean of faculties. The opportunity for "freebooting" by deans of some schools at the expense of others—opportunities which had arisen because a number of the schools had been acquired by the university as already established and previously independent entities—were now sealed off. The president and dean of faculties drew the reins of central control tighter than they had been before and consolidated the authority of the central administration in managing the university's educational affairs. In contrast to previous years, there was less direct presidential intervention in hiring, promoting, and determining salaries within the individual schools, but firmer centralized direction in setting standards and in formulating and supervising educational policies for the university as a whole.

*Dr. Miller's
Aims*

One of President Miller's primary objectives was to implement and accelerate his predecessor's policy of raising the quality of the faculty. Another was to improve and expand the physical facilities on both campuses. The war years and the postwar flood of students had put an extra strain on university facilities. Referring to the Evanston campus as it appeared in 1949, Miller later recalled, "We were run down—physically run down—living in Quonset huts, going to school in Quonset huts."[9]

To accomplish the first of these aims the university would need to raise faculty salaries and improve both teaching and research facilities. The main library on the Evanston campus badly needed more space and materials. And, as the annual deans' reports made abundantly clear, every one of the schools required both additional space and new equipment. There was no doubt about the new president's commitment to academic excellence nor about his awareness of how this could be achieved and maintained. What remained to be seen was how successful he would be in finding the financial resources necessary for the realization of his plans.

In his inaugural address of October 7, 1949, Miller stressed the importance of privately endowed universities which were able, because of their independence, to provide an environment in which free inquiry could flourish:

> The privately endowed university has contributed immeasurably to our civilization. It developed hand in hand with the system of American enterprise and, indeed, cannot exist in any other economic climate. It still remains one of the allies of those who believe in our democratic society and our traditions of individual freedom. Thinking men will insist today, as they have since 1851, that it be generously supported and kept strong and independent.

The president's strong commitment to private institutions made him reluctant during the early years of his administration in particular to accept public monies except for research purposes. He feared that the use of federal grants for salaries or construction might make Northwestern vulnerable to government interference. This aversion to seeking public funds was shared by Kenneth Burgess during his twenty-two years of service as president of the board of trustees. Subsequently, President Miller modified his position on this issue, but he never ceased to guard fiercely the independence of the university.

Fund-Raising Efforts

The resources available to President Miller for the realization of his plans were limited. Undergraduate tuition was $480 a year and gifts to the university had totaled only $1,562,586 in 1948 and $1,579,584 in 1949. The value of the endowment as of August 31, 1949, was $60,307,804.[10] Clearly these resources would need to be substantially increased even if only the most pressing of the university's needs were to be met, let alone more ambitious undertakings.

Eckstein Bequest

In 1951 Northwestern received an unexpected bequest from the estate of Mrs. Elsie S. Eckstein who, together with her husband, Louis Eckstein, had long been a devoted supporter of musical life in the area.* Income from the fund, known as the Elsie S. and Louis Eckstein Music Endowment Fund, was designated for the benefit of the School of Music, to be used for "furthering generally the understanding and enjoyment of music."[11] Because of these broad terms, the money was available for a wide variety of uses. Over the next twenty-five years President Miller's administration was to succeed in attracting more than $270,000,000 to Northwestern, including large gifts by individual donors, cumulative contributions gathered in the course of specific drives, and grants from foundations and government agencies.

---

*On October 26, 1953, the president reported to the trustees that the value of the bequest was just over $4,000,000.

As early as the 1930's President Scott had proposed a fund drive as part of the university's Centennial celebration in 1951. President Snyder carried the idea forward, but it was not until after Miller became president in 1949 that definite steps were taken to develop a complete Centennial program. It was conceived of as both a drive for funds and a series of academic events.

Centennial Campaign

President Miller announced the fund drive in a letter to the faculty, spelling out what the money would be used for.[12] The goal was to raise $8,250,000, of which $2,500,000 was to be for endowment; $3,000,000 for a new classroom building on the Evanston campus; $2,000,000 for an evening study hall; and $750,000 for a field house. Any balance was to be used for additions to the Medical and Law school library holdings and equipment for the Music and Dental schools, as well as professorships and scholarships.

A committee of the board of trustees was asked to take an active part in the campaign which was placed under the direction of the vice president and director of development, Jay Gerber. Faculty, students, and alumni also participated in the drive. In his letter to the faculty the following summer, Miller reported that the senior class of 1950 had given $8,500 toward scholarship endowment and that the students had agreed to pay a special activity fee of $5.00 annually for five years to go to the fund for the field house, the aim being to raise $40,000 a year over the five-year span.[13]

The academic part of the Centennial celebration was planned by a faculty committee working in concert with a coordinating committee. The latter included representatives from all segments of the university community as well as alumni, with A. C. Van Dusen, assistant to the president, assuming the role of overall coordinator.[14] In all, 372 members of the faculty served on the committees that planned the meetings, convocations, and conferences which approximately 60,000 people attended.[15]

Academic Celebration

The academic festival began with a Founders' Day convocation on January 28, 1951, and ended with another Founders' Day convocation a year later. A special ceremony on February 4, 1951, honored founder John Evans, whose grandson and great-grandson, John Evans II and John Evans III, were present. In the course of the year Northwestern organized six conferences on topics of major interest: International Understanding and World Peace; Science, Technology, and World Resources; The Arts in Modern Society; Problems of an Aging Population; Communications; and Individual, Group, and Government in the Modern Economy. The roster of distinguished speakers included men from many areas of public and academic life. Among them were Gordon Dean, chairman of the Atomic Energy Commission; Arthur Goldberg, then legal counsel for the AFL-CIO; Emmanuel Goldenweiser, Federal Reserve Board economist; Sumner Schlichter, professor of business economics at Harvard; Philip Hauser, population expert on the faculty of the University of Chicago; and historian Jacques Barzun of Columbia University. Concerts, theater productions, and an art exhibit were prepared and presented by Northwestern faculty and students and drew enthusiastic audiences from outside as well as from within the university community.

The Centennial Convocation of December 2, 1951, represented the climax of the celebration. On that occasion the university gave awards to 100 outstanding men and women from the six states of the original Northwest Territory. Recipients of the awards were chosen for having made "a substantial contribution to society." Nominations were made by faculty, staff, students, and alumni of Northwestern, representatives of chambers of commerce and federated women's clubs in each of the states involved and by faculty members of other Big Ten universities. These nominations were screened by a committee composed of Wheeler Sammons, the publisher of Marquis *Who's Who*, Robert C. Preble, director of Encyclopaedia Britannica, Inc. and General Robert E. Wood, chairman of the board of Sears, Roebuck and Company.

Among those receiving awards were persons who had distinguished themselves *Awards* in the professions, the arts, theater, music, public affairs, politics, religion, athletics, and academic disciplines. They ranged from writers Carl Sandburg, John Dos Passos, Thornton Wilder, and Edna Ferber, to United States Senators Paul H. Douglas, Everett Dirksen, and Robert A. Taft; from actor Alfred Lunt and actress Lynn Fontanne to architect Frank Lloyd Wright and Nobel prize winning chemist, Harold C. Urey; from Bishop Wallace E. Conkling to Henry Ford II; from Robert Maynard Hutchins, ex-chancellor of the University of Chicago, to that university's ex-football coach, Amos Alonzo Stagg. As the recipients prepared to come forward to receive their awards, the audience was asked to hold its applause until all the certificates had been presented. All went as planned until A. A. Stagg appeared, then the crowd burst into loud applause for the "Grand Old Man" of the Midway who had for so long been Northwestern's arch foe on the athletic field.

The university's alumni and friends were sufficiently impressed not only by what Northwestern had already accomplished but by what it had the potential to achieve in the years ahead that by January 25, 1952, the president was able to report that the Centennial campaign had been concluded successfully with a total of $8,405,952 pledged and subscribed, thereby exceeding the original goal. A major achievement was the raising of $3,000,000 for the classroom building which was to be called Kresge Centennial Hall with $500,000 coming from the Kresge Foundation to begin with, a further $1,000,000 later, and $1,500,000 from 6,000 individuals including trustees, alumni, faculty, students, and friends. A substantial gift from another donor, Foster G. McGaw, made possible a much-needed field house which was to be named McGaw Memorial Hall.[16]

Six years later Northwestern celebrated its 100th Commencement by inviting the presidents of the private universities in the Association of American Universities to receive honorary degrees. Sixteen of those invited were on hand for the occasion on June 16, 1958.* The Commencement speaker was President C. W. de Kiewiet of the University of Rochester.

Though the Centennial drive had been successful, it soon became obvious that a long-range program for funding was necessary. President Miller presented such a plan to the trustees in 1955. It set no specific time limit nor did it recommend an

*The presidents of Brown; California Institute of Technology; Catholic University; University of Chicago; Clark; Columbia; Duke; Harvard; McGill; New York University; University of Pennsylvania; University of Rochester; Stanford; Tulane; Vanderbilt; and Washington University.

*Long-Range
Plan of 1955* immediate high pressure campaign, but it did name a target figure of $138,500,000, of which $40,000,000 was to be earmarked for faculty salaries. Among the items to be financed by this drive would be a new dormitory and various other facilities on both campuses. Some of the money would be used for student aid.[17]

By the late 1950's it had become apparent that if the physical facilities of the Evanston campus were to be improved, it was imperative that the university acquire additional space. At the time the campus east of Sheridan Road was confined to the relatively narrow strip of eighty acres along the lake shore, bounded by Sheridan Road on the west and on the north and south by land belonging to the city of Evanston or private owners.

In 1959 President Miller asked the university's business manager, William S. Kerr, to explore the alternatives for future expansion. These narrowed down to three: moving westward across Sheridan Road into Evanston; building an "asphalt campus" by crowding new structures onto existing space and eliminating green areas such as Deering Meadow; or going eastward into Lake Michigan.

After studying these options at some length, Kerr's staff came to the following conclusion: the acquisition of land to the west of the campus would impair the university's relation with Evanston because it would take valuable real estate off the tax rolls; crowding the existing campus with new buildings would destroy its open and spacious character. This left one other course, to expand eastward by filling in part of the lake. Moreover, it was estimated that this could be done at only one third of what it would cost to buy land in Evanston.

*The Plan for
a Lakefill
Campus* The idea of a lakefill campus was not new. As far back as 1893 there had been a plan which "called for filling in a section of the lake for a polo field, a small boat harbor, and other recreational facilities."[18] It had been discarded because shortage of space was not an acute problem in those days. In the 1930's there had been some renewed discussion of a similar plan but the idea was dropped when the university began to feel the impact of the depression. In 1960, however, the plan went forward.

After studying the recommendation for expansion onto lakefill, the president accepted the proposal, obtained approval from the trustees, and on October 14, 1960, publicly announced that the campus would be extended eastward approximately 1,000 feet, adding about seventy-four acres of new land at a cost of approximately $5,200,000. He emphasized that the fill portion of the plan would be paid for entirely from new funds and would in no way affect the $138,500,000 required for the 1955 plan which included improved faculty salaries.[19]

As finally approved, the plan called for the purchase from the state of Illinois of 152 acres of submerged lake land at the cost of $100 per acre. Of this amount, 74 acres was to be filled in as soon as it was feasible, the remainder to be left for future development. There was much red tape to be cut before the university obtained permission to proceed with this venture, since approval had to be secured from the Evanston city council, the Cook County board, the Illinois legislature, the governor of the state, and the U.S. Corps of Engineers. Obtaining approval from the city and county did not prove difficult, but securing permission from the state legislature turned out to be more complicated. Since the state owned title to the lake bed Northwestern's use of the latter required a specific amendment to existing state statutes.

Northwestern University lakefront development bills were introduced into both houses on February 7, 1961. Both Alban Weber, the university counsel, and Business Manager Kerr spent a great deal of time lobbying in Springfield. Their efforts were rewarded when the bills received unanimous approval—by the Senate on March 25, and the House on May 11, 1961. Such unanimity in the legislature was a rare event indeed! Governor Otto Kerner signed the measure on May 26, 1961, and the Army Corps of Engineers issued a permit for the new campus construction on September 6, 1961, the report indicating "that the lakefill area is sufficiently removed from established lake shipping routes as to pose no problem."[20]

With these legal hurdles overcome, the next problem was how to pay for the project. As Dr. Miller later recalled, on Christmas eve 1961 he was sitting at home wondering what to do with seventy-four acres of lake bottom under nine feet of water when the telephone rang. The voice at the other end informed the president that a friend of the university wanted anonymously to pledge $4,000,000 for the lakefill project. Now the plan could be put into effect. *The Christmas Eve Call*

In October 1962, responding to a suggestion that faculty be brought into the planning procedure, President Miller appointed a Faculty Planning Committee, chaired by Professor Clarence L. Ver Steeg of the history department, to propose how the new campus was to be arranged and laid out.* There had been no such comprehensive plan for the development of the campus since the early years of the university's history. A Special Community Planning Committee, composed of trustees, administrative officers and associates had been established by the trustees in 1955 to concern itself with the deterioration of the areas adjacent to the Evanston campus. The committee had held several meetings during 1955-56 to consider such problems as zoning, traffic flow, and street widening and had invited Evanston city officials to several of the sessions.[21] But it was in no way concerned with the kind of long-range planning on which the Faculty Planning Committee now embarked under the energetic leadership of Professor Ver Steeg. *Faculty Planning Committee*

The Faculty Planning Committee concerned itself with the future physical aspect of the Evanston campus as well as with the educational goals which the new facilities were intended to promote.† A major objective was to insure that new buildings would be sited according to a comprehensive plan which made sense both from a functional and aesthetic viewpoint. The committee in time spawned a number of subcommittees which specialized in dealing with subjects that ranged from architecture to para-education.[22]

The vice president for planning and development, Franklin Kreml, enthusiastically supported the activities of the Faculty Planning Committee knowing that its work was vital to the success of his own endeavors. Dean Wild asked Ver Steeg and his committee to meet with Kreml and with Vice President and Business Manager Kerr so that their respective efforts in planning and financing the con-

---

*A precedent for this had been set in 1960 with the formation of the Faculty Planning Committee for the Library also under the chairmanship of Professor Clarence Ver Steeg (see page 279).

†See pages 279 and 280 for details of the plan.

struction of the new campus could be coordinated.[23] Letters from Dean Wild and Vice President Kreml to the faculty kept the latter informed about the work of the Faculty Planning Committee. As the committee approached the conclusion of its task, Dean Wild asked it to report to the administration through the faculty's Committee on Educational Policies as a way of establishing an exchange of ideas among these two important faculty committees,* the administration, and the Department of Planning and Development.[24]

In June 1964, the Faculty Planning Committee's report passed for review to the Administrative Policies and Planning Committee composed of senior administrative officers with Jeremy Wilson, director of the Department of Planning, as secretary.† This committee prepared the final recommendations to be submitted to President Miller. On December 6, 1966, the president laid the plan before the board which endorsed it unanimously.[25]

Between the appointment of the Faculty Planning Committee in October 1962, and the trustees' endorsement of the plan four years later, numerous administrators and faculty members cooperated in the complex process of producing the First Plan for the Seventies, with the Faculty Planning Committee and the Committee on Educational Policies coordinating faculty input and the Administrative Policies and Planning Committee coordinating input from the administration.

First Plan for the Seventies   At a special news briefing on December 13, 1966, the president announced the First Plan for the Seventies to the public. It called for a campaign to raise $180,000,000 for the improvement of Northwestern's academic and physical resources in five years, with $35,000,000 slated for academic programs and the balance for construction. Throughout its five-year term, the plan received some criticism for concentrating so heavily upon "bricks and mortar," but the president and the planners felt that without a suitable physical environment and adequate facilities many of the university's educational aims could not be carried out. Actually donors responded more to people and programs than building plans—for of the more than $181,000,000 raised only $70,000,000 was for buildings, the remainder going toward faculty salaries, student aid, programs, and research.

The plan called for an increase in undergraduate enrollment from 6,000 to 6,500 and an increase in full time graduate enrollment from 1,900 to 3,000. It proposed that financial aid for undergraduates be increased from covering 22 percent to including 34 to 35 percent of the student body and that aid to graduate students be increased by 66 percent. The plan also recommended additional scholarship aid for medical, dental, and law students.

To encourage closer relations between students and faculty by providing smaller classes, the planners urged that 110 new members be added to the faculty. They also recommended that the salaries of the existing faculty be raised. Curricular changes proposed by the plan emphasized interdisciplinary studies and the need for more fine arts programs, tutorials, seminars, and independent study options.

*For discussion of the major faculty committees during this period see pages 284 through 287.
†The Administrative Policies and Planning Committee was established in September 1964 to channel the administration's contribution to the First Plan for the Seventies.

In addition to housing facilities for 1,000 graduate and 1,200 undergraduate students, the plan called for the construction of eight major buildings on the Evanston campus and the remodeling of five existing facilities.[26]

Between December 1966, and December 1971, President Miller, Franklin Kreml and his staff, and the trustees, friends, and alumni of Northwestern worked with great determination to achieve the $180,000,000 goal. Their labors were rewarded. On January 10, 1972, it was announced that in addition to the target amount, the drive had brought in an extra $1,500,000.[27]

Friends and Alumni

During his term, President Miller received substantial help in the development program from numerous organizations of alumni and friends who were interested in the university as a whole, or in a particular school or activity. These organizations included the Northwestern University Associates, the John Evans Club, and the Alumni Association.

Associates

The Northwestern University Associates—established, it will be recalled, in 1928 to enlist the friendship of leading Chicago industrialists, businessmen, and professional people who had not attended Northwestern—continued to flourish during the Miller years under the leadership of Elmer Stevens and Tilden Cummings. At quarterly luncheons in Chicago, faculty and occasionally students presented lectures, panel discussions, and other informative programs to the Associates on subjects ranging from medical research to student attitudes. Like the John Evans Club, the Associates have an annual festive Waa-Mu dinner and theater party attended by 250 to 300 members and spouses.

In 1974 the Associates had 350 members—about 25 candidates nominated by the trustees' committee on Associates being invited to membership annually. While, as a condition to their acceptance of membership, Associates are not solicited for funds for the university, they frequently give significant assistance in opening doors for the university's fund-raising staff and volunteers.

John Evans Club

The idea for the John Evans Club, organized as what is known at most universities as a "support group," was introduced in 1952 by Vice President and Business Manager Harry L. Wells. Two years later the club, with membership limited to alumni,* was officially organized with fifty-eight founding members, each of whom had either donated a lump sum of $10,000 or had pledged to give $1,000 per year for ten years.†

Members of the John Evans Club were invited to participate in the life of the university by attending lectures, plays, concerts, and other university functions. Additionally, the club has an active social program, including an annual formal dinner, a post-graduation brunch, a pre-football game luncheon, a ladies' luncheon and a pre-performance dinner followed by the Waa-Mu show. By 1974 membership in the club had grown to 472 and in the twenty years since its founding, John Evans Club members had contributed $62,395,000 to Northwestern.[28]

A number of other support groups, with somewhat lesser gift requirements, have followed in the wake of the John Evans Club in various schools and divisions

---

*A few non-alumni "special friends" were voted to membership in the first few years of the club's existence.
†In September 1974 this was changed to a commitment of $15,000 over a period of fifteen years or a bequest of $25,000, and non-alumni were admitted on the same basis as alumni.

at Northwestern. The John Henry Wigmore Club, supporting the Law School, was founded in 1962; the G. V. Black Society, concerned with the Dental School was organized in 1965, and the Nathan Smith Davis Club, devoted to the Medical School, in 1966. In the 1970's several of the Evanston schools also decided to establish separate alumni associations similar to those which had done such good work on behalf of the Chicago schools. The Graduate School of Management developed its own alumni organization with a Dean's Council for special donors.

Special Interest Alumni Special interest groups formed recently include NUMBALUMS (Northwestern University Marching Band Alumni) organized in 1973, who came to enliven the annual Homecoming festivities; the Friends of Art, also organized in 1973; the Library Council, established in 1974; and the Music Society, founded in 1975.

The years 1954-55 brought marked changes in the organization and conduct of alumni relations. In 1954 the Alumni Association eliminated the payment of dues as a requirement for membership largely in response to alumni complaints about double solicitation each year by the Alumni Association for dues and by the Alumni Fund for a gift. At the same time all alumni relations were placed under the administration of a single director responsible to the vice president for public relations (later development).

Alumni Relations In 1955 the Alumni Relations Department moved to the John Evans Center at 1800 Sheridan Road, where it remains to this day. Two new programs, established in 1956, set up a system of regional leadership and responsibility for a variety of alumni activities, including assistance in student recruiting as well as fund raising. For those particularly interested in Northwestern's athletic programs, the Benchwarmers group was created in 1957 by Stuart Holcomb, director of athletics. Both this group and members of the Touchdown Club, founded later by Athletic Director W. H. H. (Tippy) Dye, gave generous support to the programs of the athletic department.

When membership in the Alumni Association was opened automatically to all alumni, the Alumni Fund became the single gift solicitation agency for the university. The number of contributors to the Fund grew steadily from 1954 until 1964, when more than 18,000 alumni—about 20 percent of the total alumni body at the time—sent donations to it. In the course of the following eight years, however, the fund suffered a steady decline in contributions, reaching bottom in 1972. The fall-off was attributed to various causes, including suspension of the publication of the *Alumni News* in the summer of 1969, discontinuation of the class representative system, reduced alumni club activity, annual turnover of the staff director of the association for the six years from 1965 to 1971, and the student disturbances at the close of the decade. By 1971 publication of the *Alumni News* was resumed.

In 1972 Ray Willemain, university personnel director and an employee of the university since his graduation in 1948, was appointed director of alumni relations by Vice President Fields, a former director of the Alumni Fund. On Director Willemain's initiative, responsibility for the *Alumni News* and for the Alumni Fund was transferred from University Relations and the Department of Development, respectively, to the office of Alumni Relations. In addition, alumni club programs were re-emphasized and the class representative system was brought back. Moreover, he moved to decentralize the conduct of alumni relations by encouraging all schools of the university to have their own alumni organizations, activities and fund raising programs. The organization of the Wigmore, Black, Davis, and other individual school alumni clubs were examples of this new direction in alumni relations as was the establishment of the Young Alumni Council in 1971. Composed of alumni out of school one to ten years, the Council was organized in response to the younger generation's request for special programs adapted to their needs and financial status.

Meanwhile, the Associate Alumnae continued to sponsor a number of women's activities such as the fall Woman's Day at Northwestern—attended by 550 in 1974—as well as a series of continuing education courses. The organization also raises money for scholarships in connection with the sale of tickets to the Waa-Mu Show. *Associate Alumnae*

One of the most significant alumni events has been the annual Alumni Awards Ceremony at which distinguished alumni are honored by the Association. The Alumni Medal is the highest honor accorded, followed by a number of awards which recognize achievement in a profession or field of endeavor (Merit) as well as for loyal service to the university and the Alumni Association (Service).[29]

Gifts to the university from the business community showed significant growth during the Miller years. In 1950-51, corporate gifts totaled approximately $500,000. By 1973-74, corporations were providing Northwestern with some $2,651,911 in annual support. *Corporate Gifts*

During the Centennial campaign (1949-52), corporate giving was primarily at the local level. Then, spurred by a 1953 decision by the New Jersey Supreme Court that it was within the rights of corporations to make gifts for which the corporation received only indirect benefits, many businesses established their own foundations and philanthropy became more sophisticated.

In the course of the 1960's, Northwestern expanded its corporate solicitation to the national level, and during the five-year campaign for Northwestern's First Plan for the Seventies, when support from the business community reached its height, corporations contributed a total of $15,400,000. Some of the major gifts and pledges received during this period included: $600,000 from Standard Oil (Indiana); $300,000 from both International Harvester and Commonwealth Edison; $250,000 from two major Chicago banks—Continental and First National —and Inland Steel; $200,000 from Field Enterprises; and $150,000 each from IBM and Texaco.[30]

While President Miller concentrated upon raising funds for the university from individuals and corporations, the responsibility for dealing with foundations fell largely upon the dean of faculties. Dean Wild worked with the school deans, members of the faculty, and fellow administrators in approaching foundations to obtain support for a large variety of educational projects. This was a genuinely cooperative effort: sometimes the initiative came from a dean, sometimes from faculty members and sometimes from the dean of faculties himself. Success in obtaining funds obviously depended both upon the merits of the proposal and on the foundation officers' confidence in the university administration and faculty. *Foundation and Government Grants*

To establish such confidence in Northwestern's academic and administrative staff Dean Wild made a point of maintaining a close relationship with foundation representatives and arranged for them to visit the university to observe it at first hand. However, various other members of the university community also played crucial roles in securing particular grants. To give just a few examples, in 1952-54 President of the Board Kenneth F. Burgess and President Miller spearheaded the approach to the Kresge Foundation which resulted in a grant of $1,500,000 for the construction of Kresge Centennial Hall. Similarly, the 1956 grants from the Commonwealth and Markle funds which made possible the inauguration of the six-year medical program, were largely due to the efforts of Dean Richard H. Young of the Medical School and his energetic associate dean, John Cooper. The Kellogg Foundation grants in 1969 for the Center for the Teaching Professions and the School of Education were obtained through the combined efforts of President Miller and Dean B. J. Chandler of the School of Education. Robert H. Strotz, who had succeeded Simeon Leland as dean of the College of Arts and Sciences in 1966, was chiefly responsible for securing half a million dollars for a chair in the humanities from the Avalon Foundation that year. The dean of the School of Journalism, I. W. Cole, was instrumental in obtaining a $1,000,000 grant from the Gannett Foundation for Urban Journalism and a matching $1,000,000 grant from the Ford Foundation in 1972. At the Technological Institute both Dean Harold B. Gotaas and Dean Walter S. Owen assumed leadership in sponsoring proposals and projects calling for foundation assistance.

Offices Concerned with Research As the importance of securing grants for research and educational projects became evident a number of offices were set up to specialize in dealing with potential sources for funds. John A. D. Cooper,* associate dean of faculties and dean of science, assisted in organizing the Office of Research Coordination in 1964.[31] Five years later the Foundation Research Planning Office was set up under the aegis of the vice president for development, Franklin Kreml, further to encourage the effective exploration of grant possibilities from private foundations and government agencies.[32]

In 1971 Northwestern gave additional recognition and encouragement to research by establishing the post of vice president for science and research. Dean Walter S. Owen of the Technological Institute was chosen to fill this post. He, in turn, set up the Office of Research and Sponsored Programs which combined the functions of the Research Coordination Office and the Foundation Research Planning Office.[33] The administrator reported directly to the vice president for science and research. His role was to encourage faculty to submit grant proposals and to cooperate with administrators in pursuing financial support for research from public and private funding agencies.

In 1973 the post of vice president for science and research was redesignated as that of vice president for research and dean of science. Elected to this position at that time was David Mintzer, a member of both the College and the Technological Institute faculty since 1962 as well as associate dean of the latter.

---

*The post of dean of science was created by a vote of the trustees at their meeting on June 10, 1963.

In the course of the Miller years, Northwestern succeeded in obtaining support for a considerable number of projects from various foundations. One of the largest grants received by the university came from the Ford Foundation in 1956-57. Totaling $7,658,000, it included $4,958,000 to be used for faculty salaries and $2,700,000 for instruction in the Medical School. Shortly thereafter—in 1960 —the same foundation agreed to underwrite the Master of Arts in Teaching program. Other programs at Northwestern funded by the Ford Foundation during these years included International Legal Studies, Inter-Societal Studies, Urban Affairs, Criminal Law and Police Advisory Programs, African Studies and Urban Journalism. In all these endeavors, which often took many months and involved numerous trips and voluminous correspondence, Dean Wild was ably assisted by the school deans—especially Dean Simeon Leland of the College, Deans Harold Havighurst and John Ritchie of the Law School and those mentioned earlier, as well as by various faculty members who had excellent foundation contacts of their own. All told, Northwestern received a total of $16,878,686 from the Ford Foundation in the course of the Miller years.

During this same period, the Carnegie Foundation funded projects ranging from political science curriculum revision in 1953, to an education-psychology program in 1957 and a teacher education program in 1966—in all totaling $1,626,475. Other foundations which also gave substantial support to various Northwestern projects included the Commonwealth Fund, the Sloan Foundation, the John A. Hartford Foundation, the Robert R. McCormick Trust, and the Russell Sage Foundation. Northwestern received support as well from numerous government agencies, including the National Science Foundation, United States Office of Education, Advanced Research Projects Agency, and the National Endowment for the Arts and Humanities.[34]

In 1949 when President Miller assumed his post outside grants for research from government and other sources totaled $2,060,894. For 1973-74 the amount was $31,294,481 with the federal government providing $27,697,560 of this sum.[35]

The university's success in attracting grants led to a great burgeoning in the volume of research carried out at Northwestern, but it also raised some problems. Chief among these was to what degree the faculty should be expanded on the basis of grant money which could not be counted on as a permanent financial resource. What would the university's commitment be to such faculty when the grant money came to an end? Because of their awareness of the difficulties that would ensue if the university became overly dependent on the amount of overhead money accruing from government research grants, the administration and the trustees kept a watchful eye on the volume of such research. In spite of these precautions the sharp curtailment in federal spending that followed upon the downward turn of the economy in the early 1970's, did have an unfavorable impact on the university, especially on the Graduate School, many of whose students were dependent on faculty research funds and government fellowships for financial support. Nevertheless, the university continued to support research to its fullest ability.

A shortage of all resources during and after the war brought construction to a halt, the only structures to be built on the Evanston campus during Snyder's term

Lindheimer Astronomical Research Center, designated as "outstanding" in its class by the American Institute of Architects, one of the North Shore's better known landmarks

Rebecca Crown Center, completed 1968, housing the university's chief administrative offices

Circular reading area and open stacks in one of the University Library's towers (top); a view of the University Library from the main entrance of Norris University Center

Construction
1949-1974

being the Northwestern Apartments in 1946 and the Cresap Laboratory, an extension of Swift Hall, which opened in 1949. Given the rapid increase in enrollment in the early postwar years this lack of construction resulted in severe overcrowding in every area of university life from living quarters to classrooms and laboratory space.

The building program of the subsequent twenty-five years was to transform the physical aspect of the university in a most dramatic fashion, particularly the

NEW BUILDING CONSTRUCTION AND MAJOR REMODELING 1949-1974
Evanston Campus

Educational Buildings and Lakefill

Cresap Laboratory	Biological Sciences	1949	$ 472,051
Van deGraaf	Physics Accelerator	1952	402,409
Ipatieff Laboratory	Chemistry	1953	48,101
Kresge Centennial Hall	CAS-Classrooms & Offices	1955	1,656,709
Kresge Underground	Storage	1955	289,298
Searle Hall	Student Health	1960	1,019,271
Opera Workshop	Music School	1961	28,897
Tech Library Addition	Science & Engineering Library	1961	430,391
Tech Physics Addition	Science & Engineering	1963	266,109
Tech East Addition	Science & Engineering	1963	6,638,099
Music Library Building	Music School Library	1963	65,075
Alice Millar Chapel	University Chapel	1964	3,220,657
J. Roscoe Miller Campus	74 Acres for Campus*	1964	7,950,906
Vogelback Center & Computer	Computing Center & Computer	1964	2,354,349
Lindheimer Astro. Center	Astronomy	1966	1,472,741
Tech Addition	Chemistry	1969	245,750
University Library	Library	1969	12,552,379
O. T. Hogan	Biological Sciences	1970	6,328,935
Cresap Lab Refurbishing	Biological Sci. & Psychology	1971	964,332
Leverone Hall	Graduate School of Management }	1972	11,196,506
Education Building	School of Education		
Frances Searle Building	Communicative Disorders	1972	6,786,011
Scott Hall Remodeling	Student Affairs & Poli. Sci.	1973	1,074,662
			$ 65,463,638

Residences

Sargent Hall	Dormitory	1950	$ 1,623,081
Shepard Hall	Dormitory	1952	737,121
Bobb Hall	Dormitory	1955	780,027
McCulloch Hall	Dormitory	1955	780,027
Elder Hall	Dormitory	1959	1,678,251
Shepard Hall Addition	Dormitory	1960	325,833
Allison Hall	Dormitory	1960	2,097,486
Dryden Hall (Purchased)	Married Students Apartments	1960	1,152,201
Land for Engelhart Hall	Graduate Housing	1967	501,240
Engelhart Hall	Graduate Housing	1970	5,475,177
Foster-Walker Complex	Dormitory	1972	6,556,749
			$ 21,707,193

Other

McGaw Hall	Auditorium	1952	$	1,398,786
Plant Maintenance Building	Buildings & Grounds	1958		354,121
Ticket Office	Athletic Department	1959		89,854
Sports Center	Athletic Department	1963		1,270,371
Rebecca Crown Center	General Administration	1968		3,502,780
Central Utility Plant	Heating & Air Conditioning	1968		4,057,020
Norris University Center	Student Union	1972		8,637,648
Dyche Stadium (New Turf)	Athletic Department	1974		698,300
Blomquist Recreation Center	Student Recreation Center	1974		559,811
				$ 20,568,691
				$107,739,522

SOURCE: Department of Planning Report #44, January 1975 and January 1976.

*In 1968 a ten acre addition at the south end of the lakefill was completed.

Evanston campus. It was carried out in two phases: the first in the 1950's, the second in the 1960's and 1970's, developing in concert with the construction of the lakefill campus. As the names of many of the buildings on the Department of Planning's list of New Building Construction and Major Remodeling 1949-1974 indicate, several friends of the university made very large contributions to this endeavor (see above). Numerous others made possible the construction or furnishing of particular facilities within the new buildings.[36]

Several prominent Chicago architectural firms participated in the planning of the buildings which transformed both campuses during the Miller years, including Holabird, Root and Burgee; Skidmore, Owings and Merrill; Loebl, Schlossman, Bennett and Dart; Andrew L. Heard and Associates, Ltd.; Jensen and Halstead Ltd.; C. F. Murphy and Associates; and Bertrand Goldberg Associates.

Evanston Campus: Dormitories

The first of these firms set the pattern for the nine dormitories constructed during this period, beginning with Sargent Hall which opened in 1951. In 1960 the university purchased the former Oak Crest Hotel which was renamed Dryden Hall and designated for the use of graduate students. The long-time concern of Evanston residents that the university owned too much tax exempt land was reawakened by the university's purchase of the Oak Crest Hotel. Vice President Kerr responded by pointing out that during the period 1950-1960 the university had sold sixty-eight separate pieces of real estate in Evanston with a total value of $2,187,850, all but three of which had been returned to the tax rolls.[37]

Kresge and McGaw

The first of the major classroom buildings to be erected in the postwar period was Kresge Centennial Hall, completed in 1955. The only other building put up on the Evanston campus during this decade was McGaw Hall which provided the first proper facilities for indoor spectator sports events since the razing of the old Patten Gymnasium in 1939. Possessing a floor space of 54,000 square feet, McGaw Hall was described at the time of its completion as "the largest auditorium north of Chicago's loop."[38] In August 1954, the Second Assembly of the World Council of Churches was held there and at a special convocation arranged on this occasion, the university awarded an LL.D. degree to President Dwight D. Eisenhower.

Searle Student Health Center   The construction of buildings whose prime feature was their economical and practical use of space at a reasonable cost, met Northwestern's most pressing need for dormitory, classroom, office, and laboratory facilities in the postwar period. With these most urgent requirements satisfied, the university could take a longer view, paying more attention to aesthetic considerations. As one commentator noted, "The building of the fifties was to meet the needs of the present; the building of the sixties . . . progressively aimed toward the goals of the future."[39] In April 1961, the Searle Student Health Center opened its doors providing the university health service with adequate facilities for the first time, including an outpatient clinic as well as a forty-four bed infirmary.

Tech Additions   The space available to the Technological Institute increased substantially during the early sixties. The stack capacity of the science and engineering library was doubled with the completion of a two-story addition in 1961; while two years later the massive Tech East addition was completed. Planning for this larger addition had begun in 1959 when Northwestern was awarded a contract by the Advanced Research Projects Agency of the Department of Defense "for basic research and graduate education in materials." The cost of the addition was met in large part by funds from the Murphy endowment, supplemented by grants from the National Institutes of Health and the National Science Foundation. At the time, Dean Harold Gotaas cited three reasons for the expansion: growth in graduate programs; increased research (the dollar volume of research at Tech had increased ten times during the previous decade, reaching $3,100,000 in 1963); and the growth of interdisciplinary education. Since the opening of the building in 1942, three new departments and two major interdisciplinary programs had been added.

Coon Sports Center and Anderson Hall   The athletic department also improved its facilities at this time with the construction of two buildings adjacent to McGaw Hall. One, the Byron S. Coon Sports Center, included tennis courts, an ice rink and a clubroom containing the Thomas King lounge. The other, the Harold H. Anderson Hall, housed team rooms, offices, handball courts and workout rooms. Completed in 1963, the Center was designed by the firm of Skidmore, Owings and Merrill.

Alice Millar Religious Center   The fall of the same year saw the dedication of the Alice Millar Chapel and Religious Center, made possible by a gift from Mr. and Mrs. Foster McGaw. The main chapel is named for Mr. McGaw's mother, Alice Millar, and the smaller Jeanne Vail Meditation Chapel is named for a daughter of Mrs. McGaw. The third building in the complex, Parkes Hall, is named for Dr. William Parkes who in 1952 donated the land the buildings stand on. The complex was designed by Jensen and Halstead. The themes symbolized in twelve striking stained glass windows which adorn the main chapel were proposed by a faculty committee appointed by Chaplain Ralph Dunlop. Alumni Charles W. Spofford and his wife gave the Aeolian Skinner organ to the chapel.

Basic to the development plans which determined the second and major phase of the building program of the Miller years was the decision to build the $7,950,906 J. Roscoe Miller Campus on lakefill. Skidmore, Owings and Merrill was the firm commissioned to carry out this massive undertaking. Once governmental approval for the project was received, the university asked for bids for construction of the campus and on March 5, 1962, awarded the contract to the low bidder, the Mary-Missouri Construction Company Joint Venture. The contract called for stone and steel piling for a dike around the periphery of the project (the stone core with rocks to be brought from a quarry near Romeo, Illinois, to be transported by truck and then barge via the Chicago Sanitary and Ship Canal) as well as for sand for the fill behind the steel and stone breakwater.

Construction began on July 11, 1962, and suddenly, without warning, Northwestern found itself engulfed in a nightmarish controversy.[40] It turned out that the Mary-Missouri Company had contracted with the Bethlehem Steel Company to obtain the sand from a harbor which the steel company was having dredged in Porter County, Indiana, and President Miller was deluged by letters and calls accusing the university of conniving with the steel company and the construction company in a scheme which would destroy the Indiana sand dunes, an area treasured by biologists, geologists, nature lovers, and vacationers.

Lakefill Controversy

Typical of the letters which poured in was one from a prominent Evanstonian which urged the university to buy up the contract and use "free fill from the Sanitary District." To this and similar letters the president replied that the university had not known the source of the sand fill when the contract was signed, that it had since asked that the contractor obtain a release from the steel company, but that this had proved impossible. Since Northwestern was bound by contract, there was nothing to be done.[41] In response to the torrent of angry protest the university sent out a form letter explaining that Northwestern had had no dealings whatsoever with the steel company and that, in any case, the sand was coming from the bed of a harbor—not the dunes—which was being dredged by a company over which the university had no control.[42]

On July 25, 1962, the president of the trustees, Wesley M. Dixon, received a delegation from the Save the Dunes Council demanding an end to the "destruction of the dunes."[43] Earlier, this council had issued a "Call to Arms" to save the dunes and on April 10, 1962, Senator Paul H. Douglas of Illinois made a public statement to the effect that Northwestern "should use fill from the Sanitary District's deepening of the Cal-Sag Canal, and that only those with a wanton sense of cruelty can proceed now that a superior alternative lies open." The barrage of letters and calls continued over the summer and fall of 1962, coming from such groups as the American Society of Landscape Artists, the Garden Club of Oak Park and River Forest, the Prairie Club, and the Voice of Indignant Citizens Everywhere. Some of these organizations demanded to meet with the university's board of trustees, and went so far as to send petitions to President Kennedy.[44]

All this clamor was most disturbing and disheartening to the members of the university community and inevitably dampened enthusiasm for the new campus. What was particularly dismaying to President Miller and his colleagues was the feeling of being caught in a disagreeable situation which was not of the university's making and over which it had no control, legal or otherwise. Above all, university leaders and spokesmen were distressed because the public outcry was based on misinformation.

Frances Searle Building for Communicative Disorders, completed 1973, winner of a Distinguished Building Award from the American Institute of Architects

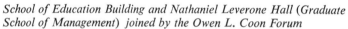

School of Education Building and Nathaniel Leverone Hall (Graduate School of Management) joined by the Owen L. Coon Forum

O. T. Hogan Biological Sciences Building, completed 1970

Pick-Staiger Concert Hall, completed 1975, first building of the new performing arts complex under construction on the lakefill campus

Much to the university's relief, an editorial in the *Chicago Sun-Times* of April 24, 1963, came to Northwestern's defense and proceeded to set the record straight, pointing out "that directing abuse at Northwestern University . . . is like abusing a home builder because his contractor obtained his lumber from a forest preserve." Continuing, the editorial pointed out that the sand was being removed to create a deep water harbor and was not coming from the site for a steel mill, that the Dunes Council was trying to preserve the area as a park but that the bulldozers were already at work, that there was no good reason why Northwestern should be denied the use of the sand "which must go somewhere" and that such use by the university was "a fine one."

Dedication of J. Roscoe Miller Campus

In due course the tumult subsided and on October 7, 1964, with the fill completed, the new campus was dedicated and named the J. Roscoe Miller Campus. Adlai E. Stevenson II being the chief speaker.* It was a windy afternoon with the sand being blown about in swirls by strong gusts from the south. As he stood on the roof of the newly constructed Vogelback Computing Center building facing an audience of approximately 4,000 people spread out on the new fill below, Mr. Stevenson had a difficult time keeping a firm hold on his manuscript. Not only the wind, but an injured and bandaged index finger on his right hand (the consequence of an earlier romp with his dog) weakened his grasp. When he was well into his address a sudden blast of wind ripped away three pages of the speech. "Well, that's a break for you!" Mr. Stevenson told his audience. The speech, though abbreviated, was enthusiastically received. The missing pages were ultimately picked up in Wilmette by a young boy who has treasured them ever since!

Vogelback Computing Center

The building whose roof had served as the speaker's platform for the dedication of the J. Roscoe Miller campus, Vogelback Computing Center, was the first to be erected on the new campus. Northwestern had begun to make use of computers in 1949 and in 1957 had established a computing center in Dearborn Observatory. The rapid improvements in computer technology led the university to replace its equipment every three or four years and the computer with which Vogelback opened, the CDC 3400, was five times faster than the machine (IBM 7094-1961) it replaced. The center, formally opened in February 1965, is named for William E. Vogelback of Chicago, an industrial engineer and a Northwestern Associate. A major conference room in the center is named for Ode Jennings, a Chicago manufacturer.

Lindheimer Astronomical Center

Two years later the Lindheimer Astronomical Research Center, the first structure built entirely on lakefill was completed. Located on a sandy spit of land jutting into Lake Michigan at the northeast corner of the Miller campus, the twin-towered structure with its two white domes commands an unencumbered sweep of the northern and eastern sky. The observatory was named after Chicago philanthropist Benjamin Lindheimer. One of its 70 foot towers supports a 40″ telescope, the other, a 16″ telescope. Designed by the firm of Skidmore, Owings and Merrill, the center was recognized as the outstanding building in its class in the annual

---

*Ten more acres were added to the campus in 1968 to provide space for the Center for the Fine and Performing Arts called for by the First Plan for the Seventies.

Distinguished Buildings competition of the Chicago Chapter of the American Institute of Architects.

The keystone of the expansion program of the late 1960's was the University Library. It was the product of three years of hard work by a faculty planning committee headed by Professor Clarence Ver Steeg who had proposed the building of a modern library after a sabbatical year spent working in the Widener Library of Harvard University. The final plans were drawn after extensive consultation among architects, the faculty, and the administration. Ground was broken for the library on September 9, 1966, and the building was dedicated on October 21, 1970.

The New Library

Designed by Walter Netsch, Jr., of Skidmore, Owings and Merrill, the library is a five-story structure composed of three connected circular towers. The upper three stories contain nine open stack radial research rooms, each organized around a group of related subjects to encourage investigation of the collection. Herein is housed the library's main circulating collection. Each room has closed and open studies for faculty and graduate students and desks for undergraduates. The second floor houses the reserve room, student lounge, poetry and browsing room, listening room, and the core library. The latter, a major innovation, is a non-circulating duplicate collection of about 50,000 volumes of basic importance in the different disciplines. The first floor is taken up by library administration, a periodical room, a reference room and the card catalogs, while the newspaper-microtext room and a map collection are housed in the basement. The new towers are connected with Deering Library, which is an integral part of Northwestern University Library.

The new library was a crucial element in the expansion program not merely because of its size and inherent value, but also because the imaginative and bold planning that had gone into creating it was now directed toward developing a comprehensive plan for the entire campus. As noted earlier, the chairman of the Library Faculty Planning Committee, Clarence Ver Steeg, went on to head the all-university Faculty Planning Committee which played a central role in the development of the First Plan for the Seventies.

Under this plan the J. Roscoe Miller Campus was to be divided into three intellectual zones: north, a science-engineering complex; center, a social science complex; and south, a humanities-fine arts complex. A student center and all-campus lecture center were to be built in the middle of the campus, and dormitories were to expand along its outskirts. This zoning served to focus both immediate and future goals.[45]

The Campus Plan

The proposal to move Northwestern's scattered administrative and business offices into a central complex was announced in 1961, predating the Plan for the Seventies. Construction of the complex was begun in 1965 and completed three years later. It was named the Rebecca Crown Memorial Center in honor of the late wife of Colonel Henry Crown, Chicago industrialist. He and his sons—John, Lester, and Robert—were its principal donors. Set on a spacious plaza ten feet above Clark Street between Chicago and Sherman avenues, the Crown Center faces south along Orrington Avenue toward the heart of downtown Evanston. In addition to offices, conference rooms, and workrooms, the Center houses Hardin Hall, which is used for meetings of the trustees and the University Senate

Rebecca Crown Center

as well as for lectures and other occasions. It was named after John Hardin, former president of the board.

O. T. Hogan   Architect Walter Netsch, Jr., who had designed both the new University Library and Rebecca Crown Center, was also the designer of the O. T. Hogan Biological Sciences Building, largely financed by Chicago insurance executive O. T. Hogan. The initial impetus for this building came from the Faculty Planning Committee which predicted in 1963 that biological research would expand considerably in the near future. Planned by a biology faculty committee chaired by Professor Robert C. King, the five-story building was designed around a central utility core which provided a high ratio of usable space. Special facilities include equipment to control air circulation, a machine shop, specialized laboratories and greenhouses with separate temperature controls.

Leverone   The connected buildings of the Graduate School of Management and the School
and   of Education which opened in the fall of 1970 were yet another important addition
Education   to the campus. The management building is named for Nathaniel Leverone, donor. The Graduate School of Management and the School of Education share the connecting Owen L. Coon Forum, which was largely financed by the Coon Foundation. Designed by Loebl, Schlossman, Bennett and Dart, these structures for the first time provided excellent facilities for the two schools on the Evanston campus.

Norris Center   One of the top priorities urged by the First Plan for the Seventies was the construction of a student center. A successful alumni campaign for the purpose was capped by a major gift from Lester and Dellora Norris in memory of their son, Lester Norris, Jr., an alumnus and trustee. Also designed by Loebl, Schlossman, Bennett and Dart, and completed in January 1973, the Norris University Center commands a magnificent view of Lake Michigan. It consists of six levels—two of which are constructed below ground—and includes a cafeteria, book store, game room, the Dittmar Memorial Gallery, conference rooms, offices of student organizations, lounges, and the 350-seat McCormick Auditorium.

Frances Searle   In some ways the Frances Searle Building for the department of communicative
Building   disorders is a model achievement of the First Plan for the Seventies. Built on the J. Roscoe Miller campus lakefill it was named after the wife of John Searle, president of the board of trustees from 1964 to 1970. In 1973 it earned a Distinguished Building Award from the Chicago Chapter of the American Institute of Architects for its designer, Walter Netsch, Jr. of Skidmore, Owings and Merrill.

Blomquist   Andrew L. Heard and Associates designed the Blomquist Memorial Recreation
Building   Building, named for the late Edwin and Juliette Renken Blomquist, both Northwestern alumni, whose bequest made possible the sports building. Blomquist was a trustee, and both he and his wife were members of the John Evans Club. Built of split concrete block to give the effect of stone, the 18,700 square foot building includes three artificially-surfaced 90-foot square courts which can be used for basketball, volleyball, dance and other indoor team or individual recreational activities.

July 1973 saw the breaking of ground for the Pick-Staiger Concert Hall, adjacent to the Norris Center. Designed by Edward D. Dart of Loebl, Schlossman, Bennett and Dart, the building was made possible by gifts from Albert Pick, Jr., chairman of the board of Pick Hotels Corporation, and Charles G. Staiger. The building is dedicated to Mrs. Pick, who attended the School of Music, and to Mr. Staiger's former wife, the late Pauline Pick Staiger, who was Albert Pick's sister.

Pick-Staiger Hall

Two additional buildings will be constructed adjacent to Pick-Staiger Concert Hall, thus forming an arts complex. The first, financed by a 1974 grant from the Joseph and Helen Regenstein Foundation, is the Regenstein Hall of Music. Plans for the second, a theatre for the School of Speech, have been under consideration ever since the Annie May Swift Theatre (built in 1895) was declared unsafe for audiences. A national committee to conduct a fund raising campaign for the theatre was organized in 1974.

Regenstein Hall

A major landscaping and improvement project on the new campus undertaken in 1974 included construction of new entrances to the campus at both the north and south ends, a two-mile network of lighted bicycle and pedestrian pathways, a visitors' parking area, new lighting for all the parking lots, and the planting of shrubbery and trees throughout the Miller campus.[46]

The only building erected on the Chicago campus in the 1950's was the Morton Medical Research Building, named after Mrs. Margaret Gray Morton, widow of Joy Morton and mother of Sterling Morton of the Morton Salt Company. Designed by Holabird, Root and Burgee, the seven-story building's chief feature was the adaptability of its interior spaces to different types of research. Dedicated with great fanfare in June 1955, it was the first new medical building to be erected by the university since the completion of the Montgomery Ward building in 1926.

Chicago: Morton Building

The 1960's saw a significant expansion in the facilities of the Chicago campus. The construction of a separate heating plant in 1960 freed three floors of Wieboldt for conversion into classroom space. Combined with the addition of a new two-story wing to Wieboldt Hall, this opened up eleven classrooms to the School of Commerce in 1962. The new wing was named Evening Study Hall.

The same architectural firm designed the next two additions to the Chicago campus, one to the Law School, the other to the Medical School. McCormick Hall, a three story L-shaped classroom and library building was ready for use by the Law School in 1962. A substantial grant from the Robert R. McCormick Trust helped finance this much needed facility.

McCormick Hall

The completion in 1965 of the Searle Building to be used for teaching and re-search, marked a monumental step forward for the Medical School. It was financed by a grant from the National Institutes of Health as well as by additional gifts and grants from various foundations, corporations and individuals, including John G. Searle, then president of the board of trustees. Built in contemporary style, the fifteen story building added 170,000 square feet to the Medical School. At its dedication in the spring of 1965, President Miller noted that the Searle Building provides Northwestern with "the finest medical teaching facilities available anywhere and will give new impetus to our research and medical education programs."[47]

Searle Building

Although the addition of the Morton and Searle wings to the Ward building greatly increased the research facilities of the Medical School, President Miller saw a need to coordinate the activities of the Medical and Dental Schools with the affiliated hospitals on a more systematic basis. As early as 1946 President Snyder had envisaged a comprehensive medical center and now what had at first seemed a somewhat grandiose plan began to be transformed into reality.

In September 1960 Dean Richard H. Young of the Medical School was appointed director of what would thereafter be known as the Medical Center.[48] Simultaneously, a committee including representatives from the boards of the affiliated hospitals and the university was formed "to coordinate planning and staffing with a view to utilizing their resources with the least duplication and waste and the greatest possible cooperation between them (the hospitals) and the university as a medical teaching and research center."[49]

The Medical Center In 1966 the Northwestern University Medical Center was organized as a separate legal entity by Northwestern together with seven hospitals which had become affiliated with the university in the course of the previous sixty-six years: Chicago Wesley Memorial Hospital in 1899; Passavant in 1925; Children's Memorial Hospital in 1946; Evanston Hospital in 1950; the Veterans Administration Research Hospital in 1950; the Rehabilitation Institute of Chicago in 1960; and the Chicago Maternity Center (nucleus of the future Prentice Women's Hospital and Maternity Center) in 1966.*

The purpose of the Medical Center was "to foster joint effort to provide centralized facilities and to improve teaching, research and patient care within the existing framework of private medicine and independently operated institutions."[50] A planning and development committee began to draft proposals to implement these aims in 1967. They included the construction of new buildings for the Rehabilitation Institute and the Women's Hospital and Maternity Center with a Psychiatric Institute also to be housed in the latter structure. The two new buildings were to be located east of Passavant on land donated by the university. These plans increased the complexity of the Medical Center's space requirements and underlined the need for additional land if its long-range needs were to be met.

In 1968 the Center's planning committee proposed to the board of trustees that the city parking garage at the southwest corner of Fairbanks Court and Superior Street be purchased as a site for a new facility to house the medical and dental clinics as well as the hospitals' outpatient clinics. The following summer President Miller, alerted to the possibility that the garage might be sold to a developer for a highrise apartment building, took the initiative and obtained the trustees' approval for the acquisition of the eastern two-thirds of the parking garage site. Then accompanied by Vice President Kreml and James Oates, a life trustee, the president went directly to Mayor Richard Daley of Chicago with a proposal that the city sell the garage to the university.[51]

Though the president and the mayor had established a friendly relationship over the years, the mayor had to consider the political repercussions of the sale of city property to a private organization. President Miller made the point that the new facility would provide additional and much needed health care for a wide segment of the city's population living in the surrounding area, and succeeded in obtaining a favorable response from the mayor. It was agreed that the negotiations would be

*Northwestern Medical School students also receive clinical training at Cook County Hospital and at Hines and Downey Veterans Administration hospitals.

carried forward by the corporation counsel, Ray Simon, acting on behalf of the city and by Franklin Kreml (subsequently John Fields), James Oates, and Hilton Scribner (chairman of the trustees' committee on educational properties) acting for the university.

The detailed proposal from the university to the city of Chicago for the purchase of the garage was drafted early in 1972. It affirmed that the new facility would provide ambulatory outpatient care through medical and dental clinics as well as a central emergency room. It would also include quarters for a centralized pathology and laboratory program in which both the university and the hospitals would participate. Construction of the new health services facility was to commence within five years of the receipt of title to the land. In addition the university promised to build a new parking facility on the university-owned block to the south of the city garage, construction to be initiated within twelve months of the signing of the agreement. The City Council accepted the proposal and passed an ordinance approving the sale of the garage property to the university for $7,200,000, with the actual transfer to take place on January 1, 1973.[52] *Northwestern's Proposal to the City*

Dean Richard H. Young had relinquished his position as director of the Medical Center in August 1969, because of ill health, and had been replaced by Ray E. Brown as executive vice president of the Medical Center and professor in the School of Management. Brown, who had had extensive experience in hospital administration at the University of Chicago and at Duke University, came to the Medical Center from Boston where he had been executive vice president of the Affiliated Hospitals Center, an affiliate of the Harvard Medical School.[53] Supported by President Miller's personal commitment to the Center, the new director moved energetically to carry out the ambitious plans devised for it.

Shortly before Brown assumed his duties, plans for the Center received an enormous boost in the form of a $10,000,000 gift from Foster McGaw, a Northwestern trustee and long-time friend of President Miller. Captured by the president's account of the Medical Center's potential at a board meeting, Mr. McGaw decided to help realize the proposed plans. In recognition of his generous support, the name of the Northwestern Medical Center was changed to Northwestern-McGaw Medical Center.[54] When the gift was announced, President Miller made it clear that the money was to be spent primarily for land and physical development and not for operating expenses or individual hospitals or schools. In 1972 Foster McGaw made a second gift of $10,000,000 for the Center and this time his wife, Mary, participated in the arrangement. This led to a further change in the name of the Center to The McGaw Medical Center of Northwestern University.[55] *The McGaw Gifts*

In the meantime faculty committees in the Medical and Dental schools in collaboration with hospital representatives and the planning committee engaged in extensive planning not only for the proposed new facility but also for the reallocation of space and activities in existing buildings.[56] Brown's efforts to avoid duplication among the hospitals led to agreements for centralized purchasing, for common kitchens and laundry, a single computer, a central blood bank, a centralized mortuary, centralized oxygen facilities and common arrangements for the housing of staff, interns, and residents.[57]

Northwestern Memorial Hospital These moves to improve hospital services and effect financial savings culminated in the merger of Wesley Memorial Hospital and Passavant Hospital on September 1, 1972, into a single hospital under a common board. The original names were retained as pavilion designations but the new entity was called Northwestern Memorial Hospital. John Sturgis, who headed Wesley, and John Stagl, who headed Passavant, moved through a thicket of historical obstacles and prejudices to achieve the merger within a relatively short period of time.[58]

Faculty and students had complained for years about the antiquated and deteriorating condition of the medical clinics in the Ward building. Indeed, the clinical faculty balked at supervising students in such quarters and students, in turn, were reluctant to pay much attention to clinical experience under such depressing conditions. The educational program of the Medical School began to suffer as did the quality of the care available to outpatients. To remedy the situation and to attract more practicing physicians to teach in the Medical School, it was decided to inaugurate a group practice. Dr. Oglesby Paul was named director of the group, effective January 1, 1973.[59] The university went on to purchase and renovate a building at 222 East Superior Street to house the group practice, and a policy board, with Vice President Mack as chairman, was formed to establish the responsibilities and relationships of the group practice to the university.[60] By the summer of 1974 the program was well under way.

Rehabilitation Institute In late 1971 construction of the new home for the Rehabilitation Institute of Chicago commenced. Designed by the architectural firm of C. F. Murphy and Associates, the eighteen story building was completed in the spring of 1974. Serving as both a training and research facility, it houses the Medical School's department of physical therapy, the prosthetics and orthotics center of the department of orthopedic surgery and the department of rehabilitation medicine.

Prentice Women's and Psychiatric Institute The firm of Bertrand Goldberg Associates designed the building—begun soon after and scheduled for completion in 1973—to house both the Prentice Women's Hospital and Maternity Center and the Northwestern Institute of Psychiatry.* At the time that he made his first major contribution to the Medical Center, Foster McGaw stated, "My wife and I believe in the tremendous potential of Northwestern as a great medical center . . . I am convinced that it can and should be the greatest medical center in the world."[61] By 1974 considerable progress had been made toward this lofty goal.

Changing Role of Faculty Committees The active participation of faculty representatives in the development of the First Plan for the Seventies represented both a step forward during a period when such participation was called for by faculties in many institutions across the nation and a return to the customs of Northwestern's very early years when an overall shortage of staff required all hands to perform a large variety of tasks. In the intervening years as administration and faculty became more numerous each group tended to become more specialized in its activities.

At the time that Dr. Miller became president there was only one significant university-wide committee, the General Faculty Committee, created by the Univer-

*Ownership of the building was transferred from the university to Northwestern Memorial Hospital prior to its completion.

NEW BUILDING CONSTRUCTION AND MAJOR REMODELING 1949-1974
Chicago Campus

Educational Buildings

Morton Building	Medical Research	1955	$ 1,280,218
Wieboldt Hall Addition	Classrooms	1962	1,179,335
McCormick Hall	Law School	1962	1,639,368
Searle Building	Medical Research	1965	9,231,124
NU Medical Associates Bldg.	Group Practice	1974	
(Purchase)			1,396,476
(Remodeling)			1,820,625 (not final)
(Equipment)			500,000 (not final)
			$17,047,146

Other

Heating Plant	Chicago Campus	1960	$ 2,556,472
City of Chicago Parking			
Garage (Purchased)		1973	7,319,290 (not final)
NU Parking Garage	Chicago campus parking	1973	4,889,943 (not final)
Land			708,055
			$15,473,760
		Total	$32,520,906

Source: Department of Planning Report #44, January 1975.

sity Senate in 1939. Committee members were elected by the faculty of each school to serve for a three-year term. The Senate empowered the committee "to consider any matter of general university policy on its own initiative or matters referred to it by the faculty of any school, by individual faculty members, by the President, the Dean of Faculties or by the Deans. . . . The committee, however, shall have no power to commit the Senate or any of the separate faculties."[62] During the 1950's the committee concerned itself largely with what might be termed the working conditions of the faculty, making recommendations to the administration on such issues as faculty salaries, medical, life and disability insurance, tuition rebates for faculty children, and privileges for retired faculty.

In general, academic and budgetary decisions were made by the administration with no formal input from the faculty. There was one exception to this—Dean Simeon Leland of the College of Liberal Arts consulted with a committee elected by the faculty in planning the annual budget for the College.

When committees including faculty members were consulted—as in the case of search committees to recommend candidates for administrative positions or standing committees such as those on the library, financial aid, lecture series, honorary degrees, and intercollegiate athletics—the faculty serving on them were appointed by the president. This situation changed markedly in the 1960's and early 1970's when younger faculty in particular, supported by some outspoken older faculty leaders, began to press for a greater share in academic decision making.

The central administration, in the spring of 1964, responded by establishing the university-wide Committee on Educational Policies to be composed of nine mem-

Committee on Educational Policies bers (including the General Faculty Committee chairman ex officio), appointed by the president from a list of nominees, two for each position, submitted by the General Faculty Committee.

In a directive to the new committee Dean Wild outlined its charge "to assist the administration and represent the faculty on major educational problems," the hope being that the committee "will carry forward the momentum generated by the Faculty Planning Committee," that it will coordinate other committees' activities, such committees "to be regrouped under this committee, that it will take the initiative in presenting educational problems" and that "it will be a major point of reference in dealing with academic issues."[63]

At its first meeting on October 17, 1964, the Committee on Educational Policies moved to establish a Faculty Committee on Admissions responsible to the CEP.* During the next decade the latter went on to deal with a large range of issues including curricular changes, general education courses, classified research, the residential colleges, a faculty associates' program, and financial aid to students.[64]

University Senate In November 1964, the University Senate, first organized in 1928, voted to increase its own membership from full professors and second term associate professors to include first term associate and second term assistant professors as well. In 1971, the Senate proceeded to admit first term assistant professors also. This brought the total of eligible members to nearly 900.[65]

Following the initial move to expand Senate membership, both the General Faculty Committee and the Senate acted to enlarge faculty participation in the decision making process at Northwestern. In 1965, for example, the General Faculty Committee and the Committee on Educational Policies appointed a joint subcommittee of six—the Committee on Committees—which was charged with the task of recommending the names of faculty members for appointment to certain committees. In 1970, however, it was the University Senate which initiated new procedures for the appointment of search committees to insure "sufficient participation by elected representatives of the faculties involved. These procedures shall be approved by the GFC in the case of university-wide positions and by the school and faculty in the case of individual school positions." This resolution was accepted in principle by the administration with the proviso that it would apply primarily to academic appointments.[66]

Senate Steering Committee In 1968 the Senate had taken an important step when it voted to change the procedure according to which the president and dean of faculties customarily assumed prime responsibility for preparing the agenda for University Senate meetings. Instead the Senate moved to establish the Faculty Senate Steering Committee "to serve as its instrument in scheduling meetings and preparing agenda." Membership consisted of the chairmen of the GFC, CEP, and Faculty Planning Committee, a representative of the administration, and one faculty member elected at large by the Senate for a three-year term.[67]

---

*This move was a response to mounting pressure from the faculty for a broader based recruitment of the student body, the complaint being that the Northwestern undergraduate student body was too homogeneous in composition and that more minority students should be recruited.

Even more important was the Senate's vote—on May 21, 1970—to establish a *Budget and* Budget and Resources Advisory Committee (known as BRAC) to participate with *Resources* the chancellor, president, and other administrative officers "in every phase of pre- *Advisory* paring the annual budget and participate and advise in the preparation of the long- *Committee* range (three year) budget." The committee was to be composed of three members of the General Faculty Committee and four other members drawn from the faculty at large. In view of BRAC's importance its chairman was to serve as a member of the Senate Steering Committee. The administration agreed to work with BRAC: it would explain its allocation of resources to the committee and in turn consider BRAC's recommendations in making its plans.

As far back as 1938 the university had established a committee to deal with the *Northwestern* non-academic aspects of student life.* In the 1950's this was superseded by the *Community* Council on Undergraduate Life, which, in response to the conditions of the late *Council* 1960's and early 1970's (see page 327), was replaced by yet another body, the North-western Community Council.† Composed of three appointed members of the ad-ministration, seven elected faculty and seven elected student representatives, the Council was assigned "the duty . . . to consider all factors of student environment and all phases of student development outside the classroom." More sweeping was the authorization in paragraph 2 of the Statutes' section on Northwestern Com-munity Council to "recommend university policy with a scope which can broadly be described as the quality of life within the university community. It is appropriate therefore that NCC be empowered to investigate any area of policy that the council members deem proper." Further, NCC reserved the right "to . . . legislate on any issue . . . within its jurisdiction regardless of what action has been taken by another formal organization."

The establishment of the NCC added yet another element to the already com-plicated committee structure of the university. Jurisdictional lines became blurred and the administration was faced with the delicate and difficult task of dealing fairly with numerous faculty groups among which the lines of communication and authority were not easily distinguishable. How to sort out recommendations from the GFC, FPC, CEP, SSC, BRAC, and NCC became a serious concern for the administration. In an effort to clarify the situation, the Senate moved to empower the faculty's Senate Steering Committee "to act as a coordinating committee for all university committees" and "to assign tasks to the various committees in such a way as to avoid needless overlapping functions" as well as "to assure that important issues are referred expeditiously to the appropriate committee."[68] Though the SSC made every effort to carry out this mandate, its attempt to coordinate the activities of so many diverse groups was not always successful.

One of the most far-seeing contributions made by a faculty committee was a *A Community* comprehensive report entitled, *A Community of Scholars*, published in two parts, *of Scholars* the first in the fall of 1968 and the second in the spring of 1969.[69] Prepared by

*The Council on Personnel Work and the Board of Personnel Administration created by Article VII of the University Statutes, April 26, 1938.

†Article V, section 5, University Statutes, 1953 and 1957; Article V, 5b, in revised University Statutes, December 2, 1971.

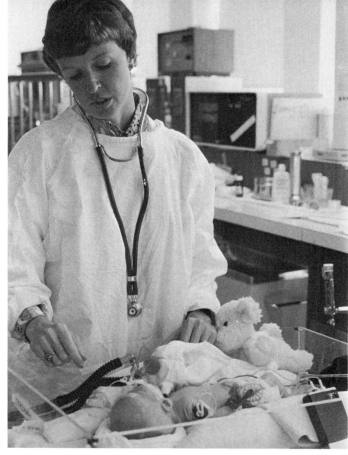

*Medical student in
nursery at Children's
Memorial Hospital*

*A programmer playing chess against a fast-thinking opponent, the
CDC 6400 computer, in Vogelback Computing Center*

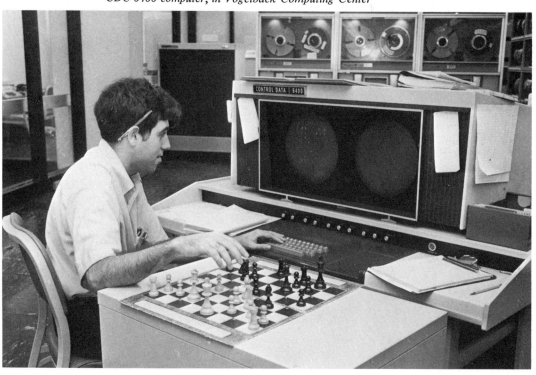

*Archeology students at the Koster site near Kampsville, Illinois,
where signs of fifteen prehistoric civilizations have been unearthed*

Professor Jean Hagstrum, it was widely hailed for offering major guidelines for future planning. The University Senate took the initiative in creating a Committee on Curriculum and Teaching to implement the proposals made in the report.[70] And many of these were in fact carried out in the course of the next few years.

The president and his fellow administrators believed that the primary requirement for a sound academic program is a first rate faculty, and that such a faculty could be counted on to devise a curriculum which would meet the changing needs of students and make the most of the resources available to the university. Thus, in the course of the Miller years, administration and faculty worked closely together to make the curricular changes which seemed necessary and desirable. Some of these—such as changes in the general course requirements for undergraduates and for Ph.D. candidates—affected the university as a whole; others affected individual schools or segments of schools.

A number of the innovative programs were underwritten by foundations and outside agencies because the faculty who proposed them and the programs themselves were of a caliber that promised that the outcome would be of more than local interest. This was the case, for instance, with the six year medical program, the senior tutorial program in the Law School, the revision of the School of Education curriculum and the changes made in the School of Commerce.

Curricular Changes in the Schools

To describe in detail the curricular changes that were made in eleven schools over a period of twenty-five years would require more space than is here available. However, a sense of the general direction of curricular changes during this period can be obtained by a brief glance at the various schools.

One of the first major curricular changes at the undergraduate level stemmed from the recommendations of the faculty General Education Committee appointed in 1954 at the suggestion of Dean Wild.[71] With the support of a $30,000 grant from the Carnegie Foundation the committee developed a program in general education which it recommended to all the undergraduate schools on the Evanston campus.[72] Its intention was to give greater breadth to the undergraduate programs of the professional schools by making available to their students the basic courses already established in the College of Liberal Arts. Whereas previously the only non-specialist courses taken by many undergraduates of the professional schools were freshman English and physical education, after the fall of 1957 such undergraduates could choose, in addition to their major, courses from four general areas. One area encompassed art, literature and music; another, the social sciences; the third, history, philosophy, history and literature of religions; and the fourth, science and mathematics. The program was administered by the General Education Committee which evaluated the general education courses proposed by faculty members.

The College

Also in the mid-1950's, Dean Leland of the College had made strenuous efforts to improve the quality of teaching and research in the sciences. With strong financial support from the administration he had increased the size of the faculty in the science departments, making new appointments at both senior and junior levels. In undertaking this task Dean Leland had the advice and support of Paul

Klopsteg of the Technological Institute, who had been appointed as consultant for science and research planning in 1960.[73]

In 1963 the dean and faculty of the College of Liberal Arts recommended to the president that the name of the College be changed back to the College of Arts and Sciences. In passing this recommendation on to the trustees' committee on educational policies at a meeting held November 25, the president endorsed it noting that "It is felt that the title will be more descriptive of the work and interests of the College." The committee approved the recommendation which came before the trustees at their meeting of December 2. An affirmative vote on that occasion made the change of name effective as of that date.

The recommendations for undergraduate education presented in *A Community of Scholars* were responsible for a number of the changes made in subsequent years. In 1972 the College instituted a three-year B.A. program. The requirement in the natural sciences and mathematics was reduced from two years to one, and freshman English was replaced by an Introductory Studies program. Faculty from all six science departments developed and taught a series of courses designed for non-scientists, while the addition of many new courses gave students a wider range of choices. Other innovations during this period included the option of an *ad hoc* major, which encouraged students to tailor major programs to their individual needs if their special interests were not satisfied by one of the established programs; independent study, which enabled students to engage in special study and research under faculty supervision; and undergraduate seminars which made it possible for students to engage in research and discussion on advanced topics in a context which called for a high degree of participation by members of the seminar.

The report also led to the establishment of an all-university Committee on Teaching and a teacher evaluation program in the College. Five new interdisciplinary centers were created and an African-American Studies program established.[74]

In 1966 Dean Simeon Leland retired. During his twenty years as dean of the College he had worked closely with the central administration to raise the standard of teaching and scholarship in the College to a new level. His vision and energy left an indelible imprint on its character. His successor, Robert H. Strotz, had been educated at Duke University and the University of Chicago before joining the economics department at Northwestern in 1947. Following Strotz's appointment to the presidency in 1970, associate dean Laurence H. Nobles served as acting dean until the selection of Hanna H. Gray as dean in 1972. Educated at Bryn Mawr College and Harvard, Dean Gray came to Northwestern from the department of history at the University of Chicago, remaining in this post two years. She was succeeded in 1974 by Rudolph H. Weingartner, a graduate of Columbia College and University and chairman of the philosophy department at Vassar College prior to his appointment to Northwestern.[75]

Between 1949-50 and 1973-74, enrollment in the College grew from 2,918 to 4,046 (see Table 7-1). During the same period the full time faculty in the College grew from 242 to 393, with an additional 28 part time members.[76]

TABLE 7-1
N.U. STUDENT ENROLLMENT, 1949-1974 (Selected Years)

Academic Year	1949-1950			1956-1957			1966-1967			1973-1974		
	Full Time	Part Time	Total	Full Time	Part Time	Total	Full Time	Part Time	Total	Full Time	Part Time	Total
EVANSTON CAMPUS												
College	2,720	198	2,918	2,134	198	2,332	3,154	80	3,234	3,949	97	4,046
Graduate	1,009	393	1,402	1,137	131	1,268	2,010	827	2,837	1,992	448	2,440
Music	744	118	862	355	80	435	420	101	521	475	54	529
Speech	873	12	885	782	23	805	683	25	708	974	33	1,007
Technological Institute	838	35	873	900	148	1,048	750	27	777	795	24	819
Commerce—Business-Management	1,553	8	1,561	889	11	900	550	7	557	533	4	537
Journalism	497	12	509	491	16	507	553	13	566	713	11	724
Education	507	18	525	664	26	690	443	42	485	255	39	294
TOTAL	8,741	794	9,535b	7,352	633	7,985	8,563	1,122	9,685	9,686	710	10,396
CHICAGO CAMPUS												
Medical	724	8	732	538	84	622	538	—	538	710	—	710
Law	457	9	466	404	9	431	522	—	522	555	—	555
Dental	456	—	456	431	—	431	355	3	358	451	—	451
Commercea—Business-Management	525	8,791	9,316	383	850	1,233	282	675	957	—	988	988
Journalism	4	535	539	—	—	—	—	—	—	—	—	—
University College	25	5,497	5,522	—	—	—	—	—	—	—	—	—
Evening Division	—	—	—	14	9,566	9,580	7	7,083	7,090	95	3,555	3,650
Graduate	74	644	718	62	435	497	106	200	306	123	25	148
TOTAL	2,265	15,484	17,749c	1,832	10,944	12,776	1,810	7,961	9,771	1,934	4,568	6,502
GRAND TOTAL	11,006	16,278	27,284	9,184	11,577	20,761	10,373	9,083	19,456	11,620	5,278	16,898
Summer School	—	(1950)	6,978	—	(1957)	5,249	—	(1967)	5,882	—	(1974)	5,328

SOURCE: Office of the Registrar.

aUndergraduate majors in Chicago Division of School of Commerce registered in Evening Divisions after 1954.

bThere were 3,022 veterans enrolled in classes on the Evanston campus.

cThere were 7,298 veterans enrolled in classes on the Chicago campus.

The Graduate School   In 1951 Dean Arthur R. Tebbutt, who had been dean of the Graduate School since 1944, resigned. As his successor would point out some years later, it was Tebbutt who had had to deal with the problems raised by the great expansion of postwar years. "He organized a staff capable of managing an operation of growing complexity, he fought laxness in the handling of programs of study, and he insisted on high standards of admission."[77]

The man who made this assessment, Moody E. Prior, would himself bring many talents and great energy to the deanship following Tebbutt's retirement from the post. A Northwestern alumnus with a Ph.D. from the University of Chicago, Prior was John C. Shaffer Professor of Humanities and English and had taught at Northwestern for twenty-four years when he became dean of the Graduate School. He also had behind him a long career as a leading member of numerous committees in the course of which he had developed a remarkable ability for distinguishing the significant from the trivial as well as a knack for reconciling conflicting views and personalities. These skills served him well in his new position, in which he remained until 1964.

In his very first report Prior declared "There can be only one reasonable goal for a graduate school at Northwestern: it must aim at the highest quality possible in the students it admits, in the training it offers, in the faculty of which it is composed, in the research it encourages."[78] In the course of the next thirteen years Dean Prior bent all his efforts to fulfilling these aims.

One of the most significant changes was the liberalization of the doctoral program in 1958.[79] In essence, the registration and credit requirements for doctoral students were revised to allow a greater degree of flexibility in work after the first year of graduate study had been completed. Instead of being required to register for a set number of credit hours with a fixed limit on the number of courses taken each quarter, graduate students were permitted to simply register for courses and to do as much or as little in them as they chose except for certain basic courses required by some departments. The purpose of this was to encourage doctoral candidates to acquire a broader background than was possible under the previous system of narrowly prescribed courses in their particular fields. The change was enthusiastically accepted and elicited many inquiries from other graduate schools. Indeed, a number of these subsequently modified their own programs along the same lines.

Some years earlier the requirement of a reading knowledge of two foreign languages for all Ph.D. candidates was changed to one foreign language required by the Graduate School. Individual departments might require a second foreign language if that seemed a necessary qualification for a Ph.D. in that particular discipline.

Innovations

To make doctoral programs less standardized and allow advanced students more freedom, the university introduced the designation of resident in research for students who had completed all formal requirements short of their dissertations. This enabled such students to maintain full time student status and to enjoy the use of library and laboratory facilities at a lower than regular tuition rate. This type of registration could be continued until the student had earned his or her degree as long as he or she was actually present on the campus and doing full time research or writing the dissertation. This innovation received favorable notice in a symposium on graduate study printed in the spring 1959 issue of the *Journal of Higher Education.*

In 1952 a reciprocal arrangement between the University of Chicago and Northwestern was worked out whereby advanced students from each were permitted to register for courses in the other institution without formal admission or payment of additional tuition. This agreement meant that the two universities need not duplicate their efforts in specialized areas but could make use of each other's resources. It was a forerunner of the educational exchanges of later years under the auspices of the Committee on Institutional Cooperation, known as CIC. As an additional means of making the best possible use of existing resources, Dean Prior was instrumental in establishing several interdisciplinary programs which consolidated facilities for research available in several different areas—the Geotechnical Center, the Center for Metropolitan Studies and what would eventually become the Transportation Center.

STUDENTS AT WORK

Viewing an exhibit of African art from the university's Melville J. Herskovits collection

Students in International Law Moot Court competition

University Symphony at work in the Arne Oldberg Rehearsal Room of Pick-Staiger Concert Hall

Robert H. Baker, associate dean of the Graduate School and a member of Northwestern's chemistry department since 1941, became dean of the Graduate School in 1964. He had been primarily responsible for all aspects of graduate admissions.[80] As graduate dean until 1975 he maintained the high standards of the Graduate School both through the period of plentiful funding for research during the 1960's and of shrinking resources during the 1970's.

In the course of the Miller years the Graduate School met in rather dramatic ways the goals set for it during the Snyder administration. Increased faculty strength and improved library, laboratory, and computer facilities helped attract growing numbers of good students as did the availability of fellowship money and housing. Indeed, between 1960 and the early 1970's aid to graduate students rose from under $1,000,000 to more than $7,000,000, the university's contribution rising from $100,000 to $1,500,000 during this period. These factors combined to thrust Northwestern into the forefront of research activity and doctoral training. In 1949-50 the combined Graduate School enrollment on the two campuses had been 1,083 full time and 1,037 part time students; in 1973-74 it was 2,115 full time and 473 part time students—most of the part time enrollment being on the Chicago campus (see Table 7-1). Moreover, whereas in 1949-50 Northwestern had awarded 132 Ph.D.'s, in 1973-74 it granted 364. Over the whole span of the Miller years, 5,516 Ph.D.'s were earned by students in the Graduate School.[81]

Increased Enrollment

One of the unhappy aspects of university life for several decades had been the rift between the College of Liberal Arts and the School of Education. While the College faculty accused the Education faculty of dwelling on hollow techniques without paying attention to the basic fields of knowledge, the latter criticized their liberal arts colleagues for assuming that knowledge of a subject automatically transformed a graduate into an effective classroom teacher. In 1956 in an attempt to heal this breach Dean Wild invited Dean E. T. McSwain of the School of Education and Professor William Hunt, chairman of the psychology department in the College, to meet with him. As he recalled later, he began by saying, "Surely you two have something in common as a basis for collaboration." They did, and the result was an agreement which made the course in educational psychology the joint responsibility of the two schools and led to a joint appointment of a faculty member who was familiar with the latest developments in psychology on the one hand and with education as a profession on the other. Financed by a grant of $156,000 from the Carnegie Corporation, this venture set the pattern for similar joint undertakings not only between the School of Education and the College of Liberal Arts but among other schools as well.[82]

School of Education

In a further move to bring about a closer relationship between the College and the School of Education, Northwestern developed a program leading to a Master of Arts in Teaching degree (M.A.T.). Initially financed by a grant of $325,000 from the Ford Foundation the program went into effect in 1961.[83]

B. J. Chandler became dean of the School of Education in 1963. Educated at the University of Texas and Columbia Teachers College, he had been a member of the faculty since 1956, having come to Northwestern from the Virginia School Boards Association and the University of Virginia.[84] Under his leadership the entire teacher training program was revamped and by 1965 the School of Education had devised a totally new curriculum known as the Tutorial-Clinical Program in Teacher Education. It called for the virtual elimination of methods courses. Instead, students selected a major or majors in the arts and sciences combined with tutorials in education as well as with practice teaching from their freshman year on. Students in this program assumed responsibility in the schools as practice teachers and teachers' aids.[85] This completely new way of training teachers had a widespread effect in educational circles throughout the country and brought the School of Education from the periphery into the very center of university activities. The faculty of the school almost doubled to forty-five full time and eleven part time members in 1973-74.[86]

Enrollment in the School of Education reached a peak of 690 in 1956-57. As the school age population began to decline, however, and it became evident that the demand for teachers would be decreasing, enrollment in the School of Education followed a nationwide downward trend.

Center for Teaching Professions

In 1969 Northwestern established the Center for the Teaching Professions with a grant from the W. K. Kellogg Foundation of Battle Creek, Michigan. Of the total of $2,481,190 to be received over a six-year period, $981,190 was assigned to program operations and the remainder for building construction. The purpose of the center was to improve the teaching of both the faculty at Northwestern and of graduate students planning to become teachers and to help other educational institutions and professional organizations improve their teaching programs as well. B. Claude Mathis, professor of education and psychology since 1956, and associate dean of the Graduate School since 1964, became director of the center.[87]

Commerce-Business

Joseph M. McDaniel, a member of Northwestern's faculty since 1947 was named dean of the School of Commerce in 1950 but resigned the following year. Ernest C. Davies, a faculty member since 1925 then served as acting dean until the appointment of Richard A. Donham as dean in 1953. Educated at Harvard, Donham had taught at the school since 1940. In the course of his administration—in 1956—the School of Commerce changed its name to the School of Business to give a more accurate indication of the scope of its curriculum. At the same time the graduate division assumed the name of Graduate School of Business Administration and continued to offer the degree of Master of Business Administration.

Graduate School of Management

Donham resigned in 1965 and was succeeded as dean by John A. Barr, until then chairman of the board of Montgomery Ward and Company and a Northwestern trustee.[88] Under his guidance, faculty, alumni groups, and an advisory council composed of forty leading Chicago businessmen considered the advisability of a major change in the program of the School of Business and finally recommended that the school discontinue all undergraduate education.[89] The last undergraduate class was admitted in 1966 and graduated four years later. Meanwhile, in 1969, the school changed its name to the Graduate School of Management and expanded its curriculum to include specialized management training in such areas as hospital administration,* public administration and the

---

*This program, first established in 1943, was suspended in 1962 but reincorporated into the program of the Graduate School of Management in 1969.

administration of non-profit organizations. In 1974 the Graduate School of Management and the College of Arts and Sciences announced a new program which made it possible for students to earn a B.A. and a Master of Management degree in five years instead of the usual six.[90]

As Table 7-1 shows, enrollment in the School of Commerce on both the Evanston and Chicago campuses declined markedly after the mid-1950's when the returning veterans had completed their education. After 1954, undergraduate majors on the Chicago campus were registered in the Evening Divisions. Following the phasing out of the undergraduate program in 1966 the graduate enrollment increased steadily to nearly 550 full time students by 1973. The decline in undergraduate enrollment and the eventual conversion to graduate work only, led to a corresponding reduction in faculty.[91]

In 1957 I. W. Cole became dean of the Medill School of Journalism. A graduate of the University of Illinois, he had been director of the School of Journalism at Pennsylvania State University before coming to Northwestern. Under his aegis the school became substantially larger, the enrollment of full time students growing from 491 in 1956-57 to 713 in 1973-74 (see Table 7-1). The faculty remained about the same: of the total of forty-one in 1973-74, twenty-three were full time and eighteen part time.[92]

Medill School of Journalism

While the undergraduate program remained essentially the same, with considerable stress on liberal arts courses as a foundation for the journalism degree, the graduate program developed in several ways. To begin with, the program for the degree of Master of Science in Journalism became entirely professional in emphasis. Secondly, with the support of a $1,000,000 grant from the Ford Foundation in 1966 and a matching grant from the Gannett Foundation in 1972, the school established a program in Urban Journalism in which students received special preparation for understanding and reporting on all aspects of contemporary urban life.

As noted earlier, the fortunes of the School of Music were much improved by the Eckstein bequest which became available in the early 1950's and converted the school from one with very limited resources to one which had the funds not only to transform its physical plant but to raise salaries, appoint additional faculty, bring in guest artists, attract promising students with scholarship aid, and introduce new and innovative programs.[93]

School of Music

In 1951 George Howerton, who had earned his Ph.D. at Northwestern and had been a member of the music faculty for twenty years, became dean of the School of Music. He served in this post for another twenty years. His successor, Thomas W. Miller, who had been educated at Westchester State College, Pennsylvania, the East Carolina University and Boston University, came to Northwestern from East Carolina, where he had been both a faculty member and dean.

Following several months of investigation and planning by the Faculty Conference of the School of Music, Dean Miller introduced the first sweeping revision of the undergraduate curriculum in many years. The result was a flexible program adaptable to the specific abilities and needs of the individual student. Under the new plan, the curriculum was divided into three parts: the basic studies program in which the entire faculty was involved and which offered students the background which all musicians should have; professional studies, directed by the department offering the student's specialty; and a considerable number of optional courses from which the students were free to choose what interested them most. This new curriculum, leading to the Bachelor of Music and to the Bachelor of Music Education degrees, was implemented in the fall of 1972.

Proximity to Chicago provided students with opportunities for professional performing experiences and in the 1970's the school formed an association with the Ravinia Festival which led to the development of many activities and courses given in conjunction with the summer program at Ravinia in Highland Park.

Arts Festivals sponsored by the university in 1967 and 1968 brought concerts by the Chicago Symphony Orchestra to the campus. The orchestra's performance in Cahn Auditorium included works composed by members of the music school faculty. On October 24, 1971, a special recital was given by Boris Goldovsky, director of the New England Opera Company, and Sherrill Milnes, leading baritone of the Metropolitan Opera and former Northwestern School of Music student, in recognition of the university's acquisition of the Moldenhauer collection of musical manuscripts which had been gathered in Europe by Hans Moldenhauer. The program consisted of works by composers whose scores were in the collection.

As in the case of all the schools, the School of Music reached a peak in enrollment around 1949-50 with 744 full time and 118 part time students. Thereafter registration declined then began to rise again in the 60's. By 1973-74 full time registration was 475 and part time 54 (see Table 7-1). Over the same period the faculty increased in number from a total of seventy-one to a total of eighty-seven. A sizeable number of the latter were instrumentalists with the Chicago Symphony who taught at the School of Music on a part time basis.[94]

*School of
Speech*   In 1957 the School of Speech, still under the guidance of James H. McBurney, adopted the General Education program, dropping its courses in non-professional subjects and requiring its students to register in the College for courses in the humanities, the arts, the social sciences, and the sciences. Some students took courses in schools other than the College as well, especially in the School of Education. For a number of years the School of Speech experimented with a special honors program for highly qualified freshmen and sophomores. Under an intern program for juniors and seniors in radio, TV and film, for example, selected students were assigned to TV stations and spent one quarter in a working situation.

The opening of the Frances Searle Building enabled the department of communicative disorders to broaden its research programs. The facilities provided by this building provided new opportunities for both undergraduate and graduate students in this highly specialized field and the department's high reputation continued to grow.

In 1972, Roy V. Wood was appointed dean of the School of Speech. Educated at the University of Denver where he also taught, Wood had joined the Northwestern faculty in 1967. One of his major problems as dean was the closing of the theatre in Annie May Swift Hall in 1972, because it was no longer safe for use. While the theatre department was able to use Cahn Auditorium for its productions,

WAA-MU

*Ann-Margret (second row,
fourth from left)
in the 1960 Waa-Mu Show,
"Among Friends"*

*Warren Beatty
in the 1956
Silver Jubilee
Waa-Mu Show*

plans were made to raise money for a new theatre building which, it was estimated, would cost about $6,500,000.

During the mid-1950's registration in the School of Speech dropped from its postwar high. But in the late 1960's and early 1970's it began to climb rapidly and reached a new high of 974 full time and 33 part time students in 1973-74 (see Table 7-1). During the same period, the full time faculty increased from thirty-nine to sixty-seven, while the part time decreased from fifty-six to five.[95]

Technological Institute   The strained relations that had developed between the central administration and the Technological Institute before Snyder's retirement continued through the early years of the Miller administration. In 1953, when Donald H. Loughridge was appointed to succeed Ovid Eshbach as dean of the Institute, the president hoped that the new dean would be able to raise the amount and quality of research and graduate training carried out at Tech. A graduate of the California Institute of Technology, Loughridge had taught for many years at the University of Washington, but had also served on the Manhattan Project and as assistant director of the Division of Reactor Development for the U. S. Atomic Energy Commission.[96]

But instead of improving relations between the Tech faculty and the central administration the appointment of the new dean led to an open rift. In his endeavor to carry out his charge to expand research and increase the number of graduate students, Dean Loughridge antagonized his faculty and in the fall of 1955 the five departmental chairmen of Tech approached the president and dean of faculties and demanded that the dean be asked to resign.

President Miller and Dean Wild had earlier become aware of the friction between the dean and his faculty and had advised him to be somewhat more conciliatory. On the other hand, since the dean's goals for Tech accorded with those of the administration, President Miller was reluctant to dismiss Loughridge and so informed the chairmen. Because he hoped to be able to work out an accord between the dean and the chairmen, the president specifically asked the latter to take no further steps without consulting him. Instead, the chairmen, on the afternoon of the day they had met with the president, returned to his office and resigned their chairmanship as a group. This put Dean Loughridge in an impossible position and in December 1955 he submitted his resignation.

The administration was thus confronted with the unenviable task of finding an acting dean who could carry on while a search was made for a successor to Dean Loughridge. Into the breach stepped former Dean Eshbach who asked that the former chairmen be reappointed. President Miller was adamant in his refusal to do so because he believed that restoring the chairmen to their posts would make it difficult to secure a new dean from the outside, since any candidate would be loath to accept an offer that might put him at the mercy of a group of chairmen who had successfully toppled his predecessor. Equally important, as far as the president was concerned, was the chairmen's challenge to his own authority. At the same time, President Miller made it quite clear that whenever a new dean was selected he would be free to reappoint any or all of the former chairmen as he saw fit. With considerable skill, Dean Eshbach managed to fulfill his obligation without the help of the chairmen. Under his benign guidance the acrimony died down and the situation stabilized.

In 1957 Harold B. Gotaas, who had received his graduate training at Harvard and had served on the faculty of the University of California at Berkeley since 1946, was appointed as the new dean of Tech, remaining in that post for twelve years.[97]

Significant academic developments came rapidly at Tech under the leadership of Dean Gotaas. In 1957 the school adopted an alternative to the five-year cooperative program, namely, a four-year program of purely academic content. An innovative move in 1970 introduced a special engineering program for freshmen. Instead of taking the conventional courses in the separate disciplines in the sciences, freshmen studied subjects like physics and chemistry in intense blocks, the content of these blocks having been designed specifically to meet the needs of engineering students. *Curricular Changes at Tech*

At the same time the Institute became increasingly a center for graduate studies and research. The number of graduate students quintupled during Dean Gotaas' regime, rising from approximately 100 to about 500. The faculty was encouraged to seek grants for research with the result that research interests expanded greatly, assisted by the appointment of Professor Burgess Jennings as associate dean for research.[98] The development of a Materials Research Center and a Biomedical Engineering Center provided conspicuous examples of a special concern for scholarly growth. To the faculty were added professors who had distinguished reputations as researchers and promotions inside the faculty were granted to those with a flair for scholarly studies as well as for teaching.

In 1969 Walter S. Owen, director of materials science and engineering at Cornell since 1966 and before that dean of engineering sciences at the University of Liverpool, England, became dean of the Technological Institute. During his two years in that position he continued the policies initiated by his predecessor. When Owen became vice president for science and research in 1971, Professor David Mintzer became acting dean until the appointment of Bruno A. Boley in 1973. Educated at the City College of New York and the Polytechnic Institute of Brooklyn, Boley had taught at Columbia University and Cornell before coming to Northwestern.[99]

In spite of its internal troubles, the Technological Institute maintained its enrollment rather steadily during the Miller years, as Table 7-1 shows. Its peak registration of 900 full time and 148 part time students came in the mid-1950's. By 1973-74 the enrollment had stabilized at 795 full time and 24 part time students. Over the same period the faculty more than doubled from a total of 66 in 1949-50 to 136 in 1973-74.[100]

Richard H. Young who became dean of the Medical School in 1949, remained in that position until 1970. In the course of his administration the Medical School instituted a special six-year medical program in a bold attempt to shorten the traditional training period of four years of college, four years of study for the M.D. degree and another three years for residency and training in a specialty.[101] *Medical School*

Funded by substantial grants from the Commonwealth and the Markle foundations, the program called for the simultaneous admission of twenty-five superior high school graduates to the College and the Medical School. After two years in

Aerial view of Chicago campus looking southeast from Chicago Avenue showing (in lower half of photo) the buildings of the Law, Medical, and Dental schools, the Evening Divisions, and the Managers' Program as well as of member institutions of The McGaw Medical Center of Northwestern University

the College, which devised a new premedical program for the purpose, these students moved without a break and with assurance of Medical School admission into the four-year M.D. program on the Chicago campus.

Following Dean Young's retirement, James E. Eckenhoff was appointed dean of the Medical School. Educated at the University of Kentucky and the University of Pennsylvania, he joined the faculty of the latter institution in 1945 remaining there until he moved to Northwestern twenty years later. Before becoming dean he had served as chairman of the department of anesthesia.[102] Both Dean Young and Dean Eckenhoff were involved in the development of the Medical Center during the late 1960's and early 1970's.

In 1974 the Medical School instituted new programs in Allied Health and Nursing Education and appointed an associate dean to head them. This was intended to provide a means for coordinating programs in medical technology, nursing, physical therapy, prosthetics, orthotics, and respiratory therapy.[103] As noted earlier, the school also inaugurated a group medical practice staffed by faculty members as a means of improving the quality of clinical instruction.

Enrollment in the Medical School declined after the mid-50's once the postwar press of veterans had passed, dropping to a total of 538 in 1966-67. But by 1973-74 registration had rebounded to 710 (see Table 7-1). Between 1953 and 1973 the full time Medical School faculty grew from 59 to 252, while the part time paid faculty grew from 9 to 96. The no-stipend faculty rose from 497 to 1,019.* The striking increase in full time paid faculty reflected the administration's commitment to the development of the school and the Medical Center.[104]

On September 29, 1959, the Medical School celebrated its Centennial. On this occasion honorary degrees were awarded to eight outstanding scientists at a morning convocation in Thorne Hall where Conrad A. Elvehjem, president of the University of Wisconsin and a biochemist whose research had made possible a cure for pellagra, was the chief speaker.† The celebration included a colloquium on the afternoon of the 29th followed by a Centennial Awards dinner that evening at which merit awards were conferred upon twenty Medical School alumni and service awards upon eleven departmental chairmen of the Medical School.[105]

Dental School

Between 1953 and 1972 George W. Teuscher served as dean of the Dental School. Teuscher had received both his D.D.S. and his Ph.D. from Northwestern and had been a member of the pedodontics department before he became dean.[106] During his administration the Dental School made significant changes in its program.

Long term rivalry between the Medical and Dental schools had resulted in the Dental School's having its own departments of anatomy, chemistry, pathology, etc., while a few floors below in the same building, the Medical School maintained similar, though larger, departments. This not only constituted a waste of resources but also meant that it was difficult for the small preclinical departments in the Dental School to attract research funds and good faculty. In 1963 the combined

---

*No-stipend faculty are practicing physicians who are on the staffs of the hospitals affiliated with the university. Usually they participate in the clinical training of medical students.

†In addition to the speaker the recipients were Dr. Charles H. Best, codiscoverer of insulin; Dr. Shields Warren; Dr. Horace W. Magoun; Dr. Irvine McQuarrie; Dr. Joe Vincent Meigs; Dr. Isidor S. Ravidin; and Dr. William S. Tillet.

Interior of Alice S. Millar Chapel showing the magnificent stained glass chancel window

Residence hall mural evokes the psychedelic art of the 1960's

*Foster-Walker Undergraduate Housing Complex, opened
in the fall of 1972, housing more than 600 students*

*Norris University Center, headquarters for most student organizations
and scene of a variety of campus events and activities*

efforts of Dean Young of the Medical School, Dean Teuscher of the Dental School, and Professor James Hampton of the anatomy department in the Medical School, brought about an agreement to combine the two anatomy departments into a single one which would serve both schools.[107]

In the ensuing years similar mergers were arranged in other areas of preclinical training. In the long run this move made good academic sense and proved most constructive; more immediately the merger raised "housekeeping" problems the solution of which required both time and patience.

When Dean Teuscher retired in 1972, Norman H. Olsen became dean of the school. Educated at the University of Idaho, Creighton University, and Northwestern, he had served on the faculty of the Dental School since 1954.[108]

Over the years the physical facilities of the Dental School had deteriorated and become outmoded to a point that placed the school's accreditation by the American Dental Society in jeopardy. Indeed, for a brief period the school was put on probation until the central administration with the strong support and cooperation of Dean Olsen was able to secure a return of full accreditation by committing itself to provide new facilities for the Dental School in a new building in the Medical Center complex.

In 1973 the Dental School established a multiphasic clinic which brought together faculty and students from all the clinical departments and provided every dental student with the opportunity to learn about all the dental disciplines in addition to specializing in a particular area. This innovative program included students who were being trained to become dental assistants.

The administration of the school pursued a policy of placing dental faculty in the affiliated hospitals with a view to providing dental students with hospital experience. The Dental School also administered the Cleft Palate Institute which included faculty holding joint appointments in other schools, chiefly the Medical School and the School of Speech.

Enrollment in the Dental School dipped between the mid-1950's and mid-60's, then rose again to its early postwar peak of just over 450 (see Table 7-1). The size of the faculty increased markedly during these years. In 1953-54 the Dental School faculty consisted of seventeen full time and forty-eight part time paid members and twelve no-stipend faculty. Twenty years later the school had sixty-nine full time paid faculty, fifty-four part time paid and thirty-nine no-stipend faculty.[109]

Law School　　Dean Harold Havighurst retired from his administrative post at the School of Law in 1956. His successor, John Ritchie III, had been educated at the University of Virginia and at Yale Law School and had served as dean of the Law School at the University of Wisconsin and, before that, at Washington University in St. Louis.[110] Within three years of his arrival, in September 1959, the School of Law celebrated its Centennial.

The celebration began several months ahead of time with the laying of the cornerstone for the Robert R. McCormick Hall on May 7, 1959. Supreme Court Justice John M. Harlan was the principal speaker. A year later this three-story addition to the school which included space for classrooms as well as for the Owen L. Coon Library, was dedicated at a Centennial Convocation at which the honorary degree of Doctor of Laws was conferred upon Chief Justice of the Supreme Court, Earl Warren; Associate Justices Tom C. Clark and John M. Harlan; Dean Erwin L. Griswold of the Harvard Law School; Dean Frederick D. G. Ribble of the University of Virginia Law School; and Lord Cyril John Radcliffe, Lord of Appeals in Ordinary of Great Britain.[111]

Between 1964 and 1966 the School of Law undertook a thorough evaluation of its curriculum as a result of which several significant changes were made in its program. The basis for these changes was "the realization that excellent legal education must provide greater individual training for students than is possible through traditional large unit instruction." In the course of the next two years the faculty revised the curriculum so that while the first year's work was completely prescribed, the second and third years were elective within certain limitations. One unusual and important innovation was the Senior Research Program for third year students. This allowed students to pursue individual research under close supervision of a faculty member on a subject of mutual interest to both. Projects ranged from ones requiring traditional library research to ones calling for empirically oriented field work.

Curricular Changes

In the fall of 1968 the school introduced a unique course entitled Poverty Law and Practice Clinic which offered instruction in the legal problems of the poor, first through classroom instruction and then through the servicing of clients at legal aid offices in Chicago. The course involved faculty members, the Chicago Legal Aid Bureau, psychiatrists and social workers.

The following fall, the School of Law joined other major law schools in the country in substituting the Juris Doctor (J.D.) for the Bachelor of Laws (LL.B.) degree previously awarded. The faculty recommended and the trustees agreed that the J.D. degree would be awarded retroactively to holders of the LL.B. upon application.[112]

The relevance of the social sciences to the law was given recognition in the pioneering of a combined Ph.D. program in law and the social sciences in 1969. This program received a generous grant from the National Science Foundation in the summer of 1974 for a study of the utilization of social science data by the Supreme Court. Another interdisciplinary program given in conjunction with the Graduate School of Management led to the award of the J.D. and M.M. degrees.[113]

The scope, variety, and flexibility of the school's offerings accelerated the impressive increase in the number of applicants for admission. With a freshman class deliberately limited to 175, the school had received 1,295 applications in 1968; applicants for the class entering in the fall of 1973 numbered 2,700.

In 1972 James A. Rahl, an alumnus of the College and the School of Law and a faculty member since 1946, became dean. A scholar with an international reputation, he had been active in planning the curriculum revisions of the late 1960's.[114]

Enrollment in the school dipped slightly during the mid-1950's then rose to reach an all time high of 555 in 1973-74 (see Table 7-1). The growth in the size of the faculty between 1953-54 and 1973-74 was also impressive—from eleven full time and ten part time to thirty full time and twenty part time paid members.[115]

These accounts of specific curricular developments merely touch on the long list of changes initiated by the various schools during this period. Fundamental alterations in both degree requirements and grading methods whereby progress toward degrees would be measured in terms of courses rather than credit hours, and pass, no-credit grades would be permitted, were recommended in votes of the University Senate and adopted by the school faculties in the late 1960's.[116]

University College In 1948 E. T. McSwain, professor of education, became dean of University College. At that time responsibility for the teaching of evening courses and the granting of the appropriate diplomas and degrees was shared by three schools: University College, the School of Commerce and, to a lesser extent, the School of Journalism. Financial waste, duplication of administrative functions and lack of coordination in planning the courses to be offered were inherent in this arrangement. Most of the Liberal Arts, Speech and Education courses came under the jurisdiction of the dean of University College who recruited a number of his faculty on an overload basis from the College of Liberal Arts faculty; most of the Commerce evening courses were taught by Commerce faculty as part of their regular teaching load; Journalism relied heavily on professional journalists from the outside to teach evening classes. A more coordinated evening program seemed desirable.

Evening Divisions The move to consolidate the organization of evening studies began in 1950 with the creation of a unified secretariat and a joint curriculum committee. A more radical step three years later replaced the amalgam of University College, Commerce, and Journalism evening courses with the Northwestern Evening Divisions under the direction of a dean.[117] Daniel R. Lang, associate dean of the School of Commerce and director of its evening classes became the dean of the Evening Divisions at this time.

Under the new system each of the Evanston schools assumed responsibility for offering evening courses in its area on the Chicago campus and retained control over both the curriculum and the requirements for degrees in that area. In 1957 it was decided to offer these evening classes on the Evanston as well as on the Chicago campus.

Enrollment in University College and the Chicago campus courses in Commerce and Journalism ran high in the postwar periods, and at the time of the reorganization was still around 10,000. Succeeding years saw a marked decline in registration in the Evening Divisions, for the most part because of competition from public institutions which required virtually no tuition. In 1973-74 the enrollment was 3,650 (see Table 7-1). Nevertheless, Northwestern remained committed to its Evening Divisions believing that it had long offered and would continue to offer a valuable service to the Chicago community by providing the kind and quality of evening courses not available elsewhere.

In 1972 Martha S. Luck became dean of the Evening Divisions. She had been associated with the university since 1940 and had served both as executive secretary of University College and as assistant dean of the Evening Divisions.[118]

Summer school sessions continued to offer a wide variety of courses at both the undergraduate and graduate levels during the Miller years. Taught for the most part by the regular faculty of the College of Arts and Sciences and the schools of

Education, Music, and Speech, the summer courses attracted large numbers of *Summer* students. Some were year round students wishing to complete their schooling *Sessions* earlier by attending summer session. Others were already employed but wished to supplement or advance their education by means of summer courses. Although there was some decline in summer school registration after the 1950's, the peak of veteran enrollment, the sessions continued to draw over 5,000 students throughout the Miller years (see Table 7-1).

During the 1940's the Summer Session had been administered by a director, a faculty member who might serve in this capacity for one or two summers. From 1949 through 1952, A. C. Van Dusen directed the sessions, then in 1953, William C. Bradford, a member of the School of Commerce faculty since 1947, assumed this responsibility. The following year he was named dean of the Summer Session, a post he continued to hold throughout this period, though in the meantime he also became assistant, then, associate dean of faculties and, in 1971, associate provost.[119]

The creation of various interdisciplinary centers between 1948 and 1974 offered an additional stimulus for faculty research. Many of these centers were organized as a result of faculty initiative. As the dean of faculties noted in a report to the president: "Such centers, when initiated by faculty persons who are seeking closer collaboration with colleagues in regard to the study of common problems, are a healthy sign of academic weariness with too much departmentalization, and deserve encouragement as a means of bringing professors into closer working harmony regardless of traditional administrative divisions."[120]

The first to be established was the Program of African Studies in 1948, followed *Interdisciplinary* by the Geotechnical Center in 1952, and the Metropolitan Studies Center in 1953. *Centers* Three years later, the Traffic Institute was joined to the Transportation Center which was formed at this time.* The Computer Center was established in 1959. The next decade saw the organization of the Materials Research Center in 1960; the Biomedical Engineering Center in 1961; the Center for Urban Affairs in 1968;† and the Center for the Teaching Professions in 1969. The Center for the Interdisciplinary Study of Science and Technology was formed in the same year. In 1970 the Health Services Research Center was established and two years later the Center for Experimental Animal Resources and the Center for Mathematical Studies in Economics and Management Sciences.

In all but one case, the directors of the centers reported to the vice president for research and dean of science. The director of the Center for the Teaching Professions, however, was responsible to the dean of the School of Education. The faculty members who participated in the activities of the centers usually came from more than one school.

Northwestern had several other centers, institutes, and programs which functioned somewhat differently from the university centers mentioned above. The Cancer Center in the Medical School and the Gannett Urban Journalism Center in the Medill School of Journalism functioned almost entirely within the jurisdiction of

*The Traffic Institute became an independent entity again in 1974.

†In 1969 the Urban Affairs Center absorbed the Metropolitan Studies Center.

those schools, while the Cleft Palate Institute, staffed by faculty from the School of Speech, the Medical School, and the Dental School was affiliated with the latter for administrative purposes.

Perhaps one of the most interesting collaborative efforts undertaken by Northwestern faculty is the Archeological Field School, the largest in the country, directed by Professor Stuart Struever. In seven years of excavating at a site in Kampsville, Illinois, members of the archeological team unearthed fifteen prehistoric civilizations. Their discoveries included a village dating back to 5100 B.C. which, according to Professor Struever, gives us "the best chance we have had to learn about the early archaic Indian peoples."[121] In studying these ancient peoples and their civilization the Field School of Archeology draws on the knowledge of faculty from diverse disciplines.

Two special programs, the Canadian Studies Program and the International Studies Program were established in 1974. The Council of International Studies program sponsored the award of scholarships for study abroad to eight undergraduates in the summer of 1974, the funds being supplied by the Richter Memorial Fund.[122]

The creation of these interdisciplinary centers and programs during the Miller years offered a wide range of new academic possibilities to students and provided the opportunity for a pooling of faculty and other resources.

Encouragement of Research High on the list of the Miller administration's priorities was the encouragement of an increase in the amount and scope of research carried on at Northwestern. To this end the administration allocated whatever resources it could to improving research facilities, from acquiring a computer to building a new library and new laboratories. But it must not be thought that all these developments stemmed from administrative initiative alone. Far from it! There was a constant interaction between faculty groups and members of the administration, and in the case of the computer and the library the faculty provided the impetus for action. As early as 1950 an eager group of young faculty took Dean of Faculties Wild to lunch and asked his support in the acquisition of an analogue computer. Dean Wild, being new on the job and unfamiliar with this type of research device, made no comment, but some years later another faculty group told him emphatically that "unless Northwestern obtained a computer soon it would be no better academically than a second-rate high school." Though deeply impressed by this vigorous presentation, the dean of faculties was neverthelesss concerned about finances. "But where is the money coming from?" he asked. To this, one of the faculty group retorted, "Well, that's your problem."

In due course the administration appointed a faculty computer committee and set about finding funds. On November 1, 1957, Northwestern opened the Computer Center with a 650 IBM computer as its first acquisition. Eight years later the center moved its operations to new headquarters in the specially constructed Vogelback Computing Center.[123]

As noted earlier, the building of the new library on the Evanston campus was also in large part the result of faculty initiative. The administration had long known that Deering Library was inadequate for a university which aspired to improving

the quality of scholarship at both graduate and undergraduate levels and as early   *The Library*
as 1952 President Miller had urged the trustees' committee on educational properties to consider the construction of a new library, but no action had followed.[124]
When Professor Clarence Ver Steeg took up the cause in 1960 the administration
appointed a faculty Library Planning Committee with Professor Ver Steeg at its
head. Under its chairman's indefatigable direction, the committee undertook to
devise a scheme which would actively aid users of the library instead of merely
providing more storage space for books. When the library was completed in 1970
it became clear that the planners had achieved their aim.[125]

The vast expanse of the library's physical plant was matched by a substantial
growth in its book and periodical holdings. As already indicated, University
Librarian Jens Nyholm had begun to increase acquisitions during the Snyder years
and continued to receive substantial support from the Miller administration for
his endeavor. In 1968 Nyholm retired. In the course of his twenty-three years as
librarian the continued holdings of the Northwestern libraries had grown from
736,000 volumes to 1,196,000; a staff of 60 had expanded to 170; and the budget
for the libraries had increased from $200,000 to $2,000,000.*

From 1968 to 1971 Thomas R. Buckman headed the Northwestern library.
Educated at the University of the Pacific and the University of Minnesota, he had
served as director of the University of Kansas Library before coming to Northwestern. During his tenure the new library building was completed and the various
collections moved into their new quarters. Buckman revised the organization of
the staff, dividing responsibility among several assistant university librarians who
reported to the university librarian.

John P. McGowan, who became university librarian in 1971, had long been
associated with Northwestern. Educated at Hunter College, Columbia University,
and New York University, McGowan had served as librarian of the Technological
Institute from 1955 to 1959, then returned to Northwestern after seven years as
director of the Franklin Institute in Philadelphia.[126] In the course of his administration, the University Library automation project with which he had experimented
at Tech was introduced into the library with the result that all technical processes
and circulation control became fully automated.

The size of the Northwestern holdings continued to grow under Buckman and
McGowan's administrations and by 1973-74 had risen to 2,349,369 volumes, of
which 1,661,396 were on the Evanston campus. By 1972-73 the library ranked
seventeenth among the seventy-eight major research libraries in the United States
and seventh among private institutions on the list.

In addition to increasing its own holdings, the library further augmented its
offerings by becoming a member of the Mid-West Inter-Library Center, which, in
1965, became a national organization known as the Center for Research Libraries.
By purchasing and holding materials which are used rarely, by serving as a deposit
center for items that member libraries find difficult to house, and by circulating

---

*This account is based on Rolf Erickson's article "Northwestern University Libraries" in the *Encyclopedia of
Library and Information Science.*

311

volumes from member libraries among the faculty of the cooperating institutions, the center performs an invaluable service. John McGowan played an active role in arranging for the center's purchase of learned journals which in some libraries absorb at least a third of the total budget.[127]

Special Facilities While the physical construction of additional laboratory facilities on the Evanston and Chicago campuses has been discussed elsewhere some further elaboration is called for here. On the Evanston campus, the installation of a language laboratory in 1959 enabled the foreign language departments to modernize the teaching of languages.[128] Of more than local interest was the opening of Frances Searle Hall which enabled the department of communicative disorders of the School of Speech to carry on its highly distinguished and internationally recognized teaching and research in the fields of audiology and language disorders under the direction of Professor Raymond Carhart.[129]

Facilities for research in the sciences and engineering on the Evanston campus were augmented by the construction of the Lindheimer Astronomical Research Center, the O. T. Hogan Biological Sciences Building, and the Biomedical Engineering Center, chiefly funded by the Advanced Research Projects Agency and the Institutes of Public Health.*

MURA To accommodate the expansion of research in physics an addition to the physics wing of Tech was completed in 1961. By that year the volume of research in the nuclear field alone was so large that a full time radiologist was employed to check safety regulations on both campuses under the supervision of a faculty committee.

As a member of the Midwestern Universities Research Association (MURA) which was formed in 1955 with Atomic Energy Commission sponsorship and support, Northwestern had an opportunity to have faculty members participate in the design of the high-speed accelerator authorized by the AEC. However, the project ran into difficulties and the university found it difficult to provide the kind of personnel needed to take part in the type of design envisaged. Following years of controversy over the design and location of the proposed MURA accelerator a more promising development came in 1965 with the establishment of the Argonne Universities Association of which Northwestern was an original member. At Argonne National Laboratory many faculty members found research facilities in science and engineering that were not available on campus.[130]

URA Northwestern also joined in the formation of the Universities Research Association and on December 16, 1966, the Atomic Energy Commission announced that Weston, Illinois, was to be the site for an accelerator laboratory with a 1200 BEV accelerator to be built at a cost of $243,000,000 under URA auspices.[131] Access to these types of national and regional facilities greatly enhanced the opportunity for expanding Northwestern's research programs. Until the Weston accelerator was authorized many scientists in the Midwest felt themselves at a great disadvantage compared to their colleagues on the Atlantic and Pacific coasts where high energy accelerators had long been available at Brookhaven, New York, and Berkeley, California.

---

*By July 1, 1972 the total federal funding for ARPA at Northwestern came to $15,456,000. *Annual Report of Director of Northwestern Program*, Professor Donald Whitmore, 1972.

*Chicago campus: the Medical School's Morton Building, completed 1955
(foreground), and Searle Building, completed 1965*

On the Chicago campus the completion of the Morton Research Wing in 1955 and of the Searle Building in 1965 vastly expanded the laboratory and research space available to the Medical School. Opportunities for research will be further enlarged by the housing of the Rehabilitation Institute, the department of obstetrics and gynecology and the Psychiatric Institute in the new buildings of the Medical Center.[132]

Northwestern University Press

Yet another stimulus to the faculty's scholarly activity was the expansion of the scope and operation of the Northwestern University Press in the late 1950's. The Press had been legally incorporated in 1922 but its activities were confined primarily to the publication of journals associated with the law such as *The Illinois Law Review*, the *Journal of Law and Criminology*, the *Journal of Air Law*, the *Journal of Radio Law* and the *American Journal of Political Science*. Meanwhile in 1935 the university had established the Northwestern University Studies under the aegis of the Graduate School to publish books written by the faculty. In 1956 Dean Moody E. Prior of the Graduate School urged that either a fully active university press be established or that the Studies be discontinued since the existing arrangement was no longer viable. The president chose the former course and reorganized the press into a fully functioning venture with a director, a board composed of representatives from the faculty and administration, and a university subsidy. A year after the Press absorbed the Studies the decision was made to expand the scope of publications by including books written by authors not connected with the university provided these works were related to the research interests and activities of the Northwestern faculty.[133]

During the next fifteen years the Northwestern University Press published scholarly books on a wide range of subjects as well as several series—notably in African studies, philosophy, and English—which received national recognition. In the early 1970's, however, the administration began to phase out the operation of the press, for the most part restricting its activity to the publication of manuscripts that had already been accepted.

Tri-Quarterly

In 1958 the university, through the College of Liberal Arts, became the sponsor of a literary magazine, the *Tri-Quarterly*, founded and edited by Professor Edward B. Hungerford of the English department. To begin with it was chiefly a local faculty and student venture, but after Professor Hungerford retired in 1964 it became almost entirely a faculty and staff operation. Under the editorship of Charles Newman, the *Tri-Quarterly* became national in scope and authorship. A special supplement in the summer of 1968 provoked considerable controversy among members of the university community, some of whom found the contents in poor taste. The resultant dispute was eventually settled with the help of a faculty committee. The *Tri-Quarterly* has gone on to achieve favorable national recognition in literary circles.

The Faculty

When Henry Wade Rogers became president of Northwestern in 1890, the faculty numbered approximately 110; by the time J. Roscoe Miller became president almost sixty years later, it numbered 2,122.[134] It had been some time since the president could stroll about the Evanston or Chicago campus greeting professors and students by name. President Miller did come to know some faculty members through their service on various committees and though he was seldom able to be at the faculty meetings of the individual schools he regularly presided over the sessions of the University Senate. But the major responsibility for dealing with faculty he delegated to Dean of Faculties Wild and the deans of the individual schools.

On less official occasions at receptions and dinners which President and Mrs. Miller gave both at their home and at the university, they came to know some of the faculty members on more informal terms. One service that President Miller performed for faculty members which was highly valued by them was his readiness to act as "medical interpreter" for them and their families when they faced a serious medical problem. Without interfering with the doctor-patient relationship, he would make inquiries of the physician on the case and translate the medical terminology into layman's language for the anxious patient and his or her family. His genuine concern and desire to help earned him the affectionate title of "the good doctor" from those he helped.

From the very outset Dr. Miller had declared that raising faculty salaries would *Salaries* be one of the top priorities of his administration. In the course of his tenure, the salaries did indeed increase from a non-competitive level to one which put Northwestern on a comparable footing with the top ten in the country. In 1949 the average salary of a full professor at Northwestern was $7,828; by 1973-74 it was $27,935.* Of course, some of this rather spectacular increase was to be attributed to the inflation of the late 60's and 70's; nonetheless, the real income of the faculty also increased substantially during this period.

By 1955-56 the improvement in salaries was sufficiently striking to attract a so-called "accomplishment grant" of $1,898,500 from the Ford Foundation, the largest such grant awarded out of the nearly half billion dollars that the Foundation distributed throughout the country for the specific purpose of raising faculty salaries. This sum was added to the general funds, expendable at the discretion of the president and trustees. In addition, Ford awarded the university $3,059,500 as added endowment, the income to be used for faculty compensation. At the same time, Ford granted $2,700,000 to the Medical School for instructional purposes, making an over-all total of $7,658,000 to Northwestern in one year.[135]

By 1959 Northwestern's AAUP faculty salary rating had risen from C to B and by 1961 the university led the Big Ten and was among the top nine institutions nationally with an A ranking. During the following twelve years Northwestern remained among the top ten nationally.[136]

In determining compensation for the faculty, the administrators worked closely with the General Faculty Committee on the one hand and the Educational Policies Committee of the trustees on the other hand. Increasingly compensation came to include more than salaries, embracing as well a whole range of fringe benefits. These included an increase in the university's contribution to the Teachers' Insurance and Annuity Association and the establishment of major medical, group life, disability, and travel insurance programs.[137] Characteristically, young faculty members tended

---

*These figures are for full time professors on a nine-month basis and do not include the Medical and Dental schools.

to be more interested in cash raises, while older members, concerned about approaching retirement and rising taxes and medical costs tended to prefer nontaxable fringe benefits.

Retirement   One of the issues which had long concerned both the faculty and the administration was the mandatory retirement age of sixty-five. As early as 1952 the General Faculty Committee asked that this be raised to sixty-eight or seventy, and the question continued to be discussed during the years that followed.[138] In recruiting new faculty and retaining existing faculty Northwestern found itself at a disadvantage compared to institutions with a higher age limit, since raising the retirement age to sixty-eight meant substantial pension benefits based upon the final three years of service. After careful consideration by the trustees and the administration, it was decided in 1956 to raise the retirement limit to sixty-eight effective September 1, 1957.[139] The raising of the retirement age combined with higher salaries and improved fringe benefits put Northwestern in a good position to keep its own distinguished faculty from leaving and to attract talented new faculty from other institutions.

Revision of Promotion Procedures   As part of the central administration's effort to improve the quality of faculty throughout the university, the dean of faculties effected a major revision in the promotion procedures employed in most of the schools. Until this intervention, promotion tended to be based principally on the recommendations of departmental chairmen to the deans of the schools. The Medical School, however, followed a more rigorous course of evaluation, with the dean appointing an *ad hoc* committee of faculty members from outside the candidate's department to make an appraisal of his qualifications and achievements. The committee then passed its evaluation on to the dean. This increased the likelihood of a more objective and wider-based evaluation than the purely departmental recommendations common in the majority of the other schools.

The dean of faculties urged the other schools to adopt a procedure similar to the one followed by the Medical School in whatever form seemed appropriate given the variation in the sizes of the different faculties. Thus, in the schools with a relatively small faculty, such as Law and Journalism, the dean of faculties called on all the full professors to participate in making the recommendation for or against promotion. Most of the other schools, however, eventually adopted the use of *ad hoc* committees as part of their procedure. In the case of the College, with its very large faculty, there was an intermediary step, the faculty electing a panel of colleagues from which the dean of the College selected the members of various *ad hoc* committees. The next step also varied from school to school. In some, the dean acted directly on the recommendation of the *ad hoc* committee; in others he or she submitted the committees' recommendations to all the full professors of the school or division* for a vote before making the final recommendation to the central committee for promotions.

Not only did this new procedure bring in the judgment of faculty outside the candidate's immediate department, but at times it also brought in evaluations from

---

*The faculty of the College of Arts and Sciences is organized into three divisions: I. Physical Sciences; II. Social Sciences; III. Humanities.

distinguished faculty in the candidate's field at other institutions to whom the *ad hoc* committee addressed inquiries about his or her work. This effort to insure objective procedures was particularly important when it came to granting tenure, since this commits a university to keeping a faculty member at the institution for the remainder of his or her working life except under highly unusual circumstances. *Given the long-range fiscal implications of promotion to tenure it is not surprising that the dean of faculties spent much time reviewing the status of all nontenured faculty with their respective deans to insure that those who were not considered likely prospects for tenure were given due warning of nonreappointment.

One of the criteria for promotion at any major academic institution is evidence that the candidate has made a contribution to his field of knowledge. But research and writing require long blocks of time and freedom from other responsibilities and here the administration's encouragement of research proved helpful to faculty. Northwestern's policy on faculty leaves had been flexible and continued to be so. Leaves were granted on the basis of proposals submitted by the faculty member, with the length of the leave and the accompanying financial arrangement varying according to the applicant's particular circumstances. In some cases the university supplemented Guggenheim, Fulbright, American Council of Learned Societies and similar fellowships awarded to faculty by outside foundations and agencies; in others it made available funds to cover part or all of a leave which might range from a quarter to a full year.

It is not possible to list here the many honors, awards and other forms of national and international recognition which have come to members of the Northwestern faculty in all the fields in which teaching and research are carried on at the university. But it can be said that among participants at national and international meetings of learned and professional societies the faculty of Northwestern is well represented as it is in the learned journals of the different disciplines. A significant outside evaluation of the quality of Northwestern's faculty appeared in 1970 in a report of the American Council on Education. In that report Northwestern University was ranked eleventh among the top twenty private universities in the country on the basis of having eighteen academic departments which rated among the top twenty in their disciplines.† This appraisal from an objective source not only supplied confirmation of the university's rising reputation but also furnished the central administration with information which proved helpful in its long-range planning and allocation of resources.

Reminiscing about the early years of his term as president, Dr. Miller admitted that he had been very reluctant to spend money on administrative help, preferring to channel it into faculty salaries and new facilities for faculty and students. But in time it became obvious that more help was needed to manage the increasingly

Expanding the Administration

---

* According to the AAUP regulations to which Northwestern adheres this includes gross misconduct or financial collapse of the institution or a significant part of it.

† The ranking of the top twenty was as follows: Harvard, Stanford, University of Chicago, Cornell, Yale, Princeton, University of Pennsylvania, Columbia, The Johns Hopkins University, Massachusetts Institute of Technology, Northwestern, California Institute of Technology, Washington University at St. Louis, New York University, Brown, Brandeis, Case-Western Reserve, Duke, Rochester, and Rockefeller University. Department of Planning Summaries, 1972-73. See "A Rating of Graduate Programs" by Kenneth D. Roose and Charles J. Anderson, *American Council on Education, 1970.*

DISTINGUISHED VISITORS

*Composer Dmitry Shostakovich,
who received an honorary
degree from Northwestern
in 1973, shown with
Professor Irwin Weil*

*Charlton Heston (left) national chairman for the theatre-interpretation building campaign with John E.
Fields, vice president for development, and Roy V. Wood, dean of the School of Speech*

Sir Michael Tippett
attending the American premiere
of his opera, "The Knot Garden,"
at Northwestern in 1974 with
Don L. Roberts, music librarian (at left)

Composer John Cage rehearsing with students in Lutkin Hall, 1975

large and complex institution and new positions were established to deal with the manifold aspects of university life. While it would take too long to detail every administrative addition during this period, several of these illustrate the ways in which the administrative roster had to change to accommodate to new situations.

In 1939, for example, Northwestern had enrolled 39 foreign students. By 1949 this number had grown to 154, and it became necessary to appoint a foreign student adviser. Over the next fifteen years the foreign adviser's office grew in importance and expanded the scope of its activities as the number of foreign students and foreign faculty increased. In 1966 the adviser's office was renamed Office of International Programs and Scholars. By 1973 there were 683 foreign students and more than 100 faculty members from other countries at Northwestern.[140]

Another new office created to meet a changing situation was that of university registrar of the Evanston campus. Until 1953 each of the Evanston schools had taken care of its own registration procedures, record keeping, the checking of degree requirements, and all the duties associated with a registrar's office, but by then it had become evident that centralization of these functions was highly desirable. Miss Katharine George, a Northwestern alumna who had been primarily registrar of the College until this time, now became the first full time university registrar. In 1954 the university registrar's office computerized its activities and took over several additional functions, including the assignment of classrooms, the preparation of time schedules and the editing of the calendars in the school bulletins.[141]

Yet another central administrative post, that of director of the Equal Opportunity Office, was created in 1971, this time in response to a federal requirement that affirmative action be taken by universities receiving federal funds to give women and members of minority groups an equal chance for university jobs. Professor Raymond W. Mack, then director of the Center for Urban Affairs, and university counsel William Thigpen drew up the affirmative action program which was accepted by the university in October 1971.[142]

A different kind of new post was established in 1974 when Northwestern appointed its first professionally trained university archivist.[143] Patrick M. Quinn, who was appointed to this post, had worked as an archivist at the State Historical Society of Wisconsin and at the University of Wisconsin. Prior to this Quinn's two predecessors, Florence Stewart and Deva Howard, had cared as best they could with limited resources for the documents and papers which constitute a record of the university's history. Presidents Scott, Snyder, and Miller had all appointed committees whose charge it was to encourage an interest in the university's history and to ensure the preservation of its records. The appointment of a professional archivist, however, marked a step forward in the administration's commitment to maintain a record and keep alive a sense of Northwestern's past.

The Transition
In the late 1960's President Miller decided that the size and structure of the central administration required reappraisal in view of the increased complexity of the university's business and his own and Dean Wild's approaching retirement. To this end he employed the services of professional consultants whose report was, in essence, approved by the board of trustees on March 10, 1969.

The report recommended that two positions—those of chancellor and provost—be added at the top level of administration and that a third—that of vice president for the health sciences—be added at the next level. The chancellor would become the chief executive, while the president would deal with the day to day affairs of the university. The report also recommended that the provost become the chief academic officer, with the vice president and dean of faculties, the vice president for health sciences, the university librarian, and the director of planning all reporting to him. The vice president for health sciences would act as the liaison between the growing Medical Center, the Medical School, and the Dental School on the one hand and the central administration on the other.

The recommendations made by the report were carried out in large part over a period of three years. In 1969 Dr. Miller was given the title of chancellor, remaining president as well until the selection of Robert H. Strotz as president in 1970. At the same time Dean Wild was appointed provost, remaining vice president and dean of faculties until the latter position was filled by Raymond W. Mack in 1971.[144]

President Strotz, who had been dean of the College of Arts and Sciences since 1966, was selected by a search committee which consisted of eighteen members. Of these, nine were trustees appointed by the board; four were faculty members elected on a university-wide basis; three were students—two undergraduates and one graduate student—representing the student population; and two alumni, namely the president and vice president of the Alumni Association, appointed by the president of the board of trustees. The inclusion of faculty and students as participants in the presidential selection process was a departure from previous procedures for the appointment of top officers. An equally representative committee recommended the appointment of Raymond W. Mack, director of the Urban Center since 1968, as vice president and dean of faculties. Educated at Baldwin-Wallace College and the University of North Carolina, Dean Mack had been a member of the sociology department since 1953.

The final administrative transition again occurred in several stages. In 1973 Provost Wild retired; in 1974 Chancellor Miller retired. In 1974 Raymond W. Mack was appointed provost and the position of vice president and dean of faculties was eliminated. Similarly the position of chancellor lapsed upon Dr. Miller's retirement.

The post of vice president for health sciences was filled in 1970 by Dr. Robert B. Lawson who had been chairman of the Medical School's department of pediatrics since 1962. He was succeeded in 1973 by Dr. Oglesby Paul, a noted cardiologist and member of the medical faculty since 1963.

In 1975 the central administration of the university included the following officers: the president; the provost, designated as second in the line of authority to the president; the vice president and business manager; the vice president and controller; the vice president for research and dean of science; the vice president for health sciences; the vice president for student affairs; and the vice president for development.

In 1973 the Northwestern University Staff Advisory Council was organized to serve as a channel "for communication between the university's administration and its non-academic employees on both campuses." The fourteen members of the council

Staff Advisory Council

321

named by President Strotz represented a wide range of job categories. The president expressed the hope that the council "would assist the Administration in developing compensation policies to make the University more attractive as an employer" and that it would "serve as a sounding board for the President on questions and decisions concering the staff."[145]

Faculty Club The General Faculty Committee proposed a plan to establish a Faculty Club in the university-owned Franklyn Bliss Snyder home in 1965. The administration enthusiastically supported this proposal believing that it was important for the faculty to have an informal place to meet. Following extensive remodeling of the house, the Club opened in 1966 as a luncheon place with facilities for special functions and dinners.[146]

The Circle The University Circle continued to bring together the wives of faculty and staff for a variety of activities. In addition to monthly luncheon meetings featuring invited speakers and entertainment, the Circle sponsored trips to nearby places of interest as well as a variety of special interest groups. Once a year husbands were invited to join members for an evening of entertainment which might include skits on university affairs presented by members of the faculty and staff, or dinner and theater parties. These activities provided one way in which faculty and administration wives and families from the different schools could meet.

Student Life and Activities Between 1949-50 and 1973-74 the total number of students enrolled on the Evanston campus rose from 9,535 to 10,396, with a dip to 7,985 during the mid-50's when the postwar enrollment of veterans came to an end. On the Chicago campus full time enrollment declined from 2,265 to 1,934, though registration in the professional schools remained much the same in the 1970's as in 1949-50, the drop being chiefly in the Evening Divisions (Table 7-1).

The composition of the student body changed dramatically during the mid-1960's as the result of strong pressure from the faculty. A new admissions director, Roland J. Hinz, was appointed in 1965 to be succeeded two years later by William Ihlanfeldt.* The effects of new recruiting and admission policies became evident in a remarkably short time. Whereas previously the freshmen had come primarily from upper-middle-class, white, Protestant backgrounds, the new policies led to the enrollment of a much more heterogeneous student body.† Encouragement of students from low-income families to enroll at Northwestern had to be accompanied by an expansion of financial aid. As tuition increased (from $480 per annum in 1949-50 to $3,180 in 1973-74) the danger arose that the campus might become polarized between the children of the very rich and the well-subsidized students from low-income families. To forestall such a development, the university expanded the scope of its financial assistance to include students from middle-income families.

*Appointed dean of admission and financial aid in 1972, and of student records as well in 1974.

†In a 1965 survey, 1,418 Northwestern freshmen responded to a questionnaire on race as follows: white, 97 percent; Negro, .5 percent; American Indian, .2 percent; Oriental, 1.4 percent; other, .9 percent. In 1974, 1,381 freshmen responded: white, 88.3 percent; Black, 8.2 percent; American Indian, .9 percent; Oriental, 2.5 percent; Mexican American Chicano, .6 percent; Puerto Rican American, .1 percent; other, 1.7 percent (some respondents checked more than one identification). To a question on religious preference, 1,389 freshmen in 1965 responded: 61.8 percent Protestant; 18.2 percent Catholic; 14.7 percent Jewish; 3.1 percent other; 2.2 percent, none. The answer from 1,353 freshmen in 1974 was: 31.1 percent Protestant; 27 percent Catholic; 19.8 percent Jewish; 1.2 percent Eastern Orthodox; 3.0 percent other; 18 percent none. *N.U. Department of Planning, "American Council on Education Freshman Survey," 1965-1974.*

Between 1965 and 1974 financial aid to students increased 343 percent. Indeed, in 1973-74, the university distributed $4,609,494 in financial aid to 46 percent of the undergraduates. More than 45 percent of the 1973 freshmen class came from families with an income of less than $20,000, but considerable help was also granted to students from families with incomes larger than $20,000. This assistance along with a new Income Protection Student Loan Program which allowed students to borrow up to $2,500 a year, permitted the university to maintain "a substantial middle class" in addition to increasing the minority enrollment.[147]

F. George Seulberger, who had become dean of students during the administration of President Snyder in 1944, resigned in 1952. James C. McLeod, who had been the university chaplain then became dean of students, remaining in that post for fifteen years. Between 1967 and 1970, Roland J. Hinz, who had been director of admission, served as vice president for student affairs. He was succeeded in that post by Jim G. Carleton who came from Syracuse University where he had been professor of political science and vice chancellor for student affairs. The position of dean of students, which had remained vacant since 1967, was filled in 1971 by James Stull, who had been a member of the student counselling staff.

Religious Life

The religious needs of the university community continued to be served by the university chaplain in concert with the fifteen or so religious counsellors maintained by the various faiths represented on campus. Some of the counsellors were full time chaplains presiding over their own centers; others were town clergy performing the duties of religious counsellors on a part time basis; others still were laymen faculty or townspeople. The university chaplains coordinated the various religious programs and activities as well as officiating at the Alice Millar Chapel and Religious Center.* Student interest and involvement in religious activities fluctuated during this twenty-five year period. But a sizeable number continued to avail themselves of the services, programs, and fellowship offered by the religious organizations on campus.

The 1950's

It has become a cliche to characterize the students of the 1950's as apathetic. In 1957 George M. Cohen, president of the Student Governing Board, lamented that during the 1956 presidential election campaign there had not been "a single campus-wide political program or forum." He went on to quote one of the speakers at the Ninth Congress of the National Student Association who had proclaimed,

> We are the privileged and antiseptic generation. We move in the backwater of great events, well clothed and well fed. We have become lazy on the victorious sacrifices of our older brothers and on the non-fulfillment of gloomy prophecies. . . . If destiny wishes to rendezvous with this generation, she will first have to find us.[148]

Yet this characterization was not altogether fair. When, in 1953, the Illinois legislature was considering the Broyles Bill which would require professors and teachers to take a loyalty oath, the Student Governing Board, under the chairmanship of John McKnight, issued a report strongly affirming the principle of academic freedom—hardly an apathetic gesture at the height of the McCarthy

*James C. McLeod, 1946-1951; Walter Wagoner, 1951-1955; Ralph E. Dunlop, 1955-1973; James Avery, 1973-.

era.[149] Moreover, students volunteered for a variety of community services, organizing Red Cross blood drives; initiating "Operation Evanston," which entailed several days of cleaning, painting, and repairing designated community facilities each spring; and staffing the Lawndale Project, devoted to providing counsel and tutoring for young people in a low-income area on Chicago's west side. But compared to the political activism on campus during the late 1960's and early 1970's, these were admittedly mild reactions to political and social conditions outside the university.

Sororities and Fraternities On the Evanston campus, undergraduate activities were mainly in the hands of the twenty-seven fraternities and eighteen sororities to which approximately 70 percent of the women and over 50 percent of the men belonged. Non-Greeks, including a large number of the commuters and graduate students, remained on the fringe of campus affairs despite the attempts of WOC (Women Off Campus) and MOC (Men Off Campus) to remedy this situation.

During the 1960's the desirability of deferring rushing from New Student Week to a later stage of the academic year was much debated by the faculty. Those in favor of deferment argued that this would allow students to become involved in their academic work instead of being swept away by social distractions from the moment of their arrival on campus. Secondly, it would prevent immediate separation of Greeks and non-Greeks (which resulted in a loss to both) and finally, it would allow those who wished to join the Greek letter societies time to make a sound choice. In 1967 a subcommittee of the Committee on Educational Policies, under the chairmanship of Professor Richard W. Leopold of the history department, submitted a plan for delaying rushing until the end of the winter quarter to the University Senate. At its meeting of February 1, 1968, the Senate endorsed the proposal by a large majority.[150]

Inauguration of such a drastic change in rushing, however, would have required a radical alteration in the housing and food arrangments for freshmen as well as sweeping away a tradition to which many students and alumni were very much attached. The faculty recommendation was therefore not accepted, but subsequently a plan placing formal rushing at the end of New Student Week and extending it into the first weeks of the fall quarter was adopted by the administration. When later the Interfraternity Council, with the approval of the Northwestern Community Council, endorsed informal rushing during "off hours" of New Student Week, both the General Faculty Committee and the Committee on Educational Policies expressed strong opposition, but President Strotz decided to allow the informal rushing as a modification of the deferred rushing program.[151]

In spite of changing times, certain student activities continued to draw support throughout the Miller years, though some suffered a temporary decline in popularity during the period of intense political activism. The Waa-Mu Show under the supremely competent direction of Joe W. Miller* achieved national renown as did the productions of the University Theatre, directed for many years by Alvina Krause. The School of Music offered a rich program of musical events including

*Who retired in 1975 after working for the university from 1929 on as director of student affairs, later as associate dean of students, and, finally as dean of university events.

orchestral concerts, chamber music, recitals by individual performers, choral music, and, after 1957, works by the Opera Workshop. The Dolphin Show, Orchesis, Homecoming, and May Week festivities continued to involve many students as did varsity and intramural sports and a highly successful Debate Society which brought back many honors from the National Debate Tournament.

Elections for student government brought out the campus politicians. In 1960 the Student Governing Board was replaced by the Student Senate which was designed to be more representative than its predecessor.* It included a president and vice president elected by the undergraduate student body as a whole; the four elected class presidents; four senators from each of the three upper classes and five senators from the freshman class. This new body was to be responsible "for the authorization and empowering as well as the efficient operation of all other student government organizations and student organizations."

Student Government

In 1969 the representative base was broadened even further when the Student Senate was replaced by Associated Student Government. This consisted of a forum comprising at least one senator and one alternate from each house or corridor (depending on the governing organization of the residential unit) as well as one senator for each fifty unaffiliated commuting students and an executive board composed of the president, vice president, treasurer and chairman of the permanent committees.[152]

The *Daily Northwestern* and the *Evening Northwestern* (published on the Chicago campus until its demise in 1972) attracted students with an interest in journalism and writing and kept the university community informed of campus issues and events. The *Syllabus*, published since 1885, continued to appear annually, recording the highlights of the preceding year. Its content and style varied considerably over the Miller years, reflecting the changing tastes and interests of students during this period.

Student Publications

On the Evanston campus Scott Hall continued to serve as the center for student activities, with the grill as the chief gathering place for informal conversations. In 1971 Scott Hall provided space for the Amazing Grace Coffee House, organized by students to offer rock music and other entertainment as well as low-cost food.[153]

Social Life

In 1972 Norris University Center opened its doors. Handsomely appointed and situated to command a view of the lake, the new center provided much needed space for student organizations and events. It included a cafeteria, a large book-store, a game room, an art gallery, lounges, meeting rooms, music rooms and a 350 seat auditorium which lends itself to a variety of uses for concerts, conferences, and film showings. Scott Hall was converted to house various offices including those of the dean of students and his staff and of the dean of university events. Amazing Grace moved to Shanley Hall, near Lunt Hall, which had served as a bookstore until the opening of the Norris Center.†

On the Chicago campus there was no overall student organization. The Medical, Dental, and Law School classes each elected their own class officers and had their

*S.G.B., first organized in 1934, had consisted of seven students elected by the undergraduate body as a whole.

†In 1975 it moved off the campus altogether.

own honor societies and fraternities—active and sometimes boisterous groups with headquarters in Abbott Hall. The Junior Bar Association and the *Law Review* absorbed the interest and energies of many of the law students. The evening students had their own lounge in Wieboldt Hall and organized their activities through the Lydians Club for women and the Commerce Club for men.

Two social events—the Junior Prom and the Navy Ball (renamed the Military Ball in 1952)—which had long been gala occasions, faded out during the late 1950's. Interest in formal affairs of this kind declined as students turned to more casual and less expensive forms of entertainment.

In the early 1960's an energetic group of undergraduates started the Symposium which brought a series of speakers to conferences and panel discussions on significant issues of the day to Cahn Auditorium. Organized by students, these conferences received financial and secretarial support from the university.[154] Students also organized the Adlai Stevenson Lecture Series in collaboration with the Adlai Stevenson Institute in Chicago, beginning in 1967. For a number of years this brought to the campus both scholars and officials concerned with international affairs.[155]

The assassination of President Kennedy in November 1963 united the university community in shock and grief. "The University Mourns" ran the banner headline of the *Daily Northwestern* of Tuesday, November 26. Below a lead story entitled "Late President Studied under Wild at Harvard,"* the paper listed the cancellation of most university events as students began a period of mourning. University Chaplain Ralph G. Dunlop reported that "small groups of students began filing into the new Alice Millar Chapel within 15 minutes of the first news that the President had been shot," and at special services on Sunday and Monday the chapel was filled not only with students but "professors, men in military uniforms, townspeople."

Beginning of Unrest By 1966-67 the winds of unrest that were unsettling campuses across the country began to blow across the Evanston campus as well. The fight for civil rights, a growing awareness of the scope and implications of American involvement in Viet Nam, and a mounting desire to have a greater voice in determining the conditions that governed their lives, led students to challenge the "Establishment" both on and off campus.

Among the first targets of student protest on the Evanston campus were the regulations governing conduct in the undergraduate residences. Until the mid-1960's the parietal rules specified visiting hours and the times at which women students had to be back at their residences. The students began to press for the removal of such restrictions and for the right of the residents of each unit to make their own rules, if any. In 1967 a group of student organizations prepared an open housing program which was endorsed by the Committee on Undergraduate Life.[156]

The administration granted a trial period for this program and immediately found itself under severe attack from trustees, parents, and alumni. In response

*Provost Payson S. Wild had taught in the department of government at Harvard before coming to Northwestern.

to one concerned alumna, President Miller wrote:

> I appreciate your letter about the recent decision on student open house privileges. This was a very difficult decision, even as an interim decision—made all the more so because of disinclination to allow such a change in rules for reasons we both recognize.
>
> The Council on Undergraduate Life unanimously recommended this action twice, predicated upon what they regarded to be a successful experiment with open houses here earlier this year, the substantially increased maturity and demonstrated judgment of the student body and, finally, upon the fact that such visiting privileges are granted by Northwestern's peer institutions.
>
> This recommendation of the CUL was overwhelmingly supported by the faculty, deans, and administrative officers of the University. In light of this I approved a trial period.
>
> I share your concern and am causing this trial period to be observed carefully, with detailed reports from the Office of the Dean of Students, so that I may make a fully informed final decision at the end of this academic year.[157]

Parietal Hours

In fact, the open house program was not instituted at that time. In the spring of 1970, however, after a student self-determination statement which included a reformulation of the earlier open house proposal had been approved by the newly constituted Northwestern Community Council (successor to the Council on Undergraduate Life), Dr. Miller accepted the recommendation that each residence be allowed the option to set its own parietal hours. In his letter to Professor Gilbert Krulee, chairman of the Council, accepting the recommendation, Dr. Miller warned, "It must be recognized . . . that this increase in the extent of self-determination carries with it a commensurate increase in responsibilities of individual students and their living unit governments."[158]

To add an academic dimension to life in the student residences a modest Faculty Associates Program had been initiated in 1966 with the support of the Faculty Educational Policies Committee.[159] Under this arrangement, members of the faculty volunteered to visit the dormitories, take meals there, and meet informally with the students. While this initial attempt to foster a closer relationship between faculty and students in the residences was only partially successful, the Faculty Associates Program received a new infusion of life with the appointment of a co-ordinator for the program in 1971.[160]

Residential Colleges

An even stronger move in this direction, however, was the establishment of five residential colleges in the fall of 1972. Although this possibility had been discussed informally by faculty members and the dean of faculties for some years, the precipitating factor was a report by a student-faculty committee appointed by the dean of students and chaired by Professor T. W. Heyck of the department of history.[161] Dean of Faculties Mack eagerly embraced the proposal for a residential college system developed in the report. With the support of the faculty—as voiced by the University Senate—and the central administration, he proceeded to put the plan into effect.[162]

By September 1972, five residential colleges were ready to begin their programs.

Each college had its own master as well as a roster of faculty associates. While the colleges did not offer a separate academic program for credit, they were expected to provide an intellectually stimulating environment for their residents by arranging seminars, discussions, and related activities. Two of the colleges organized their programs around specific themes—one around Community Studies, and the other around Philosophy and Religion—from which they took their names. The remaining three—Willard, Shepard, and Lindgren—chose not to commit themselves to any specific area in arranging their programs.

Student Activism
In 1962 an activist student group called Students for a Democratic Society (SDS) had been formed at Port Huron, Michigan. Over the next few years chapters spread to campuses across the country. In October 1965, following a wave of anti-war demonstrations throughout the United States, a chapter of the SDS was organized at Northwestern and accorded recognition by the Student Senate in December of that year. According to Jack Nusan Porter, who wrote an account of student protest at Northwestern:

> S.D.S. at Northwestern University merged with a local civil rights group called F.R.E.E., For Real Estate Equality, and a student group called Students for Liberal Action. Its first meeting ... drew a polyglot group of 80 people, graduate and undergraduate students, Greek and non-Greek.

Porter goes on to note that even during the following year Northwestern was still "at an early level of student activism; the issue of men's visitation and curfew hours were in the foreground."[163] It is generally agreed that this situation changed radically in the spring of 1967.

The first massive anti-war rally on campus was a Viet Nam teach-in, organized in April 1967. During the same month Ellis Pines, the newly elected head of student government who had run on a student power platform, arranged a rally on the steps of the administration building at 619 Clark Street. In an exchange with Vice President Kreml and Dean Wild, the students pressed for a say on a variety of academic issues as well as on the allocation of financial aid. As part of their protest against the American involvement in Viet Nam they asked that the NROTC program be discontinued.*

The leaders of one of the anti-war groups announced their intention to hold another demonstration—which they dubbed "Gentle Thursday"—on April 27, in front of Harris Hall. The rally would coincide with the weekly NROTC drill on adjacent Deering Meadow and the administration immediately let it be known that it would not tolerate disruption of "any authorized university event."[164] "Gentle Thursday" did not belie its name. A few balloons floated over the hedge toward midshipmen drilling on the Meadow, but the gathering resembled a student carnival more than a protest by militants.

The tone of student agitation became more strident in the course of the following year. The spring of 1968 brought demonstrations, sit-ins, and discord to academic

---

*Since the establishment of the program at Northwestern in 1926, over 1,300 students had had their education subsidized by it, receiving their commissions through the NROTC graduation. Much praised in the 1940's and 50's, the program had become one of the prime targets of anti-war protest on campuses throughout the country by the mid-1960's.

328

communities from the University of California at Berkeley to Columbia University in New York City. The immediate cause might differ from school to school, but almost invariably the crises assumed certain common characteristics as members of the university community became polarized by the reactions of the administration and, in some cases, the citizenry outside the campus.

At Northwestern the first major confrontation occurred on May 3rd and 4th, when a group of black students occupied the university's business office at 619 Clark Street. The immediate cause was the administration's refusal to accede to a set of demands submitted by For Members Only (the black undergraduate organization) and the Afro-American Student Union (the black graduate student organization) on April 22nd. The conditions that had led to the formulation of the demands, however, were considerably more complex.

Confrontation May 1968

Between 1965 and 1967 the number of black freshmen registered at Northwestern had risen from 5 to 70. In all, by the spring of 1968 there were about 160 black students on the Evanston campus, out of a total undergraduate population of 6,500 and a total graduate registrations of 2,500 part-time and full-time students.[165]

During the exchange between the black students and the administration in April it became clear that the black students had felt isolated in the midst of so many white students. This isolation had been exacerbated by hostile encounters between some black and white students. While the administration had assumed that once they were admitted black students would become integrated into the mainstream of campus life, this did not, in fact, happen. As a subsequent investigation revealed, black students at Northwestern felt "alienated from the mainstream of campus life . . . and by a foreign white mainstream that offered (in their eyes) little or no freedom of expression and movement for the black student."[166]

Feeling themselves apart from the white community, the black students turned to one another for support. A report by the University Discipline Committee which investigated one of the clashes between white and black students noted that "as the number of blacks on campus increased, . . . black students began to 'discover' each other. This gravitational movement tended . . . to provide black students with the reinforcement and support they individually needed to maintain their identity in the overwhelmingly white culture of the university and . . . contributed greatly to the sense of frustration and dissatisfaction these students felt. This getting together and discussing their plight heightened their sense of powerlessness and increased their bitterness towards the university."

This report recommended several measures to improve the racial climate, including the hiring of a black counsellor to deal with student affairs; the provision of facilities for meetings and social gatherings organized by and for black students; representation of black students on appropriate university committees; and the convening of campus-wide meetings addressed to the problems facing a predominantly white academic community attempting to adjust to the reality of a multi-racial campus.[167]

But it was already too late. When the administration announced the appointment of a black counsellor to work jointly with the Admission Office and the dean of students, effective the following September, the black students objected because

Student demonstrations: (top) spring 1967, Vice President for Development Franklin M. Kreml (left) and Dean of Faculties Payson S. Wild; (bottom) spring 1970, Mr. Kreml and Vice President for Student Affairs Roland J. Hinz (top photo courtesy alumna Lynn Davis)

Confrontations (top) give way to more peaceful encounters (below) as Vice President and Dean of Faculties Raymond W. Mack welcomes freshmen during New Student Week

they had not been included in the selection process. By this time they were already set on the course which would lead them to present their demands to the administration on April 22. These made clear the black students' conviction that only if they were accorded a share in the making of decisions on matters concerning them would their position at Northwestern be viable.

The Students' *Demands* The students demanded first that the university acknowledge its racial character and commit itself to changing its "racist structure" by providing for the following: that each forthcoming freshman class be 10-12 percent black, with at least half coming from the inner city; that the blacks alone appoint a committee to assist the Admission Office and that this committee have "shared power" in the making of decisions "relevant to black students"; that black students receive special consideration for increased financial aid and that black financial aid recipients not be required to augment aid by loans and jobs; that a black living unit be established; that more black faculty be appointed and that the black students decide who should occupy a proposed visiting chair in Black Studies; that black students must approve the appointment of any counsellor for the "black community"; that black students approve of all appointments to the proposed Human Relations Committee; and that blacks have access to the committee studying open occupancy and discrimination.

In response the administration indicated its willingness to seek the black students' advice on the recruitment of black faculty and students, but made quite clear its refusal to yield any of its power to make decisions on admission and financial aid, on curriculum, on the hiring of faculty and staff, and on housing. Reaffirming its commitment to integration, the administration stated that "while the university believes there is much to be done to assure the black student the rights and respect on this campus that he deserves, it strongly believes that organizing separate living for blacks is self-defeating and cannot contribute constructively to the academic purposes for which the university exists."

The black students immediately reaffirmed their demands and concluded by declaring, "The University either responds to our demands or we have no other alternative but to respond to its lack of response. The University has until 5 p.m. Friday, April 26, 1968, to notify us of its decision."[168]

On May 2, President Miller asked the black students to a meeting scheduled for the following day. The same day, Dean I. W. Cole and Professor Daniel Zelinsky, who served on the Committee on Financial Aid to Students and the Committee on Admission respectively, invited the students "to discuss in detail any matter relating to the admission and financial aid policies of the university." But neither of these invitations was accepted. Though the administration and representatives of the two concerned committees genuinely hoped to reconcile the differences between the university and the black students, the latter regarded these invitations as high-handed summonses from the "Establishment" expressing typical racist condescension towards blacks.

Instead of meeting, approximately 100 black students entered the business office at 619 Clark Street at 7:45 a.m. on May 3, after having diverted the security officers at the door by means of a ruse. Once inside, they chained the door. They had brought with them bedding, food and other supplies, and through their leader, a graduate student named James Turner, announced that they would occupy the building until their demands were met. Throughout the occupation, the black students inside talked to sympathizers outside through the open windows on the first floor. Indeed, several of the occupiers who were members of athletic teams kept their engagements by coming and going through those windows. *Occupation of the Business Office*

As soon as word of the occupation of 619 Clark was conveyed to members of the administration, they gathered at a building across the parking lot from the occupied building. Among those present were Vice Presidents Kerr, Kreml, Schmehling, Hinz and Wild, and Maurice Ekberg, superintendent of buildings and grounds. They were joined very shortly by a black faculty member, sociologist Walter Wallace.

Some time before, as student sit-ins and disturbances made their appearance on other campuses, the administration had prepared a plan for dealing with this kind of situation. This called for a request to demonstrators to quit the premises, to be followed—in the event that the request was not met—by an order to leave, accompanied by the warning that disciplinary action would follow if the order were not complied with. The third step called for removal of the trespassers by the university's security force, and the fourth for intervention by the Evanston police if the former proved unable to complete evacuation of the building unaided.

As the administration representatives conferred it became clear that they did not consider this prearranged plan appropriate to the occasion. In the preceding days, Columbia University had been wracked by fierce battles between students and police called to force evacuation of buildings occupied by protestors. Television screens had flashed across the nation pictures of the bloody combat. In the storm of recriminations that swept the campus in the aftermath, faculty, administrators, and students were so deeply divided that the viability of Columbia as a center of learning hung in the balance. At the University of California at Berkeley, at San Francisco State College, and at the University of Wisconsin in Madison, the summoning of police had similarly served to polarize the campus and escalate disaffection.

With these instances only too vividly in mind, the administration at Northwestern debated what course of action to follow. In a subsequent report to the board of trustees, President Miller explained what the alternatives and their potential consequences appeared to be:

The university authorities had to choose among three courses of action: One, which has had great appeal to many who were not close to the situation was to order the students summarily to leave (which they would not have done) and then to call the police; second, which was the decision followed, was to bring them out of the building through a process of negotiation, probably entailing some concessions to their demands, but none divesting the University of any of its authority. This course of action left open the possibility of a later decision to remove the students by force if the negotiation process failed. A third possibility was simply to ignore their demands and let them occupy the premises as long as they would, be that weeks or months. *The Choices*

The third possibility can be quickly disposed of. This would have resulted in such an interruption of the function of the University that it could not be tolerated. The cost of any of these alternatives was great.

Had the first—forcible evacuation—been pursued, the possibilities are estimated as follows: Since Northwestern's own security forces were inadequate in number to do the job, evacuation would, therefore, have had to be turned over to the Evanston police, who may well have needed the support of police from neighboring communities. The students within the building, accounting for a majority of the Negro students at Northwestern, would have had to be placed under arrest and removed physically. Instances of conflict would doubtless have occurred, followed by charges of "police brutality." There would have been involved not only the Negro students, but a goodly number of white student sympathizers and possibly some members of the faculty as well. In short order, protests would have become widespread not only among the white student body, activists, semi-activists, and others, but among the faculty as well. The possibility that further buildings would have been occupied by growing numbers of Negro sympathizers would have been great, and the continuation of this course of action would then have required having the police move against further groups of students and many of our own faculty members. It is quite possible that a majority of the faculty would have taken a stand in opposition to the administration as this process continued. The arrival of support groups from the Evanston and Chicago communities would almost certainly have followed. The resultant situation would probably have paralleled that which occurred at Columbia University. . . . This takes us to the second course of action, which we actually followed. It went well. The concessions that the University made were not unreasonable; and the demands that it felt it ought not to accede to were stubbornly resisted. . . .[169]

The University's Response

Such was the reasoning that called for negotiation instead of force. The group of university officers and faculty who set about drafting a response to the black students included Vice Presidents Kreml, Kerr, Schmehling, Wild and Hinz, Dean Robert H. Strotz of the College, Dean Robert H. Baker of the Graduate School, Director of Admission William Ihlanfeldt, Professor Wallace, Professor Gail Inlow, chairman of the General Faculty Committee, Professor Joe Park, chairman of the Faculty Committee on Educational Policies, and Lucius P. Gregg, Jr., associate dean of science. The deans of the schools were informed and consulted as the negotiators proceeded with their task. Vice President Hinz went back and forth between the conference room and the chained doors at 619 Clark Street, conveying messages, while two secretaries typed the tentatively agreed-upon statements. President Miller moved about the room urging speed and giving counsel. Attempts to reach the chairman of the board of trustees, John G. Searle, proved unsuccessful as he was out of town and unavailable.

A special meeting of the faculty was called for 4 p.m. in Cahn Auditorium. It was an unparalleled gathering which had no precedent in the history of the university, for it was not a session of faculty representatives but an assembly of all faculty members who wished to come. When President Miller opened the meeting, the main floor of Cahn was filled and the hall literally hummed with excitement. The president briefly explained the reason for the meeting and Dean Hinz outlined the events of the preceding hours. He was followed by Dean Wild who described the nature of the black students' demands, reported that attempts to negotiate were going forward and pledged that written accounts of the results would be made available to the faculty. There were a few statements and questions from the floor, and then the meeting adjourned. No vote was taken and none seemed appropriate at that stage. But it seemed to those present that sentiment ran roughly as follows. About a third of the faculty was extremely sympathetic to the black students' cause; about an equal proportion was opposed to the students' tactics; and the remainder appeared somewhat ambivalent. In any case, the majority seemed to favor further negotiations rather than the use of coercion.

Negotiations went on throughout the following day, Saturday, May 4th. The tone of the proceedings was cool and moderate. The university delegates learned that the black students sought recognition of their identity as blacks with a culture different from that of white society; that integration, as the whites understood it, was not an immediate goal; that the blacks did not wish to be swallowed up in white society, did not wish to lose their separate status. For their part, the black students learned a great deal about the way a university functions; that administrators do not have the power or authority to effect changes or draft edicts which ignore the statutes of the institution, the role of the trustees, and the prerogatives of the faculty in determining curriculum and making appointments. Accordingly, concessions were made on both sides.

In the late afternoon, the student negotiators returned to 619 Clark Street and secured the endorsement of their colleagues for the agreement with the administration. By 9:30 p.m. the black students had cleared the building, leaving everything in the best of order. Both sides had kept good faith; coercion and violence had been averted. *Negotiations Concluded*

In essence, the university agreed to seek the advice of black students on matters that closely touched their interests, while the students agreed to give up their demands to participate in the final decision-making on admissions, personnel, and curriculum.

Once again, President Miller's report best covers the results of the two days of negotiations:

> We indicate in the following paragraphs what the University did agree to do and, of that which has been demanded, what it did not agree to do. *President's Report*
>
> 1. Issue a policy statement deploring white racism in this country, and acknowledging its existence and extent. Granted.
> 2. Allow the black students to name half the members to a new University-wide Human Relations Committee, and approve the other members. Not granted. Instead, the administration called for a special advisory council to recommend to the University what changes in its procedures are needed to handle better the problems of black students. This council, composed of ten members selected by the president, J. Roscoe Miller, from a list of 20 supplied by the black students, "could in future years play an important role in recommending selection of members" for the Human Relations Committee, the agreement said. But for the moment, the President would make appointments in a way that elicits and recognizes the views and recommendations of the black students.

3. Assure that each new freshman class is 10 to 12 per cent Negro and, that half the black students come from the urban ghettos. Not granted. The University declared a commitment to seek at least half its new Negro students from urban ghettos. But it said it "cannot in good faith offer such explicit guarantees on class-wide quotas."

4. Institute a committee selected by black students that would assist the Admission Office in recruiting Negro students and share in decision-making authority, and pay the members. Partially granted. The University welcomed a committee to help in recruitment and said it should be paid on an hourly basis. (The committee work constitutes the work portion of students on work-study programs.)

   But it added that it "cannot permit University students to make individual admission decisions. The evaluation of a candidate's folder is confidential and a privileged communication between the candidate and the office of admission."

5. Supply For Members Only with a list of all Negro students on campus as well as names and addresses of incoming freshman. Granted.

6. Re-evaluate the process of determining and administering financial aid for Negroes and increase scholarships so requirements for part-time and summer work can be ended. Not granted. The University agreed "in principle" that the amount of aid should be increased and agreed to create a committee to advise the administration on financial aid policy and to help review individual requests for special assistance.

7. Provide separate housing facilities for black students. Granted. (Campus activity facilities were agreed to earlier.)

8. Allow black students to approve any personnel hired as counsellors for Negro students. Not granted. (The University on April 15 hired a counsellor to start in the fall quarter.)

9. Work with a committee of students selected by the Negroes on creation of a black student union. Not granted. (See 7.)

10. Give Negroes access to administration panels studying open occupancy matters and working on a new housing policy for the University. Granted.

11. Add studies in Negro history, literature and art, and give black students authority to approve Negro professors appointed to teach these courses. Not granted. The University said it agrees on the "importance of expanding studies of black history and black culture," which the dean of the College of Arts and Sciences would "urge upon his departmental chairmen for consideration."

12. Select black faculty members. Not granted.

The University added that "we welcome suggestions from the black community as to qualified potential faculty members" but noted that appointments are made by the various faculties.

In conclusion Dr. Miller added that the impression of those who had dealt with the students had been that they had a remarkable "depth of understanding for both their problems and ours. They did not appear to want to use their leadership position for personal notoriety or to want to make trouble for the sake of making trouble. . . . The Negro students staged an illegal and forceful demonstration, but they were not the brigands some sectors of the press depicted them to be."[170]

"Depth of Understanding"

The relief which followed the peaceful settlement of the dispute was rudely shattered by the banner headline on the front page of the Sunday morning edition of the *Chicago Tribune* of May 5, 1968: "Black Power Wins at N.U." The article characterized the agreement as a capitulation by the university. A scathing editorial the following day, entitled "A Sad Day for Northwestern," accused the university of having disregarded its statutory obligations and of having yielded its decision-making power to "trespassing rascals." The fact that these newspaper accounts were inaccurate and misleading in no way saved the administration from an avalanche of letters and calls, many of them vituperative. The president and his colleagues were castigated for abdicating their responsibility as administrators and for spinelessly allowing a small group of black students to dictate to the university. That the university had not, in fact, surrendered its fundamental authority was often overlooked in the barrage of criticism.

But there were also vigorous expressions of support. The president of the Alumni Association urged his fellow alumni to recognize that the university did not "release final authority in matters of academics or student life." Editorials in the *Chicago Daily News* of May 6, and the *Chicago Sun Times* of May 7, gave a more accurate account of what had taken place and so helped restore the balance. The faculty and staff gave high praise to the administration. Indeed, 425 of the 734 full time faculty on the Evanston campus had signed an endorsement of the agreement with the black students. At a meeting of the University Senate later in May, the unusually large gathering of faculty rose to give President Miller a standing ovation.

The trustees, however, were more tempered in their reactions. After several meetings at which the implications of the agreement with the black students were fully discussed, the board adopted a resolution which declared, in part, "The Board concurs in the administration's sincere effort to understand the problems of the black students' group . . . and authorizes the administration to proceed with the terms of the agreement of May 4, subject to review from time to time by the Board. The Board is satisfied that the administration properly rejected all demands that the University surrender administrative authority or faculty prerogative, and that under the terms . . . students will be consulted in an advisory capacity only." However, the trustees rejected any suggestion that Northwestern University was racist, adding that "the Board decries racism in any form." The resolution served notice that the trustees opposed negotiations of any kind "while unlawful or disruptive activity is in progress." In conclusion it noted that: "The Board expresses complete confidence in the administrative officers of the University and directs them to take prompt and effective action in case of any future attempt to engage in tactics which disrupt the orderly conduct of the University."[171]

"The Board Decries Racism in Any Form."

Thus the crisis ended peacefully with no injury to life, limb, or property and with considerable support within the university for the action taken. The peaceful resolution of the crisis set a precedent which was to stand the university in good stead during the next few years.

However, the creation of better understanding between the university administration and faculty on the one hand and the black student community on the other, could not prevent occasional incidents of a potentially explosive nature. In March 1969, a group of black students invaded the Triangle fraternity house in search of a fraternity member who had allegedly insulted a black woman student. Personal injuries and property damage resulted and the University Discipline Committee imposed penalties on the twenty-one students who admitted their responsibility for the incident. A group of black and white student sympathizers protested the penalties—which called for restitution for damages, in some cases suspension for the current academic year, in others, probation for two years—by staging a hunger strike on Rebecca Crown Plaza. The strike came to an end when President Miller personally reaffirmed "the decision and penalties authenticated by the University Discipline Committee."[172]

During 1969 and 1970 the black community on and off campus continued to press for the admission of large numbers of black students whose "total financial needs" would be met by financial aid. For its part, the university honored the commitment it had made in 1968 and recruited black students in increasing numbers. By the fall of 1973 approximately 650 of the undergraduates enrolled—constituting ten percent of the undergraduate body—were black students.[173] A black staff member had joined the Admission Office in the fall of 1971. The following year the College of Arts and Sciences formally established a department of African-American studies.[174]

Opposition to the War At the same time that the university was attempting to deal with pressures from the black community, the opposition of many students and faculty to the Viet Nam War was becoming increasingly vocal and militant. Between 1969 and 1973 the administration was confronted by a series of demonstrations in which both students and faculty participated. Led chiefly by the SDS,* the militants on campus resorted to force to draw attention to their views. Others, strongly opposed to the war, nevertheless rejected the tactics to which the militants resorted. Still others, both students and faculty, continued to support American intervention in Viet Nam. The administration saw itself as having the responsibility to make possible the expression of all the diverse viewpoints and to prevent the identification of the university with any particular position in the increasingly passionate controversy.

The militants at Northwestern, as elsewhere, directed much of their activity against the NROTC, insisting that this symbol of militarism had no place in an academic institution. In May 1969, an angry mob of demonstrators tried to block the entrance of guests to the annual NROTC review which had been moved from Deering Meadow to McGaw Hall. Evanston police had to be summoned to keep back the crowd and make way for those attending the review.[175]

Early in the fall of 1969, Chancellor Miller, anticipating further distrubances, issued a statement to all deans and faculty affirming that the university would not countenance any disruptions.[176] In mid-November, the SDS issued an "hourglass

---

*In March 1969, the Student Senate recognized the Northwestern University G.I. Student Activity Committee, which later changed its name to the Student Mobilization Committee to End the War in Vietnam.

ultimatum" demanding that the university open its investment portfolio for public inspection; that NROTC be removed from the campus; that "war related" research at the university be terminated; that trustee meetings be open to outsiders; and that a special student-faculty committee be established to oversee investments. When SDS leaders tried to force their way in to see the chancellor, they became embroiled in an ugly scuffle on the stairway with members of the security force. Frustrated by their lack of success, the group staged a sit-in at NROTC headquarters in Lunt Hall.[177] The chancellor invited SDS representatives to a meeting, which, however, proved unproductive. Although the SDS had set a January 15 deadline for a positive response to the ultimatum, that date came and went without incident.[178]

The next outbreak involved the Evanston community and created considerable strain between town and gown. In February 1970, William Kunstler, the controversial defense lawyer for the "Chicago Seven" (accused of conspiracy to create disruption during the 1968 National Democratic Party Convention in Chicago) was invited to lecture on the Evanston campus under the auspices of the Northwestern Faculty Action Committee (NUFAC). All went well until the lecture was over, at which time a relatively small number of people went on a rampage in downtown Evanston smashing windows and causing several thousands of dollars worth of damage.

Evanston citizens were outraged. The committee which had sponsored Kunstler undertook to collect money from the university community to cover at least some of the damage suffered by local merchants. The General Faculty Committee and the Committee on Educational Policies issued a statement which supported NUFAC's right to invite a controversial speaker like Kunstler to the campus but deplored the violence committed by a "small minority" and urged contributions to the NUFAC fund as an expresssion of faculty concern "and our sense of community responsibility." Approximately $1,000 was, in fact, collected.[179]

The next episode in this sequence of disturbances was a fire on the evening of April 27, 1970, which caused extensive damage to the building at 621 Foster Street, housing the department of linguistics. The police attributed the blaze to arson and the university offered $10,000 reward for information leading to the arrest and conviction of the perpetrators.[180] In due course a person was arrested and convicted for this crime.

Then came May 4, and the announcement by President Nixon that American forces were moving into Cambodia, followed by the news that four students at Kent State University had been killed by Ohio national guardsmen during a protest against the invasion of Cambodia. Nationwide, college and university campuses exploded with anger at these two developments. Northwestern was no exception. Early on the afternoon of Tuesday, May 5, the dean of faculties addressed a huge crowd of students who had gathered on the plaza of Rebecca Crown Center and read a statement authorized by Chancellor Miller. After expressing sadness over the loss of life at Kent State, the statement indicated that administration headquarters in Rebecca Crown would be closed the following day as a symbol of Northwestern's participation in the general protest.

Reaction to Kent State Tragedy

At a special meeting of the University Senate that afternoon, the chancellor deplored the tragic events at Kent State and rejected all violence whether manifested in the unnecessary extension of the war or in the disruption of "the full enjoyment of academic freedom on this campus." In recognition of the widespread concern among all members of the university community, the chancellor announced that:

> All formal scheduled classes of the University will be suspended for the balance of this week. The administrative offices of the University and the Northwestern University Library will be closed on Wednesday, May 6, in symbolic recognition of the concerns that trouble the campus. Department offices will remain open to assist faculty and students who may wish to plan special activities concerned with the problems that preoccupy us in a manner befitting our academic tradition.

This action was endorsed unanimously by the University Senate.[181]

At an evening rally of approximately 2,000 students on Deering Meadow, a proposal for a strike and the cancellation of classes was approved by acclamation. The fact that the chancellor had already taken the initiative in suspending the normal operations of the university did much to avert a possibly irreparable cleavage between the administration and the student body.

In the days that followed the university community closed ranks. As an outside observer wrote:

> Moderates, liberals, radicals and apolitical ex-leftists found themselves in unity over their outrage at Cambodia and Kent State. . . . (Many of) the faculty supported the strike which meant that the campus was together, administration, students and faculty, in opposition of the war. . . . Unity was the theme of the N.U. strike . . . and participation was geared to unity, giving everyone a strike-related activity. . . . So Greek Row leafleted, political freaks went to Washington . . . and radicals picketed. Communications between students increased, and radicals and moderates who normally shunned each other found themselves working side by side on strike committees, understanding each other a little better. There was no trashing (or) firebombing during the strike.[182]

Not all members of the faculty or student body were in agreement with the strike, of course. But the majority of both groups gave it their sympathetic support. The president of Associated Student Government, Eva Jefferson, served as a catalyst, bringing·diverse groups together, directing them to work cooperatively toward the strike goals and always stressing that violence was to be avoided.

The Barricade   Probably the most controversial feature of the strike was the barricade erected by some militant students across Sheridan Road near Scott Hall after the Evanston police had already diverted traffic away from the area. Eva Jefferson was opposed to the barricade as were her moderate followers, and the general public was highly incensed by this blocking off of a public thoroughfare. North Shore citizens criticized the university for tolerating this interference with traffic but in fact it was the Evanston police who urged restraint and made no move to take down the barrier.

In testimony before a joint Senate-House committee of the Illinois legislature meeting to investigate the causes of campus unrest, Wayne F. Anderson, Evanston city manager, stated:

> The City of Evanston decided to divert traffic from a section of Sheridan Road before any student barricade was erected. The decision was based upon the fact that the road was under construction . . . and the traffic conditions could be made worse because students were gathering to pass out leaflets. The City of Evanston was responsible for the continued existence of the barricade and could have removed it at any time the city saw fit. . . . The city permitted the barricade to exist because it was determined that the barricade served to collect and hold radical elements in the area. This worked to protect the security and order of the community. . . . The true radicals who are relatively few in number on that campus were unable to gain control . . . and were pinned down on the roadblock. We believe that a move against (it) could have played into the hands of (these radicals) and . . . would have created an incident that would have blown things up."[183]

The barricade was finally removed without any opposition, on May 13, by university employees after the city manager had stated that city workers would not be used "because it was decided to let the University clean up its own mess."[184]

On May 8, 1970, the students held a second rally in Deering Meadow. Chancellor Miller addressed the large assembly and, after reviewing the week's events, urged an end to the strike: "It is now time that we return to our primary reason for existence as a University—that of teaching, learning and research. Any other course would defeat the purposes of the past recent days."[185] The students, however, had already organized a large rally of university and high school students to be held that evening at Dyche Stadium, and Evanston officials, fearful of disorders, had asked Illinois national guardsmen to be at hand.

The university administration regarded this as an unfortunate move which might well provoke violence instead of preventing it. After discussions with city officials, the chancellor and his aides were able to persuade them to keep the guardsmen at a distance from the university. In the end, the National Guard came no nearer than James Park in South Evanston. The rally of approximately 7,000 people proceeded peacefully and neither guardsmen nor Cook County sheriff's men were called upon.[186]

Over the weekend the administration planned the reopening of classes for the following week, announcing that "full resumption of scheduled classes on the Evanston campus will occur Wednesday morning, May 13 . . . classroom buildings on both campuses will be open Monday morning, May 11, for those faculty and students who wish to resume the educational programs interrupted by the strike, including the evening MBA program."[187]

At this point, the Chicago campus which had been relatively quiet had its first *Chicago* disruption when a group of about ten Medical School students and nurses took over *Campus* the office of one of the Medical School deans, proclaiming that they were setting up a "People's Health Free University" and demanding, among other conditions, the admission to Medical School of more blacks, Spanish speaking persons and low-income whites. When the vice president for health sciences asked the students to leave, they at first refused but the following day they agreed to depart and to engage in negotiations.[188]

Following the chancellor's announcement on the resumption of classes, students and faculty balloted on Tuesday, May 12, 1970, for one of three choices. The first, entitled "New University," gave students three options: (a) full time work in anti-war activities and credit received for courses up to that date; (b) full time or part time work in restructured classes with grades and credit optional; (c) full time attendance of traditional classes with normal grading procedures. The second alternative proposed continuation of the strike. The third proposed ending the strike and returning to business as usual. An overwhelming number, 4,078, voted for the first set of options; 604 wished to continue the strike and 410 desired a return to the prestrike situation.[189]

The strike was over, but on condition that the options spelled out in the New University proposal go into effect. This called for a break with prestrike academic conditions; the continuation of efforts to bring the war to an end; and the development of courses related to the aims of the strike. For those students who desired to drop some or all of their regular course work and to obtain credit for what they had done until the time of the strike, a special grade of "T" was granted by faculty votes in all the Evanston campus schools except Journalism.[190] In the wake of the euphoria generated by the strike, business as usual was not the campus mood, but by the time school reconvened in the fall, interest in the New University options had very much diminished. When the administration announced that there would be no funding for the New University programs, efforts to revive it ended.[191]

After three successive years of springtime confrontations, the Spring Thing held on the new lakefront campus in May 1971, brought a welcome touch of festivity to Evanston as townspeople joined the university community in listening to bands, trying their luck at games, and consuming large quantities of carnival food and soft drinks.

May 1972 By the following spring, however, Rebecca Crown Plaza once more became the site of an angry demonstration. Called initially to protest an increase in board and room rates, the meeting turned into an anti-Viet Nam War demonstration, partially in response to President Nixon's announcement that Haiphong Harbor in North Viet Nam would be mined by the United States. Once again student government leaders declared a strike and militants erected a barricade across Sheridan Road. There were rallies and marches; an abortive attempt to disrupt NROTC drills at Dyche Stadium; demands that the university close down, a hunger strike by approximately 150 students; and considerable leafleting on Evanston streets.

President Strotz, while supporting the right of peaceful protest, refused to close the university. Classes were, on the whole, well attended during this period and cool heads among both student leaders and Evanston police averted serious clashes. The barricade on Sheridan Road was removed by the police without incident and by May 12, 1972—three days after the initial demonstration—the excitement had subsided.[192]

Return to Peaceful Days As the United States began its moves to disengagement, the mood on campuses throughout the country changed. What would have seemed unimaginable to an observer of the university scene in 1968-1972 had in fact happened by 1974. Interest in traditional, purely social activities began to revive. The Greek letter societies found a renewed interest in what they had to offer. A new wave of students began to show more concern for grades than for world affairs. To faculty and administrators who had been at the university in the 1950's it seemed that the wheel had come full cycle. But some things had changed forever. Nobody could still consider Northwestern a country club for the children of a privileged few.

Not only had the racial, religious and socio-economic character of the undergraduate student body changed drastically, but the number of out-of-state and foreign students had increased dramatically. Of a total of 23,630 students enrolled at Northwestern in 1950, only 194 came from overseas, 4,520 came from out-of-state and the remaining 18,926 from Illinois. By 1974, out of a total of 17,000* students, 480 came from 14 foreign countries, 5,708 from out-of-state and the remaining 10,813 from Illinois. Northwestern University had become an institution of national stature, attracting students from thirty-four states.

Athletics 1949-74

After the Wildcats' climactic Rose Bowl victory in 1949, their fortunes declined steadily. In 1951-52 a faculty committee headed by Dean E. T. McSwain of the School of Education reported that the university's high admission standards and relatively high tuition reduced the athletic department's ability to recruit large numbers of skilled players. While the other members of the Big Ten had separate schools of physical education with their own admission standards, physical education at Northwestern was taught in the School of Education which, of course, adhered to the university admissions standards. From time to time sports enthusiasts suggested that the admission requirements for the physical education division be modified so that it could be competitive with similar departments in the other schools in recruiting athletes. The university administration rejected any such move and subsequently never deviated from its commitment to a single admissions standard.

The fortunes of the football team reached a nadir in 1955 when the Wildcats ended the season in last place.† At that point the *Daily Northwestern* demanded that Northwestern withdraw from the Big Ten Conference. But President Miller emphatically opposed such a move.[193] In the first place, he believed that intercollegiate athletics, though peripheral to the basic educational aims of the institution, were a healthy and desirable aspect of the undergraduate experience. He felt, moreover, that if the university withdrew from the Big Ten Conference—of which it had been a founding member in 1896—it would disappoint significant numbers of students and alumni and would lose their support. Casting about for an alternative, he saw no group comparable in prestige to the Big Ten to which the university might attach itself, and realized that an attempt to create a new collection of intercollegiate rivals would entail an enormous amount of the administration's time and energy for years to come. Finally, even if such a new set of football opponents were agreed upon, he suspected that attendance and enthusiasm at games with unfamiliar opponents would drop markedly thus making the financial picture for athletics even more bleak. Thus he decided that Northwestern should

---

*1947-1950 marked the high point of enrollment as veterans of World War II took advantage of the educational benefits provided by the G.I. Bill.

†This and all subsequent citations of standing in the Conference are taken from the *Big Ten Record Book*, as are the scores of the individual games referred to in the text.

Action: on the balance beam and on the courts

stay with the Conference and hoped that an improved record would help to justify this decision.

Staff changes in the athletic department brought in Stuart Holcomb who replaced Theodore Payseur as director in 1956. Ara Parseghian was appointed football coach and William Rohr basketball coach during the same year.[194] To his new athletic director, Dr. Miller gave only two injunctions: "Stay within the rules and don't impair our academic standards."*

To advise and assist the director of athletics and the administration in assessing the athletics program, the president established the Alumni Advisory Council on Athletics with Thomas Z. Hayward as chairman. The council embarked on a study of the organization and curriculum of the division of physical education, comparing its program with those of the physical education departments in the other Big Ten schools.[195] As a result of this study, the council made two suggestions. First, it urged that Northwestern consider relaxing its admission standards for students enrolling in the division of physical education. Second, it suggested that the division lower its course requirements to bring them more in line with the offerings of the other Big Ten schools to their athletes. For example, while Northwestern's freshman program required Biology A, a social science course, and English A, one of the other schools let its freshman athletes count Beginning Basketball and Beginning Football and Rhetoric (as differentiated from the regular freshman English course) for full credit. Yet another required that only seven out of sixteen mandatory semester hours have sound academic content.[196]

Alumni Advisory Council Survey

Nevertheless, in spite of this evidence that Northwestern labored under a severe disadvantage compared to the other members of the Big Ten Conference, the administration refused to depart from its policy of maintaining the same standards for its physical education students as for the rest of its student population. In recruiting players, the athletic staff stressed Northwestern's academic merits and concentrated on athletes who showed promise of being able to earn a degree. Between 1952 and 1963, the athletic director reported, 138 out of 159 men who earned letters in football (88 per cent) also earned degrees from the university. This was a record unmatched by any other Big Ten school and one of which members of the Northwestern community were justly proud.[197]

During Parseghian's first year as coach, 1956, Northwestern's football team rose from last place to sixth in the Conference but sank to the bottom again, without a Conference win, in 1957. However, in the course of the next four seasons—1958-1961 —"Northwestern . . . played nearly equally within the Conference, winning 11 and losing 15. The overall mark (was) 20-16 including four straight victories over Notre Dame." Perhaps most satisfying to Northwestern supporters were the victories over Michigan, 55 to 24, and Ohio State, 21 to 0, in the fall of 1958.[198]

In 1964 Parseghian resigned as coach to go to Notre Dame and was succeeded by Alex Agase, former coaching assistant to Parseghian at Northwestern. The best years during Agase's term came in 1970, when Northwestern tied for second place with Ohio State, and in 1971, when it occupied second place alone. After the 1972 season, Agase responded to a bid from Purdue. His successor, John

*The same directive went out to W. H. H. (Tippy) Dye, who succeeded Holcomb as athletic director in 1966.

Willie the Wildcat   *Northwestern's inspiring Wildcat Marching Band*

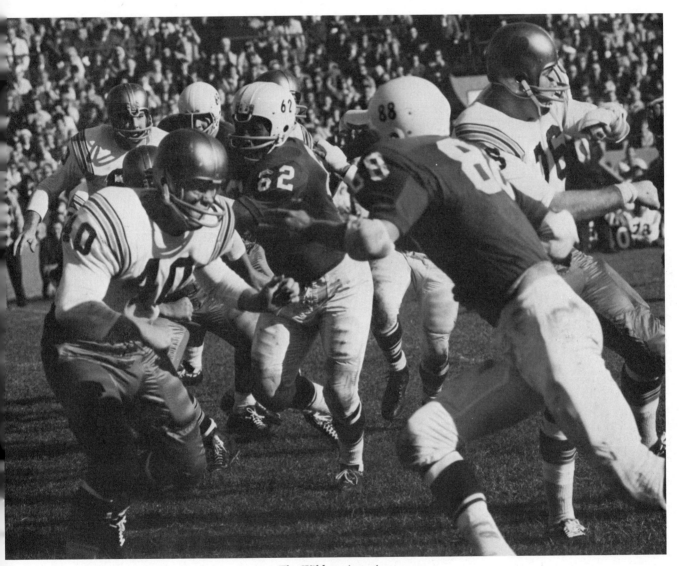

The Wildcats in action

Pont, had coached Indiana to a Rose Bowl game before coming to Northwestern. Prior to that, Pont had been head football coach at Yale. When Tippy Dye retired in 1974, Pont also became Northwestern's athletic director.[199]

Council of Ten   In 1952, the Northwestern basketball team, after twelve years of wandering and playing their home games at the Chicago Stadium and the Evanston Township High School gymnasium, finally found a permanent home in the newly completed McGaw Memorial Hall field house. The "Wandering Wildcats are Back" cheered the *Daily Northwestern*. Nevertheless, the team tended to rank in the lower division of the Conference. Best seasons were those of 1957-58, 1958-59 and 1959-60, when Northwestern tied for fourth, tied for second, and tied for third, respectively, and in 1967-68 when Northwestern came out fourth.

Northwestern did win one championship in a major sport during this period. In 1957, the Wildcat baseball team finished in first place in the Conference. This victory was particularly satisfying to Dr. Miller who enjoyed college baseball because, as he often said, "it is low pressure." During May, whether the weather was warm and pleasant or misty and cold with a frigid wind blowing off the lake, he and Mrs. Miller were often to be found seated in the stand at Wells Field watching the baseball teams compete. The crowds at these contests were always small and the atmosphere very informal, with youngsters and dogs running about on the fringe of the diamond.

Northwestern also participated in other sports on an intercollegiate basis, including tennis, swimming, track, cross country, wrestling, golf, fencing and gymnastics (though the latter two were discontinued in 1957). In tennis, Northwestern brought home eight team championships between 1936 and 1963, and several singles and doubles titles besides. The cross country team won the Conference championship in 1965. Most of these sports were also played on an intramural basis with the addition of touch football, softball, handball and bowling. Despite the fact that Northwestern teams have rarely occupied the limelight, a remarkable number of alumni have gone on to achieve national prominence in individual sports and as members of professional teams.

In 1952 the Big Ten Conference established a Council of Ten composed of the presidents of its member institutions. The council was empowered to appoint the Conference commissioner and to approve the annual budget of his office. In addition, it met each May and December to discuss whatever problems had arisen in intercollegiate athletics in the interim. This was, however, the full extent of the presidents' authority in Conference affairs; control of the rules and regulations remained in the hands of the faculty representatives and athletic directors whose respective jurisdictions had been spelled out by Conference legislation in 1951. From time to time these two bodies met together in what was known as the Joint Group.

The presidents often chafed at their inability to be more directly involved in determining Conference policy, especially as it applied to the use of the member institutions' athletic facilities. In 1964, the Joint Group of faculty representatives and athletic directors had reaffirmed Regulation III which stated that Conference athletic facilities "are not available for the conduct of admission-paid exhibitions or contests by professional sports teams or professional sports organizations."[200]

In 1971, Dr. Miller, deeply concerned about the deterioration of Dyche Stadium and the huge costs of the intercollegiate athletic program, decided to open negotiations with George Halas, owner of the Chicago Bears Football Club, for the possible use of Dyche Stadium by the Bears. Although the presidents of the University of Minnesota and the University of Illinois were also interested in making their facilities available for professional sports events, the Joint Group remained strongly opposed to such a move. Its members feared an adverse financial effect upon the Conference if professional teams were scheduled regularly during a regular season as well as "an erosion of the identity of the collegiate program by constant juxtaposition with the professionals."[201]

Disappointed but undeterred by this unfavorable response from the Conference, Dr. Miller proceeded to negotiate actively with the Bears' organization and signed an agreement on February 26, 1971, which called for the use of Dyche Stadium for eight games to be played by the Bears Sunday afternoons in the fall. But the Conference was not alone in opposing this agreement. Several members of the Evanston City Council also voiced their objections to having professional sports events in the city. In the face of this dual opposition, Dr. Miller reluctantly abandoned the plan but the possibility that Northwestern might revive the plan at some future date was left open.[202]

In the meantime, the university undertook a more aggressive public relations campaign to sell tickets for home games. Essential repairs to the stadium were made whenever funds became available. In 1973 artificial turf was installed on the field with $700,000 raised for the purpose by a group of fifty Benchwarmers and other football minded alumni and friends.

Ties with the Church

During the latter part of Chancellor Miller's administration, it became clear that the ties between the university and the Methodist Church had become so tenuous that the association no longer served any purpose. In 1972 the Methodist conferences decided to end the practice of electing Northwestern trustees. Consequently the university's board, in accordance with section 2 of the second amendment to Northwestern's charter, declared vacant "all places of trustees appointed by the Conferences."[203]

The question of whether church affiliation helped or hindered the university's ability to attract outside support—one which had deeply troubled earlier presidents like James and Harris—was no longer likely to arouse any debate. As William H. Thigpen, general counsel of the university, noted in a letter to the executive secretary of the Senate of the United Methodist Church, "The trustees and officers of the university held the view (for years) that Northwestern University was a completely non-sectarian institution."[204]

Nevertheless, despite the fact that the conferences had ceased to elect trustees to the board of the university, some ambiguity seems to have remained concerning the relationship of the university to the national office of the United Methodist Church, for the latter continued to list Northwestern as a "Methodist-related" university. To clarify the situation, Chancellor Miller and President Strotz held discussions with representatives of the church and authorized the general counsel of the university to request formally that the Senate of the United Methodist

Church remove the name of Northwestern from its list of members. The church senate complied with this request and in a letter to President Strotz dated October 14, 1974, acknowledged that Northwestern's affiliation with the Methodist church had come to an end.

Finances   Northwestern's financial record during the Miller years was impressive. Total annual budgeted expenditures, as shown in Table 7-2 and Table 7-3, grew almost

TABLE 7-2
N.U. BUDGETED RECEIPTS AND EXPENDITURES, 1949-1961

(In Thousands of Dollars)

Academic Year	1949-1950	1950-1951	1951-1952	1952-1953	1953-1954	1954-1955	1955-1956	1956-1957	1957-1958	1958-1959	1959-1960	1960-1961
INCOME												
Tuition	$ 6,815	$ 6,272	$ 6,136	$ 6,239	$ 6,241	$ 7,046	$ 7,482	$ 8,282	$ 8,168	$ 8,275	$ 9,508	$10,089
Investments	2,408	2,696	2,950	3,501	3,602	3,265	3,603	4,159	4,682	5,057	5,381	5,693
Capital Gains	—	—	—	—	—	—	—	—	—	—	—	—
Gifts	1,092	1,203	1,126	1,204	1,720	1,894	2,051	2,892	3,266	3,707	3,644	3,805
Clinics	327	370	371	412	431	465	439	523	558	580	662	712
Govt. Contracts	956	1,033	1,315	1,529	1,453	1,445	1,426	1,928	2,584	3,218	4,321	5,649
Other	4,479	4,472	4,365	4,287	4,533	4,955	5,554	5,714	6,292	6,916	7,138	7,425
TOTAL	16,077	16,046	16,263	17,172	17,980	19,070	20,555	23,498	25,550	27,753	30,654	33,373
EXPENDITURES												
Instruction, Clinics & Research	8,600	8,790	8,801	9,434	9,946	9,258	9,981	11,331	12,294	12,960	13,648	14,281
Libraries	547	553	538	550	582	595	659	760	824	845	893	980
Administration	1,321	1,340	1,262	1,154	1,011	1,167	1,251	1,341	1,544	1,685	1,861	1,871
Physical Plant	1,262	1,144	1,068	1,091	1,314	1,429	1,507	1,872	2,008	2,187	2,452	2,026
Student Aid	543	623	704	843	894	813	875	1,072	1,306	1,468	1,814	1,696
Govt. Contracts	—	—	—	—	—	1,256	1,210	1,648	2,217	2,762	3,706	4,913
Other	3,544	3,594	3,575	3,836	4,109	4,300	4,808	4,799	4,956	5,401	5,670	7,148
TOTAL	15,817	16,044	15,948	16,908	17,856	18,818	20,291	22,823	25,149	27,308	30,044	32,915
SURPLUS	260	2	315	264	124	252	264	675	401	445	610	458

SOURCE: Northwestern University Financial Reports, 1949-1961

seven times from approximately $16 million in 1949-50 to nearly $107 million in 1973-74, while total annual income matched expenditures almost dollar for dollar. Only once, in 1970-71, was there a budget deficit, and that less than 1 percent of the total budget.* Inflationary trends nothwithstanding, these figures suggest a massive growth in the scale of the university's financial operations during the quarter century since 1949.

Although declining as a proportion of the total from 42 percent to 36 percent, student tuition and fees remained the most important single source of the university's income, rising from $6.8 million in 1949-50 to nearly $38.8 million in 1973-74. During that period, individual student tuition rose from $500 to $3,180. Returns from investments that grew from $2.4 million to nearly $11.9 million continued to

---

*The deficit was charged to a budget reserve provided in previous years to meet such emergencies.

contribute approximately 15 percent to the total. Other operations—including an assortment of non-academic activities such as the housing and feeding of students, intercollegiate athletics, the bookstore, etc.—required an increase in outlay that was just less than fourfold between 1949 and 1974, while income from these activities increased at a slower rate so that the traditional "margin of profit" from these operations was reduced by a third (from 6 to 4 percent).

TABLE 7-3
N.U. BUDGETED RECEIPTS AND EXPENDITURES, 1962-1974

(In Thousands of Dollars)

Academic Year	1961-1962	1962-1963	1963-1964	1964-1965	1965-1966	1966-1967	1967-1968	1968-1969	1969-1970	1970-1971	1971-1972	1972-1973	1973-1974
INCOME													
Tuition	$12,227	$12,851	$15,438	$16,126	$18,861	$19,937	$21,143	$22,866	$24,262	$27,380	$31,673	$35,292	$38,796
Investments	5,814	6,119	6,736	6,921	7,379	7,960	8,656	9,303	9,568	10,330	9,879	10,264	11,865
Capital Gains.	—	—	—	—	—	—	—	—	1,136	1,816	2,128	2,782	2,915
Gifts	3,640	3,672	3,738	4,276	4,618	5,536	6,632	7,957	8,679	9,603	10,446	11,025	9,871
Clinics	725	701	799	793	906	1,064	1,388	1,675	1,874	2,094	2,451	2,487	2,568
Govt. Contracts	7,959	10,174	13,496	13,485	15,442	17,337	18,702	19,322	19,389	19,434	21,118	23,056	24,751
Other	7,998	8,988	9,362	9,362	10,031	11,030	12,227	12,968	14,366	15,702	15,857	16,612	17,526
TOTAL	38,363	42,505	49,569	50,963	57,237	62,864	68,748	74,091	79,274	86,359	93,552	101,518	108,292
EXPENDITURES													
Instruction, Clinics & Research	15,394	16,503	18,274	19,169	21,286	24,022	27,862	30,458	33,890	37,865	39,679	43,985	47,556
Libraries	1,111	1,195	1,390	1,473	1,724	1,790	2,171	2,306	2,765	3,618	3,872	4,173	4,396
Administration	2,090	2,344	2,784	3,128	3,529	3,543	3,918	4,311	4,882	5,748	6,273	6,549	7,214
Physical Plant	2,127	2,508	2,828	3,082	3,133	3,668	4,300	4,200	4,889	5,254	5,504	5,338	4,580
Student Aid	2,201	2,214	2,613	2,877	3,266	3,196	3,740	4,840	5,280	6,280	7,771	8,349	9,136
Govt. Contracts	6,877	8,753	11,994	11,929	13,586	15,169	16,371	16,820	16,710	16,697	18,089	19,388	21,535
Other	7,275	7,760	7,849	8,143	9,428	10,389	9,730	10,001	10,579	11,238	11,724	12,505	12,283
TOTAL	37,075	41,277	47,732	49,801	55,952	61,777	68,092	72,936	78,995	86,700	92,912	100,287	106,700
SURPLUS (Deficit)	1,288	1,228	1,837	1,162	1,285	1,087	656	1,155	279	(341)	640	1,231	1,592

SOURCE: Northwestern University Financial Reports, 1962-1974.
Included in investment income prior to 1969.

Gifts for current operating purposes showed a spectacular gain during the Miller years, jumping nearly eight times between the first five year period of 1949 to 1954 with its total of $6.3 million and the last five year period from 1969 to 1974 with its total of $50 million.*

Research contracts with federal government agencies, primarily in the areas of medicine, the physical sciences, and engineering also showed a spectacular increase between 1949 and 1974. By the latter date such income had grown to nearly $24.8 million, or 23 percent of the total, while the $21.5 million spent on government research projects made up nearly 20 percent of aggregate expenditures for that year.

Although as a percentage of the total they remained essentially unchanged, the funds allocated to the libraries expanded approximately eight times during this period: from $547,000 in 1949-50 to almost $4.4 million in 1973-74. Administrative

*Gift figures shown in Tables 7-2 and 7-3 are solely for current expenditures and do not include gifts for capital purposes such as building funds or endowment of professorships, scholarships, library acquisitions, etc.

expenditures grew at about the same rate: from $1.3 million to $7.3 million. The most significant increase occurred in the proportion of the total expended on student aid, from $543,000 (3.5 percent of the total) to $9.1 million (8 percent of the total). This increase is the more remarkable because of the drop in the size of the student body by 1973-74 from the peak reached in the flush of the postwar years when Dr. Miller first became president.

A total of just over $284 million was raised by Northwestern during Dr. Miller's twenty-five year administration. Of this amount approximately $152.3 million was in the form of gifts, pledges, and bequests from individuals; $56.3 million came from foundations; $43.2 million from corporations; and $32.4 million from other sources, principally the federal government.* A substantial portion of these funds was used to finance the extensive building program undertaken during the Miller years. As shown in Table 7-4, this led to an increase in the value of Northwestern's physical plant from almost $33.2 million to nearly $190.8 million. Other assets increased from just over $2 million to nearly $25.3 million. The major contribution, however, was to endowment, which grew from $66.2 million to nearly $209.8 million.

TABLE 7-4
N.U. RESOURCES AND LIABILITIES, 1950-1974 (Selected Years)

(In Thousands of Dollars)

Year Ending August 31	Physical Plant	Endowment	Other Assets	Total	Liabilities	Net
1950	$33,181	$66,239	$2,187	$101,607	$2,150	$99,457
1955	48,065	72,612	3,374	124,051	1,560	122,491
1960	62,223	98,739	5,630	166,592	1,947	164,645
1965	93,778	114,690	17,274	225,742	4,174	221,568
1970	136,956	179,086	17,506	333,548	13,063	320,485
1974	190,780	209,790	25,251	425,821	28,091	397,730

SOURCE: Northwestern University Financial Reports, 1950-1974.

Dr. Miller's extraordinary ability as fund raiser was the major factor in expanding the financial resources of Northwestern during his administration. One of the reasons for his success was that, as he admitted, he frankly enjoyed the task. He had had his first experience in raising funds while dean of the Medical School and found that he could count on the continued support of the friends he had made for Northwestern at that time. Recalling his fund-raising activities shortly before his retirement, Dr. Miller maintained that he had not found his task all that difficult for he had a first rate institution to recommend to potential donors.[205] But the fact remains that he had a very special talent for dealing with people and for winning their support for his goals for the university.

In his relations with potential donors, Dr. Miller was always genuine and forthright, sometimes to the point of making his development officers' hair stand on end. He would establish the general content for his goal but, as he explained, he would never ask directly for funds, leaving it to administrative colleagues or trustees to

*Information supplied by the Office of Development.

be more blunt when necessary. In his efforts he had the highly effective help of his wife, Berenice, who was a constant support in all his endeavors and traveled all over the country with him to meet alumni groups and friends of the university.

In the course of the transition years of 1971-74 when Chancellor Miller and President Strotz shared the chief administrative functions, Dr. Miller concerned himself primarily with external relations while President Strotz dealt with the internal affairs of the university. The two men quickly established close personal rapport and without spelling out specific divisions of authority worked out a congenial relationship in which each came to understand how the other desired to operate. They consulted one another and collaborated on major policy decisions so that the troublesome constitutional issue of how a chancellor and a president would carry forward the university's top administrative duties was resolved informally through a close personal understanding. Personalities, not legal niceties, were the key to the situation.

Transition and Retirement

During this period Chancellor Miller worked closely with President Strotz, the development staff, the deans, and a trustees' committee to prepare the Toward the Eighties fund drive for $177 million which was launched in February 1974. Unlike the First Plan for the Seventies, this drive placed major emphasis on current and endowment funds for faculty, the library, research, and student aid requirements, with $128 million to be allocated to these needs and the remaining $49 million to be devoted to new buildings.[206]

At the time of his retirement in 1974 Chancellor Miller could look back upon two and a half decades of continued growth in the university's endowment and physical plant. But the full measure of his achievement lay in the expansion and development of academic programs and in the quality of the faculty which was drawn to teach and carry on research at Northwestern. The university had, by virtue of those programs and that faculty and the students it could therefore attract, achieved a place of eminence as a private university such as its founders envisioned a hundred and twenty-four years earlier when they set out to establish "a university of the highest grade."

June 15, 1974, marked Chancellor Miller's last commencement as chief executive of Northwestern University. On this moving occasion the university conferred an honorary degree on Berenice Miller in recognition of her many years of devoted service to Northwestern's interests.* For Chancellor Miller came recognition of another sort. As he led the academic procession down the steps from the platform to the main aisle of McGaw Hall the rows of new graduates rose spontaneously to give him a standing ovation. Coming so soon after the troubled years of student unrest, this manifestation of support for the chancellor and the administration which had steered the university through those difficult times augured well for the future.

---

*A fuller account of her accomplishments can be found in the summer 1974 issue of *Northwestern Report.*

President and Mrs. Robert H. Strotz

CARRYING FORWARD 1974—

On September 1, 1974, Robert Henry Strotz, Northwestern's thirteenth president, took over sole leadership of the university's administration. At that time he had been a member of the university community for twenty-seven years. The first nineteen of these were spent in the economics department, after which he served as dean of the College of Arts and Sciences. In July 1970 he was elected president of the university and shared the administrative reins with the chancellor who, in accordance with the by-laws, was chief executive officer.

President Strotz received both his bachelor's degree and his doctorate from the University of Chicago. In 1953, he became the managing editor of *Econometrica*, quarterly publication of the Econometric Society, an international association concerned with the application of mathematics and statistics to economic analysis. While on the economics faculty, he published extensively in the areas of welfare economics, statistical estimation procedures in economics, and the theory of consumer behavior. While his career has been in academe, his counsel has been sought in business and industry as a member of the board of directors of a number of major national corporations and of the Federal Reserve Bank of Chicago. During World War II, President Strotz served in army intelligence in the European theater.

Soon after taking over the role of chief operating officer of the university, President Strotz, in an address to the faculty, presented his plans and expectations for the attainment of the goals set forth by the founders.

> Northwestern University is first and foremost dedicated to intellectual and cultural pursuits. It is dedicated to learning and to teaching, but beyond that it is dedicated to discovery, be it in research laboratories, practice rooms, or classrooms. There are many ancillary services and activities that characterize a fine American university, but none can ever be allowed to dominate our primary devotion to the basic academic values.
>
> As we all know, a university, unlike a small liberal arts college, is a collection of many things. It is a collection of a variety of schools and departments, of interdisciplinary programs, and of research centers. It is also a collection of undergraduate instruction, graduate and professional school instruction, and research. It embraces active extracurricular programs of intellectual and cultural sorts. Universities also provide a number of common services that are of convenience and value to their members, including residential facilities, recreational facilities, health care facilities, faculty clubs, placement services, bookstores, dining halls, sailing clubs, outing clubs, and even bulletin boards. A university

is thus often referred to as a "community," because its members share many things in common. What needs to be stressed, however, is that these many programs and activities are not simply added up to make the whole. There are many interactions among them. Like the symphony orchestra, there are not just the horns, then the violins, then the kettledrums, but there are all these things together, and the music is more than the sum of the parts. A university must be thought of not as a multiversity or a conglomerate corporation, but as an entity having its own integrity, as is the case with the symphony orchestra. There are some things we are going to want to do, even if the accountants tell us that they think we lose money doing those things. And if it costs us to maintain certain programs that are justified on the basis of scholarship and the universality of our interests, we must compensate for those financial burdens in other areas. A great library does not select its books exclusively on the basis of user frequency, nor can a great university select its faculty exclusively on the basis of enrollment data. Higher education is more than a department store. It is an institution that must do some things because of the general social and cultural advantages they bring, whether those things pay off in the marketplace or not.

Now, none of this is to say that "money doesn't matter." During recent years we have seen many of the major private universities running very substantial budget deficits. To the extent these are being eliminated, this has been achieved by cutting down on programs and faculty. Fortunately, this has not happened at Northwestern and this, I believe, gives us an opportunity to adapt more effectively to the conditions that lie ahead.

What is needed is a strategy for survival and success. Moreover, this strategy must be one that lies within the financial capabilities of the institution. For Northwestern, I feel that much that we must do is fairly clear and we have in the last few years made some important strides in the right direction.

The first element of this strategy is that we must maintain and, we hope, improve the distinction of our faculty. That is in large measure what determines the distinction and prestige of the university, and it is hard to imagine that either private contributions or students will flow into a university if its reputation is not among the best.

Secondly, and even more important, is what happens to students once they enroll at Northwestern. Do they have a satisfying experience, or are they disappointed? This depends upon several things, the most important of which is the quality of instruction and the personal attention that students receive, not only from appointed counselors and advisors, but also from members of the teaching faculty.

The third aspect of our strategy for the future must be to attend to the extra-curricular environment in which students find themselves at Northwestern. I do not wish to question the primacy of our academic concerns, but we must recognize that we have here at Northwestern thousands of young people, most of whom live on or near the campus twenty-four hours a day and seven days a week. We are not a subway school at which a student simply attends classes and reads in a library. We therefore must have a concern about the attractiveness of the total environment which is not inconsequential in the attractiveness of the university to the student.

The final component of our strategy for the future is to develop educational programs and adapt existing programs to the needs of our students. To the extent that the student's time is misspent in meeting credit and longevity requirements, we must eliminate that waste. We must also recognize that the substantial numbers of Northwestern undergraduates are not content to terminate their schooling with a bachelor's degree. We should help students effect a meaningful progression from their study of liberal arts and sciences, which is the major component of all our undergraduate programs, to the professional education that they want in order to support their career objectives.

Most components of this strategy for the future require funds, and we all know these are in short supply. But at this time to try to meet budgetary stringencies by cutting back on programs, deferring maintenance, by neglecting student services, and by reducing the size of the faculty—and, most important, its ability to respond to educational requirements—could be disastrous. This is what in fact is happening at many colleges and universities throughout the country, and I am determined that it should not happen here.

During 1974-75, the first year of the new administration, Northwestern continued to advance in many fields. Financially, it once again registered a balanced budget. As far as plant and equipment are concerned, the university dedicated several new buildings. These included the Pick-Staiger Concert Hall, which added architectural distinction to the campus and provided a new cultural focus for the community. But most striking was the publication of the report of the decennial visit of the accreditation committee of the North Central Association, which includes representatives from twelve major educational institutions across the country. After examining many of Northwestern's functions, the committee issued a detailed report on the strengths and weaknesses of the university, the summary paragraph of which reads as follows:

Among the very numerous strengths . . . it is useful to summarize certain more general items: relative affluence, program and enrollment stability, quality faculty, physical plant, library service, computing center, financial aids, admissions, preprofessional programs, professional schools, financial and general commitment of trustees, quality of students, widespread devotion to teaching improvements (illustrated by the links of the School of Education and the Center for the Teaching Professions to the rest of the University), the Evening Divisions, and the character of the Administration. We do not mean by restating only the institutional strengths to suggest an absence of interest in our areas of concern, but we do want by this summary to stress our highly favorable impressions of Northwestern as a major university notable for ability and self-confidence in using enviable financial resources to provide quality educational services to carefully selected students in well-defined areas of competency. We believe that this is what a rich private university is supposed to do. Many of us believe that in observing how well Northwestern performs its role we learned much more than we have been able to contribute by way of advice to the institution.

So, after a century and a quarter of moving forward from its provincial origins as a university for the Northwest Territory to an acknowledged position as a major national and international university, Northwestern in its 125th year could rely heavily on its past for many of the answers to the obvious problems ahead.

APPENDIXES

NOTES

BIBLIOGRAPHY

INDEXES

APPENDIX A

Presidents* Board of Trustees	Presidents Northwestern University
John Evans....................1850-1894	
	Clark Titus Hinman, D.D..............1853-1854
	Henry Sanborn Noyes, M.A.†..........1854-1856
	Randolph Sinks Foster, D.D., LL.D.....1856-1860
	Henry Sanborn Noyes, M.A.†..........1860-1867
	David Hilton Wheeler, D.D.†...........1867-1869
	Erastus Otis Haven, D.D., LL.D........1869-1872
	Charles Henry Fowler, D.D., LL.D......1872-1876
	Oliver Marcy, LL.D.†.................1876-1881
	Joseph Cummings, D.D., LL.D.........1881-1890
	Henry Wade Rogers, LL.D............1890-1900
Orrington Lunt..................1894-1897	
William Deering.................1897-1906	
	Daniel Bonbright, M.A., LL.D.†........1900-1902
	Edmund Janes James, Ph.D., LL.D......1902-1904
	Thomas Franklin Holgate, Ph.D., LL.D.†..1904-1906
	Abram Winegardner Harris, Sc.D., LL.D...1906-1916
William F. McDowell...........1906-1917	
	Thomas Franklin Holgate, Ph.D., LL.D.†..1916-1919
James A. Patten.................1917-1920	
	Lynn Harold Hough, D.D..............1919-1920
Oliver T. Wilson................1920-1924	
	Walter Dill Scott, Ph.D., LL.D..........1920-1939
Robert W. Campbell............1924-1930	
Melvin A. Traylor...............1930-1930	
Arthur Andersen...............1930-1932	
John H. Hardin.................1932-1935	
Mark W. Cresap................1935-1937	
Kenneth F. Burgess.............1937-1959	
	Franklyn Bliss Snyder, Ph.D., LL.D......1939-1949
	James Roscoe Miller, M.D., LL.D., Sc.D., L.H.D., Litt.D.....................1949-1970 ....*Chancellor 1970-1974*
Wesley M. Dixon...............1959-1964	
John G. Searle.................1964-1970	
Kenneth V. Zwiener............1970-1975	
	Robert Henry Strotz, Ph.D., LL.D.......1970-
Thomas G. Ayers...............1975-	

*In August 1972 the title President was changed to Chairman
†interim

APPENDIX B

CHARTER

AN ACT TO INCORPORATE THE NORTHWESTERN UNIVERSITY

SECTION I. *Be it enacted by the People of the State of Illinois, represented in the General Assembly:* That Richard Haney, Philo Judson, S. P. Keys, and A. E. Phelps, and such persons as shall be appointed by the Rock River Annual Conference of the Methodist Episcopal Church to succeed them in said office; Henry Summers, Elihu Springer, David Brooks, and Elmore Yocum, and such persons as shall be appointed by the Wisconsin Annual Conference of said church to succeed them; four individuals, if chosen, and such persons as shall be appointed to succeed them by the Michigan Annual Conference of said church; four individuals, if chosen, and such persons as shall be appointed to succeed them by the North Indiana Annual Conference of said church; H. W. Reed, I. I. Steward, D. N. Smith, and George M. Geas, and such persons as shall be appointed to succeed them by the Iowa Annual Conference of said church; four individuals, if chosen, and such persons as shall be appointed to succeed them by the Illinois Annual Conference of said church; A. S. Sherman, Grant Goodrich, Andrew J. Brown, John Evans, Orrington Lunt, J. K. Botsford, Joseph Kitterstring, George F. Foster, Eri Reynolds, John M. Arnold, Absalom Funk, and E. B. Kingsley, and such persons, citizens of Chicago or its vicinity, as shall be appointed by the Board of Trustees hereby constituted to succeed them, be, and they are hereby, created and constituted a body politic and corporate, under the name and style of the *Trustees of the Northwestern University*, and henceforth shall be styled and known by that name, and by that name and style to remain and have perpetual succession, with power to sue and be sued, plead and be impleaded, to acquire, hold and convey property, real, personal, or mixed, in all lawful ways, to have and use a common seal, and to alter the same at pleasure, to make and alter from time to time such by-laws as they may deem necessary for the government of said institution, its officers and servants, provided such by-laws are not inconsistent with the constitution and laws of this State and of the United States, and to confer on such persons as may be considered worthy of such academical or honorary degrees as are usually conferred by similar institutions.

SECTION II. The term of office of said Trustees shall be four years, but that of one member of the Board for each conference enjoying the appointing power by this act, and [the] term of three of the members whose successors are to be appointed by the Board hereby constituted, shall expire annually, the term of each member of the Board herein named to be fixed by lot at the first meeting of said Board, which Board shall, in manner above specified have perpetual succession, and shall hold the property of said institution solely for the purposes of education, and not as a stock for the individual benefit of themselves or any contributor to the endowment of the same; and no particular religious faith shall be required of those who become students of the institution. Nine members shall constitute a quorum for the transaction of any business of the Board, except the appointment of President or Professor, or the establishment of chairs in said institution, and the enactment of by-laws for its government, for which the presence of a majority of the Board shall be necessary.

SECTION III. Said annual conferences of the Methodist Episcopal Church, under whose control and patronage said university is placed, shall each also have the right to appoint annually two suitable persons, members of their own body, visitors to said university, who shall attend the examination of students, and be entitled to participate in the deliberations of the Board of Trustees and enjoy all the privileges of members of said board except the right to vote.

SECTION IV. Said institution shall remain located in or near the City of Chicago, Cook County, and the corporators and their successors shall be competent in law or equity to take to themselves, in their said corporate name, real, personal, or mixed estate, by gift, grant, bargain and sale, conveyance, will, devise or bequest of any person or persons whomsoever and the same estate, whether real, personal, or mixed, to grant, bargain, sell, convey, devise, let, place out at interest, or otherwise dispose of the same for the use of said institution in such manner as to them shall seem most beneficial to said institution. Said corporation shall faithfully apply all the funds collected or the proceeds of the property belonging to the said institution, according to their best judgment, in erecting and completing suitable buildings, supporting necessary officers, instructors, and servants, and procuring books, maps, charts, globes, and philosophical, chemical, and other apparatus necessary to the success of the institution, and do all other acts usually performed by similar institutions, that may be deemed necessary or useful to the success of said institution, under the restrictions herein imposed: Provided, nevertheless, that in case any donation, devise, or bequest shall be made for particular purposes accordant with the design of the institution, and the corporation shall accept the same, every such donation, devise, or bequest shall be applied in conformity with the express conditions of the donor or devisor: Provided further, that said corporation shall not be allowed to hold more than two thousand acres of land at any one time unless the said corporation shall have received the same by gift, grant, or devise; and in such case they shall be required to sell or dispose of the same within ten years from the time they shall acquire such title; and by failure to do so, such land over and above the beforenamed two thousand acres, shall revert to the original donor, grantor, devisor, or their heirs.

SECTION V. The treasurer of the institution and all other agents when required, before entering upon the duties of their appointment, shall give bond for the security of the corporation in such penal sums, and with such securities as the corporation shall approve, and all process against the corporation shall be by summons, and the service of the same shall be by leaving an attested copy thereof with the treaurer at least sixty days before the return day thereof.

SECTION VI. The corporation shall have power to employ and appoint a President or Principal for said institution, and all such professors or teachers, and all such servants as may be necessary, and shall have power to displace any or such of them, as the interest of the institution may require, to fill vacancies which may happen, by death, resignation, or otherwise, among said officers and servants, and to prescribe and direct the course of studies to be pursued in said institution.

SECTION VII. The corporation shall have power to establish departments for the study of any and all the learned and liberal professions in the same; to confer the degree of doctor in the learned arts and sciences and *belles-lettres*, and to confer such other academical degrees as are usually conferred by the most learned institutions.

SECTION VIII. Said corporation shall have power to institute a board of competent persons, always including the faculty, who shall examine such individuals as may apply, and if such applicants are found to possess such knowledge pursued in said institution, as in the judgment of said board renders them worthy, they may be considered graduates in course, and shall be entitled to diplomas accordingly on paying such fee as the corporation shall affix, which fee, however, shall in no case exceed the tuition bills of the full course of studies in said institution; said examination board may not exceed the number of ten, three of whom may transact business, provided one be of the faculty.

SECTION IX. Should the corporation at any time act contrary to the provisions of this charter, or fail to comply with the same, upon complaint being made to the Circuit Court of Cook County, a *scire facias* shall issue, and the circuit attorney shall prosecute in behalf of the People of this State for forfeiture of this charter.

This act shall be a public act, and shall be construed liberally in all courts, for the purposes herein expressed.

SYDNEY BREESE
Speaker of the House of Representatives

WILLIAM McMURTEY
Speaker of the Senate

Approved January 28, 1851
A. C. FRENCH

Attest: a true copy, March 22, 1851
DAVID L. GREGG
Secretary of State

AMENDMENTS TO CHARTER

FIRST AMENDMENT

AN ACT TO AMEND AN ACT ENTITLED "AN ACT TO INCORPORATE THE NORTHWESTERN UNIVERSITY," APPROVED JANUARY 28, 1851

SECTION I. *Be it enacted by the People of the State of Illinois, represented in the General Assembly:* That John L. Smith, Aaron Wood, Luther Taylor, and Wm. Graham, and such persons as shall be elected to succeed them by the Northwestern Indiana Conference of the Methodist Episcopal Church, be, and they are hereby, constituted members of the Board of Trustees of the Northwestern University.

SECTION II. No spiritous, vinous, or fermented liquors shall be sold under license, or otherwise, within four miles of the location of said University, except for medicinal, mechanical, or sacramental purposes, under a penalty of twenty-five dollars for each offense, to be recovered before any Justice of the Peace of said County in an action of debt in the name of the County of Cook: Provided, that so much of this act as relates to the sale of intoxicating drinks within four miles, may be repealed by the General Assembly whenever they may think proper.

SECTION III. The said corporation shall have power to take, hold, use and manage, lease and dispose of all such property, as may in any manner come to said corporation charged with any trust or trusts, in conformity with trusts and direction, and so execute all such trusts as may be confided to it.

SECTION IV. That all property of whatever kind or description, belonging to or owned by said corporation, shall be forever free from taxation for any and all purposes.

SECTION V. This act shall be a public act, and take effect from and after its passage.

THOMAS P. TURNER
Speaker of the House of Representatives

G. KOERNER
Speaker of the Senate

Approved Feb. 14th, 1855
J. A. MATTESON

I, Alexander Stearm, Secretary of State for the State of Illinois, do hereby certify that the foregoing is a true and correct copy of an Enrolled Law now on file at my office.

In testimony whereof, I have hereunto set my hand and caused the great seal of State to be affixed. Done at the City of Springfield, this 21st day of March 1855.

ALEXANDER STEARM
Secretary of State

AMENDMENTS TO CHARTER

SECOND AMENDMENT

AN ACT TO AMEND AN ACT ENTITLED "AN ACT TO INCORPORATE THE NORTHWESTERN UNIVERSITY"

SECTION I. *Be it enacted by the People of the State of Illinois, represented in the General Assembly:* That the annual conferences of the Methodist Episcopal Church, which now are or may hereafter be authorized to elect or appoint Trustees of said University, shall hereafter elect only two Trustees each, who shall also be and perform the duties of the visitors to said institution, and the place of the two Trustees last appointed by each conference is hereby vacated. The trustees elected by such conferences shall hereafter hold their office for two years, and until their successors are chosen, the term of one elected by each of them expiring annually. In case any conference having authority to elect Trustees now or hereafter be divided into two or more annual conferences, they shall have authority to elect Trustees. On the request of the Board of Trustees made at a regular meeting, any such annual conference may elect Trustees as herein provided.

SECTION II. Any annual conference electing Trustees as herein provided, having at any time refused to elect successors thereto, or resolved to discontinue or refuse its patronage to said institution, shall authorize the Board of Trustees, by a vote of a majority thereof at any regular meeting, to declare vacant the place of all Trustees appointed by such conference, and its right to appoint Trustees shall thereupon cease.

SECTION III. Any chartered institution of learning may become a department of this University by agreement between the Board of Trustees of the two institutions.

SECTION IV. This act shall take effect and be in force from and after its passage.

SHELBY M. CULLOM
Speaker of the House of Representatives

FRANCIS A. HOFFMAN
Speaker of the Senate

Approved Feb. 16th, 1861
RICHARD YATES
Governor

A true copy—Attest: Feb. 16th, 1861

O. M. HATCH
Secretary of State

AMENDMENTS TO CHARTER

THIRD AMENDMENT

AN ACT TO AMEND AN ACT ENTITLED "AN ACT TO INCORPORATE THE NORTHWESTERN UNIVERSITY" AND THE SEVERAL ACTS AMENDATORY THEREOF

SECTION I. *Be it enacted by the People of the State of Illinois, represented in the General Assembly:* That the name of that corporation created by act of the General Assembly of the State of Illinois, approved on the 28th day of January, A. D. 1851, under the name of the "Trustees of the Northwestern University," be, and the same is, hereby changed to "Northwestern University," and by that name shall hereafter be known, and in and by such name shall have and exercise all the powers and immunities conferred on said corporation by said act of incorporation, and all acts amendatory thereof.

SECTION II. In addition to the number of Trustees heretofore provided for by law, the Board may elect any number, not exceeding twenty-four, and without reference to their several places of residence; and a majority of the whole Board shall be members of the Methodist Episcopal Church.

SECTION III. No greater number shall be required to constitute a quorum than has been heretofore required by law; *Provided*, that in all called meetings of the Board, the object of the meeting shall be particularly specified in the notice to be previously given to each Trustee.

SECTION IV. This act shall be a public act, and in force from and after its passage.

F. CORWIN
Speaker of the House of Representatives

WILLIAM BREESE
Speaker of the Senate

Approved Feb. 19, 1867
P. J. OGLESBY

A true copy—Attest: February 23, 1867

SHARON TYNDALE
Secretary of State

NOTES

After initial citation the following abbreviations for Northwestern University sources are used throughout the notes. Northwestern University Archives: N.U.A. Northwestern University Board of Trustees' Minutes: T.M. Northwestern University President's Report: P.R.

CHAPTER 1

1. The leading source for the history of Chicago is Bessie Louise Pierce, *A History of Chicago*, 3 vols. (New York: Alfred A. Knopf, 1937-57). Hereafter cited as Pierce, *Chicago*.

2. Daniel Boorstin, *The Americans: The National Experience* (New York: Random House, 1965), p. 116.

3. Donald Tewksbury, "The Founding of American Colleges and Universities before the Civil War," in *Contributions to Education*, 543 (1932), p. 15. Hereafter cited as Tewksbury, "Founding of American Colleges." Also Frederick Rudolph, *The American College and University: A History* (New York: Alfred A. Knopf, 1962), p. 219. Hereafter cited as Rudolph, *American Colleges*.

4. Tewksbury, "Founding of American Colleges," p. 3.

5. Robert Howard, *Illinois: A History of the Prairie State* (Grand Rapids: William B. Eerdman's Publishing Company, 1972), p. 177; Kendric C. Babcock, "The Expansion of Higher Education in Illinois," in *Transactions of the Illinois State Historical Society*, XXXIII (1925), pp. 41-53; John W. Cook, *Educational History of Illinois* (Chicago: Henry O. Shepard Company, 1912); A. F. Ewert, "Early History of Education in Illinois—The Three Oldest Colleges," in *Illinois Blue Book, 1929-30* (Springfield: Secretary of State, 1929), p. 301; M. H. Chamberlin, "Historical Sketch of McKendree College," in *Transactions of the Illinois State Historical Society*, IX (1904), pp. 328-64.

6. Tewksbury, "Founding of American Colleges," pp. 103-11; William Warren Sweet, *Methodism in American History*, rev. ed. (Nashville: Abington Press, 1961), pp. 207-28.

7. Pierce, *Chicago*, 2:355.

8. Matthew Simpson, ed., *Cyclopedia of Methodism* (Philadelphia: Everts and Stewart, 1878), entries for Rock River Conference, Chicago. Hereafter cited as Simpson, *Cyclopedia*.

9. Northwestern Board of Trustees' Minutes, May 31, 1850 (hereafter cited as T.M.).

10. Biographical material, Founder's Papers, Northwestern University Archives (hereafter cited as N.U.A.).

11. *Daily Democratic Press* (Chicago), January 23, 1854.

12. Edgar Carlisle McMechen, *Life of Governor Evans; Second Territorial Governor of Colorado* (Denver: Wahlgreen Publishing Company, 1924), p. 62.

13. The bulk of the John Evans Papers are housed with the State Historical Society of Colorado in Denver. The Northwestern University Archives carry an incomplete microfilm of this collection as well as other Evans papers. Highly pertinent to the university's history is John Evans's "Interview given to Ashley Bancroft in 1889," typescript copy, N.U.A., original in Colorado Biography and Reference File, Bancroft Library, University of California at Berkeley (hereafter cited as Evans, Bancroft typescript). Evans has been the subject of several books, including McMechen's *Life of Governor Evans*; Harry E. Kelsey, Jr.'s *Frontier Capitalist: The Life of John Evans* (Denver: State Historical Society of Colorado and Pruett Publishing Company, 1969); and Walter Dill Scott's *John Evans, 1814-1897: An Appreciation* (Evanston: L. J. Norris, 1939).

14. Robert D. Sheppard and Harvey B. Hurd, eds., *History of Northwestern University and Evanston* (Chicago: Munsell Publishing Company, 1906), p. 465. Hereafter cited as Sheppard and Hurd, *History of Northwestern University; Dictionary of American Biography*, s.v. "Lunt, Orrington" (hereafter cited as D.A.B.); Lunt Papers, N.U.A.

15. *The Bench and Bar of Chicago* (Chicago: American Biographical Publishing Company, 1883), p. 576; Goodrich Papers, N.U.A.

16. *Daily Inter-Ocean*, March 16, 1889.

17. *The Bench and Bar of Chicago*, p. 517.

18. Founders' Papers, N.U.A.

19. Charter Committee to Michigan Annual Conference of the Methodist Episcopal Church, September 3, 1850, Founders' Papers, N.U.A.

20. See Appendix A, *Private Laws of the State of Illinois Passed at the First Session of the Seventeenth General Assembly, Begun and Held at Springfield, January 6, 1851* (Springfield: Lamphier and Walker, 1851), p. 20.

21. *Private Laws of State of Illinois, Nineteenth General Assembly, Springfield, Illinois, January 1, 1885* (Springfield: Lamphier and Walker, 1855), pp. 454, 483.

22. William S. Kerr, Vice President and Business Manager to Payson S. Wild, September 17, 1974, N.U.A.

23. Evans, Bancroft typescript, N.U.A.

24. T.M., September 22, 1852.

25. Sylvanus Milne Duvall, "The Methodist Episcopal Church and Education up to 1869" in *Contributions to Education*, 284 (1928), pp. 87-88.

26. Clark T. Hinman Papers, N.U.A.

27. Evans, Bancroft typescript, N.U.A.

28. Pierce, *Chicago*, II: 306-7.

29. *Northwestern Christian Advocate*, June 22, 1870.

30. Frances E.Willard, *A Classic Town*(Chicago: Woman's Temperance Publishing Company, 1891), p. 26. Hereafter cited as Willard, *Classic Town*.

31. Evans, Bancroft typescript, N.U.A.

32. *Daily Democratic Press* (Chicago), January 23, 1854.

33. Garrett Biblical Institute Records, N.U.A.; Grant Goodrich, "Garrett Biblical Institute," in *The Early Schools of Methodism*, ed. A. W. Cummings (New York: Phillips and Hunt, 1886), pp. 380-87.

34. *Northwestern Christian Advocate*, January 4, 1854.

35. *Northwestern Christian Advocate*, June 20, 1855; J. Wesley Jones, undated typescript, Northwestern Female College Records, Evanston Historical Society.

36. Sheppard and Hurd, *History of Northwestern University*, p. 64.

37. Arthur H. Wilde, "Opening of the University," in *Northwestern University, 1855-1905*, 4 vols., ed. Arthur H. Wilde (New York: University Publishing Society, 1905), I:166. Hereafter cited as Wilde, *Northwestern University*.

38. Rudolph, *American Colleges*, p. 165-67.

39. *National Cyclopedia of American Biography* (New York: James T. White Co., 1898-1969), s.v. "Foster, Randolph S." (hereafter cited as N.C.A.B.); also Simpson, *Cyclopedia*.

40. Arthur H. Wilde, "The First Faculty," in Wilde, *Northwestern University*, I:207.

41. Wilde, *Northwestern University*, I:227.

42. C. C. Stratton, ed., *The Autobiography of Erastus O. Haven* (New York: Phillips and Hunt, 1883). Hereafter cited as Stratton, *Autobiography of Haven;* D.A.B. s.v. "Haven, Erastus O."

43. Stratton, *Autobiography of Haven*, p. 175.

44. *Christian Republican* clippings, Haven Papers, N.U.A.

45. Stratton, *Autobiography of Haven*, p. 182.

46. Rudolph, *American Colleges*, pp. 158-61.

47. T.M., June 21, 1854; Wilde, *Northwestern University*, I:143-45.

48. T.M., June 21, 1854; *Northwestern Christian Advocate*, April 19, 1899; Wilde, *Northwestern University*, I:219-21.

49. N.C.A.B., pp. 420-21; O. F. Long, "In Memoriam: Daniel Bonbright," *Classical Journal*, VIII (February 1913), pp. 216-21; T.M., June 26, 1856.

50. Rudolph, *American Colleges*, p. 226.

51. T.M., June 7, 14, 1857; Newton Bateman, *et al.* eds., *Historical Encyclopedia of Illinois* (Chicago: Munsell Publishing Company, 1923), I:51; Blaney to Kennicott, March 16, 1858, copy in Kennicott-Bannister Papers, N.U.A.

52. N.C.A.B. s.v. "Marcy, Oliver."

53. Northwestern University catalogs for these years indicate the changing admission requirements for both the Preparatory School and the College.

54. Leslie B. Arey, *Northwestern University Medical School, 1859-1959* (Evanston and Chicago: Northwestern University, 1959), p. 74. Hereafter cited as Arey, *Medical School;* T.M., July 27, 1869; March 10, 1870.

55. Arey, *Medical School*, p. 21.

56. Nathan Smith Davis, *History of Medical Education and Institutions in the United States.* (Chicago: S. C. Griggs and Company, 1851), p. 170.

57. Thomas M. Bonner, *Medicine in Chicago, 1850-1950: A Chapter in the Social and Scientific Development of a City* (Madison: American History Research Center, 1957), pp. 44-68.

58. T.M., June 24, 1873.

59. Alfred Z. Reed, *Training for the Public Profession of the Law,* (New York: Carnegie Foundation, 1921), pp. 172-85.

60. *Catalogue of Northwestern Female College*, 1855-56, N.U.A.

61. Undated typescript, Northwestern Female College Records, Evanston Historical Society.

62. T.M., July 21, 1856; William P. Jones to N.U. board of trustees, Summer 1856; Northwestern Female College Records, Evanston Historical Society.

63. "History of the Evanston College for Ladies," undated ms. in Gold Medal Album of the Woman's College. Northwestern University, N.U.A.

64. Stratton, *Autobiography of Haven*, pp. 109-10.

65. *Chicago Times*, August 26, 1869.

66. "Proceedings," Evanston College for Ladies, April 1871, N.U.A.

67. *Chicago Tribune*, July 5, 1871; *Tripod*, July 20, 1871.

68. *Tripod*, October 21, 1872.

69. *Catalogue and Circular of the Evanston College for Ladies*, 1871-72, N.U.A.

70. James Alton James, "History of Northwestern University," unpublished typescript, chapter VIII, p. 10, N.U.A. (hereafter cited as James, "History of N.U.").

71. Frances E. Willard, *Glimpses of Fifty Years* (Evanston: National Woman's Christian Temperance Union, 1904), p. 227. Hereafter cited as Willard, *Glimpses*.

72. "Proceedings," Evanston College for Ladies, April 12, 1873, N.U.A.; Mary Earhart, *Frances Willard: From Prayers to Politics* (Chicago: University of Chicago Press, 1944), pp. 116-19. Hereafter cited as Earhart, *Frances Willard*.

73. *Evanston Index*, April 26, November 29, 1873; *Chicago Tribune*, November 25, 1873; *Tripod*, December 1873; Willard, *Glimpses*, pp. 226-43.

74. College of Liberal Arts Faculty Minutes, April 14, 1874, N.U.A. (hereafter cited as C.L.A. Faculty Minutes).

75. Earhart, *Frances Willard*, pp. 116-21.

76. Willard to Faculty, June 16, 1874, Woman's College Records, N.U.A.

77. *Evanston Index*, July 25, 1874.

78. Mary Putnam Jacobi, "Women in Medicine," in *Woman's Work in America*, ed. Annie Nathan Meyer (New York: Arno Press, 1972), p. 174.

79. *Northwestern University Catalogue*, 1860-61 (henceforth cited as *N.U. Catalogue*).

80. C.L.A. Faculty Minutes, December 22, 1856, N.U.A.

81. *N.U. Catalogue*, 1860-61.

82. "Faculty Regulations," 1865, 1866, N.U.A.

83. Lewis Elmer Sims, Letters, December 13, 1874, March 7, 1875, April 19, 1876, Class of 1879 File, N.U.A. (hereafter cited as Sims, Letters).

84. Sheppard and Hurd, *History of Northwestern University*, p. 427.

85. Sims, Letters, March 11, 1877.

86. Hinman Society Minute Book, September 11, 1857, January 24, 1868, N.U.A.

87. Otto F. Bauer, "A Century of Debating at Northwestern, 1855-1955," M.A. Thesis, School of Speech, Northwestern University, 1955, N.U.A.

88. John S. Brubacher and Willis Rudy, *Higher Education in Transition: A History of American Colleges and Universities, 1636-1968*, rev. ed. (New York: Harper and Row, 1968), p. 127.

89. Jonathan T. Howe, "The Northwestern University Fraternity System: A History, 1851-1963," Honors Thesis, Department of History, Northwestern University, 1963, N.U.A.; Alvan E. Duerr, ed., *Baird's Manual of American College Fraternities* (Menasha, Wis.: George Banta Publishing Company, 1940).

90. *Vidette*, February 15, 1878, N.U.A.

91. Walter Paulison, *The Tale of the Wildcats* (Evanston: Northwestern University Alumni Association, 1951), pp. 1-3. Hereafter cited as Paulison, *Wildcats*.

92. Sims, Letters, October 8, 1876.

93. Sheppard and Hurd, *History of Northwestern University*, p. 429.

94. Charles B. Atwell, ed., *Alumni Record of the College of Liberal Arts*, (Evanston: Northwestern University, 1903), p. 12. Hereafter cited as *College Alumni Record* (1903).

95. U.S. Census, 1860, "Population."

96. Willard, *Classic Town*, p. 193.

97. *Evanston Index*, July 12, 1873.

98. *Chicago Tribune*, July 13, 1866.

99. Hinman Society Minute Book, October 6, 1858, N.U.A.

100. J. Seymour Currey, "Lincoln's Visit to Evanston in the Year Before the War," *Proceedings of the Evanston Historical Society*, VI (July 1910), pp. 12-26; *Evanston News*, June 1, 1910.

101. Viola Crouch Reeling, *Evanston: Its Land and People* (Evanston: Fort Dearborn Chapter of Daughters of American Revolution. 1928), p. 114.

102. Willard, *Classic Town*, p. 266.

103. Merritt C. Bragdon, Diary, 1865-67, typescript, February 8, 1865, N.U.A.

104. *New York Times*, September 12, 1860; *Northwestern Christian Advocate*, September 19, 1860; Charles M. Scanlan, *The Lady Elgin Disaster: September 8, 1860* (Milwaukee: Privately printed, 1928).

105. *U.S. Census*, 1870, "Population."

106. Sheppard and Hurd, *History of Northwestern University*, pp. 169-85.

107. *Evanston Index*, July 12, 1873.

108. Harold M. Mayer and Richard C. Wade, *Chicago: Growth of a Metropolis* (Chicago: University of Chicago Press, 1969), pp. 76-77; Evans, Bancroft typescript, N.U.A.).
109. *Evanston Index*, July 12, 1873.
110. *College Alumni Record* (1903), pp. 59-116.
111. Brooks Mather Kelley, *Yale: A History* (New Haven: Yale University Press, 1974), p. 260.

CHAPTER 2

1. William Deering, Thomas Hoag, Frank P. Crandon biographical files, N.U.A.
2. D.A.B., s.v. "Deering, William."
3. Sheppard and Hurd, *History of Northwestern University*, pp. 555-56.
4. Willard, *Classic Town*, p. 377.
5. *N.U. Catalogue*, 1873-74.
6. Marcy to executive committee, June 1878, Marcy Papers, N.U.A.
7. Marcy to Lunt, June 11, 1880, Marcy Papers, N.U.A.
8. "Northwestern University versus the people of the state of Illinois," (U.S. Supreme Court Reports, October Term, 1879, vol. 99, p. 309).
9. *The Northwestern*, June 3, 1881.
10. Sheppard and Hurd, *History, of Northwestern University*, 489-92.
11. *Chicago Tribune*, October 6, 1881.
12. *N.U. Catalogue*, 1883-84.
13. *President's Report*, 1890-91, N.U.A. (hereafter cited as P.R.).
14. *The Northwestern*, March 4, 1887; James, "History of N.U.," chapter XII, pp. 16, 18.
15. Northwestern University Treasurer's Report, June 1889, p. 35, N.U.A.
16. Dearborn Observatory Records, N.U.A.
17. P.R., 1881-82.
18. T.M., June 18, 1887; July 15, 1887.
19. C.L.A., December 13, 1881; January 30, September 25, 1883.
20. W. R. Bagnall to Cummings, September 7, 1889; Phi Beta Kappa Papers, N.U.A.
21. *N.U. Catalogue*, 1876-77, 1889-90.
22. T.M., April 10, June 22, 1886.
23. *In Memoriam; Oscar Oldberg* (Chicago: n.p., 1914), pamphlet, N.U.A.
24. *N.U. Catalogue*, 1886-87.
25, T.M., May 21, 1887.
26. *N.U. Catalogue*, 1887-88.
27. Mrs. George Williams to Ellen Soulé, January 5, 1875; Henry A. Dingee to Jane Bancroft, November 28, 1877; Woman's College Records, N.U.A.
28. Residents of Woman's College to executive committee, December 13, 1886, Woman's College Records, N.U.A.
29. *N.U. Catalogue*, 1881-82; Jane M. Bancroft, "Occupations and Professions for College-Bred Women" in *Education* V (May 1885), pp. 486-95; biographical sketch, Jane Bancroft Robinson, *Notable American Women* 3 vols., ed. Edward T. James (Cambridge, Massachusetts: Harvard University Press, 1971), III: 183-84.
30. Frank M. Elliot, ed., *History of Omega and Reminiscences of N.U.* (Chicago: n.p., 1885), p. 43. Hereafter cited as Elliot, *Omega*.
31. *The Northwestern*, June 6, 1884.
32. *The Northwestern*, November 20, 1885.
33. Elliot, *Omega*, p. 43.
34. *Evanston Index*, March 6, 1886.
35. Students' Christian Association Constitution and Minutes Book, 1880-90; Y.M.C.A.-Y.W.C.A. Records, N.U.A.
36. *The Northwestern*, March 23, 1882.
37. *The Northwestern*, October 22, 1886.
38. Florence Call to "Bert," November 18, 1883; to her family, September 16, 1883 Class of 1884 File, N.U.A.
39. Florence Call to "Bert," November 18, 1883.
40. *Evanston Index*, June 5, 1886.
41. *The Northwestern*, February 15, 1884.
42. *Evanston Index*, March 2, September 24, November 19, 1889, April 5, 1890.
43. Paulison, *Wildcats*, pp. 4-5.
44. Paulison, *Wildcats*, p. 5.
45. *The Northwestern*, December 13, 1889.
46. William Etridge McLennan, "The Life Saving Crew," Wilde, *Northwestern University*, II: 257-86; *Evanston Index*, July 21, 1900.
47. *College Alumni Record* (1903), pp. 116-213.
48. *The Northwestern*, November 20, 1885.
49. T.M. June 4, 1889.

CHAPTER 3

1. P.R., 1890-91; typescript, Cummings Papers, N.U.A.
2. D.A.B., s.v. "Rogers, Henry"; *Evanston News Index*, September 6, 1890.
3. *Daily Inter-Ocean* (Chicago), February 20, 1891; *Evanston Index*, February 21, 1891. All quotations from Rogers's inaugural address are from the version printed in the *Evanston Index*, February 21, 1891.
4. Estelle Frances Ward, *The Story of Northwestern University* (New York: Dodd, Mead and Company, 1924), p. 199. Hereafter cited as Ward, *Story of Northwestern University*.
5. P.R., 1891-92.
6. C.L.A. Faculty Minutes, February 3, 1893
7. P.R., 1895-96.

8. James A. Rahl amd Kurt Schwerin, *Northwestern University School of Law: A Short History* (Chicago: Northwestern University School of Law, 1960), pp. 13-14. Hereafter cited as Rahl and Schwerin, *School of Law*.
9. *N.U. Catalogue*, 1891-92.
10. Greene Vardiman Black, "The Dental School," Wilde, *Northwestern University*, IV, p. 126.
11. Black, "The Dental School," Wilde, *Northwestern University*, IV, pp. 125-30.
12. Black, "The Dental School," Wilde, *Northwestern University*, IV, p. 134.
13. Arey, *Medical School*, p. 141.
14. P.R., 1891-92.
15. Arey, *Medical School*, p. 150.
16. Arey, *Medical School*, p. 182.
17. *Woman's Medical School, Northwestern University* (*Woman's Medical College of Chicago*): *The Institution and its Founders* (Chicago: H. G. Cutler, Publisher, 1896), p. 49; *N.U. Catalogue*, 1891-92; T.M., June 23, 1891.
18. Pierce, *Chicago*, III: pp. 22-24, 516.
19. *Evanston Index*, February 16, May 11, 1895.
20. C.L.A. Faculty Minutes, November 29, 1892; P.R., 1892-93.
21. *N.U. Catalogue*, 1890-91.
22. Oliver Marcy, "An Address Read Before the Students of the College of Liberal Arts, Northwestern University, December 1893," in *In Memoriam: Oliver Marcy* (privately printed, n.d., N.U.A.), p. 172, N.U.A.
23. *N.U. Catalogue*, 1892-93.
24. P.R., 1895-95.
25. James, "History of Northwestern University," chapter XIII, pp. 37-38.
26. *Evanston Index*, July 8, 1893.
27. *N.U. Catalogue*, 1860-61.
28. *N.U. Catalogue*, 1869-70.
29. James, "History of Northwestern University," chapter XIII, pp. 52-53.
30. C.L.A. Faculty Minutes, June 22, 1891.
31. James, "History of Northwestern University," chapter XIII, pp. 52-53.
32. *The Northwestern*, March 22, 1900.
33. C.L.A. Faculty Minutes, March 27, 1900.
34. James Lawrence Lardner, "A History of the School of Speech," unpublished ms, N.U.A. (hereafter cited as Lardner, "School of Speech").
35. *The Northwestern*, September 23, 1892.
36. T.M., July 5, 1892.
37. T.M., June 23, 1894.
38. Peter Christian Lutkin, "The School of Music," Wilde, *Northwestern University*, IV: 190-91.
39. P.R., 1892-93.
40. Ward, *Story of Northwestern University*, p. 324.
41. *N.U. Catalogue*, 1895-96.
42. Peter Christian Lutkin, "The School of Music," in Wilde, *Northwestern University*, IV: 198-99.
43. James Alton James, "The Origin and Early Development of the University Guild," ms, 1942, University Guild file, N.U.A.
44. Mrs. Anne George Millar, "The History of Our Art Collection," ms, n.d., University Guild File, N.U.A.
45. Northwestern University Settlement Papers, N.U.A.
46. J. Scott Clark, "The Coffee Club," in Wilde, *Northwestern University*, III: 90.
47. *The Northwestern*, October 22, 1896.
48. *Chicago Evening Post*, June 13, 1895.
49. *The Northwestern*, May 2, 1895.
50. *The Northwestern*, May 20, 1897.
51. Francis Martin Gibson, "The Rogers Literary Society," in Wilde, *Northwestern University*, III: 62.
52. *Evanston Index*, May 6, 1899.
53. James Frank Oates, "Fraternities," in Wilde, *Northwestern University*, III: 103.
54. *Evanston Index*, October 18, 1890, May 16, 1891.
55. Myrtle Viola Whitney, to her mother, September 28, 1890; Woman's College Records, N.U.A.
56. H. W. Rogers, "The American College Fraternities," in *Fraternity Men of Chicago*, Will J. Murdoch, ed. (Chicago: Umbdstock Publishing Company, 1898), p. 16.
57. *N.U. Catalogue*, 1895-96.
58. *N.U. Catalogue*, 1895-96.
59. P.R., 1892-93.
60. C.L.A. Faculty Minutes, June 4, 1897.
61. C.L.A. Faculty Minutes, September 17, 1897.
62. *Epworth Herald*, August 13, 1892.
63. *Syllabus*, 1895.
64. *N.U. Catalogue*, 1895-96.
65. C.L.A. Faculty Minutes, October 25, 1892.
66. T.M., October 17, 1893; C.L.A. Faculty Minutes, February 20, 1894.
67. C.L.A. Faculty Minutes, January 15, 1895.
68. Paulison, *Wildcats*, p. 7.
69. Paulison, *Wildcats*, p. 25.
70. Sheppard and Hurd, *History of Northwestern University*, p. 161.
71. Paulison, *Wildcats*, p. 27.
72. Paulison, *Wildcats*, p. 89.
73. Paulison, *Wildcats*, pp. 21, 23.
74. *The Northwestern*, November 4, 1892.
75. *College Alumni Record*, (1903), p. 40.
76. P.R., 1894-95.
77. P.R., 1895-96.
78. N.U. Treasurer's Report, 1900.

79. *Evanston Press*, June 16, 1900.
80. *Chicago Tribune*, June 13, 1900.
81. *Evanston Index*, June 16, 1900.
82. *Chicago Daily News*, June 14, 1900.
83. *Evanston Index*, June 16, 1900.
84. *Evanston Index*, July 7, 1900.
85. *Evanston Index*, June 16, 1900.
86. *The Daily News*, June 14, 1900.
87. *Chicago Evening Post*, June 18, 1900.
88. *Chicago Times-Herald*, June 14, 1900.
89. *Who Was Who, 1916-1928*, (London: A. C. Black, Ltd., 1929); James, "History of N.U.," chapter XIV, p. 51.

CHAPTER 4

1. *Chicago Evening Post*, July 7, 1900.
2. T.M., November 19, 1900; December 4, 1900; February 11, 1901; March 17, 1902; April 29, 1903; May 18, 1903; November 17, 1903; February 19, 1917.
3. T.M., May 20, 1918; October 28, 1924.
4. T.M., March 5, 1901; October 13, 1901; January 21, 1902; September 15, 1902.
5. Edmund J. James Papers, N.U.A. (hereafter cited as EJJ Papers).
6. Wilson to E. J. James, January 27, 1902, EJJ Papers, N.U.A.
7. *Evanston Press*, January 18, 1902.
8. Newspaper clippings in C. W. Pearson Papers, N.U.A.
9. *Evanston Press*, March 15, 1902.
10. *Evanston Press*, March 22, 1902; *The Northwestern*, March 27, 1902.
11. *Chicago American*, March 24, 1902; *Chicago Record-Herald*, March 24, 1902; *Chicago Tribune*, March 24, 1902.
12. Richard A. Swanson, "Edmund J. James, 1855-1925; A Conservative Progressive in American Higher Education," unpublished Ph.D. Dissertation, University of Illinois, 1906, p. 195.
13. E. J. James to F. P. Crandon, April 24, 1902, EJJ Papers N.U.A.; TM., May 19, 1902, June 14, 1904; William Dyche to Edward Swift, May 1, 1905, in William Dyche file, N.U.A.
14. T.M., September 8, 1904.
15. E. J. James to A. H. Wilde, April 8, 1911, EJJ Papers, University of Illinois Archives
16. William Andrew Dyche, "The Administration of President James, 1902-1904," Wilde, *Northwestern University*, I: 366.
17. Thomas F. Holgate biographical file, N.U.A.
18. William Deering to Miller as related to Frank Crandon, December 27, 1905, William Deering file, N.U.A.

19. *Evanston Index*, June 22, 1907.
20. Abram W. Harris to William Deering, February 7, 1907, Abram W. Harris Papers, N.U.A. (henceforth cited as AWH Papers).
21. *N.U. Catalogue*, 1911-1912.
22. Abram W. Harris to Frank M. Elliot, March 27, 1911, AWH Papers, N.U.A.
23. T.M., July 3, 1913.
24. *N.U. Catalog*, 1916-1917.*
25. Abram W. Harris to William Deering, March 5, 1907, AWH Papers, N.U.A.
26. *Evanston Index*, February 23, 1907; August 1, 1908.
27. *Evanston Index*, June 22, 1907.
28. N.U. catalogs.
29. T.M., November 22, 1910.
30. P.R., 1917-1919.
31. P.R., 1913-1914.
32. Walter Lichtenstein biographical file, N.U.A.
33. N.U. catalogs.
34. T.M., October 10, 1912; Arey, *Medical School*, p. 191.
35. Arey, *Medical School*, p. 198-99.
36. P.R., 1916-1917.
37. P.R., 1900-1901, 1904-1905.
38. T.M., September 16, 1901; Rahl and Schwerin, *School of Law*, p. 20.
39. Rahl and Schwerin, *School of Law*, p. 71.
40. T.M., February 17, 1908.
41. T.M., October 26, 1915.
42. *Daily Northwestern*, May 10, 1916.
43. William Dyche biographical file, N.U.A.
44. T.M., August 20, 1900; September 17, 1900.
45. P.R., 1905-1916; *N.U. Catalogue*, 1909-1910.
46. E. C. Sage to A. W. Harris, May 24, 1913, reprinted in TM., June 10, 1913.
47. *Northwestern Magazine*, January 1910.
48. *The Northwestern*, May 8, 1902; May 21, 1903; Y.M.C.A.-Y.W.C.A. Records, N.U.A.
49. T.M., February 11, 1901; October 21, 1901.
50. *Northwestern Magazine*, April 1904; Northwestern University Settlement Report, Winter, 1906-1907, N.U. Settlement Records, N.U.A.
51. *The Northwestern*, April 30, 1906; *Northwestern Magazine*, February 1913.
52. *Northwestern Magazine*, January 1914.
53. *Daily Northwestern*, March 21, April 18, May 1, 1914.
54. Mary Ross Potter, "The Social Situation," *Northwestern Magazine*, December 1913.
55. *The Northwestern*, January 8, April 23 1903.

*In 1913 the spelling was changed from catalogue to catalog.

56. *Northwestern Magazine*, October 1907.
57. *Northwestern Magazine*, December 1907; see also Scrapbook of Horace G. Smith, captain of the Northwestern University Debate Team, Class of 1905 files, N.U.A.
58. *Chicago American*, April 2, 1903.
59. Paulison, *Wildcats*, p. 90.
60. T.M., March 20, 1906.
61. T.M., June 18, 1907.
62. Paulison, *Wildcats*, p. 30-32.
63. Paulison, *Wildcats*, p. 92.
64. Paulison, *Wildcats*, p. 9.
65. Paulison, *Wildcats*, p. 156.
66. Paulison, *Wildcats*, p. 162.
67. Paulison, *Wildcats*, p. 131.
68. *Northwestern Magazine*, March 1914.
69. *Northwestern Magazine*, March 1914.
70. *Purple Phi Kap* (Evanston); Upsilon Chapter of Phi Kappa Sigma, X (July 8, 1947), pp. 9-10, N.U.A.; Psi Omega Chapter of Sigma Alpha Epsilon, Semi-Annual Reports, 1911, 1916, Sigma Alpha Epsilon National Headquarters, Evanston.
71. *Northwestern Magazine*, November 1910.
72. William A. Dyche, "A Study of Men's Dormitories in Universities and Colleges," January 15, 1930, typescript in Men's Housing file, N.U.A.
73. T.M., December 21, 1903.
74. See Harris correspondence, Men's Housing file, N.U.A.; also Jonathan T. Howe, "The Northwestern University Fraternity System: A History, 1851-1963," unpublished honors thesis, department of history, Northwestern University, 1963, N.U.A.
75. *She Yet Speaketh: A Memorial Collection of the Writings of Lydia A. Bartlett* (Evanston: Kimball Press, 1908), in Class of 1909 file, N.U.A.
76. Ethel Robinson Scrapbook, N.U.A.
77. Miscellaneous clippings, Coeducation file, N.U.A.
78. *Northwestern Magazine*, November 1912.
79. *Northwestern Magazine*, May 1907.
80. *Northwestern Magazine*, January 1914; December 1915; October 1911.
81. *Daily Northwestern*, September 23, October 15, 1915.
82. *Daily Northwestern*, March 30, 1917.
83. P.R., 1917-1919; Arey, *Medical School*, p. 226.
84. James, "History of N.U.," chapter XVIII, p. 10.
85. P.R., 1917-1919.
86. James, "History of N.U.," chapter XVIII, pp. 13-17.
87. P.R., 1916-1917.
88. Letter of February 1, 1975 from Gemma M. Rizner (daughter of Walter Lichtenstein) to Rolf H. Erickson, University Library.
89. Northwestern University Library Records, N.U.A.
90. T.M., June 18, 1919.
91. T.M., August 20, March 19, 1917; June 13, August 1, August 18, August 22, September 29, October 9, 1919; March 27, June 15, 1920.

CHAPTER 5

1. J. Z. Jacobson, *Scott of Northwestern* (Chicago; Louis Mariano, 1951), pp. 10, 21-22, 32. Hereafter cited as Jacobson, *Scott of N.U.*
2. Jacobson, *Scott of N.U.*, pp. 39-42, 46-48.
3. Edmund C. Lynch, *Walter Dill Scott: Pioneer in Personnel Management* (Austin, Texas; Bureau of Business Research, University of Texas, 1968), pp. 21-22, 24-27.
4. Jacobson, *Scott of N.U.*, pp. 121-23.
5. *Alumni News*, February 1939.
6. Speech File, Walter Dill Scott Papers, N.U.A. (hereafter cited as WDS Papers).
7. Speech File, WDS Papers, N.U.A.
8. P.R., 1920-21; 1921-22.
9. T.M., January 31, 1922.
10. P.R., 1921-22; T.M., May 22, 1922.
11. *Alumni News*, March 1934.
12. Interview with Thomas Gonser by Harold F. Williamson and Payson S. Wild, August 15, 1973, N.U.A.
13. Northwestern University Treasurer's Reports, 1924-1930.
14. "Memorandum on Large Donations," WDS Papers, N.U.A.
15. T.M., September 22, 1925; November 23, 1926; P.R., 1925-26; 1928-29.
16. P.R., 1928-29.
17. *Alumni News*, February 1928.
18. T.M., June 12, 1926.
19. P.R., 1926-27.
20. Minutes of Subcommittee on Committee on Development, October 18, 1928, WDS Papers, N.U.A.
21. *Alumni News*, March 1929.
22. Carl Condit, *Chicago, 1910-1929, Building, Planning and Urban Technology* (Chicago: The University of Chicago Press, 1973), p. 228.
23. James Gamble Rogers, "The Alexander McKinlock Memorial Campus Northwestern University, Chicago," *Architecture*, June 1927, pp. 301-6.
24. *Alumni News*, July 1927.
25. Arey, *Medical School*, p. 245
26. Arey, *Medical School*, p. 253.
27. *N.U. Catalog*, 1929-30.
28. P.R., 1924-25; 1930-31.

29. Arey, *Medical School*, pp. 214-15.
30. Arey, *Medical School*, pp. 360-65.
31. *N.U. Catalog*, 1920-21.
32. *N.U. Catalog*, 1924-25.
33. *N.U. Catalog*, 1924-25; "School of Dentistry, Executive Committee on Faculty Organization and Activities of the Dental School, 1891-1934," unpublished ms., pp. 10-11, N.U.A.
34. T.M., July 9, 1929; Rahl and Schwerin, *School of Law*, p. 42.
35. Leon Green, Biographical File, N.U.A.
36. Rahl and Schwerin, *School of Law*, p. 51.
37. P.R., 1924-25.
38. T.M., May 23, 1933.
39. Walter Dill Scott to William Dyche, November 21, 1920; Copy of Resolution; WDS Papers, N.U.A.
40. *Alumni Journal*, February 5, 1921.
41. H. F. Harrington to Walter Dill Scott, June 1922, WDS Papers, N.U.A.
42. Baker Brownell, biographical file, N.U.A.
43. T.M., April 27, 1926.
44. T.M., November 23, 1926; November 26, 1927.
45. *Alumni News*, February, 1929, October 1938.
46. P.R., 1922-23.
47. P.R., 1925-26; 1927-28.
48. P.R., 1925-26.
49. P.R., 1926-27; 1927-28.
50. P.R., 1929-30; 1930-31.
51. *N.U. Catalog*, 1921-22; 1929-30.
52. *N.U. Catalog*, 1920-21.
53. P.R., 1921-22.
54. Carl Beecher biographical file, N.U.A.
55. P.R., 1919-20, 1929-30.
56. Lardner, *School of Speech*, pp. 46-47; T.M., February 28, 1921.
57. *N.U. Catalog*, 1920-21.
58. Lardner, *School of Speech*, p. 51; T.M., January 18, 1927.
59. Lardner, *School of Speech*, pp. 55-56.
60. P.R., 1920-21; *N.U. Catalog*, 1929-30.
61. *N.U. Catalog*, 1920-21.
62. Colleges of Engineering Survey Report, 1926, N.U.A.
63. P.R., 1925-26; T.M., February 23, 1927.
64. T.M., April 22, 1929.
65. T.M., April 26, 1920.
66. WDS Files, N.U.A.
67. *N.U. Catalog*, 1926-27; 1929-30.
68. *N.U. Catalog*, 1919-20; 1938-39.
69. Walter Dill Scott, "The Future of Northwestern University," WDS Papers, N.U.A.
70. T.M., October 25, 1921.
71. Paulison, *Wildcats*, pp. 39, 40, 42, 196-97.
72. *Daily Northwestern*, October 22, 1926.
73. *Daily Northwestern*, March 25, March 28, April 1, 1924.
74. *Scrawl*, March 1928.
75. *Scrawl*, November 1925.
76. Bernard De Voto, "The Co-Ed: The Hope of Liberal Education," *Harper's Monthly Magazine*, September 1924, pp. 453-54.
77. Walter Dill Scott, "Northwestern Democratic," *Alumni News*, January 1923.
78. T.M., October 28, 1924; P.R. 1924-25.
79. U.S. Bureau of the Census, *Historical Statistics of the United States*, Washington, D.C., 1860, pp. 73, 139.
80. P.R., 1937-38.
81. *Daily Northwestern*, October 11, 1932.
82. *Alumni News*, December 1932.
83. Robert M. Hutchins, Memorandum May 25, 1933, Merger file, N.U.A.
84. Memorandum on educational changes and economies, Merger file, N.U.A.
85. Memorandum to members of the merger committee, Merger file, N.U.A.
86. *Chicago Daily Tribune*, November 22, November 24, 1933.
87. *Evanston Review*, January 25, 1934.
88. William Benton, *The University of Chicago's Public Relations* (Chicago: University of Chicago Press, 1937), p. 134.
89. George Craig Stewart to John H. Hardin, July 11, 1933, Merger file, N.U.A.
90. *Chicago Daily Tribune*, November 23, 1933.
91. "Report of the Northwestern University Senate Committee on the Proposed Merger Between Northwestern and the University of Chicago," N.U.A.
92. *Chicago Daily Tribune*, February 25, 1934.
93. Walter Dill Scott to Charles Thorne, March 1, 1934, Merger file, N.U.A.
94. Robert M. Hutchins, *The State of the University, 1929-49* (Chicago: University of Chicago Press, 1949).
95. P.R., 1930-31, 1935-36.
96. Rahl and Schwerin, *School of Law*, pp. 48-49.
97. *N.U. Catalog*, 1939-40.
98. P.R., 1938-39.
99. P.R., 1937-38.
100. P.R., 1932-33; 1933-34; 1938-39.
101. P.R., 1935-36; 1937-38.
102. *Daily Northwestern*, October 11, October 15, November 4, November 18, 1930.
103. Clyde J. Murley, "The Men's Union," *Syllabus*, 1929.
104. *Syllabus*, 1934; Files of the Coast Guard Life Saving Station.
105. *Daily Northwestern*, December 6, 1933; January 11, February 15, 1934.
106. *Daily Northwestern*, February 19, 1935; April 22, 1937.

107. *Alumni News*, February 1939.
108. T.M., June 12, 1937.
109. Cabell to Scott, February 22, 1936, Murphy file, N.U.A.
110. Gonser to Cabell, March 14, 1936, Murphy file, N.U.A.
111. Gonser memorandum, May 18, 1937, Murphy file, N.U.A.
112. Cabell to Gonser, May 16, 1936; Kettering Proposal for a School of Engineering, August 18, 1936, Murphy file, N.U.A.
113. Cabell to Gonser, July 3, 1936; Gonser to Cabell, July 22, 1936, Murphy file, N.U.A.
114. Memorandum, August 10, 1936, Murphy file, N.U.A.
115. Memorandum, August 26, 1936, Murphy file, N.U.A.
116. Walter Dill Scott, *Walter Patten Murphy 1873-1942* (Evanston, Illinois: Privately printed, 1952).
117. Brook's Report, August 26, 1936, Murphy file, N.U.A.
118. P.R., 1938-39.
119. *Alumni News*, February 1939.
120. *Evanston Review*, February 16, 1939.
121. Files of the Women's Athletic Association and of the Women's Building Fund, University Guild, N.U.A.
122. Typescript issued by Northwestern News Service, September 19, 1940, N.U.A.; *Alumni News*, October 1940.
123. *Alumni News*, February, 1939.
124. *Alumni News*, February, 1939.
125. *Alumni News*, February, 1939.
126. J. M. Brooks, "Northwestern University, Certain Aspects of 40 Years of Financial Progress," ca. 1959, Business Manager's Records, N.U.A.
127. *Alumni News*, April 1939.

CHAPTER 6

1. *Alumni News*, October 1939.
2. Franklyn Bliss Snyder, biographical file, N.U.A.
3. P.R., 1939-40.
4. P.R., 1940-41.
5. Edward Stromberg, Director of Public Relations, memorandum: "The Administration of Franklyn Bliss Snyder," 1950 (hereafter cited as Stromberg ms., N.U.A.); P.R., 1944-45.
6. Stromberg ms., N.U.A.
7. P.R., 1944-45.
8. Stromberg ms., N.U.A.
9. Snyder memorandum, October 15, 1942, Franklyn Bliss Snyder Papers, N.U.A. (hereafter cited as FBS Papers).
10. P.R., 1943-44.
11. P.R., 1946-47.
12. Report to trustees, February 26, 1948, FBS Papers, N.U.A.
13. F. B. Snyder to A. Hibbard, May 12, 1944, FBS Papers, N.U.A.
14. T.M., January 8, 1946.
15. F. B. Snyder to O. Eshbach, March 31, 1949, FBS Papers, N.U.A.
16. F. B. Snyder to F. D. Fagg and A. Hibbard, April 16, 1943, FBS, N.U.A.
17. F. B. Snyder to P. A. Schilpp, January 25, 1940, FBS Papers, N.U.A.
18. F. B. Snyder to Nancy Mater, September 3, 1944, FBS Papers, N.U.A.
19. P. A. Schilpp to F. B. Snyder, July 5, 1944, FBS Papers, N.U.A.
20. Student letters to F. B. Snyder, October 7, 1945; April 29, 1946, FBS Papers, N.U.A.
21. Records of the College of Liberal Arts, N.U.A.
22. M. Campbell to F. D. Fagg, January 2, 1945, FBS Papers, N.U.A.
23. Memorandum from F. B. Snyder to P. A. Schilpp, June 6, 1940, FBS Papers, N.U.A.
24. Walter A. Jessup to F. B. Snyder, June 13, 1944, FBS Papers, N.U.A.
25. Memorandum from F. B. Snyder to P. A. Schilpp, January 9, 1945, FBS Papers, N.U.A.
26. F. B. Snyder to P. A. Schilpp, November 15, 1947, FBS Papers, N.U.A.
27. P. A. Schilpp to F. B. Snyder, August 2, 1948, FBS Papers, N.U.A.
28. Owen L. Coon to P. A. Schilpp, June 30, 1944, FBS Papers, N.U.A.
29. C. MacDougall to K. Olson, March 11, 1948, FBS Papers, N.U.A.
30. K. Olson to F. B. Snyder, March 17, 1948; F. B. Snyder to K. Olson, March 18, 1948, FBS Papers, N.U.A.
31. F. B. Snyder to E. M. Hadley, May 1, 1948, FBS Papers, N.U.A.
32. Report of Vice President Gonser, P.R., 1945-46.
33. P.R., 1941-42.
34. Stromberg ms., N.U.A.
35. P.R., 1941-42.
36. P.R., 1945-46.
37. *Chicago Sunday Tribune*, March 10, 1946; *Chicago Sun*, March 10, 1946.
38. P.R., 1946-47.
39. J. M. Brooks, "Northwestern University, Certain Aspects of 40 Years of Financial Progress," ca. 1959, Business Manager's Records, N.U.A.
40. Memorandum, August 26, 1936, Murphy file, N.U.A.
41. Memorandum to himself by F. B. Snyder, August 1, 1944, FBS Papers, N.U.A.

42. F. B. Snyder to O. Eshbach, March 18, 1947, FBS Papers, N.U.A.
43. T.M., June 16, 1947.
44. Report of the Trustees' Committee, February 26, 1948, J. Roscoe Miller Papers, N.U.A. (henceforth referred to as the JRM Papers).
45. O. Eshbach to F. B. Snyder, March 4, 1948, FBS Papers, N.U.A.
46. P.R., 1946-47.
47. P.R., 1938-39, report of the dean of faculties.
48. F. B. Snyder correspondence with E. O. Melby, FBS Papers, N.U.A.
49. E. O. Melby to F. D. Fagg, June 4, 1940; F. D. Fagg to E. O. Melby, December 5, 1940; F. B. Snyder to E. O. Melby, December 20, 1940, FBS Papers, N.U.A.
50. E. O. Melby to F. B. Snyder, August 8, 1941, FBS Papers, N.U.A.
51. T.M., October 28, 1941.
52. Memoranda of Search Committee to F. D. Fagg, January 21, and March 28, 1944; memorandum of E. T. McSwain to F. D. Fagg, April 13, 1944, FBS, N.U.A.
53. P.R., 1944-45.
54. *Daily Northwestern*, January 10, 1941.
55. P.R., 1940-41 and 1941-42, reports of Director of Athletics Kenneth L. Wilson.
56. *Daily Northwestern*, October 8, 1940.
57. *Daily Northwestern*, April 25, 1941.
58. Memorandum from Paul MacMinn to Joe Miller, February 16, 1942, FBS Papers, N.U.A.
59. Letters to Snyder, February 27, 1942, FBS Papers, N.U.A.
60. *Daily Northwestern*, January 14, January 15, 1941.
61. F. B. Snyder to Richard Thurston, November 7, 1941, FBS Papers, N.U.A.
62. J. L. Rollins to F. D. Fagg, November 21, 1941, FBS Papers, N.U.A.
63. Documented by report of Joyce O'Brien to F. B. Snyder, November 6, 1941, FBS Papers, N.U.A.
64. Memorandum from H. L. Wells to F. B. Snyder, June 18, 1941, FBS Papers, N.U.A.
65. F. B. Snyder's memorandum concerning this talk, July 18, 1941, FBS Papers, N.U.A.
66. Memorandum from staff member to F. B. Snyder, November 13, 1941, FBS Papers, N.U.A.
67. Memorandum from F. B. Snyder to F. D. Fagg, August 14, 1944, FBS Papers, N.U.A.
68. Letters of H. L. Wessling to F. G. Seulberger and Wilson of the Northwestern Y.M.C.A. August 11, 1944, FBS Papers, N.U.A.
69. P.R., 1947-48, report of dean of students. *Daily Northwestern*, November 11, 1948.
70. T.M., April 8, 1947.
71. Quoted in letter from F. B. Snyder to Mrs. Edwin B. Mills, April 16, 1946; memorandum of F. B. Snyder to members of the Chicago Teachers Union, August 2, 1945, FBS Papers, N.U.A.
72. Letter from M. R. Dabner to F. B. Snyder, November 1, 1945, FBS Papers, N.U.A.
73. C. W. Freeman to F. B. Snyder, November 8, 1945; FBS Papers, N.U.A.
74. P.R., 1943-44, 1944-45, and 1945-46, reports of dean of students.
75. T.M., 1944-45; F. George Seulberger biographical file, N.U.A.
76. *Daily Northwestern*, October 9, October 17, October 19, 1945.
77. P.R., 1946-47, report of the dean of students.
78. P.R., 1947-48, report of the coordinator of veteran's education.
79. *Daily Northwestern*, November 9, 1945.
80. *Daily Northwestern*, November 15, 1945.
81. University Board of Religion Minutes, April 30, 1940, N.U.A.
82. *Evanston Review*, June 3, 1943.
83. P.R., 1946-47, report of the university chaplain.
84. T.M., June 19, 1946.
85. *Daily Northwestern*, November 23, 1948.
86. *Daily Northwestern*, January 7, 1949.
87. *The Big Ten Record Book* (Chicago: The Western Intercollegiate Conference).
88. *Alumni News*, April 1958.
89. Taped interview with Moody E. Prior (professor of English emeritus and dean of the Graduate School 1951-1964) by Harold F. Williamson and Payson S. Wild, October 1973, N.U.A.

CHAPTER 7

1. J. Roscoe Miller biographical file, N.U.A.
2. Payson S. Wild biographical file, N.U.A.
3. John E. Fields, William S. Kerr, Arthur T. Schmehling biographical files, N.U.A.
4. Payson S. Wild Papers, N.U.A. (hereafter referred to as PSW Papers).
5. T.M., June 12, 1973.
6. T.M., August 7, 1972
7. J. R. Miller letter, January 25, 1968, JRM Papers, N.U.A.
8. J. R. Miller letter to a trustee, July 17, 1962, JRM Papers.
9. Taped interview with J. Roscoe Miller by Harold F. Williamson and Payson S. Wild, October 8, 1973.
10. The University Register, 1948-49; J. M. Brooks, "Northwestern University, Certain

Aspects of 40 Years of Financial Progress," ca. 1959, Business Manager's Records, N.U.A.

11. T.M., April 23, 1951.

12. J. R. Miller to faculty, November 1, 1949, JRM Papers, N.U.A.

13. J. R. Miller to faculty, June 14, 1950, JRM Papers, N.U.A.

14. J. R. Miller to faculty, January 20, 1950, JRM Papers, N.U.A.

15. J. R. Miller to faculty, January 25, 1952 JRM Papers, N.U.A.

16. Records of the 1951 Northwestern University Centennial Celebration, N.U.A.

17. T.M., June 13, 1955.

18. William S. Kerr's account in *College and University Business*, November 1964.

19. J. R. Miller to faculty, November 11, 1960.

20. William S. Kerr in *College and University Business*, November 1964.

21. T.M., 1955-56.

22. P. S. Wild to I. M. Klotz, November 1, 1965; May 22, 1966; June 22, 1966, PSW Papers, N.U.A.

23. P. S. Wild to C. L. Ver Steeg, December 12, 1962, PSW Papers, N.U.A.

24. P. S. Wild and F. M. Kreml to faculty, November 4 and November 19, 1964; P. S. Wild to I. M. Klotz, November 1, 1965, PSW Papers, N.U.A.

25. Administrative Policies and Planning Committee Report, February 21, 1966.

26. "First Plan for the Seventies," in *Northwestern University Bulletin*, 1966.

27. *First Plan for the Seventies*, final report, University Relations publication, April 13, 1972.

28. John Evans Club files, N.U.A.

29. Alumni Relations Office.

30. Department of Development Records.

31. P. S. Wild to Administrative Council, November 2, 1964, PSW Papers, N.U.A.

32. P. S. Wild and F. M. Kreml to faculty, January 10, 1969, PSW Papers, N.U.A.

33. W. S. Owen to Administrative Council, December 8, 1971, PSW, N.U.A.

34. Office of Research and Development Records.

35. Office of Research and Sponsored Programs, Annual Report 1973-74.

36. Office of Planning and Development Records.

37. *Evanston Review*, June 16, 1960.

38. *Alumni News*, July 1954.

39. Peter Byrne, Report on Building Programs, 1974, N.U.A.

40. University Relations Release, July 1962.

41. Correspondence from J. R. Miller, July 1962, JRM Papers, N.U.A.

42. J. R. Miller to L. E. Kautz, May 1962, JRM Papers, N.U.A.

43. W. M. Dixon to J. R. Miller, July 25, 1962, JRM Papers, N.U.A.

44. Letters from American Society of Landscape Artists, May 28, 1962; Garden Club of Oak Park and River Forest, November 17, 1962, JRM Papers, N.U.A.

45. *Alumni News*, January 1967.

46. University Relations Release, January 21, 1974.

47. University Relations Release, May 1, 1965.

48. T.M., July 25, 1960.

49. P. S. Wild to J. R. Miller, July 11, 1960, JRM Papers, N.U.A.

50. University Relations Release, October 15, 1969.

51. Jeremy R. Wilson to R. H. Young, December 20, 1969; December 20, 1968; T.M., June 9, 1969; Planning Committee to Medical Center officers and directors, July 31, 1969, JRM Papers, N.U.A.

52. Jeremy R. Wilson to R. H. Strotz, P. S. Wild, J. E. Fields, J. E. Eckenhoff and N. H. Olsen, March 23, 1972; Medical Center Activity Report, November 30, 1972, JRM Papers, N.U.A.

53. Medical Center Planning Committee Report to officers and directors of the Medical Center, August 31, 1969, JRM Papers, N.U.A.

54. Medical Center Planning Committee Report, October 31, 1969, JRM Papers, N.U.A.

55. T.M., November 9, 1972.

56. Medical Center Newsletter, March 4, 1971; Ray Brown report on Superior-Fairbanks site August 1, 1972, JRM Papers, N.U.A.

57. Jeremy R. Wilson to Administrative Policies and Planning Committee, June 23, 1970, JRM Papers, N.U.A.

58. Merger Agreement, March 3, 1972, copy Northwestern University Legal Department.

59. Medical Center Activity Report, November 30, 1972, JRM Papers, N.U.A.

60. Administrative Policies and Planning Committee, November 29, 1973, JRM Papers, N.U.A.

61. University Relations Release, October 15, 1969.

62. University Senate Minutes, April 8, 1939.

63. P. S. Wild to Committee on Educational Policies, May 13, 1964, PSW Papers, N.U.A.

64. Committee on Educational Policies file, PSW Papers, N.U.A.

65. University Senate Minutes, November 30. 1964; May 11, 1971.

66. University Senate Minutes, May 21, 1920; R. H. Strotz to E. F. Perry, April 8, 1971,

JRM Papers, N.U.A.

67. University Senate Minutes, February 1, 1968.
68. University Senate Minutes, May 11, 1971.
69. Jean Hagstrum, *A Community of Scholars* (Evanston: Northwestern University), volume 1 issued September 1968; volume 2 issued October 1969.
70. University Senate Minutes, February 6, 1969.
71. Report of dean of faculties, 1954-55.
72. Report of dean of faculties, 1957-58.
73. Report of dean of faculties, 1957-58; 1960-61.
74. Report of Dean Raymond W. Mack in *Northwestern Memo*, November 1972.
75. Robert H. Strotz, Laurence H. Nobles, Hanna H. Gray, Rudolph H. Weingartner biographical files, N.U.A.
76. Statistical and Faculty Summaries, 1973-74, Northwestern University Department of Planning.
77. Report of dean of faculties, 1959-60.
78. Report of dean of the Graduate School, 1951-52.
79. Graduate Faculty Minutes, May 13, 1958.
80. Robert H. Baker biographical file, N.U.A.
81. Graduate School reports to the president, 1960-70, N.U.A.
82. Carnegie Corporation to J. R. Miller, June 28, 1959; J. R. Miller to faculty, September 1957; JRM Papers, N.U.A.
83. Report of dean of faculties, 1961-62.
84. B. J. Chandler biographical file, N.U.A.
85. N.U. catalogs.
86. Statistical Summaries, 1973-74.
87. B. Claude Mathis biographical file, N.U.A.
88. Joseph M. McDaniel, Richard A. Donham, John A. Barr biographical files, N.U.A.
89. Graduate School of Management Faculty, Minutes, May 4, 1966.
90. Graduate School of Management Faculty Minutes, February 5, 1969.
91. Statistical Summaries, 1973-74.
92. Statistical Summaries, 1973-74.
93. J. R. Miller to faculty, July 12, 1951, JRM Papers, N.U.A.
94. Statistical Summaries, 1973-74.
95. N.U. catalogs; Statistical Summaries, 1973-74.
96. Donald H. Loughridge biographical file, N.U.A.
97. Harold B. Gotaas biographical file, N.U.A.
98. T.M., June 11, 1962.
99. Walter S. Owen, David Mintzer, Bruno A. Boley biographical files, N.U.A.
100. Statistical Summaries, 1973-74.
101. Report of dean of faculties, 1960-61.
102. James E. Eckenhoff biographical file, N.U.A.
103. University Relations Release, March 5, 1974.
104. Statistical Summaries, 1973-74.
105. University Relations Release, September 25, 1959.
106. George W. Teuscher biographical file, N.U.A.
107. Report of dean of faculties, 1963-64.
108. Norman H. Olsen biographical file, N.U.A.
109. Statistical Summaries, 1973-74.
110. John Ritchie biographical file, N.U.A.
111. J. R. Miller to faculty, June 16, 1960, JRM Papers, N.U.A.
112. John Ritchie to J. R. Miller, August 1, 1968; "A Proposal for the Growth of the Northwestern University School of Law During the Next Decade, Presented by the Dean and Faculty of the School, November 20, 1968"; "Senior Research Program Off to an Impressive Start," by James A. Rahl; Inspection Report on Northwestern University School of Law, by American Bar Association, April 24-25, 1968; N.U. School of Law, Annual Report, 1971-72. All in PSW Papers, N.U.A.
113. University Relations Release, July 1, 1974.
114. James A. Rahl biographical file, N.U.A.
115. Statistical Summaries, 1973-74.
116. University Senate Minutes, May 16, 1967; May 15, 1968; November 6, 1968; February 5, 1969.
117. T.M., June 15, 1953.
118. Martha S. Luck biographical file, N.U.A.
119. William C. Bradford biographical file, N.U.A.
120. Report of dean of faculties, 1952-53.
121. University Relations Release, July 1, 1974.
122. University Relations Release, June 25, 1974.
123. Report of dean of faculties, 1964-65.
124. Report of dean of faculties, 1952-53.
125. Report of dean of faculties, 1960-61; 1962-63.
126. John P. McGowan biographical file, N.U.A.
127. *Midwestern Library News*, May 7, 1965.
128. Report of dean of faculties, 1958-59.
129. Report of dean of faculties, 1972-73.
130. J. R. Miller to Frederick L. Hovde of Purdue, June 1, 1957, JRM Papers, N.U.A.; Correspondence in MURA File, 1955-1961, PSW Papers, N.U.A.; Founders' Agreement, February 25, 1965, Northwestern University Legal Department.
131. URA By-laws adopted September 16, 1965; Report of president of URA, December 5, 1967, PSW Papers, N.U.A.
132. Files for the named buildings, N.U.A.

133. Moody E. Prior's Report on the University Press, November 1956, PSW Papers, N.U.A.

134. *University Register*, 1949-50.

135. N.U. Budget Office.

136. Annual Reports of the American Association of University Professors.

137. Reports of dean of faculties, 1949-61; N.U. Budget Office records.

138. Reports of dean of faculties, 1952-53.

139. J. R. Miller to faculty, June 13, 1956, JRM Papers, N.U.A.

140. J. R. Miller to faculty, September 1950, JRM Papers, N.U.A.; Office of International Programs and Scholars Records.

141. University Senate Minutes, February 19, 1954, report of Katharine George.

142. Report of the provost, 1971-72.

143. University Relations Release, July 1, 1974.

144. T.M., March 10, 1969; July 20, 1970; April 20, 1971.

145. *Northwestern Memo*, November 1973.

146. Faculty Club file, N.U.A.

147. Director of Financial Aid, Dan Hall in *Northwestern Report*, Summer 1974.

148. Address to students, May 15, 1957, PSW Papers, N.U.A.

149. Student Governing Board Report, February 11, 1953, PSW Papers, N.U.A.

150. University Senate Minutes, November 30, 1967, February 1, 1968.

151. University Senate Minutes, October 31, 1972.

152. Constitution of Student Senate; Constitution of Associated Student Government, PSW Papers, N.U.A.

153. Roland Olson to Dean of Students James F. Stull, September 20, 1971, PSW Papers, N.U.A.

154. Exchange of letters, P. S. Wild and Symposium Officers, October 28, November 15, 1963, PSW Papers, N.U.A.

155. Norman Miller, director of Lecture Series, to P. S. Wild, September 9, 1967; Roland Hinz to P. S. Wild, October 18, 1967, PSW Papers, N.U.A.

156. Report of Roland J. Hinz, October 12, 1967, PSW Papers, N.U.A.

157. J. R. Miller to alumni, March 31, 1967, JRM Papers, N.U.A.

158. J. R. Miller to J. C. McLeod, June 7, 1967; J. R. Miller to G. K. Krulee, April 23, 1970, JRM Papers, N.U.A.

159. M. E. Prior to P. S. Wild, June 11, 1965, PSW Papers, N.U.A.

160. Committee on Educational Policies' Subcommittee on the Academic Environment to the faculty, May 12, 1971, PSW Papers, N.U.A.

161. Report of Student Faculty Committee on Residential College, January 20, 1972, PSW Papers, N.U.A.

162. University Senate Minutes, May 11, 1971; March 7, 1972.

163. Jack Nusan Porter, *Student Protest and the Technocratic Society* (Chicago: Adams Press, 1973), pp. 47-49; hereafter cited as Porter, *Student Protest*.

164. Administration Policy Statement, April 25, 1957, PSW Papers, N.U.A.

165. Administration Responses to the Black Student Petition, April 22, 1968, PSW Papers, N.U.A.

166. Report of Victor H. Good and William E. Perkins to Admission Director William I. Ihlanfeldt, October 28, 1968, PSW Papers, N.U.A.

167. Report of University Discipline Committee, April 15, 1968, PSW Papers, N.U.A.

168. Copies of the Black Students' Demands and the subsequent exchange of statements between the students and the administration are to be found in the PSW Papers, N.U.A.

169. T.M., May 9, 1968.

170. T.M., May 9, 1968.

171. T.M., May 14, 1968.

172. University Relations Releases March 8, April 18, 1969; J. R. Miller to university community, April 22, 1969, PSW Papers, N.U.A.

173. Office of Admission Records.

174. T.M., October 18, 1971; Wild to Dean Hanna H. Gray, January 17, 1973, PSW Papers, N.U.A.

175. Porter, *Student Protest*, p. 62.

176. J. R. Miller to faculty, September 30, 1969, PSW Papers, N.U.A.

177. Hourglass Ultimatum, November 17, 1969, PSW Papers, N.U.A.; *Chicago Tribune*, November 25, 1969; *Chicago Sun Times*, November 25, 1969.

178. J. R. Miller to SDS, November 24, 1969.

179. General Faculty Committee and Committee on Educational Policies' statement to the Northwestern community, February 29, 1970; Northwestern Faculty Action Committee chairman to dean of faculties, March 10, 1970, PSW Papers, N.U.A.

180. *Chicago Tribune*, April 29, 1970.

181. University Senate Minutes, May 5, 1970.

182. *Chicago Tribune*, May 12, 1970.

183. Hearings before the joint Senate-House Committee of the Illinois legislature, December 10-11, 1970.

184. *Chicago Tribune*, May 14, 1970.

185. J. R. Miller to students at Deering Meadow rally, May 8, 1970, PSW Papers, N.U.A.
186. *Chicago Tribune*, May 9, 1970.
187. J. R. Miller to faculty and students, May 10, 1970, JRM Papers, N.U.A.
188. *Chicago Daily News*, May 11, 1970.
189. *Chicago Daily News*, May 13, 1970.
190. *Chicago Tribune*, May 14, 1970.
191. P. S. Wild to students, September 1970, PSW Papers, N.U.A.
192. *Evanston Review*, May 18, 1972.
193. *Alumni News*, January 1956.
194. T.M., December 28, 1955.
195. Thomas Z. Hayward to J. R. Miller, February 4, 1957; P. S. Wild to Thomas Z. Hayward, February 7, April 15, 1957, PSW Papers, N.U.A.
196. Stuart Holcomb to J. R. Miller, September 29, 1958; JRM Papers, N.U.A.
197. William Jauss, "Football at Northwestern," *Alumni News*, October 1962.
198. *Alumni News*, October 1962.
199. T.M., January 7, April 27, 1964; January 8, 1973.
200. *Big Ten Record Book*, pp. 210, 214.
201. Leon A. Bosch to J. R. Miller, December 15, 1970, JRM Papers, N.U.A.
202. T.M., April 12, 1971.
203. T.M., June 12, 1972.
204. William H. Thigpen to Executive Secretary of the Senate of Methodist Church, October 15, 1973, JRM Papers, N.U.A.
205. Taped interview with J. Roscoe Miller by Harold F. Williamson and Payson S. Wild, October 8, 1973, N.U.A.
206. *Toward the Eighties*, University Relations publication, February 1974.

BIBLIOGRAPHY

In researching and writing this history the authors drew heavily on the resources of the University Archives. These serve as the repository for both the official records and a variety of other documents, including presidential papers, relating to the history and activities of all segments of the university community. The archival holdings of published materials include catalogs, reports, brochures, and various student, faculty, and alumni publications. Unless otherwise indicated all of the primary sources consulted in the preparation of this history may be found in the University Archives. Other sources not included in the following bibliography are cited in the notes for individual chapters.

Primary Sources

Official Publications of Northwestern University

The Alumni Journal, 1914-1917.
Alumni News, 1921-.
Alumni News Letter, 1903-1914.
Alumni Record of the College of Liberal Arts, 1903. Edited by Charles B. Atwell.
Faculty Newsletter, 1967-1969.
Faculty Planning Committee Report, *A Community of Scholars*, volume 1 published 1968, volume 2 in 1969.
Northwestern Record, 1967-1969.
Northwestern Report, 1969-1976.

Northwestern Review, 1965-1969.
Northwestern University Bulletin, 1902-1975.
Northwestern University Catalog, 1856-1858, 1860-1870, 1873, 1876-1940, 1966-1975.
President's Annual Report, 1876-1881, 1891-1948, 1958, 1961, 1972. Prepared for presentation to the board of trustees, these included reports by all the deans and other administrators as well.
President's Report to the Faculty, 1949-1967.
Register, 1940-1963.
Treasurer's Reports, 1876-1877, 1881-.

Student Publications

Daily Northwestern, 1903-.
Evening Northwestern, 1943-1949.
The Gadfly, 1933-1934.
The Northwestern, 1881-1903.
Northwestern Magazine, 1904-1916.
Northwestern News, 1949-1970.
Northwestern University Record, 1893-1896.
The Northwestern World, 1890-1892.
Pandora, 1884.
Profile, 1949-1959.
Purple Parrot, 1921-1950.

Scrawl: A Literary Quarterly, 1924-1928.
Syllabus, 1885-.
Tripod, 1871-1880.
Vidette, 1878-1880.

Newspapers

Evanston Index, 1872-1914.
Evanston News, 1909-1914.
Evanston News Index, 1915-1942.
Evanston Press, 1889-1915.
Northwestern Christian Advocate, 1852-1940. [Garrett Theological Seminary Library.]

Unpublished Materials

Personal Papers of the following

Harris, Abram W.
Holgate, Thomas F.
James, Edmund Janes, in both the Northwestern University and University of Illinois archives.
MacChesney, Nathan W.

Miller, J. Roscoe.
Rogers, Henry Wade.
Scott, Walter Dill.
Snyder, Franklyn Bliss.
Wild, Payson S.

Unpublished Materials

Minutes of Meetings of the following

Board of Trustees and its Executive Committee, 1851-.
College of Liberal Arts (and Sciences) Faculty, 1856-.
Commerce, Business School and Graduate School of Management Faculty Minutes, 1911-.
University Council, 1902-28.
University Senate, 1928-.

Records, Files and Reports

Chicago Campus Building Files.
Class Files, 1859-.
Dearborn Observatory Records.
Evanston Campus Building Files.
Evanston College for Ladies Records.
Faculty Biographical Files.
Hinman Society Records, 1857-1870.
History of the McKinlock Campus 1915-1935, prepared by the Board of Trustees.
Library Records.
Northwestern after Twenty Years, Report dated August 1966, prepared by Simeon E. Leland.
Northwestern Female College Records, both in the Northwestern University Archives and at the Evanston Historical Society.
Northwestern University Press Releases, 1946-.
Northwestern University Statistical and Faculty Summaries, 1966-, prepared annually by the Department of Planning.
Northwestern University Settlement Records.
Northwestern University—University of Chicago Merger Files.
Phi Beta Kappa Records.
University Archives Reference Subject Files.
Woman's College of Northwestern University Records.
Y.M.C.A.-Y.W.C.A. Records.

Secondary Sources

Published Materials

Arey, Leslie B. *Northwestern University Medical School, 1859-1959*. Evanston: Northwestern University Press, 1959.

Dalgety, George S. *Evanston and Northwestern University*. Evanston, 1939.

Earhart, Mary. *Frances Willard: From Prayers to Politics*. Chicago: University of Chicago Press, 1944.

Elliot, Frank M., ed. *History of Omega Chapter of Sigma Chi and Reminiscences of Northwestern*. Chicago, 1885.

Erickson, Rolf. "Northwestern University Libraries," *Encyclopedia of Library and Information Science*, Allen Kent ed. New York, in progress.

Jacobson, J. Z. *Scott of Northwestern*. Chicago: Louis Mariano, 1951.

Kelsey, Harry E., Jr. *Frontier Capitalist: The Life of John Evans*. Denver: State Historical Society of Colorado and Pruett Publishing Company, 1969.

McMechen, Edgar Carlisle. *Life of Governor Evans: Second Territorial Governor of Colorado*. Denver: Wahlgreen Publishing Company, 1924.

Paulison, Walter. *The Tale of the Wildcats*. Evanston: Northwestern University Alumni Association, 1951.

Rahl, James A. and Schwerin, Kurt. *Northwestern University School of Law: A Short History*. Chicago: Northwestern University School of Law, 1960.

Reeling, Viola Crouch. *Evanston: Its Land and People*. Evanston: Fort Dearborn Chapter of Daughters of American Revolution, 1928.

Scott, Walter Dill. *John Evans, 1814-1897: An Appreciation*. Evanston: L. J. Norris, 1939.

Scott, Walter Dill, *Walter Patten Murphy, 1873-1942*. Evanston: Privately printed, 1952.

Sheppard, Robert D. *A Historical Sketch of Northwestern University*. Evanston, 1903.

Sheppard, Robert D., and Hurd, Harvey B., eds. *History of Northwestern University and Evanston*. Chicago: Munsell Publishing Company, 1906.

Stratton, C. C., ed. *The Autobiography of Erastus O. Haven*. New York: Phillips and Hunt, 1883.

Wells, Harry L. *Northwestern University's Evanston: An Irrevocable Trust*. Evanston, 1948.

Wilde, Arthur E., ed. *Northwestern University, 1855-1905*, 4 vols. New York: University Publishing Society, 1905.

Willard, Frances E. *A Classic Town*. Chicago: Woman's Temperance Publishing Company, 1891.

Willard, Frances E. *Glimpses of Fifty Years*. Evanston: National Woman's Christian Temperance Union, 1904.

Woman's Medical School. Northwestern University (Woman's Medical College of Chicago): The Institution and its Founders. Chicago: H. G. Cutler, Publisher, 1896.

Unpublished Materials

Barry, James J. "Ralph Brownell Dennis, Lecturer, Interpreter, and Dean of the School of Speech." M.A. thesis, Northwestern University, School of Speech, 1947.

Bauer, Otto F. "A Century of Debating at Northwestern, 1855-1955." M.A. thesis, Northwestern University, School of Speech, 1955.

Hoadley, Grace. "Significant Chapters in the History of Northwestern University, 1905-1923." Master's thesis, Northwestern University, 1923.

Howe, Jonathan T. "The Northwestern University Fraternity System: A History, 1951-1963." Honors thesis, Northwestern University, Department of History, 1963.

James, James Alton. "Graduate Study and the Development of the Graduate School, 1856-1931." Unpublished manuscript, Northwestern University, n.d.

James, James Alton. "The Origin and Early Development of the University Guild." Unpublished address, Northwestern University, May 1942.

James, James Alton. "History of Northwestern University." Unpublished manuscript, 1951.

Lardner, James Lawrence. "A History of the School of Speech." Unpublished manuscript, Northwestern University, 1951.

Luck, Martha. "History of the University College." Unpublished manuscript, n.d.

Mattern, Grace. "The Biography of Robert McLean Cumnock." Master's thesis, Northwestern University, School of Speech, 1929.

Newcombe, P. Judson. "The First Fifty Years of Speech Training at Northwestern University." Unpublished manuscript, Northwestern University, August 1961.

Sedlak, Michael W. "A History of the Northwestern University Graduate School of Management, 1908-1975." Unpublished manuscript, Northwestern University, 1976.

Swanson, Richard A. "Edmund J. James, 1855-1925: A Conservative Progressive in American Higher Education." Ph.D. Dissertation, University of Illinois, 1966.

GENERAL INDEX

Numbers in italic refer to pages of illustrations

Abbott Hall, 190, 203
   V7 housing, 207, 217, *219*
Academy, see preparatory school
Act of Incorporation, 5-6, 363-67
Adelphic Society, 28, 33
Adlai Stevenson Lectures, 326
Administrative
   Council, 255
   Policies and Planning Committee, 264 and
   note
Admissions
   athletes, 343
   early years, 18-99, 47, 51, 81-2, 111
   Faculty Committee on, 286 and *note*
   professional schools, 112; *see also school*
     entries
   student demands for, 329, 336, 338, 341
   University Council responsibility for, 119
   see also Recruitment
Adult education, 164, 193, 225-26, 308-9
African-American Studies, 291, 338
African Studies, Program of, 309
Afro-American Student Union, 329
Agase, Alex, 345
Air Law Institute, 158, 189
Alcoholic beverages, 5-6, 29, 365
Aleph Teth Nun, 125
Allison, Brent, 176
Allyn, Joseph, 57
Alpha Chi Omega, 62, 161-2n
Alpha Gamma Delta, 161-2n
Alpha Kappa Alpha, 238
Alpha Omicron Pi, 161-2n
Alpha Phi, 62, 201
Alpha Xi Delta, 161-2n
Alumnae, Associate, 267
Alumni
   Advisory Council on Athletics, 345
   Association, 66, 105, 130, 151, 266, 337
   Fund, 266
   Journal, 120
   News, 201, 266
   opposition to proposed merger, 185
   organizations, 265-67
   records, 187
   Relations, *204, 247,* 266-67
Amazing Grace, 326 and *note*
Ambrose, Lodilla, 46, 67, *124*

American
   Association of University Women, 60
   College of Dental Surgeons, 75
   College of Physicians and Surgeons, 79
   Society of Engineering Education, 233
   Student Union, 197
Anchor and Eagle, 243
Andersen, Arthur, 361
Anderson, Harold H., 199, 274
Anderson Hall, 274
Anderson, Wayne, 340-41
Ann-Margret, *299*
Anna Scott Garden, 201-2
Annie May Swift Hall, *70,* 85, 298
Archeological Field School, *289,* 310
Architecture firms, 273; *see also specific*
   firm names.
Archivist, 320
Argonne National Laboratory, 234 and
   note, 312
Armour, J. Ogden, 168
Armour, Philip, 168
Armour Institute of Technology, 168-69
Army Corps of Engineers, 263
Arrow, 89
Association of American Universities,
   112 and *note,* 170, 254
Astronomical Society, Chicago, 53-55
Athletics
   early, *32,* 34, *59,* 64, 91-3
   1900-20, 126-30
   1920-30, 171-73, *175*
   1930's, 196
   1940's, 236, 244-46
   1949-74, *334,* 343-49
   see also Baseball, Basketball, Football
Athletic Sports, Committee on Regulation
   of, 91
Austin, Frederick C., 150
Austin scholars, 150, 180 and *note*
Avalon Foundation, 268
Avery, James, 323n
Ayers, Thomas G., 361

Baccalaureate degree, 38, 66, 80
   in Business Administration, 119
   see also College

Bainum, Glenn C., 165
Baird, Robert, 57
Baker, Ralph "Moon," 172
Baker, Robert H., 295, 334
Bancroft, Jane, 57, 60
Barr, John A., 296-97
Bartlett, Lydia, 131 and *note*
Baseball
    early, *32*, 34, *63*, 64, 92
    1900-20, 126-30
    1920's, 173
    1940's, 244
    1957, 248
Basketball
    1898, 93
    1900-20, 126-30
    1920's, 173
    1940's, 244
    1949-74, 348
Bauer, William C., 167-69, 192-93
Beattie, John W., 191-92, 220, 227
Beatty, Warren, *299*
Beecher, Carl, 165, 191
Bell, James W., 195
Benchwarmers, 266, 349
Besley, Frederick A., 133
Beta Theta Pi, 33
Bethlehem Steel Company, 275
Better Understanding Week, 238
Big Ten, 91 and *note*, 92, 126, 130, 172-73
    Council of Ten, 348-49
    effect of World War II, 246 and *note*
    faculty salaries in, 315
    proposed withdrawal from, 343-45
Bimetallic League, 87
Biological Sciences Building, 272, *277*, 280, 312
Biomedical Engineering Center, 309, 312
Black, Arthur D., 117, 157, 189
Black, Greene Vardiman, 75-78, *77*, 117, 266
Black student demands, 329-38
Blanchard, Richard H., 2-4
Blaney, James, 17-18, 37n
Blodgett, Henry W., 74
Blomquist, Edwin and Juliette, 280
Blomquist Memorial Recreation Building, 273, 280
Board of Trustees, *see* Trustees
Boley, Bruno A., 301
Bonawit, Diven, 182
Bonbright, Daniel, 17, 31-32, *100*, 101, 105, *109*, 361
Booth, Henry, *21*, 22-23, *42*, 74
Botsford, Jabez, 2-4

Bradford, William C., 309
Bradwell, Judge, 24
Bragdon, Merritt C., 37
Brooks, James M., 254
Brown, Andrew J., 2-4, 35
Brown, Mrs. Andrew, 24, 34
Brown, Ray E., 283
Brownell, Baker, 160-61
Bryan, William Jennings, *104*
Buckman, Thomas R., 311
Budget and Resources Advisory
    Committee, 287
Building fund, first permanent, 39
Bunche, Ralph, 238
Burgess, Kenneth F., *247*, 248, 256, 259, 268, 361
Business
    central office for, 73
    black occupation of, 329-37
    see also business managers Dyche, Kerr, Sheppard, Wells

Cabell, E. E., 197-98
Cahn, Bertram, 201
Cahn Auditorium, *200*, 201, 217, 244, 298
Call, Florence, 63
Calumet, wreck of, 66
Campbell, Robert W., 146-47, 148n, 155, 361
Campbell, T. Moody, 215
Campus life
    1876-90, 60-66
    1890-1900, 86-93
    1900-20, 125-32
    1920-30, 171-77
    1930's, 196
    1940's, 236-46
    1949-74, 322-49
    see also student life
Campus Players, 166, 173
Canadian Studies Program, 310
Canal Street Church, 2
Carhart, Raymond, 312
Carleton, Jim G., 323
Carnegie, Andrew, 105, 106
    Corporation, 165, 178, 215, 295
    Foundation, 269, 290
    Institute, 234
CATS (Civilian Army Training), 210
Centennial
    Law School, 306-7
    Medical School, 303
    Northwestern University, 254, 260-61, 267
    United States, *26-7*
Central Debating League, 87

Chancellor, 254, 321
  see also Miller, J. Roscoe
Chandler, B. J., 295-96, 268
Chapin Hall, 131
Chaplain, 244
Charles Deering Memorial Library, *see*
  Deering Library
Charles G. Dawes home, 220
Charter, Northwestern University, 5-6, 363-67
Chicago, 1, 2, 63
  Association of Commerce, 119
  Bears, 349
  Campus
    founding, 120, 139, *140, 142,* 147
    1920-30, *152-53,* 154-61,
    post World War II additions, 220-1
    1940's, 225, 242
    1949-74, 281-85, 302, 313
    1970 disturbance, 341
  Fire, effect of, 16, 28, 37, 53
  Medical College, 20-22, *21,* 30, 58-59
    enrollment, 19, 47, 51, 59
  Maternity Center, *see* Prentice Women's
    Hospital
  Newspapers
    Chicago Daily News, 98, 337
    Chicago Evening Post, 98-99
    Chicago Journal, 103
    Chicago Sun-Times, 337
    Chicago Tribune, 154, 168, 337
      and School of Journalism, 159-61,
      190 and *note*
Children's Memorial Hospital, 221, 225,
  282, *288-89*
Children's Theatre of Evanston, 166, 192
Chi Omega, 161-162n
Circle Français, 86
Circular, 38
Civil War, 12, 18, 23, 33, 35, 37
Clara A. Abbott Trust, 217
Clark, Henry, 2-4
Clark, J. Scott, 125
Class rush, 173
Classical curriculum, 9, 17, 19-20
Cleft Palate Institute, 306, 310
Clinics
  Dental, 76, 117, 157, 242, 306
  Law, 307
  Medical, 187-88, 282-84
  Speech and Hearing, 166-67; *see also*
    Frances Searle Building
Clubs, 126, 265-67; *see also specific club names*
Coe, George, 80

Coeducation, 23-30, 49, 60
  Lodilla Ambrose's student record, 46
  and President Rogers, 82, 98
  effect on athletics, 130
  see also Women
Coffee Club, 87
Cohen, George M. (student), 323
Cohn, Henry, 84, 99
Cole, I. W., 268, 297, 332
College
  of Arts and Sciences, 268, 291-92, 308-9,
    312, 316-17
  of Liberal Arts, 57-58, 72-73, 79
    curriculum, 79-81, 119, 223, 226
    enrollment, 51, 78, 111, 113, 156, 188,
      211, 322
    1920's, 148, 162-64, 167
    1930's, 188, 191
    1940's, 213, 232, 235, 290-91, 295
    relationship to University College,
      226, 308
  of Literature, Science and the Arts, 9, 57
    enrollment, 19, 51
  of Technology, 23, 46-47
Columbian Exposition, 86
Commerce, School of, 119, 135
  enrollment, 113, 156, 159n, 188, 211, 322
  1920's, *153,* 155, 158-59
  1930's, 188, 190
  1940's, 223, 225, 227-28, 235
  1949-74, 196, 308
Commerce Building, 159, 227n
Commonwealth Edison, 267
Commonwealth Fund, 268, 269, 301
Communism, 216
Community of Scholars, 287, 291
Community Planning Committee, 263
Computer Center, *see* Vogelback Computing
  Center
Conklin, Edwin, 80
Continental Illinois National Bank and
  Trust Company, 6n, 267
Cook, Charles E., 47
Cook County Hospital, 282n
Coon, Owen L., 215
  Forum, 280
  Foundation, 280
  Law Library, 306
Coon (Byron S.), Sports Center, 273, 274
Cooper, John, 268
Crandon, Frank P., 45-46
Cresap, Mark W., 148n, 361
Crew, Henry, 80

Crime Detection Laboratory, 158, 189
Crown, Henry Colonel, 279
    see also Rebecca Crown Memorial Center
Cummings, Joseph, *42*, 46, 50, 59, 63, 69, 71, 361
Cummings, Tilden, 265
Cumnock, Robert McLean, 58, 64
    School of Oratory, 84-85, 112, 166
Curriculum
    1855-76, 16-20 and *note*, 57-60, 79-81
    1900's, 102, 105, 111
    engineering, 192-93
    1942 goals, 212
    1949-74, 264, 290-310
    see also specific disciplines
Curriculum and Teaching Committee, 290
Cutter, Irving S., 157, 185, 187, 225, 253

Daily Northwestern
    on football, 172
    on Harris resignation, 120
    on Hough, 137
    on postwar, 244
    on Rose Bowl, 246
    on student government, 236
    on World War I, 132
    on World War II, 243
    MacDougall letter, 215
    Survey of attitudes, 196, 237
    Evening Northwestern, Chicago campus, 325
    Woman's Edition, 132
Daley, Richard, 282
Danielson, Barbara Deering (Mrs. Richard), 151, 182
Darrow, Clarence, 202
Dart, Edward D., 280
Davies, Ernest C., 296
Davis, Nathan Smith, *21*, 22, 60, 78
Davis, Nathan Smith, Jr., 79, 115, 266
Dawes home, 220
Dean's Councils, 255
Dearborn Observatory, 53 and *note*, 55 and *note*, *66*
Debate
    early societies, 33
    1890's, 87
    1900's, 126
    1930's, 192
    1941, 237
    1949-74, 325
Debt-paying funds, 50-51, 52
Deering, Charles H., 147, 150
Deering, Marion Whipple (Mrs. Charles), 151, *183*

Deering, Roger, 187
Deering, William, 20, 45, 51, 71, 86, 96, 361
    on Rogers, 97
    on Sheppard, 99
    on James, 106
Deering Library, 150-51, 171, 182, *183*
Delta Delta Delta, 89n, 161-62 and *note*
Delta Gamma, 62, 161-62 and *note*, *240*
Delta Tau Delta, 89n
Delta Upsilon, 62
Delta Zeta, 161-62 and *note*
Dempster, John, 10
Dempster Hall, 34
Dennis, Ralph B., 166-67, 230
Dental
    College, 51, 59-60
    School
        1890's, 73-78
        1900's, 102, 112, 113, 117
    World War I, 135
    1920's, 148, 154 and *note*, 156-57
    1930's, 188
    1940's, 211, 225, 242
    1949-74, 303-6
    G. V. Black Society, 266
    Medical Center, 281-83
Depression, 1930's, 180-82
    effect on Medical Center, 155
    effect on proposed merger, 184
Development
    Committee on, 148-54, 187
    Department of, 187, 239, 248, 255, 352-53
DeVoto, Bernard, 176
Dewhurst, Winifred R. (Mrs. F. B. Snyder), 205
Disque, Robert, 230n, 233-34
Dixon, Wesley M., 256, 275, 361
Doctoral programs, 83-84 and *note; see also* Graduate Schools
Donham, Richard A., 296
Dormitories, *see* Housing
Dougherty, Eddie, 159-60
Douglas, Paul, 196, 261, 275
Downey Veterans Hospital, 282n
Driscoll, John "Paddy," 126
Dryden Hall, 272-273
Duncan, Robert, 147
Dunlop, Ralph E., 274, 323n, 326
Dyche, David R., 59
Dyche, William A., 105, *109*, 120, 139, 148n, 149, 160, 182, 186
Dyche Stadium, 111, 160
Dye, W. H. H. (Tippy), 266, 345n, 348
Dykstra, Clarence, 238

INDEX

Eckenhoff, James E., 303
Eckstein, Louis and Elsie S., 259, 297
Education
  Department of, 111, 156
  School of
    1920's, 169-70; *see also* College
      of Liberal Arts
    1930's, 188, 193-94
    1940's, 211, 223, 234-36
    1949-74, 268, 280, 295-96, 308-9
      admission for athletes, 343
    Center for Teaching Professions, 309
Educational Policies
  Faculty Committee on, 264, 285-87, 324
  1970 statement on NUFAC, 339
  Trustee Committee on, re faculty salaries,
    315
Edwards, Arthur R., 115
Eisenhower, Dwight D., honorary degree, 273
Ekberg, Maurice, 333
Elgin Academy, 101
Eliot, George Fielding, 237
Elliott, Frank H., 66
Ely, Richard T., 159
Endowment, 9, 38-41, 69
  statements of need, 13, 72-73, 96-97, 122-23
  1918 needs, 137-39
  1920's, 145-46, 148-50
  1930's effect of depression, 181, 186-87
  1940's, 202-3, 248
  1950, corporate gifts, 75, 267
  J. Roscoe Miller aims, 259
  See also Finances; List of Tables on
    Resources and Liabilities
Engineering
  College of, 72, 107, 111, 148
    relation to Liberal Arts, 163n, 167
  School of, 167-69
  Murphy gift, 197-98
  Enrollment, 113, 156, 188
  see also College of Technology,
    Technological Institute
Engineering Council for Professional
  Development, 192-93
Enrollment
  Effect of Civil War on, 35-37
  1875-76, 47
  1890's, 66, 81, 82 and *note*
  1900, report to trustees, 96
  effect of depression on, 181
  post-World War II, 222-23, 243
  1949-74, 322, 329, 338, 343
  see also List of Tables, Enrollment
Epworth Herald, 90

Equal Opportunity Office, 320
Equitable Assurance Society, 95
Eshbach, Ovid W., 230-34, 300
Evans John, *xiv*, 2-3, 6, 8-9, 35, 39, 45, 50,
  260, 361
  see also John Evans
Evans, W. A., 62
Evanston, 6, 8, 9, 54, 63-64, 115
  Relationship to Northwestern before
    1900, 35-37, 86, 90
    1900's, 103, 110
    on proposed U. of C. merger, 185
    on Viet Nam disturbances, 339-41
    on Chicago Bears, 349
    Operation Evanston, 324
    possible expansion into, 262
    Spring Thing, 342
  see also taxation
Evanston
  College for Ladies, 24-28
  Hospital, 282
  Waterworks, 37
Evanston
  News Index, 37, 98, 131, 137, 168
  Press, 103
  Review, 185
Evening Divisions, 308-9
  see also Adult Education, University
    College
Evening Study Hall, 281
Executive Committee of Board of Trustees,
  6, 11-12, 98, 103
Experimental Animal Resources, 309

Faculty
  early, 16-20
  1890's, 57, 66-67, 72, 79-80
  community criticism of, 103
  1920's, 177-78
  effect of depression on, 181
  opposition to U. of C. merger, 185-86
  World War II, 207, 210
  enlargement of graduate schools, 227
  1949-74, 256, 258-58, 314-17
  committees, 284-91
  sympathy with blacks, 334, 337
Faculty Associates Program, 327-28
Faculty Club, 322
Faculty Planning Committee
  biological sciences building, 280
  lakefill, 263 and *note*, 264
  Library, 279
  Senate Steering Committee, 286-87

Fagg, Frederick D., Jr., 158, 190, 205-7, 214, 255
Fayerweather, Daniel B., 53, 96
Fayerweather Hall, 52, 53, 217, 220, 229
Fellowships, 171, 227, 295, 317
Field Enterprises, 267
Fields, John E., 255, 266, 283, *318*
Fighting Methodists, 172
Finances
  1876-90, 45-50, 66
  1890-1900, 72-73, 93-96
  1900-20, 121-23, 136
  1930's, 180-82
  1940's, 221-23
  1949-74, 258, 350-52
  see also List of Tables, Receipts and
    Expenditures, Resources and
    Liabilities
Financial Aid, 264
  for heterogeneous student body, 322-23
  for black students, 329, 336, 338
First Methodist Church, 4, 27
First National Bank, 267
First Plan for the Seventies, 264-65, 267, 268n, 279-80, 284-86
Fisher, Waldo, 172
Fisk, Herbert, 82
Fisk Hall, *70*, 136
Flickinger, Roy C., 162
Football, 34, 64, 91 and *note*, 92
  1900-20, 88, 126-30, *128*
  1920's, 172-73
  1930's, 196
  1940's, 244-46
  1949-74, 343-48, *347*
For Members Only, 329, 336
Ford Foundation, 268, 295, 297, 315
  total grants, Miller years, 269
Foster, John H., 9
Foster, Randolph Sinks, 7, 12, 18, 361
Foster Farm, 8-9, 11
Foster House, 220
Foundation grants, 267-69
  see also specific foundations
Foundation Research Planning Office, 268
Founders, 2-5, 11, 363-67
Fowler, Charles H., 12-13, 16, 26, 28-29, 55, 361
Frances Searle Building, 272, 276, 280, 298, 312
Fraternities, 62, 87, 89, 173, 196
  housing, 107, 130-31
  rushing, 324
  Scrawl article on, 176

World War II use of, 220, 238, 243
  see also Greek letter societies, specific clubs
Freedoms Foundations, 246
Freeman, Charles W., 189, 225, 242
Friends of Art, 266

Gage, Lyman, 20
Gamma Phi Beta, 62, 161-62 and *note*
Gannett Foundation, 268, 297
Garrett Biblical Institute, 4, 10, *15*, 24
Garrett, Eliza Clark, 10
Gary, Elbert H., 118 and *note*, *142*
  contributions, 147, 148
Gary Library, 147-48, *152*, 155, 221
General Assembly, Illinois, 263
General Education Board, *see* Rockefeller Foundation
General Education Committee, 290
General Faculty Committee, 284-87, 322
  faculty compensation, 215-16
  rushing policy, 324
  on NUFAC, 339
Gentle Thursday, 328
Geographical diversity, 96, 311
George, Katharine, 320
Geotechnical Center, 293, 309
Gerber, Jay J., 260
G.I. Bill, 211
Gilmer, Thomas, 117
Goodman, 11, 17
Goldberg, Bertrand, 273, 284
Golf team, 173
Gonser, Thomas A., 148-54, 187, 197-99, 254
Goodman, Benny, 237
Goodrich, Grant, *facing 1*, 2-4, 24
Gotaas, Harold B., 268, 274, 301
"Go U Northwestern," 127
Government funds, federal, 269, 274
  NIH, 281, 312
  ARPA, 312n
  1949-74, 351, 352
Graduate Record Exam, 227
Graduate Schools, 83-84, 112
  1920's, 159, 170-71
  1930's, 194-95
  1939-49, 212-13, 226-27
  1949-74, 292-95
  federal fund cutback, 269
  see also Enrollment Tables
Graduate Studies, Board of, 112
Grand Pacific Hotel, 39, *52*, 95
Grand Prairie Seminary, 101
Grant, Ulysses S., 80

Gray, Hanna H., 291
Gray, John H., 80
Greater Northwestern, campaign, 147
Greek Letter Societies, 33-34, 89, 125,
    243, 324
Green, Leon, 158, 190n, 223-224
    report on merger, 184
    support of court-packing, 189
    on sit-down strikes, 189-90, *247*
Greenleaf, Luther, 20
Greenleaf, Mrs. L. L. 24
Gregg, Lucius, P., Jr., 334
Grosscup, Peter S., 118
G.V. Black Society, 266

Hadley, Edwin M., 216-17
Hagstrum, Jean, 290
Hahne, Ernest, 196
Haiman, Frank, 244
Hall, Zadoc, 2-4
Hamrin, S. A., 225
Haney, Richard, 2-4
Hanley, Dick, 172
Hardin, John H., 182, *183*, 279-80, 261
Harper, William Rainey, 98
Harrington, H. F., 160, 190
Harris, Abram Winegardner, *100*, 106-20
    passim to 132, *109*, 361
Harris, Norman W., 107
Harris Hall, 107, *109*
Hartford, John A., Foundation, 269
Hatfield, James Taft, 57, 103
Hatfield, Robert H., 50-53
Haven, Erastus O. *7*, 24-28, 72, 361
Havighurst, Harold, 56, 224, 269, 306
Hayford, John, 111, 133, 167
Hayward, Thomas Z., 345
Hazing, fraternity, 238
Health Services Research Center, 309
Heard, Andrew L., 273, 280
Heilman, Ralph E., 158-60, 190
Herskovits Collection, *294*
Heston, Charlton, *228*, 218
Heyck, T. W., 327
Hibbard, Addison, 164, 191, 213-14
Hines Veterans Hospital, 224, 282n
Hinman, Clark T., 6-8, *7*, 10-11, 17, 361
Hinman Society, 28, 33, *36*
Hinz, Roland J., 322, 323, *330*, 333-34
Historical Association, NU, 86
Historical Society, Evanston, 220
Hoag, Thomas, 45, 93 and *note*
Hobart, Emily Hatfield, 162
Hobart House, 162

Hobbs, James B., 55
Hogan, O. T., 280, 312
Holabird, Root, and Burgee, 273, 281
Holcomb, Stuart, 266, 345
Holgate, Thomas F., 80, *100*, 105-6, *109*,
    120, 126, 133-37, 206, 361
Homecoming, 130, 173, 266, 325
Hotchkiss, Willard E., 119
Hough, George Washington, 55
Hough, Lynn Harold, *100*, 137-39, 361
Housing
    early, 30-35, 53
    women's, 102, 106, 107, 161-2, 201
    in Y.M.C.A., 125
    1900-20, 130-31
    World War II, *208*, 220, 243
    black students, 238-42, 332-36
    1960's restrictions, 326-28
    First Plan, 265
Howard, Deva, 320
Howard, Earl D., 119
Howerton, George, 297
Hughes, James M., 235-36
Hungerford, Edward B., 314
Hunt, William, 295
Hutchins, Robert Maynard, 212, 243, 261
    Proposed U. of C. merger, 182-86

I.B.M., 267
Ihlanfeldt, William, 322 and *note*, 334
Illinois Society of Public Accountants, 119
Illinois Trust Safety Deposit, 95
Indiana Street chapel, 2
Industrial Club of Chicago, 119
influenza epidemic, 135
Information Service Office, 255
Ingalls, Frederick A., 150
Inland Steel, 267
Inlow, Gail, 334
Institute for Research in Land Economics
    and Public Utilities, 159
Institutional Cooperation, Committee on, 293
Intercollegiate Conference of Faculty
    Representatives, *see* Big Ten
Interdisciplinary Centers, 291, 293, 309-10
Inter-Fraternity Council, 238, 324
International Harvester, 267
International House, 239-40
International Programs and Scholars, 320
International Studies, 310
Interracial Commission, student, 238
Interracial Group of Evanston, 239
Intervention, World War II, 237
Isolationism, 1930's, 196-97; World War II, 237

J. Roscoe Miller Campus, 281
  table of construction, 272-73
  see also Lakefill Campus
James A. Patten Campus, 151n
James, Edmund J., *100*, 102-5, 130-31, 361
James, James A., 80, 112, 170-71, 194-95
James, Mrs. James A., 201
Jefferson, Eva, 340
Jennings, Burgess, 301
Jennings, Ode, 278
Jensen and Halstead, Ltd., 273, 274
Johannesen, Berenice, *see* Miller, Berenice
John Evans
  Center, 244, *245*, 266
  Club, 265 and *note*
John Henry Wigmore Club, 266
Johnson, Frank D., 79
Jones, J. Wesley, 23-24
Jones, William P., 23-25
Journal of Air Law, 158, 189
Journalism, School of, 159-61
  1930's, 188, 190
  1940's, 221, 225, 229
  1949-74, 268, 297, 308
  Gannett Urban Center, 309-10
  MacDougall, 216-17
  see also List of Enrollment Tables
Jubilee Memorial Fund, 105-6
Judson, Philo, *15*, 23, 35, 38

Kappa Alpha Theta, 62, 161-62 and *note*
Kappa Delta, 161-62 and *note*
Kappa Kappa Gamma, 62, 161-62 and *note*
Keith, Effie, 236
Kellogg Foundation, 268, 296
Kendall, Arthur I., 157
Kennedy, John F., 217, 325
Kennicott, Robert, 18 and *note*
Kent, Raymond A., 162-64
Kent State tragedy, 339-41
Kerr, William S., 254, 263, 273
  sit-in, 333-34
Kettering, Charles F., 198, 232 and *note*
King, Robert C., 280
Klopsteg, Paul, 233, 234
  engineering curricula, 290-91
Koch, Theodore W., 136, 151, 182, *183*
Koch Memorial Gardens, 236
Koster site, *289*, 310
Krause, Alvina, 324
Kreml, Franklin M., 255, 268, *330*
  Faculty Planning Committee, 263-65
  Medical Center, 282-83
  demonstrations, 328, 333-34

Kresge Centennial Hall, 261, 272-73
Kresge Foundation, 268
Krueger, Maynard, 196
Krulee, Gilbert, 327
Kunstler, William, 339

Lady Elgin wreck, 37
Lakefill Campus, *252*, 262-63, 272, 273n
  J. Roscoe Miller Campus, 274-79
Lang, Daniel R., 308
Lang's Army, 133-35
LaSalle Street property, 6, 39, 95-96
Latham, Helen Babcock, 148n
Law
  Department of, 9, *42*
    see also Union College of Law
  School, 73-75
    1900-20, 102, 112-13, 118
    1920's, *142*, *152*, 157-58
    1930's, 188-90
    1940's, 221, 223-24, *247*
    1949-74, 281, *294*, 306-7
    John Henry Wigmore Club, 266
  see also list of Enrollment Tables
Lawson, Captain Lawrence, 66
Lawson, Robert B., 321
Leachman, Cloris, *228*
Leland, Simeon E., 213, 226, 269, 285
  curricula, 290-91
Leopold, Richard W., 324
Levere, William C., 89n
Leverone (Nathaniel) Hall, 272, *276*, 280
Leverton, Garrett, 166
Lewis, Leland "Tiny," 172
Liberal Arts, *see* College
Library, 20, *36*, 67
  1890's, 80, 83, 86
  separation from College, 112, 136
  consolidation, 221, 225, 236
  Education curriculum, 236
  University Library, *271*, 272, 279, 310-12
  Council, 266
  Law, 118, 306
Library of Living Philosophers, 214 and
  note. 215
Lichtenstein, Walter, 112, 136
Lifesaving Crew, 27, 64-66
Lifesaving Station (U.S. Coast Guard), *63*, 196
Lincoln, Abraham, 3, 4, 35
Lindgren Foundation, 197
Lindheimer (Benjamin) Astronomical
  Research Center, *270*, 272, 278, 312
Linn, Alphonso, 37

INDEX

Linnaean Society, 87
Literary societies, 33, 62
Literature, Science and the Arts,
   see College
Little Red Schoolhouse, 159, 227n
Locke, Oren Edwin, 85
Locy, William A., 80
Loebl, Schlossman, Bennett, and Dart,
   273, 280
Long, John H., 115
Long, Omera Floyd, 80
Louckes, Vernon, 182
Loughridge, Donald H., 300
Lowry, Tim, 172
Luck, Martha S. 308
Lunt, Cornelia, 85-86
Lunt, Orrington, *facing 1*, 2-4, 45, 50, 72, 361
   location of university, 8-9
   gifts, 83, 96
   see also Orrington Lunt Library
Lutkin, Peter C., 85, 111-12, 164-65
Lutkin Hall, *218*, 220, 244, *319*

McBurney, James H., 230, 298
McCarn, Ruth O, 238-39
McCasky, Isaac, 12
MacChesney, Nathan W., 120, 151, 172
McCormick, Marion Deering (Mrs.
   Chauncey), 151, 182, *183*
McCormick Co., R.R., 160
McCormick, Robert R.
   Hall, 281, 285, 306
   Trust, 269, 291
McDaniel, Joseph M., 296
MacDougall, Curtis, 216-17
McDowell, William F. and Mrs., *109*
McGaw, Foster G., and Mrs., 260, 274,
   283-84
McGaw Medical Center of N.U., 283
McGaw Memorial Hall, 260, 272, 273, 348
McGowan, John P., 311-12
Mack, Raymond W., 254, 284, 320, 321,
   327, *331*
McKinlock, George A., *142*, 146n
McKnight, John, 323
McLeod, James, 244, 323 and *note*
MacMinn, Paul, 238
McSwain, E. T., 225, 235, 295, 308
MacVicar, Helen Avis (Mrs. Bernard
   DeVoto), 177
Management, Graduate School of, 280,
   296-97
Maney, George A., 193

Mann, Thomas, 197
Marcy, Oliver, 16, 18, *42*, 46-50, *66*, 361
   on College of Technology, 23
   on Liberal Arts, 55-57, 73
Markle Fund, 268, 301
Marshall, John S., 59
Mary-Missouri Construction, 275
Mason, William S., 150
Massasoits, 89 and *note*
Master of Arts in Teaching (MAT), 295
Materials Research Center, 309
Mathematical Studies in Economics and
   Management Sciences, 309
Mathis, B. Claude, 296
Mayer, Rachel, *142*, 148, 150
Mayer Hall, 148, 150, *152*, 155
Mayo, A. O., 30
Medical Center, 220-21, 309, 314
Medical Corps Hospital Unit, 133, 224
Medical School, 73, 78-79
   1900-20, 112-15
   World War I, 133, 135
   1920's, 148, 154-56
   1930's, 187-88
   1940's, 220-21, 224-25, 242, 255
   1949-74, 268, 281-84, 301-4, 316, 341
   see also List of Tables on Enrollment
Medill, Joseph, 160
Medill School of Journalism, *see* Journalism
Melby, Ernest O., 193-94, 234-35
Menges, Theodore, 75
Men's Union, 173 and *note*, 196
Methodist Church, 2-5, 10, 17, 363-67
   Relationship to N.U., 96, 98, 105, 110
   sever relationship, 255
Methodist Conference, 5, 255, 363-67
Methodist Women's Home Missionary
   Society, 72
Metropolitan Studies, Center, 293, 309
   and *note*
Military service, World War II, 210
Millar (Alice) Chapel, 274, *304*
Miller, Berenice (Mrs. J. Roscoe), *250*, *252*,
   253, *257*, 353 and *note*
Miller, H. H. C., 99
Miller, J. Roscoe, 215, 221, 225, 242, *250*,
   252, *257*, 253-353, 361
Miller, Joe W., 173, 324 and *note*
Miller, Thomas W., 297-98
Milton H. Wilson Campus, 151
Milwaukee Railroad, 9, 37
Mineralogical Journal Club, 87

Minorities, 75
  1940's, 238-42
  1960's, 329-38
  numbers enrolled, 322n
  see also Women
Mintzer, David, 268, 301
Montgomery Ward Memorial Hall, *140*,
  147, 154, 284
Morrison, Paul H. 229
Morton, Joy and Margaret Gray, 221
Morton Building, 221, 281, 285, *313*
Moulton, E. O., 195
Mount, Leighton, 173
Murphy, C. F., and Associates, 273, 284
Murphy, Walter Patten, 193, 197-99
  bequest, 222-23, 230, 248
Murphy Foundation, 199, 230-34
Museum of Natural History at N.U., 18, *54*
Music clubs, 87, 111
Music, Conservatory of, 30, 78, 85-86
Music, School of, 85-86, 90
  1900-20, 112-13, 125
  1920's, 150, 156, 162, 164-65
  1930's, 191-92
  1940's, 211, 220, 227, 235-36
  1949-74, 259, 297-98, 309, 324
  see also Tables of Enrollment
Music Society, 266

Nathan Smith Davis Club, 266
National Defense, 207
National Guard, 341
National Institutes of Health, 281
National Science Foundation, 307
Naval ROTC, 207, 220
  protested, 328, and *note*, 338
Navy Civilian Service Award, 246
Netsch, Walter, Jr., 279, 280
Newman, Charles, 314
Nobles, Laurence H., 291
Norris, Lester and Dellora, 273, 280
Norris University Center, *305*, 325
North Central Association, 357
Northern Oratorical League, 87
North Shore Music Festival, 107, *108*,
  110-11, 164, 165
Northwest Territory, 1
Northwestern, 62, 63, 64, 89
  on Annie May Swift Hall, 85
  on housing, 130
  see also Daily Northwestern
Northwestern Apartments, *218*, 220
Northwestern Christian Advocate, 125

Northwestern Community Council, 287, 327
  on rushing, 324
Northwestern Female College and Preparatory
  Department, 23-25
Northwestern Institute of Psychiatry, 284
Northwestern Library News, 236
Northwestern Magazine, 130-32
Northwestern Memorial Hospital, 284
  and *note*
North Western University, spelling change, 5n
Northwestern University Associates, 151-54,
  199, 265
Northwestern University Building, 102
Northwestern University Faculty Action
  Committee (NUFAC), 339
Northwestern University Foundation, 151, 171
Northwestern University Press, 314
Northwestern World, 89
Noyes, Henry Sanborn, *7*, 11, 12, 17, 361
Noyes, Mrs. Henry, 24
Nuclear Physics, 312
NUMBALUMS, 266
Nyholm, Jens, 236, 311

Oak Crest Hotel, 273
Oates, James, 182, 282-83
O'Brien, Joyce, 239
Occupations of graduates
  1859-76, 38
  1876-90, 66
  1891-1900, 90-91, 91n
  1930's, Speech, 192
Odgers, J. Hastie, 148
Old Clark Street Church, 2, 6, 10
Oldberg, Oscar, 59, 115
Old College, *facing 1*, 10, 20, 82 and *note*, 169
Olsen, Norman H., 306
Olson, Kenneth, 216, 229
Oratorical contests, 87, 126
Oratory, School of, 84-85, 112-13, 166
  see also Cumnock, Speech
Orrington Lunt Library, 83 and *note*, 86
  and *note*, 112
  other uses, 220, 229
Ossoli Literary Society for Women, 33
Owen L. Coon Foundation, 215
Owen, Walter S., 268, 301

Pacific Hotel Company, 39
Pacifism, 176, 196, 214-15
Pandora, 62
Panhellenic Council, 238
Panic of 1857, 39
Panic of 1873, 41, 45-50

Park, Joe, 334
Parkes (William) Hall, 274
Parseghian, Ara, 345
Passavant Memorial Hospital, 148, 155,
   282, 284
   see also Northwestern Memorial Hospital
Patten, James A., 103, 139, 361
   gifts, 107, 130, 144
Patten Gymnasium, *68*, 107, *108*, 111,
   130, 199n
   New Patten Gymnasium, *219*, 220
Patterson, Joseph Medill, 160
Paul, Oglesby, 284, 321
Payseur, Theodore, 345
Pearson, Charles W., 57, 103
Pearsons Hall, 131
Pedagogy, Department of, 111
Pepper, Claude, 244
Pharmacy
   Illinois College of, 51, 59, 73
   School of, 73-74, 78, *114*
      1900-17, 96, 102, 112-13, 115-17
      transferred to U. of Illinois, 136
Phi Beta Kappa Society, 58
Phi Delta Theta, 33, 62
Phi Kappa Psi, 33, 62
Phi Kappa Sigma, 33
Philippines annexation, 96, 98
Pi Beta Phi, 89n, 161-62 and *note*
Pick, Albert, Jr., 280-81
Pick-Staiger Concert Hall, *277*, 280-81, *294*
Pines, Ellis, 328
Police
   Evanston, 196, 333, 338
   International Chiefs of, 196
Pont, John, 348
Porter, Jack Nusan, 328
Posey, Rollin, 225
Potter, Mary Rose, 126
Pratt, Willie, 37
Preble, Robert C., 261
Prentice Players, 166, 173
Prentice Women's Hospital, 282, 284
Preparatory School, 6, 8, 18, 47, *70*
   Academy, 82, 113, 135-36
Presser Foundation, 165 and *note*
Prior, Moody E., 292-93, 314
Professional Schools, 9, 20-23, 30
   1880's, 47, 58-60, 63-64
   1890's, 73-74, 96
   1900-20, 111-119, *116*, 139
   1926 move to Chicago campus, 154-61
   1949-74, 295-307
Progressive Party, Illinois, 216 and *note*,

Prohibition amendment to Charter, 5-6, 365
Prohibition Club, 87
Provost, 254, 321
Public Relations, 187, 254
   Information Service Office, 255
Publications, student, 62
Publicity Department, 146, 187
Purple, 93
   football team, 172
Purple Oak, 201

*Quarterly Journal of Land and Public
   Utilities*, 159
Quinn, Patrick M., 320

Race relations, *see* Minorities
Rahl, James A., 307
Ravinia Festival, 298
Raymond, James, 85
Rebecca Crown Memorial Center, *270*,
   273, 279
Recruitment
   of athletes, 345
   of black students, 336
   Bonbright recommendations, 101
   of students, 6, 18, 19, 47, 49, 51, 81-82
   of heterogeneous student body, 322-23
Regenstein Hall of Music, 281
Registrar, 320
Rehabilitation Institute, 282, 284
Religion
   1850-90, 5, 17, 31, 62, 72, 90
   1890-1900, 90-91
   1900-20, 110, 125
      Pearson controversy, 103
   1920's, 177
      Scott view of, 144
   1940's, 244
   1949-74, 323
      questionnaire, 322n
Religion, Board of, 244
Religious Counsellors, Association, 244
Research and Sponsored Programs office, 268
Richter Memorial Fund, 310
"Rise Northwestern," 127
Ritchie, John III, 269, 306-7
Roberts, Don L., *319*
Robinson, Ethel, 131
Rock (The), 177
Rockefeller Foundation, 123
   contributions, 145 and *note*, 146-48, 162
Rogers, Emma (Mrs. Henry), 72, 86, 162
Rogers, Henry Wade, *70*, 71-99, 118, 361
Rogers House, 162

Rogers, James Gamble, 146, 151, 154, 160-62, 168, 182
Rogers Literary Society, 87
Rohr, William, 345
Rollins, J. L., 238
Roosevelt, Theodore, 103, *104*, 126
Rose Bowl, *240*, 244
Rush Medical College, 3, 9, 18, 22
Russell Sage Foundation, 269

Salaries, faculty
  1890-1900, 57-58 and *note*, 66
  in College
    1920's, 162, 163
    1930's, 164, 226, 191
  Effect of 1930's depression on, 181
  post-World War II, 213-14, 222, 264, 314-15
Sammons, Wheeler, 261
Sandburg, Carl, 237, 261
Sargent, Fred, 199
Sargent Hall, 272-73
Save the Dunes Council, 275-76
Schneider, Herman, 198-99, 230 and *note*
Scholarships
  perpetual, 6, 9, 10
  tuition, 101
    for graduate students, 171
    for war veterans, (WWII), 242
    for study abroad, 310
    for black students, 336
Schilpp, Paul A., 214-15
Schmehling, Arthur T., 254, 333-34
Science Curriculum, 17, 20
  in College of Technology, 23
  in Medical School, 22
  in 1890, 58
  in Technological Institute, 232
  see also Engineering, College
Science and Technology, Center for, 309
Scott, Anna Miller (Mrs. Walter D.), 143, 145, *257*
Scott, John A., 80
Scott, Walter Dill, President, 119, 133, *142*, 143-203, *183*, 205, 260
Scott Hall, 199-202, *200*, 217, 325
Scrawl, 29, 176
Scribner, Hilton, 283
Searle, John C., *252*, 256, 280, 281, 361
Searle Building (Chicago), 281, 285, *313*
Searle Student Health Center, 272, 274
  see also Frances Searle Building
Selective Service, 207, 237
Senate, Student, 325, 328

Senate, University, 178, 184, 285-90
  on rushing, 324
  on black negotiations, 337
  on Kent State, 340
Seulberger, F. George, 243, 323
Shaffer, John C., 147
Sheppard, Robert D., 57, 86, 93-95, 101, 120
  and Rogers resignation, 99
  and Dawes home, 220
Sheppard Field, 93
Sheridan Road, 64,
  Barricade, 340-41
Sigma Alpha Epsilon, 89n
Sigma Chi, 33
Sigma Nu, 89n
Simmonds, James P., 157
Simon, Clarence T., 166
Sims, Lewis Elmer, 31, 34
Skidmore, Owings and Merrill, 273-74, 278
Sloan Foundation, 269
Snowball fight, 238
Snyder, Franklyn Bliss, 194, 195, 197, 205-249, 257
Social Science Club, 87
Sororities, 62, 89, 161-62, 173, 196
  see also Greek letter societies
Soulé, Ellen, 30, 57
Sound Money Club, 87
Special Committee on an Important Problem (U. of C. merger), 182
Speech, School of
  1920's, 166-67
  1930's, 188, 191
  1940's, 223, 230, 235
  1949-74, 298-300, 308, 309
  see also Enrollment Tables
Speech Re-Education Clinic, 166-67, 192
  Communicative Disorders, 312
  see also Frances Searle Building
Spencer, Edward, 37 and *note*
Spofford, Charles W. and wife, 274
Spring Circus, 173
Stadium Corporation, 161
Stagg, Amos Alonzo, 261
Stagl, John 284
Staiger, Charles G. and Pauline Pick, 280-81
Standard Oil of Indiana, 261
State National Bank, 45-46 and *note*
Steering Committee, Faculty Senate (FSSC), 286-87
Stevens, Elmer, 265
Stevens, Samuel N., 194
Stevenson, Adlai E. II, 252, 278
Stewart, Florence, 320

INDEX

Stewart, George Craig, 149n, 185

Stout, John E., 169, 193

Strawn, Silas H., 154, 199

Strotz, Robert H., 254, *257*, 268, 291, 321-22, 334, *345*, 349, 353-57, 361

Struever, Stuart, 310

Student Council, 126, 173

Student Defense Committee, 237-38

Student Governing Board, 237, 242, 323, 325

Student Government, 126, 236, 325

Student Life
   1850-80, 14, 30-35, *46, 88, 92*
   1900's, 105-7, *114, 124, 128-29*
   1920's, *174-75*
   1930's, 196, *200*
   1940's, *204,* 208-9, *228,* 236-46, *240-41*
   1949-74, *271, 288-89, 294, 299, 304-5,* 322-49, *330-31, 344, 346-47*
   see also Campus Life, Coeducation Women

Student Religious Council, 244

Students Army Training Corps (SATC), *134,* 135

Students Christian Association, 60, 63

Students for a Democratic Society (SDS), 328, 338-39

Stull, James, 323

Sturgis, John 284

Summer School, 112
   1920-30, 170, 188
   1949-74, 308-9
   see also Enrollment Tables

Sunday, Billy, 64

Swift, Gustav, 85, 107

Swift Hall of Engineering, 107, 111, *116,* 220

Swimming team, 173

Syllabus, 62, 89, 131, 325

Tanes, Isabella, 176

Tappan, Henry, 2

Taxation of University Property, 6, 365
   attempt to remove exemption, 38, 41, 50
   Harris on exemption, 110
   Stadium Corporation not exempt, 160
   effect of proposed U. of C. merger, 184-85
   Oak Crest Hotel purchase, 273

Teachers Insurance and Annuities Association, 178, 315

Teaching Professions, Center for, 296, 309

Tebbutt, Arthur R., 226, 292

Technological Institute
   1940-49, 230-34, 236
   grants, 268, 274
   1949-74, 300-301, 311-12
   see also Engineering, College of Technology, Enrollment Tables

Technological Institute Building, 199, *204,* 217, *231,* 274
   Murphy gift, 222 and *note*

Temperance, 5-6
   WCTU, 29

Terry, Arthur Guy, 125

Teuscher, George W., 303-4

Texaco, 267

Thalian Players, 173

Theatre, 65, 166, 192

Thigpen, William, 320, 349

Thistlewaite, Glenn, 172

Thomas, Norman, 202, 237

Thorne, Ellen, *142,* 147

Thorne Hall, *152,* 182

Touchdown Club, 266

Toward the Eighties, 353

Traffic Institute, 196, 207, 309 and *note*

Transportation Center, 196, 293, 309

Traylor, Melvin, 148-49, 185-86, 361

Tremont Hotel, 102, *116,* 118

Tribune, see Chicago newspapers

Tripod, 33-34

Tri-Quarterly, 314

Trustees, Board of, 5-6, 10, 28, 45, 349
   Charter, 363, 366
   on Rogers's resignation, 97-99
   and Jubilee Memorial Fund, 106
   establish Board of Religion, 244
   Committee on Technological Institute, 232-33
   relationship with Snyder, 248; with Miller, 255-56
   Committee on Associates, 265
   policy statement on sit-in, 337

Turner, James, 333

Undergraduate Life, Committee, 326-27

Union College of Law, 22-23, 30, 58-59
   enrollment, 19, 47, 51

United Nations Week, 1946, 244

Universities Research Association, 312

University Circle, 201-2, 217, 322

University College, 188, 194, 221
   1940-49, 225-26
   1949-74, 308
   see also Enrollment Tables

University Council, 74, 119-20, 178

University Day, 64, 119

University golf course, 220

University Guild, 86 and *note,* 201, 217

University Hall, *15,* 40, 83

University of Chicago
  original
    Law Department, 22-23
    Observatory, 53-55
  present, 71, 98, 118, 212
    proposed merger, 182-86
    doctoral exchange, 293
University seal, 206
University Settlement Association, 86, 125
University Staff Advisory Council
  (NUSAC), 321-22
University Theatre, 166, 192, *228*, 230, 324
Urban Affairs, Center for, 309 and *note*

Vanderblue, Homer B., 227-29
Van Dusen, A. C., 254, 260
Vaughan Veterans Hospital, 224
Ver Steeg, Clarence L., 263-64, 279, 311
Veterans, World War II, 242-43
Veterans Administration Research Hospital,
  221, 282
Viet Nam
  opposition to, *330-31*, 338-42
  teach-in, 328
Vogelback Computing Center, 272, 278, *288*,
  309-10
V7 Reserve Midshipman's Training, 207
V12 Navy College Training, *204*, *208*, 210

Waa-Mu, 173, 201, 217, *228*, 242, 265-67,
  299, 324
Wagoner, Walter, 323n
Wallace, Henry A., 216 and *note*
Wallace, Walter, 333-34
Walter P. Murphy Foundation, 199, 230-34
War Benefit Fund, 242
Ward, Elizabeth, *142*, 147-48, 150, 157
Ward, Winifred, 166
Ways and Means Committee, 41
Weber, Alan, 263
Weil, Irwin, *318*
Weingartner, Rudolph H., 291
Wells, Harry L., 186, 248, 265
  1947 report, 222 and *note*
Wesley Memorial Hospital, 217, 220, 224,
  282-84
Western Association of Collegiate Alumnae, 60
Western College Baseball Association, 64
Wheeler, David H., 13, *15*, 24-25, 57, 361
White, Henry, 80
Wieboldt, William A., *142*, 148
Wieboldt Foundation, 148, 150
Wieboldt Hall, 148, *153*, 154-55, 159
  addition, 281, 285

Wigmore, John Henry, 74, 118, 133, 157, 158n
  John Henry Wigmore Club, 266
Wildcats, 172
Wild, Payson S., *330*
  biography, *endpiece*
  dean of faculties, provost, 253
    passim to 353
Willard, Chester E., 243
Willemain, Ray, 266
Williamson, Harold F., biography, *endpiece*
Willard, Frances E., 25-30, *26*, 35, 162
Willard Hall
  old, 34, 126, 131, 162, 217
  new, 162
Wilson, Jeremy R., 264
Wilson, Milton H., 86, 102, 125
  contribution, 137, 144
  bequest, 150, 164, 171, 191
Woman's Suffrage, 30
Woman's College Building, *26*, 29-30, 34, 86
Woman's College of N.U., 28-29, 60, 62
Woman's Medical School of Chicago, 78-79,
  96, 113
Women, *59*, *88*, *128*, *240-41*, *344*
  early education, 10, 23, 49
  early student life, 24, 29, 60, 90
  Law School policy on admittance, 75
  admitted to School of Pharmacy, 75
  in medicine, 79, 157
  enrollment, 82, 102
  housing, 131, 161-62
  Bernard DeVoto, 177
Women's Athletic Association, 173, 201
Women's Building Fund, 201
Women's Educational Aid Association of
  Evanston, 25
Wood, Robert E., 261
Wood, Roy V., 298-300, 318
World Council of Churches, 1954, 273
World War I, 127, 132, *134*, *138*
World War II, 155, *204*, 207-10, *208-9*, 220,
  236-44, *247*

Yearbook, 62
Y.M.C.A., 63, 90, 125, 173, 177, 238
Yoakum, Clarence S., 164
Young, Abram, 57
Young Alumni Council (NUYAC), 267
Young, Richard H., 255, 282-83, 268, 301-3
Y.W.C.A., 63, 90, 125, *129*, 173, 177

Zelinsky, Daniel, 332
Zeublin, Charles, 86
Zwiener, Kenneth V., 256, 361

INDEX OF TABLES

Northwestern Student Enrollment

Table 1-1	1855-1876	19
Table 2-1	1876-1890	51
Table 3-1	1890-1900	78
Table 4-1	1900-1910	113
Table 4-2	1910-1920	113
Table 5-1	1920-1930	156
Table 5-5	1931-1939	188
Table 6-1	1939-1949	211
Table 7-1	1949-1974	292

Budgeted Receipts and Expenditures

Table 1-2	1869-1876	40
Table 2-2	1877-1890	67
Table 3-2	1890-1900	94
Table 4-3	1900-1910	122
Table 4-4	1910-1920	123
Table 5-2	1921-1930	179
Table 5-4	1931-1939	180
Table 6-2	1940-1949	221
Table 7-2	1949-1961	350
Table 7-3	1962-1974	351

Resources and Liabilities

Table 1-3	1868-1876	41
Table 2-3	1876-1890	67
Table 3-3	1890-1900	94
Table 4-5	1901-1920	136
Table 5-3	1921-1939	179
Table 6-3	1940-1949	223
Table 7-4	1950-1974	352

New construction and remodeling, Evanston,
   1949-74, 272
New construction and remodeling, Chicago,
   1949-74, 285

INDEX OF ILLUSTRATIONS

John Evans, xiv
Grant Goodrich, facing p. 1
Orrington Lunt, facing p. 1
Old College, facing p. 1
Clark T. Hinman, 7
Henry S. Noyes, 7
Randolph S. Foster, 7
Erastus O. Haven, 7
Student regulations, 1866, 14
David H. Wheeler, 15
Philo Judson, 15
University Hall, 15
Nathan S. Davis, 21
Henry Booth, 21
Chicago Medical College, 21
Charles H. Fowler, 26
Frances E. Willard, 26
Woman's College, 1879, 26
Centennial Celebration, Evanston, 1876, 27
First Methodist Church, Evanston, 27
Baseball team, 1875, 32
Old Gym, 1876, 32
Hinman Literary Society, 36
Library, University Hall, 1875, 36
Oliver Marcy, 42
Joseph Cummings, 42
Law School, Class of 1877, 42
Student Record, Lodilla Ambrose, 46
Class of 1879, 46
Grand Pacific Hotel, 1887, 52
Fayerweather Hall of Science, 52
Evanston, 1880, 54
Museum of Natural History at N.U., 1887, 54
Tug-of-war Champions, 1890, 59
Women athletes, 1880, 59
Women's dormitory room, 1880, 59
Baseball team, 1889, 63
Lifesaving Station, 1890, 63
Dearborn Observatory, 1889, 66
Old Patten Gymnasium, 68
Annie May Swift Hall, 70
Henry Wade Rogers, 70
Fisk Hall, 70
Dental School, 1890's, 76
Dental Clinic, 1890's, 76
Dr. Greene Vardiman Black, 77
Women's tennis team, 1890's, 88
Jesse Van Doozer and Albert Potter, 88
   1896 halfbacks
Senior Class Play, 1894, 88

Lakefront, 1890's, 92
Old Oak, 1898, 92
Daniel Bonbright, 100
Edmund J. James, 100
Thomas F. Holgate, 100
Abram Winegardner Harris, 100
Lynn Harold Hough, 100
President Theodore Roosevelt, 1903, 104
William Jennings Bryan, 1903, 104
Old Patten: North Shore Music Festival, 108
Alumni Luncheon, 1907, 109
Harris Hall, 109
Evanston Livery Stable, 114
Junior Class Day, 1908, 114
School of Pharmacy Student Parade, 1903,
   114
Tremont House, 116
Swift Hall of Engineering, 116
Lodilla Ambrose, assistant librarian,
   1904, 124
Northwestern University Band, 1904, 124
Botany field trip, 128
Football team, 1903, 128
Women's basketball team, 128
Hard at play, circa 1903, 129
Y.W.C.A. student conference, 1915, 129
Students' Army Training Corps, 134
Recruiting, World War I, 134
Rifle Practice, 138
Red Cross Chapter in Fisk Hall, 1917, 138
Montgomery Ward Memorial Building, 140
Major Contributors, Chicago campus, 142
Entrance, School of Law, 142
Thorne Hall, 152
Levy Mayer Hall and Elbert Gary Library,
   153
School of Commerce in Wieboldt Hall,
   1926, 153
Lincoln Street beach, 1921, 174
University Circus, 1928, 174
Roaring Twenties, 175
Tennis team, 1920's, 175
Women's athletics, 1920's, 175
Cornerstone laying, Deering Library, 1932,
   183
Charles Deering Memorial Library, 183
Men's Quadrangle; Scott Hall, Cahn
   Auditorium, 200
Alumni Day Parade, 204
V12 trainees, 1943, 204

Temporary buildings, World War II, 208
Naval aviation cadets, 1943, 208
Commencement, 1947, 209
World War II memorial service, 209
Northwestern Apartments, 218
Lutkin Hall, 218
Abbott Hall, 219
New Patten Gymnasium, 219
Cloris Leachman, University Theatre, 228
Paul Lynde and Charlotte Rae, Waa-Mu, 1948, 228
Charlton Heston, University Theatre, 228
Technological Institute, 231
Delta Gamma Sorority House, 240
Rose Bowl Rally, 1949, 240
Women's Quadrangle, 241
John Evans Center, 245
Snow on south campus, 1945, 245
Commencement, 1945, 247
Alumni Day, 1946, 247
Chancellor and Mrs. J. Roscoe Miller, 250
Lakefill campus dedication, 1964, 252
Aerial view, Evanston campus, 252
Franklyn B. Snyder and J. Roscoe Miller, 257
Mrs. W. D. Scott, Mrs. F. B. Snyder and Mrs. J. Roscoe Miller at 1949 inauguration, 257
J. Roscoe Miller and Robert H. Strotz, 1970, 257
Lindheimer Astronomical Research Center, 270
Rebecca Crown Center, 270

University Library, 271
Frances Searle Building, 276
School of Education and Nathaniel Leverone Hall, 276
O. T. Hogan Biological Sciences Building, 277
Pick-Staiger Concert Hall, 277
Medical student at work, 288
Student at the computing center, 288
Koster Site, Kampsville, Illinois, 289
Student examining African art, 294
International Moot Court competition, 294
University Symphony rehearsing, 294
Ann Margret in Waa-Mu Show, 299
Warren Beatty in Waa-Mu Show, 299
Aerial view, Chicago campus, 302
Alice Millar Chapel interior, 304
Residence hall interior, 304
Foster-Walker Housing Complex, 305
Norris University Center, 305
Chicago campus, Morton and Searle Buildings, 313
Dmitry Shostakovich with Professor Irwin Weil, 318
Charlton Heston with John E. Fields and Roy V. Wood, 318
Sir Michael Tippett and Don Roberts, 319
John Cage in Lutkin Hall, 1975, 319
Student life, 1967-70, 330-31
Action in gyms, on courts and playing fields, 344
The Northwestern Wildcats, 346-47
President and Mrs. Robert H. Strotz, 354

ABOUT THE AUTHORS

Harold F. Williamson earned his B.A. at the University of Southern California and his Ph.D. at Harvard. After teaching at both Harvard and Yale he joined the Northwestern department of economics in 1948 remaining there until his retirement in 1969. From 1970 to 1973 he was resident scholar at the Eleutherian Mills History Library in Wilmington, Delaware. He returned to Northwestern in 1973 to become director of the Northwestern University History Project.

An active member and former president of the Economic History Association, he also served as secretary-treasurer of the American Economic Association, and was a founding member and president of the Business History Conference.

Mr. Williamson is the author or coauthor of several books including *Growth of the American Economy; Winchester—The Gun that Won the West; Designed for Digging: The First 75 Years of the Bucyrus-Erie Company; Northwestern Life: A Century of Trusteeship;* and *The American Petroleum Industry.*

Payson S. Wild earned his B.A. at the University of Wisconsin and his A.M. and Ph.D. at Harvard. Between 1929 and 1949 he taught in the Harvard department of government. From 1943 to 1946 he served as associate dean of the Graduate School of Arts and Sciences and from 1946 to 1949 as dean. In that year he came to Northwestern as vice president and dean of faculties, becoming provost in 1969. He retired from this post in 1973.

Between 1938 and 1946 Mr. Wild also served on the staff of the U.S. Naval War College. From 1944 to 1948 he was president of the Massachusetts U.N. Association. Mr. Wild is a member of the American Academy of Sciences and the author of *Sanctions and Treaty Enforcement* and a U.S. Naval War College series, *International Law Situations.*

Since his retirement, Mr. Wild has continued to teach part time in the political science department at Northwestern. He is a trustee of the Art Institute of Chicago and a member of the committee on long-range planning of the Evanston Historical Society.

NORTHWESTERN UNIVERSITY: A HISTORY 1850-1975
DESIGNED BY MIRJANA HERVOIC.
COMPOSED BY A & P TYPOGRAPHERS, INC.
SET IN MONOTYPE TIMES ROMAN AND TIMES ROMAN ITALIC.
TABULAR MATTER SET IN
NEWS GOTHIC CONDENSED AND BOLD CONDENSED.
PLATE WORK AND PRINTING BY PHOTOPRESS, INC.
PAPER: GLATFELTER OFFSET, VELLUM FINISH.
BOUND BY THE ENGDAHL COMPANY.